Previous Book by Harry N. MacLean

In Broad Daylight

QUANTITY SALES

Most Dell books are available at special quantity discounts when purchased in bulk by corporations, organizations, or groups. Special imprints, messages, and excerpts can be produced to meet your needs. For more information, write to: Dell Publishing, 1540 Broadway, New York, NY 10036. Attention: Director, Special Markets.

INDIVIDUAL SALES

Are there any Dell books you want but cannot find in your local stores? If so, you can order them directly from us. You can get any Dell book currently in print. For a complete up-to-date listing of our books and information on how to order, write to: Dell Readers Service, Box DR, 1540 Broadway, New York, NY 10036.

Once Upon A Time

A True Story of Memory, Murder, and the Law

Harry N. MacLean

A DELL BOOK

For Mike and Pat MacLean,
Keepers of a Safe Harbor

Published by
Dell Publishing
a division of
Bantam Doubleday Dell Publishing Group, Inc.
1540 Broadway
New York, New York 10036

ISBN: 0-440-21716-4

Reprinted by arrangement with HarperCollins Publishers, Inc.

Printed in the United States of America

Published simultaneously in Canada

August 1994

10 9 8 7 6 5 4 3 2 1

RAD

Acknowledgments

I<small>N ONE SENSE THIS BOOK IS ABOUT THE MURDER OF A</small> little girl in Foster City, California, in 1969, and the trial of her alleged murderer in Redwood City in 1990. In a much larger sense this book is about the nature of human memory, an elusive and still little understood function of the mind. The effect of trauma on the memory process, particularly in a child, and the ability of the mind to isolate the trauma are key themes because the murder charge is based on a memory supposedly repressed for twenty years. The tendency of the personality to repeat and reenact childhood traumas is a theme woven inextricably into the search for the truth in the trial of the alleged murderer.

In coming to understand the various processes and dynamics of the mind, I spoke with many psychiatrists, psychologists, social workers, and other professionals in the mental health field, to whom I am greatly indebted. I would particularly like to mention Dr. Stephen White, an author and clinical psychologist in Boulder, Colorado, whose contribution to this book, both as a friend and a professional, is immeasurable. His ability to translate psychiatric concepts and jargon into understandable terms and bring them to bear on the facts of this story was invaluable, as was his support during the long journey of researching and writing this book. I am also grateful to Dr. Michael Weissberg, an author, psychiatrist, and member of the faculty of the University of Colorado School of Medicine, for his suggestions and wise counsel.

I would also like to thank Cinde Chorness, a San Mateo reporter, who shared her insights and knowledge unstintingly and who contributed to the development of the manuscript in countless ways. Without her unrelenting encouragement and support, I could easily have wandered off to a less difficult and challenging story. Her name might well belong on the jacket of this book.

HarperCollins was kind enough to hire Alice Price, a Denver freelance writer and editor, to edit the manuscript. Alice did a masterful job of straightening out some serious kinks, relocating stray scenes, fixing bad grammar, and persuading me to cut several beloved, but fanciful, paragraphs.

I would also like to thank Neil Chethik for his valuable research assistance; Suzanne Snider for her secretarial and administrative support; Diane Gonzolas for her editorial suggestions; and Tom Austin and Jean Obert for once again allowing me to live and write in their beautiful house on Kealakekua Bay, Hawaii.

I hesitate to list the contributions of many of the individuals whose stories are told herein, but obviously many of them gave generously of their time and energy, for which I am extremely grateful.

Finally, thanks to my mother and father and a blessing on the spirits of Jules Roth, a friend and healer, and Sharon Galleher, my sister and guide.

Once Upon
A Time

An asterisk (*) indicates the use
of a pseudonym.

Part One

September 1989

MARY JANE LARKIN STOOD AT THE FRONT OF THE classroom and looked out at the sea of small faces staring up at her. Her hands rested lightly on her wooden desk, the same one she had used for the past twenty-five years in teaching fourth and fifth grades at Foster City Elementary School. Next to her hands lay her open grade book, with the students' names neatly printed in ink in alphabetical order, and pencils, bottles of glue and stacks of paper.

Things had changed over the years at the school—a lot more Asian faces filled her classroom now—but some things remained the same, like the row of black iron coat hooks on the back wall and the small metal desks with the wooden lift-up tops which had been in her classroom when she started almost a quarter of a century earlier. Her students today were certainly more sophisticated, with cable television and home computers, but they were still kids, innocent and unwary. You couldn't tell them often enough about strange men in unfamiliar cars with open doors and dolls on the front seat and what might happen if they got too close. Fourth- and fifth-graders had brief attention spans and short memories, and they still believed that the world was a safe place. There was one way, a way she had used at the beginning of every class since 1970, to convince them otherwise. What had happened in the fall of 1969 had ripped the veil of innocence from everyone's eyes. Although reliving that time brought back many of the horrible feelings, it was the best way she knew to make sure it didn't happen again. Mrs. Larkin closed her attendance book and pulled herself together to tell them the story.

"Many years ago I had a girl in my class who disappeared," she began, thinking back on the time when Foster City was a small, isolated community. Only one neighborhood had existed then, and it was populated by young families with lots of children and mothers who stayed at home and kept house and greeted their kids after school with a snack. Life was simpler and safer; kids either walked or rode their bikes to school, and in the afternoons they played at each other's houses or in the vacant lots until dinnertime. Mary Jane Larkin had six children herself, and while she had reminded them often about strangers, she worried more about them getting sick or falling off the bars on the playground. It wasn't like that any more, of course; in the past eight or nine years it seemed that missing children on the peninsula had become almost commonplace.

"Her name was Susan Nason," she continued, "and they found her two months later, kidnapped and murdered up by the reservoir." Susan had been so frail, so small, there just didn't seem to be much to her. But with her blue eyes and reddish hair cut in bangs and pulled back from her ears, she was a bubbly and lively child. Mary Jane had never forgotten Susan, not in all these years. Back then there was no grief counseling for students or teachers after a tragedy and everybody just dealt with it in their own way. "School must go on," had always been her attitude, and she had come to class smiling and cheerful.

"Now I don't want to scare you . . ." she insisted to her students. "This is a safe community and you all come from nice homes and loving parents." The tiny community had changed after Susan disappeared. The children no longer walked to school with friends; parents either walked or drove them in the morning, and at 3:00 P.M. the adults would be bunched up outside the door waiting to pick them up.

But her fourth-graders hadn't really reacted to the tragedy, at least not in an obvious way, even after Susan's body was found. Mary Jane didn't mention Susan to her students and they didn't ask about her. Children at that age didn't quite grasp the meaning of death. They may have understood that Susan wouldn't be at school that day, or the next, but not that she would never be anywhere again.

". . . But you know there are bad men in the world who want to do bad things to children. And they want little boys too, not just little girls. You must never, ever get in cars with strangers." Strangers. Whiskery people from other places intruding into their small, safe community to snatch their children and do them harm. It had to be someone who came from somewhere else just for that purpose, because there was no other reason to be roaming the town's streets; there were no movie houses or bars or restaurants. Perhaps it had been a construction worker—there were lots of houses being built then—coming back for a child he saw walking home from school one afternoon.

"She used to sit in one of these very desks," Mary Jane would say, trying to make Susan real for them. Every year the kids would get excited and insist on knowing which desk was hers, worried that they might be sitting in it.

"Is her desk haunted?" one would ask, and the others would giggle.

That night in the fall of 1969 when Mary Jane learned that Susan was missing, she thought maybe the child had gone to play at a friend's house and fallen asleep, or maybe she had gotten mad and run away and was hiding in the bushes somewhere. Mary Jane didn't believe, like some of the other teachers, that Susan had drowned in a lagoon. In the early hours of that evening she had been sure Susan would turn up and everything would be fine again.

Always, always, some child asked: "Did they find the person who did it?" And always she had to tell them: "No." In all this time they had never found the person who killed Susan.

November 21, 1989

Inspector Charles Etter of the San Mateo County District Attorney's Office had received the first call from the man four days earlier. He said that his wife had just told him she had witnessed a murder twenty years ago. She knew the murderer, the husband said, and the victim had been her best friend, but she was afraid to say anything because the murderer had told her he would kill her if she ever told anyone. He wanted to know what would happen if she came forward and her testimony was all they had. The man would say only that his first name was Barry and that the killing had taken place in San Mateo County. Barry was clear on one fact: he wanted the perpetrator of this horrible crime dead.

Gray-haired and only a year away from retirement, Etter was a solid investigator, but not a star. The receptionist had steered the caller to him because he was the only inspector in the office when it came in. Calm, reassuring, and nonthreatening, Etter turned out to be the perfect person for the call.

Barry had called Etter back a few hours later that first day. He wanted his wife to talk to Etter so he could assure her that she would be well treated. A soft-spoken woman got on the line and Etter explained to her she wouldn't get passed around in the bureaucracy and cautiously urged her to tell her story. The woman seemed reassured, but said she wanted to think about it over the weekend.

Barry called again on Monday and forcefully lectured Etter about the pitiful failures of the criminal justice system. Etter listened politely and tried to assure him that the case wouldn't be mishandled, while probing gently. Barry began leaking details: the killer, whom he wouldn't name, was a relative; the killer had even raped his own children; his wife's mother had once been married to the murderer. He was concerned that a cocaine charge against his wife when she was seventeen would affect her credibility. Finally, after stating that his wife could provide facts about the murder that hadn't been publicized, Barry began bargaining: His wife would tell everything about the crime if she had the final decision on whether or not to file charges. Etter declined immediately. Barry continued to hammer him about the risks of coming forward, and Etter continued to reassure him as best he could. Finally, Barry's wife, apparently sick of the discussion, called him away from the phone.

This morning Barry had called with a new offer: His wife would tell Etter where the killing happened, when it happened, and give the name of the victim, and then the cops could examine the evidence. If they found any physical evidence to tie someone to the crime, then she would provide the name of the killer. Etter, speaking in his usual unflappable, avuncular tone of voice, accepted this offer immediately.

The man's wife picked up the phone, and asked coyly, a slight challenge in her voice:

"Well, have you figured out what case this is on your own?"

"No, no. We haven't," replied Etter, matter of factly.

"Okay. It was in Foster City, her name is Susan Nason."

Etter pressed a little:

"As I understood your husband, you were gonna tell us what happened that day."

The woman turned away from the phone and angrily demanded of her husband why he had said that she would give all the details. She had nothing more to say. Etter heard voices in the background and then the woman came back on the phone and agreed to give a brief account of the killing. Her voice was firm and confident as she recounted that she had been in the car with the person who committed the crime and that they had picked Susan up across the street from her house. They had driven to a wooded area on the road to Half Moon Bay and there she had watched from the front seat as the man had raped her friend in the back.

Then the woman's voice dropped slightly, became softer:

"And, after that, we were all out of—out of the car, and

Susan was sitting down and I was standing by the car, and she was sitting—I can't give you an exact distance. I would say like maybe fifteen feet, twenty feet from the car, and she was sitting on, like a little tiny hill, or maybe it was a rock. She was sitting on something that was slightly elevated. And he hit her" (here her voice hesitated, and caught in her throat) "on the head with the rock and she brought her hand up to her head and he hit her again and she had a—blood went everywhere. She had a ring on her hand, and it—it crushed the ring on her hand." Her voice wavered and skipped.

Etter asked her what happened next.

"Well, this part's real fuzzy for me because I have sort of a half-memory of this."

"Um-hum?"

"Of that he made me help him put something over her. A mattress."

"Did he leave the body there?"

Her voice slipped to a whisper.

"Yeah."

"At the same spot where he had hit her?"

"Yeah," she murmured weakly, as if about to slip away.

Etter held her like an anchor.

"Okay, and then what happened?"

"Well, I was screaming. I . . ."

"You were screaming?"

". . . and he pushed me on the ground . . . and held me down and told me that he would kill me . . . and that no one would ever believe me. Okay?" Now, almost as if she were on the ground again, hearing the horrible sounds from the murderer's mouth, her words began to rush out: ". . . If anyone ever did believe me they would say that I was a part of it, and that they would put me away, and they would blame me for this, and that he would kill me if I ever talked about it."

"And how old were you at this time?" asked Etter.

"I was eight," the childlike voice fluttered back.

November 30, 1990

Detective Sergeant Bob Morse, the head of the Crimes Against Persons unit in the sheriff's office, had been working full-time for a year on the Susan Nason homicide. Tonight he sat at the far end of two tables pushed together in the center of the Broadway Cocktail Lounge, surrounded by his buddies, mainly other cops, or former cops, and a few assistant D.A.s. His gray suit jacket was tossed over the back of a chair, the cuffs of his white shirt were rolled once, and his red tie had slipped an inch or two. A bottle of Michelob sat half-empty in front of him. The jury on the Nason murder was out. The lawyers had completed their closing arguments this morning, and deliberations had begun after lunch. Now there was little to do but wait. And drink.

The Broadway was where cops in Redwood City waited while they drank. Directly across the street from the Hall of Justice, the tavern was in the corner of an odd, triangular gray building, next to a bail bonds-woman's office and a Christian Science reading room. Inside the lounge, the bar area to the left was well lit, and off to the right, in the shadows, black Naugahyde booths lined the walls. The cops usually sat at the bar or at the center tables, pushing them around to adjust to the comings and goings of fellow officers.

Although a few reporters, lawyers, and various other sorts patronized the Broadway, the place was known as a cop bar. The cops gathered there regularly after work, sometimes during work, and drank and told stories and recounted tales of battles past and present and others yet to come. The Broadway was a contemporary temple for various male warrior rituals. Here victories were celebrated and defeats mourned.

Tonight Detective Morse was predicting victory.

"We got the fucker!" he exclaimed, leaning forward into the light. "I'm telling you, the sonofabitch is going down!" Gray-haired and of average height, Morse did not cut a particularly imposing figure. Everyone, including his superiors and even some judges, referred to him by his nickname, "Bones," which alluded to his skinny rear end, or "negative ass," as he put it.

But his green eyes were lively and intense; on occasion, they flattened out, acquiring an almost serpentine cast.

Across the table sat Morse's partner, Bryan Cassandro, a seasoned tri-athlete and winner of the 1988 San Mateo County Policeman of the Year Award. In over fifteen years together the two of them had investigated and prosecuted more than one hundred murder cases, losing only two, both of which losses Morse attributed to weird juries. Cassandro also had his jacket off, cuffs rolled up and tie loosened, and he was drinking a Coors. Cassandro's thick, well-trimmed hair had over the years turned from black to mostly white, as had his mustache, but his clear blue eyes gave him a perpetually youthful look. Women found him shy, but cute. He had a reputation for being detached, unemotional. He watched his partner gesturing his confidence, and when another cop asked him whether he agreed with Morse, Cassandro said simply, "Yeah, sure."

A deputy D.A. ventured that he couldn't see anything worse than a hung jury; just no way there could be an outright acquittal.

"You guys don't get it!" urged Morse, his eyebrows jumping in amazement. "This guy is dead!" He caught the waitress's eye and circled his finger over the empty bottles and glasses on the table for another round. The table was filling rapidly with empties.

"Have you looked at the jury?" he demanded of the others. "We got the banker, I know he's with us. And the nurse? She's been with us from the beginning. You just have to look at her. And the pediatrician? The doctor? Jesus, I can't believe the defense left him on. He's the foreman and he'll bring the others along. I'm telling you," he said, grabbing a new bottle and leaning back in his chair, eyebrows twitching again, a smile playing across his face, "this guy is going down."

Cassandro looked steadily at his partner, a hint of a ruddy grin spreading behind his mustache, then raised the beer to his mouth and drank deeply.

The others became quiet. What the hell—if Bones said the man was going down, the man was going down.

A THUMB OF LAND JUTS OUT FROM THE MIDSECTION OF California to form a gradually narrowing peninsula. San Francisco sits on the tip and at the bottom sprawls San Jose. Most of the land in between constitutes San Mateo County, which is bounded on the east by the San Francisco Bay and on the west by the Pacific Ocean. A range of mountains runs down the thumb slightly to the west of center, and small beach communities like Half Moon Bay and Moss Beach dot the Pacific coast.

San Mateo County is home to 570,000 people but it consists of only 44 square miles. For the most part, the twenty-two cities in San Mateo form an elongated bedroom community for San Francisco, and to a lesser extent San Jose; the county ranks as one of the wealthiest per capita in the country. The towns run the socioeconomic gamut, ranging from the wealthy Hillsborough, perched in the hills overlooking the bay, to East Palo Alto, a wretched black ghetto only a few miles from Stanford University, but the overwhelming character of the county is very conservative; so conservative that San Mateo County is often times referred to as Orange County North.

Foster City, one of the bayside communities, is not a real city. It doesn't have any outskirts or alleys; any taverns, railroad tracks, or parking meters; any telephone poles, warehouses, dime stores, or pool halls; or a main street with movie theaters and a post office. Instead, Foster City, a planned community, has underground utility lines, divided boulevards, shopping centers, bikeways, parks, lagoons crossed by gracefully arched bridges, and glorified, look-alike tract homes. Aesthetically pleasing to some, Foster City is antiseptic, soulless, to others.

Thirty years ago Foster City didn't exist. In 1958, a wealthy Oklahoma businessman bought what was then Brewer's Island and dredged up enough sand and shells from the bay to solidify the land and support a city of 36,000 people. The first homes were built in 1963, and by 1964 several residents had moved in. The first-comers, who considered themselves modern-day pioneers, were young families with children, and the husbands worked blue- and white-collar worker jobs. The houses, priced from $20,000 to $30,000, were usually their first.

In the early years, the scene in Foster City was bleak: the wind blew in harshly from the northwest five and six hours a day and kicked up the sand which filtered in through the window screens and collected on the sills and the floor. There was not a tree or a hill to be seen, only large stretches of flat, empty land, overrun with weeds and thousands of jackrabbits. The town was still an island with only one way off. Many of the residents had come here to get away from the big cities of San Francisco and San Jose, and Foster City, rough as it was, felt homogeneous and safe, a small clearing on the edge of an urban forest.

As Foster City grew, it seemed the perfect place for raising families. On warm afternoons housewives sat on the benches by the side of the newly dug lagoons and traded recipes and talked about starting a Brownie troop while their children played happily at the water's edge. On the weekends couples worked on landscaping their lawns and organized BYOB gatherings for Saturday night. Kids roamed the neighborhood, riding their bikes to and from each other's houses and the small beaches on the bay, playing pick-up baseball and building forts in the vacant lots after school. By 1969, nearly 12,000 people lived in Foster City, although three-quarters of the land still lay vacant.

The Nason family moved into Foster City in 1967. Their single-story house on Balclutha Street had four bedrooms and faced inward and toward the backyard, with the garage serving as the main entrance from the street.

Donald Nason was a slender, gregarious salesman for an industrial partition company in Redwood City. His wife Margaret, a thin woman with wavy brown hair and glasses, was quiet, almost shy, a homemaker who loved to cook for her family, sew for her children, and work on her painting and pottery. Shirley, the oldest daughter, born in 1959, had brown hair like her mother and was quiet and a little moody. Her sister Susan, born in the fall of 1960, was quite different; with reddish-blond hair and freckles dotting her nose and cheeks, she was, to her parents anyway, a sprite, blessed with seemingly limitless energy and smiles.

Shirley and Susan often had friends over to play dolls after school and Margaret sometimes served them dishes of ice cream as a special treat. Other days the girls would go to their friends' houses and string beaded friendship rings or play kickball in the street or tag among the houses. On hot summer afternoons the girls would sell lemonade from a small wooden stand in front of the Nason house. Both girls were Brownies, and Margaret gave generously of her time and artistic talents to their troop.

Shirley and Susan had a very short walk to Foster City Elementary School, which consisted of nine portable buildings in the middle of a large asphalt field surrounded by a chain-link fence. Some days they walked through a vacant field directly across from their house, but usually they crossed over Balclutha and went half a block north and turned right on Ranger Circle. In the middle of the circle they turned off onto a path that led through the fields directly to the school playground. Occasionally, the two would be accompanied by several other girls, including Eileen and Diana Franklin, who both had red hair much brighter than Susan's and lived around the corner from her on Harvester Drive.

September 22, 1969

MARY JANE LARKIN, SHORT WITH DARK RED HAIR and sparkly blue eyes, loved children and enjoyed teaching. She always welcomed fall and the beginning of school. She missed the kids over the summer and looked forward to learning the new names and faces. This was her third year at Foster City Elementary, and she liked the school and the community. Everyone was new here, and the parents were enthusiastic and eager to volunteer for school activities.

By the third week of school in 1969, her class, consisting of seventeen girls and twelve boys, had settled into a familiar routine: math, reading, and social science in the morning, then science, art, and physical education in the afternoon. During recess, the kids played on the jungle gym and bounced balls off a high wooden wall in a primitive sort of handball. Girls were required to wear dresses to school, so if they wanted to play on the bars, which most girls did, they had to wear shorts underneath their dresses. Girls also wore good shoes to school— often brown or black buckle shoes called Mary Janes—so on days that the class had physical education they brought their tennis shoes to school with them. Usually the girls kept them under their assigned hook on the coatrack in the back of the room.

Some of the children tore out of the classroom the minute the three o'clock bell rang. Others took their time gathering their things, making sure they had all their books and papers and notes to give their parents. Susan Nason, the girl with the freckles who seemed so little, almost frail, was one of the last ones to leave on this Tuesday afternoon. On her way out of the room she spotted a paper bag with tennis shoes in it next to Celia Oakley's desk.

"Look," the youngster said excitedly to Mrs. Larkin, "Celia forgot her shoes. Can I take them home to her?"

"Well, okay," responded the teacher, "but just be sure you go home first." Most kids were under strict instructions to go straight home from school unless there was a planned activity.

"I will," Susan assured her. "I know where Celia lives, it's not far from my house." The little girl picked up the sack, tucked her books under her other arm, and bounced out of the room.

Margaret Nason had come home from visiting a friend around noon that day, and a few minutes later a neighbor dropped by to chat. When she left, Margaret began working on a dress she was sewing for Susie's ninth birthday, which was on Saturday. The dress was almost half-finished, and when Susie popped in the door shortly after three, Margaret was working on the side panels. Her daughter was so excited about her birthday that she had wanted to start decorating the house that day, although the party was still four days away. The plans were to take Susie and her friends roller-skating, which was all the more exciting because Susie hadn't been to the rink before. In another room, hidden from Susie's view, were her presents: a bright carry-all bag, a little doll dress kit, brightly colored crayons, and other treasures concealed in birthday wrappings and bright ribbons.

Susie was carrying books under one arm and a paper sack in the other when she greeted her mother. She showed her a scrape on her arm, then opened the sack for her inspection and explained that the tennis shoes belonged to a classmate, Celia Oakley. She wanted to take the shoes to Celia right away. Her daughter seemed to know where her friend lived, so Margaret said yes. She thought little of it as Susie whirled out the door, paper bag in hand.

Shirley was just arriving home as her sister was leaving. She asked Susie where she was going and Susie explained her mission. Shirley hadn't reported in yet so she couldn't go along, but the two girls talked and agreed that Susie would come right home and the two of them would play together. Shirley went inside and waited.

Susan headed up the block and stopped at a house on the corner of Balclutha and Matsonia and knocked on the door. Suzanne Banks opened the door and greeted the little girl standing on her step. The girl held up a paper bag and explained that it contained her daughter Celia's tennis shoes, which she had forgotten at school. Mrs. Banks explained to her that she had the wrong house, that the Oakleys lived a few houses away on Matsonia. Mrs. Banks helpfully walked Susan down the street, pointed out the Oakley house to her, and watched as Susan walked up to the front door. When the door opened, Mrs. Banks turned away and called for her nine-year-old daughter Linda, who was playing in the vacant lot across the street, to come home.

Celia Oakley, a tall, slender girl with straight brown hair, answered the doorbell when Susan rang, but she did not invite her classmate in to play. She thanked her and accepted the shoes. She watched as Susan walked away, then closed the door. Soon Celia left to play with her friends.

Margaret was surprised when Susie did not come right home after her errand; her youngest daughter was always starving after school, but she had been in such a hurry earlier that she had forgotten her snack. Margaret wasn't worried. She figured her daughter had probably stayed at Celia's house to play. She always asked permission before going to a friend's house to play, but in this instance she would know that her mother would know where she was.

About 4:00 or 4:30 P.M., Margaret felt a slight twinge and called the Oakley house. An older sister answered, and when Margaret asked if Susie Nason was there, the girl said she didn't know any Susie. Celia wasn't home, so Margaret asked the girl to have Celia send Susan home when the two of them returned. Margaret called a little later and another sister answered the phone and said that Celia wasn't due home until 6:00 or 6:30.

Margaret decided it was past time to begin looking for her youngest daughter. She called Don at work and told him Susan hadn't come home, then went to the garage and got out her bike, noting that both Shirley and Susan's bikes were in their usual spots. She rode to the places Susie usually played, and then to areas where she didn't play, even up north to Flying Cloud Isle in the middle of the lagoon. She stopped by the Oakley house and found one of Celia's sisters, who hopped on her bicycle and joined her in the search. The two of them rode around to all the places that Celia played looking for the two girls, with no luck. When they returned to the Oakley house, Celia was there, alone.

"Have you seen Susan?" asked Margaret, a bad feeling beginning to creep over her.

"Susan who?" Celia responded.

"Didn't Susan Nason bring you some shoes this afternoon?"

"Yes," she replied.

"Didn't she stay and play with you?"

"No."

Margaret's heart sank. Something was very wrong: Susie would never stay out this late. She rode home quickly. Don was there, but no Susie. She sent Shirley to a neighbor's house and the two parents renewed the search, Don prowling the streets in the car, Margaret pedaling the neighborhood on her bike. She stopped people on the street and asked if they had seen Susie, and she retraced her daughter's route, knocking on doors. Eventually she found Mrs. Banks on the corner, who told her she had given Susie directions to the Oakley house. By then dusk had settled in. Margaret, weary and frantic, decided to return home and call the police.

The Foster City police and fire departments were combined into a single department of public safety which consisted of sixteen officers, all of whom performed both functions. It was not unusual for a fire truck to respond to a call from a resident complaining about a neighbor's loud party. Most of the calls involved vandalism, shoplifting, or a home burglary. In the fall of 1969, there had been no serious crimes in Foster City; no murders, not even a robbery.

Lieutenant William Hensel was the supervisor in charge of law enforcement on the evening of September 22. Hensel had served seven years as a fireman in Millbrae, a town several miles north, before coming to Foster City, where he had risen quickly in the ranks. When the dispatcher advised him of the call about a missing child, he immediately drove to the Nason home. He knew Donald Nason well. The man had a serious drinking problem and had had several encounters with the law, including one DUI. Hensel first had to rule out the possibility that harm had come to the girl in her own home, or that she might be hiding somewhere in or around the house. He and another officer searched inside and out, including the attic and the yard, and found nothing. Margaret's story seemed to make sense and she said that Don had not been home when Susie left the house to return the shoes. They asked Don to come in the next day for a polygraph test, and he agreed. By the time the two cops left, Don was inebriated.

Hensel drove to the Oakley house and confirmed that Susan had dropped off the shoes and left around 3:15 P.M. He immediately notified police chief Gordon Penfold and put out an all-points bulletin for a missing girl, four feet three inches tall with a slight build, blue eyes and brown hair, freckles across the bridge of her nose, wearing a blue print dress, brown shoes, and a turquoise ring with a silver band. Hensel called in the off-duty officers and they went door to door on the block, retracing Susan's steps. They lost track of her somewhere on Balclutha, not too far from her home.

Lieutenant Hensel soon rejected the possibility that Susan had run away from home. Margaret told him about the upcoming birthday party and said that Susie was also due to begin ballet lessons the very next day, something she had wanted to do for a long time. She was "happy clean through," Margaret assured him. Over time, Hensel would develop a slightly different picture of the missing child. Away from home, Susan was kind of a loner, with only one or two friends. She was self-conscious about her freckles, and other kids at school and in the neighborhood teased her, sometimes viciously. She was an average student and well behaved. The latter point was important: she was not a problem child, she did as she was told, and her parents had told her many, many times not to talk to strangers. Margaret was adamant that Susie would never have gotten in a strange car without a fight.

After a few hours, when he turned up nothing on the block, Hensel returned to the station and, along with another officer, began to organize a major search. He called in the reserve officers, who numbered over thirty, and notified the San Mateo County Sheriff's Office. He focused primarily on Susan's neighborhood, dividing it into grids, and assigning teams of five people to each segment. They began going door to door, searching yards and garages and empty fields. Of particular importance were the many construction sites: a half-finished house, a partial foundation, or a stack of lumber would be an easy place to stash a small body. The edges of all the lagoons would have to be walked, inch by inch.

Hensel called the principal of the school and asked her to meet him at her office. When she arrived, she dug through the records and gave him pictures of Susan and her classmates and the names of her friends. She also called Mary Jane Larkin and asked her if she had any idea where Susan could be. Had she been kept after school? No, Mary Jane said, but she had given Susan permission to take a classmate's tennis shoes home to her.

Mary Jane drove to the school and went straight to the office, where several of the teachers had gathered, and then walked to her classroom and unlocked the door. She went in and looked around, although she knew Susan couldn't possibly be inside. Standing by her desk, she pictured Susan asking her about the shoes, then picking up the sack and skipping out. She went outside with some of the other teachers and poked around in the bushes, a silly thing to do, she thought later, but she had to do something. Finally, she went home, certain she would find Susan sitting at her desk in the morning when the bell rang.

As the cops went door to door, they asked the residents to help in the search and soon more than 100 people had volunteered. Many searchers worried that the girl might have drowned. Across the street from the Oakleys, behind the houses, was a lagoon, and perhaps she had stopped there to play. Neighbors walked the shorelines with flashlights. Others formed long lines and strode silently through the fields, sweeping the ground with their lights, kicking the weeds. Some deputy sheriffs rolled in a huge 360-degree platform light and drove through the fields illuminating the night like a giant firefly. One volunteer crawled into manholes and shone his flashlight down the tunnels and was sliced open by a shard of glass for his efforts. Neighbors organized to comb the parks and the school grounds.

As the night wore on, Hensel stayed in touch with the Nasons. Don continued drinking and eventually crumbled and began crying. Margaret, revealing a deep inner strength, held together and assisted in whatever way she could.

Some of the volunteers were convinced Susan would be located quickly: a call would come that she had been found asleep in the bedroom of a friend's house. But by the early morning hours, those hopes had dimmed substantially. Finally, at 4:00 A.M., the majority of the volunteers were released and asked to report back at 8:00. Some stayed and searched through the night on their own.

News of the disappearance spread fast in the tight little community, and by morning Foster City was bustling with a myriad of efforts to find Susan. More than 100 people gathered early at the public safety department to resume the search, and others simply linked up with their neighbors and walked the fields and parks by their houses. Wherever people went that morning, they looked on top of, behind, and under everything they saw. The sheriff's office sent over bloodhounds, and their handlers, after holding pieces of Susan's clothing to the dogs' noses, loosed them in the vacant lots and the parks and along the shorelines. One dog showed considerable interest in a spot along the lagoon across the street from the Oakley house, returning to it time and again, but turned up nothing. A team of divers from Hamilton Air Force Base arrived and began diving the lagoons close to the Nason house. A Coast Guard helicopter skimmed the waters and hovered over vacant fields, looking for recently disturbed dirt that might indicate digging. Small boats patrolled the waters of the lagoons. Searchers were assigned to scour the entire island, and by midmorning more than 200 people had joined in.

The fire trucks were backed out of the garage at the public safety building and parked on the street, and long tables were set up and plates of food laid out for the searchers, creating a strange picniclike atmosphere. Neighbors converged on the Nason household with baskets of food and offers of assistance. Rumors swirled that Susan had been found in Central Park Lake and that she had been seen riding on the back of a motorcycle with a tall blond man. Workers at the nearby racetrack were suggested as likely kidnappers. Crazy calls flooded the police department, several of them from angry wives pointing fingers at suspicious-acting husbands.

The police found several people who said they had seen Susan after she set out on her errand. Sharon Fuls, a blond fourth-grader who lived up the street from the Nasons, and a friend had been riding their bikes up Balclutha to Sharon's house when they saw Susan walking in the same direction on the sidewalk, carrying some sort of paper in her hand. The two girls used to tease Susan, probably because she was so tiny and shy and had so many freckles, and as they rode by they yelled something like "Na-na-na-na-na!" Then they rode to Sharon's home, put up their bikes, and roller-skated on the sidewalk in front of her house.

Sharon's mother was standing in front of her house a short time later when she saw Susan walking on the other side of the street. She called over to the child and invited her in for a cold drink. Susan said no, she had to return some tennis shoes to Celia Oakley and then go right home.

A few minutes after Sharon and her girlfriend began roller-skating, Mrs. Fuls was overcome by a strange feeling that something very bad was happening close by. She called the girls and told them to play in the backyard, then went into the kitchen where she could keep an eye on them from the window.

At 4:00 P.M. that afternoon Annette DeNunzio was standing in the front window of her house on Matsonia watching for her interior decorator. She noticed a little girl with blond hair walk by and turn up the walk to the Oakley house. A short time later the same little girl walked by in the opposite direction. As the girl passed in front of her window, Mrs. DeNunzio saw a blue station wagon with cardboard boxes piled in the rear window driving by in the same direction. A man in a yellow shirt was behind the wheel.

By late afternoon, as the island was covered and the likely possibilities eliminated, people began to sense that, whatever had happened to Susan, she was most likely no longer on the island. The realization that their haven had been violated by the worst sort of crime, a child-kidnapping, began to sink in and reverberate throughout the community.

When Susan was not at her desk in the morning, Mary Jane Larkin decided to treat it as a simple absence and penned an "a" by her name. Her mind kept wandering back to the last time she had seen Susan, and each time the scene played the same: it had been Susan's idea, not hers, to take the shoes to Celia, and, even though she had approved the errand, she had insisted that Susan go straight home first. The detectives came and talked to Mary Jane after school and she explained to them about the shoes. It unsettled Mary Jane when they asked her for a sample of her handwriting.

Susan's disappearance seemed to frighten some parents more than their children. In many homes the next morning moms and dads sat their kids down and lectured them about not getting into strangers' cars. From now on, the youngsters were never to walk anywhere without a buddy. There would be no more playing in the vacant fields and they should always stay in view of a friendly neighbor's door.

Other parents didn't want to alarm their kids by painting a picture of death for them at such a young age, at least until they knew what had happened to Susan, so they warned their children to be careful and assured them that she would probably be found.

In the beginning, some children didn't comprehend all the commotion. Susan was just somewhere she wasn't supposed to be and she would be in real trouble when they found her. Others internalized their parents' fears and became terribly frightened for themselves: they connected her disappearance with the Zodiac killer, the serial murderer on the loose in the San Francisco area; or they became convinced that a monster lay coiled under their bed or in their closet ready to jump on them while they slept. One child visualized Susan hiding in the garbage can outside her bedroom window.

Residents formed prayer groups to ask for the little girl's safe return. The Safeway store kept platters of food on the tables at the firehouse for the searchers. The FBI was called in for consultation. The Nasons sent Shirley to San Francisco to stay with her grandparents.

The police interviewed and re-interviewed the neighbors, but Lieutenant Hensel decided against questioning the children directly; he was worried that policemen in uniforms might scare them. Instead, he asked the school to have the teachers talk to the children to see if they knew anything.

The case hit the media that afternoon. TV stations showed a color picture of Susan on the evening news and the *San Mateo Times* carried the disappearance as their top story with the headline: FEAR FOSTER CITY GIRL IS VICTIM OF KIDNAPPER. Beneath it ran a picture of Susan, her hair neatly parted, bangs curling over her forehead, a slight gap between her front teeth.

The founder of Foster City offered a reward of $1,000 for the safe return of the girl. Donald Nason's employer pitched in with an offer of $10,000 for information leading to her safe return, and within a few days his offices had become a hub of activity, with employees calling radio and television stations up and down the peninsula, trying to keep the story alive and Susan's picture on the evening news.

Margaret and Don began to cling to the theory that a childless couple had kidnapped their daughter and that she was safe and sound in the couple's home, possibly in another state. One sighting had Susan in New Jersey. TV cameras and reporters converged on the Nason home. A distraught Margaret went on camera and pleaded for her daughter's return: "Please bring her back," she said softly into the camera, "please bring her back."

As the days passed, frustration began turning to despair.

Police reported they had run down more than 200 leads but had not come up with "a damn thing." One official opined helpfully that the only way to keep kids from getting in a stranger's car was to brainwash them. Margaret Nason kept insisting that Susie would have obeyed her instructions not to go with strangers, but finally admitted to one reporter that her daughter loved dolls and animals and someone with a kitty and a good story could probably entice her into a car.

Ann Hobbs, a classmate of Susan's, told the police a startling story. The previous Friday she had been approached by a man in a blue station wagon in front of the school. The middle-aged driver was wearing a suit and had "a large nose that was pushed in on the side and turned up in the front" and "ears that stuck out beyond his head" and "brown hair with white showing in the edges." The man had gotten out of his car and said he knew her parents and offered her a ride home. Ann could see mud on the floor and a pistol lying next to the pedals. When he opened the rear door, Ann saw several dolls on the seat: one or two were new, a few had scratches on their faces, and one had a broken arm. Also on the rear seat lay a white sweater, and cardboard boxes were piled up in the windows. Ann Hobbs ran home.

On Wednesday the *San Mateo Times* ran a story on this lead, and Don Nason's employer printed a flier with the now-familiar picture of Susan, her description, and a notation about the blue station wagon. The flier was distributed by volunteers up and down the peninsula. Lieutenant Hensel began running blue station wagons through the Department of Motor Vehicles.

By the end of the week, the police abandoned the search of the island and concentrated on the possibility of an abduction. Hensel kept six men on the case and began checking the register of convicted sex offenders, calling them one by one and making them account for their whereabouts the previous Tuesday afternoon. Cops staked out the neighborhood and noted the cars driving by between 4:00 and 5:30, then called each of the 100 owners and asked them if they had seen anything out of the ordinary on September 22.

In an interview on Friday, the day before her daughter's birthday, Margaret, wearing white glasses with pointed rims, her brunette hair puffed into a bouffant, tearfully held up for the cameras the dress she had sewn for Susie's birthday party and begged whoever had taken her to bring her back. She graciously thanked the many people who had helped in so many ways in the past few days: those who had prayed for Susan, walked the fields looking for her, brought food to their house, dropped by to offer comfort, even mowed their lawn.

Hopes were raised the following week. Two girls in Belmont, a nearby community, were accosted by a man in a blue station wagon, and they managed to get his license number. He checked out as Aaron Patterson, an illustrator from San Jose, and he matched the description of the man given by Ann Hobbs. Ann identified him from a photograph and Patterson was arrested and his house searched. In a lineup a day or so later, the two Belmont girls picked him out, but Ann didn't. The cops tried fervently to tie him into the Susan Nason case, but he passed two polygraph tests, and they couldn't place him in Foster City.

Five or six psychics called the police and offered their assistance in finding Susan. Each one came over to the Nason house and handled a piece of her clothing or a toy. One lady held a blouse of Susan's to her forehead and closed her eyes and then pointed on a map to a dump just north of Half Moon Bay Road in the mountains. Another used a darning needle and a piece of yarn to pinpoint the girl's location at a lake south of Foster City. Hensel and Morgan took them all seriously, and the cops went charging off to whatever place the psychic indicated, always without results.

For a brief moment, the horrible ordeal looked like it might be over. On September 30, the Nasons received a letter demanding $30,000 for the safe return of their daughter. In words cut from a newspaper, the sender threatened to cut off Susan's fingers one by one and mail them to the parents if the ransom wasn't paid.

Kidnapping for money had always been considered an un- likely possibility, since the Nasons were not wealthy, but Margaret and Don were euphoric: they believed they were going to get their daughter back safely. Even the cops were hopeful. Don Nason was instructed to put the cash, which his employer had provided, in a sack and drop it off in the doorway of a tavern in San Francisco. On the appointed day, Don drove to the spot with an agent hiding under a blanket in the rear seat. The cops had staked out the tavern with cops dressed as garbagemen and bums. Don put the money in the doorway and left. The sack lay untouched for hours. Finally, one of the cops instructed Don to return and pick up the money, but somebody forgot to tell the cops in disguise what was going down. In a scene from the Keystone Kops, Don picked up the sack, returned to the car, and a garbageman in wing-tipped shoes rushed him and slammed a gun up against the side of his head. The agent under the blanket, thinking that either the kidnapper had shown up or Don was being robbed, popped up, jacked a shell into the chamber of his shotgun, and stuck it in the face of the agent/garbageman. Numerous other cops sprang from their hiding places, guns drawn, and only at the last instant did someone realize that all of them there were good guys. Donald Nason was severely shaken.

The alleged kidnapper sent a second note, saying he had spotted the disguised cops and giving new instructions for a drop. This time, Don, wired for sound, went alone. As he was walking away from the drop, he saw a man approach and pick up the sack. He spoke into the mike, and the cops converged and arrested the man. Although he was indeed the note-sender, the cops soon determined that all he knew about the Susan Nason case was what he had read in the newspaper.

As the days and weeks passed and autumn deepened, the cops continued checking out leads. They methodically ran down each and every incident involving a missing child or child molestation in Northern California for similarities and continued to interview and interrogate known sex offenders. The officers went to the school and talked to the kids about safety and strangers. Residents established a block parents program: silhouettes of a man and woman in the front window meant the house was a refuge and that a child in trouble should run to the door and ring the bell.

The Nasons still clung to the image of their daughter safely in the home of a disturbed couple.

4

October 31, 1969

I<small>N THE WEEKS SINCE</small> S<small>USAN'S DISAPPEARANCE,</small> F<small>OSTER</small> City had tried to get on with life. People still talked about the missing Nason girl, but with less intensity and frequency. Susan wasn't discussed in the classroom; the kids seemed to go on about their lives and Mary Jane Larkin continued to write an "a" by her name every morning. But her absence was a presence. Parents' patrols were still watching children walking to and from school. One little girl was scared every time she went outside her house alone. Walking on the sidewalk, she would hear the sounds of a car pulling to a stop behind her and take off running through the yards as fast as she could go. She saw blue station wagons at every corner. "Officer Bill" came to the school and talked about cars and candy and strangers so often that some kids began calling all policemen "Officer Bill."

One day Donald Nason decided to look for his daughter himself. He and a friend followed Half Moon Bay Road through the foothills and up to the lakes in the watershed, thinking that uncivilized country might be a likely spot. The two men parked not far from a pulloff overlooking the lakes and hiked around in the hills for several hours looking for her.

Margaret ran into Kate Franklin, a neighbor's daughter who lived around the corner on Harvester Drive, and mentioned to her that no one had come over to play with Shirley since Susan had been missing and she was lonely. Kate gathered her sisters Janice and Eileen and went over and played with Shirley.

Donald Nason's employer increased the reward from $10,000 to $20,000 for the safe return of the girl and the conviction of her kidnapper.

The cops kept looking for the stranger who had penetrated the territorial sanctuary of Foster City: the fiend who had wandered down from San Francisco or across the bay from Oakland and either talked or dragged Susan into a car. They continued to work the known-pervert files and check on other missing child cases and to follow up on leads, but got nowhere. In Pacifica, a small town north of Foster City, a small boy who had a habit of wandering away from home disappeared again and the papers started covering the cases in the same article: "No Clues to Missing Youngsters." As the weeks, and then months, went by, Lieutenant Hensel stayed on the case full-time, still expecting, for some reason, to find Susan alive.

THE PENINSULA WIDENS GRADUALLY AS IT DESCENDS FROM SAN FRANcisco to San Jose and the temperature warms just as gradually. San Jose can bake in dry heat while San Francisco shivers in chilly fog. In the middle of the thumb, around San Mateo and Foster City, the weather is nearly Mediterranean: bone dry in the summer, occasional rain from October through May. During the summer months the cool air rolls in from the Pacific and collides with the warm air from the valley to create a dense, dark fog that blankets the coastline and occasionally slides up and over the mountain range and down to the edges of the bay cities. Some days, the fog will spill down Half Moon Bay Road to Crystal Springs Lakes and soak the huge stands of cypress trees until they shed quarter-size drops of water into puddles on the pavement. In the fall, when the valley has cooled off and the fog has receded, the days in the mountains are usually crisp and sunny.

Crystal Springs Lakes lie in the middle of a spectacular, near-pristine wilderness area. The high ridge of mountains running down the peninsula forms the western edge of the San Andreas Valley, which was condemned in the early 1900s for use as a catchment basin for the peninsula. Dams and reservoirs were constructed and the valley was flooded, creating a

15-mile-long, 23,000-acre watershed. The watershed was turned into a game refuge and placed off limits to the general public. The lakes, which sit on top of the San Andreas Fault, shine like elongated sapphires in the rolling green hills.

Few people knew the watershed like Ephe Ray Bottimore. At six feet five inches and 208 pounds, the pleasant, soft-spoken Bunyanesque figure had thick arms and large hands and walked with a lumbering gait. His great-uncle and father had been watershed keepers and Bottimore grew up in a house on the north end of the preserve. He went to work there himself shortly after World War II and raised his family in a house on the edge of the south lake.

Bottimore's job, along with the other nine keepers, was to patrol the watershed and make sure everything was OK. He checked the level of the reservoir every morning, then jumped in his pickup and drove the back roads, checking fences and spillways and running off hunters and fishermen. He loved to park his truck and roam the wilderness for hours. Some of the other keepers called him "the Snoop" because he was so curious.

Bottimore had read about the disappearance of the Nason girl and watched it on TV, and the cops had been out looking around the watershed several times in the past two months, once or twice tromping along behind psychics who claimed they knew where the body was, but they hadn't found anything. Bottimore wasn't exactly looking for the little girl, but he had a suspicion and he was definitely keeping an eye out for her.

Maybe he was suspicious because he had found seven or eight corpses in the watershed over the years. Once, after he spotted a car unattended by a gate for several days, he started snooping around and eventually noticed a purse hanging on a snag by the water's edge. He called the sheriff, and the divers came out and pulled the body of a little girl from the shallow water. Her mother later floated to the surface in the north lake. He learned that the woman and her husband had been fighting over the custody of the little girl. The cops figured the mother and her daughter had driven to the lakes and parked and walked down the hill right into the water.

In the 1950s, Bottimore noticed an empty car parked on the roadway over the dam and stopped to investigate. He found a polished wooden cane hanging on the railing, and down below he saw an elderly man fully dressed in his summer suit and Panama hat and glasses floating face up in the water. Another time, a black man had been murdered in the area and the police were convinced his body was somewhere on the watershed. After the cops gave up their search, Bottimore began looking himself and finally found the man halfway down a remote hillside. He had slid down from the top and wrapped around a tree.

The morning of December 2, 1969, dawned clear and bright, and Bottimore was up and about early, policing his preserve as usual. Around ten o'clock, he was heading down from the ridge on Half Moon Bay Road toward the lakes when he decided to turn into a pulloff on the south side of the road just at the bottom of a tight S curve. The pulloff, about a mile and a quarter up the hill from the lakes, was large enough for two or three vehicles and people frequently parked there because the spot provided a spectacular, panoramic view of the valley. Standing on the edge, he looked down the hillside and over the south lake, which was embroidered with dark green cypress groves. Up the hill, the coastal oak grew twisted and bent from the ceaseless efforts of the strong winds sweeping down off the ridge.

People also stopped at the pulloff to go to the bathroom and dump trash. A narrow trail led down from the lip of the pulloff through the coyote shrub and poison oak and was always littered with beer cans, milk cartons, and paper bags. Over the years, people had pushed a variety of appliances and furniture over the edge; two cars had even made the journey. The trail ended in a small clearing, which was obscured from the road by the brush.

Just as he had done on countless other occasions, Bottimore decided to walk down the trail and look around. The leaves of the ubiquitous poison oak bushes had fallen off, making it easier to see the ground. He stopped and glanced over at a box spring not too far from an old stove. He had seen the spring before; it was an old-timer, a simple wooden frame enclosing rusty coils, the kind that probably had never had any material on it. Brush was piled on top of the frame, which lay at a 45° angle to the ground. Years ago he had spotted a rattlesnake right in that same spot. Bottimore had never paid the box springs any mind before, but today he walked over for a closer look. He leaned over the frame and through the coils and the brush he saw a small brown skull with a hole in the side. A chill shot through his body. He could tell the skull was human and guessed it was a child's. Probably the Nason girl. There wasn't much left of her, but he looked closer, and when he noticed bones and pieces of multicolored material that looked like a dress, he figured it was her for sure. Without touching a thing, not even the brush, Bottimore walked back up the trail and radioed his office and told them to call the sheriff's department.

A sheriff's deputy was on patrol in the area when he received the call to go to the pulloff. When he arrived, Bottimore led him down the hill and pointed to the box spring. Beneath the brush, the deputy could see the badly decomposed skeleton of a young girl. She was lying on her left side, with her left leg drawn up under her and her right foot outstretched. A white bobby sock was on her left foot, and a brown shoe lay near by. Beneath the multicolored material covering her torso was a pair of denim cutoffs. Her head was devoid of flesh and hair, exposing a black hole on the right side of her skull behind her right ear. What little flesh remained on the bones was discolored and mummified. A small dental retainer lay in the dirt. Not far from the skull sat a large rock.

Like Bottimore, the deputy had little doubt as to who lay under the spring. He also knew that when the press found out, they would come charging up the hill and invade the crime scene. He decided to stay off the air. He climbed up the slope to his car and drove a half mile up the hill to Skylawn Memorial Park and used the phone inside to call the detectives in the sheriff's office.

Soon, other officers arrived and their cars crowded onto the pulloff. Criminalists began surveying the crime scene and collecting evidence. A photographer took pictures of the undisturbed body beneath the springs. Then the body was uncovered and placed in a canvas bag and carried up the hill.

Ephe Ray Bottimore watched the bag being loaded into the ambulance for transportation to the morgue. The chill that had taken hold of him earlier had dissipated, and now he felt very sad. He thought of his own two daughters and tried to imagine what the girl's parents would soon be feeling. At least they would finally know what had happened to their little girl, which would be some sort of a relief. He left the scene in order to make more room on the pulloff for the cops and also to collect himself. He went home for lunch and told his wife what had happened.

5

DR. PETER BENSON HAD GRADUATED FROM YALE Medical School in 1958 and completed his residency in pathology at the University of California in San Francisco in 1962. He went to work immediately for the San Mateo County Coroner's Office, and was still employed there as a forensic pathologist on the afternoon of December 2, 1969, when he was called to the hospital to perform an autopsy on the remains of a white female child.

Benson performed his task carefully and methodically, describing in detail the various items of clothing: the multicolored dress, which had stains consistent with blood or tissue fluids, the denim cutoffs, the white underpants, the white sock and brown buckle shoe. While removing the A-line dress, he found hidden in the folds of the material a small rock with blood and hair on it and a fingernail attached to a clump of hair. The body was skeletonized, but a small amount of dried and hard tissue remained on the arms and legs and the right hip area, which showed signs of bruising. He estimated the time of death as some three to six months earlier.

He noted the injury to the skull: a dumbbell-shaped defect above and behind the right ear, measuring approximately two by five inches, with fracture lines radiating away from the edges. The defect had irregular contours and appeared to be the result of a severe blunt trauma, perhaps caused by two blows. In his opinion, either the small rock or the large rock found close by could have produced the injury.

The body's right hand was severely distorted. The convex contour of the hand had been flattened, leaving it almost concave. The back of the hand also showed tissue damage, and several of the long metacarpal bones as well as one wrist bone were missing. The tips of all four fingers were gone and some of the bones of the index, middle, and ring fingers were missing. Benson had two possible explanations for this damage: Either insects and animals had been attracted to the hand because of the damage and the animals had carried off the bones, or the animals had simply done the initial damage themselves and then taken the bones. The fact that the left hand was intact and showed no signs of damage suggested the former possibility. Certainly the condition of the white metal ring on the middle finger of the right hand supported the conclusion that the hand had suffered injury. The petal-like oval setting in the center was empty and distorted and the underside of the band was flattened, as if it had been resting against something hard when the setting was smashed. A small, undamaged ring with four blue stones was on the left hand.

The location of the injury on the right rear of the skull and the damage to the right hand and the ring suggested the possibility that the hand had been injured while being used in a defensive or protective manner. The location of the skull injury also suggested that the girl's head was bent downward when the blow was struck.

A detective from the sheriff's office was present for the autopsy, as was a photographer who took color pictures of the remains. The detective noted that the stitching on the dress appeared to be homemade. Susan's dentist arrived around 5:30 P.M. with X-rays and a plaster mold he had made of her mouth for the retainer. He examined the skull on the table and found marked similarities between the teeth and the X-rays and mold. A second dentist was called in, and after examination and consultation, the two dentists made a positive identification of the corpse as the body of Susan Nason.

Gordon Penfold, the Foster City chief of police, had been called to the autopsy. Gathering up the two rings, a piece of the dress, and the panties, he drove to the Nason home on Balclutha in Foster City. Margaret Nason immediately recognized the material and her stitching on the hemline—she had bought the fabric in Lake Tahoe and made the dress herself—and said the panties looked like Susan's. The crushed silver ring with the missing stone had been a gift from Susan's grandmother. Shirley had received an identical ring which she was still wearing. There was no question in anybody's mind now that the body found up in the hills overlooking the lakes was Susan's.

Don was at the office working on a big contract due to close the next morning when Margaret called him and told him of the policemen's visit. The blood drained from his face and he turned to a co-worker and said: "They found Susan."

The papers played the story big the next day. On the front page the *San Mateo Times* ran the familiar gap-toothed photo of Susan and a picture of a deputy at the pulloff on Half Moon Bay Road. The paper also carried pictures of Susan's family: Margaret, in her bouffant hairdo, sitting on a couch, looking down forlornly at a doll and two stuffed animals cradled in her arms; Donald, slender and stern, standing beside his wife, his arm resting on her shoulder; Snoopy, the family poodle-dachshund, sitting contentedly on the floor. Donald told the media that he had always hoped that his daughter had been kidnapped by someone who wanted a little girl. Then he broke into tears.

"It seems like you warn them so many times," he said, "but it is just not enough. It seems to go in one ear and out the other. They probably think parents should warn them about important things, not trivial ones."

Margaret also accepted responsibility for her daughter's death.

"I guess all mothers warn their daughters because they were once little girls and just about every girl is approached by some kook at some time," she told reporters. "I guess I just didn't warn Susan enough."

Since the body had been located in unincorporated San Mateo County, the sheriff's office had primary jurisdiction, although the deputies and the Foster City police worked together the first few weeks. At a press conference on Wednesday morning, December 3, the day after the discovery, the police revealed that Susan had been found lying at the bottom of a thirty-five-foot embankment under a partially overturned mattress and that she had died from a skull fracture, possibly from a three-pound rock found nearby. The papers noted additionally that a ring and a brown buckle shoe and white sock had been found close to the body. The sheriff opined that the body must have been carried or thrown to the spot where it was found. Chief Penfold exhibited a piece of Susan's red, green, and blue print cotton dress for the reporters. A local TV station ran footage of Ephe Ray Bottimore standing on the pulloff looking out over the lakes and gesturing in the direction of the clearing.

A captain in the San Mateo Sheriff's Office took charge of the investigation and ordered a thorough search of the crime scene on Thursday morning. The team, which included Lieutenant Hensel, scoured the area and collected everything within five feet of where the body had lain, including the box spring, a hubcap, beer cans, barbed wire, bottles, and several bone fragments. The cops also collected soil and rock samples and picked up broken pieces of brush. Then they shoveled all the dirt within an immediate radius of the body through a box with a wire mesh screen, coming up with several more bone fragments. Sunglasses and a house key were found further away. A deputy supervised a search of the pulloff and the roadway by three inmates on the work furlough program. One inmate came up with several items of interest: a blue chambray work shirt, a green fur-lined cap, and a green one-quart bottle, all spotted with what appeared to be blood. Several deputies came up with cases of poison oak.

The cops told the reporters they had found several interesting objects at the crime scene, but wouldn't say what they were. An assistant sheriff mentioned the rock found in the dress and cited it as support for the theory that the body had been dragged to the spot. For the first time the papers reported that the ring on Susan's right hand had been smashed.

The cops responded to all the calls and checked all the leads. One man called and reported that he had seen a fellow parked in a Toyota Scout near the turnoff the night Susan disappeared and that three weeks later he spotted buzzards circling the area. A gravedigger at Skylawn cemetery reported that on the evening of September 22 a man had approached him in the cemetery with a gun. Comparisons were made with a case in Florida in which a little girl had been killed in the same manner. Police asked local hospitals and clinics to be on the lookout for people who had sought treatment for poison oak. Foster City police announced their continued adherence to the theory that a child molester had come into the community, enticed Susan into his car and taken her off the island and killed her.

At Hensel's request, the coroner severed Susan's right hand from her body. Since several of the fingers were missing, Hensel wanted to be able to match the hand with any fingers an alleged kidnapper might send in. The hand was placed in a jar filled with formaldehyde and placed on a shelf in the evidence room of the Foster City Department of Public Safety.

RING TELLS MUTE STORY OF STRUGGLE, one headline blared on Saturday morning. NASON GIRL FOUGHT AT HER GRAVESIDE, cried another. The captain had laid everything out for the press: The silver ring had been smashed from an oval shape into an elliptical shape, he said, indicating that Susan had placed her hand over her head to protect herself from a blow with a rock.

"It appears as if she tried to struggle and defend herself," the captain explained. "It looked like she struggled as her assailant beat her over the head. It took some force to bend the ring the way it was." He also told reporters that they had found the missing setting stone, a small topaz, close by where Susan had lain, indicating that perhaps she had been killed at her grave site.

"THANK GOD THEY FINALLY FOUND HER," THOUGHT MARY JANE Larkin when she heard the news. She stopped writing an "a" by Susan's name and began leaving the space blank. For the Nasons, the waiting and the wondering were over. No more question marks about where she could be, no more looking for her in the malls, bushes, parking lots. The parents who really suffered the most, Donald would realize, were those whose child was never found: They could never let her die inside themselves.

Many parents told their children of Susan's death at the dinner table. A few youngsters had heard a rumor at school that Susan had been thrown over a cliff and smashed her head on a rock. Some reacted very little, perhaps because in their minds she was already gone. Others felt a renewed terror.

Ephe Ray Bottimore kept snooping around. He was immune to poison oak, and since most of the deputies weren't, they asked him to keep an eye on the site and notify them if he found anything. A few days after Susan was found, Bottimore came across a rat's nest not far from the body. Knowing how rats pack things away, he kicked it open, and found a piece of carpeting, a rag, and a license plate. He turned the items over to the sheriff's office and they ran a check on the license plate, but nothing came of it.

One of the psychics had led the Foster City cops to a dump down a road only half a mile up the hill from the pulloff. The spot was so close that Hensel ran a check on the lady to determine where she had been on the night of September 22.

On several of the arched bridges in Foster City, somebody painted the words "I killed Susan Nason" in large red letters.

THE FUNERAL FOR SUSAN NASON WAS HELD DECEMBER 9, ONE WEEK after her body was found, seventy-seven days after she was killed. A minister from the Seventh-Day Adventist church performed the service. In addition to the family, seventy-nine mourners attended, including a four-man honor guard from the Foster City police. Donald Nason's boss served as a pall-bearer. Mary Jane Larkin, the school principal, and one other teacher attended the service and sat together in the rear of the small chapel. Mary Jane, who had heard about arsonists returning to the scene of the crime, kept an eye out for anyone out of the ordinary.

Outside, Lieutenant Hensel and another officer sat in their police car and also looked for anybody who seemed out of place and meticulously jotted down the license plate number of each vehicle that pulled into the chapel parking lot. They noted without interest the license plate of a tan Volkswagen van.

The brief service was, for Mary Jane, almost unbearable. The chapel seemed so small and dark, and the white casket at the front, surrounded by beautiful flowers, so tiny and doll-like. She cried and shook throughout the service. She couldn't imagine the pain the poor Nasons must be feeling. On the way out of the chapel, the three wobbly teachers leaned on each other for support.

Skylawn Memorial Park, just up the hill from the gravel pulloff, straddled the spinal ridge of the coastal range. To the east, you looked out over scrub-covered hills and down to the lakes, and, if the sky was clear, you could see to the curving shoreline of the bay and the edge of Foster City. To the west, the silvery Pacific Ocean spread out to meet the sky. A "view lot" looking out over the Pacific was considered the most desirable and was therefore the most expensive. The cemetery had donated a view lot for Susan. The wind streaked in from the ocean, blowing relentlessly up the hillside, even on sunny days. In the summer the cold fog hung on the ridge like a wet shroud for weeks on end, immune to the staggering wind, obscuring the light.

But December 9 was a sunny day. Few mourners had made the trip from the chapel up the hill past the gravel pulloff to the cemetery. Hensel sat in his squad car noting license plate numbers. Men's ties whipped over their shoulders and women's dresses flattened against their legs as the minister intoned the final words and Susan Nason was lowered into the ground. People left shortly after the brief ceremony, the rough wind, if nothing else, discouraging them from lingering. The Nasons went home to an empty house; perhaps they weren't aware of the custom of mourners visiting the family after the funeral, or perhaps people simply couldn't handle any more.

Margaret Nason wrote a note to the people at the cemetery thanking them for their many kindnesses. For a few moments, she told them, as she stood on the sunny, windswept ridge overlooking her daughter's grave, she felt closer to heaven.

A marble stone was later inscribed and laid at Susan's head:

SO SMALL, SO SWEET, SO SOON
Susan Kay Nason
1960–1969
Forever in Our Hearts

Margaret and Don would leave Susan's room undisturbed for years.

6

November 22, 1989

AFTER THE WOMAN ON THE PHONE HAD GIVEN INSPECtor Etter the name of the victim, he immediately contacted Marty Murray, a deputy district attorney and experienced homicide prosecutor, and brought him up to date. Murray contacted Bob Morse in the sheriff's office, and the two of them sat down and listened to the tapes of Etter's phone calls. They noted with interest the hesitation and fear in the woman's voice. She did not sound like a kook, a woman on some mission of vengeance or destruction.

Morse remembered the Susan Nason case—he had been a patrol cop in Menlo Park when it happened, and it had come up occasionally over the years—and when he heard the tapes, his juices began flowing. He could tell the truth from bullshit when he heard it, and what this woman said sounded a hell of a lot like the truth. The next step was to check the evidence, see what remained after all this time and how it stacked up against what the woman said, so he stopped by the desk of his partner, Bryan Cassandro, and told him they might have a hot lead on a twenty-year-old unsolved murder. Morse and Cassandro knew how the tasks would be divided: Cassandro would handle the physical evidence and Morse would deal with the woman and her husband.

Cassandro figured there was a good likelihood that the evidence in this case had been thrown out or misplaced over the years—it had happened before—so it was with some trepidation that he went to the property room to see what remained. A quick look revealed that several of the storage bags had disintegrated and the tags had fallen off many of the items, but, to his surprise, most of the actual evidence appeared to be there: the A-line dress, the two rocks, a small brown shoe, a white sock, a plastic vial containing a small, distorted silver ring, a pair of underpants, and the autopsy photos. He could easily re-tag and re-bag all of the evidence.

Cassandro and Morse went over the evidence and the old files carefully and their excitement grew as they realized that the woman's story matched the evidence: Susan had been found in a wooded area near a lake on a road to Half Moon Bay; her skull had been crushed with something like a rock; the top of her right hand been smashed as if it had been raised in a defensive gesture; Susan's body had been hidden under a mattress.

Morse reviewed the coroner's file carefully, to see if the woman might have pieced together her eyewitness account by reading newspaper articles of the murder. But the article in the file made no mention of a damaged hand or a bent ring or a mattress. That did it for Morse: the only way the woman could have known of these items was if she had witnessed the crime. She had to be telling the truth. He reported his finding to Marty Murray, and they both waited anxiously for the next phone call.

For Morse and Cassandro, this could be the case of a career, but putting the facts together and proving the case would be difficult and tricky. First they had to convince the woman to give her name; without her they had nothing more than a bunch of boxes of evidence and twenty-year-old files stacked on their desk. She was obviously quite shaky and Murray and Morse were very worried that she might be scared off. With what they now knew, the matter had become even more urgent. Murray and Morse were ready to take over from Etter.

The first call of the day came at 1:35 P.M. Murray and Morse were waiting in Etter's office.

"Hi, this is 'Mrs. Barry' calling!" the woman said when Etter answered.

"Hello, Mrs. Barry, how are you today?"

"How did it go, did you get anything?"

"We did, and I am personally very excited about it. And very seldom do I get excited."

"Excited, and you seldom get excited!" the woman exclaimed. "Wait a second, Barry, why don't you get on the extension. My husband wants to hear this, okay?"

"Okay."

"But you're not, I don't want you to give me any details or anything that would impair my memory in any way, that would make me an invalid . . ."

"We're not—we're not going to do that."

Etter told her she had to have been an eyewitness to the murder.

"What!" the woman exclaimed.

Etter said that Martin Murray, their top prosecutor, was in the room and was very interested in the case. He would be handling it and wanted to talk to them.

Murray, in his calm, sober manner, sought to assure the woman that her family would not be exposed to the killer if she came forward. The cops would not contact the suspect until they had definitely decided to prosecute him. They would divulge her name only after they had launched an effort to put the man in prison, and they would charge him with first-degree murder, which would mean a minimum of twenty years.

The woman insisted on knowing if she had told Etter anything that wasn't public knowledge.

"What I can tell you," Marty responded, "is you have told us things that in my opinion only a person who saw the crime would know."

She was either there, Murray explained further, or the person who committed the crime had told her the details.

Murray told them he was assigning the best cops available to the case. Leading the investigation would be Detective Sergeant Bob Morse, the most experienced homicide cop in the county. A police officer for over twenty-five years, Morse had investigated more than 200 homicides, many of them "body dump" cases from San Francisco, and he hadn't lost a witness yet. He had even solved one case where he began with nothing but a skeleton that had been laying out in the woods for two years.

Barry and his wife continued to express concern over their own safety, worrying that the cops would contact the suspect and that he would come after them.

"We're not foolish enough," Murray said, slightly exasperated, "to jeopardize you or to jeopardize a lawsuit or false arrest claim, unless we're pretty well convinced that we're gonna win it. Okay?"

"Okay, what do you want me to do now?" the woman said suddenly.

Murray said he wanted to send two police officers down on the Saturday after Thanksgiving, to interview her.

Barry began to agree, but the woman panicked.

"Wait, I need to think about this for a minute. These are gonna be police officers?" she asked, clearly worried.

"Well, yeah," Murray scrambled, concerned that he might have blown it, "they are police officers, but they're plainclothes detectives; they don't operate in uniform. They look like businessmen."

"I have a general distrust of police officers," she explained. "I'm afraid. Not from anything I've done, I just don't like them."

The woman then said she would like a few minutes to think about the Saturday visit. Murray didn't want to let her off the phone without getting her name and address, but she refused, insisting that she would call back in half an hour.

"Okay," Murray agreed. "Can I do one thing? Can I have you talk to Detective Morse for just five minutes?"

"Sure," Barry agreed.

Murray had played his ace and Morse was ready for the play. He knew that in every murder case convincing the witnesses to trust you, to believe that you weren't going to bleed them and leave them hanging in the wind, was critical, just as was convincing them that victory was inevitable. This situation was a little trickier than usual, but he would go about it naturally, intuitively, the way he always did.

"Look," he began after introducing himself, "I've been working for the county sheriff's office for seventeen years. I've been doing this a long time. Way over two hundred homicides."

The woman was clearly impressed and Morse moved in quickly.

"We've never lost a case, I'm telling you that flat out. Check it out, you'll find it's true.

"We have a good reputation," he continued easily, smoothly, "and you can ask any lawyer, any judge, or any district attorney around here: we have never lied to anyone, I have never had a witness intimidated or hurt, we have never once ever burned somebody in the newspapers or not kept our promises. And, from my point of view on this, now, you know I'm not a lawyer, but I've worked with these guys on hundreds of cases, believe me, this sounds like a case this guy is going to prison on."

Like a good salesman, Morse schmoozed the husband and wife a little, telling them how intelligent and impressive they were, then he pushed forward.

"Let's get going on this guy," he urged. "Let's put him in prison. The safest thing for you is for us to get this guy and book his butt right into jail."

"I agree," replied Barry, warming to Morse's approach.

"Don't worry about the killer getting out and coming after you," he assured them. If bail was set at all, it would be astronomical: bonds in the amount of five to ten million dollars were not uncommon in San Mateo County. Barry liked the sound of those figures.

But still the couple wanted to talk by themselves.

"We do everything we can possibly do [for our witnesses]," Morse pressed. "We care about you, we honest to God do."

"Okay. Etter told you what I told him on the phone yesterday?" the wife asked.

"Yes."

"And you believe that I was an eyewitness to this?"

"Absolutely," Morse shot back. "There's no question in my mind whatsoever that you were present there."

Like a good therapist, Morse assured them they would feel a lot better once they came forward with the details.

"Here's the approach I like to use, you guys, okay? And I'm not B.S.ing you here, okay? We use the team approach. All right. We're a team. We operate like a team. Marty's the quarterback. We're the players, all right?"

"Yeah," agreed Barry.

"You know, we're good friends to have, but we're really shitty enemies."

"Good," Barry said, starting to sound like a one-man audience at a revival meeting.

"Okay," Morse continued, "and we know what we're doing, and we got a lot of influence and a lot of friends, and believe me, no matter how much money this guy's got, we got more. No matter how many friends he's got, we got more."

"Yeah, I hope . . ." Barry began, but Morse cut him off.

"We're more powerful than he is. He wouldn't make a pimple on our butt."

"All right," said Barry.

"Okay," said his wife, promising to call them back in a few minutes after she and her husband talked about it.

Morse knew they would call back. The husband was sold, he was sure of that, and he sensed that he had a lot of influence over his wife.

THE PHONE RANG AGAIN AT 2:35 P.M. ETTER PICKED IT UP.

"Hi, this is Eileen calling."

"Irene?"

"Eileen."

"Eileen. And this is Mrs. Barry?"

"Yep."

"I see. Eileen, what's your last name?"

"It's hyphenated, it's Franklin . . . hyphen Lipsker."

"Eileen, thank you very much, we certainly appreciate that. What's your birth date?"

"Eleven twenty-five sixty. So, they have to say Happy Birthday to me on Saturday."

After obtaining her address, Etter passed the woman back to Morse. He made arrangements for Saturday's visit, then quickly went after one more fact. He did not want to wait until Saturday to find out the name of the murderer. If she gave it up now, she couldn't back out later. He wanted to speed things up a little, he explained to her, to get their computer working on the case. Would she give him the killer's name? Eileen passed the phone to Barry.

"Okay, you want the information now?" Barry asked.

"No, I just want his name so I can start the computer background information."

"Okay, but you're not going to contact him until you're sure you got a case?"

"You have my word of honor."

"Because, otherwise, we're . . ."

"You have my word of honor."

"His name is George Franklin . . . It's her father."

Morse reassured Barry again, relying on his football analogy: Drop back ten and take it easy. Nobody was going to let them down. The team was going to kick some butt. The team was going to get her father off the streets and in the slammer.

Barry offered one last piece of information: Another person had witnessed George Franklin pick up the little girl and she wanted to testify.

"Oh well, that just put the cherry on the cake right there," Morse said.

ONCE THE WALL CRACKED, THE DAM BURST. EILEEN CALLED MURRAY a few hours later and volunteered that the other witness was her sister Janice. She had been in the van that afternoon and her father had made her get out when they stopped to pick up Susan. Her father had beaten her mother, she continued, and sexually abused two of her sisters, and once he had held her (Eileen) down while a black man raped her in exchange for drugs. She hadn't reported the killing until now, she explained, because her father had threatened to kill her. The information she was giving them about the killing now was a result of therapy she had undergone in the past twenty years.

7

THE FRANKLINS WERE ONE OF THE FIRST 100 OR SO families to move into Foster City. In 1964, George and Leah bought a just-completed, four-bedroom, single-story house at 678 Harvester Drive. Like the Nason house around the corner, the main entrance to the house was through a two-car garage, which opened onto the street. There were no street lights, the only trees consisted of twigs tied to sticks, and dirt swirled across the street from the vacant lots, but the house was still a definite step up from the Franklins' previous house in San Mateo.

To a casual observer, the Franklins might have seemed a typical family in the new community. The parents were young, with five children, and probably had the same dreams for the future as everyone else. George, the father and a fireman in San Mateo, was a burly and boisterous man, good-looking in a rough sort of way with a big smile and bushy reddish-brown hair that sprouted like an afro. His wife Leah had long black hair and well-defined features. On the heavy side, she wore scant makeup and favored long dresses that fell to her ankles, similar to those of the hippies in Haight Ashbury. Some of her extra weight was undoubtedly due to having had five children in six years.

Kate, the first child, was born in June 1958, when her parents lived in San Bruno. Her hair was dark brown, almost black, like her mother's, but it was thick and wild like her father's, and her eyes were a soft sea green. Kate was a quiet, serious child, her mother's favorite.

Next came Janice, born in June 1959. She had brown eyes, glossy chestnut hair, and sharp features like her mother. Janice was a spirited child, a rebel and mischiefmaker. Then came Eileen, born in November 1960, a cute little redhead, a surefire attention-getter, and always Daddy's favorite. George Jr. followed in March 1962. He had woolly blond hair but not the stocky build of his father. As the only boy, George was always under the gun. Finally came Diana, born in June 1963, a redhead like her older sister Eileen, whom she idolized. Very shy, Diana was the baby of the family. George and Leah would later tell their children that they had kept having babies because they wanted a boy. After Diana, who was supposed to be Andrew David, George had a vasectomy.

A closer look at the family would have revealed small differences from their neighbors. George, unlike other fathers, wasn't around home much. Coming and going, he would greet his neighbors with a wave and a hearty hello, but he wasn't a part of the community, not a Lion or a Scout leader. Part of the reason was undoubtedly his schedule as a firefighter. He worked in twenty-four-hour shifts beginning at eight in the morning and he painted houses with other firemen on his days off. He also worked on the fire truck at the Belmont racetrack and occasionally sold life insurance. When he was home, the tan Volkswagen van was in the garage, and neighbors would see him loading cans of paint and ladders into it on his way to a job. His van was easy to spot because of the Confederate flag on the rear bumper. Leah drove a newer, red Volkswagen van.

To some neighbors, Leah didn't seem to be around much either, although she was. She raised her kids differently from the other mothers in the small community; she appeared to almost turn them loose and let them run wild and fend for themselves. They would come around to a neighbor's house with their long frizzy hair and messy clothes to play or have milk and cookies, and while they were always polite enough, they often had runny noses or dirty faces and their table manners were atrocious. Leah didn't seem to know where they were from one hour to the next. Kate, the oldest daughter, looked after them; she was in charge of their comings and goings, herding them home in time for dinner, breaking up their fights. Leah, who seemed awfully young to have so many children, was often at the library or at home reading.

The Franklin residence was different as well. George and Leah had painted the outside a medium brown with chocolate trim, giving it a definite masculine tone. The yard was messy and full of weeds. While others in the new community were busy landscaping their lawns, planting grass and trees and evergreen bushes, the Franklins let their lawn grow wild. Some exasperated neighbors even talked about cleaning up the Franklin yard and planting some bushes in it themselves.

Inside, the house was dreary. The furniture was large and heavy and tattered from the abuse of five kids. The rugs and drapes, also dark, were usually closed. The house was often a disaster. In the kitchen, dirty dishes were piled high in the sink, pans sat on the stove, and the floor was unswept. Sewing projects were stacked up on the kitchen table. Clothes and books and papers were scattered throughout the living and family rooms.

Two families came to know the Franklins better than most. Tom and Maureen Poeschel met George and Leah in 1960, when the two men had worked together in a Safeway. In those days, a family could just get by on a grocery clerk's wages, particularly if he earned premium pay by working evenings and weekends, which George did whenever he could. Tom found the bushy, red-haired George to be a likeable guy. He was gregarious and had a sharp wit, and played the down-home, beer-drinking southern boy to the hilt. He would refer to himself as a typical southern red-neck shit-disturber and talk about how you should save your Confederate money because the south was going to rise again. A couple of times when he returned from a trip to his hometown in Virginia he brought back moonshine in Mason jars and passed it out to a few of his friends.

But George kept people at a distance. You never knew what he was going to do or say; he enjoyed shocking people, arguing for the sake of arguing, and he would embarrass you in front of other people just to get a reaction. George also had a damn short fuse. Some little thing would bug him and he would turn beet red and explode. George had no use for blacks. He was always calling them dumb niggers this or dumb niggers that. He could also be really crude. The high school was just a few blocks away and the sixteen- and seventeen-year-old girls came in after school for candy and pop, and George would constantly try to hustle them, making smart, suggestive remarks. If anyone objected, George would grin and say in his cocky way, "Hell, I'm just a good old boy from the south who doesn't know any better." On occasion, George would brag about his female conquests.

George treated his family poorly, particularly his children. They acted like whipped puppies around him. If one child made a noise and he yelled, they would all freeze in their tracks and wait to see what happened next. And they never talked back or sassed him. The boy, Georgie, seemed to bear the brunt of his dad's anger. George would yell and call his son stupid and take a swipe at him with his foot as he walked by. Since Georgie was his only boy, you might think he would do things with him, like Little League or Boy Scouts, but he didn't. Georgie seldom played with the other kids and was sometimes dressed absurdly in bib overalls.

In all the years Tom knew Leah, she never looked him in the eye when they talked. If he said something to her—regardless of the topic or where they were—she would look away, off somewhere, as if she wasn't listening, but he could tell she heard him because she would eventually respond. It seemed like she didn't want to be exposed to the world's eye.

When Maureen Poeschel talked to Leah, she didn't look away as she did with Tom, but she did something equally as odd: she closed her eyes. Some people shut their eyes for a second or two while talking to collect their thoughts, but when Leah closed her eyes she kept on talking. She would open them for a few seconds, then close them again, and keep them closed for several more minutes while she finished her thought. Maureen wondered if she was trying to shut something out, or to avoid something unpleasant inside herself.

George made no secret of his feeling that the role of women was to keep house and raise children. He talked down to Leah as if she were just a dumb broad and Tom never saw any affection or rapport between the two of them. Leah was usually at home, which was one reason Tom couldn't understand why the house was always so dark and such a mess.

Financially, George looked after his wife and kids. Tom sold him his first life insurance policy and, over the years, sold him two more. George believed in security for his family and always kept his policies paid up.

When the Franklin children came over to the Poeschel house, they always seemed a bit downtrodden. The girls weren't well dressed or well kept, and were not as perky and lively as other kids their ages. Eileen, the older of the two redheads, particularly seemed to be unhappy, often standing around by herself, eyes downcast. They were very well behaved, obedient children, except that the boy was sometimes naughty. Kate, the dark-haired girl with the discernible Irish cast to her pretty round face, seemed to be doing the best of all the children. She was very poised and always happy to stop and chat with you.

The Franklins reminded Denise, the oldest of the Poeschel children, of the Addams family; the girls in their homemade dresses and long frizzy hair and the mother without any makeup, always wearing Birkenstock-type sandals, her dark hair falling loosely down her back or pulled back in a ponytail, and the boy, an outsider who tried to act tough but couldn't pull it off. Denise went to the Franklin house only once, and she didn't like it; the place seemed tiny for so many people, and it was dark and smelly, as if it needed to be aired out.

Denise didn't want to play with the Franklins, and when she had to because they were at her house, she was too embarrassed to tell her friends about it. (She played with Susan Nason a couple of times, usually when her mother, who was a Brownie leader with Susan's mother, sent her over on an errand, but she wouldn't admit that to her friends either.) Freckle-faced Eileen was withdrawn and homely and her red hair was always messy, as if her mother had neglected to brush it in the morning. Although Eileen went on the Brownies' field trips and to day camps and made crafts with the rest of the girls, she didn't really fit in. Janice didn't have the wild hair, but she thought she was really cool. She wore lipstick and smoked in the bathroom in the sixth grade. Most of the kids stayed out of Janice's way. One time the boy Georgie wet his pants at school and his mother had to bring dry clothes to him. The kids teased him and he got in a fight and the other boy chipped one of his front teeth. Kate was different from her siblings. She was pretty, almost exotic-looking, and artsy. She seemed very sure of herself, as if she knew who she was and where she was going.

RON MUNIER WORKED IN THE SAN MATEO FIRE DEPARTMENT WITH George Franklin, and his wife Fay gave lessons in ballet, modern dance, and jazz in a studio in her house. The Franklin girls were among Fay's first students when she opened the studio in 1965. First Kate and Eileen attended, then Janice came for a while, and finally Diana joined. Although the Franklins lived only a few blocks away, Leah drove her children to and from class three or four times a week, showing up in her red VW van full of kids, and she almost always stayed to watch her children practice, rather than dropping them off as many mothers did. She seemed to enjoy her girls, and was very relaxed and patient with them. Kate, who looked so much like her, was her special joy. Kate had always been called Cathleen until one day before class, Leah announced proudly that the two of them had decided the night before that from now on she would be called Kate.

Leah never missed a performance and she sewed all of her girls' costumes beautifully. Fay never had to call and ask Leah about the slippers or the tutus; if the program called for four changes of costumes, Leah had four costumes ready.

Fay had met Leah when the two families lived around the corner from each other in San Mateo in the early sixties. They served together on the women's auxiliary for the fire department and traded baby-sitters and went shopping for sewing materials. Leah would say that she liked to sew because it was the one thing she did that stayed done. She was dumpy then, and her children were a little wild, but she tried hard and did her best. Leah's life wasn't easy: in addition to five kids, she handled the books for a rental property and took in sewing to make ends meet.

Fay and Leah had begun attending the College of San Mateo in 1963, soon after Diana was born. Leah was obviously very intelligent and determined to complete her education. If the class she wanted was full, she would walk down the hall until she found another one that appealed to her. She always seemed to be up, looking at the bright side of life. Although Leah never talked about her personal life, Fay knew there were problems at home and she wondered about Leah's ability to isolate them, to wall them off. It was almost as if she had a shut-off valve.

All the Franklin children, except one, seemed to have a place in the family. Kate, beautiful and talented, was her mother's helper (she had helped toilet-train Diana). Eileen was the red-headed pixie, full of energy and an attention-getter, although she definitely had her morose, pouty side. George, who didn't dance, was the only boy among all the girls. Diana, not quite as cute as the others and a little pudgy, clung to her mother. Only Janice, who had long, slender arms and legs, seemed to have somehow slipped through the cracks. She didn't enjoy dancing and seemed to move about in a shadow.

George Jr. was always on the social periphery. He kept to a very small group of friends. Fay's daughter, Bonnie, liked him in a way, but she would never have gone out with him. She appreciated his sense of humor, although at the same moment she would be laughing at one of his frequent and horrendous puns, she would be saying *Oh God!* to herself. The Tom Waits quotation under his picture in the high school yearbook—"I'd rather have a bottle in front of me than a frontal lobotomy"— was typical George.

The other kids knew that George wet his bed, even when he was eight or nine. Often you could smell the urine-soaked sheets when you walked by his room. They teased him about it —one time they were playing soldier with garbage can lids and sticks and George spit on a girl because she had called him a baby and a bed-wetter—but he still wanted to play with them. The Franklin children burned incense in the house, perhaps to cover up the smell.

HEIDI WAS THE ONLY GIRL IN A FAMILY WHO LIVED ACROSS THE street from the Franklins. Her mother didn't like Heidi playing with the Franklin kids—she thought the family too odd—but Heidi loved the adventure. They made army forts in a vacant lot and watched television and rode bikes and played house. Heidi learned about sex from the Franklin children when she was nine. She had been told nothing at home, and the Franklin girls explained to her that the girl has this and the boy has that and this was how you did it. One afternoon she played house at the Franklins' and George was allowed to play because they needed a man. Janice was the director and she decreed that Heidi and George were married. Heidi didn't want to be married to George, but she didn't mind as long as they only sat around and drank tea from imaginary teacups.

Then Janice announced that Heidi and George were going

to make babies and instructed Heidi to lie down in the bed and take off some of her clothes and George to lie down on top of her and kiss her. Heidi knew this wasn't right and suddenly she wanted to go home, but the girls told her the game wasn't over and she couldn't leave. They pushed her down and said, "No, no," like it was still a game, and she got scared and cried and begged to be let out of the room. When they still wouldn't let her go, she began struggling and screaming, hoping that their mother would hear and rescue her. Finally, she made it to the hallway and yelled for help. The others pulled her by the hair and called her a crybaby. When she made it at last to the living room, their mother was sitting in the chair reading a book as if she hadn't heard a sound. Heidi yelled at her, "Didn't you hear me screaming?" but the woman still didn't respond. Heidi fled the house in tears. She stayed away for a long time.

8

GEORGE THOMAS FRANKLIN WAS BORN ON JUNE 24, 1939, in Bassett, Virginia, a community of 3,000 people nestled in the foothills of the Blue Ridge Mountains in southeastern Virginia, about fifty miles south of Roanoke. Bassett, the second largest town in rural Henry County, lies scattered along the banks of the Smith River at the end of a narrow valley. In 1902 J. D. and C. C. Bassett started a sawmill in the small settlement, and in a few years the brothers began making furniture from the fir, oak, and pine trees that grew in abundance in the heavily forested, hazy-blue hills. Because the valley was so narrow, the town could grow only along the river, and four-block-long factories and company housing soon stretched out north and south of the community. Bassett was a company town in every sense of the word: residents attended the J. D.

Bassett High School, lived in company housing, worshipped in Bassett-built Baptist churches, and played in recreation centers (one for whites and one for blacks) built by Bassett Furniture. The unincorporated town had no local government, and the police and fire departments were provided by the company.

Bassett was, if not in the deep south, at least in the heart of the old south. During the Civil War the men had fought proudly for the Confederacy and today some of these soldiers' great-grandsons make moonshine in copper stills back in the hills and hollows and occasionally hold Ku Klux Klan rallies under twenty-foot burning crosses in clearings deep in the backwoods. The Baptist religion is woven into the fabric of everyday life in the community. Women frown on cursing, and social and political events are not scheduled for Wednesday night when good Baptists should be in church. There is a Methodist church in town, but Catholics and Jews are few and far between.

George's grandfather, the first George Thomas Franklin, grew up on a farm a few miles south of Bassett in the latter part of the nineteenth century. Originally the farm had been a plantation and George Thomas's grandfather had worked the land with slaves. George Thomas was an ambitious man and he left the farm to begin a road-contracting business. With mules and steam-powered shovels, he carved out hundreds of miles of winding roads in the hilly countryside, connecting farm to farm and farm to market. He was, by all accounts, a hard, rough man, meaning he drove his men and animals to their limits and suffered no opposition and accommodated no weakness. One of his favorite sayings was, "If you kill a mule, buy a new one. If you kill a nigger, get a new one." His workers did what they were told, when they were told.

In his early twenties George Thomas married Maybelle (usually pronounced Mabel) Thomasson, the daughter of a local well-to-do farmer, and as was the custom, they began raising a large family. Maybelle was a heavy woman with a round face and a gentle disposition. She was a Primitive or

"Hard chair" Baptist, a strain that believed in absolute predestination.

Under George Thomas's savvy gaze and heavy hand, his business grew, and soon he amassed enough capital to buy 540 acres of prime bottom land from the Bassett family along the Smith River in south Bassett. He built a large, six-bedroom frame house across the road from the river, which became known as the Franklin home place. George Thomas and Maybelle had nine children, six boys and three girls, and gave them names like Wilda, Neval, Onas, Flick, Easterbird, Orval, and Marant. George Thomas drank heavily—up to a quart of liquor between dinner and the time he went to bed—and he ruled the household with an iron fist. Maybelle was known to be assertive, but at home she was completely submissive to her husband. She told a friend she would never be caught sitting down when George walked came in the house. When she heard a female relative say something back to her husband, she said later that George would have slapped her on the head if she had said that to him. His word was absolute law, and the children lived under that law. The slightest misbehavior could bring a switch or a belt. More than once he lined his offspring up against the wall and whipped them with a belt for no apparent reason. With his indulgence, Maybelle raised her brood in the Primitive Baptist Church.

The Franklins became highly respected in Bassett and Henry County. They were one of the two or three wealthiest families in the area, and George Thomas served for many years on the county board of supervisors, a powerful political position.

Onas Cyril Franklin was born to George Thomas and Maybelle in 1905. Most of the other children managed to make something of themselves, either by working for their father on road construction or going into the service, but Onas was the black sheep. He was unpleasant, meanspirited, swore constantly, and had little regard for anyone else's thoughts or feelings. He also drank heavily and made moonshine in the hills. But as a young man he was handsome, and when he was twenty-six he met Hattie Jarrett, a girl nine years his junior, who had been raised on the old Jarrett plantation seven miles down the road. Hattie was in fact related to Onas: her great-grandmother was the daughter of William Franklin, who was Onas's great-grandfather. Hattie was also one of nine children and she was a pretty girl with dark brown eyes, naturally curly brown hair, and beautiful white teeth. Hattie was a little silly (she could never learn to drive, and when her nephews tried to teach her, she would inevitably throw up her hands and say, "Oh, I just can't do it!"), and she talked a lot (ran on at the mouth, some would say), but she had a good heart and was generally well liked. At seventeen, she hadn't been off the farm much, and she got to know Onas Franklin when he came around with her older brothers. Onas proposed on their first date, and she accepted immediately. She had always dreamed of children and a house with a lawn and flowers.

Hattie and Onas had four children: Virginia Belle, Isis, Annette, and George Thomas, who was named after his grandfather. After three girls Hattie had wanted a boy very badly, and she was ecstatic when George was born. Since so many children in the Franklin family had been named George in honor of their wealthy forebear, young George Thomas was called "George T." As her youngest child and only boy, George T. was always his mother's favorite. She loved all of her children, but she favored her little freckle-faced, red-headed son. She fussed over him constantly and took him with her everywhere. George T. was also close to his sisters, particularly Virginia Belle, the prettiest of the three, who looked after him a good deal.

Onas, who stood around five feet seven inches and wore bib overalls, glasses, and a cap, walked around with a good-sized chip on his shoulder and left little doubt that he thought most people were SOBs. His cold demeanor and rough manner kept people at bay, and he became somewhat of a loner. According to one story, which is legend in Bassett, one night he and another brother picked up a woman and had her in the back of a pickup driving down the road, when Onas got so mad at her that he pushed her out the back and watched as she was run over and killed by a car a few yards back.

The only person Onas seemed to truly care for was his mother, Maybelle, whom he treated with respect and affection. He was attentive to her, stopping by the home place almost daily and talking to her for hours. Maybelle, for her part, seemed to think that her husband was particularly brutal to Onas and she tried to make up for the abuse by giving him extra money and attention.

As one cousin would say, Onas was a drinker, not a worker. His heavy drinking started when his father died in 1936. For a while he drove dump trucks for his older brother Flick, but after Flick died, he was unable to keep a job. Onas bootlegged a little of his moonshine, but most of his energy went into drinking it. As a provider, he was close to worthless; as a father, he was a terror. The children stayed well out of his way, not out of respect, but out of fear. George T. was beaten viciously by his father, both with a belt and a fist. By the time he was in high school, George T. was taller than his father, but he still kept a baseball bat in his room for protection. To some, it seemed that Onas was taking out his treatment by his father on his own family, particularly his boy. Onas took what he wanted when he wanted it; on several occasions he violently forced his wife to have sex with him in front of the children. When the physical abuse became really severe, Hattie would grab the children and flee in the night to a relative's house.

The elder George Thomas Franklin had built a large two-story brick house about a mile down the road from the home place for Onas and Hattie. The family managed to live well because Hattie sold off pieces of the land one by one to cover their expenses. In his will, George Thomas left substantial sums of money to each of his children. When the money and the land were gone, Maybelle helped out Hattie and her family financially. She well knew the sort of man Onas was ("Don't ever leave Onas alone with the girls," she once warned Hattie), but as a mother she couldn't see him abandoned, and she made Hattie promise not to leave him, at least until after Maybelle had died. In exchange, Maybelle promised Hattie that she would take care of her and the children as long as she lived.

In the afternoon, Hattie could be seen in a pretty dress and makeup walking her boy down to the home place to visit Grandmother Maybelle. George T., always a little heavy, was, to appearances anyway, a mama's boy, perhaps because there was little choice. He clung to his mother, and often seemed to prefer her and his sisters' company to that of the neighborhood boys. Maybelle, seeing the way Hattie fussed over him, said to her one day, "Why Hattie, he's just your little flower pot." Soon, George T. became known as "Hattie's Little Flower Pot." Hattie spoiled her only son: whatever George T. wanted, George T. got, and when he would harass or hit one of his sisters or otherwise misbehave, he was seldom scolded or punished. He wasn't a sissy exactly, as much as he was a boy doted on and spoiled by women. When his cousins would run off to ride their bikes or go fishing, he often stayed behind with his mother and sisters. The youngster seemed more comfortable in the company of females.

Sometimes the cousins would gather to spend the night at the home place. According to family legend, there were two ghosts living in the house, Bloody Head and Raw Bones, and on some nights they could be heard dragging their chains across the floor. A favorite game of the cousins was to see if George T., who was terrified by the story, could stay the entire night. After lights were out, the cousins would gather upstairs in one of the large bedrooms, and one would begin telling the story while another dragged a chain across the floor. A third would shine a flashlight on a cardboard skeleton hung on a door as the door was slowly pulled closed with a rope. Despite George T.'s promises, he never made it through the night. Somewhere in the story, he would get so scared that, much to the delight of his cousins, he would bolt from the room and run a mile home in the dark.

For all of the turmoil at home, George T. did not appear to be a troubled or disturbed youngster. To the contrary, he seemed, to his classmates and family, to be an ordinary, happy child. In fact, people remembered George T. as consistently happy, a jolly red-haired kid who was always smiling and teasing others and telling jokes. Some thought him the friendliest of the four children. He did not pick fights on the school grounds, sulk in the classrooms, steal candy from the grocery store, or vandalize houses. He never lost his temper or lashed out in anger. He acted out a little in class, but that was simply due to his boisterous, expressive nature. He loved to pick on the girls, pulling their hair and tickling them, but not in a particularly bullying manner. His favorite time was in the afternoon when he listened to "The Lone Ranger" on the radio. George T. would skip dinner rather than miss the program.

George T. did well in school and was especially interested in Confederate history, which he read extensively on his own. He also undertook to read the encyclopedia, and within a couple of years had read every book in the set.

George T. was never "one of the boys" in high school. Football was the primary school activity and a defining factor in the adolescent social structure. George T. was on the team, but despite his broad shoulders and sturdy legs, he never amounted to much as a player. George T. didn't run with the boys who drank and drove cars and pursued girls, either. In fact, George didn't drink at all in those days, and no one remembers him having a girlfriend, not even a casual date. George T. did kiss the girls, though. He and a friend would approach a girl in the halls or on the school grounds and one would say laughingly, "You hold her arms so I can kiss her," and they would argue about whose turn it was, until finally one of them held her while the other kissed her.

George T. participated in few school activities. Hattie had raised her children in the Baptist Church, so George T. had joined the High Y, a Christian youth group. On weekends and during the summer George T. worked at a lumber yard with one of his cousins. George saved his earnings to buy a red 1940 Ford convertible. When he had enough money, he bought the car with plans to fix it up and drive it to school his junior year. But George didn't attend high school in Bassett his junior year. With little explanation to his cousins, he moved to California, leaving the prized convertible behind.

Maybelle finally passed away in 1956, outliving her husband by twenty years. True to her word, she had provided for Onas's family, including clothes and food for Hattie and the children and college tuition for Isis. Within six weeks of Maybelle's death, Hattie decided to leave Onas and Bassett. Onas was furious when he learned of her plans, so she hurriedly packed up the children and left town. While Hattie and Virginia Belle and Annette headed for Florida, everyone agreed that George T. should go west and live with Isis, who had married an Annapolis graduate and moved to San Bruno, California. He wanted an education and the plan was for him to finish high school and, with his brother-in-law's help, attend one of the military academies.

While the separation from his father had to be a relief for George T., leaving his mother must have been hard. He would later tell his children that his mother Hattie had won a beauty contest as the prettiest girl in Henry County. His father, on the other hand, was the meanest man in the county.

George T. came back to Virginia only for an occasional visit. When Onas died destitute and drunk in a trailer behind the home place in 1975, George and Virginia Belle were the only children who returned home for his funeral.

9

AT AGE FIFTY-FOUR, BOB MORSE HAD TRAVELED A long road to his position as head homicide detective in San Mateo County; the tattoos on his right forearm never let him forget how far. He had carved them in himself with a needle when he was a thirteen-year-old kid growing up in a blue-collar district of San Francisco, the son of a merchant sailor who was at sea most of the time. The ragged blue letters going across his arm said PEP, for his best friend, and PEG marched raggedly down, sharing the E. MOM was stitched across the biceps of his left arm. Morse had frequently walked the wrong side of the line as a youth. In second grade he and an older boy broke into an elementary school and trashed the place; afterwards, he was blamed for all the trouble in the neighborhood. In high school he wore his hair in a duck-tail, hung out with street gangs, and had an attitude that got him in a lot of trouble. He was thrown out of school for smashing a varsity basketball player in the eye and then threatening to knock the gym teacher on his ass if he messed with his duck-tail one more time. After finishing continuation school, where the bad boys went, and thinking about the amount of pain he was causing his mother, he joined the Air Force as a preventive measure.

He completed eight years in the Air Force, during which time he married an English girl and was busted from corporal to private, then returned to San Francisco in 1963. He worked for UPS and drove a bread truck until one day he saw an advertisement for policemen in Menlo Park and thought, "What the hell? It's got to beat peddling bread." Except for being pulled off the Menlo Park motorcycle patrol for twice dumping his motorcycle—he never quite got the hang of a two-wheeler—he did well and made sergeant in three years. He divorced his wife, with whom he had had two children, and soon remarried. To complete his education, he attended the College of San Mateo and eventually received his B.S. from the College of Notre Dame. Looking for a bigger pond, he joined the San Mateo County Sheriff's Office in 1972, where he put in his time on patrol and in the jail before moving to the detective bureau. Once in homicide, it was clear Morse had found a home, and within a few years he had earned a reputation as a thorough, honest homicide dick who never lied or misled anybody. Local defense attorneys respected him as a wily investigator but a straight shooter. Everybody in the courthouse, in local government, knew Bob Morse and Bob Morse stories. He was considered a good guy and a cop who didn't lose cases.

Morse felt that he understood the ordinary citizens of his county and what was important to them. He would speak of San Mateo juries with respect and something akin to affection.

He knew that the cases he and his partner so painstakingly put together would not be tried in front of a panel of San Francisco-esque bleeding hearts. San Mateo jurors were reasonable people who would do the right thing; and so would the judges on the bench. In the fall of 1989, more than half of the judges sitting in San Mateo Superior Court, where felonies are tried, were former prosecutors. Many of them had tried cases investigated by Morse and Cassandro.

SAN MATEO COUNTY IS NOT A GOOD PLACE TO COMMIT MURDER, OR more accurately, to be tried for murder. San Mateo is one of the wealthiest counties in the country, consisting mainly of middle- and upper-middle-class, well-educated commuters. The peninsula offers its residents an escape from some of the big-city problems like large welfare rolls and high crime rates.

The prosecutors in San Mateo County are very much aware of the socioeconomic status and conservative bent of their jury panels. At one time seventy percent of the prospective jurors in the county had indicated that they would have no qualms about imposing the death penalty in appropriate cases, while only thirty percent of the prospective jurors in San Francisco and Marin counties to the north were similarly disposed. The prosecutors also see San Mateo juries as more amenable to convictions based on circumstantial evidence than in other, more liberal counties. Since 1983, ninety percent of the people charged with murder in San Mateo were convicted. Only six or seven murder cases go to trial each year, but of those, only one defendant in ten walks away free. In some circles, San Mateo is known as a "hanging county."

Marty Murray, the assistant district attorney on the Franklin case, was a twelve-year veteran with the D.A.'s office. He was responsible for the presence of two of the eleven San Mateo County inmates on California's death row and very proud of both convictions. Handsome, well dressed, and very straight, Murray has a calm, composed demeanor, belied occasionally by a biting wit. He is extremely methodical and able to express complex thoughts clearly and in straightforward sentences.

Highly respected in legal circles, he has had considerable success in trying first-degree murder cases.

After listening to Etter's tapes, Murray remained skeptical that a prosecution would result. Eileen certainly seemed credible on the phone, quite interesting, really, and so far her story seemed to fit the evidence; but there were many, many problems to overcome, not the least of which was that the crime occurred more than twenty years ago. Still, what she had told them was sufficient to begin an investigation, and the first step was to talk to her in person. Murray was pleased that Morse and Cassandro were assigned to the case. He knew from past cases that if anybody could get to the bottom of a story, it was Bob Morse. His reaction, and that of his partner, would be pivotal in the initial prosecutorial decisions.

November 22, 1989

After the phone call from Eileen the day before Thanksgiving in which she had implicated her father, Morse told Cassandro they needed to go to Canoga Park to talk to her in person. Cassandro set about making the plane reservations, renting a car, and locating a map for directions to Eileen's house. Bryan Cassandro was the sort of person who knew everything he was going to do the minute he woke up in the morning. Cassandro went about his tasks methodically and planned his moves meticulously. If he and Morse intended to interview a witness across the bay in the morning, Cassandro came to work carrying a map with the route to the person's house highlighted in yellow and the house marked in red. The witness's phone number and address would be printed neatly on the bottom. Although Morse was a sergeant and head of the unit and Cassandro still a detective, they worked together as equals. Each did what they were good at, combining their strengths and compensating for their weaknesses. Cassandro's mind and memory for details were balanced by Morse's intuitive feel for a case.

Morse would conduct the interview with Eileen, not only because he had established some rapport with her, but because he was the lead detective on the case. He would ask the questions and Cassandro would keep track of the answers and fill in what Morse missed. The two cops worked well together, and had, for example, developed an excellent good cop, bad cop routine: Morse would storm from the room during an interrogation, swearing that he had been lied to for the last time and was finished screwing around with the bozo and he was on his own now; Cassandro, who had been sitting there silently, his blue eyes staring intently at the suspect, would say, "Jesus, you just pissed off the wrong guy, you're in bad trouble now. We still might be able to do something, but you got to be straight with me." The two were proud of their confession rate, which was, by all accounts, impressive.

Cassandro remembered the Nason case. He had been a rookie cop in the patrol division of the sheriff's office when the little girl from Foster City disappeared and was later found near the reservoir, but he hadn't thought of her for years—there had been no new leads since he had become a detective. He had skimmed the reports before their trip but he hadn't studied the case from beginning to end. There would be plenty of time for that if they decided to pursue George Franklin.

Cassandro had to admit that he was somewhat apprehensive about the woman's story. Why had she come forward now? What the hell had she been doing with this information for twenty years?

10

IN THE SUMMER OF 1956 GEORGE MOVED IN WITH HIS sister Isis and her husband in San Bruno, a blue-collar community across the highway from the San Francisco airport, and began his junior year at a large public high school. His mild southern drawl drew some teasing from his classmates, and he made a point, in his loud boisterous way, of his background: he was, by God, a rebel from Virginia. George was friendly and outgoing, but being a new student in a large school he had little impact. His only activity was football. He made the team as a reserve guard, but as in Bassett, he didn't play much.

Although George had never met his grandfather, he had heard as a boy how hard he had worked and how successful he had been. He would tell friends that his grandfather had made a lot of money, but his worthless father had blown every cent of it. George seemed determined to emulate his grandfather and demonstrate that he was more than a drunkard's son. If he couldn't get into a military academy, he would go on to college somewhere else.

George began working after school and on weekends as a bagger at a supermarket in Burlingame, just south of San Bruno. After a few months he noticed a woman and her attractive daughter, who was usually dressed in the brown uniform of Mercy High School. The mother thought the young bagger, with his reddish-brown hair and broad shoulders, was cute, and one afternoon, after she had passed through his line and left the store, she mentioned him to her daughter. The daughter went back in the store and picked up a pack of gum and passed through his line again. Much to her delight, the bagger put the gum in a sack and carried it to the car for her. She gave him her phone number.

Leah, the eldest of three daughters, was born to Leo and Marie DeBernardi in 1940 in San Francisco. Leo, a post office worker, was Italian Catholic, and Marie was English-Irish. When Leah was ten, the family moved to Burlingame, a middle-class community with a large Italian Catholic population. The DeBernardis lived in a small white house with yellow shutters and closely trimmed hedges. Our Lady of the Angels Catholic Church, with its stark steeples and gold and turquoise dome, dominated the neighborhood. Leo and Marie were died-in-the-wool, toe-the-line Catholics who adhered rigidly to their strict beliefs. (Janice would later mockingly remark that her grandparents undressed in the dark and slept in separate beds.) They raised their daughters in the same tradition and sent them all to the parish grammar and high schools.

Leo was very quiet—it was rare to hear him speak at all—and remote. According to some, he was not a giving person, not a father who hugged his kids or otherwise demonstrated affection for them. His role in the household was as provider and disciplinarian. While Leo worked at his postal job in San Francisco, Marie stayed at home, cooking and caring for the children. She played the organ in the church, and the family attended mass once during the week and again on Sunday.

The lives of the three DeBernardi girls revolved around the family and the church. Their parents stressed education, particularly reading, and books were everywhere in the home. All three girls were smart and did well in school and all were expected to go to college. Jean, the youngest, was the smartest and her mother's favorite. Susan, the middle child, was the prettiest, or at least the most vivacious; she certainly attracted the most boys. Leah and Susan were extremely competitive, and their mother seemed to encourage their rivalry. In front of Leah, Marie would say how cute Susan was and how well she had done in school. Seldom did she ever lavish the same praise on her oldest daughter. More than once she punished Leah for crying by locking her in a dark closet. The two sisters disliked each other intensely and carried the animosity into adulthood. Leah, the least favored daughter, was an unhappy child.

Leah attended Mercy High School, a Catholic girls' school on the grounds of the Sisters of Mercy Convent. Mercy held joint functions, such as sock hops and proms, with two Catholic boys' schools close by. Kissing for more than a few seconds was wrong, and "going all the way" was a mortal sin, although there always seemed to be one or two girls each year who left school pregnant, bringing great shame on their fathers' names.

In her high school yearbook picture, Leah was neither attractive nor unattractive. She wore her dark hair short, allowing a few locks to fall over her forehead, and she had a long graceful neck and oval mouth. But her eyes slanted downward slightly at the outer corners, giving her a sad, almost melancholy, look.

One classmate remembers Leah harshly: "Poor dear, she was very homely and unpopular. We never saw her parents. She was very alone. Leah never went to dances or football games. We were mean to her. By that I mean we just ignored her. But also she just wasn't *present,* she just *wasn't there.* She was a big girl and she always wore her blouses buttoned up to her neck and her skin was bad. I wouldn't have any idea what her arms looked like. She had a pointed face with lips that were always tight and pursed together."

Other, more charitable classmates remember Leah as average-looking and recall that while she was never in the most popular group, she had friends. Of one thing there was no dispute: Leah was easily one of the brightest students in the class of sixty-five girls. She was always very alert and well prepared in class. She was considered to have great potential, and everyone assumed that she would go on to college. (For her part, Leah didn't particularly care for Catholicism or Mercy High; she would say that she learned more on her way to and from school than she did at school.)

Leah did have dates, although her boyfriends were usually from the public schools. For a while, she was going out with a boy from South San Francisco, then suddenly, in the middle of her senior year, she announced to her best friend Kay Ballard that she had met a new boy and fallen in love. His name was George Franklin and he went to public school in San Bruno. He was a handsome boy who laughed a lot, she said, and had an easy, natural charm. Although at seventeen Leah was a year younger than her new boyfriend, she would graduate in the spring of 1957, a year ahead of him.

Leah's family had been proud and her friends envious when she was awarded a prestigious math and science scholarship to Lone Mountain College, a Catholic women's college in San Francisco. They were all quite shocked when she announced one day that she was going to get married after high school. Kay and others tried to change her mind—she was so smart and would do so well at Lone Mountain, they told her—but she was adamant: She was in love and she was going to get married and that was final. She seemed happy, and she and

George did make a lively, attractive couple, but Kay began to notice that George seemed to have some sort of influence over her. She had been so determined to go to college, to live up to her parents' expectations, George must have somehow changed her mind.

It was an odd match, this burly, smiling eighteen-year-old Baptist redneck from Virginia and this reserved, seventeen-year-old Italian Catholic girl from California.

Kay Ballard was dating a young man named Stan Smith during this period. In July they received an invitation to a dinner party at the DeBernardis' in celebration of George and Leah's engagement.

The happiness and goodwill all came to an abrupt end in October when Leah announced to her parents that she was pregnant. The DeBernardis were horrified—such things just did not happen in good Catholic families. There was only one thing to do: George converted to Catholicism and in November the couple was married in the rectory of Our Lady of the Angels Church.

Marie was severely disappointed in her oldest daughter. Later she would mention in front of Leah that her sister Susan had made the right choices in her life; rather than getting pregnant like her older sister, she had kept her head and gone right on to college.

The relationship between the DeBernardis and George deteriorated quickly. George had no use for their religion, their values, their heritage, anything about them, and he let his feelings be known. The sentiment was mutual: he was tolerated at family occasions as Leah's husband, the father of her children, but her family resented his sulking behavior and arrogant attitude. Susan was bothered by Leah's submissive behavior toward him. George figured his in-laws thought they were better than he was. He would get even in later years by cutting his wife off from her family and forbidding his children to visit their maternal grandparents.

The newlyweds lived in San Bruno while George attended high school and Leah prepared for her baby. On June 25, 1958, Cathleen Victoria was born. George's dream of attending a military academy had evaporated, but on November 4, 1958, he joined the Marine Corps Reserve, 7th Infantry Battalion. After six months of training, he served in the Reserves as a rifleman and radio operator, winning a promotion to corporal, and was discharged in January 1965.

After the marriage, George continued to work in the produce department at the grocery store and took courses at the College of San Mateo, finally earning enough credits to obtain his high school degree in 1961. At the store, he became acquainted with the chief of the San Mateo Fire Department, who had also worked in the store as a youth. The chief talked George into taking a test to become a fireman, and in March 1961, George joined the San Mateo Fire Department as a probationary employee.

FIREMEN LED A GOOD, ALBEIT DANGEROUS, LIFE. THEY DIDN'T GET paid much, but they had good perks, such as four days off in a row to go fishing or work other jobs, crisp blue uniforms that attracted the girls, and the respect and gratitude of the community. Firemen would say they had two families: one at home and one at the station. On their shifts, they slept, ate, and worked together. Hours of boredom could be interrupted in an instant by a call to a raging second-story structural fire where a man's life depended on the skills and courage of his mates. Though not as tightly knit as cops, the families of firemen socialized together, gathering on weekends for baseball games, picnics, and dances. Wives and kids stopped by the firehouse on holidays with presents and food.

In this completely male milieu—while you couldn't come to work drunk, it was macho to come to work badly hung over—the ultimate question was: How are you in the crunch? Where're your guts? George Franklin quickly earned a reputation as a solid firefighter, a man not afraid to be the first in the building with an ax or a hose. When it was time to fight fires, George was there. He was capable, strong, and aggressive. Because of that, a lot of other characteristics could be overlooked.

It was impossible, however, to miss the huge chip on

George's shoulder. Beneath the boisterous, good ol' boy, slap 'em on the back attitude lay a deep, swirling anger that could erupt at the slightest provocation. One fireman made the mistake of giggling when he and George were bidding on a painting job, and afterwards, as they were walking from the house, George flared at him: "You stupid bastard! You can't do things like that! You have to keep an image!" George loved to tease, but he couldn't take it himself. Although he would make fun of his background, he didn't see the humor when his fellow firemen teased him about being a rebel from Dixie or imitated his southern accent.

Arrogance permeated George Franklin's attitude. In the view of some firemen, George thought that because he read a lot of books and knew a lot of thirteen-letter words he was smarter than the next guy. He was extremely opinionated on everything that came up and, while he might listen to someone else, in the end, the way he saw things was the way they were. If you disagreed with him, or challenged him, he would cut you up verbally. His words dripped with contempt if he thought you were a candy-ass.

Not that George couldn't be likeable. He had a gift of gab and could really bullshit and spin yarns. Particularly in the early years, there was an easygoing side to him that could laugh at the world and its problems. But there was always the other part of him. He used to say that people who tried to walk the fence ended up with pickets up their asses. You were either on one side or the other; you were either for him or against him. Disloyalty from a friend was unforgivable.

One of George's friends in the department thought that his attitude stemmed from an old-fashioned, deep-seated inferiority complex. All the bullshit, the arrogance, was a cover for what lay buried underneath. George, he figured, was severely repressed. Even that silly grin of his—he would stand in the doorway of the lounge and rock back on his heels and grin at the world, or was it the fools *in* it—was a barrier between you and him, between him and himself.

George worked hard. When he finished a twenty-four-hour shift at 8:00 A.M., he would paint for twelve hours, go home, go to bed, and report for another twenty-four-hour shift in the morning, and repeat the cycle day after day. His family wasn't going to live like Okies, he would say. His children would always have decent clothes and the best medical care and they would receive an education—the one he never received—and make something of themselves.

Leah would occasionally bring the children to visit George at the station. It was obvious that he completely dominated his wife, who, in her long hair and ankle-length dresses, seemed to hover about in the background. He was always running her down around the firehouse, referring to her as "that narrow-minded Catholic dago bitch," or "that Catholic dago slut."

Unlike most parents, George didn't seem to take much pride in his children; he would refer to them as "ungrateful brats" and his daughters demeaningly as "princesses." All the girls could talk about, it seemed to him, was clothes and makeup. He seldom mentioned his son.

When George undertook a project, he pursued it with a stubborn single-mindedness. He had a definite feel for the real estate market, and he was about ten years ahead of his time. In the early sixties the market in California hadn't taken off yet, and George got in the game early. He saved the money he made painting houses and working at the racetrack and bought a house in the shore-view area of San Mateo. He fixed up the place and rented it out and bought another and did the same with it. He was famous for lowballing. He would tell an agent to make an offer of $30,000 on a $50,000 house. If the agent refused to make the offer, George would find one who would. Every now and then he would get the house at his price.

George had no intention of remaining a fireman. He did not seek rank or authority over others, and he never took a test for a promotion. Riding on the back of a fire truck was something he did along the way to becoming a real estate mogul.

George was a controversial character at the station. Some firemen disliked him intensely and wanted nothing to do with him, some liked him and became his friends, and others figured the easiest way of getting along with him was to stay out of his way.

Of those firemen who liked him, it was most often because they looked up to him. George was smart and shrewd and spoke up for himself and didn't take anything off anybody. Bill Mann came on the force a few years after George and liked the older man immediately. Bill was a go-along, get-along sort of guy, and when he ran into his mentor's arrogance and insecurity, he never challenged him. If the two of them were to split a pie, he would tell George to take however much he wanted. George would initially take two-thirds, and then feel badly and split it equally. George did care about what people thought about him, but he avoided rejection by appearing not to care.

George and Bill spent a lot of time carousing and drinking in the early years, but even when he was drinking George seldom talked about himself. He would spout opinions and ask Bill endless questions about himself, but he never revealed what was going on inside him. George saw the world as a hostile place, and he was determined never to show his weak side. A friend today could be an enemy tomorrow.

George was very active in union activities and was, in Bill's opinion, a brilliant organizer. He was relentlessly critical of the administration and its policies and he never hesitated to needle the brass. George belittled those whom he saw as sucking up to their superiors. Under the collar on his blue shirt, he wore a pin that said: "FUCK YOU."

George's moodiness and antagonism settled in as he drank, and his drinking increased steadily. He had a strange habit of drinking one type of drink for a month, and then never having it again. If you offered him last month's drink, a rum and Coke, he would mock you for being behind the times. He would show up at work smelling of booze and looking like hell, but the drinking never seemed to impair his performance as a fireman.

Almost from his first day at work, George became known as the horniest guy in the firehouse. He had an insatiable sexual appetite and was, literally, always on the make. He was compulsively promiscuous and completely indiscriminate. Although his announced preference was for fat women—"Bring me a fat broad!" he would say—any woman would do. Most of George's girlfriends were second rate, at least in the eyes of the other firemen. They joked that George would screw women other guys wouldn't go near. "If the bush rattled, George jumped on it," his fellow firemen cracked. Or, "Crippled, blind, or crazy, they were all the same to George." Or, "Anything between eight and eighty would do for George."

Women usually said hello to a man in a fireman's uniform, and George made the most of their trust. He hit on any woman who came into view. He combined his gift for gab and charm with a redneck crudeness "Are you here to fuck or fuck around?" he might ask a woman shortly after meeting her. "If you're here to fuck around, then hit the road." He would go into a tavern with his buddies and begin at one end of the bar and work to the other, asking each woman in turn if they wanted to fuck. Sometimes he got slapped, sometimes ignored, and occasionally he got lucky.

One afternoon in the mid-sixties he and another fireman were driving down the main street of San Mateo and George ordered his mate to pull over next to an attractive woman in a fur coat walking down the sidewalk. George jumped out, and talked her into the back seat of the car. She turned out to be pregnant, but within a few minutes, he was having intercourse with her.

In another incident, the two men had gone to a house to bid on a painting job. George wandered off to inspect the house with the owner's thirty-year-old daughter. Soon George came into the room puffing and upset. Pulling his partner aside, he explained that he had been having sex in a back room and the woman had passed out on him. "What should we do?" he asked. His partner excused himself, went back and found the woman lying on the floor, just beginning to come around. George had known her less than ten minutes.

One friend theorized about George's indiscriminate sexual behavior: "George would say or do anything to get a woman into bed, and his charm worked on lots of different types. It didn't matter to him what the woman looked like. Any of them were acceptable physically, and none of them were acceptable mentally. All women were cunts. If you see women that way, it doesn't make any difference what they're like. Just as long as they walk or crawl."

This man didn't want George around his wife or daughters. "George," he told him one day, "if you go near my wife or girls, I'll kill you." Rumors circulated in the department that George was sleeping with the wife of one of the chiefs.

Another fireman summed up George's attitude toward women in fewer words: "Women were just holes to George."

George's hostility toward women became more overt when he drank. At firemen's dances, George would have a drink or two and start swearing luridly in front of the wives: fuck this, cocksucker that. At the dinner table at a friend's house one evening, he turned to the wife when she joined in the conversation and barked, "Shut the hell up, who cares what you think!" Another wife whom he had insulted in similar fashion instructed her husband not to bring him home any more.

George could be vicious when teased about the quality of the women he took out. One evening when the taunting began, he silenced the table by saying loudly, "Yeah, I may take those fat pigs out and fuck 'em, but at least I don't marry 'em like you guys do!"

George seldom bragged about his conquests around the firehouse the way some men did. He just went out and screwed the women and let the other guys talk. George didn't show any particular preference for young women or any interest in little girls. He might have had a porno magazine or two in his locker, but none of the firemen he worked with, or later lived with, recalled him showing any sexual interest in children.

Some firemen were amused by George's behavior and attitude. A few were deeply offended. One supervisor was genuinely repulsed by the man. "George was crude, a real asshole," he would say. "Driving down the street, he would make a remark about every woman he saw, regardless of who he was with. 'See that fat chick over there?' he'd call out, pointing. 'I'd sure like to fuck her!' Age made absolutely no difference to him. 'Old enough to bleed, old enough to butcher.' " George Franklin might have been a good fireman, but, in this man's opinion, morally he was down in the sewer with the worst of them.

George did not try to hide his infidelities from his wife. One afternoon he came home and talked Leah into the bedroom and then while making love to her asked if knowing that he had just slept with one of his tenants turned her on.

George also made no secret of his racial prejudice. When he was moving out of his house on Second Avenue in San Mateo, the new renter sent a black mover over with furniture before George was completely moved out. George lost it. "No nigger is coming into my house while I'm still here!" he yelled and the black man, who said he was just doing what he was told, left with the furniture.

George eventually became a serious malcontent in the fire department. He had a hard time with anybody who had authority over him, and he pushed every rule and regulation to the limit. He let his hair grow out into a bushy afro until his hat perched on top. He also grew a mustache, which was against the rules. One of his favorite phrases was "prima donna," which he used for anyone who tried to tell him what to do or thought he was smarter than he was.

His friends could sense the mean streak coursing beneath the surface. He could be intimidating, but he never raised his hand or made a fist, or even threatened to strike somebody. At the station, George relied on his mind to get what he wanted.

11

GEORGE FRANKLIN STRUCK LEAH FOR PERHAPS THE first time in 1963. She was sitting on the couch drinking a glass of wine when he whacked her on the head with the back of his hand. In those early days, the violence was intermittent. After an incident, peace would return and life would go on for weeks or months before he exploded again.

With each baby, Leah seemed to become more overwhelmed by the roles of wife and mother. Her weight ballooned and she took on a blimpy look; her hips broadened, her arms turned to flab, and her face became round as a pumpkin. By the time Diana was born, she was close to 200 pounds and her clothes draped her like a tent.

By 1967, George's anger ruled the household, either through its presence or by its absence. The art of living had become the task of survival. Violence, in a variety of forms, had become commonplace. There were, to be sure, still periods of relative peace and tranquility in the household, just as there were moments of genuine affection between George and his children. In the summer, for example, the family would go to Leah's parents' cabin in Calaveras and George would hike with his children and play with them in the lake, tossing them high in the air and laughing at their shrieks of delight. He shepherded his children to Disneyland and rode on the rides with them. He bought the children bikes and stuffed their Christmas stockings with presents. He could also be romantic and surprise Leah with roses and a negligée on their anniversary. Sometimes on Sunday morning he would get up early and cook a huge breakfast of freshly baked rolls and eggs and sausage, or, if he had been home recently, a Virginia-baked ham. Days, occasionally even weeks, would pass without incident.

But, as Kate would say, you never knew. A tranquil scene could erupt into a hellish nightmare in an instant. Her father would be sitting in his chair in the family room drinking bourbon and Coke and take a dislike to a child's attitude or posture, or become irritated at the squabbling of two siblings, and yell and rap the offender on the head with his knuckles, or, if sufficiently provoked, whip his belt from his pants and lash the back of the child's thighs. Usually you got whacked where you stood, even in front of your friends. Except for George Jr.—he was often taken to his room for special treatment.

No one ever ended up in the hospital, but the children suffered welts and split lips and bruises. If you were ever questioned about the marks on your legs at school, you were to tell the teacher or nurse exactly what you had done to deserve them.

Dinner inside the Franklin household on Harvester Drive was seldom a fun or festive occasion. If George was in the middle of a twenty-four-hour shift, the scene was somewhat relaxed and Leah would serve the kids tuna fish sandwiches or hot dogs. But if George was off-duty, the children were in their seats at the dinner table at the appointed hour and Leah would prepare a hot meal such as a roast with a salad and vegetables.

The family ate together at the large Formica table in the kitchen. If their father was relaxed and sober, the kids chattered noisily through dinner, but when his mood was sour and the atmosphere distorted by the pressure of his barely latent rage, the children waited fearfully for the games to begin.

"Cathleen," her father would begin, his dark brown eyes glaring at her from beneath his heavy brows. He usually began with her, probably because she was the oldest, and at these moments he always called her Cathleen.

"Here we go," she thought, "here we go again. Hold on."

"What did you learn in school today?"

Kate usually had an answer prepared, an anecdote about history, her father's favorite subject, something like, "Today we learned the story of Pocahontas," or, "Today we read the story of Paul Revere's ride." The point was always to keep your answer short and simple and get off the hook as quickly as possible because the slightest miscue could set him off.

Bad table manners could really provoke him. If he caught you reaching for food or chewing with your mouth open, his thick forearm would jerk back and a fork would slice through the air and smack you sharply on the head. Often he seemed to inflict pain randomly, and that was the worst part—you never really knew when you were going to get hit.

If Kate got whacked, she just sat there. She did not say ouch, she did not whimper, or cringe, or raise her hand to her head. To react at all was only to invite more pain. She kept her head down and absorbed whatever came her way.

Around the table George would go, in a grisly form of family round robin, looking for someone to fault, to punish. During Kate's turn, her siblings would sit rigidly in their seats, taut with anticipation, heads down, wondering what to say when their turn came. Diana, who probably got smacked less than anybody, could easily draw his wrath at the table. Even the Irish sheepdog, Benjamin, got his share.

He might turn to you and grill you about something you had allegedly done or failed to do that day. "Your mother told me you were late for school," or, "Your mother told me you were rude to her." You had no hope then because you knew Mom was not going to bail you out.

Sometimes, when several children got whacked in a row, Leah would intercede: "George, that's enough," she would say. He might back off, but usually he would bellow at her, "Leah, don't you ever interfere while I'm disciplining my children!"

When he raged, the children stayed in their chairs, not moving, until formally dismissed. Then they would get up and begin clearing the table and loading the dishwasher and putting things away in the drawers and cupboards until they could slip quietly away.

DIANA, AS THE YOUNGEST, MAY HAVE RECEIVED LESS THAN HER share of abuse, but fear was laid down in her system long before she could talk, perhaps even when she was *in utero*. As a result, she experienced the world through a desensitizing haze. To teachers and classmates, she appeared quiet and painfully shy, and not very smart. She had difficulties in school from the beginning and everyone, including her mother, assumed she had some sort of learning disability. She had minimal social interactions outside the family.

Diana wasn't completely immune. Her father inflicted emotional violence on his youngest child. One afternoon when she was in second grade, he asked her what time it was, and when she couldn't answer he told her he would ask her again when he came home the next afternoon and if she didn't know then he would beat the shit out of her. Under Kate's tutoring, she was able to safely answer him the next afternoon.

When Diana hadn't learned how to tie her shoes, her father again threatened her. She practiced and practiced, but couldn't learn to make the bows, and when he approached her the following afternoon, she was so scared she burst into tears. He ridiculed her for her failure, but did not strike her.

When Diana was five, she walked into the family room without a top on and, noticing her father sitting in his chair, crossed her arms over her chest.

"Goddamn it, Diana," he yelled from his chair, "I'm your father, take your arms down!" He looked mean when he yelled at her; his features were immobile, his eyes dark and cold.

Diana was traumatized by her father's violence to her siblings. On one occasion, he hit George Jr. in the face with his fist and bloodied his nose. Another time he made all the children watch while he beat Janice with a belt as she lay on her stomach on the floor of her bedroom, pinned there by his foot. He lashed her repeatedly, bringing the leather strap down time and again on her flesh, striping her back and shoulders a bright red. Leah intervened (one of the few times, some of her children would later say), and told her husband to stop, and George smacked her across the face and continued whipping Janice. When he finished, he ordered Janice to get up and walk in front of the other children so they would get a good look at the welts and understand that the same would happen to them if they misbehaved. Diana was haunted for years by the piercing, inhuman screams emanating from Janice as she lay on the floor. Sometimes, she would think, life might be easier if she was beaten more herself.

Diana noticed that whenever her parents went out in the evening, her father invariably beat the children when they returned. For no apparent reason, he would take off his belt and line them up against the wall and whip them one by one. Years later Diana would joke that whenever her father was feeling in a sadistic mood, he would say to his wife, "Come on, Leah, let's go out tonight."

At school, Diana simply checked out. She sat in the classroom in a dead fog. At the end of the day, the clanging of the bell pulled her out of the fog and she picked up her books and left, only to slip back into the heavy mist the next morning. She developed a serious reading problem, and her siblings drilled her with flash cards after school.

Diana depended on her sister Eileen. Eileen made sure Diana got up on time in the morning and helped her pick out clothes and get dressed for school; Eileen made sure she had her sack lunch in her hand when she walked out the door; Eileen read to her; Eileen explained things to her and took her every place she went, even with her friends; Eileen looked out for her, protected her. Eileen was her guardian angel.

Diana was happiest when she and Eileen shared a room. If they were separated she would take her blanket and pillow and sleep on the floor by her bed. Diana looked like a miniature Eileen, except that her hair was a deeper, more vibrant red.

IF DIANA HANDLED LIFE IN THE FRANKLIN FAMILY BY WITHDRAWING, Janice handled it with anger. She argued constantly with Kate, her roommate, and fought viciously with her mother. On several occasions, Leah, in an attempt to dissipate her daughter's anger, took her outside and gave her empty liquor bottles to smash against the side of the house. In one of their many battles, Leah hit Janice so hard with a hairbrush that she chipped her tooth.

Janice always stood up for herself. If somebody threw a clod of dirt at her as she walked through the vacant lot on her way to school, she would throw two back. If that didn't take care of the problem, she would lock the offender in the outhouse until he cried. While she had her friends, the more popular girls in school saw her as tough and kept their distance from her.

Janice had memorized her father's schedule and the first thoughts in her mind when she awoke in the morning were, "Where is he today? How soon can I get out of the house? Will he be here when I come home from school?" She would sort through her mind to see where her father was in the shift sequence. If he was coming off a shift, 8:00 A.M., he would be home around 8:15 A.M., and since she left for school no later than 8:30, she would see him for only a few minutes. If he was going on duty, he would leave around 7:30 or 7:45, so it might be possible to avoid him altogether. She dreaded his days off. He would be painting and fixing houses and hanging around the house getting drunk, hassling everybody. If he heard her footsteps in the hallway or the slamming of a cabinet door in the kitchen, he would yell out, "Janice!" and then maybe nothing would happen, or a foot might fly out and smack her in the thigh, or a hand would whack her in the back of the head. Sometimes he would just stare at her with those cold eyes—she could see and feel, but never understand, the hatred in them—daring her to look away, locking her to him, until her eyes burned with pain. She stood there too terrified to talk, move, even cringe. Whatever she did could make the air whistle. It was like walking through a mine field.

Janice saw her mother as essentially useless. She was just never *around,* she never *did* anything. The house was a mess and the laundry was never done. Janice would wear a dress again and again before putting it in the hamper for fear she wouldn't see it again for weeks. Her mother was mean too, telling her how she hated her children and how they had ruined her life. Leah, as far as Janice was concerned, was a bitch.

Janice's only friend within the family was her younger sister Eileen, and even that relationship was tenuous. Janice observed how close Eileen was to her father. The two of them were always together. He even had a nickname for her, "Pooh." Janice watched as Eileen and her friend Susan sat on his lap and played games with his belly button. She also noticed how clever Eileen was at playing up to him, working into his moods and good graces. She couldn't understand Eileen's connection with him: If she were really Daddy's little girl, she couldn't be trusted. Her father was a monster, and how could you trust anybody who consorted with a monster? Janice also resented the fact that Eileen got knocked around less than the others. Eileen seemed to be the only person in the family whom her father liked.

Janice could not handle the suffering her brother Georgie

endured at the hands of their father. He would punch and slap him and heave him crashing into the furniture and Georgie would scream and scream and the awful cries would ring in her ears. Janice was tough and could take her licks, but she couldn't tolerate what happened to her little brother. Her father deserved to burn in hell for what he did to that poor boy.

GEORGE JR. HAD A HARD TIME AS THE ONLY BOY IN A HOUSEFUL OF girls. He was blamed for everything. If an argument started, it was George's fault; if something was missing, George had taken it. Most often, his sisters didn't allow him to play with them, and he had no natural ally in the household. In the ever-shifting alliances (only Eileen and Diana were constant), he was usually odd kid out. The only benefits to being the only boy were that he didn't have to wear hand-me-downs and he had his own room.

George was obedient to his father and tried hard to live up to his standards, but he could never please him. His mother didn't help: sometimes when he misbehaved, she would take him to the fire station to be punished.

> Georgie Porgie, puddin' n' pie
> Kissed the girls and made them cry.

The neighborhood kids sang out the old nursery rhyme relentlessly to taunt George. They made up other cruel, disjointed verses just for him.

> Georgie Porgie wet his bed
> and turned his sisters' hair all red.

His father joined in the mockery, calling his son "Pee Brain" and "Pissy Doodle."

TO OUTSIDERS, KATE MIGHT HAVE BEEN THE VIVACIOUS DAUGHTER, her mother's favorite, the responsible older sister, the good student, the quiet girl with a good sense of herself, but Kate saw herself quite differently: In her eyes she was the outsider, the child who didn't want to play in the family games, who wanted to be left alone, who was afraid to feel close to anybody in the family.

Kate knew abuse as a normal part of life. Occasionally, there was a point to her father's violence—some distorted form of discipline for a bad report card, in which case she would get whacked only once. Other times the brutality seemed random and there might be two or three or five whacks in a row. When he began swinging, she would crouch slightly and raise her arms to protect her head and face, leaving her in a grotesque standing fetal position. Her father was a big man, stocky and solid, with a barrel chest and broad shoulders, and his dark eyes instilled terror in her heart. "Look at me," he would insist. Once he began hitting her, she never knew how long the beating would last, or sometimes, when it was over, how long it had lasted; it always seemed to go on forever.

Kate was terrified by one particular tactic of her father's. If she had set the table wrong or given an incorrect answer to a question, he would raise his arm in the air as if to strike her, and if she flinched or raised her arm or pulled away, he would become furious and scream, "Do you think I'm going to hit you?"

She said nothing, of course—what was the right answer? Yes? No? I don't know?—and he would yell anyway, "Goddamn it, you'll know when I hit you!" and then he would whip his massive arm back again as if to strike her and she would try her best to freeze, to not move a muscle or even close her eyes. But the horrible part was she could get cracked in the head even if she didn't flinch.

Her mother was no help. When the violence began, Leah didn't rush in to deflect the anger or the blows, or take her away to a safe place; she didn't do anything except stand there and watch, like some ghostly bystander. Worse, on occasion Leah would actually serve a child up to her husband by telling him things the child had done wrong. Kate learned early in life that she had to look out for herself; her safety was in her own hands.

Kate didn't see herself as her mother's favorite. She resembled her mother and she helped her with chores and looked after the other kids, but she didn't feel close to her. Actually, her mother didn't have a favorite; as far as Kate could see, she wasn't capable of having that sort of relationship with any of her children. She was an obese, inert form that never seemed to be doing anything: she would sit at the breakfast table drinking coffee, stirring only to rise and make another cup, until the morning was nearly gone. She just didn't seem to *be* there most of the time.

Kate received her first severe beating when she was six. Her mother and Janice were in her bedroom with her when, for some reason—she could never remember why—her father grabbed her violently by the head and threw her over her bed and into the wall. Her small body flew through the air and crashed face first into the wall, then fell and crumpled into a heap on the bed.

Kate adopted a very deliberate strategy of staying out of everyone's way and minding her own business. She kept her thoughts to herself and her mouth shut. Her father would often say in frustration that he had no idea what his oldest daughter was thinking, which was just fine with her.

Kate avoided the public areas where Janice or Eileen could pull her into a squabble. If she felt danger in the air, she retreated immediately to her room. She would pile Janice's stuff on her bed and throw her clothes into the closet, then plop down on the floor and lean up against her bed and open to her place in *Little Women,* or *Gone with the Wind,* her two favorite books, and slip off to another place, lost to herself and the world for hours.

Eileen could be dangerous because of her limitless need for attention. She certainly received a lot of attention from her father, and whatever Eileen wanted, Eileen got. (Kate didn't begrudge Eileen her special status; in her mind, being either parent's favorite was neither an honor nor a blessing.) Eileen was also a little policeman, an instigator. For no reason, she would begin recounting some incident to her father, something that Kate had said or done, or some place that she had been that she wasn't supposed to be, and Kate would say to herself, "Oh no, don't talk about that, please don't bring that up," but it would be too late and Eileen would go on and Kate would be held to answer for whatever she had supposedly done. Although Eileen could be cute and endearing, particularly when she was with Diana, she definitely enjoyed stirring things up and being the center of the storm.

IF GEORGE FRANKLIN LOVED ANYBODY IN THE FAMILY, IT WAS HIS Pooh, the third daughter and first redhead in his brood. He liked to tell her that when he first saw her red hair and held her in his arms, he knew some day she would break his heart.

Eileen was the sort of child whom adults and children saw differently. To her ballet teacher, she was a cute little redhead. To her classmates, she was a homely red-haired girl with freckles who didn't belong. They teased her and taunted her and called her names. She could be an emotional attention-getter. Once during recess she fell on the playground and screamed and screamed as if something terrible had happened to her when it was really nothing more than a scrape. She did have a few friends: Susan, who the children also teased because of her freckles and hair and because she wet her pants, and Janice, a girl who was ridiculed because of a crippled leg. The three outcasts sat at the same table and ate lunch together at school and often walked home together.

At age eight, Eileen was very small and had tiny wrists and ankles. She wore her red hair long and straight, letting it fall down over her shoulders almost to her elbows. Her face was oval-shaped, with full cheeks and a broad forehead. Beneath a heavy brow were deepset, large brown eyes. Freckles the color of her hair masked her face from her brow to her chin, and buck teeth gave her a slightly chipmunkish effect. Cute to adults, certainly beautiful to her father, she was homely to herself and her schoolmates.

Eileen relished her position as Daddy's favorite. Sometimes when he came home from work in the morning, she would talk him into giving her a ride to school, even though it was only a few blocks away. In the belly-button game, she would sit on his lap and they would poke at each other's navel until somebody gave in and laughed. Eileen adored her father and thought him the most handsome man in the world. When she had a stomach ache and stayed home from school, he would take her on painting jobs with him. They would go to a restaurant and sit in a booth and he would flirt with the waitresses and she would feel so proud of him. While others made fun of her looks, he told her time and again how beautiful she was. She was in love with her father, and he with her.

Eileen knew that her mother didn't love her. She neglected her. Eileen recalls that when Eileen was about nine years old, she fell ill at a summer camp. The nurse called her mother and told her Eileen was very sick and that she must come for her right away. Her mother finally arrived two days later in the car with the other children. Then she complained about having to come at all and was mad at Eileen for being sick, and when they arrived home, she went inside and left her daughter in the car. Eileen, in intense pain, crawled into the house and went to bed. When her father came home from the fire station in the morning and found her terribly ill, he was furious with his wife and immediately took Eileen to the hospital. The doctors found that her appendix was ready to burst and told Eileen she could have died. Her mother was so angry at her she refused to visit her in the hospital.

Her father was her teacher, as well as her protector. He taught Eileen his philosophy of life and tried to impart rules to live by: "You should always tell the truth," he told her again and again, "for the truth will set you free; A coward dies a thousand deaths, a brave man only one. You should be frank and honest with people, and tell things the way they are. And you should travel and see the world, it's a fascinating place."

IN SOME WAYS, GEORGE FRANKLIN WAS THE MORE NURTURING PARent. If he was around in the morning, he would make sure the children had breakfast before they went to school and check to see if the girls' shoes matched their outfits. When Janice had her night terrors and saw her nemesis, the "boogey bathtub monster," coming for her in the dark and ran and hid in her closet, her father was the one who saved and comforted her. He encouraged his children to take dance lessons and to study and watch the news and read history. George Franklin had great aspirations for his children.

In Leah's mind, she was another casualty of George's moods. She watched her husband's temper erupt and the blows rain down on her children's heads and bodies, and she felt them pound on her own body too. But most of the time she felt helpless. She was engaged in a struggle for her own survival. He was dumping a lot of his hate and spite on her, and it was all she could do to hold herself together.

Leah couldn't understand why her life and her home were disintegrating. She kept hoping things would return to the way they were in the early years of her marriage. She knew her parents had had difficulties, but they were committed to their marriage and urged her to stay in hers. Even though she was not raising her children as Catholics, she felt the constraints of the church's prohibition against divorce. She felt locked in a horrible situation with nowhere to turn: How would she survive in the outside world, she wondered, if she couldn't survive within her own four walls? If *she* wasn't safe in her house, how could she protect her children?

In her own struggle for survival, Leah seemed to deny the full reality of what was happening; she created an attitude, a persona, that didn't fully integrate all aspects of experience into her consciousness. When she had coffee with her friends, she was cheerful and everything seemed to be great: she was fine and the children were fine. She tried to live away from the reality of her home life. As one friend observed, she had the ability to flip a switch in her mind.

Leah did, however, methodically pursue her education, taking one course each semester. Initially she went to night school and took courses in psychology, then she focused on real estate and began taking courses toward board certification. When all of the children were finally in school, she switched to day classes. In her view, she was attempting to obtain the economic freedom to fend for herself and her children, but several of her children bitterly resented her schooling. In their view, when she left for class in the evening, she was abandoning them to predictable violence and violation. Janice felt that her mother cared more about school than her children. She didn't dare interrupt her or make a noise while she was studying.

Leah's fragile, overburdened structure eventually collapsed. The pressure of having five children, keeping the real estate books, going to school, living with a psychologically and physically abusive husband, and constructing and maintaining a persona to cope with it all finally overwhelmed her. In 1967 she had a nervous breakdown and was admitted to Twin Pines Hospital in nearby Belmont. She stayed several months and received electroshock therapy, a technique used for the deepest, most intractable types of depression. In 1968 she suffered a relapse and was readmitted for a brief stay. For years after, she took Lithium.

12

November 25, 1989

THE TWO DETECTIVES, MORSE AND CASSANDRO, FLEW from San Francisco to Burbank on the Saturday after Thanksgiving, Eileen Franklin's twenty-ninth birthday. On the flight down, they talked little. Morse went over some reports and Cassandro read the newspaper. They had done this hundreds of times before. They weren't out to get all the facts that the woman supposedly knew about the killing, to dredge every detail from her mind. Their task was quite simple: Confirm in their own minds that she had witnessed the killing and determine whether or not she would be a credible witness in front of a jury.

After getting lost once, the cops arrived at the house on Blythe Street in Canoga Park, a middle-class suburb of Los Angeles. Eileen, the good hostess, invited them in and served them coffee. They talked to Barry for a while, about how much they hated L.A., but when it came time to turn to the topic at hand, Morse asked him to leave.

Morse, aware of Eileen's dislike for cops, approached the interview delicately and let her tell her story in her own words. "Start in the morning," he suggested, "and just tell us what happened that day."

"Well, the way I remember it, my father was driving my sister Janice and I to school, and directly around the corner from my house, I saw my friend Susan just leaving her house, beginning to walk to school, and I asked my dad if Susan could get into the car with us. And he stopped the car, and he let Susan get in, and he made my sister Janice get out. And then he drove around like he was going to take us to school, and actually went up into the front of the school, and then he said that we were going to play hooky that day.

"We drove for some time and I remember going past the reservoirs, like the way you drive up towards Half Moon Bay, and we drove out—I think he told me we were driving to the woods on a fire road, or something like that, because he was a fireman and the fire trucks went up there to check on the area and we drove up there and stopped the car. It was a Volkswagen van and it had two front seats with an open area you could walk between and in the back there was a wooden platform made of plywood with a mattress on it. It was not a twin size mattress but it was a larger mattress. And we got out of the car and were just walking around and then we were in the car and Susan and I were bouncing on the bed and playing and running up and back in the car and then my dad came in and started to play with us, just friendly playing. After a little bit of this I was in the front seat and my dad pinned Susan down with her legs hanging off the edge of the bed up towards the front seat and he held her two arms up with both of his hands and with his elbows straddling either side of her body he began to rub back and forth on her in a humping motion, and he continued to do this and I watched from the front seat back to where they were and I got really scared when I looked directly at Susan. He had pulled her skirt or her dress up and there was something white underneath it, which would have been a slip or an undershirt or something white was underneath it, and I got really scared and just rolled up in a ball until he stopped, and then he got up and walked out of the car, and, after a little while Susan and I both got out of the car, and she was crying a little bit, but not a real lot. Just a little bit. And she walked a distance from the car to where there was like a point or a peak in the way the ground was formed, and she was sitting there, you know, sitting on a rock or sitting on something that was slightly elevated, and I was standing next to the car, and I picked up something off the ground. Something that had fallen off the tree. I was just looking at it. And when I looked up, my father had a rock in his two hands, and he was maybe two or three steps away from her and was approaching her. He was not directly in my line of vision. It was—that was more over to the right. And he had the rock above his head, and he was proceeding—he had his right arm and right leg forward when I looked up, and I could see the sun coming through, and I screamed and Susan looked up, and she saw my dad, and she looked instantly at me and brought her hand to her head. I think both hands to her head. And he crushed the rock down against her head where her hands were. And I had stopped screaming for just a second and I heard the sound of the rock crushing her head. And he did a second blow, and then I think I started screaming again, because he came to me and I must have started running because he grabbed me when I was running and knocked me onto the ground and held my face down into the ground and told me that I had to be quiet or he was going to kill me. And he held me down like that and I was crying and he told me that if I ever told anyone about this he would kill me, and that if I tried to tell anyone that they would never believe me that this happened, that they would know that I was a part of this. But it was my idea for Susan to get into the car. And that they would take me away and put me away like they had put my mother away in a mental home."

Her father, dressed in tan Levi corduroy pants, a white T-shirt, and a wool Pendleton, had taken a spade from the van and dug down by the body and then come back and told her to help him take the mattress out of the van and said, "Goddamn it, Eileen!" when she wouldn't do it. She got in the car and curled up and put her head down. Her father returned, took off the Pendleton, got in the car, and they left. She told him that they shouldn't leave Susan there because she would be cold and afraid, but he said nothing. They drove home and she went right to her room. Her sister Janice comforted her, and she might have told her what she had seen.

Morse tried to clear up two serious problems with the story. First, the location. He asked her again where they had been, and she said they had driven off the main road for a while on a dirt road wide enough for fire trucks to use and stopped at a place where she could see three trees in a zigzag line. Morse, prompting her, asked if they had parked on a turnout. No, Eileen replied, they had left the main road and driven for several minutes along a bumpy, dirt road before stopping.

Second, the time of day.

"Are you absolutely certain," Morse asked her, "that you didn't go to school that day?"

"No, I thought that—that—it's possible that I went home for lunch and that this happened when we were returning to school from going home for lunch. But that's—that's possible. When we got home, it was still light outside. But I don't really remember if this was on the way to school, or on the way back to school from having lunch. I just know it was on—I was en route to school—to Foster City School."

Morse asked her about her father. He was a violent man, she said, who had beaten his wife and children. One time Eileen had walked into her parents' bedroom and saw him holding a gun to her mother's head. He had also sexually abused several of his daughters. Janice had told her that her father had had sex with her on several occasions and that sometimes when she woke up at night he was having sex with Kate. Eileen remembered him putting his finger in her vagina when she was six or seven, and she had a horrible memory of him helping another man rape her. They had been in a flat in San Francisco and her father and another man were doing drugs and her father had held her down and put his hand on her shoulder while the other man raped her. On one of the walls was a picture of Jimi Hendrix.

"What did he look like, this person who raped you?" Morse asked her.

"He was dark-complected and had like an afro-style hairdo."

"Was he a black man?"

"Yes."

Morse asked whom she had told about the killing.

"I told my therapist."

"Anyone else?"

"I told some of my family."

"Which members of your family did you tell this?"

"Well, because you came today, I made it a point to tell some people before it started in the last couple of days. So, I've told my mother, that's Leah Franklin, I told my sister Kate, my sister Janice. I just mentioned it to my brother. I didn't go into any details with him. I told two of my aunts on my mother's side.

". . . And I told—I told my husband and we told his immediate family."

"Through the years . . ."

"Yes?"

". . . Did you tell your girlfriends?"

"No. I ha—I've never told anyone."

"You never mentioned this to anyone through the years?"

"As far as I know, I've never mentioned this to anyone."

"Why are you coming forward now, with this information?"

"Well, for several reasons."

"Okay."

"My memory had become very vivid of it, not as vague. I really feel that I owe something to Susan and to her family, and I think that my father really needs help and is a dangerous person. He shouldn't be around helpless people. And just to—to do the right thing. It's—you know—the honest, right thing to do."

Later, Morse asked her:

"Did you ever want to tell anybody where she was?"

"No, I was really afraid. I was really afraid."

"Did it sort of die off, then? Dwindle away?"

"After her body was found, I was afraid for a little while, and then, I just had to basically get on with my life. I had to keep functioning in order to keep this going. The lie going."

Eileen did not mention that she had just recently remembered the killing.

Eileen questioned the detective: Do you believe me? Do you think I saw my father kill Susan Nason? Yes, the two cops assured her, they believed her. They explained that they would have to talk to Marty Murray to determine what the next step would be, and there would be more questions for her and they would have to try to corroborate her story, but yes, they believed her. In the meantime, she should try to remember more details. She said she would.

The detectives talked with Barry briefly, mainly to get a sense of him and to placate him for being excused earlier. Barry said that years earlier Eileen had told him about her best friend in Foster City who had been murdered, and about a week ago she told him she had witnessed the killing. Barry also didn't mention anything about Eileen's having forgotten the killing for twenty years. Barry seemed solid to Morse, just like a supportive and concerned husband should be.

"Do you believe her?" Cassandro asked Morse in the car on the way to the airport.

"Yeah," Morse responded.

"I do too."

Cassandro had been impressed with Eileen's demeanor during the interview, and by her description of the smashed ring and the rock, details she couldn't have known unless she had been at the murder scene. He had thought of asking her to take a polygraph test, but rejected the idea: trust was a big thing with her, and such a suggestion might well jeopardize whatever goodwill had been developed.

On the way home the two detectives talked about the likelihood that Franklin had committed additional murders. A man who would do this once would do it twice, three times, or more. They would check it out.

*   *   *

MORSE SHOWED UP IN MARTY MURRAY'S OFFICE EARLY MONDAY morning.

"Do you believe her?" Murray asked him immediately.

"Absolutely," the detective responded without hesitation.

"What sort of a witness will she make?" Murray continued.

"Dynamite."

Murray decided to launch a full-scale investigation. He felt both trepidation and excitement over the prospect of prosecuting the case: trepidation because putting together the facts would be a monumental undertaking; excitement because of the possibility of solving a horrible crime that had been on the books for twenty years. He would brief District Attorney Jim Fox because of the extensive publicity the case would undoubtedly generate, but he felt sure that his boss's response would be the same when he told him Morse's evaluation. He also knew that if Morse had answered either of the two questions in the negative, the case would almost certainly have died on the spot.

November 27, 1989

Morse and Cassandro had expected to interview Janice at Eileen's house on Saturday, but she had left for the peninsula earlier. On Monday, she came into the sheriff's office and gave the two detectives a statement. She described a household of pervasive violence and sexual abuse.

". . . When I was in . . . about third or fourth grade, my father would come into the bathroom while I was going to the bathroom and tell me how to fold the toilet paper and wipe myself and stand there and watch me, and tell me to pull the lips of my vagina apart. And I thought . . . the guy was a fanatic about dusting the floorboards and stuff, but I thought he was going too far, and it was like 'leave the bathroom,' but . . . I didn't realize really, until later, that that was, you know . . . it made me very uncomfortable at the time."

She said that he also "used to have me sit on his lap, and

he'd pretend like he was hugging me and stuff like that, but he'd be putting his hands in my panties. . . ."

After Susan was killed, according to Janice, the drinking and violence and sexual abuse in the household escalated dramatically. She told of a night when she was in seventh grade and she was home alone with her father. "Go upstairs, take your clothes off, and lay on my bed," he told her. Then he followed her up the stairs. "Close your eyes and put your legs up," he ordered.

Her father tried to penetrate her vagina with his penis, but it wouldn't go in, so he had her perform oral sex on him instead and ejaculated in her mouth.

She had finally told her mom about the incident when she was fifteen, after her father had moved out of the house, and Leah's only response had been to take her to see a psychiatrist.

Although Janice didn't think her father had abused Diana, she knew he had sexually abused Kate. The two girls shared a room together, and she had seen her father come in for Kate.

For Morse and Cassandro, this confirmed George Franklin's incestuous, pedophiliac behavior. A man who would molest his own daughters would also molest one of their friends, and a man who would molest one of their friends might panic afterwards and kill her to shut her up. Morse and Cassandro were more convinced than ever that George Franklin had killed Susan Nason.

Morse asked her about a 1984 statement she had made to the Foster City Police in which she said that she suspected her father of murdering Susan Nason. She had told an officer that on the night Susan disappeared she remembered her father being at home around 4:00 P.M. and that he had sat in his chair drinking the rest of the evening. In effect, she had provided her father with an alibi, and the police had not pursued the matter. Now, she explained to Morse that her estimate of the time in 1984 had probably been wrong. She was so scared of her father as a child that she had never come home until the last possible moment before dinnertime, which was usually around 5:30 or 6:00, so it couldn't have been until around then that she saw him sitting in his chair.

Then Janice delivered a serious blow. She didn't remember seeing Susan after school on the day she disappeared. Maybe she had seen her get in the van, but then again maybe she hadn't; she just couldn't be sure. With that, the "cherry on the cake" that Eileen and Barry had promised the cops suddenly vanished.

13

By 1971, GEORGE'S LONG HOURS ON THREE JOBS were beginning to pay off, and he and his family began moving up in the world. They sold the small house on Harvester and built a large two-story house on Beach Park Boulevard, a much nicer street which ringed the eastern perimeter of the island. The house had a vaulted ceiling, and the second floor provided a dramatic view of San Francisco Bay, which was just across the street on the other side of a small levee.

This house was also decorated in masculine colors: brown and black shag carpeting, dark gold walls, and black wrought iron stair railings. The children had separate bedrooms which they were allowed to decorate in their favorite colors, except for Eileen, who slept in the loft overlooking the living room. George Jr.'s room was downstairs next to the laundry room.

But life in the Franklin family hadn't changed. Leah read voraciously and took classes in humanistic psychology, but continued to be the absent, neglectful mother, at least in the eyes of her children. Janice, the troublemaker, fought constantly with her mother, and Kate remained the house recluse.

Most mornings Kate arose early and left without eating in order to avoid her father and her siblings. Eileen, closer than ever to her dad, was still an instigator, still dangerous, the one who would say, "I'm going to tell Daddy!" if she knew you were fibbing about what you did after school. Kate took a circuitous route to school and on her way home she would often stop and look for seashells and sit on the narrow beach and write in her diary or read. She had few friends and cared little for her classes, although she received good grades. School was mainly a better place to be than home.

Kate planned her daily life around her father's schedule, which she knew by heart. If he was going to be home after school, she would find activities lasting until dinner. If he was going to be around in the evening, she would line up baby-sitting jobs. There was little reason to be at home: her father was dangerous and her mother, at best, was in complete emotional shutdown. Looking forward to the day when she could leave home and begin her own life, Kate carefully saved the money she earned baby-sitting and working in a plant store after school.

One morning she arose late and heard her father and mother talking in the kitchen. She heard her name and realized her mother was telling him something she had done wrong. He turned and yelled, "Cathleen!" She walked slowly to the kitchen.

"When I get home this evening," he said to her, his burly arms and broad chest looming over her, "I'm going to beat the hell out of you." And then, as if to make sure terror was firmly instilled in her heart, he added, coldly, evenly, "That should give you something to think about today."

Kate did not react to his threat. Knowing better than to protest or explain, she turned and left. But her heart was frozen at school. She could not think of anything except what was going to happen when she got home. "What am I going to do?" she asked herself again and again. By lunchtime she had an answer. On the way home from school, she stopped at a convenience store and called the Foster City police station.

"My father told me when he gets home tonight he's going to beat the hell out of me," she told the officer on the phone. He asked what she had done and she told him as best as she knew.

"Okay," the officer said, "has he ever hit you before?"

"Yes," Kate answered.

"What time does he usually get home?"

"At six," she replied.

"We'll have an officer there," he promised.

After Kate hung up, she felt tremendous relief. The cavalry was on the way. She arrived home around 4:00 P.M. and went upstairs to her room and put on her robe and waited. Finally, she heard her dad's voice boom up the stairs.

"Cathleen!"

"Here we go," she thought. She walked to the head of the stairs and looked down. Her mother and father were standing in front of the open door. She couldn't always tell from her dad's appearance if he was drunk, but she didn't sense the weird, scary energy that meant he had been drinking heavily.

A police officer stood outside on the steps. He was gray-haired and overweight, not the sort of hero she had been waiting for.

"Cathleen, get down here!" her father yelled, immediately taking charge of the situation.

"Did you call the police today?" he demanded.

"Yes," she replied.

"Did you tell them I was going to hit you?"

"Yes," she repeated.

Then the police officer finally spoke. Without asking Kate any questions, he told her, "You know, we can't do anything until he injures you. So far he hasn't done anything wrong."

"Oh no," Kate thought, a sinking feeling overwhelming her, "Oh no. Why didn't you tell me this before? Why did you come at all? This time," she prayed, "I really hope he kills me and gets it over with."

"They're my kids and I can do whatever I want to them!" her father yelled at the elderly policeman and slammed the door in his face.

"Go up to your room," her mother said quickly to Kate. Trembling, Kate started up the stairs and made it as far as the third step before a thick hand reached out and grabbed her by the shoulder and yanked her back violently. Down the stairs she flew until her shoulders and then her head crashed on the tile floor, knocking her unconscious. When she awoke, she was lying on her bed, sobbing. Her mother was sitting beside her, asking her if she was okay, but not touching her. Kate's head, her back, her entire body ached for days.

Kate didn't tell anybody at school what had happened, nor did she ever call the police again. Sometimes her mother would make excuses for her father—"He's been drinking," she would say, "he really didn't mean it"—but not this time. The incident was never discussed again.

In high school, Kate smoked cigarettes and a little pot—who didn't?—but it was a minor distraction. She was, as one classmate put it, "normal." Not in the most popular group, but not an outsider either. She had her small group of friends—an odd mixture of blue-collar and Hillsborough students who listened to FM radio, read books, went to dances at St. Timothy's Catholic School, and attended Yes and Rod Stewart concerts. But mostly the group was quiet and unobtrusive, like Kate. She was in the drama department and worked on sets and had a role in one play, but, other than tutoring reading at a nearby elementary school, that was her only activity.

She didn't have any boyfriends, and with the exception of a mild crush or two, didn't particularly care. Although she tried her best to leave her home life behind when she stepped out the door in the morning, she often slipped into depressions that lasted for days. Despite her lack of interest, Kate graduated high school six months early.

Sometimes Kate would come home and find her father sitting in the dark in his chair by the large window. He would sit there hour after hour, drinking steadily, smoking cigarette after cigarette, listening to Hank Williams Sr. on the stereo and staring out over the bay. "How sad," she would think, "he's really so lonely." In those moments, Kate would feel her own isolation, and almost against her wishes, her own deep longing for a close, warm family.

As Diana grew older, she assumed Kate's position as mother's favorite. Her new role probably began when she was home alone with her mother and the other children were in school, although she remembers mainly sitting around the house by herself with nothing to do. Being her mother's favorite meant little anyway—perhaps an extra dress or a blouse at Christmas —because her mother didn't really relate to her any more than she did to the other kids. Her mom wasn't much of a toucher or hugger; even when Diana was grown, she received only stiff, formal embraces from her. She experienced her mom's mean streak, too. When Leah got mad, she would tell her children she hated them for having ruined her life.

Diana lived in fear of her father. He sat in his chair and ordered her to fetch drinks for him. Every half hour she would take his glass to the kitchen and mix a bourbon and Coke, three-quarters bourbon and one-quarter Coke. She was always very careful around him: she might receive the fewest blows, but he could hurt her in other ways. That cold, hard look he gave her, as if she wasn't really a human being, as if she wasn't worth loving, hurt her deeply.

In seventh grade, after her father had left the house, Diana began to open up. She talked more and finally made a friend. But even then, she didn't feel as if she had her own identity: If her friend bought a dress, Diana would immediately go out and buy the same one; if Eileen liked a song, Diana would learn the words. But at least she had found her voice.

Diana's life changed in another way: Eileen, her role model, introduced her to drugs. Diana had smoked pot before—it was everywhere in junior high—but nothing more, and then when she was twelve, Eileen introduced her to acid. She knew Eileen did a lot of drugs in high school. She took psychedelics four or five times a week and was high on something, uppers or downers, almost every day. One time Eileen overdosed on pills and was taken to the hospital. Eileen told her she had taken two reds and didn't get high so she took two more and still didn't get high, and after another two she finally passed out. Only much later would Diana learn that Eileen characterized this episode as a suicide attempt.

The first time Eileen gave Diana acid, the two of them went with a friend, who was also high, to an orthodontist's office. Diana and Eileen were sitting in the waiting room when the drug took effect, and the two of them began giggling so hard they had to leave the room and wait outside by the car. Diana loved the feeling of the drug; it pulled her from the dead fog into open space and made her feel alive.

Eileen still included Diana in her activities. On some evenings, Eileen carried a bag of amyl nitrates in her purse and she would break open a capsule while she was dancing and sniff it and pass it back and forth with her friends.

Diana's red hair took on a rich auburn hue and she grew more attractive than Eileen. She took great care with her appearance, paying particular attention to her makeup and clothes. She lied about her age and went out with men in their twenties. High school boys seemed like kids to her.

Diana smoked enough pot to stay stoned most of her sophomore and junior years. She and her friend cut classes regularly and went to malls looking for boys. When she did go to class, she was usually loaded. In her junior year, the principal called her in and said she had fallen so far behind in her classes she would either have to take makeup classes or transfer to a special school to study for her GED. Not about to take the makeup classes, Diana transferred to the special school. She found the place intolerable and dropped out altogether. Like her role model Eileen, Diana would not obtain her high school diploma.

JANICE WAS THE OUTGOING DAUGHTER IN THE FAMILY. SHE LAUGHED and talked easily with people, whether she knew them or not. She was no more popular than Eileen, but her attitude about her exclusion was different. She had her own friends and they thought of themselves as independent and free thinkers. Janice was the first girl to wear black fingernail polish and black lipstick to school. Some of the other kids snickered behind her back about how much makeup she wore, calling her "the Makeup Queen," and some thought she looked cheap. But they would never have said it to her face: Janice had a hard edge, a "don't mess with me" attitude that intimidated most of the students.

In the eighth grade Janice's grades dropped dramatically and she began hanging around with the bad crowd. They smoked cigarettes and used foul language and experimented with drugs. She and her friends did things other girls only talked about, and they earned reputations as loose girls. Over the lunch hour or after school they would sit in the park and smoke and drink wine or beer, sometimes brandy.

By ninth grade, Janice had developed the figure of a young woman. She was taller than Eileen and longer-limbed, and her fine chestnut hair hung to her waist. She had the fine features of her mother, and red lipstick gave her a flashy air. She began skipping school with her friends and chasing boys.

Janice and her mother screamed at each constantly. In some of their worst yelling matches Leah would call her "Lady Cunt!"

THE FRANKLIN GIRLS SEEMED TO KNOW MORE ABOUT SEX THAN THEIR peers. One classmate spent the night at their house and said that the sisters talked constantly about sex. They described intercourse and how you did it, although they didn't actually say they had done it themselves. Janice told her their dad had said it was all right for Confederate men to rape their wives.

EVEN GEORGE JR. SEEMED SEXUALLY PRECOCIOUS. ONE DAY AFTER school when a friend was over, he threw open the door to Eileen's room and said, "Hey, do you want to have sex with my sisters? Everybody else does!"

To many classmates, George Jr. was a nerd, a goofy-looking boy with few friends. He had an unruly afro, a strange look in his far-apart eyes, and a high-pitched voice. He was so uncoordinated in sports that when he tried to kick the soccer ball, there was no telling where it would go. If you asked him what his dad did, he would puff up with pride and say, "Firefighter!" Sometimes he tried to act tough, but he couldn't pull it off. The boys continued to make fun of him, and girls shied away from him.

George fought back in his own way. He developed an ironic, somewhat cynical sense of humor and learned to play into his strangeness. He would quote W. C. Fields and wear bright yellow jackets and loud pants to school. He proposed that it would be a smart idea to acquire real estate on the moon.

One day in eleventh grade, the students in history class were supposed to give oral reports on their projects. When it came George's turn, he walked to the front of the room with his binder held to his chest, and once at the podium, he dropped his arms to reveal the words "FUCK YOU" printed in large letters on his T-shirt. The students broke up and the shocked teacher ordered him back to his seat. When George received his high school diploma at graduation ceremonies, he kissed the superintendent on the cheek while he shook his hand. His classmates were not surprised.

14

ASSISTANT DISTRICT ATTORNEY MARTY MURRAY wasn't surprised that Eileen hadn't told anybody about the murder for twenty years. Sometimes the secrets of childhood abuse or trauma lasted a lifetime. He was curious, though, as to why she came forward when she did. He speculated that as a child, fear had kept her silent. As a teenager, she probably realized she should tell someone, but couldn't bring herself to do it. What day was she going to pick to ruin her life? Now that she was married and had children, the right moment had come. Murray was very curious to meet Eileen: she seemed unusually articulate and, even over the phone, very compelling.

Eileen's story made sense to the prosecutor. Mrs. Nason had been so certain in the 1969 interviews that Susan would not have gotten into a car with a stranger (and a stranger would have been crazy to snatch a child in isolated Foster City), but Susan would surely have gotten into a van driven by her best friend's father, particularly if that best friend opened the door and called to her. However, Murray was concerned about the discrepancy between the two sisters' stories: Did Janice see Susan get in the van or not? Eileen had been so certain that Janice had been in the van when she and her father stopped for Susan. Murray thought he might be able to use the inconsistency to demonstrate that Eileen and Janice, who were living together in the fall of 1989, hadn't put their stories together.

Murray continued gathering facts. He called the San Mateo Fire Department and determined that Franklin had not been on duty on the afternoon of September 22, 1969.

He also called the Nasons, who were still living in the same house on Balclutha. He explained to Margaret that there had been a development in the murder of her daughter and he would be sending two detectives out to speak to her and her husband. There was a long silence on the other end of the phone. Finally, in a gentle, gracious voice, Margaret replied that she would be glad to talk to the detectives and help in whatever way she could. "Thank you," she said softly at the end.

Morse and Cassandro then drove to the Nason house and by the time they arrived, Margaret was crying. Morse asked if they knew the Franklins and if Susan had played with Eileen. Yes, Margaret told them, Susan and Eileen had been best friends. Morse warned them that the press would be all over the case if there was an arrest.

After hearing the detectives' report, Murray decided it was time for Morse and Cassandro to pay a visit to George Franklin.

First, though, they had to find him. Eileen hadn't seen her father in five years, but thought he lived in the Sacramento area. Cassandro called a detective in the Sacramento police department and asked for an address. Franklin's only listing was a post office box number, but the records revealed that he had called in recently on a vandalism complaint and given an address on Fair Oaks Boulevard in Carmichael, a suburb on the northern edge of the capital city. Murray drafted a search warrant based on an affidavit by Morse in which the detective noted, among other things, that Eileen knew facts she could not have known unless she had witnessed the killing. Morse also attested that, in the opinion of another detective who was an expert on child molestation, George Franklin was a pedophile.

Morse was ready to move. He wanted to demonstrate to Eileen that when the cops said they were going to do something, they did it. He was also concerned about the public safety. Pedophilia was a repetitive type of behavior: a man who did it once did it again and again. God only knew what Franklin had been up to in the past twenty years. With search warrant in hand, he and Cassandro took off for Sacramento.

Morse always gave a suspect a chance to speak before arresting him, and he definitely wanted to hear what George Franklin had to say. Morse hoped, prayed, that he would waive his rights and talk to them. He and Cassandro were good at extracting confessions and the ones they extracted held up in court. (In a recent California Supreme Court decision, *People v. Beardslee,* the court heaped praise on Morse and Cassandro in obtaining confessions from the defendant, a multiple murderer. The court described their behavior as "exemplary," noting that the two detectives "scrupulously protected the defendant's rights.") He figured Franklin to be a smart guy, and the smart guys were the easiest ones to break. They were so sure they knew more than you and couldn't wait to prove it. You turned their intelligence against them. You made them see the truth of their situation with their own eyes. As he and Cassandro drove to Sacramento, about an hour and a half northeast of Redwood City, Morse thought about how it would go if only Franklin would talk to them.

What do you mean, you hardly knew the girl? We have witnesses who say she sat on your lap and you were fondling her. What are you talking about? Is everybody lying here except you? Be logical—would you believe that? Haven't we treated you with respect? Well, then, you treat us with some respect and don't feed us that bullshit.

Morse was not above lying. He wouldn't risk jeopardizing

the entire confession with a maze of deceptions, but he would tell a small lie, or perhaps two, to get to the truth. You always had to make the defendant believe you knew everything and never let him know what you didn't know.

What happened? Are you a cold-blooded murderer? Or did you lose your temper? Did you have a problem and you don't have it any more? Now is the time to be truthful, George.

The two cops showed up at the Sacramento sheriff's office shortly before seven on Tuesday morning. They reviewed the search warrant with the local cops and then headed out to Carmichael, hoping to catch George Franklin in bed.

FAIR OAKS BOULEVARD IS THE PRINCIPAL ARTERY LEADING FROM Sacramento to Carmichael. A few miles over the line, the street takes on a blue-collar tone, with fast food joints and strip malls squatting a few feet from the curb. In the midst of this, on the west side of the street, is Wooded Village, an apartment complex not unlike thousands of other complexes in California: two-story stucco buildings with one- and two-bedroom thin-walled apartments, carpeted in green shag and opening onto tiny balconies in the back.

The complex manager, Diane Wiegert, an attractive bleached blonde in her mid-forties, had rented a second-story studio apartment overlooking the pool to a well-kept, gray-haired man in October 1988. He had said he was interested in Wooded Village because he wanted to be close to American River College where he was attending classes. He sought a quiet place where he could study undisturbed in the evening. She checked him out and his credit report was R-1, the highest possible rating and the best she had seen in many years of managing apartments. He owned property in Hawaii and had bank accounts in several cities, as well as a variety of loans and credit cards. She verified the balance in his bank account and called several creditors. The man paid every month right on time.

The tenant, George Franklin, was a pleasant-looking man, although his thick gray hair and lined face made him look older than his fifty years. He was stocky and seemed to be in good shape. Often he would wear white pants, slip-on sneakers, a light-colored pullover, and a captain's hat—he had a white one and a blue one, both trimmed in black with gold insignias—as if he were the captain of a ship. That was kind of his attitude—I'm in charge of my life and I'm happy with the way it's going. George was almost always upbeat. He would burst into her office and say with a broad smile, "Diane, I'm so glad to be free! Isn't it a gorgeous day?" It seemed almost as if he had rediscovered life and was really enjoying it for the first time.

Diane never had any complaints from the other tenants about George. In fact, he was quite responsible: If he saw that somebody's car had been vandalized, he would call the police; if a railing needed repairing, he would mention it to her, but very politely.

George did keep somewhat erratic hours. He was in and out during the day, and in the evening he either studied or was off working on a real estate deal. Sometimes he would be gone for days at a time—he had another place in Nevada City—and then other times he would be around every day for a week. The only bitter streak she saw in him was when he talked about his family. "My wife was mean to me, Diane," he would say, "and I'm glad to have her off my back. I tried to do what I was supposed to do, but it was never enough." She knew he had children, but he never talked about them, other than to say, "I raised mine, that's it. I'm glad I don't have to give any more." He didn't smoke or drink, not a drop, hadn't for several years, and he talked about what alcohol had done to him, how it had held him down. "I was real sick for a long time," he would tell her. He seemed to be starting over, and getting sober and divorced had been the keys to his liberation.

George had a certain arrogance in his manner, the attitude of a self-made man: "I've put my life together and what you think about it doesn't matter a whole lot to me." But he also had a gentle side, as well as a deep lonely streak. He didn't seem to need, or want to need, anybody. Sometimes he would sit out on his deck by himself for hours, quiet and withdrawn, staring off into the distance in a deep melancholy.

George was also a serious student, determined to complete his studies and become an educated man. He was taking courses in algebra and English, but history was his true love. He would come into the office all excited, waving an essay he had written on some historical figure, and say, "Isn't this terrific? Look, I got the highest grade in the class!" His papers were always well written and flowed easily. He had files on everything, and his apartment was crammed full of books and boxes and filing cabinets.

Diane would hear George comment on the pretty girls in the complex, but he wasn't handsome enough to attract them, not that it seemed to bother him. He never said anything crude and was certainly never personally suggestive to her. He had a girlfriend or two, pleasant-looking women in their forties. They didn't stop by too often, probably because his place was so cluttered.

Diane appreciated George's positive attitude toward life. He would get so excited when he had learned or done something new. He wanted to travel, to visit and absorb strange places. He looked forward with almost a childlike exuberance to the world of experiences ahead of him, to the opportunity to catch up on what he had missed in life, to learn and grow. In constant refrain, he would say how grateful he was that he was healthy and free.

15

FOSTER CITY WAS TOO SMALL TO HAVE ITS OWN HIGH school. Some students went to school in Burlingame, but most of them attended San Mateo High, which in the mid-seventies had around 800 students. Like all high schools, San Mateo High had well-defined social groupings. The "popular" crowd was the sons and daughters of the wealthy residents of Hillsborough. The serious students wore slacks and carried their books home after school and sought scholarships to Stanford and Berkeley in physics or math. The vocational students took woodworking and shop, knowing that high school would be the end of their formal education. The jocks hung together, but also belonged to other groups. The stoners, the rebels, smoked pot and thumbed their noses at everyone else. The misfits milled around the edges in ones and twos.

Eileen Franklin's appearance alone would have disqualified her from the popular crowd in high school. She wore her thick orange hair short and parted in the middle, and dark freckles splotched her face. Her father's rough features, particularly his heavy brow, gave her a coarse look. While some of the girls wore blouses and skirts or cord pants and sweaters, she often came to school in tennis shoes, boy's pants, and T-shirts.

Her lack of activities would have disqualified her, too: she didn't play softball or join the band, although she had played French horn in junior high; she didn't write for the paper or the yearbook; she didn't sing for the choir or act in the drama club. About a third of the students at San Mateo High came from Foster City and many of them had gone through elementary and junior high school with Eileen. Those who had ignored or tormented the homely redhead back then did not invite her into their little subgroup in high school either.

Many students in her class barely knew Eileen existed. If they saw her once or twice a year, it was only a passing glance in the hallway. Even some of the nerds wanted little to do with her. One senior student had always thought she was quite weird, but after she came up to him one day in the hall and said in his face, for no apparent reason, "Jesus loves you!" he avoided her completely. (Eileen had been "born again" prior to her drug phase. In this period she attended three or four meetings a week and talked Christianity constantly.) Eileen seldom dated and appeared at very few parties.

In Eileen's mind, the other students shunned her because of her homely looks and ratty clothes, but a few of her classmates saw Eileen as the source of her own alienation. In junior high she had been angry and hostile, with a "Don't come near me" attitude, which had antagonized some of her classmates. Without provocation, she would say strange things to other students, such as the time she accused a girl to her face of being a lesbian. If her classmates had picked on her, it was because she had provoked them.

In high school, some of her classmates also thought she could have been accepted if she had only made an effort and been a little friendlier herself. Instead, she seemed to shun the others. She walked in the halls with her head down and ignored you if you said hello to her, or if she couldn't ignore you, she would look right through you when she said hello. While some of the Hillsborough students dressed fashionably, many other students came from middle-class and blue-collar families and wore jeans and sweatshirts to school. Eileen didn't dress any worse than those students. In the view of these girls, whatever isolation Eileen experienced in high school, she brought on herself.

Toward the end of her sophomore year, Eileen finally found a home. For the first time in her life, she belonged. None of the four or five other students in this small clique belonged to any other group, and they seldom mixed with other students. Both boys in the group were gay, and when the crowd was together, they loved to draw attention to themselves by acting out in class and talking about sex in a loud and provocative manner. Alone, they were much quieter.

Initially, Rick, a member of the group, didn't care for the gawky, withdrawn redhead. But by their junior year, the two had become fast friends. He had a car, and would drive over and pick her up and take her roller-skating and to the movies. In the evenings Rick and Eileen and the others would frequent the Answer, a gay bar in San Mateo. Eileen soon became comfortable with the gay crowd. They asked little of her and paid her unlimited attention.

As Rick and Eileen got to know each other, Rick opened his heart to her and found her kind and receptive. They talked about marriage as if they were boyfriend and girlfriend, but they were never intimate. Rick got a kick out of the way she liked to put on lots of lipstick and then hug somebody and leave lip prints on their shirt or blouse.

Rick could tell that money was very important to Eileen. She never said it in so many words, but she talked frequently about her intentions of marrying a rich man. She seldom discussed her father, although she and Rick would occasionally stop by the fire station to see him.

Rick's parents owned a house on the delta of the Sacramento River, and they allowed their high school sons and daughter to visit their place on weekends and holidays. Eileen's little group went there many times over the years. One weekend when they were playing cards with Rick's parents, Rick encountered Eileen's uncouth side. Eileen, unhappy with her hand, yelled out, "Eat me raw!" Rick had been terribly embarrassed. It didn't surprise Rick's older sister, who thought Eileen seemed a little rough. She didn't like the way Eileen was always seeking attention, acting sweet, and sucking up to her.

During the day, students known as "the Bellevue crowd" gathered across the street from the school. Over the lunch hour they came to buy and sell pot and get stoned. While the stoners—the hard-core smokers who got high before school, during breaks, and after school—made up the core of the Bellevue crowd, other students hung around the corner off and on. At one time or another, all of the Franklin children except Kate made the Bellevue scene. Janice, with her good looks, fast reputation, outgoing personality, and hard attitude, fitted in easily. George, the odd duck with the bizarre sense of humor, found birds of a feather in the stoner crowd. He enjoyed sitting on the grass in a circle with his friends, and occasionally one or two of his sisters, smoking dope.

Eileen alone would not have been welcomed in the Bellevue crowd, but with her new friends there was a place for her. The shy redhead, who by now was smoking Benson & Hedges Menthol Lights, could be almost boisterous when she was with her friends, as if saying to the others, "Now, look, I have friends!" A friend's father owned an apartment down the street and occasionally the group would go there during the day and get high. One semester she and her friends were all in the same course, and on the day they were to give oral reports they went to the house and got stoned before class. They giggled uncontrollably as one by one they stood and gave their barely coherent reports.

The wallflower began her gradual transformation into a cactus flower toward the end of high school. Todd, the other gay in her crowd, whom Eileen considered to be extremely handsome, asked her to the prom her junior year, and her mother took her shopping and they bought a white, strapless dress like the one made famous by Marilyn Monroe. She had her hair cut into a Dorothy Hamill–style bob. She put on eyeliner and shadow to accent and deepen her large eyes. She and Todd doubled with Rick and his date. She would say later that when Rick told her how beautiful she was that evening, she felt attractive for the first time in her life.

But dates with straight boys were still hard to come by.

Eileen didn't graduate from high school, a failure she remained defensive about well into adulthood. She blamed it on her mother, who, she said, dressed her so poorly that much of the time she was too embarrassed to go to class.

Although she didn't graduate, Eileen attended her senior class party, as did Jack Belcher,* who also was not graduating. In class shortly after Susan died Jack had said out loud that it was probably just as well that she was dead because nobody liked her anyway. In high school he was reviled by most students, existing even further beyond the pale than Eileen. His classmates called him names like "loser," "geek," "deviant," and "horny pervert," because he was gross and chased every girl in the class. The night of the party some students discovered Jack and Eileen in the bushes drunk and groping each other. The other students were hard on Eileen anyway, and this incident severely damaged what reputation she did have. Getting caught in the bushes, wasted, with a slob like Jack, was extremely bad form.

Eileen thrived on the attention of her gay friends. They adored her and loved dressing her up and making a fuss over her and taking her to their parties and bars. Eileen particularly

liked Rick's family, which was very close knit and did many
things together, and she spent a lot of time at his house. She
confided in Rick's mother and told her many stories about how
her own family hated and mistreated her. Rick's mother, however, did not reciprocate the affection. In fact, she didn't find
Eileen a particularly nice person and was not at all happy
about her son's friendship with her. She recalled one incident
in particular when Eileen lied to cover up for Rick when there
really was no need to—and she had no use for liars. Indeed,
she even once described the girl as "a pathological liar." And
the girl was never quiet: she had something to say about everything and everybody. Rick's mother figured if Eileen was telling her about the woman across the street, then she was telling
the woman across the street about her. She had heard that
Eileen was a tramp and slept around and then told stories. She
didn't want her son associating with that sort of girl.

Rick's parents moved to Honolulu in 1980, a few years after
their son graduated. When Eileen learned that Rick planned
to visit them over Christmas that year, she called Rick's
mother and asked if she could come too. Rick worked on his
mother until she finally gave in. Rick decided not to go at the
last minute, but Eileen went anyway. Rick's father, who flew
on the same plane with her, was a little startled when she
announced in mid-flight that she was pregnant. "Is it Ricky's?"
he asked. "No," she assured him, "the father of my child is a
very wealthy man and we plan to be married."

Eileen stayed for two weeks and was a miserable house
guest. She was sick every morning, moaning constantly and
talking about how her parents hated and didn't understand
her. She explained again to Rick's mother that the child's father was very wealthy and was going to marry her.

A few days after she returned home, Eileen called Rick's
mother and told her that her mother had disowned her and
her father said he never wanted to see her again. Not only that,
the wealthy man had left her. "Strange," thought Rick's
mother, "that she's telling me all this. Poor thing must not
have anyone else to talk to." A short time later Eileen called
again and confided that she had had a miscarriage and had

become so ill in the hospital she had almost died. Afterwards, her mother had come to the hospital and forgiven her and said she could come home. She had also met another very rich man, a millionaire, and was going to marry him.

In 1989, when Rick's mother heard of Eileen's charges against her father, she vividly recalled Eileen's falsehoods and her belief that the girl was a pathological liar, and she flat-out didn't believe Eileen's story that she had seen her father murder a little girl twenty years earlier.

16

In January 1974, Leah finally told George to leave. she had called each of her children into her bedroom separately and told them she was thinking of divorcing their father and asked what they thought. Janice was dumbstruck that her mother had to ask—hadn't she lived in the same house with them for the past fourteen years? For Kate, the physical and sexual abuse had become so severe that she told her mother she would leave if her father didn't. Leah said later that she had decided her husband had to go after he had beaten one child so severely she feared one day he would cause a permanent injury. (Several of her children insist that Leah threw their father out only after he finally beat *her* up.) George didn't object—he had been around home less and less anyway, sometimes staying away for three or four days at a time, cruising in the van. He left the next day.

On April 11, 1974, George Franklin filed a petition for divorce in the Superior Court of San Mateo County. He did not seek child custody. The couple by then had acquired five rental properties in the Shoreview area of San Mateo which were valued at $150,000 and their Beach Park house had appreciated to $70,000. They entered into an agreement for child support and property division which provided that, in lieu of spousal support, Leah would receive the Beach Park house and one of the rental properties. George was also ordered to pay a total of $450 a month in child support. A final decree of divorce was issued on November 12, 1975, seventeen years and one day after their marriage.

Leah claims that even after George left, she would come home to find him in the house screaming and yelling at the children. The children, who then ranged from ages eleven to seventeen, recall the separation quite differently. While their parents fought continuously over money after he left, his anger and abusive conduct, at least toward them, dissipated completely. He would come into the house, chat with them, conduct his business with Leah, and leave. From their perspective, it was almost as if the violent current in the household was discharged when the connection between George and Leah was broken.

Leah was bothered by George's new girlfriend. He had become involved with an attractive twenty-year-old checker at the supermarket, Sharon Martinez,* an outspoken and independent woman with two children. George bought a duplex in Mountain View with Sharon, and in 1976 they moved into the upper unit. He frequently picked up one or two of his children on Friday and took them to Mountain View for the weekend. The children liked Sharon, and when they returned home talking about what a good time they had had with her and their father, Leah became furious. One time Diana brought home a gingerbread house that Sharon had made for her and on seeing it Leah angrily smashed the creation to pieces. Leah was particularly appalled, perhaps even morally offended, that her husband had become involved with a woman who hadn't finished high school and who had two illegitimate children. She would tell Kate how embarrassed she was to go to the mall and be seen in public after it became known that her ex-husband was living with that woman and her bastard children.

Leah did not handle the divorce well. She had never been a serious Catholic as an adult and she and George had not fulfilled their promise to the priest who married them to raise their children in the Catholic faith, but she couldn't shake off her upbringing. She well knew that in the eyes of the church, as well as in the eyes of her parents, her marriage was a failure.

Rather than experiencing relief that her husband was finally gone, Leah felt guilty and depressed. She had begun drinking early in the marriage—Burgundy mainly—and some of the most violent incidents had occurred when she and George were both drunk. Now her drinking increased. Frequently she drank by herself until she passed out on the couch. Then Kate would have to rouse her mother from her stupor and walk her upstairs and put her to bed.

In 1976, after thirteen years of determined effort, Leah finally graduated with honors from San Mateo College. She obtained a real estate license and had been working with a local company. She soon quit, however, and enrolled in the San Mateo Law School. Some of her children later bitterly charged that she took the settlement money intended for their college education and used it for her legal education and a luxury cruise.

Despite the misery George Franklin had inflicted on his children, everyone but Kate continued to be involved in his life. Janice lived with her father and Sharon in Mountain View for almost a year while she attended school. Later, as an adult, she invited him to live with her. When Diana was twelve, she accompanied him to a real estate convention in Sacramento. George Jr. worked for his father in the early eighties when he owned an apartment complex in Sacramento. Eileen celebrated her nineteenth birthday by traveling with him to Mexico in the same van he owned in 1969 and would later describe the trip as one of her favorite birthdays. She also worked in his real estate business for a while and visited him several times when he lived in Hawaii. One winter Janice and Eileen drove with their father across the country in the van to Florida to visit his mother and sisters.

Kate stayed away from him. She had no illusions about her father and no desire to have any sort of relationship with him. When he came to Beach Park to pick up his children for the evening or a weekend, she would make sure to be baby-sitting or working at the plant shop.

By Christmas 1977, George Franklin was no longer an enthusiastic fireman, if he ever had been. Not many fellow firefighters or captains were enthusiastic about George Franklin, either. The decline probably started in the winter of 1974, about the same time he and Leah separated. The collective bargaining agreement between the firefighters union and the city of San Mateo had expired in July of that year and relations between the two parties had deteriorated rapidly. George Franklin was appointed to the strike steering committee and quickly became a leader. He was an effective rabblerouser and organizer, passionately urging the hard line and the use of activist tactics. By the time the union went on strike in August, George was one of the loudest voices in the union hall. His anger and resentment, which had heretofore seethed below the surface in public, had finally found a legitimate target, something other than his wife and children.

When the firemen walked out, the governor called in the forestry workers to run the fire stations. George organized the picket lines around the stations and led the chant of "Scabs!" when supervisors and forestry workers crossed the lines. He angrily shook his fist and yelled for those inside to come out and fight.

Franklin also engineered one of the most brilliant maneuvers of the strike. He threw pickets around the racetrack and the pari-mutuel clerks refused to cross the line, closing the track for two days and depriving the city of tax revenues. The city came back to the table with a new offer which the union readily accepted.

When the firefighters returned to work, some union leaders realized that it was important to get past the hard feelings and begin healing. George Franklin, though, couldn't let go of the bitterness. Having thrived in the adversarial arena, he stayed hooked in the feelings that went with the struggle. He taunted the chiefs and encouraged others to persist in their disputes with management. He was elected vice-president of the union and he took full advantage of the right that, in his view, the position gave him to aggravate the supervisors.

In October 1976, George injured himself at work. He was leaning back in a chair in the station when the spring broke and he fell hard on the floor. He was put on disability for an injured disc for almost a year, during which time he grew a beard, put on weight, and took on the appearance of a wolf man. He returned to work in 1978. If his attitude had been bad before the injury, it was horrible now. He waged a vendetta against the administration and charged the captains and chiefs to their faces with being incompetent assholes who had to kiss ass to get their promotions. He began to develop strains of paranoia: everything in the department that irritated him was a personal attack. In the sixties, he had enjoyed screwing with his superiors' heads, jerking them around, but now he was genuinely surly and mean. He also began alienating his friends one by one. If you disagreed with him once, he turned on you instantly. You were either for him or against him, and if you were against him, fuck you and the horse you rode in on. He drank even more than in the past, and when he drank he became even moodier and more paranoid.

George and Sharon rented out the duplex and purchased a house together. But as George's drinking worsened, the two of them began leading separate lives. Finally, Sharon got fed up with coming home to a drunk every night and ended the relationship. When George learned that Sharon had asked Bill Mann's advice on the real estate division, he cut Mann, his longtime pupil and admirer, out of his life. Bill felt sorry for George: in the worst period of his life he was throwing his friends away. He reminded Bill of a dog who gets hit by a car and in the pain and confusion chews his own leg off.

George was also frequently stoned on the job. By then he had moved to Sacramento, and while driving to work with another fireman he would roll and smoke joints. At the station he stepped out back and got high.

After his return to work, George slipped while pushing a gurney up a hill and reinjured his back. He sought permanent disability and the department fought his request doggedly. His attitude in this period became so foul that many people simply avoided him. If you were to ask him in passing, "How are you?" he might say nothing, or he might respond, "Why do you want to know?" If a captain said, "Hi," to him, he would say, "Fuck you, talk to my lawyer."

He hired a lawyer to fight the department, and in 1978 he received permanent disability, which amounted to around $1,000 a month. Between his fight with the department, his hostility toward his friends, and his rejection by Sharon, which appeared to wound him deeply, George had become a bitter, isolated man. As one fireman would say, his world got smaller and smaller until finally there wasn't room in it for anyone but himself. He refused to attend his own retirement party, and when his colleagues came to get him, he threw them out of his house.

17

LEAH FRANKLIN WAS SITTING AT HER DESK IN HER law office in San Mateo when Eileen called her in October 1989 and asked her if she had noticed any changes in her after Susan was killed. Leah said she wasn't sure, but she would get out the family albums and look at the photos and see what she could remember. Eileen was incensed at her mother's response: What sort of a mother would not notice changes in her daughter after her best friend was murdered?

A few days later, Eileen called her mother again. This time she announced that she had seen her father murder Susan Nason twenty years earlier. Leah had long suspected that her former husband had killed Susan, had even accused him of it to his face in 1978, but hearing Eileen say she had seen him kill Susan, God, it felt like someone had dropped a bomb on her!

"No!" she cried.

"What do you mean, 'No'?" Eileen demanded angrily. "I am telling you what I saw, and I am telling you because I expect you to believe it. I am telling you the truth!"

"Well, I didn't say, 'No, I don't believe you,'" Leah responded quickly, "I said no because I am so sorry and so surprised that you were there and saw it."

Leah didn't doubt her daughter: she knew what sort of a man George Franklin was. But she wondered how she was going to deal with it if Eileen went public with her charge, how she was going to get through what would surely be a horrible ordeal. She decided to simply put the entire matter out of her mind.

A short time later Eileen called again and told her mother that she had visualized the killing while under hypnosis.

Kate was seven and a half months pregnant when Eileen called to tell her about the killing. It was the Monday before Thanksgiving 1989, and Kate's in-laws were visiting. Eileen asked if it was all right if Barry listened in on another line. "Sure," said Kate.

"Kate," she said then, "I'm going to tell you something that's going to change your life."

"It's going to change your life, your husband's life, your mother- and father-in-law and grandmother-in-law's life, everybody's life."

Eileen sounded very excited, strangely exhilarated. Kate half expected her to say she had won the lottery.

"I saw Dad kill Susan Nason!"

"What!" Kate shot back, stunned.

"I was riding in the van with Dad on the way to school and Janice was with us and we saw Susan and I said, 'Oh, Dad, won't you please stop, let's give Susan a ride!' And he said, 'Fine,' and he stopped and made Janice get out of the van and Susan got in and then we drove into the woods."

"Stop!" Kate interjected. "I don't want to know the details!"

Whatever was going on here, Kate didn't want any part of it. Her instinct told her the less she knew about what her sister was saying, the better. She refused to get pulled into one of

Eileen's crazy dances—there had been plenty of them in the past ten years and they were always destructive, full of bitterness and anger—and they were even crazier when she and Barry did them together. Kate had just recently relearned that lesson. Only a few weeks earlier, she had invited Eileen and Barry and their kids for Thanksgiving dinner, and when Eileen said they had to go to Barry's parents' house, Kate had suggested that his parents come up too, the more the merrier. Eileen said she would talk to Barry and call her back.

A couple of days later, not having heard, Kate called and Barry answered the phone. "Hi Barry, this is Kate," was all she had said before he launched into a vicious twenty-minute diatribe against the entire Franklin family; on and on he raged about how their mother was insane, their father was a perverted criminal, George Jr. was a fag, and Diana was retarded. Kate was stunned, but she listened wordlessly. She had experienced Barry's screaming before, but this was over the edge, even for him. Finally Kate asked if she might speak with Eileen.

"Eileen, are you coming for Thanksgiving dinner?" Kate asked, trying to start the conversation anew.

"No," Eileen had responded bitterly. "Barry and I decided my family has never given a damn about me and there is no reason to start now."

"I love you too," Kate said stiffly. "Goodbye." Kate had tried years ago to resign from her family. The one serious mistake she kept repeating in her life was refusing to give up hope that someday her family would become emotionally civilized. At moments like this, she realized it never would be. The rage was everywhere, woven into every fiber of the familial existence.

Now, here was Eileen on the phone only weeks later, all excited, telling her that their father had killed her best friend twenty years ago.

"Eileen, are you sure?" Kate asked.

"Yes, I was having nightmares and I went back into therapy, and then I had a dream and that's when I saw Dad kill Susan."

"A dream," Kate thought.

"I called the D.A.'s office," Eileen continued, "and they told me I knew things only an eyewitness could have known."

"So what happens next?" Kate asked.

"I'm going to talk to the D.A.'s office again on Wednesday," she replied.

Then Barry broke in.

"Isn't it great!" he demanded. He was as exhilarated and excited as Eileen.

"Great?" Kate wondered.

"Now your father will go to prison and get the help he needs," he continued.

"For rehabilitation," Eileen chimed in.

"Rehabilitation?" Kate thought. "In the American prison system?"

Kate slipped into a kind of shock, saying very little so as not to upset the others in her small house.

"What do you think?" Eileen finally asked.

"Eileen, are you sure?"

At that, Eileen came completely unglued and began screaming almost incoherently.

"You . . . mean . . . you . . . don't . . . believe . . . me?" she screeched.

"Eileen, you have to be sure about this," insisted Kate.

"Well, what do *you* think we should do?" Eileen asked.

"Eileen," Kate tried to say calmly, "you and Barry are both adults, you do what you think is best."

Barry and Eileen were obviously in one of their frenzies and Kate wanted no part of it. "No," she thought, "I'm not going to get pulled into their hysterical jig."

"I don't want to deal with you two on this," she finally said.

Eileen reiterated that they were going to talk to the cops again in a few days. They would let her know what happened.

"Yes, keep me posted," Kate responded, and hung up. She walked outside onto the deck of her small house for air. Her husband followed her out and she recounted the conversation to him. "Eileen's crazy," he said. Her in-laws, aware that she was upset but not wanting to pry, treated her gingerly the rest of the evening. As Kate drifted off to sleep that night, Eileen's story floated loosely in her consciousness. At 3:00 A.M. she awoke and began sorting things out. One thing didn't make sense: Eileen said they picked Susan up on the way to school, but hadn't she in fact disappeared after school?

Eileen called again on the Wednesday before Thanksgiving and told Kate that the prosecutors were going to pursue the case.

"Does it look like a good possibility of a conviction?" Kate asked.

"Yes," Eileen responded.

Kate called Eileen on Saturday, November 25.

"Hi, Eileen, I wanted to call and wish you a Happy Birthday. How are you?"

"How do you think I feel?" Eileen demanded, "I just spent four hours talking to the detectives *on my birthday*!" Her tone was bitter and self-pitying.

"That's it," thought Kate. "Everyone is a target for Eileen's wrath." Eileen had always felt that nobody in the family loved her and she was going to use this opportunity to vent her rage over her horrible childhood. You couldn't pay Kate enough to listen to that stuff.

"Sorry I asked," she said, " 'Bye."

As the days passed, Kate became confused and ambivalent, unsure of her thoughts and her feelings about Eileen's allegations. Had her father killed Susan? Was he capable of murder or was Eileen just imagining things—working through all of her childhood pain? Kate couldn't say her father was incapable of killing Susan. She had suffered mightily at his hands and had witnessed the damage he had inflicted on others and she believed him to be a man who could willfully make an immoral choice. Yet . . . Eileen had always stirred things up—always thrived in the eye of the storm.

18

November 28, 1989

THE CAR CARRYING MORSE AND CASSANDRO AND A
Sacramento officer pulled into Wooded Village at 7:20 A.M.
Tuesday morning. The cops wound their way through the complex, eventually finding the swimming pool, and climbed the
steps to Unit 226. Morse rapped on the door. No response. He
knocked again, and waited. Still no response. They left and
checked out the parking stall for Unit 226. Empty. The detectives went to the office and told the manager to have Franklin
give them a call when he got in, they wanted to talk to him.

Back at the station, the Sacramento cops called Allison
Bender,* a former girlfriend of Franklin's whom Morse had
learned about from Eileen. Allison was an attractive, successful Sacramento businesswoman and the local cops knew and
liked her. She came to the station and explained congenially
that she had met George in the fall of 1978 in Santa Cruz—he
had picked her up on the boardwalk—and they had eventually
lived together for six months. She terminated the relationship
because of his excessive drinking and one incident of violence.
Yes, she remembered his Volkswagen bus with a platform and
mattress in the back. No, there had been no pornography or
weird sex.

Around 11:00 A.M. George Franklin called the police and
said he was home. Once again, the cops drove to Wooded
Village and walked up to the deck outside Unit 226. This time
when Morse knocked on the door, it opened, and in front of
him stood a beefy man in baggy, dirty sweats. His gray hair and
beard were thick and shaggy. To Cassandro's eye, he was a far
cry from the image of a retired fireman, and he appeared a
helluva lot older than fifty. Morse thought he looked like a

wild man who had come in from the woods. Morse and Cassandro identified themselves as San Mateo detectives, showed their shields, and asked if they could come in. No, replied Franklin, he would talk to them outside.

"We have a new captain," Morse explained to Franklin, who had now stepped out onto the deck, "and he's reviewing all the old cases in San Mateo County, and we picked up the Susan Nason case since it's never been solved."

"Am I a suspect?" the gray-haired man asked immediately.

"Just like that," Cassandro thought, not, "Oh yes, I remember her," or, "She was that poor girl who used to play with my girls and disappeared," but just, "Am I a suspect?"

"Yes," replied Cassandro, in his usual straightforward style.

"Do I need an attorney?" Franklin asked.

"That's up to you."

"Have you talked to my daughter?"

"We will," replied Cassandro, even more surprised by this question than the previous one. An innocent man would ask, "Why are you talking to me?" or, "Is there something new?" A man wouldn't ask, "Have you talked to my daughter?" unless he was scared about what his daughter might have said.

Both cops thought it imperative to get Franklin away from his natural habitat.

"We would like you to come down to the station with us," Morse said. "We'll bring you back when we're through."

"Okay, do I need a lawyer?" Franklin inquired again.

"It's up to you," Cassandro repeated.

Looking at the man, Cassandro had the strange feeling that Franklin had been expecting them, as if he had always known somewhere inside that one day his favorite daughter would grow up and tell someone what she had seen and the cops would come knocking on his door.

Franklin asked if he could make a phone call and Cassandro said okay, then followed him inside to make sure he didn't pull anything. Franklin sat on the edge of the bed while he dialed. Cassandro could hear his conversation:

"Gladys," he said into the phone, "the police are here and

they want to talk to me about an old murder case. What do you think I should do? Okay, I'll call you back."

Franklin sat in the front seat of the police car with the Sacramento detective and Morse and Cassandro sat in the back. Traffic on Fair Oaks Boulevard was heavy, and as the trip stretched out, Morse saw his chances for a confession slipping away. You never wanted to give a suspect the opportunity to think; the more they thought, the less likely they were to waive their rights and talk to you. Trying to distract Franklin, Morse started chattering with the driver about his son's playing basketball and football and his work in the Police Olympics. Franklin said nothing.

At the sheriff's headquarters they put Franklin in an interview room and started a tape. Morse read Franklin his rights from a Miranda card and asked him if he understood.

"If I'm being read my rights, then I'm under arrest?" Franklin asked.

"We read rights to everybody," Morse responded, sensing that his worst fears were coming true. "If you want an attorney, then that's up to you. But, did you understand these rights?"

"Would you read them again, please?" Franklin asked.

Morse ran over them again.

"Insofar as I understand it, I think I better have a lawyer."

"Okay, buddy, that's it for you," Morse thought. People who invoked their rights always made him suspicious; a man with nothing to worry about wouldn't hide behind a lawyer. But he had learned something: Franklin apparently didn't have an alibi; he didn't say, "Hey look, guys, I was painting a house in Mountain View that day," or, "I was working the dog track that afternoon." Morse told all suspects that if they cooperated with him, he would work as hard to clear them as to convict them and he meant it. If Franklin had given an alibi, Morse would have stopped the process and sent him home while he checked it out. But Franklin had to say something, give him something to work with. Hell, so far the guy had seemed completely unperturbed by the whole thing.

Exactly one minute before noon on Tuesday, November 28,

1989, less than a week after Eileen had identified her father as her best friend's killer, Morse placed George Franklin under arrest for the murder of Susan Nason.

He ordered him to stand and lean up against the wall. Franklin complained that his back hurt.

Morse told Franklin that he could be booked in Sacramento, in which case they would be back to pick him up in five days, or he could agree to be booked in San Mateo County and they could leave that afternoon.

"I need a lawyer," Franklin replied. "I don't even know how to answer a question like that. I'm in a state of shock."

The latter statement had a false ring to Morse. Franklin didn't act like a man in a state of shock; he was too calm, too relaxed. Morse explained the option to him again.

"This is bizarre; I didn't do it. I didn't do anything," Franklin protested.

Finally, a denial, Morse thought, but still no explanation, only a flat statement, like it was something he thought he should say under the circumstances.

"We offered to listen to your side of the story," said Morse, slightly exasperated, "but you obviously don't want it that way. It's up to you. We acknowledge your rights, we don't mess with anybody's rights."

Franklin refused to agree to being taken to San Mateo County, repeating that he was in a state of shock and wanted to talk to an attorney.

Morse served him with the search warrant and asked him for the keys to his apartment and truck so they wouldn't have to break in.

"Well, I'm obviously in your power here," Franklin said, handing him the keys. "What can I do?"

A Sacramento officer came in and led Franklin away, and Morse and Cassandro left once again for Wooded Village to see what they could find.

Morse had decided he had probable cause to arrest Franklin when he refused to give them an alibi or some alternative explanation. The prosecutor would have to make the decision whether or not to formally charge him with the crime. Under

California law, Murray had forty-eight hours to charge or release Franklin. If he released him, his record would stay clean.

Morse knew he needed additional evidence to corroborate Eileen and Janice's statements before Franklin could be charged with murder. Marty Murray was a damn good prosecutor, and he had backed them unmistakably on this case so far, but they would have to give him something more, something to substantiate that Franklin was the type of man his daughters said he was, or he would have to be released.

The cops arrived back at Unit 226 at five minutes before one and used Franklin's key to enter the apartment. They took Polaroid pictures of the interior and for the rest of the day sorted through every box and file in the apartment. They also searched Franklin's 1988 Nissan pickup. On the rear bumper was a sticker with a picture of a large screw, followed by the word GUILT.

WITH LESS THAN FORTY-EIGHT HOURS TO MAKE THE DECISION whether or not to formally charge George Franklin with the murder of Susan Nason, Marty Murray reviewed the situation. There were serious problems: The murder occurred twenty years ago, which meant faded and faulty memories and scanty physical evidence; the case would rest on the credibility of a twenty-nine-year-old woman's recollection of what she saw as an eight-year-old girl. Children's, and even adults', memories of what they saw or experienced a month earlier were tricky enough in a court of law, much less a memory that was twenty years old.

Viewed from another perspective, Murray felt he had a strong case. First of all, he had an eyewitness to the murder, which was unusual, and the best homicide dick in the county said she would be great in front of a jury. Her recall of the details matched the physical evidence in most respects, and the inconsistencies and variations gave her story the ring of truth. Some of the facts were deadly accurate, some were plausibly accurate, given the vagaries of an eight-year-old's memory, and some didn't fit at all, like the time of day of the killing. The inconsistencies demonstrated that she hadn't gone to the newspaper files and stitched together a story. A completely accurate story would have been more suspect. To Murray's ear, her story sounded right, like it was being replayed through the eyes of an eight-year-old by an articulate twenty-nine-year-old. And when he listened to the tapes of the phone calls, he had the feeling that Eileen wanted to get the murder off her conscience and that she would be really just as happy if nothing happened. If Murray had said to her, "Sorry, we can't do anything with a twenty-year-old case," she would have said, "Thank you," and gone on her way. No, this woman was, at best, a reluctant accuser.

Also, what possible motive could she have for lying? She didn't stand to make any money from the accusation, and she sure wasn't doing it for the publicity. This poor woman was going to have to reveal the most intimate details of her life, dredge up horrid memories and bare her very soul before the world in a court of law.

Her story didn't stand totally uncorroborated. She reported facts, supported by evidence, like the crushed ring and the mattress, that she could not have known unless she had witnessed the killing. And the items Morse and Cassandro had found in Unit 226 demonstrated that her father had a long-standing sexual interest in little children. Whether such material would ever be admissible in court was another matter.

Finally, George Franklin, given the opportunity, had not presented another view of the facts. If he had been somewhere else that afternoon, he certainly would have said so.

Murray didn't underestimate the difficulties of the prosecution, and he was well aware that many prosecutors would be extremely reluctant to file a charge on this evidence. But he felt he had a reasonable probability of obtaining a conviction. Equally important, he believed that George Franklin had murdered Susan Nason.

Murray picked up the phone and called Eileen and told her that her father had been arrested, was in custody, and that he expected to charge him with first-degree murder.

"Oh my God!" she exclaimed. "They didn't hurt him, did they? Did he say anything? Did he confess to the killing?"

When Murray told her he hadn't confessed, she expressed her fear that he might be released on bond and come looking for her; he had property in Sacramento and Hawaii and could probably raise a lot of money quickly. Murray said he would seek a bond of two million dollars and he promised to let her know if and when he made bail. "Please tell me the second he gets out," she pleaded, "because if he does, I'm taking my kids and going into hiding."

Murray told her that Mrs. Nason had been informed of the arrest.

"Is she mad at me?" Eileen asked plaintively.

"No, why would she be?" Murray replied.

"For not coming forward sooner."

19

ON THE MORNING OF NOVEMBER 28, WHILE THE COPS were knocking on George Franklin's door, he was driving down from Nevada City, a historic gold rush town about eighty miles north of Sacramento. George had rented three rooms in the attic of a gray frame house trimmed in red which sat on a hilly, rundown street lined with ramshackle cottages and overgrown yards. Marilyn Kedslie owned the house and, more than a year earlier, had answered an ad in the *Foothill Trader,* the local shopper, from a man seeking a place to live. He described himself as a nonsmoker, nondrinker, with no pets. Marilyn preferred to rent the attic to a single man, because women were so helpless when it came to fixing things.

Marilyn liked George immediately. He told her he was a full-time student and planned to move up to Nevada City permanently when he finished his studies. He had a real estate license and intended to establish himself in business. Until then, he would come up mainly on weekends and holidays.

George frequently stopped and talked to her elderly mother and dropped off AA literature, religious tracts, and Lillian Vernon catalogues. Her mother liked him, as did Marilyn's children and grandchildren. He was an excellent tenant, paying the $200 a month rent three months in advance and occasionally helping out with small chores.

As George settled into his weekend life in Nevada City, he started planning ahead for his permanent move. He put an ad in the *Foothill Trader* saying that he was looking to associate with an established real estate company. Ginny Gage, a crusty middle-aged woman who owned her own real estate firm, answered his ad. Ginny liked everything about George Franklin except for his beard and thought he looked quite handsome in his glasses, which he wore only to read. George was more of a gentleman than many preachers she knew, and he was articulate and well read. He could talk knowledgeably about any subject that came up and he spoke with perfect grammar and diction.

Soon after they met, he began sending her cards, often pencil sketches with religious messages, or thank-you notes with happy-face stickers on them. He typed copies of his recipes from his fire department days and gave them to her.

To Ginny, George seemed to have his life all together. He enjoyed cooking and spending most of his evenings alone. He was excited about moving up to the area permanently and buying some land for himself. He placed ads in the paper for kits for dome houses and log cabins. The man seldom spoke of his personal life, other than to mention in passing that he had a wife and five children, whose names or ages he never mentioned. He seemed like a man who wanted to open a new chapter in his life.

George Franklin was returning to Carmichael the morning of November 28 because he had two classes at American River College that day: United States History in the afternoon and

California History in the early evening. It would never occur to George to miss a class. He was always the first one in the classroom and the last one to leave.

Professor Bill Chambers was used to seeing George already in his seat when he entered the classroom. In his thirty years of teaching, Professor Chambers had never had a student like George Franklin. American River College was a two-year community college and most students were in their mid-twenties. A few older women attended, usually mothers coming back to school after raising their children, but he saw few men in their fifties. Rarely did the students evidence any real interest in the subject matter. George, on the other hand, had a genuine thirst for knowledge. He always sought to understand the material at least one level beyond the textbook presentation.

In the fall of 1988, George had taken his first class from Professor Chambers, entitled "History and Geology of the Mother Lode," which focused on the gold rush and its modern implications. George became fascinated with the topic and began reading in the area on his own. He went to Chambers's office one evening after class and brought copies of related articles from *Smithsonian* and *Audubon* magazines, which he apparently subscribed to, and talked about them with great enthusiasm. "I'm really enjoying this," he would say; "where should I look next?" He became fascinated with the Donner Pass party and the Overland Trail along the Platte River, and he searched widely for articles on the topics.

"Now, I don't mean to get us off the track," George would say in class, "but would you elaborate a little more on this line, what Jackson was really like in his attitude toward the Indians?" And off the class would go on a ten-minute journey. It was a type of inquiry Chambers would never get from other students: the man genuinely sought to understand. He wanted knowledge for knowledge's sake.

George didn't need to try to impress his professor; he averaged 91.7 percent on the quizzes, and he received the highest of the three A's awarded in the course. He wrote very clearly and coherently, a good deal better than most of the students.

The other students seemed drawn to George, in spite of the age difference. Maybe it was his enthusiasm for the course, or maybe it was just his general positive attitude. He always had plenty of energy and an active sense of humor. His classmates obviously trusted his judgment: On the day before a test, Chambers would come in and see the students questioning him about what he thought would be covered and asking to look at his notes.

Once, when George stopped by Chambers's office, he made a bitter remark or two about his divorce, but he didn't seem consumed by that or anything else in the past. It seemed to Chambers as if his oldest and best student was hitting his stride for the first time in his life.

Chambers received a note of appreciation from George during the spring class in which George referred to himself as a southern Democrat who firmly believed that people got the government they deserved. When people become uninvolved in the political process, he stressed, they have no right to complain when they become bit players in a B movie "upstaged by Bonzo and his co-star, Ronnie Righteous." He also enclosed a bookmark containing the prayer of St. Francis, which read: "Lord Make Me An Instrument Of Your Peace: Where There Is Hatred, Let Me Sow Love; Where There Is Injury, Pardon; Where There Is Doubt, Faith; Where There Is Despair, Hope; Where There Is Darkness, Light; Where There is Sadness, Joy."

Professor Chambers had been delighted when George signed up for two classes in the fall of 1989. His star pupil had received an A the previous spring and he was once again enlivening the classroom discussion with his inquiring mind.

Chambers received a Thanksgiving note from George on November 21, a few days before the holiday. George had enclosed a copy of an article from the *Sacramento Bee* written by a minister who called for a "deep thanksgiving for the freedom of the spirit." George liked the article for its tolerant attitude and tied it into the class's recent study of the Constitution and the freedoms guaranteed therein. Although he was a "heretic" from the Baptist Belt of the south, he was also a card-carrying member of the ACLU, and he was appreciative of the freedoms he felt obliged to protect and defend.

"For the blessings of freedom, I am grateful," he closed, "and, Sir, I wish you a very happy and peaceful Thanksgiving."

20

GEORGE FRANKLIN SPENT TUESDAY NIGHT, THE 28TH, in the Sacramento jail. On Wednesday he was transported to the Hall of Justice in Redwood City and booked on suspicion of first-degree murder.

The public relations officer for the San Mateo County Sheriff's Office knew that the reporters, who worked in the press room on the first floor of the courthouse, would eventually discover Franklin's arrest by flipping through the booking slips on the fourth floor, so around 3:30 P.M. he called the press room and said he had a story. Within a few minutes his office was filled with the "cops and courts" reporters from the *San Francisco Chronicle,* the *San Francisco Examiner,* the *San Mateo Times,* the *San Jose Mercury,* the *Peninsula Times Tribune,* and the *Bay City News,* a local wire service. The officer did not tell them much: A Sacramento man had been arrested on a tip in the 1969 murder of Susan Nason of Foster City. He refused to identify the source of the tip, but noted that Franklin, a former San Mateo fireman, would be arraigned Thursday afternoon in municipal court.

The media scramble began. The *Mercury* put four reporters on it, the *San Mateo Times* two. The afternoon papers were mad because Franklin had been arrested on Tuesday and they hadn't been told until Wednesday, too late for their deadline. Reporters hunted up the clips from 1969, skimmed the facts, then called the Nason household in Foster City for quotes.

Television mini-cams set up on the Nason front lawn and reporters banged on the front door. Other scribes contacted the fire department, searching for profile information on Franklin. The reporter for the *San Francisco Chronicle* discovered that the "tip" had come from one of Franklin's daughters, who claimed to have witnessed her father kill Susan, and the *Chronicle* broke the story in the Thursday morning edition. The PR officer eventually confirmed for the other reporters that the tipster was one of Franklin's daughters and a former classmate of Susan's, but refused to disclose her name. Reporters located the 1974 Franklin divorce file in the clerk's office, in which the daughters' names and ages were listed, and began tracking them down.

Donald Nason spoke to the press for the family. The pain from the reopened wound was evident on his face. "It's never over until it's over," he said, expressing the family's shock and relief on hearing of the arrest. "The worst part," he was quoted as saying, "was waiting for her to be found. Until you know that, you can't even begin mourning. As far as finding out who did it, we always felt it would be a matter of time." He barely remembered the Franklins, but praised the daughter for coming forward and said it must have been very painful for her all these years. He worried some about whether she could hold up under the ordeal. He found solace in the fact that the accused killer wasn't a stranger as he had assumed for twenty years, that it had been a neighbor who had snatched his youngest daughter from in front of her home. This meant he and his wife hadn't failed to properly warn Susie against strangers and that Margaret had been right when she said her daughter would never get in the car with a stranger. "But," he asked plaintively, "how do you guard against someone you know?"

A veteran cops and courts reporter for the *San Jose Mercury* was on hand at the arraignment Thursday afternoon. That morning she had obtained some of the daughters' addresses from the Department of Motor Vehicles. She had also called Leah's law office, but had not gotten through to her. She reached George Jr.'s answering machine, and chuckled over his weird message that he was off to Colombia looking for some snow. Kate, she learned, lived in an upscale mountain suburb populated by well-to-do professionals. The reporter made her way to Courtroom 7-E, the "in-custody" courtroom where arraignments were held, and which was now crammed elbow to elbow with press. The *Chronicle*'s identification of the tipster had cranked up the story, and print, radio, and television people had stormed the small courtroom. A bulletproof Plexiglas shield separated the spectators from the rest of the room, shutting off air circulation and making the public section hot and stuffy. Six prisoners were led in, each one wearing identical orange T-shirts and orange pants. Shiny chains encircled their waists and bound their wrists and ankles. Five of them were linked together, but Franklin, the high-profile defendant, stood alone. He would go first.

The reporter saw Bob Morse sitting next to various other detectives and assistant D.A.'s who were anxious to get a glimpse of the already-famous George Franklin. She had known Morse for many years and liked and respected him. He could be a bit crusty until you put in your time on the crime beat and he got to know you and decided that "you could hold your mud," which was cop talk for not betraying a confidence. After that, he always played it straight with you. She was amazed that despite all the horrible stuff he had seen and all the rotten human beings he had dealt with over the years, he hadn't developed a shell and turned weird and withdrawn like a lot of cops. He had an ego, but it wasn't in the least offensive, and he had a wicked sense of humor that spared no one, least of all himself.

The reporter took a long look at Franklin. He seemed very big and powerful, easily strong enough to smash a child's skull with a rock. He definitely stood out from the riffraff who had been in the dock many times before. His bearing had a certain wild power to it and it gave her the creeps.

She had never heard of the lawyer from San Francisco who entered his appearance on Franklin's behalf. Doug Horngrad stood a little over six feet tall, had black hair, and wore horn-rimmed glasses. He was obviously not a native Californian, probably a transplant from New York or Boston. He seemed a cut above some of the local lawyers who attended the arraignment in polyester suits and battered briefcases. He handled himself well.

She watched as Franklin was formally charged with first-degree murder. At Horngrad's request, the judge continued the matter until the following Wednesday for entry of plea and setting of bail. Then Horngrad asked the judge to issue an order prohibiting all law enforcement officials and potential witnesses, including Franklin family members, from talking to the press. He argued that pre-trial publicity would make it impossible for his client to get a fair trial. The reporter watched in dismay as the judge issued the gag order and sealed the court documents, including a list of the items seized under the search warrant.

She approached Morse after the hearing. He wanted to talk to her, but couldn't. "You'll see," he said, leaning into her as if he were taking her into his confidence, his green eyes twinkling and his eyebrows jumping, "we got great stuff on this guy."

Friday's papers carried the same freckle-faced, gap-toothed picture of Susan Nason that had run twenty years ago. Next to it was a picture of George Franklin, an image of unrepentant evil: his heavy black brows protruded over deep eyes that stared off in a cold, remorseless gaze; the corners of his mouth slashed downward like black sickles, and deep creases in his cheeks disappeared into an unkempt beard; clumps of white hair swirled out from the side of his head like horns. If ever a man looked capable of bludgeoning an eight-year-old girl to death, this man did. The pictures and the story of his arrest ran in newspapers from one end of the state to the other.

Saturday would mark the twentieth anniversary of the discovery of Susan's body in the hills overlooking Crystal Springs Reservoir.

CALIFORNIA COULD NOT PUT GEORGE FRANKLIN TO DEATH FOR THE killing of Susan Nason. He would have to be tried under the laws in effect in 1969, and the death penalty in effect in California at that time had subsequently been ruled unconstitutional. In Murray's view, George Franklin was certainly deserving of the death penalty and he would have sought his execution without hesitation had he been able. The fact that Franklin had killed Susan during the commission of a felony, child molestation, would have met the requirements of the current statute. In lieu of the ultimate penalty, Murray would settle for nothing less than a conviction for first-degree murder. Absolutely no plea bargaining. This case was up or down. Either George Franklin had killed the little girl with premeditation or he hadn't killed her at all.

When Murray first saw Franklin, the man looked so scruffy and wild that he thought he might be deranged. Murray knew he had been a hard drinker, and he worried that the defense might argue that he was subject to alcoholic blackouts and couldn't be held responsible for his actions.

At the continued arraignment on December 6, Franklin, with Horngrad at his side, entered a plea of not guilty. Murray asked for bail in the amount of two million dollars, and the judge set a hearing on the matter for the following Wednesday.

A *Los Angeles Times* reporter was the first to reach Eileen. He figured she was the most likely of the sisters because she was the same age as Susan; he had found her address through the Department of Motor Vehicles. When he called her at home, she confirmed that she was the accuser, but said she couldn't talk about the case. However, she said, she and her husband Barry had had a business relationship with the *Los Angeles Times* and she thought the paper was a class organization, so when the time came to talk she would give him her first in-depth interview. A short time later, a reporter for the *Mercury* showed up at her door, but she didn't speak with him either. Barry, on the other hand, was not so reticent. He indicated that he and Eileen were quite anxious to talk to the press. They had agonized for a long time over the decision to call the authorities and finally came forward because of their compassion for Susan's parents.

At the bail hearing the following Wednesday, December 13, Marty Murray reiterated his request for a two-million-dollar bond. Then he dropped a bombshell. In support of his argument that Franklin should not be allowed on the streets and that he had good reason to flee the jurisdiction, Murray stated that items recovered in the search indicated that the defendant had shown a sexual interest in children for the past twenty years. This was good stuff for the press, titillating corroboration of the daughter's story, and would receive big play in the next day's papers.

Arthur Wachtel, Horngrad's law partner, protested to the court that the items recovered in the search did not in any way connect his client with the commission of the crime and asked that bail be set for $50,000. He said there were people in the courtroom prepared to testify as to his client's good character and the fact that he wasn't a danger to the community. Then the defense dropped a bombshell of its own: The government had previously cleared George Franklin in the killing of Susan Nason. Another daughter, Janice, had gone to the police in 1984 and said she suspected her father of the crime, but she had also said he had been home after 4:00 P.M. or 4:15 which, in effect, provided him with an alibi. The two sisters lived together in Canoga Park and Janice had undoubtedly told Eileen of her suspicions in 1984, and now Eileen claimed to have witnessed the killing. The sisters, the defense was suggesting, had cooked up the story.

The judge wasn't impressed with Wachtel's argument. He set bail in the amount of two million dollars and continued the gag order. Over the next two weeks, attorneys for the media continued to argue for a lifting of the gag order, and finally, on December 27, the judge, with Murray's concurrence, limited the order to attorneys and law enforcement officials. Witnesses were now free to talk about the case.

After the gag order was lifted, Cinde Chorness of the *San Mateo Times* was the first to reach Eileen. The accusing daughter told her she would have to check with Barry before talking. Eventually, both proved more than eager to speak with her. In fact, the reporter had difficulty that first night getting through Barry to Eileen. He hogged the phone and told Chorness that he was the first person that his wife had told of the killing. He also explained that Eileen and Janice were both convinced that their dad had killed Susan, and that they had "put their two stories together." When Barry finally put Eileen on the line, she provided only sketchy details of the killing. The *San Mateo Times* had been the family newspaper, Eileen told her in the first call, and when she decided to give an in-depth interview, it would be with a reporter from that paper. Later, Chorness spoke with her frequently and was surprised at how available she was and how she was never in a hurry to get off the phone.

Barry took charge of the phone that first evening, juggling calls, leaving some reporters on call-waiting while talking to others. Scribes from two papers didn't make it through Barry to Eileen at all. The reporters soon began making fun of Barry because of his continuous posturing and the fact that he would never shut up. He was, in one reporter's words, "a schmuck."

While Eileen would not discuss the details of the killing, she did speak freely and dramatically about the tragic implications of the killing for her life:

"I don't think I'll ever lead a normal life again," she said to an *L.A. Times* reporter. "I'm not just a witness to a crime, I'm a witness to a crime that my father committed—the same man who is the father of all my brothers and sisters and is the grandfather of my children." She insisted that she had told her story to all of her siblings and none of them had doubted her.

She and Susie had played together, she went on, and ". . . were kindred spirits. We had somewhat the same features and were bonded by the torment from the other kids because of our reddish hair and freckles. I guess what I really lost was the ability to feel safe making friends," she said. "I developed this fear of loss and became a real loner after that."

A few days later a reporter for the *Mercury* called Eileen to follow up the story.

"Wait a minute," she said, "I think we're mad at the *Mercury*." She turned from the phone and asked her husband, "Barry, aren't we mad at the *Mercury*?"

"Yes," a male voice replied.

"We're mad at the *Mercury*," she confirmed. "I'm not going to talk to you."

21

IN THE FALL OF 1981, GARY HIRATO HAD BEEN A member of the San Jose police force for almost four years. He had transferred to the vice squad the previous spring, and he considered it a good assignment. Hirato, a short, good-looking man of Japanese ancestry in his early twenties, had been nicknamed "Boom Boom" by the other vice cops in honor of the two nuclear bombs dropped on Japan in World War II. He handled it with good humor.

Vice handled gambling, drug, and alcohol offenses and commercial prostitution, which included call girl rings and massage and escort services. Street whores were handled by another unit. Outcall services advertised in the newspapers and took out ads in the Yellow Pages. You could even clip a coupon for an extra hour for every two you purchased. The pimps insisted they were legitimate businessmen and would talk on the phone only about escort or massage services. If you mentioned sex, they would disclaim any knowledge and sometimes become outraged and greatly offended. The only deal they wanted to talk about was fifty dollars for a massage, plus a tip for the girl. Many of the pimps even had their girls sign statements swearing they had specifically been told not to have sex with the customers.

For the girls, taking calls at home from their pimp was more civilized than standing on street corners sticking their heads in dark car windows and negotiating sex acts. A massage girl could still get in sticky situations, but at least she wasn't walking the streets with ice picks or hat pins in her purse as protection against her customers. Most of the girls carried beepers, and they were sent on calls up the peninsula and across the bay to Berkeley and Oakland. San Jose was right on the southern edge of the Silicon Valley, which was booming in 1981, and business was good. Hirato guessed around 35 or 40 services were running close to 500 girls.

Hirato's partner Alex Cruise was a tall, lanky Panamanian of Hispanic-African descent, who had worked vice for three years. He was bilingual and spoke in a deep, mellifluous baritone. He had the language and moves, the jittery attitude, of a legitimate street dude, probably a result of having worked vice in New York City for three years.

Cruise felt sorrier for the street whores than he did for the massage and escort girls. The street ladies came from tough backgrounds and led hard, often dangerous lives, while many of the escort girls were middle-class housewives or professional women trying to earn a few bucks on the side, often to support a drug habit. But they were all taking their chances.

The real goal of these busts was to nail the pimp and put him out of business. The charge against the girls, solicitation for an act of prostitution, was only a misdemeanor. Pimping was a felony. The cops always tried to turn a girl on her pimp, but most of the time the girls kept their mouths shut and did their time. Out of a hundred prostitution busts, Hirato had nailed the pimp only twice.

On November 3, 1981, Hirato was thumbing through the ads in a local rag that specialized in personals in anticipation of setting up a bust. He selected an ad and dialed the number.

"Sin-su-al Massage, may I help you?" the black male voice answered.

"Yes," Hirato began, "I would like to know something about your . . . ad . . . here I got in your paper."

"Okay sir, we're now called a massage service and we're strictly outcall. We charge fifty dollars per hour for a full body massage and we accept cash, Visa, and MasterCard. Our girls serve residences, motels, hotels in Santa Clara, San Mateo, and Southern Alameda counties," the man said as smoothly as if he were selling a rug-cleaning service.

The man told Hirato that he could have a girl at his motel in thirty to forty-five minutes. Hirato drove to the Easy 8 Motel and booked Room 102. The Easy 8 wasn't as bad as its name implied. Vice used a variety of motels, but stayed away from the real sleazy ones.

Hirato called Sin-su-al again to say he'd gotten a room. The man asked him for details.

"Okay, my name is Gary Hiroshima." It wasn't the first time Hirato had used the name of this bombed-out Japanese city, but nobody had ever picked up on it. Neither did this guy. Hirato gave him the room number.

The man said he would call Hirato back in half an hour to confirm the appointment and then send a girl over to his room.

"Okay, how long will it take once you call me, 'cause I don't have much time?" Hirato knew from experience that prostitutes were habitually late.

"It'll take about half an hour."

Hirato pressed him, telling him he needed to be finished by five. The only problem would be the traffic, the man told him, because they were getting close to rush hour. Also, the girl he had in mind lived in Palo Alto, an upscale community twenty miles north of San Jose.

The woman received the call around 3:30 in her Palo Alto apartment. She already had plans for the evening and wasn't anxious to do the job, but Frederick, her pimp, said he was in a bind, so as a favor to him she agreed to go. She grabbed her purse and hopped into her yellow 1980 Ford Fairmont and left for the Easy 8 Motel, running into some traffic on the way. When she arrived, she stuck her purse under the front seat of the car and looked for Room 102.

Inside the motel room, Hirato had planted a high-powered mike in the wastebasket. Cruise sat outside in his car with a wire into the mike. His 110 flash camera was loaded and ready.

While he waited, Hirato ran over the scene in his mind. Sometimes he acted nervous like this was his first time cheating on his wife, other times he acted like he was in a rush. If the girl seemed antsy or suspicious, he would joke that he was too young or too short to be a cop. He knew that legally there must be an agreement of sex for money and one overt act in furtherance of the agreement. After the girl agreed, he would give her the money, which had been photocopied, and then have her remove her clothes. He would remove his clothes if necessary, but never touch her. Absolutely never. Once she was naked, he would give the prearranged signal to his partner, who would come busting in with flashbulbs popping. The tape captured her words and the film her body. If it was done right, the case would never go to court. The prosecutor could always play the tape and hold up the photos to the jury and ask, "Why would this girl be naked if she was only going to give this man a massage?" Most girls eventually pled out.

Hirato heard the knock on the door and rose to answer it.

"Hi," he said pleasantly, a little taken aback by the girl standing in front of him. Many of the massage girls were in their late twenties or early thirties, usually a little less rough-looking than street whores, but this one was young and pretty, almost innocent. Her red hair was long and striking.

"Hi, Gary?" the woman asked.

"Yes."

"I'm Eileen."

"Oh, hi, Eileen, how are you doing?" he answered, stepping back so she could come in. She was wearing an attractive floral print dress, low cut but not too revealing.

"Pretty good, how are you doing?"

"All right . . . So . . . pretty warm today."

"It's beautiful."

"It's nice, so ahh . . ."

"I have to get the money for the massage," Eileen interrupted, obviously ready to get down to business, "and let them know I'm here."

Hirato knew that, as a general rule, the cop wasn't supposed to mention sex first. He was supposed to let the girl bring up the topic so she couldn't later claim entrapment, but some of the girls were wise and they would play word games with you: What is it you want? A good time. What is a good time to you? I don't know, what is it to you? On and on. The rules were a little more relaxed in massage cases, and Hirato decided to get straight to the point.

"There's the phone right there if you want to call. Mmmm, I

didn't . . . uh . . . I didn't really want a massage. I'd rather get laid. Is that okay?"

"It depends on if you can afford it or not," Eileen responded coolly.

This girl was not strung out, Hirato thought. She seemed very calm, very sure of herself. If anybody was nervous, it was him.

"Well, well," he stammered.

"Okay," she continued, " 'cause they sent me out to give a massage. The money for the massage I give back to them and I get five dollars to pay for my gas." Eileen was explaining the necessity for a "tip."

"Five dollars?" Hirato repeated.

"Sure, sure, but that doesn't keep me from making a thousand a week," Eileen bragged, apparently wanting to assure her customer that he wasn't getting a cheap prostitute, or an unsuccessful one.

Hirato was skeptical of her claim—massage girls usually only turned four or five tricks a week, although with her youth and good looks, she might be able to do more.

He had to get her to say the magic words.

"Okay, well . . . it's . . . fifty—fifty dollars for a massage?"

"That's strictly a massage, okay?"

"Okay, go to it," Hirato said, indicating the phone. "I've got my wallet here."

"Okay, let me call and let them know I'm here."

She walked over to the phone.

"Hi, this is Eileen," she said into the receiver. "You'll hear from me in an hour. The traffic is a bear. Okay, 'bye. My, I'm sorry. . . . Yes, Cherie, goodbye."

"Who's that?" asked Hirato, acting like a first-timer.

"Oh, one of our bosses."

"Oh, he's not your pimp or anything like that?"

"I don't have a pimp," Eileen responded forcefully. "I'd have to give all the money to a pimp."

"Yeah, I know," Hirato responded. "Let me ask you this

. . . Do you make guys use a rubber?" At least he could make clear what they were talking about.

"Mmmm," began Eileen, "if . . . okay, if the person doesn't want to use them, I have to charge them a little extra to get a check-up."

This gal was no cherry, a beginner, Hirato thought. This chick knew what she was doing.

"Okay, well . . ."

"There's the whole bit. I can't take the pill."

"Oh, okay."

"I don't have a body that will accept it."

"Oh, I see," said Hirato.

"I think you're in a hurry, aren't you?" Eileen asked.

"Well, kind of, yeah. I thought you were going to get here faster."

"I'm sorry, the traffic was really bad."

"Okay, will you . . . how much . . . you said you have to charge extra for a . . ."

"Okay," began Eileen, finally getting to the specifics, "it's fifty dollars for a massage. Okay? And . . . God, I don't know . . . a hundred more."

"A hundred more?" Hirato asked. "Do you usually charge a hundred dollars?" It was a very reasonable figure, he knew. Street whores usually did five or six tricks a night at $35 apiece, but massage girls could get $50 to $150.

"I've charged two to three hundred," retorted Eileen, apparently offended that this john would think $100 was a lot of money for her, "but you're young, you know. I don't know if I can get away with it." Like any good salesman, she was trying to convince her customer that he was getting a good deal, a special deal.

"Well, I've got a hundred and twenty."

"Okay."

"Why don't I let you keep twenty dollars?" Eileen was already going to be down $30 from her stated price, but she was apparently unable to stand the thought of leaving her customer broke.

"Well, I've got a credit card, okay?"

"Well no, but that's not fair 'cause you'll have to eat or something." At this rate, after she kicked back to the pimp, she would get only $50.

Hirato rewarded her generosity by opening the jaws of the trap a little further.

"So, a hundred dollars to get laid then?"

"Sure."

"Okay."

Hirato pulled out his wallet and handed Eileen the $100. Having learned that he couldn't afford the extra $25, she handed him a condom and asked him if he would mind using it.

Eileen knew she should try to get the customer to begin disrobing first—some cops hesitated to take off their clothes—but she was in a hurry to get on with her plans for the evening, so she went ahead and slipped the dress over her head and lay down on the bed.

As soon as she was completely naked, Hirato gave the prearranged signal.

"Boy, I wish my friends could see me now!" he said loudly.

Cruise, who had been following every word in the car, grabbed his camera, strode rapidly to the room, and burst in the door. He began snapping pictures of Eileen lying on the bed.

Hirato watched as Eileen desperately pulled a sheet over herself to avoid the sharp flashes of light bouncing around the room. Some of the more jaded girls just sat there when it came down, staring at the cop, at the camera, resigned. A few would begin screaming at the cops. Others would get angry at themselves: "I knew it! Goddamn it, I just knew it!" Some of the newer ones, the younger ones, would cry. When the flashbulbs stopped popping, Eileen's hands flew up to her face and she burst into tears. Her eyes seemed to just open up and pour forth. She had never expected this to happen.

Looking at her, Hirato wondered what such a pretty girl was doing here. Some of the girls, he knew, were lesbians, and many of them had been sexually abused as children. Some of them were ice cold. None of them enjoyed it. This girl seemed a little different from the others.

Hirato placed Eileen under arrest for solicitation of an act of prostitution. As soon as she was dressed, he handcuffed her hands behind her back and asked for identification. She told them it was under the front seat in the car. Hirato knew it wasn't uncommon for the girls to leave their purses in the car to avoid being ripped off by a customer. They left the room and walked to her yellow Fairmont. On the front seat Hirato found various papers with guys' names and addresses on them, also something commonly found in the possession of outcall girls. In the purse he found Eileen's identification, her check-book, three paper bundles containing what looked like cocaine, a glass tube, and a razor blade. A lot of the girls used drugs and dealt to their customers, although the tube and blade and the relatively small quantity led Hirato to believe the coke was just for Eileen's personal use.

They put Eileen in the cop car and drove her to the station. Along the way she recovered enough to mock Hirato for offering her a cigarette: How the hell was she supposed to smoke when her hands were cuffed?

At the station the cops booked Eileen and charged her with possession of cocaine, a felony, and solicitation, a misdemeanor. She was fingerprinted, photographed, and processed. The young woman who peered into the camera for a mug shot was not the same woman who had been bragging a short time earlier about how much money she charged an hour. Her carefully brushed out hair now hung limply to her shoulders. Only a hint of the original styling was evident in the wave which fell raggedly over her right eye. Reddish wisps stuck out here and there, a few clinging to the fair skin above her breast. Her eyebrows arched over round eyes, in a look reminiscent of her father. Her lips were slightly parted, as if to form words of protest or explanation. No tears streaked her freckle-free complexion; no look of shame or fright or contrition fixed her face; no flicker of humiliation or pain constricted her features. Instead, her face was curiously open, accessible, almost calm, although her eyes conveyed a focused and eerily flat look.

Something else hovered in that look—a shadow of defiance, perhaps, mixed with relief and gratitude.

Cruise and Hirato questioned Eileen and she identified her pimp. They knew Frederick—he had been busted earlier for operating a business without a license. They filled out the paperwork on her and went back to the vice unit. Hirato didn't track his cases as they wound through the system. He busted a girl and brought her in and booked her and went on about his business. If the D.A. needed him for anything on the case, he knew where to find him.

AFTER EILEEN WAS BOOKED, SHE WAS TAKEN TO ELMWOOD, THE women's jail outside San Jose, where she was strip-searched and thrown in a cell with the other prisoners. A few hours later she was released on her personal recognizance and a promise to return on November 17 for her arraignment.

Once out, Eileen turned to Aunt Sue, Leah's younger sister, for support and guidance. Sue had no idea of the abuse that had permeated her older sister's household for so many years until Eileen showed up on her doorstep in late 1981 with tales of prostitution, drugs, and childhood abuse. She was not surprised that Eileen was coming to her rather than her mother. She was horrified, however, at Eileen's sexual behavior and drug use, which Eileen admitted were out of control. Sue counseled her niece to take control of her life and look at who her friends really were. She was nothing more than an economic unit to her pimp and, as for her gay friends and their promiscuous and drug-oriented lifestyle, she should ask whether they really had her best interests at heart. She must accept responsibility for her behavior, and that meant not bashing her parents over the head with her prostitution arrest —she should keep that fact to herself.

Eileen also called Kate soon after her arrest, distraught over her legal problems and destitute. She had no money and an empty refrigerator. Kate and her husband Allen* brought bags of groceries to her apartment in Palo Alto, which she was sharing with a gay friend. She told them only about the cocaine charge, and Allen, a lawyer, counseled her to retain and follow the advice of a good criminal lawyer. Since this was her first offense, she might get off easy.

Sue contacted a prominent lawyer she knew who agreed to have a young associate handle Eileen's case under his supervision. Eileen pleaded not guilty, and on February 22, 1982, after a series of continuances, the court conducted a preliminary hearing. The judge found probable cause to believe that Eileen had solicited an act of prostitution, but to Eileen's great relief, he determined that the cocaine had been seized pursuant to an illegal search and dismissed the felony charge.

In the beginning, Eileen had wanted to go to trial, but as the date drew near and she realized that the prosecution intended to use the photographs from the motel room, she changed her mind. Unable to face the prospect of the pictures becoming public documents, she pled guilty to the solicitation charge and received a fifteen-day suspended jail sentence and a $750 fine, which she was allowed to pay off in monthly installments. She understood that if there were no further offenses for five years, her record could be cleared.

EILEEN WAS DETERMINED TO TURN HER LIFE AROUND. ALTHOUGH SHE talked to her pimp about going back to work, she followed her Aunt Sue's advice and decided against it. She knew she needed to get off cocaine, and she began cutting back.

Eileen had been dating three men, all older and all wealthy, but none of them really appealed to her. Then, a few days after her prostitution arrest, a fifty-year-old successful real estate salesman got her number from Diana and called and asked her out. Although not particularly attractive—one co-worker described him as Ichabod Crane with a hair transplant—he was very smooth and a polished ladies' man.

Eileen was captivated by him: he drove a gorgeous red Ferrari and was wealthier and more thoughtful than her other three suitors. The romance caught fire and soon she was deeply involved. The realtor found Eileen exciting and he respected what he saw as her straightforwardness, her honesty with herself and others. He sensed the toughness in her, but he saw it as a mask developed to protect a deeply sensitive nature.

She was a little shy, but she had considerable poise and mixed easily with his older friends. He saw her as a woman who, at twenty-one, had done a good job of putting her life together, a woman with strong common sense, street sense, who was very capable of making good choices and directing her own life. He loved the strength and tenderness in her, a combination he rarely found in women.

Eileen and the realtor dated for about a year and a half, until he decided he wanted to focus exclusively on another relationship he was in. Maybe he and Eileen could get back together if and when that was over. Eileen was crushed. She had counted on getting married, and felt abandoned and betrayed by his decision—he was no better than the other men in her life.

22

IN JUST OVER TWO YEARS, EILEEN HAD EVOLVED FROM one of the homeliest girls at San Mateo High School into a beautiful hooker in San Jose. She had gone from having no confidence in herself and feeling extremely unattractive to selling her sexuality to whoever could read the newspaper and dial a phone number. It had been a disjointed path.

After high school, she had moved in with Janice and found a job as a receptionist at the REMAX real estate office in Foster City. She had few if any girlfriends, except for Diana, and continued running with the gay crowd, which had expanded well beyond her high school friends. After work she would meet her gay friends in the San Mateo bars and often party on into the evening, drinking, playing pool, dancing, and doing drugs until closing time.

Jeff Munson, a gay who had just moved to town and worked

at a local bank, was introduced to Eileen by a friend one evening at the Answer. He was immediately impressed: she
seemed to know a lot of people and what was happening. He
liked her attitude, too: she was sarcastic and enjoyed making
snotty, rude remarks about other people. The two hit it off and
soon began sharing confidences and telling each other their
problems. Eileen talked a lot about her mother, who she
claimed had thrown her out of the house, but little about her
father.

Jeff noticed admiringly that Eileen usually managed to be
the center of attention. She had a flamboyant way about her, a
dramatic flair, and the gays responded by showering her with
adoration and affection.

Eileen often mothered Jeff. After he was an eyewitness to a
robbery at the bank, his roommate was scared to come home
because the robber was out on bail. Eileen came to his apartment with flowers and told him he was her hero and stayed
with him for several days. Soon, however, Jeff came to learn
another side to Eileen: she was a woman of many faces, a
master of disguises. She could create a mask or a persona for
any situation in order to get what she wanted. She was also
quite clever at manipulating people in such a way that they
didn't know they had been manipulated.

Eileen and Jeff spent more and more time together until
finally they moved in together. They became even closer, leaving their doors open between the adjoining bedrooms, unless
one of them had an overnight guest. If Jeff had a guest and
Eileen didn't, she would throw open his bedroom door early in
the morning and sing a wake-up song to him and his partner.
The two of them talked about getting married.

Eileen may have found the affection of gay men to be a
welcome alternative to the sexual attentions of straight men,
but during this time she also plunged into a period of intense
promiscuity. If she wasn't in the gay bars, she was in the
straight bars picking up men. She would sleep with a man
merely because he offered to take her to a hotel, a new experience. One Saturday morning a relative showed up at her apartment just as she came dragging in, disheveled and depressed.

She explained that the night before she had gone home with a man she had met in a bar and had had to walk home because he refused to give her a ride.

The AIDS epidemic had not yet hit and, in Eileen's circle at least, constant, indiscriminate sexual activity was the norm. Everyone was acting out sexually and there was almost a challenge to see how much sex you could have with how many people in how little time using as much alcohol and as many drugs as possible. It was a time, Jeff would think later, when everyone was defining their self-worth in terms of their sexuality. Eileen fitted perfectly into the scene—her friends lavished their approval on her loose sexual behavior and daily drug use.

Eileen was not completely without direction. She knew what she wanted—nice clothes, jewelry, trips, cars, all the things that money could buy—and she was determined to marry a rich man in order to get them. She had sought jobs that would give her exposure to wealthy men. Real estate on the peninsula had become one of the hottest markets in the United States, and there was no better place to meet financially successful men than sitting behind a desk right inside the front door of a major real estate office, like REMAX. For several months she dated the owner of a swanky restaurant in the area. He was married and twenty years her senior, but he had money and status in the community. Although she was under age, she would sit at the bar and order drinks as she pleased, making it clear to the bartenders and waitresses that she expected to be treated with deference because she was the boss's girlfriend.

Eileen had left the homely, freckled redhead behind in high school. Now she was pretty and sexy, or at least trying her best to be. She wore her hair shoulder length, with one wave falling seductively over her right eye. As she talked, she would give the wave a graceful but provocative toss. The manager at REMAX thought Eileen was trying to transform herself into a sultry red-headed Marilyn Monroe. She swayed her hips slightly as she walked, and when she spoke on the phone or over the intercom her voice was low and breathy. Her blouses were either low cut or open to the second button, revealing expanses of white flesh, and her skirts were tight and short.

Several of the real estate agents in the office complained that Eileen dressed too provocatively and showed too much skin for a business office.

In 1979, Eileen made her first appearance on television. Three years earlier, she had become acquainted with a female television reporter, and now this reporter was doing a series on teen suicide. The reporter's message was that teenagers shouldn't despair, there was life after adolescence. Eileen had told her about her suicide attempt (the same one she told Diana was an unsuccessful attempt to get high), and when the reporter asked Eileen to go on camera and talk about her experience, Eileen readily agreed. The clip is short but moving.

As the scene opens, Eileen is walking across a field toward the camera. The sun is shining brightly, highlighting the rich golds and greens of the meadows. She smiles and waves to the reporter, then her hand breezily flips back the lock of hair over her right eye, opening her youthful, innocent face to the light. She is wearing a sleeveless white, vestlike top with muted green stripes and a deep V neckline. The vest fits snugly and the top button is open. Beneath the bottom button, the vest cuts away, revealing her bare midriff. Her green, knee-length skirt clings tightly to her shapely hips and thighs, but is pulled into sharp creases across the front by an oddly protruding stomach. She clutches a black purse in her left hand and moves easily, confidently, in white high heels over the uneven ground toward the camera.

In a calm voiceover, the reporter, an attractive woman in her early thirties with short brown hair, explains that Eileen works as a secretary in a real estate office. As Eileen draws closer, the reporter intones more seriously that Eileen is a friend she would never have made if Eileen had succeeded in killing herself three years earlier at age sixteen. Eileen and the reporter hug somewhat awkwardly and turn and begin walking arm in arm through the trees. A blue lake fills in the background as the voiceover explains that Eileen had passed out after swallowing an overdose of sleeping pills and had been taken to the hospital. Eileen's soft, childlike voice breaks in to say that at the hospital she had swallowed medicine to make herself throw up.

The two women sit facing each other at a picnic table and the camera closes in slowly on Eileen: her golden-reddish hair frames her soft face; her smooth, freckleless countenance is open, her brown eyes clear and trusting. A small gold cross adorns her neck. She appears absolutely guileless. One cannot imagine a suicidal pain ever coursing through this sweet, waif-like soul.

The reporter asks Eileen if she had regretted not dying.

"Yes," she responds, unhesitatingly, "I was very angry that my decision to end my life had been taken out of my hands." Her closed hand rises dramatically to her chest in time with "my life," and her face becomes appropriately somber at the end of the sentence. Her pretty brown eyes darken as she explains that she had seen a psychologist after the attempt but was unable to open up and tell him what was really wrong inside. As the reporter tells us that time and the mere keeping of appointments with the therapist had helped Eileen deal with the pent-up feelings behind this violent act, Eileen suddenly becomes happy and a beautiful warm smile spreads across her face, revealing white, even teeth. The wind blows lightly in her hair, and the branches overhead wobble and scatter patches of light softly over her face.

The reporter summarizes that Eileen was helped by finding more mature friends, opening herself to the needs of other people, and developing a sense of self-worth through helping others. Then she asks the closer: "Are you still resentful you weren't left to die?"

The highlighted wave has now fallen forward, partially covering Eileen's eye, but she doesn't brush it back. Her chin tilts down and shadows appear under her eyes. The cross now lies at a crooked angle on her chest.

"I'm very glad I'm still here," she responds, looking warmly at the reporter. "I love life too much now." The little girl's voice has become strong and sincere, as if she is trying to convince the reporter of the beauty she now sees in life. "I realize there is more good in life than all the heartache and pain that goes with growing up." Her lower lip catches between her teeth as she leans forward searching for the reporter's response.

THE PROTRUDING STOMACH, SO APPARENT IN THE FILM CLIP, WAS probably early evidence of Eileen's pregnancy, an event which had caused quite a stir in the Franklin family. Although some siblings doubted that Eileen could name the father, Eileen had told Diana she had gone to her lover and told him of the pregnancy and he had wanted nothing to do with her or the baby. She had demanded money from him and he had called her a whore and denied the child was his. One evening as the two sisters left a restaurant, Eileen spotted his car in a parking lot and took a car key from her purse and tore a groove down the side of the car from the front fender to the rear tail light.

From the very beginning, Eileen was determined to keep the baby. She had always dreamed of having children and she didn't believe in abortion. She considered herself to be pro-life and she moralized to others that it was simply wrong to take the life of an unborn child. In her mind, she was young but she was smart, and she would keep the child and raise it by herself.

Everyone in the family was opposed to Eileen having the baby, but no one was more adamant than her mother. Leah, who had become pregnant herself at seventeen, condemned Eileen for her behavior. In a vicious letter, she disowned Eileen and told her that she was no longer welcome in her home. The letter devastated Eileen, and in her pain she called Kate, who listened sympathetically to her tale. At the time, Kate thought perhaps Eileen viewed a baby as someone who would give her the love she had never received at home. Later, she would wonder if the whole scene wasn't simply another attention-getting play, or a way of spiting her mother. Whatever the reason, Eileen had the whole family in an uproar, and as usual, she was whirling in the center of the storm.

Eileen's pregnancy certainly earned her father's attention. He was now living with Allison Bender, the Sacramento businesswoman. Eileen visited her father frequently, and Allison was moved by their closeness. They touched frequently and hugged and sat next to each other on the couch. George had long talks with his favorite daughter and counseled her on what to do with her life. She considered being a model, until she accepted the fact that at five feet two, she was probably too short. He urged her to come and live with him and work on his properties and learn the real estate business. She thought about the idea for a couple of weeks, then rejected the offer.

George was adamantly against Eileen having the child. He believed that she could do and become many things, but not if she tied herself down at age nineteen with a baby. He put an incredible amount of emotional energy into trying to change her mind. Week after week he reasoned with her: You are too young, he would say, you don't have a husband or an education, you really don't know anything about the world or raising a baby, and you won't have any way to support it.

As the months passed and Eileen's pregnancy began to show, she became more determined than ever to keep the baby. All of her siblings urged her to have an abortion, although Diana was very careful about the way she expressed her opinion. Her older sister's love was still terribly important to her, and while Diana hinted at what she thought might be the right thing for her to do—she knew Eileen was humiliated at going to work "showing," and she was obviously not capable of raising a child by herself—she would not risk that love by openly opposing or arguing with her.

In his campaign to change Eileen's mind, George organized a family gathering at Kate's apartment. Everyone attended except Leah, who could not stand to be in the same room with her former husband. One by one, the participants went over their arguments, coupling them with reassurances of their love for Eileen. George made the most moving statement. "Eileen," he said softly, tenderly, "I understand you want the child, but the child should be with someone you love, it should be a love child." He stroked her hair gently. "The child should be an expression of love between you and the father."

Eileen held fast.

As she progressed into her second trimester, George frantically searched for a hospital that would perform the abortion.

Finally, Leah came up with an idea. She knew that Eileen was without a car and that she had enjoyed her stay in Hawaii, so she offered her a trip to Hawaii and $1,000 for a new car if she would have the abortion. Eileen accepted. Only a few weeks short of six months, and barely within the legal limits, Eileen had an abortion. She told other people, including Rick's mom, that she had lost the baby. She bought a car, went to Hawaii, and Leah accepted her back as her daughter.

Eileen felt guilty and remorseful over having aborted a fetus that might well have been viable. She seemed to turn her feelings about herself and what she had done against her family. She became furious with her father and her siblings and announced that she wanted nothing more to do with any of them. They hadn't supported her when she really needed them; they were the family that had never really loved her as a child and had now abandoned her in her moment of crisis as a young woman.

Diana was stunned and hurt by Eileen's attacks. While she hadn't urged Eileen to keep the baby, she had never criticized her either, and she had tried to be supportive through the entire ordeal. But she learned that with Eileen, love was conditional. Everything was black or white, all or nothing. You were either for her or against her, and if you were against her, the hell with you.

23

MARY JANE LARKIN WAS SOUND ASLEEP WHEN THE radio switched on at 6:00 A.M. and the familiar male voice began rattling off the day's news. The name of Susan Nason reached her through the sleepy fog, and then something about a man having been arrested for her murder. "George Franklin," she thought she heard the man say. She jerked wide awake. George Franklin? She sat up in bed and grabbed the phone and called the Foster City Police Department. She explained to a detective that she had been Susan Nason's teacher in 1969.

"I think I heard on the radio that someone had been arrested for her murder," she told the detective.

"That's right," he told her, "the man's name is George Franklin. Used to be a San Mateo fireman. They arrested him up in Carmichael yesterday."

"My God," she thought, "after all these years," and it hadn't been a stranger who had plucked little Susan from their midst; it had been a friend, a neighbor.

Mary Jane had driven by the Nason house twice a day for fifteen years, until the school moved, and every time she passed she would glance unwillingly at the house and wonder what the passage of time meant for the Nasons. The cops had kept the tragedy alive for her—every three or four years a detective would come to her room after school and review the facts with her. She always had to explain about girls wearing shorts under their dresses back then and that the kids put their tennis shoes by their desks because there were no lockers. After every visit she would replay the events of that afternoon in her mind. God, what if she hadn't insisted that Susan go home first? She would have been whacked-out in some mental hospital long ago. Maybe she shouldn't have allowed Susan to take the shoes at all, should have told her to leave them there for Celia to find the next morning, but how could she have known? How could anybody have known?

Mary Jane didn't doubt that George Franklin had killed Susan. It all made perfect sense. She had never believed that Susan would have gotten in a stranger's car—they had warned the kids too many times—and as a fireman, George Franklin could easily have been around home after school. After she saw his picture in the paper, it made her skin crawl to think of that heavy, creepy man, molesting that tiny doll-like figure. She knew that Susan would have run away if she could have.

Mary Jane, a practicing Catholic, began to pray for the conviction of George Franklin.

There were only six or seven teachers left from 1969, and they gathered in the lounge the day Franklin's arrest was announced and compared details of what they remembered about Susan's disappearance. Back then the teachers had purchased a wooden bookcase with a metal plaque inscribed "In Memory of Susan Nason" on the front, and many people had given books dedicated to Susan to the library.

Now, in the lounge, the older teachers brought the newer ones up to date on the details. Mary Jane's view soon became the consensus: George Franklin was guilty. When the teachers learned the next day that one of his daughters had accused him of murder, they were even more convinced: Why in the world would a daughter say such a thing about her father if it wasn't true?

Mary Jane told her students about the arrest. She didn't want to scare them, so she didn't tell them the identity of the killer, but the next morning several children who had seen the story on television reported to the others that Susan had been killed by her best friend's father.

GLADYS WAS GEORGE FRANKLIN'S ACCOUNTANT. HE HAD LIVED WITH her and her husband and son in Carmichael for more than a year prior to moving into his apartment in Wooded Village. George had been as straight as they came: a nonsmoker, nondrinker, very quiet. Most of his energy went into studying for his classes at the college. Gladys had been shocked when he called her that Tuesday morning and said the police were taking him to the station for questioning in regard to an old murder. When he had called her again about six that evening and said he had been arrested for murder and would be taken to San Mateo the next day, she couldn't believe it. The George she knew could never have committed such a crime, and if for some reason he had done it, he would never have been able to live with it all these years. An honest and forthright person, he would have said, "Yes, I did it, and I have to pay for what I did." She believed him when he told her he was innocent, and agreed to help him. Wednesday night Gladys drove to the San Mateo jail and George executed a power of attorney authorizing her to handle his personal and business affairs for six months. Several days later, when Bryan Cassandro called her for an interview, she politely but firmly refused to speak with him.

HATTIE FRANKLIN LEARNED OF HER SON'S ARREST WHEN HIS PICTURE flashed on her television screen. She couldn't understand what was happening until he called her the next day and told her he was innocent and everything would be over soon. Ever since fleeing her husband in the mid-fifties, Hattie had lived with her daughters in Florida, sewing and keeping house and looking after her grand- and great-grandchildren. George T. had been a good son, calling and visiting frequently over the years. She had last seen him on her birthday two years earlier. She had met all of his children except Diana, and they all seemed happy. George Jr. had stopped in before he went in the service and Eileen had stayed with her for two months when she was fifteen. Eileen also stayed in touch with her, even sending her a T-shirt with "Hattie's Little Flower Pot" printed on it. Hattie knew that Eileen had called her shortly after the arrest, but Hattie's daughters, all of whom believed fervently in their brother's innocence, wouldn't let her speak to her.

Hattie told her son on the phone that she believed in him and loved him dearly.

WHEN PROFESSOR CHAMBERS WALKED INTO CLASS ON TUESDAY, November 29, he was surprised to see George Franklin's empty seat. When he didn't show up again on Thursday, Chambers became more concerned. Then he saw the headlines in Friday's *Sacramento Bee:* "SHE TURNS IN HER FATHER IN '69 SLAYING." Under it ran the malevolent picture of George, where his matted hair was brushed up in horns and his hard, deep eyes stared into the camera lens. Chambers saw something different in the picture: A beaten man whose strength and exuberance and love of life had been sucked right out of him. On

George's face he saw a look of incomprehension: What's happening to me?

Chambers wondered if maybe the guy was a Jekyll and Hyde, or maybe his personality had changed in twenty years and he didn't remember killing the girl. Christ, maybe George did it. Chambers had never socialized with him and had no idea what he was really like. Still, he felt bad for him.

The following Tuesday, the third class without George, a female student muttered, "God, I wonder where George is?" Another student who had seen the story on television told her about his arrest, and then the word spread quickly. First his classmates reacted with disbelief; then it was, "Christ, I was sitting right next to him," and, "I always thought he was kind of strange."

TISH TYLER, A SACRAMENTO HAIRDRESSER, HAD MET GEORGE Franklin in the fall of 1988 when she answered an ad in the personals placed by a man calling himself the "Silver Fox." George had romanced her, bringing her candy and flowers, sending her cards, and gazing longingly into her eyes before kissing her. She might have gotten more involved if George had been able to perform sexually. As it was, the only time he could get an erection was when she called him "Daddy," and even then he couldn't maintain it long enough to achieve penetration. Sometimes he would apologize and say he was tired; other times he would laugh and say that when he turned fifty, his dick had developed a mind of its own. Just a few months after breaking up with him, a friend called and said that George been arrested for murder, then Tish saw his picture in the paper.

Tish didn't know what to make of the murder charge. George was certainly strange, but she'd never seen the slightest hint of violence in him. In the ten months she had dated him, she'd never even seen him get angry. She decided to write him a letter in jail.

DIANE WIEGERT, THE APARTMENT MANAGER, HEARD ABOUT George's arrest from some tenants who had witnessed his being led away by the cops. She didn't believe George was capable of murdering a little girl. Maybe he had done it while he was drunk—he had been sick from alcohol for many years—but that was a long time ago and maybe he'd forgotten it. The daughter bothered her; why did she wait all these years? Diane suspected the daughter was setting up her father, probably for money.

The tenants talked about how George would sit on his balcony and watch the pool parties and wave hello, but never come down. No one ever heard him swear or make lewd remarks about women, and he never made a move toward any of the children. In the afternoons the schoolgirls would sit on the stairs leading up to his place and do their homework and giggle. He would come out and say, "Hi, how are you kids today?" and they would chatter back and scootch aside to make room for him to walk by. The kids liked him. Diane's son loved him: he would come running into the office yelling, "George is home!" No, in Diane's mind George was innocent.

MARILYN KEDSLIE, GEORGE'S LANDLADY IN NEVADA CITY, SAW George's orange-suited image flash on television in a news preview before a commercial, and asked herself, "Why George, what have you done?" Then the announcer told her. Two days later the detectives from San Mateo came to her door with a search warrant. They asked her if George had approached her grandchildren or ever taken any children upstairs to his apartment. No, she told them, nor had he ever approached her. They left a receipt listing the pornographic items taken from his apartment. It was all a surprise to her; he sure wasn't that sort of a man around her or her family.

A few days later a woman and a boy from Carmichael showed up in a pickup and began hauling away George's belongings.

24

BOB MORSE WASN'T SURPRISED BY WHAT HE AND CAS-
sandro found when they searched George Franklin's apartment. Guys like Franklin were repeaters and collectors.
Pedophiles liked pictures and magazines and they wrote letters
and joined clubs.

Among the documents seized from the residences were a
series of articles about young girls having sex with their fathers. In "Oral Dad," a young girl lies in bed and fantasizes
about the "glorious sight of her father's mouth filled with her
tits." Finally she goes to his room and seduces him. In "First
Long Kiss," the father fondles his daughter and then has her
masturbate him until he ejaculates onto her breasts. In "Please
Dad, Do It for Me," a father enters his twelve-year-old daughter's bedroom and finds her masturbating and helps her finish.
In "Little Squeals of Desire," the mother introduces her
daughter to sex with her father.

Morse and Cassandro also confiscated a book entitled *Animals as Sex Partners.* On the cover is a woman on her back
being approached by a bulldog and inside are stories of sex
between humans and various animals, including flies, cats,
cows, and deer. *Forbidden Sexual Fantasies* contains chapters
on incest, bestiality, and rape. One drawing depicts a fish
swimming toward a woman with her legs open.

George subscribed to several dating and swinging newspapers. In one ad, circled in pencil, a woman sought a man who
loved children and enjoyed life. In *News Letter for Sexual Ad-
venturers,* a girl named Eileen is sitting clothed, on a ledge,
smiling, with her knees up and spread apart. Eileen, the caption explains, was eighteen but sounds younger.

A series of letters from Donna* were laced with sexual overtures and pedophilic references. One began, "Hello my delicious 'Daddy,'" and proceeded to describe her fantasies about sex with a dog, group sex, and incest. She explained that her fantasy would have been more pleasurable if only her "Daddy" had been next to her. Donna signed off, "Take care, Daddy." In a card dated only a few days before Franklin's arrest, Donna wrote: "Thank you for a very nice couple of afternoons. I especially love being close to you, Daddy. How delightfully wicked knowing I'm fucking Daddy's cock and his warm, naked body is next to mine. Que fantastica." She added that she was considering his proposal to have sex with a dog.

The detectives uncovered a trove of photographs, some of which were as yet undeveloped. One series showed a black woman holding her dress up and exposing her sex while sitting, squatting, and kneeling on the ground. In another, a masked white woman stands with her foot on a chair using a dildo on herself. The same woman is also shown performing oral sex on an unidentified man. A black girl is pictured naked in a bathtub. In one photo, a toy white lamb with a black face stands on a bed surrounded by dildos. There's one of Franklin, in boots and gray underwear, standing bent over in the kitchen, his smiling face looking out between his thick hairy legs, mooning the world; and another of him holding a dildo next to the vagina of a nude woman in a picture.

The cops also found a large collection of pornography and paraphernalia: videos such as "Meats," "The Best of Big John," and "Spots"; books entitled *The G Spot, Lusty Dusty,* and *Altar of Venus;* more than twenty-three dildos, many of them later described by the prosecution as "child-sized."

Perhaps the biggest find for the detectives was the names and phone numbers of George's girlfriends. In talking to them, Morse and Cassandro unmasked the personality of a man obsessed with sex with young girls and animals. In the mid-1980s, George Franklin answered a lonely hearts advertisement that described a Christian woman with an eight-year-old daughter. According to the woman, Pamela*, Franklin insisted that when they were making love she should call him "Daddy" and he would refer to her as his "naughty little girl." When she revealed to him that she had been molested by her father, Franklin asked her about the details of what her father had done to her and insisted that she talk about the specifics while they were having sex. Franklin questioned her about her daughter's breasts and pubic hair, and asked her to take photos of her daughter asleep with her legs spread, exposing her vagina. He explained that he belonged to the René Guyon Society, which advocated children having sex at a young age and had as its motto: "Sex before eight, or else it's too late." He told her that a young girl's first sexual experience should be loving and caring, and that she was depriving her daughter of a beneficial experience if she didn't let him have sex with her before her eighth birthday. He explained that girls between the age of seven and ten often came on to him by sitting on his lap and rubbing against his groin. She told the detectives he had asked her to procure little girls for him for sex.

Carol*, another sex partner who met George through an advertisement, said that during their relationship he referred to himself as "Daddy" and to her as his daughter. He would call her his "incestuous little girl," and ask, "Daughter, do you like that?" while they were having sex. She was supposed to act like a child and give her age as eight or nine when he asked. Sometimes George would grab Carol's wrists and pin her arms over her head with one hand while he tickled her and said, "Be quiet and do what Daddy says." During sex he would ask her if she had ever had sex with her father. She told the cops that George said he had sex with girls under ten several times, twice with the consent of the mother, and that he used to pick up teen-age hitchhikers in the sixties and seventies and exchange alcohol and drugs for sex.

To another woman he explained that he enjoyed having fellatio performed on him by a dog and asked her to have sex with a dog in front of him. He told her he had had sex with the young daughter of a woman he was dating, and when the woman asked why the girl didn't report it, he had responded, "Because she liked it."

Mixed in with the letters and photos were various notes and

comments, mostly written to women, that revealed George's conversion to sobriety, adoption of the principles of metaphysics, and his struggle with the issues of co-dependency. He advocated taking control of one's life as opposed to being controlled by other people. A color analysis of his personality done in March 1988 concluded that in the past he had let other people take advantage of him, but that recently he had learned to examine others' motives more carefully before reaching agreement with them. George wrote, "I have allowed it. Masada shall not fall again." His diverse interests become strangely mixed in one letter addressed to a woman. At the top he wrote: "Whimper, Daddy what are you going to make me do now? Moan, Whine." Below it read, "Now when you say or think 'that's the way I am' you're really reaffirming it. That's how I choose to be. The more you resist change the more difficult it becomes. . . . It's all around you. You simply don't see it. Self-esteem is right in front of you. Go for it. Love, George." To another woman, he quoted a Chinese proverb: "The fire you kindle for your enemies often burns you more than them."

Morse and Cassandro could not have cared less about George Franklin's philosophy of life, but the materials and letters confirmed their belief that Franklin was a man who had lusted after and abused little girls, and who had used mothers as an avenue to their daughters. In Bob Morse's view, when George Franklin said to a woman, "Hello, I'm George, pleased to meet you," he was really saying, "Hello, I'm George, and I'd like to fuck your daughter."

Now that George Franklin was formally charged with murder and securely in jail under a two-million-dollar bond, Marty Murray began looking down the long road ahead. He knew, as all good trial lawyers knew, that preparation wins cases. The intricate puzzle of what had happened twenty years ago would have to be assembled methodically and meticulously; each piece would have to be held up to the light and viewed from every perspective; every document assembled and catalogued; every person remotely involved interviewed once and possibly twice; every empty space filled with facts. Experts would have to be located, theories developed, negatives disproved. All questions had to be asked and answered. The law had to be studied and fashioned to fit the facts and the prosecution's theory of the case. Weaknesses had to be uncovered. Surprises could kill you.

A trial is like a drama involving a struggle between good and evil, right and wrong, a play whose specific goal is supposedly the divining of the truth to ascertain guilt or innocence. On the courtroom stage, two different versions of reality are acted out for the jury, each one represented as the truth. Everyone is a player: the lawyers, the witnesses, the judge, the bailiff, even the media. The roles, while tightly defined, leave substantial room for creative interpretation. Because the prosecutor has the burden of convincing the jury of the truth of his version, he is the director of the first act. The reality he creates, the version of events he spins, must be sufficiently convincing or the play won't go forward.

"Facts" are the building blocks of the various realities. Each side insists that the facts point inexorably to their truth. Pure, indisputable facts are always hard to come by, but nailing down twenty-year-old facts is even more difficult.

As the prosecutor, Marty Murray would supervise the investigation and direct the efforts of the two homicide detectives, and he knew that the critical scene in this play would be a re-enactment of September 22, 1969. The jury would have to relive that day through the prosecution's eyes, from beginning to end. Murray sat down with Morse and Cassandro and divided up the chores.

Cassandro was assigned the task of locating the more than 100 witnesses from the 1969 investigation. He talked to the homicide cops from back then, all of whom were retired, and pored over volumes of files, carefully noting every name, then tracked the people down one by one through a network of computer files. Just locating the witnesses—there was only one he was unable to find—took over three weeks. Then he had to set up and conduct the interviews.

Cassandro knew the prosecution had to rule out other suspects in Susan's murder, so he kept an eye out for someone lurking between the lines in the old reports. He knew the blue station wagon could present a problem. Ann Hobbs had said a man in a blue station wagon had tried to pick her up a few days before Susan's disappearance, and a woman and her daughter claimed to have seen a blue station wagon in the area moments after Susan left Celia Oakley's house. If the defense could patch together a plausible theory that Susan had been abducted by a man in a blue station wagon, the jury might wonder just enough to find a reasonable doubt. He was also worried about the "Susan sightings," the people who claimed to have seen Susan in the neighborhood at 5:00 P.M. or 5:30, after George Franklin was at home. By court order, Cassandro would have to give the names and addresses of the 1969 witnesses to the defense, but he fully intended to try to get to every one of them first. He wanted to lock the witnesses into a story on tape early so the defense couldn't lead them into changing their stories on the stand. It was hard for a witness to flip on you if you could read his or her own words back to them.

Morse reviewed the 1969 facts with Cassandro. In his mind, the Foster City police had botched the investigation from the very beginning. The very first thing you did in a missing person case was re-create the person's last day, minute by minute; find each and every friend and associate and ask when they last saw the person, what they were doing, what they said, how they looked. You didn't conduct house-to-house searches, or fly helicopters with searchlights over the island, or send dogs sniffing through the fields, or submerge divers in the lagoons *unless you had some reason to*. Susan Nason's murder could have been solved within hours of her disappearance. The failure to interview Eileen Franklin was unconscionable: What eight-year-old girl wouldn't have remembered seeing her best friend murdered by her father when asked by a cop three or four hours later? The corroborating evidence would have been right in front of them. Imagine the pain the Nasons would have been spared, imagine the years George Franklin wouldn't have been walking around a free man, if that evening one policeman had thought to ask Margaret Nason the name of Susan's best friend and then walked around the corner to 678 Harvester Drive and talked to her.

Morse knew the Foster City cops felt bad about it—one of them had even cried on the phone when he interviewed him—and, when he got over his anger, he felt bad for them. Besides, as Morse was soon to realize, the San Mateo Sheriff's Department had screwed up badly back then, too.

Morse never doubted that Franklin would pay the price for his crime. He believed in the psychology of success, and part of his job, as he saw it, was to create a sense of the inevitability of victory. The detectives met every morning at 8:30 in the back room of the Court House Café across from the municipal courthouse. At this morning ritual, a sober counterbalance to the gatherings at the Broadway Lounge after work, the cops drank coffee and talked about their cases and shared ideas. Here, among his peers, Morse was forceful. "Franklin did it and we're going to kick his ass," he would announce. "And I'll tell you what else—that isn't the only girl he murdered. That sonofabitch will never see the light of day."

He also pumped up the principal witness. Eileen had to be made to feel secure. If she wobbled and blew her lines, their case was finished. She was strong, but she was also weak, and she needed continual reassurance. He would tell her time and again how tough she was, how he had faith in her, how well she was going to do in court, how courageous she was for coming forward.

25

I N NOVEMBER 1989, DOUG HORNGRAD HAD BEEN IN the private practice of law for only four months. He had graduated from the Golden Gate University Law School in 1980 and immediately gone to work for the public defender's office in Marin County, where he had interned in a clinical program his senior year. As a public defender, he had defended hundreds of cases ranging from homicide to rape to drug dealing. He had a knack for attracting high-profile cases which received a lot of publicity, leading his colleagues to nickname him "Hollywood Horngrad." He left the public defender's office in 1989 to go into partnership in San Francisco with Art Wachtel, who had been a year ahead of him in law school. In the fall of 1989, he was waiting for his first big case as a private attorney.

Horngrad didn't look like he belonged in California and, even after twelve years, he still refers to himself as "from back east." At six feet two, with straight black hair and horn-rimmed glasses, he had a certain literary air about him, as if he would feel more comfortable reading Blake on a bench on the Boston Commons or arguing Hegelian philosophy from a podium in a Harvard classroom. He wore slightly baggy suits and walked with a slight forward tilt.

Horngrad, the only son of Jewish parents, grew up in Queens, where he attended high school until his family moved to Connecticut. He majored in political science at Boston University, then began graduate school at American University in Washington, D.C., before deciding that law was his calling and heading west.

Horngrad was urbane and witty and unfailingly polite. He lived in a fashionable three-story Victorian row house in San

Francisco with his wife, whom he had met in law school. He compensated for living on the West Coast by reading five or six newspapers a day and twelve to fifteen magazines a week. He devoured pulp detective novels by the box.

Horngrad thoroughly enjoyed being his own type of lawyer —on days he wasn't in court he would arrive at the office in baggy khaki pants, tennis shoes, and an open collar—and he prided himself on employing an eclectic assortment of San Franciscans as secretaries and assistants—gays, Asians, social activists. Like many criminal lawyers, he thrived on the art and intensity of trying cases, but he seemed to be unafflicted with the successful litigator's oversized ego and overbearing personality. He processed most experiences through a wry sense of humor, and his behavior belied a belief that courtesy is not inimical to the presentation of an aggressive defense.

As an old-fashioned east coast liberal, Horngrad was firmly dedicated to the traditional civil libertarian values, the most important of which is the primacy of the individual vis-à-vis the government. To Horngrad the government is inherently oppressive and the courts are the final battleground to protect and guarantee individual freedoms. In court he often referred to the prosecution as "the government." On the couch in his office sits a pillow given to him by his mother, who fled Nazi Germany before the war. On the pillow is crocheted: "There is no situation of human misery that can't be made worse by the presence of a police officer." Unlike many defense attorneys, Doug Horngrad could never have been a prosecutor.

DOUG HORNGRAD HAD HANDLED OVER 2,000 CRIMINAL CASES WHILE in the Marin County Public Defender's Office and he listened to his client's stories with a cynical ear, but also, he would say only partly facetiously, with a forgiving heart. Sometimes his clients would break down and confess the crime to him, other times they would admit to some things and deny others, occasionally they would withhold information and lie to him. Often they would proclaim their complete innocence. He had developed over the years an ability to peer through the smoke and discern the truth.

His first contact with the Franklin case had been a phone call from a friend of George Franklin, a former firefighter and protégé of Franklin's who had gone on to get his law degree and who asked Horngrad to represent his jailed friend. Franklin had just been booked into the San Mateo County jail that morning, and all Horngrad knew when he drove down to Redwood City that night was that his prospective client had been charged with a very old murder. He immediately learned from Franklin that the crime involved the murder of a young girl in Foster City in 1969, but Franklin had no idea who had accused him of the horrible crime.

"I don't know why I'm here," he told Horngrad, "I didn't do it. I'm innocent." It would become George Franklin's mantra: "I didn't do it. I'm innocent."

Horngrad picked up a copy of the *San Francisco Chronicle* the next morning and read that one of Franklin's daughters had accused him of the murder. Believing that he should tell George the news before he picked it up in the jailhouse, he drove immediately to Redwood City. He sat across the table from his client in the lawyer's room of the courthouse and told him that one of his daughters claimed to have seen him kill Susan Nason. Which one?

"Janice," Franklin told his lawyer. "It has to be Janice. She's always hated me."

Over the following days and weeks, Horngrad spent hours with Franklin going over his background and the family history. He had given his daughters plenty of reason to hate him —hate, Horngrad would soon learn, resonated throughout the Franklin family—but that didn't add up to murder. Horngrad felt that Franklin withheld nothing from him. When he looked into George Franklin's eyes that first morning, and every time afterwards, he sensed he was coming clean. Absolutely, unequivocally, without qualm, condition, or hesitation, Horngrad came to believe George Franklin innocent of the murder of Susan Nason.

Proving it would be another matter. He agreed with a friend who said that defending an accused child molester in the nineties was like defending an accused Communist in the fifties.

* * *

A COMMON VIEW AMONG CRIMINAL LAWYERS IN SAN FRANCISCO WAS that the prosecution in the Franklin case faced a difficult if not impossible task. Whatever physical evidence existed at the time was probably gone, and even recent, adult memories could be turned upside down and shredded by a skillful attorney. True, an eyewitness was always the most compelling direct evidence, but the prosecutor would have to corroborate the daughter's story in some essential aspect to convince twelve people beyond a reasonable doubt that this former fireman with no previous criminal record had viciously murdered a young girl twenty years earlier.

Horngrad could not, and did not, take this viewpoint. As he looked into the case, he soon learned that he would be entering the battle with several serious handicaps, stemming in part from the contents of the boxes of material taken by Morse and Cassandro from his client's apartments and in part from the fact that his client's former wife and all of his children, not just the one making the accusation, as well as a former girlfriend, loathed him for the abuse and pain he had allegedly inflicted on them in the past. Horngrad knew he had a major tactical struggle on his hands and that, like the cops, he would essentially have to reinvestigate the entire 1969 case. He hired Steve Schwartz, a private investigator, to work almost full time, obtaining records and interviewing witnesses, and he assigned a paralegal to assist in the detailed discovery effort he would soon launch.

From the outset, Horngrad was concerned about the trial venue. He had yet to try a case in San Mateo County, but he was very well aware of the county's reputation. San Mateo cops filed their cases first and put them together afterward, and the prosecutor charged high and went for the maximum penalty. Out of the eight bay area counties, San Mateo was widely viewed in the defense bar as the most difficult county for a criminal defendant to get a fair shake. Horngrad visualized San Mateo as the Gulag to the south, a place where the innocent could be found guilty because of an overzealous government and a compliant citizenry. He knew that the case would attract massive pre-trial publicity, most of it undoubtedly unfavorable to his client, which would make it even harder to find fair-minded jurors. To preserve his right to argue for a change of venue later, he would have to attempt to stem the flow of publicity now, and thus he sought the gag order on attorneys, cops, and potential witnesses.

After beginning his investigation, Horngrad was given one explosive piece of information by George Jr. which, if true, could dispose of the entire case.

In August 1989, George Jr. told him, Eileen had called him in San Francisco and invited him down for a visit. She even offered to buy his plane ticket. George Jr. didn't consider himself close to Eileen, although over the years they had spoken on the phone frequently. He understood Eileen's deep hatred for both of their parents and considered his father to be an abusive alcoholic. Although he agreed with his siblings that he and Janice had been beaten the worst, he hadn't gotten as obsessed by the abuse as Eileen and Janice. In recent years, it seemed Eileen had become absorbed with her childhood, and Janice, who hated their parents with a terrible vengeance, had completely stripped a gear. That sister was crazy, totally untrustworthy.

George Jr. accepted Eileen's invitation and soon after his arrival, when he and Eileen were alone in the kitchen, she suddenly announced that she was undergoing hypnotherapy. The next evening she told her brother that during one session she had visualized their father killing Susan Nason. Her therapist would confirm her story.

George wasn't completely flabbergasted. He knew Janice had gone to the cops and accused her father of the murder in 1984. Not that he believed Eileen. His first reaction was one of disbelief: "Boy," he thought, "they're out to pin this one on Dad for all the lousy things he did to them."

He didn't think Eileen would exactly fabricate the story, he just wasn't willing to take her word for it. He knew his sister too well. George viewed himself as something of a twentieth-century man, someone who relied on reason and intellect to solve problems and sort out life, and he would need a lot more evidence than Eileen's hypnotically retrieved memory to convince him that Susan Nason had died at their father's hands.

Nonetheless, George Jr. understood his sister's pain, and he was sympathetic and supportive. This was a very serious matter, he responded calmly, and they needed to be sure. She and Barry were on their way to Europe, and he urged her to go on the trip and think about it. Call him when she got back, and if she was still convinced of her father's guilt, they could do a little research, poke her story with a stick and see what it looked like up close.

George Jr. didn't hear from Eileen again until one day in late November when he came home and punched his answering machine and was startled to hear her voice telling him that their father had been arrested for the murder of Susan Nason. A few days later she called again, this time with some questions: Had he talked to the defense? Yes, he had. Had he given her father's lawyers a statement? Yes again. Upon hearing that, Eileen suddenly changed her story. She had not really been under hypnosis when she remembered the murder, she explained; actually she had recalled the crime in regular therapy. If the police ever asked him, would he please not tell them about the hypnosis story?

Horngrad was delighted to hear about the hypnosis. For years police had used hypnosis in an attempt to jog witnesses' memories, particularly in eyewitness identifications, and many states had ruled out such testimony because of the inherent suggestibility of the human mind in a hypnotic state. Experts had ascertained that memories could be created and implanted in the unconscious mind during hypnosis and that memories recovered during hypnosis were unreliable. In the fall of 1989, the California Supreme Court followed suit. In the *Shirley* case, which arose in San Mateo, the court held that the testimony of a witness who had undergone hypnosis for the purpose of restoring her memory was inadmissible. Thus, if Eileen had recovered the murder memory, in whole or in part, while under hypnosis, she would be prohibited from testifying as to the contents of that memory in court, which meant that George Franklin would walk. The possibility wasn't that far-fetched—hypnosis was a commonly used therapeutic technique to retrieve and integrate traumatic childhood memories that had supposedly slipped from the conscious mind.

The prosecution would be hurt either way by Eileen's statement. If she hadn't been hypnotized but had told her brother that she had been, then she was an admitted liar. Not only that, she had attempted to induce her brother to lie, perhaps perjure himself, to cover up her lie. Liars do not make good witnesses—jurors often decide that if somebody lies about one thing, the person might well lie about others.

Horngrad began an immediate search for the hypnotist. He issued subpoenas seeking the names of all the therapists that Eileen, Janice, or Barry had seen in the past twenty years. The prosecution fought the subpoenas as too broad, and the court ordered that only the names of therapists with whom Eileen had discussed her father or the killing of Susan Nason need be disclosed. Eileen gave up the name of Kirk Barrett, the therapist she had been seeing in 1989 and who used hypnosis in his practice, and some time later she admitted that she had also seen another therapist, Katherine Rieder, in 1988 and 1989.

Horngrad was convinced that Eileen had told her brother the truth in her kitchen. Somehow, in between the time she told her mother and her brother that she had been hypnotized and her follow-up call to him, she had learned of the inadmissibility of a memory retrieved under hypnosis and changed her story. Perhaps her mother, a San Mateo lawyer, had told her of the *Shirley* case. Horngrad had a private detective in Los Angeles call the hypnotists in the Los Angeles Yellow Pages and say that a friend of his had recommended a hypnotist to him but he had forgotten the name of the clinic—had Eileen Franklin ever been a patient there? No luck.

Horngrad also focused on Eileen herself. In the end, the entire case would rest on her word, which meant that discrediting her would be a critical theme in the defense strategy. Eileen and Janice were claiming that their father had abused them as children, and he needed to explore the theory that the murder charge was some sort of a revenge conspiracy by the two sisters, or the possibility that Eileen had unconsciously created a false memory of the murder. Eileen's emotional structure, her mental processes, her memory, indeed her entire psychological history, formed the very narrow foundation for the allegation, and he needed a mental health professional to chart her mind and speak to its soundness, to evaluate her and spot any delusional propensities or character or thought disorders, any evidence of a psychopathology that could provide a context for why she was hurling this bizarre charge at her father. Was she crazy? A pathological liar? Was she delusional? A multiple personality? Horngrad greatly needed a full psychiatric evaluation, and he filed a motion with the court asking that she be ordered to submit to one.

In the *Ballard* case, the California Supreme Court reviewed a lower court decision in which the defense had sought a psychiatric examination of a woman who claimed that a doctor had raped her after administering drugs to her in his office. The court, while not ordering the examination, affirmed the principle that in a sexual assault case the trial judge had the discretion to order a psychiatric evaluation of the complaining witness if the case rested upon her uncorroborated testimony. In response to that decision, and after being subjected to intense lobbying by prosecutors and women's groups, the legislature enacted a statute prohibiting a judge from ordering a psychological examination of a victim or witness in a sexual assault case for the purpose of assessing his or her credibility.

Horngrad believed that the statute didn't apply in this instance since his client was charged with murder, not sexual assault, but since the prosecutor was resisting his motion he would have to wait for a court ruling.

26

September 1988

Debbie Gaerlan was startled when she saw Eileen Franklin sweep into the ballroom of the AMFAC Hotel with her friends. Gone was the shy, homely person she had known in high school and in her place was an attractive young woman. Somehow in the past ten years, the freckled oddball had blossomed into a stunning beauty.

Debbie and her high school friends had begun talking about a ten-year class reunion the previous year. Debbie had taken charge and selected one member from each of the old cliques and asked them to serve on a committee, which began meeting once a month. She had called many of her classmates herself.

"Hi, Eileen," she had said when the woman picked up the phone at the Canoga Park number, "this is Debbie Gaerlan, and I'm calling about our high school reunion next year."

"How did you get my phone number?" Eileen snapped.

Debbie explained that a friend who worked for a law enforcement agency had run all the classmates' names through the computer and come up with addresses and phone numbers.

"Well, what if I had a police record?" Eileen demanded.

Debbie thought the response odd, but went on to explain that a committee had been formed to organize the reunion. When Eileen heard the names of the members on the committee, she became upset—the popular students who had run the school ten years ago were still in charge and she had been left out again.

"It's too bad that I'm not on the committee," Eileen complained, "because I own a limousine service and I could have a limo pick up all the members of the committee and take them to the hotel."

Debbie suggested that wasn't too plausible since Eileen lived in southern California and the reunion would be in Burlingame.

"I'm not that ugly duckling any more," Eileen said enthusiastically, "I look a lot like Fergie."

Debbie had been sure that Eileen wouldn't come to the reunion, given her bitterness about not being included in the planning.

Eileen walked right up to Debbie in the ballroom, which was decorated elegantly in a black and white motif, and told her what a great job she had done on the reunion and how fantastic the place looked. Debbie couldn't get over the change in Eileen; the outcast with the strange friends who used to slouch down the hall in her bell bottoms was now poised and confident, very much aware of and pleased with her newfound femininity. The two chatted for several minutes and Eileen told Debbie about her two children and how proud she was of them.

A few weeks before the party, Donna Dupont had received a phone call from one of Eileen's gay friends saying that the old high school group was getting together at his house for a few drinks before the reunion dinner and that Eileen was coming up from Canoga Park. Donna was excited; she had had very little contact with her high school friends over the years and looked forward to seeing them. The host served champagne and hors d'oeuvres at the pre-party gathering. Donna hadn't seen Eileen since graduation, and she felt almost intimidated by the striking young woman in the obviously expensive, dark green gown (although the satin cape draped around her shoulders was perhaps a little too much for the occasion). Well-applied makeup disguised most of her freckles and highlighted her brown eyes, but most of all it was her hair: the orange haystack had grown into a magnificent red mane which cascaded over her shoulders and tumbled luxuriously to her waist.

Donna said a brief hello to her at the cocktail party, but

Eileen spent most of her time talking with the host. After a few glasses of champagne, the old friends piled into their cars and drove to the hotel.

Inside the ballroom, everyone clustered in their former cliques and Eileen's group commandeered a table just inside the door. In the center of each table, on a small mirror, sat a glass vase filled with two roses. A small bottle of wine with a reunion label stood by each place.

Others admired Eileen the swan.

"Look at Eileen," one woman said to her friend. "Isn't she beautiful?"

"Amazing," the other responded, "how she's changed."

Her classmates noted how confidently she walked up to people and greeted them and engaged in conversation. She seemed anxious to talk about her two children, her successful husband, their limousine service, and their house in Los Angeles. "See," she seemed to be saying, "see how well I've done?"

Karen Hewes, who had known Eileen since grade school, remembered her as timid and passive during most of high school, then a little vampy or slutty at the very end. Karen stopped by her table to say hello to the group. Eileen turned to her and asked, "Oh, would you like to see a picture of my children?"

Without waiting for a response, Eileen opened her wallet and allowed at least ten pictures in plastic sleeves to unfold and tumble down. At first, Karen thought maybe she was kidding—showing pictures at reunions was such a horrible cliché, everybody bragging and trying to impress each other—but it was apparent that Eileen was quite serious. One by one, she described each child in each picture, explaining where they were and what they were doing. She even pointed out her husband. Karen indulgently admired the kids and exclaimed how cute they were, then walked away shaking her head.

When dinner was over, most people, as if on cue, stood up and began mingling outside their groups. Soon the music started and a few people danced. Eileen continued to socialize assertively, talking about her children and the business she owned in Los Angeles. Eventually a little snickering began around the edges, a few comments here and there about the string of photographs falling from her wallet, her successful life and wealthy husband, the airs she was putting on.

It seemed to Donna that Eileen was trying hard to impress her old classmates and gain the acceptance she had been denied in high school. Donna was reminded of an old movie about an extremely unattractive woman who had been mangled in a car accident and had undergone massive reconstructive surgery from which she had emerged quite beautiful. When the woman returned to the town where she had grown up, all the men who had ignored her as a girl pursued her ardently, and she began killing them one by one. Eileen was not out to kill anyone, but she was definitely out to prove something.

Toward the end of the evening, Donna was standing with the old group and the talk turned to where they might go after the dance, perhaps to Donna's house. Donna turned to Eileen and made some innocuous remark, but to her surprise, Eileen looked right through her as if she hadn't heard her. Donna tried again, and this time Eileen, still expressionless, looked beyond her, as if she didn't exist.

"Excuse me," Donna asked, demanding her attention, "have I done something to offend you?"

"A lot of these people weren't very nice to me in high school," Eileen murmured.

"That might be," Donna responded with growing irritation, "but I wasn't one of them, was I?"

Eileen repeated how mean the others had been to her in school, then walked away. Donna was upset. Even with all of Eileen's changes, her new looks and her money, she was still carrying a grudge. The party was almost over and she must not have received the reactions or attention from her former classmates that she wanted or thought she deserved. It was a little sad, really, Donna thought.

A photographer had been hired to take photos of the reunited friends and Debbie Gaerlan later assembled the pictures from the evening into a reunion yearbook and mailed a copy to all the attendees. On the first page she listed those who had come but whose pictures were not included. Eileen Franklin's picture was missing, and her name was not listed. She had been overlooked again.

BY ALL APPEARANCES, EILEEN HAD INDEED FINALLY ATTAINED HER dream. She was married to a computer consultant, who, while not rich, made around $120,000 a year. She had two children, Jessica, four, and Aaron, one, and she lived in a spacious, 3,220 square foot house at the end of a cul-de-sac in a middle-class suburb in the San Fernando Valley. The house had a large, modern kitchen, four bedrooms, including a huge master bedroom with a fireplace, three baths, a recreation room, and a family room. One wall of the living room was hidden behind a home entertainment center packed with the latest in stereos, televisions, and VCRs. The fenced-in backyard contained a Jacuzzi, a swimming pool with tiled edges, a rock garden, and a treehouse. In the side yard Eileen and Barry had set up a slide and swing set. In the driveway sat a long, dark green 1982 Mercedes SL with a sun roof, compact disc player, and car phone, and next to it was a new, similarly equipped BMW. Sometimes in the drive sat a white Lincoln limousine, which always caused a stir in the neighborhood when it appeared. Eileen drove the Mercedes.

Eileen had a live-in nanny or au pair, whom she paid $500 a month, and she paid $560 a month to have Jessica in an upscale private school. She incurred $720 a month in psychotherapy bills, and her closet was filled with expensive clothes.

But the dream was only that, an illusion. The house, private school, swimming pool, fancy car, nice clothes, were the payoff for living in an emotional prison. Far from what Eileen had led her classmates to believe, she was, by her own description, living a nightmare. She was experiencing the bitter rewards of a truly Faustian bargain.

Eileen complained to others that her sex life with Barry was very unsatisfactory. At the most they made love once or twice a year, and those instances were perfunctory. She told Diana that she had had an intense affair with the husband of a couple with whom she and Barry were friends, but that the man eventually broke it off because of the awkwardness he felt when the four of them were together. She laughingly told her sister that Barry had had an affair with a woman named Diana.

In November of 1988, a few months after the high school reunion, Eileen suffered a miscarriage. According to Eileen, she was shattered by her family's reaction to her tragedy: Barry told her that he was relieved because he didn't want any more children; her mother replied only that she already had two children; and her mother-in-law was hurt that Eileen hadn't told her she was pregnant. Everyone had plenty of words for her, but no sympathy, which left her feeling lonely and depressed. Her weight gain—she claimed fifteen pounds, Diana thought it was more like forty-five—only increased her depression.

According to Eileen, she had attempted twice to get out of her marriage, but each time she returned without filing for a divorce. Finally, on July 15, 1988, just a few months before her class reunion, she filed for divorce in the Superior Court of Los Angeles. In a sworn affidavit, she told about living with an emotional tyrant, a man obsessed with money, a man who psychologically abused her as well as his son, and was insanely jealous and ruled the household through intimidation and fear. She asked the court to issue an order directing Barry to move out of the house immediately, not come within 100 yards of her and her residence, and not to contact, molest, strike, threaten, sexually assault, batter or telephone or otherwise disturb her peace. She asked that the order be issued without notice to him, because he had threatened repeatedly that if she ever left him, he would take their daughter and she would never see her again. She also worried that he would dissolve the corporation and take the assets, leaving her with nothing but the empty house and the bills. If he had notice of any hearing, she argued, he might explode in a tirade of anger at her or the children and whisk Jessica away into hiding and run off with all their money.

According to Eileen's affidavit, Barry yelled and screamed at her daily. He had a practice of waking her in the middle of the night and angrily interrogating her about bills. At 3:00 A.M. one night the previous March, when she had just fallen asleep after tending to her ill son, he had woken her and grilled her about a late charge on a bill. Several days later he had awakened her at 5:00 A.M. ranting and raving about a parking ticket she had received, and in April he woke her at 2:30 angry and upset over a nine-dollar interest charge on a credit card.

Barry was extremely jealous and controlling. He interrogated her daily about telephone calls she received, demanding to know whom she was speaking with and what was discussed. He even seemed jealous of his son Aaron, whom he was apparently content to leave with Eileen in the event of a split. Aaron, then twenty months old, had asthma and often awoke during the night vomiting. When Eileen rose to care for him, Barry would become angry and yell at her. One night he came into Aaron's room just after Eileen had rocked him to sleep and put him in his crib. After waking Aaron, he yelled something like, "Why are you still with him? He is never going to grow up. You coddle him."

On numerous occasions, Eileen alleged in the document, Barry overreacted to the children's behavior and yelled at them, often for whining or crying. Once, when Aaron was sitting on the floor and put his bare foot in a bowl of ice cream which Barry had given him, Barry "became furious, yelling at the child, 'You stupid jerk boy, you bad boy,' etc. . . ." When Jessica tried to interfere, Barry responded, "Aaron is a stupid jerk boy and we don't like him."

All the yelling and screaming and outbursts were causing Eileen a great deal of "stress, nervousness and anxiety as well as a lack of sleep." At a minimum, she asked the court to order her husband to stay out of the master bedroom so she could get some rest.

According to Eileen, Barry had totally lost it when he learned that she was thinking of filing for divorce. He raved for nearly two hours before leaving the house. Then he called her and said he intended to dissolve the corporation, remove her name from the bank account, and put the house up for sale. She had two choices: She could either forget everything, or they could work things out themselves. When she told him she had retained a lawyer, he began "ranting again, claiming that I had a scum-sucking attorney."

On July 15, the judge entered a temporary order restraining both parties from transferring or concealing any property or taking and concealing either of the two children. Barry was allowed to continue to live in the house, but Eileen was granted the exclusive use of the extra bedroom. The judge also restrained Barry from molesting, threatening, or striking Eileen, or otherwise disturbing her peace. Copies of the order were delivered to the Los Angeles Police Department.

The court eventually set the matter for hearing on January 9, 1989, to consider custody and support issues. On December 14, Eileen filed an amended financial declaration. She had paid her "scum-sucking lawyer" $7,000 and sought reimbursement from Barry. The parties failed to appear on the scheduled date and the matter was removed from the calendar.

A FEW MONTHS LATER, IN APRIL 1989, EILEEN CALLED KATE AND invited her down for a visit, saying she wanted help decorating her house and offering to buy her plane ticket.

Kate was wary of Eileen's invitation. After two disastrous incidents with the family a few years earlier, both ending in bitter accusations and hurt feelings all around, she had pulled away again to a safe distance, at one point going so far as to change her phone number. She had relented in the past year or so, and had even begun spending time with Leah, who had remarried and lived close by; and while she hadn't seen Eileen in four or five years, she had talked to her several times on the phone. Last fall Eileen had been in town for her ten-year reunion and called Kate asking for help with her makeup for the dinner-dance. The two of them had also chipped in to buy Janice a dress for her reunion. So, when Eileen had invited her down to help redecorate her house, Kate, despite her misgivings, had accepted.

On the way from the airport to Eileen's house, Eileen pointed to the home of a successful Hollywood producer she knew. She told her sister that she and Barry had begun attending expensive Hollywood charity events in order to meet producers, directors, actors, and other Hollywood people, because they felt it would be important for Jessica and Aaron to be exposed to these people as they grew up. At one $1,000-a-plate dinner, they had been seated next to the producer and his wife, and had gotten along so well they had subsequently been invited to the producer's house for dinner. But the evening had been a disaster because Barry had argued boorishly with the guests and jumped up every five minutes to make a phone call. Eileen had been terribly embarrassed.

On entering the Canoga Park house, Kate immediately had a sudden sensation of familiarity, as if she had been there before. As she walked around the house and looked out the windows she gradually realized that it reminded her of their old house on Beach Park: like that house, this one was a glorified tract home, similar to every third house on the block, and like that house this one had dark rugs and masculine colors, and it was messy, with stacks of paperwork on the kitchen counters, clothes on the couch, dishes in the sink. Kate half-expected to turn around and see her mother sitting insensate at the kitchen table drinking coffee.

Barry was polite to her. The U.S. economy was going to fall apart very soon, he said, and he intended to sell the house and the cars and hold on to the cash. His consulting contract with the *L.A. Times*, which had been extremely lucrative, was almost completed and he was trying to move his computer consulting business to Switzerland for tax reasons. One potential European contract had fallen through, and the future was uncertain. As usual, Kate thought, everything with Barry was money, money, money. It was the way he related to the world.

Kate looked around the house with Eileen and made a few decorating suggestions. Eileen had already picked out the curtains for the dining and living rooms, so Kate suggested moving one of the heavy dark pieces in the living room. "Oh, Barry would never let me move that," Eileen objected. Kate suggested painting the kitchen or changing the window coverings, and again Eileen declared that Barry would never allow the changes. "Okay," thought Kate, "I won't say anything more, but why exactly am I here?"

Very soon Kate began to wish she wasn't there. She began feeling as if it were old home week, as if she was a child again and living in the midst of chaos. Eileen and Barry fought constantly. "Eileen, get your ass in here!" Barry would scream from the office, or, "Eileen, get the Goddamn kids out of here now!" The timbre of his voice, the intonation, the self-righteous irritability—it was her father all over again. When the mail came, Barry would open it and yell at Eileen about the bills, and then demand to know if she had made all of her assigned phone calls. Eileen yelled and screamed back. Anger, rage, reverberated throughout the house as it had when Kate was a child. There was no pleasure in anything, and the constant tension made everything an ordeal. If Eileen was going for Japanese takeout, she and Barry would bicker for twenty minutes about what to order. If Barry yelled that Eileen had lost a document, she would respond sneeringly, "It's right there, Barry, right under your nose!" All communication resulted in conflict. "My God," Kate thought the first evening, "Eileen is reliving her mother's life. She still thinks this abuse is normal, that this is the way families are. She's repeating her childhood as an adult, she's married our father!"

The only time Eileen mentioned their family was when she announced to Kate that neither Janice nor their father was welcome in her house any longer. Janice owed Eileen money and she smoked in front of the kids. Their father had said something weird about Jessica and Barry refused to permit him in the home any more.

By the second day, Kate, with her low threshold for conflict, was a nervous wreck. True to her childhood pattern, her response to the emotional violence was to flee the scene. In a thinly veiled excuse which she was sure Eileen saw through, Kate told her sister that she had a great many things to do at home and would have to leave a day early. When she finally stepped out of Eileen's car at the airport, she felt tremendous relief; by the time she was inside the terminal, she was so happy to be released from her past that she felt like kneeling and kissing the floor. Still, she couldn't help wondering why she had been invited in the first place.

27

AFTER GEORGE FRANKLIN WAS ARRESTED, EILEEN called prosecutor Marty Murray constantly, sometimes three and four times a day. She had an apparently insatiable need to talk about the crime, her memories, her past. Murray didn't want to receive new information from her over the phone—if issues developed in the trial about how her memory evolved, he might end up being called as a witness in his own trial—so he urged her to wait until a third person was present or a tape recorder was running. He knew that refusing Eileen's offer of new facts or ideas was a delicate matter—she, far more than most witness/victims, needed to develop trust and confidence in the prosecution. She also needed reassurance that she wasn't crazy.

Although Eileen viewed her history with men as one of unremitting betrayal and treachery, she still needed a hero, and heroes were men. Morse and Cassandro, as cops, were disqualified, but Marty Murray was strong, even-tempered, consistent. He had kept his promise to her that he wouldn't reveal her identity until her father was safely in jail, and he had obtained a bail that had kept her father behind bars. She turned to him for feelings of safety and comfort.

Murray, for his part, encouraged her questions on procedural matters, of which she had an endless supply: When would the case come to trial? What was a preliminary hearing? When would it be set? How long would it take? Who would pay for her airfare to San Francisco? Where would she stay? What should she do about the subpoenas? What medical records did she need to turn over? Would her past problems come to light?

Despite the new life Eileen had created for herself, the prostitution conviction had hovered like a shadow around the edges of her existence. Barry had eventually found out, and how he found out was a matter of great dispute in the Franklin family. Within months of their marriage in 1984, Eileen had fled her new husband, taking with her the baby, the VCR, and a large sum of money. In his effort to track down his wife, Barry called Kate and Allen. He was hysterical, and Kate and Allen drove down to San Jose to comfort him. While Kate prepared dinner, Barry told Allen that he had hired a private detective to find Eileen and he had uncovered her prostitution conviction. According to Eileen, when Barry finally found her, he told her he knew about the prostitution conviction and that he intended to sue for custody of Jessica unless she came home. Eileen was not surprised that Barry would stoop so low as to blackmail her with her past and threaten her with loss of her daughter to get his way, but nonetheless she felt she had no choice but to comply—she had been "checkmated," she would later say—and she returned home. Apparently looking for someone else to blame for her misfortune in having to return to her marriage, Eileen called Kate and Allen and viciously accused *them* of telling Barry about her prostitution conviction. Later she called Diana and accused *her* of telling Barry.

Although Eileen believed that if she went five years from the date of her conviction in 1982 without another violation, she could apply to the court in San Jose to have her record sealed, she did nothing until the spring of 1989, seven years after the conviction and four or five months after she later claimed to have visualized the killing of Susan Nason. In apparent anticipation of going forward to the police with her story, she contacted a San Jose probation officer who, on June 20, petitioned the court on her behalf, swearing that Eileen had complied with the sentence of the court, was not serving a sentence for any offense, and had lived an honest and upright life. On July 13, the court, in accordance with California law, ordered that the plea of guilty be vacated, a plea of not guilty be entered, and the charge dismissed. The court did not order, however, that the record of the conviction be sealed.

When Morse and Cassandro had taken Eileen's statement in November 1989, she asked them whether they had run a check on her. They had, but had found nothing, and she did not tell them of the conviction. Believing that she had successfully escaped from her past, that she had shrugged off that period in her life like an old skin, Eileen had been ecstatic. She would be able to go forward into the struggle as the untainted wife and mother.

Thus she was horrified when Marty Murray informed her later that the defense had requested her rap sheet and that when he pulled it he found a misdemeanor conviction for prostitution. Murray assured her that he would only inform the defense of the existence of a misdemeanor conviction—not the nature of the offense—and would argue before a judge that the offense itself need not be revealed because it was not relevant to her truth or veracity.

IN ADDITION TO ALL THE DAILY CALLS FROM EILEEN, MURRAY WAS also hearing from a variety of women who had read about the case in the papers and had a story to tell about George Franklin.

The Franklins' baby-sitter, who had been thirteen in 1967, told Murray that one evening when George Franklin was taking her home, he pulled over in San Mateo and began questioning her about her sexual activities with boys. The baby-sitter's younger sister had a similar experience with Franklin: he sat very close to her in the car and, while driving slowly, questioned her about what she did with boys.

Another woman called Murray and said she had some photographs that George Franklin had given her several years before to keep for him and she wanted to mail them to Murray. He explained that that wouldn't do because if he ever needed to use them in court he would have to explain where they came from. The woman said she would drop them off at his office, and while she wouldn't give him her name, she would leave a phone number he could call if he absolutely had to get hold of her. Murray agreed. A few negatives were in the package and he had them developed. In one picture, George, who looked in his mid-thirties and had bushy red hair, was smiling his broad smile in front of a cake that read: "WELCOME HOME GEORGE." In another he was sitting naked on a couch with his legs spread wide and one hand pulling a condom off his penis.

Most interesting were three pictures of one woman. The first one was a high school yearbook photo of an innocent-looking girl with a round, open face, broad shoulders, long brown hair, and a large bust. A gold pendant rested on her maroon sweater. In the second picture the girl, older now, is lying naked on her back on a quilt on a couch, her legs open and her large breasts falling across her chest and stomach. Her eyes are closed and one hand is between her legs. In the third, her knees are pulled up to her shoulders and in between her legs is a large German shepherd standing on his hind legs. His front paws are next to her armpits and his pelvis is pressed against her vulva.

Morse and Cassandro tracked down three other former girlfriends who said Franklin had expressed interest in them having sex with a dog in his presence. He had bragged to one of them that young girls often came on to him; in one instance, a twelve-year-old niece had flirted with him at a wedding until he finally "had to poke her." One of his favorite sayings was, "The younger they are, the sweeter the meat."

Carolyn Adams told the prosecution she had been involved with George for over three years in the mid-eighties. He had beaten her and tried to get her to procure other women for him and to participate in group sexual activities. She had left him in 1987 when he told her that he had had sex with his daughter.

Jean DeBernardi, Leah's youngest sister, told Morse that when she was seventeen, George had grabbed her in the kitchen, kissed her roughly on the mouth, and stuck his hand inside her dress and fondled her breasts.

Leah's other sister, Sue, claimed that when she was in high school, George had grabbed her wrists and held them over her head with one hand and fondled her breasts with the other.

Murray analyzed these reports and pondered how he might get the information into evidence. The state had charged Franklin with first-degree murder and, in California, first-degree murder could be proven two ways. In the simplest fashion, the prosecution attempted to prove that the defendant killed a person with malice aforethought, i.e., that the murder was willful, deliberate, and premeditated. The second way is under the felony murder rule, which states that a person who kills another person, even if unintentionally or accidentally, while committing a felony is guilty of first-degree murder, as long as he had specific intent to commit the other felony (and even though he could not be prosecuted for the felony because of the statute of limitations). If a man was driving a car while holding a woman against her will (felony kidnapping) and the car swerved off the road into a tree and killed the woman, the man would be guilty of first-degree murder, even though he had not intended to kill her.

Murray had charged Franklin with both intentional first-degree murder and felony murder, the felony being the commission of a lewd and lascivious act upon a child, Susan Nason. A lewd and lascivious act is defined in California as any touching of the body of a child under fourteen with the specific intent to arouse, appeal to, or gratify the sexual desires of either party.

Thus, Murray could establish first-degree murder either by proving that Franklin intentionally and with premeditation killed Susan Nason by smashing her head with a rock, or by proving that he molested her in the back of the van before her death. Under either theory, he would have to prove specific intent to commit the act.

"Uncharged conduct," "prior acts," and "prior crimes" all amount to the same thing in criminal law: alleged misconduct by the defendant which the prosecution would like to put before the jury as circumstantial evidence to prove that he committed the crime in question. This is one of the trickiest areas in criminal law because the evidence of past crimes (for which the defendant may or may not have been convicted or even charged) can obviously be highly prejudicial, and at best it does nothing more than raise an inference that the defendant committed the crime for which he is being tried. In their most common form, prior acts are allowed into evidence because they are similar to the one under consideration. If the defendant is charged with raping a woman in the back seat of his car in a cemetery on Saturday night while holding a bread knife to her throat, the prosecution might seek to have three other women testify that he raped them in the back seat of his car in a cemetery, even though he was never charged with those crimes. The issue would be whether the circumstances of the uncharged rapes are similar enough to the circumstances of the charged rapes to raise the inference that they were committed by the same person. (In the rape trial of William Kennedy Smith, the judge disallowed the testimony of three women who claimed Smith had previously assaulted them on the grounds that the circumstances were not similar enough to the Palm Beach offense.) In California, if the uncharged conduct is offered to establish the identity of the killer, it must be similar and specific enough to establish that the current crime bears the defendant's "signature."

California law also allows evidence of uncharged conduct to prove other facts, such as motive, opportunity, intent, plan, knowledge, or absence of mistake or accident. The court must weigh the probative value of the uncharged conduct—the strength of the inference—against the prejudicial effect the evidence is likely to have on the minds of the jurors.

California law also specifically prohibits the admission into evidence of other crimes or wrongs to prove the defendant's disposition or propensity to commit the act in question. Thus, the prosecution cannot attempt to prove that the defendant has a criminal mind or possesses a tendency to commit criminal acts, that he is a "bad guy." The prosecution cannot show, for example, that a defendant charged with first-degree murder is a brawler and a drug abuser. A jury might be too inclined to find, as Judge Benjamin Cardozo wrote in 1930, that "A quarrelsome defendant is more likely to start a quarrel." This prohibition against "character evidence" has one major exception: If the defendant himself puts his character in question; if he takes the stand and testifies, or even strongly implies, that he is a good guy, an upstanding citizen, the prosecution is entitled to counter this testimony with evidence of his bad character.

The effect on the jury of character evidence can be devastating, and a great many defendants, in order to make sure it doesn't come in, do not take the witness stand. Under the Fifth Amendment, the defendant need not take the stand, and even if he does he is safe from this type of evidence as long as he doesn't put his character in issue. However, good prosecutors are skilled in the art of eliciting a "good character" statement from a defendant, and even the wariest, smartest person can be tricked into it, because it doesn't take much. All a defendant has to say is, "Oh, I would never do anything like that," and the prosecution may be entitled to throw in whatever facts it has (evidence of child pornography, or bestiality, for example) to show that he is indeed the sort of person who would do something like that. So the prosecution will often amass information showing what a disreputable, deviant, or abusive person the defendant is, not so much in hopes of actually getting the facts in evidence, but as a way of keeping him off the stand.

Murray knew he needed more evidence than Eileen's twenty-year-old memory to convict her father of murder. He expected to find, and did find, evidence that George Franklin had a sexual interest in young girls. He could prove that he was a violent man who beat his wife and children and sexually abused his daughters. He knew Franklin liked to hold girls' hands by the wrists over their heads while he fondled them, as Eileen said he had done with Susan in the back of the van; as Sue DeBernardi said he had done to her when she was seventeen; as Carol said he had done to her. His team had indexed and boxed a pornography collection that demonstrated a range of perverted sexual interests from bestiality to a desire to view the sex organs of eight-year-old girls. Murray and the cops knew that the outcome of the case might very well depend on how much of this "uncharged conduct" they could persuade a judge to let a jury see and hear. The pornography and bestiality would probably keep Franklin off the stand, but that wasn't enough: they wanted the jurors to see the sickness of Franklin's soul. They wanted Franklin the monster, not Franklin the retired fireman, sitting in the courtroom with the jury. Murray knew that admissibility of uncharged conduct was, to a large extent, discretionary with the judge, and some judges were extremely strict about not allowing it in, feeling that such evidence was often highly prejudicial. He was aware that it would take some very persuasive and highly creative lawyering to get the true picture of George Franklin before the jury.

28

In late December 1989, Eileen told Marty Murray that she was coming to the peninsula to see her mother and would drop by his office. Murray was looking forward to meeting her. While he trusted Morse and Cassandro's judgment that she would be dynamite in front of a jury, he wanted to size her up in person for himself. She had told him on the phone that her shoulder-length red hair made her quite distinctive-looking, but recalling her comment about using a therapist for weight control, he expected to find a moon-faced heavy redhead sitting in the waiting room of the district attorney's office; instead, he found a beautiful, poised woman. He told her that she was far more attractive than he had expected, gorgeous in fact. Obviously pleased, she laughed somewhat coyly and asked, "Why, what did you think I would look like?"

As well as being somewhat taken with her personally, Murray was pleased professionally. Eileen was not only lovely and articulate, she came across as very sincere. Her affect was quite appropriate—when she said sad things, her eyes welled up with tears. By the end of the meeting he was convinced that the jury would believe her. To top it off, she was completely clean—she had no financial or other improper motive for coming forward.

Murray had been concerned when Eileen told him in early December that she and Barry had hired a Los Angeles entertainment attorney, Bill Simon, to represent them. She explained that she was being hounded by agents, movie producers, television producers, and authors, all wanting to do her story, and they were driving her crazy and invading her privacy. Now she could send them all to her entertainment attorney. That made sense to Murray. He himself had received calls from all sorts of producers—some of whom he learned later had grossly misrepresented themselves—for a variety of shows and he wanted nothing to do with them. He sarcastically told one tabloid that he could imagine the Franklin story being sandwiched in between a piece on a woman who had Elvis's baby in a spaceship and one on a two-headed chicken. Now when these characters called and asked for Eileen's number, he could send them to the lawyer. It didn't occur to him that Barry and Eileen and their entertainment lawyer would actually begin negotiating book and movie deals. She had assured him that she would never take any money for her story.

Murray received another jolt from Eileen when she told him that she had only recently remembered the murder. Murray was immediately skeptical of the new version. In the taped telephone conversations she said that she hadn't reported the killing earlier because her father had threatened to kill her and she told Murray on the phone that the information she was giving them was the result of therapy over the past twenty years. In her November interview with the detectives, they had asked her why she was coming forward now and she had replied that her memory of the killing had recently become more vivid.

Murray knew how important it was to Eileen for her story to be believed, and she had expressed concern that the Nasons might be mad at her and she might be in trouble herself for not coming forward earlier. She also worried that people would think badly of her for keeping the solution to this horrible crime to herself all these years. All of these concerns would be ameliorated if she had forgotten the killing soon after it happened and had spoken up within months of remembering it. Murray was also skeptical of the concept of repression. In his view, her loss of the memory for twenty years would be harder to explain to a jury than her keeping it to herself.

"People will understand that you didn't come forward all these years because you were too frightened," he assured her, "it won't hurt the case."

"No, no," she said, "I really didn't remember it until recently."

"Think about it," he urged her, "people will understand that you were just too scared to come forward."

He assured her that if the repression story was a defense against feelings of guilt, it wasn't necessary. He fully expected her to change her story at some point before the trial.

Eileen shocked Murray again when she called to tell him that she wanted to see her father.

"I love my father," she had said, "and he brought me up to tell the truth. I want to go see him and tell him that I love him, and if he loves and respects me he won't make me get up there and go through a trial but will admit what he has done."

Murray did not particularly like the idea, but he knew he had to play it very carefully. He couldn't stop Eileen from doing what she wanted to do, but it could not look as though she was visiting her father on behalf of the prosecution. George Franklin had an attorney and it was not legal for a law enforcement person to question him unless his attorney was present.

"I can't tell you to do it," he responded to her, "I can't approve it, suggest it, or even encourage it. If you see him, you're on your own, I'm not even going to arrange it for you. I'll give you a name to call, and that's it. Just remember," he stressed, in case she had missed his point, "you are not my agent."

Eileen, who had not seen her father in four years, visited him in jail and, according to Eileen, they had a very tender twenty-five-minute conversation. She found him very handsome, as always, and she told him she had always loved him.

She didn't believe that he had premeditated the killing of Susan, but believed it was probably a situation that had gotten out of control. He had to pay the penalty and, if he loved her, he would confess. She appreciated the special treatment she had received as his favorite child, and she was grateful for his saving her life when she had appendicitis. He had taught her that the truth would set her free, she reminded him, and now the truth could set him free. In jail, he would be free from his need to hurt people. She pleaded with him not to be a hypocrite and a liar as well as a murderer. If he loved her he would confess.

George Franklin didn't confess to his "Pooh," not then or ever. George Franklin said very little to his favorite daughter that afternoon in the jail visiting room; indeed, it was what he didn't say to her that the jury would remember so clearly when they sat in judgment on him almost a year later.

Eileen had one final surprise for Murray. She had decided to appear on NBC's "Today Show." She wanted his advice on what she should and shouldn't say in front of the camera. Murray was very upset—publicity was already a serious problem and he was hoping that the sources would dry up and the story would die down. He didn't want Eileen or Barry talking to *anyone,* and he particularly didn't want Eileen telling her story to a nationwide television audience. The prosecution was still assembling its case, and he wanted to construct it behind a wall of silence and let the public learn the facts as they unfolded in the courtroom. Whatever she or Barry said now could come back to haunt them. Extensive publicity could also result in the case being moved to another county, and Murray very much wanted to try this case to a San Mateo jury.

29

EILEEN WOULD LATER CLAIM THAT SHE HAD NO IDEA that her charge against her father would generate such massive publicity. She envisioned a few articles in the San Mateo area press, perhaps, but little more. She would say she was overwhelmed and completely unprepared for the intense national media interest in the story—unannounced visits from television crews and the phone calls from morning to night. According to her, she never wanted to talk to any of them; she didn't want to be on television, have her picture in *People* magazine, write a book, or have her life made into a movie. She only wanted to be left alone. She hated the idea of the story becoming public property; it was a matter between her, her father, the legal system, and Susan, and she wanted it kept private. More than anything, she cherished her privacy.

Nonetheless, she gave interviews to at least three newspapers within an hour of the judge's directive lifting the gag order on December 27. In two of the interviews, Eileen gave the reporters hot information: She said she had just recently recovered her memory of the murder through a "flashback." She explained to a reporter from the *San Jose Mercury News* that a few days after she saw Susan murdered, she had forgotten the crime. When her body was found, she had been "really terrified," then forgot it again. Afterwards, when she walked by the Nason house, she would veer off to the far sidewalk without knowing why. She hadn't remembered the murder until a few months earlier when she had begun having flashbacks of the slaying. After deciding that the flashbacks were real, she told her husband, who called the authorities.

She told a *Los Angeles Times* reporter that she had "blocked out" the memory of the killing after it happened and that she went to the police after having flashbacks of the murder, which included an image of her father bludgeoning Susan to death with a rock. She wouldn't discuss any more facts because she wanted to keep the memory accurate—"I know what I remember and I don't want anything to influence my memory."

Prosecutor Murray was very disturbed when he read Eileen's statements to the press, particularly her use of the term "flashbacks" to describe her memory. Not only was she giving information to the defense that it would otherwise not have had, she was fueling the media frenzy. Eileen told him that it was Barry, not her, who had used the word "flashbacks." Barry was also to blame for the growing media storm. She would walk in the room and find him talking on the phone with reporters, giving them details about her memory and discussing her feelings about her father. He gave long interviews to CNN and CBS. He was making these facts up, she told Murray, and she had asked him again and again to stop talking to the press, but he refused. Barry became even more stimulated by the attention of the Hollywood producers. He talked at length with them about "The Eileen Franklin Story," and explained what his and his wife's demands were for a movie deal. Eileen insisted that she wanted nothing to do with any of these deals —the idea of making money from Susan's death was repulsive to her—but she was powerless to shut her husband up.

To many members of the press, Eileen did not behave like someone surprised or upset by the amount of media attention she was attracting. While she claimed to be unsophisticated in press matters, she would sometimes demand, after giving an interview, that the article be read to her over the phone for her approval; if the reporter refused, she would insist that her quotes be read back to her for accuracy.

In one interview, Eileen was answering questions coolly and calmly while Barry kept nagging and interrupting her in the background; finally she lost it and turned and yelled, "Barry, shut the fuck up!" Other than getting past Barry, the reporters never had any difficulty talking to Eileen. In fact, they were surprised at the ease with which she could be reached, even after she had hired an entertainment attorney supposedly to handle media calls. Her number was listed in the phone book and remained unchanged. The reporters never reached an answering service and, if they left a message on her machine, she called them right back. Eileen never seemed too busy to talk.

Eileen's "flashback" comment to the *San Jose Mercury News* and *Los Angeles Times* gave the story the hook it needed to explode from a local news item to a national media event. It was one thing to come forward and charge your father with murder; it was quite another to say that you had completely repressed the brutal slaying for twenty years because your father had threatened to kill you. The image of a twenty-nine-year-old wife and mother of two living the American dream in a Los Angeles suburb one day receiving horrifying, unbidden images of her father bashing her best friend's head in with a rock twenty years earlier—and such images forming the basis for a first-degree murder charge against her father, a former fireman with no previous offenses—would prove irresistible to the national media. When Eileen presented herself and her playmate in 1969 as two little freckled outcasts bonded together in the pain of rejection and isolation because of their red hair, and herself as a person suffering an inability to trust anyone because of the tragic loss of her friend, she gave the story the perfect grab-you-in-the-gut dimension. And while Eileen told the reporters that this long-forgotten memory had just recently intruded into her consciousness, she didn't reveal *how* or *why* the memory had returned. The world wouldn't hear about the "trigger" for the memory until she testified at the preliminary hearing.

The story might have died down if Eileen had not decided to give the exclusive interview to NBC. According to Eileen, Barry set the process in motion by telling a friend of his, a television cameraman, about her repressed memory of the killing. The cameraman told his brother, Chuck Scarborough, an NBC anchorman in New York, who, when he learned that Eileen had not given any television interviews, became excited over the possibility of a major journalistic coup. Eileen says she was persuaded to do the interview by assurances from

Chuck and Barry that the interview, which would be broadcast on the evening national news and the "Today Show," would kill the interest in the story and the media would then leave her alone. If she gave an interview to one major network, they explained, the other networks would go away and the media interest in general would die. NBC would abide by whatever conditions she set. The interview appealed to Eileen because it would give her a chance to prove to the world that she was normal. Eileen also used Barry's intense desire to have the show done to shut him up: if she agreed to do the interview, he would have to stop talking to the press. Barry agreed.

Horrified at the prospect of his star witness telling her story to millions of people instead of to a jury, Murray pleaded with Eileen not to do the "Today Show" interview. She could seriously jeopardize the case, he insisted; only harm could flow to the prosecution from her appearance on national television. Eileen stubbornly refused to listen. She had already made up her mind to go on television and nothing Murray could say was going to change it, even his predictions that her behavior might help her father go free.

Murray certainly wouldn't advise Eileen on negotiating terms with NBC, because that would tie him into the project, the last thing he wanted. He did insist, however, that she not watch the segment. It would undoubtedly recount the facts of the killing, and it was important to keep her memory as uncontaminated as possible. Murray wanted her to be able to say on the stand that she had not read any newspaper accounts or watched any television reports of the case.

Eileen dictated her own terms for the interview to NBC: She would not discuss the events of the case, her relationship with her father, whether she had ever been physically or sexually abused, her memory, or what may have "triggered" her memory. Her children must not be recognizable, the interview must be conducted outside of a studio, and only the interviewer, cameraman, and absolutely necessary technical or production support would be present. NBC agreed without hesitation; they could easily lay out the facts of the case with old clips, interviews with other key people, and a narrator. What they needed was the voice and face of Eileen Franklin. As yet, she was a visual unknown. NBC would have the first image of the living victim, the accuser.

Eileen located what family photographs she could find for use in the show, and called Diana and asked her if she had any pictures NBC could use. Diana declined to cooperate in the venture. Barry called Don Nason and urged him to give an interview to NBC.

BRYANT GUMBEL INTRODUCED THE SEGMENT BY ANNOUNCING THAT A fifty-year-old retired fireman in California would be appearing in court that day (January 22, 1990) for a crime that had shocked Foster City twenty years ago. "The break in the case," he proclaimed, "may have been as shocking as the crime itself." Stressing their "exclusive interview," Gumbel turned to Chuck Scarborough, who had Don Nason in front of a television camera in his living room.

Don hadn't wanted to do the interview—he and Margaret had separated a few weeks after the arrest and she was refusing all interviews—but he had given in to Barry's pressure. People who hadn't seen Don for ten years, and remembered him as the thin, handsome salesman of the sixties, were shocked by the white-haired, corpulent man on the screen. Don hadn't stopped drinking since Susan's death, and he had recently undergone major surgery. The TV screen filled with an unhealthy man frozen in the pain of his daughter's murder: his eyes, peering out from a mass of flesh, were wet and burning; his voice raspy, halting. Scarborough, a middle-aged man nattily dressed in a double-breasted raincoat, worked to bring Don's pain to the surface for the camera with questions like, "Tell me what sort of a child Susan was."

The gap-toothed picture of Susan appeared on the screen as Scarborough explained that the day she was murdered, Susan had gone home from school to play with her best friend, Eileen Franklin, and then the camera cut to Eileen, who was sitting alone on a couch. She was wearing a simple blue turtleneck with no jewelry. She smiled radiantly as she described how close she and Susan were because of their red hair and how they had been picked on by their classmates.

Then Scarborough intoned that Susan didn't return home after playing with Eileen, because "that evening Susan Nason vanished." After getting Don Nason to admit that he felt despair over his daughter's disappearance, Scarborough cut to himself standing across the highway from a clearly visible pulloff he described as being on Highway 92, which runs by the Crystal Springs Reservoir. Then the cameras showed clips from December 2, 1969, of the same gravel pulloff filled with cops and cop cars. Ephe Ray Bottimore was standing on the lip of the pulloff looking at a clearing some twenty yards down the hill. In the clearing lay a white object, a sheet lying on top of something. Scarborough explained that the body was found in the ravine under a discarded mattress.

When Scarborough said that Eileen recovered her memory of the murder only three months earlier, the camera closed on Eileen and the radiant smile faded into a somber, slightly pained look. She explained that only a few years earlier she had begun to remember unpleasant experiences from her childhood. Scarborough told the viewer that images of her best friend being molested and beaten to death with a rock inexplicably began flashing through Eileen's mind. "With equally terrifying clarity," he intoned dramatically, "she also saw the killer."

"Once I remembered it," Eileen said sadly, "and remembered it as accurately as I think I do, I realized that my father"—here her voice quivered slightly—"had murdered Susan." After consulting a psychologist, Scarborough reported, Eileen became convinced that she had repressed the memory for twenty years.

Scarborough then interviewed Dr. Lenore Terr, a San Francisco psychiatrist, who explained that repressed memories of painful experiences can be recovered by a smell, the time of year, a sound, or "because one's own child is the age one was at the time of the event in the first place."

Scarborough asked Eileen why she had repressed the memory, and she responded softly that her father had threatened to kill her and have her put away. It had been difficult to confront her husband with her memory, she explained with a strange, inappropriate smile, and she was embarrassed to say that it had taken her many, many weeks to tell him.

The camera shifted suddenly to Barry, who was sitting on Eileen's left. His small, almost beady eyes were set close together over a large mustache, giving him a walrus look. Responding on cue to his name, he proclaimed that "My wife did one of the most difficult and courageous things that anyone in society could do. She came forward after witnessing a terrible crime and she turned her father in to the authorities." The scene of the caring, supportive husband was seriously marred by the look on Eileen's face as Barry talked; staring right at him, she appeared almost nauseated, as if hearing him brag about her courage could make her ill.

The screen then filled with a startlingly attractive image of Janice in a blue sweater. She explained that she had gone to the police in 1984 because her instincts and suspicions told her that her father was a killer and a dangerous person who should be taken out of society. The police hadn't been able to do anything with her charge, Scarborough explained, until her younger sister came forward with her eyewitness account of the killing.

The camera shifted to George in the courtroom in orange pants and T-shirt looking like a wild man. He was conferring with Horngrad while they waited for his case to be called. Then Scarborough asked Eileen what it felt like to turn in her father. Eileen, pausing dramatically, said that it hadn't been all black and white, she hadn't turned her father in on a whim. Hovering on the verge of tears, her voice shaking, she said she came forward because she owed it to Susan.

The segment closed with the camera focused on the tears brimming in Don Nason's eyes while Scarborough read aloud a poem about life and death ("Don't mourn for me, I am not dead") which he had noticed on the Nason refrigerator door and which Don had refused to read himself.

A brief version of the interview aired that evening on the "NBC Nightly News," and was introduced by Tom Brokaw, who shook his head in fascinated dismay over the bizarre story. Hundreds of affiliates around the country ran abbreviated versions on their late evening news, exposing Eileen to millions more viewers. Eileen may have intended the interview to discourage the other networks, yet she herself tells how subsequently she agreed to give an interview to the "CBS Evening News" on the condition that the interviewer, camera operator, and technicians in the room all be women—conditions which the network refused. The publicity certainly didn't discourage the tabloid newspapers or television shows: Janice gave an interview to the tabloid *Star*, reportedly for money, and Eileen continued to be pursued by "Inside Edition" and "A Current Affair," the latter promising her a personal meeting with Maury Povich. According to one tabloid TV staffer, Eileen countered that she would consider an interview, but only if the show flew her to New York and bought her a mink coat. *People* magazine and the weekly news magazines picked up on the story, and several newspapers carried pieces about the NBC interview.

Eileen had come a long way in a few weeks. From the uneducated housewife trapped in a loveless marriage to an abusive husband, stashed away in an unkempt middle-class house in Southern California raising two kids and running her husband's business out of an upstairs office, she was now sought after by and negotiating with television producers, literary agents, talk show hosts, authors, and reporters from the biggest newspapers in the country, many of them telling her how strong and courageous she was.

Eileen was learning to trust her entertainment lawyer. He was talking about selling her "life rights," which would be a package deal, a book and a movie tied together to maximize profits. Eileen was defensive about her lack of education, but she had always wanted to write and she saw this as an opportunity to begin. She began keeping a diary of her thoughts and feelings for the day she would tell her story in print.

Eileen was very impressed with the number of producers who were interested in making a movie about her life. She was determined to keep absolute control of the book and the movie, including the script and the casting—she wanted the right persons to play her sisters and her children, for example —and she and Barry began the tedious process of interviewing and ranking each of the producers. Barry was impossible in the meetings—it was hard for him to accept that for the first time in their relationship she was the focus of attention, not him— and he kept telling everyone how much money he made. One of the highlights for Eileen, though, was when she met Henry Winkler, the Fonz, who owned one of the production companies.

One producer was appalled at the dog and pony show, the process of being interviewed by Eileen, the victim/subject, and her husband to see how her company stacked up. The producer had had to make a presentation and answer questions as if she were a contestant in some sort of a talent show. She couldn't figure out what this beautiful woman was doing with this little schlepp of a husband who talked on and on about how much money he made and how they really didn't need the money, that wasn't why they were interested in a movie. The two of them had been really organized; they knew just what they wanted, which was a lot. They made incredibly outrageous, greedy demands. Eileen had even insisted on consulting fees for her sisters Janice and Diana. The producer didn't like Eileen and she sure as hell didn't believe her story.

30

DIANA, NOW A TALL, SLENDER TWENTY-SIX-YEAR-OLD, was working in the cosmetics department at Macy's in San Francisco when Eileen called to tell her their father had been arrested that morning. She was shocked and also very hurt that her sister had waited until the last possible minute to tell her—

only a few hours before it would appear in the paper. But Diana believed her sister instinctively. Eileen would not make something like this up, and she had no doubt that her father was capable of committing murder. The man was a monster.

Diana hadn't heard from Eileen for several years, with the exception of one phone call the previous summer. The alienation had begun, in Diana's mind, when Eileen met Barry. Barry ran down Eileen's family, constantly telling her what "a bunch of idiots and fucked-up people" her parents and siblings were. In Diana's view, Barry was an absolute pig. In the middle of dinner he would flip on the television and begin watching it, as if no one else was there. Eileen told her about how embarrassed she was to have people over because Barry would begin screaming at her in front of the guests. Eileen stayed with him for the money and the kids—if they split, she knew Barry would seek custody of Jessica.

Before Barry came into the picture, Eileen and Diana had been as close as ever. The two striking women would hold hands in a restaurant or walking down the street, the way they had as children on the way to school. Diana had been so traumatized by her sister's prostitution conviction that she had stopped eating and had lost twenty pounds in two weeks, but she had stuck by her. (Diana was somewhat irritated, though, when she learned that Eileen had been wearing one of her dresses when she was busted.) Then Eileen called after she had left Barry the first time and said that Barry had found out about the prostitution conviction and was blackmailing her with the loss of Jessica if she didn't return home. Eileen was upset that Kate's husband, Allen, was siding with Barry, and Diana made a snide remark that she thought Allen may have been hitting on her when they drove to Wyoming to his parents' cabin. Eileen, apparently to get even with Allen for siding with Barry, called Kate and accused her husband of trying to sleep with Diana. The incident caused a huge uproar in the family—even Leah got into the act, calling Kate and blasting her for her husband's behavior. Diana and Eileen hadn't spoken until Eileen had called a few months earlier.

Now, Eileen's phone call at work had upset Diana and she

immediately went home and called Eileen back and told her that she remembered her father sticking his tongue in her mouth when he kissed her as a little girl. When Eileen called her again the next morning, Diana read to her word-for-word a newspaper article in the *San Mateo Times* about the arrest, which recapped the facts of the murder and specifically mentioned that Susan had disappeared while playing after school and that her body had been found in a ravine off Highway 92 not far from Crystal Springs Reservoir. "Diana," Eileen had said excitedly, "this is going to be the biggest story ever to come out of San Mateo County."

Diana had never been close to Kate or Janice—she considered Janice to be the most unstable of the siblings, very moody and unpredictable—but she and George Jr. were friends. She enjoyed his cynicism, his way of turning ordinary things upside down and laughing at them.

George Jr. knew firsthand what a conscienceless bastard their father was, but he doubted he was capable of murder. George Jr. had become very suspicious of Eileen and her motives, particularly when he saw how she had really cranked up the story, talking to the newspapers, going on the "Today Show," selling her "life rights" for movies and books. There had been no good reason for any of it other than to finally get all the attention she had always craved. He was furious with her for laying open the family to the ravenous eye of the media. Initially, he had intended to stay neutral, sifting through the facts as they became available and reaching his own conclusion, but as time went on he gradually moved closer to his father's camp. He simply could not convict his father on Eileen's word alone. He and Diana argued about the case frequently and then finally stopped discussing it. Their father wasn't worth destroying their friendship.

As soon as George Jr. had indicated the slightest doubts about Eileen's story, she and Barry marked him as a traitor; soon they suspected him of trying to ferret information from her to give to the defense and branded him a spy. Eileen began to berate Diana for continuing to have anything to do with their brother. Diana, always vulnerable to Eileen's anger and usually willing to do anything to please her, held fast. She loved Eileen, but she loved her brother too, and she would not give him up.

In the early months after the arrest, Diana visited Eileen several times in Canoga Park, usually when she knew Barry would be in Switzerland. If Barry was at home, everything was crazy. He complained constantly about Janice and demanded to know when she was leaving. Janice and Eileen made sure to hide the mail under Janice's mattress because Barry gave Eileen the third degree over even the smallest household bills.

During one of Diana's visits before the preliminary hearing, she and Eileen and Janice watched the tape of the "Today Show." Diana had seen it once, but she wanted to see it again. The three sisters went upstairs to Eileen's bedroom while the nanny watched the kids below. Watching Eileen pop the tape in and automatically click rewind, it was obvious to Diana that this wasn't the first time she had seen it. Eileen explained that she wasn't supposed to watch the show and that if anybody ever asked, Diana should say that Eileen had left the room when the tape started. "Watch," she said, and got up and left the room. But she came right back in and, except for a few seconds here and there, watched the entire tape. When Janice came on, the sisters found one of her mannerisms so funny that Eileen, who had the controls, played it again and again while they all laughed.

Diana had no doubt that she was supposed to lie on the stand if asked whether Eileen had watched the "Today Show."

31

IN THE EARLY PART OF 1990, MURRAY REALIZED THAT
he was carrying too many cases. In August 1989, just a few
months before Barry had called the police, the district attorney
had assigned him two complex first-degree murder trials. Murray had handled the preliminary hearing for one of the cases in
September and the trial was set for January 1990. The preliminary hearing for the other was set in May, and most likely the
case would be set for trial in the fall. Massive amounts of
additional preparation were still required for both cases.
Horngrad was making it clear that Franklin wanted to go to
trial as soon as possible, which probably meant the fall. As
things stood, that meant Murray would have to handle two
preliminary hearings and three first-degree murder trials in a
nine-month period.

Murray was also becoming burned out on his work: the
twisted pathology of the defendants and the intense pain of
their victims had worn him thin, and he was seriously considering a lucrative offer to go into private practice. All of which
meant he had to make a move. Giving up Franklin made the
most sense because it hadn't been fully worked up yet. There
were only two attorneys in the office he considered capable of
handling Franklin and, in January, after obtaining a conviction
in one of the other cases, he approached one of them, Elaine
Tipton, a senior attorney with extensive experience in the prosecution of sex crimes, about helping him out.

In the winter of 1990, Elaine Tipton, thirty-seven, had been
with the district attorney's office for ten years. She had grown
up one of five children in a middle-class Catholic family in
nearby Menlo Park and had graduated from Hastings Law

School in San Francisco in 1980. She had spent several years prosecuting sex crimes—rape, sexual assault, child abuse—and had earned a reputation as a prosecutor who identified, perhaps more than usual, with the victims. Murray saw her as tough, highly focused, and extremely thorough.

Other members of the D.A.'s office agreed that Tipton was a superb trial lawyer. She was well organized and had an emphatic but balanced style. Jurors related well to her, and in a close case how the jurors felt about a lawyer could easily make the difference. She was particularly skilled on cross-examination, calmly using logic and reasoning to shred opposing witnesses. She knew that female prosecutors traditionally have a tough time on cross-examination before a jury—they had to be tough without being bitchy—and Tipton managed that well. She also had a penchant for answering every question that might arise in a juror's mind, whether or not it was asked.

Tipton's first big case had been the murder trial of Danny Mickle. In 1983, Mickle, who had two previous convictions for sex offenses against young girls, molested and stabbed a twelve-year-old girl in a motel room, then torched the building to cover his crime. The girl had died of the stab wounds, but not before surviving at least forty minutes in the burning building. Under Tipton's tutelage, a jury convicted Mickle of first-degree murder in 1984. In 1986, she convinced a different jury to send him to the gas chamber.

In the legal community, prosecutors are divided into two camps: those who have obtained death sentences and those who haven't. With Mickle, Tipton moved into the elite circle of those who have, becoming the first female prosecutor in San Mateo County to earn the honor. A few months before the Franklin case arose, Tipton had been promoted from deputy to assistant district attorney and assigned the responsibility of supervising the attorneys in municipal court. She was also the first woman in San Mateo to achieve that position. Tipton was confident of her abilities in the courtroom. She had never lost a felony trial.

Tipton knew Murray was thinking of leaving the office for another position, and she had approached her boss and expressed her willingness to take the Franklin case if Murray left. When Murray asked Tipton which of his two cases she preferred, Tipton picked Franklin. She would soon realize how naive she was about the arduous and hazardous journey that lay ahead of her.

Murray and Tipton entered into a transition phase in which Murray continued to handle some matters, including the constant emotional hand-holding of Eileen, while Tipton gradually took over others. Murray began hinting judiciously to Eileen that a change might be in the works, but assured her she would be a part of any such decision. The plan was to have Tipton begin developing a rapport with her, and then, when they felt Eileen was ready, formalize the transfer.

One of Murray's tasks was to respond to Horngrad's motion to have Eileen psychiatrically evaluated. Murray felt he had solid grounds to resist the motion because the underlying felony in the felony murder charge was child molestation, a sex crime, which would bring it within the purview of the statute. But another strategy tempted him. He was convinced that Eileen was not a wacko and that an objective evaluation would find her free of any mental disorder. Why not launch a preemptive strike and have her evaluated themselves and put the evidence of her mental competence in front of the jury? Murray discussed it with the district attorney, and the boldness of the move tempted him too. But ultimately, they decided they had fought too long and too hard to protect witnesses in sex crime cases from the intrusive probings of psychiatrists to change their position now, so Murray opposed the motion. Horngrad argued that the statute did not apply in this case because the charged crime was not a sex offense, and that Eileen's mental processes were the sole foundation of the case. The judge denied Horngrad's motion for an evaluation.

TIPTON WAS EXTREMELY PLEASED THAT MORSE AND CASSANDRO were on the case. She had worked with them on previous cases —one gang rape, several sexual assaults—and they were a great team. Morse provided the spirit, the humor, the gung-ho, let's-kick-their-ass-attitude, while Cassandro, not without his own sense of humor but far more reserved, kept more to himself and went about the business of nailing down the facts. Tipton was compulsive and knew that eventually she would have to examine every fragment of evidence, talk to every witness, and study every item in Franklin's porno collection herself, but she also knew she could trust these two detectives to pull all the pieces together for her.

Morse and Cassandro began doing just that. They had identified the woman in the photograph with a German shepherd and called her several times for an interview. Alice* kept putting them off, and, after the ninth or tenth time, the detectives drove down to see her unannounced. On the way, they joked that maybe they should have brought Cassandro's German shepherd, Cato, along to soften her up a little.

Morse questioned Alice about Franklin's sexual interests. She denied that he had engaged in or shown any interest in bizarre or kinky sexual activity. As far as she knew, he was a normal guy sexually.

"Give me the photos," Morse said to Cassandro.

"Is this you?" he asked, handing her the high school photo.

"Yes," she responded.

"Is this you?" he asked again, showing her the photo of a woman on the couch with her legs spread.

"Yes," she said. "So what? There's nothing wrong with it."

"Is this you?" he asked one more time, showing her the picture of the dog hunched over the woman.

"Oh God," she said, "I must have been drunk."

Morse pressed her. "Is it right for men to engage in sex with eight-year-old girls?"

"No," she replied, "they can't consent."

"What about dogs?"

"You're right," she said, "they can't consent either."

On the way back to Redwood City the detectives joked about what they were going to tell Tipton about the interview. "Elaine," they would say to her straight-faced, "you wouldn't believe it. Right over the mantelpiece in her living room was a large picture of a German shepherd, and beneath it was the inscription, 'To Alice, Love Fido.'" Elaine would love it.

* * *

ONE OF THE MANY TASKS ON THE LONG LIST FOR THE DETECTIVES WAS to interview all of the 1969 cops, and they quickly located Lieutenant William Hensel, the Foster City policeman who had directed the initial investigation.

Hensel had left Foster City and law enforcement in 1971, but he had stayed in touch with the Nasons over the years and visited them frequently. He felt sorry for the whole family. Soon after Susan's body had been found, Don had applied for a gun permit, saying that whoever killed Susan might come after him too. Hensel recommended against issuance of a license because of Don's drinking. Don was intelligent and a terrific salesman, and he would close his deals by noon and begin drinking at lunch and never go back to work, but he could always function the next day. The Foster City cops who picked him up usually just took him home when they realized who he was. Don was obsessed with the fact that Susan's killing had never been solved and his mind seemed to whir continuously with the details of the crime.

Margaret handled the loss much differently. She had been the perfect housewife, staying at home and keeping an immaculate house, sewing Shirley's clothes, cooking, and serving as a den mother. She seemed to have come to terms with the tragedy; her attitude seemed to be, "Susan's gone, we found her body, maybe someday her killer will be captured, there is nothing I can do about it, I need to get on with my life." She found solace in her artwork.

For years Margaret had viewed her husband's drinking with understanding and acceptance: if that's what he needed to do to deal with his pain, then that's what he needed to do. When Hensel stopped by the Nasons' a few weeks after Franklin's arrest, he learned that at Margaret's request Don had moved out. Odd why it happened then, he thought. Hensel knew Margaret was religious, more so in recent years, and he learned that the minister and some of the parishioners had helped her realize she didn't have to continue to live in his shadow. But he sensed something else; it was almost as if the bond that had held them together was their daughter's unsolved murder, or perhaps their shared sense of responsibility for her death. Maybe when they were able to visualize the murderer and realize that they hadn't failed Susan, their reason for being together dissolved.

Hensel felt terrible for Shirley Nason. He knew how badly she had suffered. Even after Susan was buried and gone, she remained the center of the family. Shirley had paid her own price for the tragedy—one time, probably a year after the killing, she had wandered into the fire station in a daze asking if anyone had seen her sister Susan. Maybe she was one of the reasons Don and Margaret had stayed together. In recent years, Shirley had been doing much better.

Hensel had been shocked when he first heard of the arrest— a neighbor!—but it made so damn much sense: somebody Susan knew and trusted. Who would ever have suspected a fireman who lived right around the corner?

Hensel felt guilty, too. When he reviewed the old reports, the Franklin name was everywhere: George had been a search volunteer, Janice had been interviewed twice, the Franklin vehicle had gone to the funeral home and cemetery. But they had missed him. They had been looking for a stranger. So much pain for so many years.

Morse, who had been so infuriated at the incompetence of the 1969 police investigation, lightened up when he saw how bad Hensel felt. Hensel also had additional information for him: On September 22, 1970, the one-year anniversary of Susan's death, he and another officer had gone to Skylawn Memorial Park and sat in their car all day and wrote down the license plates of all the vehicles that drove near or stopped by Susan's grave. When the cops located the list, right there in black and white was the license plate of George Franklin's van: VXJ707. Morse checked with Leah and she said she had not visited the grave that day. He asked Karyn Weis, Ephe Ray Bottimore's daughter who worked at the cemetery, to check the records, and she confirmed that there had been no funeral on September 22, 1970. The cops were excited: the list proved that Franklin had returned to the grave of his victim in some macabre one-year anniversary celebration of his grisly deed!

The detectives finally got around to another item far down on their long list of things to do: checking the 1969 newspaper articles. The fact that Eileen knew details she could not have known unless she were an eyewitness to the killing was, of course, critical to the prosecution's case: it had been a big reason why Murray and the cops had believed Eileen in the first place; they had relied on it in their affidavits for the search warrants for Franklin's apartments, and they had cited it to the district attorney as one of the primary bases for charging Franklin. Only an eyewitness could have known of the rock, the crushed ring, the mattress.

The detectives soon came across the clippings of the press conference held by Chief Penfold and the sheriff the day after the arrest, in which they revealed that Susan's body had been found under a mattress at the bottom of a thirty-five-foot embankment and that she had died from a skull fracture, possibly from a three-pound rock found nearby. The article noted that the cops had found a ring, a brown buckle shoe, and a sock close to the body. Next day's article gave the specifics: a silver ring had been smashed from an oval shape into an elliptical shape, indicating that Susan had placed her hand over her head to protect herself from a blow with the rock. Morse and Cassandro read the headlines: RING TELLS MUTE STORY OF STRUGGLE and NASON GIRL FOUGHT AT HER GRAVESIDE. All the papers, including the *San Mateo Times,* which had been delivered to the Franklin household, had repeated the facts of the mattress, the rock, and the smashed ring, day after day.

32

TIPTON WAS SEVERELY SHAKEN WHEN THE DETECTIVES told her about the 1969 articles. The linchpin of her strategy was to have been affirmative proof that Eileen knew certain facts—facts which she had stated on tape to Etter in the very beginning—that she could not have known *unless she had witnessed the killing.* Tipton had planned to stress in Eileen's testimony two or three central facts—the rock, the ring, the mattress—and then introduce the 1969 articles devoid of those facts. The proof wasn't airtight, but almost. In her opening and closing statements she would have asked the jury how Eileen Franklin could possibly have known these facts unless she had witnessed the killing.

Now, with all the critical facts in the public domain, that strategy was out the window. She would have to prove her case by inference and implication. Eileen would testify in great detail about her memory of the killing and Tipton would corroborate her testimony by putting on the physical evidence—the rocks, the photographs, the dress, the brown shoe, the ring— which matched Eileen's account. Then she would ask the jury: "What is the likelihood that Eileen either read or unconsciously absorbed this information as an eight-year-old child and then it suddenly popped up in her mind twenty years later, or that she intentionally learned it so she could come in here and tell you a lie today?" This question would be nowhere near as powerful as the original one, she knew quite well, but it was not without some power. This new strategy would, however, leave her star witness much more exposed to defense attacks.

There was another question that Tipton knew would hang in

the courtroom, demanding an answer, just as it had in everyone's mind who had heard Eileen's story: Why would she take the stand and accuse her father of this horrible crime, put herself through this horrible ordeal, if it weren't true? Horngrad's dilemma, and she was anxious to see how he dealt with it, would be whether or not to try to answer this question. He almost had to, yet if he did, he could very likely serve up his client to the jury on a silver platter.

HORNGRAD HAD KNOWN OF THE DETECTIVES' MISTAKEN CONCLUSION about the newspaper articles from almost the very beginning. In his view, it was a perfect illustration of over-zealous cops busting somebody without doing their homework, digging themselves into a serious hole and then not having the guts to climb out and admit their mistake. The case should never have been filed in the first place and, when the erroneous assumption upon which it was based had surfaced, it should have been dismissed forthwith by the prosecution.

One of private detective Steve Schwartz's initial tasks had been to determine if Eileen had looked up the old 1969 clips before coming forward. He contacted the morgues of all the newspapers in the area, as well as the public libraries, to see if they kept records of who came in to look at old newspapers. None of them did. Eileen could have come and gone with no one knowing.

ANOTHER SHOCK WAS IN STORE FOR THE PROSECUTION. THE PRELIMInary hearing had been rescheduled for May 21 and in early May Tipton and Murray decided it was time to interview Eileen again and formalize the transfer of the case. The two women hadn't met, but when Eileen sensed that Tipton might prosecute the case, she had flattered her by telling her that maybe it would be easier to tell her story to a woman and that she had heard that Tipton was a very, very good prosecutor.

On May 11, Bob Morse, Marty Murray, and Elaine Tipton visited Eileen in Canoga Park. According to Eileen, she felt a "delightful thrill" that she could finally talk to them about the things that had changed or become clearer to her in the past few months. She proceeded to explode a bomb in their faces. After thinking about the incident in which her father had held her down while a black man raped her, she had realized that the rapist *wasn't really black,* he was white. Not only that, she recognized the face of the white man: it was Stan Smith, her godfather (the man who had attended George and Leah's engagement party with Kay Ballard). She had been confused about her attacker's identity because her father had held her head in such a way that she was forced to look at a poster of Jimi Hendrix on the wall.

"You know," she asked her visitors, "how if you stare at something for a long time and then look away, the image of that object stays in your vision?" That's what had happened, and as the radiating colors and superimposed image of Jimi Hendrix had faded, Stan Smith's face gradually became clear to her.

She explained that her mother had once told her that Stan Smith had confided in her that he had trouble teaching sixth grade because he was attracted to the girls. She had seen Smith only once after the rape. She had been at an Alateen meeting, which she was attending because of her father's drinking problem, and when she approached him he had become frightened and walked away.

Then the hypnosis issue raised its ugly head again. Aware of the law prohibiting the admissibility of statements retrieved under hypnosis, Murray had very early asked Eileen if she had been hypnotized. She had said no. Cassandro had asked her in the Canoga Park interview and she had denied it again. The defense had kept insisting in their discovery motions in January and February that Eileen had been hypnotized, so Murray had finally asked Eileen whether she had ever *told* anyone she had been hypnotized. Apparently figuring that George had ratted to the defense, Eileen had admitted she had told her brother she had recovered the memory under hypnosis. Today Murray asked her the question again, on the record, and she said she had lied to George in order to persuade him to believe her. She did not feel bad about the lie because the part about the murder was true. Eileen did not mention that she had told her mother the hypnosis story.

Eileen also explained that she wanted to change two facts in her story. The first one would clear up a major discrepancy: She had thought about the crime scene and realized that what she had seen was a *silhouette* of her father standing over Susan with a rock in his hands. That meant that the sun was starting to go down and therefore the killing had to have taken place in the afternoon, not in the morning as she had told Morse and Cassandro on their first visit.

Also, she was now sure that she had seen Janice in an open field near the spot where she and her father had stopped to pick up Susan. She was not sure if Janice saw Susan get in the van, or whether Janice might have actually gotten in the van herself.

Then Eileen told the prosecution, for the first time, how she had recovered the memory. Describing a trigger remarkably similar to one suggested by the psychiatrist on the "Today Show," she said she had been sitting on the couch in the family room and her daughter, who looked very much like Susan, had been playing with her friends on the floor. Her daughter had glanced up at her from the floor, and Eileen had envisioned Susan looking up at her the instant before her father brought the rock down on her head. On Susan's face had been a look of betrayal.

Tipton's case had suffered serious damage. When the prosecution filed the charge, it had a credible eyewitness to the murder who knew facts not in the public domain and another witness who saw the victim get in the perpetrator's car at the time of her disappearance. Now the key witness was an admitted liar on an important point in her story—how she retrieved her memory—and she no longer knew any facts not in the public domain. And the second witness was in a field, not in the van. She had also shifted her story on the time of day because she had *thought* about her father's silhouetted figure and realized now that it *had* to be in the afternoon.

The most troubling switch of all, however, was the identity of her rapist. "Holy fuck!" Cassandro had thought when he heard the switch from an unknown black man to her white godfather, "How in the hell are we going to explain that?" It was one thing to confuse the time of day, quite another the color of the perpetrator. What did that say about the stability of her mind? Her mental processes? What other significant facts could change? Were these "facts" or just momentary perceptions? Was the whole case built on shifting sand?

As concerned as Tipton now was about her case, her belief in her star witness was not shaken. In fact, she was more convinced of her credibility after the interview in Canoga Park than before. Tipton had tried enough cases and heard enough stories to develop an instinct for the truth when she heard it. As she listened to someone tell a story, she could sense whether the person had experienced those facts or picked them up somewhere else, what came from within and what from without. In this case, it was the little things, the details, the quirks, the peccadillos, that gave Eileen's story the ring of truth: her father holding Susie's hands over her head, pinning her arms down and saying, "Now, Susie, Now, Susie"—how could someone fabricate that sort of detail? Eileen saying, "I remember him knocking me to the ground, and then he put me on his knee and said, 'It's over now, it's over, you have to forget this ever happened' "; and then his threats—" 'If you tell anyone they'll blame you because it was your idea' "; Eileen's thinking while they were driving home from the murder site about poor Susie, cold and dark, all alone. Is there somebody on this planet who could really make up those details? If Eileen had really wanted to nail her father, why hadn't she described an actual act of sexual intercourse or oral copulation in the van?

Tipton figured the defense could propose two possible explanations for Eileen's story. One, Eileen had read the information in the papers when she was eight years old or picked the facts up through some sort of osmosis listening to others talk about it over the years; or, two, she had researched the facts and put together the story as an adult in order to nail her father. In either case, why would she have gotten the time of day wrong? The most often-repeated fact in the stories, usually in the first line or two, was that Susan disappeared *after* school. And all the media described Susie as wearing a blue dress when she disappeared, and yet Eileen was unable to describe the color of Susie's dress. If she had concocted the story, why wouldn't she have gotten those two basic facts right? The argument that she could have intentionally left these facts out in order to make her story *more* credible seemed preposterous. And if she had fabricated the rape story, why had she made herself vulnerable by changing the man from black to white? Why not just leave him black?

33

BARRY ELIOT LIPSKER WAS BORN IN 1947 TO AARON and Lea Lipsker in Burbank, California, a suburb of Los Angeles. When he was still a child, the family moved to Billings, Montana, where his father opened a sporting goods store and where Barry and his younger sister and brother attended high school. When his father's business went under, the family returned to Los Angeles, then moved to England where his dad sold insurance to American servicemen. Barry and one of his brothers formed a rock band which toured American bases in Germany and Viet Nam.

In 1969, Barry joined the Air Force and was stationed in Germany, where he married a German woman. He received extensive training in computers in the Air Force and from 1969 to 1970 worked as a computer technician at NORAD with secret security clearance. After his discharge, he stayed in computers, working first as a civilian for the Marine Corps, and then from 1972 to 1975 as a civilian computer analyst with security clearance for the Department of the Navy. In 1975 he moved into the private sector and worked as a computer technician for a software company in Reston, Virginia, until 1982.

Barry eventually returned to California, and after attending junior college, graduated from California State University in Fullerton. He and his wife were divorced after twelve years of marriage, without children. Barry was working in computer sales for Computer Corporation of America in 1982 when he met Eileen Franklin. He was thirty-five, she was twenty-one.

Eileen was employed by a company that managed one of the condominium developments in Foster City, which had in recent years grown considerably and become a haven for Yuppies with Porsches, BMWs, and high-tech, well-paying Silicon Valley jobs. Barry, who lived in one of the condos, fit the bill perfectly, except he drove a white Mercedes. Although Barry wasn't as rich as Eileen's other three boyfriends, he bragged about how much money he was going to make, and although he wasn't particularly attractive—five-feet eight, on the heavy side, with dull brown hair and small eyes—she was impressed with his strong mind and the breadth of his knowledge, including his world travels. She claims to have resisted his advances for months. Once she went out with him he paid her constant and avid attention. He was very persistent, and he told her exactly what she wanted to hear: "I love you, I'll take care of you, we'll make lots of money and have a good time." Barry was also ready for children, and so was Eileen.

In later years, when Eileen came to detest the very traits in Barry she had admired in the beginning (his persistence would become pigheadedness, his reasoning facility made him cold and unfeeling), she would say she resented him for taking advantage of her vulnerability. But fresh from her prostitution conviction and drug problems, she saw Barry as someone who would take over her life and give structure to it. Barry, a hyper, high-energy person with high blood pressure, who was controlling by nature, was more than happy to oblige.

According to Eileen, she didn't love Barry when she met him, when she moved in with him in 1982, when she had a child by him in 1983, or when she married him in 1984. Eileen has never claimed to love Barry; their relationship was always an arrangement: You give me what I want out of this world—security, attention, money, babies—and you can have me in exchange. Barry was obsessed with money, and she had no doubt he would one day be wealthy. She used to fantasize about how much money he would make. He promised to buy a Mercedes for her if she quit smoking. She quit, and he bought her the car.

In October 1983, Eileen and Barry bought a $150,000 house in the southwest section of San Jose, a little east of Los Gatos where the Santa Cruz Mountains rise from the valley floor. In a middle-class neighborhood, the attractive 1900-square-foot house had a nice yard and a pool. Barry upgraded Eileen from the Mercedes to a silver DeLorean with the gull-wing doors, which Eileen loved to take cruising in the nearby hills. On December 23, Eileen gave birth to Jessica, whom she nicknamed "Sica." Eileen claims that her family was ashamed of her for having a child out of wedlock with a Jewish father, and boycotted her and the new baby. (Kate remembers it more as Eileen withholding her child from her family as some sort of a payback for the abortion.) Her mother sent Eileen another letter disowning her and refused to visit her and the baby, even though Jessica was her first grandchild. (Leah would not see her granddaughter until 1986, when Eileen brought her to Leah's mother's funeral.)

By Eileen's telling, Barry had been pressuring her to get married, and she finally gave in and married him on Valentine's Day, February 14, 1984. The brief ceremony was conducted by a justice of the peace, and the only family member in attendance was her father, who had just recently come back into her life after a period of estrangement, and his girlfriend Carolyn Adams.

Eileen remembers that Barry's behavior toward her changed soon after they were married: He began to view her more as a possession than a person, they communicated only on a superficial level, and they made love only once every three or four months. Money held more appeal to Barry than sex, and he was busy devising his plan to go into business for himself and make real money as a computer consultant. When she complained about his lack of attention to her and the baby, he would say something like, "Look how hard I'm working! What more do you want? Look at the money I'm making!" Barry yelled at her and she yelled back.

Eileen made several attempts to get out of her marriage—in fact, her marriage could be seen as a series of attempted breakouts, ending each time with her being brought to heel by a manipulative, blackmailing, ruthless husband. (An alternative explanation offered much later by Eileen for staying with Barry was that she was "frozen into inaction" because, like so many other women, she had no choice.) After she left Barry for the first time, he had his first heart attack and he told her the attack was her fault for having left him, so she came home. Later, when they were still living in San Jose, Barry decided that they should move to Los Angeles because his business was developing in that city. Eileen balked because she had grown to like San Jose. Barry had another heart attack and on the emergency room table he told Eileen that the stress of traveling back and forth to Los Angeles had caused the attack. "You did this to me," he told her. Shortly afterwards, in 1984, they moved to Manhattan Beach, a suburb of Los Angeles.

Eileen turned to her father for relief from her loveless marriage and unfeeling husband. Now sober, George began paying attention to his third daughter, not just because she had his grandchild, Eileen would later insist, but because he genuinely cared for her. She relished regaining her status as Pooh, the favorite child, and he gave her the attention and affection she wasn't receiving from Barry. When he visited, she confided to him her marital problems, including Barry's refusal to stay in counseling—he would go one or two times and then quit—and she even said that there would be a room for George in their new house if he would like to live with them. The old bond between them, according to Eileen, "was coming through with a fresh intensity."

He wasn't exactly the loving grandfather, though. One day in 1984, he was playing with Jessica on the living-room floor when Eileen left the room for a few moments. Eileen claims that when she returned, he had placed her daughter on a coffee table and pulled her labia apart with his thumbs while he looked inside her vagina. He explained that he was only admiring his beautiful granddaughter, whom he thought was pretty and sexy. Although Eileen would say that the incident bothered her for days, she subsequently allowed her father and his girlfriend to baby-sit Jessica.

Despite her father's sexual abuse of her daughter, and despite her knowledge that he had sexually abused two of her sisters and physically abused all of his children, Eileen and Jessica went on a trip with him. Life with Barry had once again become intolerable and Eileen launched another escape attempt. She withdrew half of the money and in their bank account and was preparing to leave the house with Jessica when her father appeared on her doorstep and announced that he was on his way to Las Vegas and had stopped by to say hello. Eileen viewed his appearance as "divine intervention" and asked if she and her daughter could come with him. George, who had arranged for the use of a condo in Las Vegas, agreed immediately and the three of them piled in the van and took off.

Barry went crazy when he learned that his wife had fled with their daughter and half their money and in the company of her father. He called around frantically trying to track her down and eventually reached Janice. Janice had never wavered in her belief that her father was a monster, a child molester, and a murderer. Janice was also frustrated by, if not jealous of, her sister's renewed relationship with their father: their closeness —and her exclusion—had bothered her as a child and it made even less sense to her as an adult. For years she had been hammering Eileen with their father's sins of the past, insisting that he hadn't reformed or shown an iota of remorse in his life, and that he was the same mean, perverted bastard he had always been. Janice claimed that he had even tried to feel her up in the receiving line at Kate's wedding (although Kate recalls there was no receiving line at her wedding), and made sexually suggestive remarks to her as an adult. Why the hell was Eileen having anything to do with him?

Janice, who had no more use for Barry than Eileen's other

siblings, made common cause with him when she learned of her sister's flight. She had had enough of "this Daddy's little girl shit." Seeing a way to bust that father-daughter relationship once and for all, she told Barry she had better get his daughter away from her father because he was a confirmed child molester.

Barry won the struggle with George for Eileen's favor by once again threatening her. He told her he had hired Marvin Mitchelson, the famed Los Angeles palimony lawyer, and he was going to charge Eileen with absconding with corporate funds and illegally transporting Jessica across state lines unless she returned. Eileen came home with Jessica and the money.

Upon her return, Barry insisted that her father be forever banned from their house. Eileen agreed, and when he showed up sometime later, she turned him away. She did not see him again until her jailhouse visit.

But her father's absence didn't improve Eileen's marriage. Barry still played by Barry's rules and Eileen felt subjugated to his needs and desires. She wondered who she would be if she ever broke free from him—Who was she really?—and determined that one day she would divorce him. She stayed with him now for the sake of her children. Barry had told her he couldn't relate to his children until they were five or six and old enough to reason and they were her responsibility until then.

Life with Barry wasn't all bad: Eileen had gone to Europe several times and broadened her range of interests considerably; she had cleaned up her life and used no drugs and very little alcohol; and they both had become hard-core vegetarians, which bothered only Barry's mother, who complained that her daughter-in-law couldn't even cook her son a kosher meal. Eileen had also become an integral part of Barry's work. While he traveled and developed the business, she worked in the home office and kept the books and did the paperwork.

Eileen finally had everything she wanted; the problem was, she had it all with the wrong person. She still didn't love Barry. He was remote and cold and controlling and she had no feelings for him. She and Janice called him "the Mind Police" because he demanded to know what she did every minute of the day, who she had called, and where she had been. Eileen had been furious with him for calling the district attorney's office, and for telling his parents and family about her memory without her permission. To her pained dismay, he had even told the story to the people in the Swiss town where they were moving.

She told Barry that, with their insipid sex life, she would inevitably have to take a lover. She had plenty of offers, that was for sure, and she had been looking around for the right man for some time when the memory had suddenly returned. She thought maybe she had found the right person, but then when the news of her accusation broke, he referred to her as "damaged" and she turned away from him.

She promised herself that from now on, when she was out of this marriage, she was going to stop going out with older men. The maximum age would be thirty-five. She had a habit of picking assholes and was going to be a little smarter the next time.

Part Two

Part Two

34

THE PRELIMINARY HEARING IS SCHEDULED TO BEGIN on Monday, May 21, 1990. In some respects a preliminary hearing is like a dress rehearsal: All the characters are present and dressed in their courtroom clothes and manners; witnesses are brought in to tell their story in front of a black-robed judge who is elevated in height, and hopefully wisdom, above everyone else; clerks with loud phones and thick files, deputies with gold badges and wooden-handled guns, and stenographers with blank looks and steadily tapping fingers are standing or sitting in their designated places to direct and record the event, while the defendant, brought over in chains, sits cloaked as the Accused and watches the drama of his life unfold before rows of reporters who will retell the story daily to the world in print and pictures.

In other respects, the prelim, as it is called, is an abridged version of the play; its sole purpose is to determine if the full play will be performed. It focuses not on whether the defendant is guilty or innocent, but on whether there is sufficient evidence to believe that a crime has been committed and that the defendant committed it; whether he shall be held to answer to the charge another day on another stage. The mini-play is performed to a judge, not a jury, so the theatrics and emotional appeals, the rising voices, pointing fingers and rolling eyeballs, are missing, and the atmosphere, while solemn, is more informal than were a jury present, which demands strict role adherence at all times. The result, at least in San Mateo County, is usually a foregone conclusion: The municipal court judge almost inevitably holds the defendant over for trial.

The prelim, like the grand jury, was designed as a protection against over-zealous prosecutors, and most prosecutors don't like it much. The hearing requires them to prematurely show their hand, while the defense may simply poke around and fire test shots and reveal little of their case. But even prosecutors can test their strategy, observe their witnesses on the stand, obtain some early evidentiary rulings, size up their opponents, and get a feel for their own and the other side's weaknesses during the prelim.

In the case of *The People of the State of California v. George Thomas Franklin,* Prosecutor Elaine Tipton is anxious to test her primary weapon, Eileen Franklin. After the collapse of the "she knew things only a witness could know" strategy, the case rests solely on Eileen's credibility, and Tipton wants to find out exactly how tough Eileen is, whether she will stand up or collapse in the cauldron of cross-examination. She is, after all, an admitted liar whose story shifts and evolves from month to month, a classic target for a skilled cross-examiner to discredit and break down. Other than her eyewitness, Tipton will put on the bare minimum of evidence: no detailed allegations of uncharged conduct, no pornography, no former girlfriends. Tipton has narrowed her witness list to four, the bare minimum: Dr. Peter Benson, Margaret Nason, Ephe Ray Bottimore, and Eileen Franklin. At the prelim, less is definitely more.

Horngrad knows that unless he can establish that Eileen has been hypnotized, his chances of getting the charge against his client dismissed at this early stage are slim. For him, the prelim is an opportunity to probe and pick around in the heart of the prosecution's case and to size up the accuser in person, and to begin thinking of how to handle her in front of a jury. He views his opportunity to question her under oath now as something akin to exploratory surgery, except that when he finds out what is wrong, he fully intends to expose, not fix, the problem. The prelim is also an opportunity to put Eileen on the record, to make her lay out the details under oath in statements which he can later hold up to her in mock confusion before the jury should she change her story. He will question her to the limits of the judge's patience.

May 17, 1990—Thursday

One question must be addressed before the prelim can begin: Who will be the audience? NBC filed a motion in April 1990 to allow the hearing to be televised. The network is anxious to follow up its dramatic "Today Show" piece with visuals of actual testimony for its nightly newscasts. In a hearing before Judge James Browning, Jr., an entertainment lawyer from Los Angeles argues on behalf of NBC that television coverage would serve the purposes of the First Amendment. Tipton and Horngrad both oppose the motion: Horngrad argues that live coverage will taint the jury pool and diminish his client's right to a fair trial; Tipton argues that the presence of a camera will intimidate her principal witness, Eileen Franklin. NBC, who so graciously acceded to Eileen's conditions for the "Today Show" interview, now turns her participation against her: Eileen willingly went before their television cameras once to talk about the murder, the lawyer argues, and thus it is unlikely that she will be intimidated by telling it again in front of a camera. On April 11, Judge Browning grants NBC's request for a pool camera, specifically noting Eileen's voluntary interview on the "Today Show."

Tipton files a motion for a rehearing on the issue and argues that NBC misrepresented Eileen's participation in the interview. She produces letters from Eileen and Janice to prove her point. In her letter, Eileen describes how she was harassed mercilessly by the media—screamed at, given cookies, and sent flowers—and how she politely asked the reporters not to contact her any more. She had become "frightened for the privacy and safety of my family," and says that "as the mother of two small children who do not know the details of the case, I did not know how to shield my children from the press." She only agreed to the interview after NBC's assurance that an exclusive interview would reduce media interest. Eileen goes on to say that she doesn't want to testify about private and painful incidents in front of a camera. Pleading on behalf of the Nasons, her young children, and her paternal grandmother (Hattie, George's mother), she asks that her right to privacy prevail.

Tipton also argues, with a straight face, that since Eileen did not give her correct name on the "Today Show," she had really appeared on the show "quasi-anonymously." She urges the court to think of Eileen's children, who will turn on the television and see Mommy talking about this horrible event.

Horngrad argues, also with a straight face, that he would hate to see the trial moved to another venue because of pretrial publicity, and NBC's lawyer counters that the public's right to know outweighs a witness's right to privacy.

Judge Browning, a former U.S. Attorney from Northern California, is considered intelligent and fair. He has a narrow face, a pencil-thin mustache, wavy gray hair, and wears clear-frame glasses. Unfailingly polite, he leans back in his chair like a concerned uncle and listens attentively as the attorneys rehash their points.

The judge is not impressed by the Franklin sisters' letters: they are eloquent, he says, but irrelevant. If intimidation of a witness were sufficient grounds for excluding cameras, they would always be excluded. Furthermore, if Eileen doesn't want her children to watch their mother on television, she should turn off the TV. As for the defense, it is required to produce rational evidence that the television cameras would prejudice the defendant's right to a fair trial and it hasn't done that. Motion to reconsider denied.

Just as everyone in the press starts to relax, Horngrad pulls another trick from his hat: Having lost the motion to exclude cameras, he moves to have the entire hearing closed on the grounds that it will involve some incredibly sensational testimony that may not be admissible at trial and will receive so much media coverage that it will be impossible to find twelve unbiased jurors for the full trial. Judge Browning seems surprisingly amenable to the motion and schedules arguments for Friday morning.

Media interest is building: the word is out that Eileen will testify on Monday and that the so-called "sensational" testimony is about sexual abuse. Reporters rehash stories about past dealings with Eileen and Barry. One reporter remarks that the whole story had died down in January until Eileen cranked it up again on the "Today Show." Eileen seems like a voluntary martyr, the reporter says, a victim who is thriving on all the attention and publicity. The sense in the press room is that Franklin probably killed the girl, but the prosecution is going to have a hell of a time proving it. The reporters are frustrated because they know so little: the attorneys won't talk to them, the return on the search warrants is still sealed, and now Horngrad is trying to close the hearing for Eileen and Janice's testimony.

May 18, 1990—Friday

Horngrad, the pale intellectual in a baggy suit, stands behind the table next to Franklin and argues again that some of the testimony, apparently to be introduced by him, will be so sensational that his client will never receive a fair trial. He suggests that he be allowed to summarize the testimony for the judge in his chambers, just the two of them.

Tipton rises to respond. She is an attractive, trim blonde, well coiffed in an anchorwoman-style hairdo. There is a certain harshness to her, though, bordering on brittleness; perhaps it is her thin mouth, or her eyes, which harden easily, or maybe it is just pre-trial tension. This is Tipton's biggest case, and she is clearly unprepared to deal with the intense media coverage. She announces to the court that the district attorney "stands mute" on the closing of the hearing, meaning she is perfectly willing to have the press excluded.

After a phalanx of media lawyers argue against the closing, Horngrad retreats to the judge's chambers and privately outlines the evidence, which consists mainly of Eileen and Janice's testimony about the physical and sexual abuse suffered at the hands of their father. He knows Tipton won't put this evidence on at the prelim, and he very much wants an opportunity to examine Eileen about the allegations in some detail. He wants to pin her down on the black man/white man rape and he wants to see how she holds up under aggressive questioning. But he can't do it in front of the world: it would appear that he was condemning his own client and he would have a hard time complaining later about pre-trial publicity when he seeks to have the venue changed.

The judge announces, to the utter surprise of the lawyers and the press, that he is going to close the hearing for the testimony of Eileen and Janice Franklin. The hearing will begin Monday morning with the other witnesses while the media attorneys appeal the judge's decision to Superior Court.

May 21, 1990—Monday

By Monday morning, the media are ravenous, particularly the television reporters and news photographers. They desperately need visuals. None of the papers have any stills of the star witness and NBC has the only footage. Outside, a huge NBC truck is parked next to the courthouse with its dish aimed at a satellite in preparation for worldwide transmission of the mini-play. Inside, print reporters bump into photographers loaded down with cameras and technicians carting boxes of equipment; television producers wander in and out of the courtroom asking people who they are and shouting, "What's happening, what's happening?"; radio reporters grasp their microphones tightly and look about anxiously for someone to interview for the noon news; freelancers for *Glamour* and *People* magazines try to catch up on the latest developments. Everywhere the buzz is about Eileen: When will she show up? Will she testify today? What triggered her memory? Was she sexually abused? The local reporters, who know Eileen won't appear today, take their usual seats in the first two rows, notebooks open, pens in hand, and calmly await the opening gavel.

By 8:15 A.M. television has taken over the hallway: tin boxes striped in red and yellow tape litter the floor; miles of red and black cord are piled by the courtroom door; TV monitors, all showing the same picture, are stacked three rows high along the wall. Technicians are busily plugging things in, taping cord along the hallway and into the courtroom, hooking up lights in the jury box, and cursing. Someone shouts, "Which way is she coming in?" and the hubbub of voices rises excitedly. A technician yells, "Where's the Goddamn videotape?" A string of orange-clad, chained-together prisoners snakes through, unfazed by the circus.

The municipal court building, constructed in 1905, was severely damaged in the earthquake of 1989. Inside, the elegant domes and arched ceilings held up by massive pillars have been weakened and several panes of stained glass are missing. The main entrance to the courtroom is sealed as a hazard, and the only public entrance is through the side door at the top of the back stairs. The TV reporters direct their cameramen to aim their cameras over the railing and down into the stairwell, providing a bright welcome for anyone ascending.

The deputy sheriff serving as a bailiff arrives and is irritated that the equipment has been set up inside the courtroom without his supervision. He announces that he has been up since four-thirty shooting at the range. Knowing he has favors to dispense, the reporters laugh at his jokes.

The courtroom is ornate, with blue rugs and oak benches and railings. Behind the bench, the hills of the Santa Cruz range, barren and brown from the unrelenting drought, are visible through a high, arched window. The clerk and deputy banter and gossip with the press about Franklin. He doesn't eat much, they say, and has lost over forty pounds. He is a model prisoner, but asks for a lot of things like law books and writing materials. The deputy argues briefly with the clerk over the placement of the still cameras in the jury box. The clerk tells him the judge has approved it.

Outside, at 8:55, another string of orange-clad prisoners, with one deputy in front and another behind, clambers noisily up the stairs in their chains, and gets almost to the top before someone recognizes the man at the end in a suit who is not chained to the others. "That's Franklin!" someone yells and cameras swivel and lights go on and shutters click in a flurry. Franklin looks with deep eyes into the madness for a second, then back at the shoulders of the prisoner ahead of him.

Horngrad has obtained a court order allowing his client to appear in the courtroom without chains and in civilian clothes, and Franklin is led in front of the spectators to the defense table where he is uncuffed and unshackled. He is wearing black bifocal glasses with small white whirls on the stems and his hair has been neatly trimmed. The creases over his thick, dark eyebrows are deep, his hands heavily veined. His skin shows a yellow tinge in the overhead lights. He seems uncomfortable in his suit, like a longshoreman at an opening night. He talks animatedly with Horngrad, then his gaze wanders to the hills through the window. He stares noncommittally at the judge when he enters.

Franklin looks healthier on the television monitors in the hallway, which are left permanently trained on him until the hearing starts. His red tie shows up well against the blue suit. With all the equipment set up, tested, and working, the technicians are enjoying themselves, drinking coffee and eating doughnuts. They revel in their lack of responsibility for the content of the story, and they spout their already-formed opinions—"If I were on the jury, I would hang the sonofabitch," and, "He sure looks like a child molester, doesn't he?"—even though they haven't heard a word of evidence. One sums it up: "Why in the hell would a daughter say this about her father if it weren't true, for chrissakes?"

Counsel tables are lined up next to each other: at the far end, close to the deputy, sits George Franklin, then Horngrad and his partner Art Wachtel, then Cassandro, Morse, and, farthest away from Franklin, Tipton. She has on red lipstick and is wearing a black skirt and a black and white checked jacket. One of the reporters quips, "Someone said Elaine smiled the other day."

The prosecution's first witness is Dr. Peter Benson, the pathologist, who holds the same position he did in 1969 when he performed the autopsy on Susan Nason. Benson has not forgotten the case over the years. Whenever he drives on Highway 92 to Half Moon Bay he thinks of her as he passes the narrow pulloff where her body was found. Benson likes his work, but is frightened by the capacity for violence in human beings. He doesn't watch bloody movies or read violent books. What draws him to his work is the challenge of putting together the pieces of the puzzle. Bodies speak with varying degrees of eloquence about what happened to them.

On the stand, Benson appears old, sallow, almost bloodless, as if he's spent far too many hours under bright indoor lights in a dark basement and not enough in the California sunshine. Since 1963, he has performed more than 15,000 autopsies and testified as an expert witness in 500 cases. He's never testified on a twenty-year-old autopsy before, but under Tipton's questioning he calmly and confidently recounts the state of Susan Nason's body: the advanced decomposition, the bare skull, the few remaining tissues, hard and dry. He describes the bruises on her right leg and the dumbbell-shaped defect on her skull above and behind her right ear. Either the small rock with blood and hair on it which he found nestled in the folds of her dress, or the one found near her body, could have caused the fatal injury. The damage to her hand and the flattened ring indicate she may have been trying to defend herself, and the location of the defect on her skull indicates her head was bent downward when she was struck.

George Franklin takes notes while Benson talks. Franklin's gray head bends over the autopsy photos when Tipton lays them on the table in front of Horngrad before offering them into evidence.

On cross-examination, Horngrad does little with Benson except to suggest that fewer than or more than two blows could have caused the injury and that possibly the injuries could have resulted from a fall.

MARGARET NASON ENTERS WEARING A TURQUOISE-COLORED, BELTED dress and a pearl necklace. Margaret has a job and lives in San Mateo. She has desperately wanted to talk to Eileen and tell her that she believes her and that she's not angry at her, but the district attorney has cautioned her that she mustn't speak to Eileen until the trial is over. Over the years, Margaret has dealt with the pain of Susie's death by pushing her favorite memories of her out of her mind. Since Eileen has come forward, she has often thought of the last few moment's of Susie's life, how horribly alone she must have felt. Margaret pictures Franklin standing with the rock raised over Susie's head and she cries out, "Run, Susie, run!" but Susie is frozen to the spot. Margaret feels the rock smashing into her daughter's head.

Under Tipton's gentle questioning, Margaret recounts the day of her daughter's disappearance and tells how Susie came home shortly after three with Celia's tennis shoes and left to return them and never came home. She and her husband told the girls many times never to accept rides with strangers and she is sure Susie never would have. Susan and Eileen had been good friends and played together frequently.

Art Wachtel cross-examines Mrs. Nason. Wachtel, California born and raised, is the antithesis of his partner. In his mid-thirties, he is boyish-looking except for his silver hair, a few locks of which inevitably fall over his tanned forehead. His suits are expensive and well tailored and he drives a yellow Porsche. He speaks softly, somewhat hesitantly.

He, too, is very gentle with Mrs. Nason. She admits telling reporters in 1969 that, given the right story, Susie might have gotten in a car with a stranger. He establishes that Shirley had been in the house when the police came and talked about the case, and that Janice had continued to play with Shirley after Susan's death.

"Ephe Ray Bottimore!" the deputy calls into the hallway. "That's the guy who found the body," one reporter whispers to another. Ephe's wavy hair is gray now, but at six feet five and 208 pounds he is still an imposing figure as he lumbers through the door and up to the clerk to be sworn in. He retired five years ago and moved up north with his wife, but misses the watershed dearly. One of his daughters, Gale, has been hired as the first female watershed keeper and tramps his old trails and drives his old roads. He comes down frequently and travels the territory with her, except now, instead of her getting out and opening the gates for him as she did when she was a little girl, he opens them for her. He was surprised when he got the call from the cops a few months ago and, while he is anxious to help, he is also ready for all the excitement to be over. He's weary of the phone calls from the press and visits from process servers.

Bottimore's affability is apparent on the stand. His hands are huge, and the suit coat binds at the shoulders. Tipton takes him through the day he found the body. He has grown slightly deaf and several times has to ask for the question to be repeated. He describes the site as a clearing about thirty feet down the hill from the lip of the pulloff and tells about the moment he spotted the skull of a child under a box spring. Elaine and Wachtel go back and forth with him on how much traffic there was on the road in 1969 as opposed to now, and he opines ruefully as to how there is an accident almost every day now on 92. Franklin, who has been sitting expressionless, unblinking, occasionally pursing his lips, smiles at the comment and makes a note on his pad.

When Bottimore leaves, there is only one prosecution witness left, and the Superior Court has not yet ruled on whether or not she will testify in private or public. Judge Browning recesses court to await the decision.

George Franklin is cuffed and shackled before being led out and as he leaves, he says politely, "Excuse me, excuse me, please," to reporters and others who have gathered in his way. The deputy, irritated at the interference with his charge, calls out, "Clear the way! Clear the way!" From now on, he announces loudly, no unauthorized persons will be allowed in front of the bar.

On Tuesday morning, the Superior Court rules that the Franklin sisters will testify in open court. Horngrad, it says, can't have his cake and eat it too.

The preliminary hearing is scheduled to resume at 1:30 P.M. Thursday afternoon, May 24.

35

MORSE KNEW THAT THE CASE DEPENDED COMPLETELY on Eileen, and he felt that under his and Murray's tutelage she had come a long way. The real problem was not Eileen but her husband Barry. In recent weeks, the prospect of movie and book deals had grown like a huge tumor on the heart of the case, and Barry seemed to be the person behind it all. Morse knew how to get people to do what he wanted, even when he was dealing with pimps and drug dealers and murderers, but he absolutely could not control Barry. The guy had been a hero in the beginning and then money and greed had taken over and he had turned into a raving asshole. Barry thought he was smarter than anyone else and he absolutely would not listen to reason. He argued against all common sense that Eileen's making money from the case would not hurt the prosecution. If Morse could have figured out a way to get him out of the picture, he would have. His behavior was putting an incredible strain on the key witness.

Morse grew so angry with Barry one day that his partner had to step in and mediate. But even sure and steady Cassandro finally lost it and, much to his own surprise and dismay, ended up yelling at Barry to "get the fuck out of here!"

Marty Murray had had no more success with Barry. While Tipton was busy handling a myriad of details before the prelim, Murray, who had remained closely involved in the case,

MISSING
CHILD

SUSAN NASON

9 YEARS OLD

Missing from near her home since September 22, 1969.

4' 5", 60 pounds, light brown medium length hair, fair complexion, heavy with freckles across nose, wearing blue print dress, white bobby sox, brown shoes.

A vehicle possibly linked with her disappearance described by 9 - 12 year old children is a 1961 or 1963 light blue Station Wagon, possibly Ford, License possible X-- ---. Cardboard cartons in load area obstructing view into rear area, possibly taped up against rear windows.
Private Lic.
4 Door

DEPARTMENT OF PUBLIC SAFETY
FOSTER CITY, CALIFORNIA
(415) 341-6582

The poster circulated around San Mateo, California, after eight-year-old Susan Nason disappeared. (Courtesy *Peninsula Times Tribune*)

Ephe Ray Bottimore in 1969 looking at the site where he found Susan's body. (Courtesy *San Francisco Examiner*)

Don and Margaret Nason (holding Snoopy) in 1969 after learning that Susan's body had been found. (Courtesy Walt Lynott, *San Francisco Examiner*)

George Franklin as a fireman.

Leah Franklin at age 18.

George Franklin holding his first child, Kate.

Janice (left), Kate (right), and Eileen Franklin (center) in their ballet costumes. (Courtesy Norm Coleman)

Eileen Franklin, age eight.

The Franklin family (minus Kate) at Disneyland in June 1969, three months before Susan Nason's disappearance. Front row (left to right): George Jr., Diana, Eileen, and Janice. Back row: Leah and George Sr. (Courtesy Kate Franklin)

George Franklin, Jr., in high school.

Kate Franklin in high school.

Eileen Franklin (left) and her younger sister Diana in 1990.

Eileen Franklin at age 19, before she bloomed. (Courtesy Kate Franklin)

Barry, Eileen, and their children, Aaron and Jessica. (Courtesy Stephen Ellison, *People* magazine)

Leah Franklin in 1990.
(Courtesy Kate Franklin)

Detectives Bryan Cassandro (left) and Bob Morse. (Courtesy Mike Russell, *San Mateo Times*)

George Franklin at the time of his arrest in November 1989. (Courtesy Mike Russell, *San Mateo Times*)

Douglas Horngrad, Franklin's chief defense attorney. (Courtesy Russell D. Curtis, *The Recorder*)

Arthur Wachtel, Horngrad's partner, who assisted in Franklin's defense. (Courtesy *The Recorder*)

Prosecutor Elaine Tipton (center) with the detectives who investigated the Franklin case, Bryan Cassandro (left) and Bob Morse. (Photograph by the author)

George Franklin arriving at the courthouse for his preliminary hearing. (Courtesy P. F. Bentley, *Time* magazine)

Eileen Franklin at the preliminary hearing demonstrating her image of her father killing Susan Nason. (Courtesy John Green, *San Mateo Times*)

The many faces of Eileen Franklin at the preliminary hearing.
(Photograph directly above courtesy P. F. Bentley, *Time* magazine;
other photographs courtesy John Green, *San Mateo Times*)

Janice Franklin at the preliminary hearing. (Courtesy Mike Russell, *San Mateo Times*)

Judge Thomas McGinn Smith, who presided over the Franklin trial.

George Franklin (right) with his attorney Douglas Horngrad at the trial. (Courtesy Mike Russell, *San Mateo Times*)

The photograph of Susan Nason introduced into evidence at the trial.

Eileen's daughter, Jessica, also from evidence.

Detectives Cassandro and Morse in the paper bags they wore to Tipton's office the morning after Horngrad's closing argument. (Photograph by the author)

From left: Elaine Tipton with Shirley and Margaret Nason talking to the press after the verdict. (Courtesy Mike Russell, *San Mateo Times*)

Mary Jane Larkin, Susan's fourth grade teacher, in 1989, standing by the bookcase donated to the school in Susan's name. (Courtesy Barbara Vogt, *Foster City Progress*)

baby-sat Eileen and Barry for her. Murray had become very upset when he learned of the negotiations for movie and book deals—there went the unsullied witness, the accuser with only the purest of motives—and he had repeatedly asked Eileen not to sign anything. Eileen explained that she wanted to control the contents of whatever was written or produced, and that Barry and her L.A. entertainment lawyer had convinced her that if she signed movie and book deals it would ensure that no other deals would be made.

A few weeks before the prelim, Murray had gone to the number two man in the D.A.'s office and suggested that, because of the damage the book and movie deals had done to the case, they should consider dismissing the charge against Franklin. Eileen and Barry had even visited a criminal lawyer in Los Angeles for advice on whether the book and money deals would damage the case, and Eileen had undergone practice questioning by him. The supervisor agreed that Barry was way out of line and had given the defense valuable ammunition. Murray also talked to Tipton about dismissing the charges and she agreed that the book and movie deals had done serious damage to the case. But she reached into her desk, pulled out a picture of Susan Nason, laid it on her desk, and said, "This is why we have to go forward."

For her part, Tipton found Barry insufferable. He demanded that everything go the way he wanted it to and he had intruded his opinion and agenda into the process at every turn, trying to convert the prosecution into the "Barry Lipsker Show." She had tried to convince him that the case wasn't about Barry Lipsker, that something much larger than money was at stake here, but to no avail. She and Barry finally had a shouting match in the hallway in the district attorney's office, much to the amazement of the other attorneys, who knew Elaine Tipton as very calm and controlled. She yelled at him to back off, that this case was not about him, that it was a criminal case, not a civil case, and he didn't control it, the prosecution did. Couldn't he see the additional strain his constant harassment was causing his wife?

Murray tried to keep Eileen calm during and after the

shouting match, but he eventually blew up at Barry himself. He was sick at the idea of the two of them making any money from the death of Susan Nason. The three of them were sitting in his office on Thursday morning, May 24, a few hours before Eileen was scheduled to go on the stand. Although Eileen had insisted on going ahead with the book and movie deals, she had said she would give the money to charity. Barry disagreed.

"We'll have to discuss it," Barry said.

"She just said she wasn't going to keep any money," Murray insisted angrily. "What gives you the fucking right to make money off the fact that your wife had the misfortune to witness her best friend getting killed twenty years ago?"

"Well, they're coming to us," Barry answered.

"What gives you the right," Murray demanded again, "to make that decision for her? I've had witnesses who were rapists, thieves, and murderers who weren't as determined to destroy a case as you. And for what? For money!"

"I don't think it will hurt the case," Barry insisted.

"I'm telling you it could swing the case. We have a witness with pure motives and you're perverting it for money! Let's just eliminate it!"

"Eileen and I will discuss it," Barry replied.

When Eileen said that she didn't want to keep the money, Barry protested, "But, Eileen, we might need it for the children's education."

In the middle of the blow-up, Barry yelled at Eileen for not returning to the hotel and ironing his shirt.

"Get a grip on it," Murray said to him, "can't you see she's facing the most difficult day of her life?"

Finally, Murray lost control completely and yelled at Barry that he was "a fucking parasite." He threw him out of his office and told him never to come back.

Eileen suggested that she testify that she would give the option money to charity but that she hadn't decided what she would do with the rest of the money, which would be a much larger amount. Murray argued that such an approach would look deceptive to the jury and that she should just make a decision about the money once and for all.

Murray later realized it was probably just as well that he didn't try the Franklin case. After learning that Eileen and Barry had consulted the L.A. criminal attorney, acting as if he and Tipton had to scrape the cow shit off their shoes before going into court, and after watching the way Eileen played off Barry and gave the impression that everything was his fault, he might have had a difficult time getting back on track for the trial.

36

May 24, 1990—Thursday

Shortly after 1:15 p.m., Eileen, accompanied by Morse, Cassandro, and Murray, leaves the Hall of Justice and walks across the street to the municipal court building. Tipton, determined that Barry won't accompany his wife to the courtroom, has banished him from her office and leaves him sitting in the waiting room while she and Eileen and the cops slip out a side door.

In her first public appearance, Eileen throws the world a fashion curve: instead of the beautiful, long-haired look of the "Today Show," she has achieved a stark, severe look. Her hair is pulled back tightly into a French braid and she is wearing a blue suit trimmed in white with a pearl necklace and earrings. Her cheeks are heavily rouged and her eyes are made larger by blue eye shadow.

A few still cameras catch Eileen outside the courthouse and, as she enters the building, the television cameras, lights blazing, point down the dark stairwell in search of her. She ascends the steps with a frozen, scared look on her face. Inside the courtroom, the pool camera and two stills lie in wait for her in the jury box as she walks in hesitatingly, eyes wide like a deer, and sits with Murray and the two cops in front of the bar.

Shutters click sporadically around the courtroom. Eileen looks confused, disoriented, perhaps because of the television lights. She whispers something to Morse, and he smiles back at her. Her father enters, but they don't look at each other as he walks in front of her on the way to the defense table.

Some observers don't recognize George Franklin at the defense table today. They are looking for the orange-clad mountain man with the black eyes, heavy beard, and the tousled hair, but what they see instead is a football coach or a hardware store owner dressed in a white shirt and blue suit. He takes notes and chats with Steve Schwartz, Horngrad's private detective, who sits behind him.

The resemblance between father and daughter, seated only a few feet apart, is compelling. Eileen is a female version of her father: broad forehead, large eyes, heavy brows, strong chin. At some angles she appears almost mannish. *Glamour* magazine will describe her as cadaverous and desexualized. The pool camera, only a few feet away, stays locked on her face, focusing on the slight scar across the bridge of her nose that she says she incurred when she fell out of a window as a child.

Horngrad seizes the initiative and demands a hearing on whether or not Eileen has been hypnotized. While he and Tipton argue before the judge, Eileen stares innocently off into space. Her father looks up at her quizzically. Horngrad is allowed to question her, and Eileen testifies that she has never been hypnotized but that she had told her brother she had been. She admits, apparently for the first time, that she also lied to her mother about being hypnotized. The press is startled by her admissions: a self-confessed liar is a very shaky foundation for a first-degree murder charge.

Tipton rises to lead Eileen through the account of the killing. She asks Eileen who was her best friend in fourth grade.

"Susan," she says softly.

"Susan who?" Tipton asks.

"Susan Nason," Eileen replies, tears suddenly coming to her eyes, lips quivering.

As Eileen recounts the day of the killing, she becomes what

one journalist would describe as "otherworldly." Indeed, she seems to regress into the persona of an eight-year-old girl as she recounts how excited she had been when she saw Susan across the street and convinced her father to stop and pick her up. The excitement fades rapidly, however, when she describes the van pulling over in a wooded area. Dramatic pauses begin to punctuate her narrative. The most sensational moment of the day, at least from the camera's viewpoint, occurs when Tipton asks:

"Will you show us what position your father's hands were in when you saw him holding the rock?"

"He had both of his hands up above his head like this," Eileen replies, raising her arms and holding her hands over her head in a large oval, "turned this way." As if on cue, shutters click all around the courtroom like a thousand startled cicadas, then camera motors whine and the cicadas click again and keep whirring and clicking until she lowers her arms. The image of her round, pained face framed in her upraised arms as she imitates her father's killing stance will flash on television screens and be portrayed in newspapers around the country.

Tipton cleanly closes her questioning a few moments later by asking:

"Eileen, did you see the defendant kill Susan Nason on September 22, 1969?"

"Yes, I did," she answers firmly.

Only then does the press realize that Tipton is not going to ask her what triggered the memory, which, along with any sexual abuse, is what everyone is waiting to hear. Tipton is not eager to get into the question of repressed memories at the prelim and she has left that for Horngrad to develop as he chooses.

Early in his questioning, Horngrad touches on the trigger, and Eileen provides the leads for the next day's articles.

"Well, I was sitting on the sofa in my family room, and I was holding my son. And my daughter was playing on the floor with some of her little playmates. And my daughter said something to me which caused me to look down at her, and I matched her gaze. And at that moment she very closely resembled Susan. And I remembered seeing Susan sitting there and seeing my father with a rock above his head."

Horngrad, who is being very deliberate and gentle with Eileen, moves closer to her, then suddenly complains to the judge about the television camera sticking in his face. The cameraman shoots back that it would be easier for Horngrad to move than him, and finally Tipton objects that Horngrad is practically "sitting on the witness" and demands that he get back to counsel table where he belongs. Horngrad, ever gracious but willing to argue any point, talks the judge into allowing him to sit in seat number ten of the jury box so he can have a "conversation" with the witness.

When the lawyers are arguing, Eileen has to look down or to her right to avoid looking either at her father or into the camera. Franklin sits rock still, ~~as~~ if posing for a painting, as he watches his favorite daughter accuse him of molestation and murder.

Under Horngrad's questioning, Eileen alternates between weakness and strength, sometimes sitting back in her chair and responding softly, uncertainly, other times leaning forward and challenging him, mocking him with his own words. Occasionally she smiles at him winsomely, almost flirtatiously, and her face opens up like a calm sea. Moods flit across her face like clouds across the face of an autumn moon: a youngster dutifully answers, "yes sir, no sir," to an adult's questions; a girl turns to the judge and asks for protection from the big man; a suffering victim tearfully recounts painful details; an articulate, intelligent adult defines terms, draws careful distinctions, and tries to sidestep questions; an angry woman lashes back at her persecutor for his cruelty, for not understanding her. Before answering, Eileen sometimes flutters her eyelids, or runs her tongue in between her upper lip and teeth, the very mannerism of Janice's which had so amused the three sisters when they played the tape of the "Today Show."

Marty Murray walks Eileen from the courtroom at the end of the day, guiding her gently with his hand in the small of her back.

May 25, 1990—Friday

Today Eileen is dressed in black. Her red hair is combed out and spreads from one shoulder to the other and falls to the middle of her back. She seems more powerful, strong. After some reflection, the reporters agree that her lies haven't hurt her much. Her father watches her intently as she walks to the stand.

On the way to court, a female photographer had asked her to pose for a picture and Eileen waved the woman off. Morse suggested that if she posed for her, the photographer would leave her alone.

"What paper are you from?" Eileen had demanded.

"From a French magazine," the woman answers.

"I hate the French," Eileen said to her contemptuously. Nevertheless, under Morse's prompting, she posed for the picture. After watching Eileen testify, the reporter comments that she is coldhearted and false, a horrible actress.

On the stand, Eileen corrects her earlier testimony when she said she had told her therapist Kirk Barrett in March of 1989 about her memory of the murder. She has reviewed her records with Tipton and now remembers she told him of the killing image in June. In spite of his explanation of the concept of repression, Eileen says she still doesn't understand how a memory could return after twenty years.

Eileen quarrels with Horngrad over his use of the word "image" in describing her memory, because it reminds her of the word "imagine" and that isn't what she did; likewise she objects when he uses the word "phenomena" to describe her memory loss and recovery, because her memory process was normal, not phenomenal.

Always courteously, never raising his voice, Horngrad, working without notes, meticulously pins her down on the details, and when she becomes angry or exasperated with him for turning her in circles, he backs off immediately, and then comes forward again, slowly, gently, so as not to appear to provoke or antagonize her. She watches him very intently as he frames his questions. When she senses danger, she closes her eyes for several moments and pauses before answering.

Tipton appears to be caught off guard by Horngrad's unyielding but courteous style and several times she is late in rising to her feet to protect her witness. Once Marty Murray, who is still shepherding Eileen to and from court, has to lean forward and spark her into objecting. Tipton appears to be playing catch-up.

The avuncular judge is solicitous of the star witness. When Horngrad circles in too close, Eileen turns pleadingly to the judge and he backs Horngrad off.

Tipton felt bound under California discovery rules to inform the defense of Eileen and Barry's consultation with the Los Angeles criminal lawyer, and Horngrad now turns eagerly to the topic. Eileen waives the lawyer-client privilege and explains that she and Barry flew to L.A. Tuesday night and met with the lawyer on Wednesday.

"And whose idea was it to see Mr. Price?" Horngrad asks her.

"It was Barry's idea."

"And did Barry consult with you before he made this appointment to see Mr. Price?"

"No."

Both Barry and Eileen hoped to use the interview to their own purposes:

"Well, my hope was that this attorney would convince Barry that, that it was not beneficial to the case to accept money even though I simply don't want the money. Whether it's beneficial or not, I simply don't want it. My hope was the attorney would convince Barry not to take it. And Barry's hope was to convince me to take it."

The L.A. lawyer advised her not to take any money for her rights. Her disdain, if not contempt, for Barry is clearly evident. She tells Horngrad she has made up her mind: whatever money she receives for her movie rights will go to charity.

Horngrad asks about book deals, and she says irritably that she knows an unauthorized book on the case is being written. She insists that she hasn't talked to anyone about doing her own book, but then says that she may be going ahead with a book but only to stop the unauthorized book. Finally, she admits that she has in fact talked to a literary agent and an author, but there have been no negotiations, no agreements, and no one has offered her money. She certainly would not seek to control the contents of the book.

Tipton, severely aggravated by the effect of the book and movie deals on her case, becomes irritated when Horngrad asks Eileen for the name of the author who is "employing" her. Whirling on the press corps, where Eileen's author, William Wright, is sitting, Tipton contemptuously describes the writer as "some hack . . . out there taking notes as to what Ms. Lipsker is testifying to. . . ." At the break, Morse, knowing that "hack" is not a journalist's favorite word, comes back and smooths ruffled feathers. For the rest of the hearing, reporters refer to each other as "hacks."

Horngrad keeps coming back to hypnosis, convinced that it reveals Eileen's duplicity. He presses her on how and when she learned that hypnotically induced testimony was not admissible in court. She says she doesn't know, it may have been from the L.A. lawyer she saw just before telling Barry of the murder memory, or possibly her mother, she's just not sure.

When Horngrad asks if she told George Jr. she was mad at him for talking to the defense, she bares her teeth in an angry outburst.

"Well, when George . . . said that anything I said to him he was going to report back to the defense, I would say that it made me a little bit angry."

"Why?" Horngrad inquires innocently.

"Because I am—believe that my conversations are private conversations, and that if you had something you wanted to ask me, you could have called. And I don't think you need to send my brother in as a spy, to imply he is having a private conversation with me, then tell me that he is not."

Suddenly she smiles, apparently pleased with the success of her attack on her tormentor. Horngrad appears wounded that she would think him capable of such devious behavior.

Horngrad finally gets to the heart of his cross-examination:

the numerous changes in her story about the day of the killing. He needs to pin her down now as to when and why her memory changed. Eileen explains that the changes in her account were not as much the result of mistakes as they were "miscalculations." She realized she had been guessing, giving estimates of what happened twenty years ago, particularly on times and distances. She had been only eight years old then, and didn't have a good concept of time and distance and space as she has now.

First, the largest discrepancy: the time of day. She changed her mind, she explains, from morning to afternoon shortly after her first interview with Morse and Cassandro the previous November. She had thought about it and realized morning didn't make sense.

". . . The more I thought about the sun being behind my father, when I saw his frame with the rock up, I thought how can that be morning, unless it was very early morning. Maybe I was mistaken and it was afternoon."

Horngrad establishes that her memory of the day hadn't actually changed, rather she had *thought* about it and realized her original recollection had to be wrong. Reason, in other words, had overruled her memory.

Horngrad expresses his incredulity that Eileen hadn't told the prosecution about the change in the time of day until May 9, some six months after the first version. Eileen becomes rattled, defensive. She rolls her eyes in exasperation at Horngrad's relentless pounding on the same point.

Second: Janice in the van. Originally, Eileen told Marty Murray on the phone that Janice was in the van with her and that her father made her get out when they stopped to pick up Susan. She made the same statement on tape to the cops when they visited her a few days later. In her May 9, 1990, statement to Tipton and the detectives, she had backed off and said that she remembered seeing Janice in an open field near the spot where her father stopped to pick up Susan. She testifies now that Janice was indeed outside of the van. She isn't sure when her memory changed on this fact, maybe in January, but more likely over a period of time. Then she wanders all over the landscape on Janice's location.

"The more I concentrated on it and tried to be certain of how the event exactly happened, the less certain I felt about whether Janice had been in the van or out of the van. And the less certain I felt about it, the more I tried to concentrate on it and remember it."

"And?" Horngrad prods her.

"After—over a period, I would say several weeks, that I just —it seemed more and more clear to me that I remembered seeing her outside the van, and that I am just unclear of—as to whether she was inside first or what. I tend to think she was outside. And I don't know why I thought she was inside before."

"Well, you just said now you are unclear. So can you tell us now was she in the van?"

"I don't know if she was in the van."

"Is it possible she was in the van according to your memory now as you sit here today?"

"It's possible."

Horngrad thinks he understands why Eileen's memory on Janice's location has changed. In 1986, Janice had told her that she had gone to the police in 1984 and accused their father of murder, and after Eileen had gone forward in 1989 she suddenly realized that Janice would certainly have told the police in 1984 if she had been in the van or seen Susan get in it, and of course Janice had not told them that. Janice had also probably mentioned to Eileen that she had told Morse and Cassandro in her November 1989 statement that she hadn't been in the van.

However, Eileen insists that, although Janice has been living in her house for eight months, she has never discussed her murder memory with her. She has no idea whether Janice is saying she was in or out of the van.

Third: the dirt road. Eileen had originally told the detectives that they had bumped along a dirt road, something like a fire road, for several minutes before pulling over. On direct examination, she had testified that they had driven on a paved road and pulled off onto an unpaved section and parked. On cross, Eileen dismisses the dirt road statement as the inaccurate perceptions of an eight-year-old and states she has no idea when her memory changed from dirt to paved.

Horngrad figures the bumpy dirt road changed to paved road for the same reason that morning changed to afternoon: Eileen watched the "Today Show" in which the narrator says that Susan was kidnapped after school and in which a picture of the narrow gravel pulloff along Highway 92 is shown. She also has undoubtedly read recent newspaper accounts containing both facts. Eileen has denied watching all but a few seconds of the "Today Show"—she testified that she got up and left the room when it came on, and says she hasn't seen Barry's file of newspaper clippings about the case. Horngrad doesn't believe her on either point.

Horngrad next focuses on additions to and subtractions from her memory. Eileen had said for the first time on direct examination that after the killing, when she was sitting in the van, she saw the cars going by and thought to herself, "If they only knew what was going on in here as they drive by me now."

Eileen admits that while originally she said the trip in the van from start to finish took from two to three hours, she now says that it's more in the area of an hour and fifteen minutes.

She has also originally told the police that she thought Susan had something in her hand when they stopped to pick her up, but now, although she has tried very hard to remember, she can't say for sure whether she did nor not.

Horngrad asks if there is anything else about the events of Susan's death that she didn't mention on direct. Yes, last month she realized she had seen her father throw something, a shoe, maybe.

He asks her about the blue flower pattern dress that Susan was wearing when she disappeared.

"I don't think I ever said anything to anyone about a blue flower pattern dress," she says confidently.

"As you sit here now, what do you recall, if at all, Susan wearing that day?"

"I think that she was wearing a dress."

"What color?"

"I am not sure."

"Have you any idea of the color?"

"I don't know," Eileen begins, and then leans forward in a look of bitter triumph and demands sarcastically: "Did you just feed it to me? Did you just tell me what it was?"

Horngrad, nonplussed, tries to turn his error into advantage by asking her: "Could I affect your memory that way?" Tipton objects that Horngrad is trying to perform a psychology experiment on her witness, and Judge Browning sustains the objection.

In his exploration, Horngrad stumbles on a possible gold mine. Eileen insists that she still doesn't know the site of the molestation and killing, and Horngrad asks her, for no real reason, if she has recently been on Highway 92 in the area of Crystal Springs Reservoir. She was in the area last Friday, she says. Tipton, knowing what Horngrad is about to inadvertently uncover, objects on the grounds of relevancy.

Overruled.

"Why were you out there, Ms. Lipsker?"

"Because I went out there to look for something."

"What? What were you looking for?"

"A road."

"What road?"

"I don't remember the name of it."

"And why were you looking for this road?"

Tipton objects again as to relevance, and all Horngrad can say is, "Oh boy."

Objection overruled.

Horngrad thinks Eileen had been looking for the dirt road that she originally told the cops they had traveled on before the murder.

"And was it a road that you thought you were confusing—"

"No."

"When you told the prosecution initially that you were driving on a dirt road?"

"No."

"Well, why were you looking for this road that you have

driven down with your father near Crystal Springs Reservoir? Why did you do that?"

"Because I thought that I had seen him bury something out there, and I wanted to look for it."

"Find anything?"

"No, sir."

"Who was with you?"

"My husband and Bob Morse."

"What was it you thought your father had buried?"

"A diary."

Horngrad knows that Leah had told the prosecution that many years earlier George had said he had put his life story in a journal, sealed it in wax, and buried it on Star Hill Road. But he had no idea that Eileen and the cops had gone looking for it and, in a sidebar conversation with the judge, he bitterly attacks Tipton for withholding the fact of the failed search from the defense.

Eileen testifies that a few weeks after the arrest, Jean DeBernardi, Leah's youngest sister, had said to her, "Why don't you guys try and find the diary that your father wrote?" Eileen then called her mother, who confirmed the story of the diary. It had occurred to Eileen that her father might have confessed in the diary to killing Susan. A couple of months ago, in March or April, she suddenly recovered a memory of her father digging and burying something, and so she put two and two together and figured she might have seen him burying the diary. She had decided to try to find it.

She testifies that when she and Barry and Morse were driving on the road a few nights earlier, she pointed to a place that looked like the spot where she saw her father burying something and they stopped.

"Did somebody dig?" Horngrad asks.

"Yes."

"Inspector Morse over here?"

"No."

"Who?"

"We let Barry," Eileen says, smiling broadly, either at the image of Barry digging or the fact that she got him to do her dirty work. A flicker of amusement passes among the local press.

"As you sit here now and you see this in your mind, Eileen," Horngrad proceeds, using the familiar for the first time, "can you describe the area where your dad did the digging?"

"In front of some trees."

"How many trees?"

"I believe three."

For Horngrad, it is a startling example of how Eileen's mind could create a false memory. After her father is arrested, she learns that he has written a diary in which he may have confessed to the killing. Desperate to have her story corroborated and to avoid going through a public trial and having her past revealed, she suddenly has a memory of him digging and burying something in the woods and concludes that it may well be the diary she has heard about. It also appears that the memories of the killing and the burying may have run together: in both of them, she remembers her father digging and in both of them she remembers three trees in the foreground.

Horngrad knows this nugget won't get the case dismissed, but it is certainly valuable information on the creative processes of Eileen's mind.

As the afternoon draws to a close, the judge realizes that Horngrad has no intention of finishing his cross-examination that day or any time soon and that, with his methodical, searching, pick-the-statement-apart style, he could very well go on for another week. He politely informs Horngrad that he may close off questioning of Ms. Franklin-Lipsker, who has been on the stand for a day and a half, after one more hour.

The testimony concludes for the day with Eileen's statement that she scoffed in 1986 when Janice told her she believed her father had killed Susan Nason.

"Were you angry with her for having gone to the police?"

"I don't think I was angry with her."

"Didn't you feel love for your father then in 1986?"

"I think I have always felt love for my father."

37

May 29, 1990—Tuesday

THE HALLS ARE EMPTY THIS MORNING, DEVOID OF cords and monitors and men with headsets and television cameras. The San Francisco reporters are noticeably absent. The Franklin hearing is being seriously upstaged by Mikhail Gorbachev, who is appearing today at Stanford University, only a few miles down the road.

One big city reporter comments that Eileen thinks she is as smart as Horngrad and can see where he is going with his questions. She tries to hold herself in check, then loses it and lashes out at him. In his view, she is not coming across well at all. Another reporter comments that, on the phone, Eileen was aggressive and took control of the conversation, while on the stand she is more passive, compliant.

Eileen arrives looking poorly. She is wearing a black jacket with yellow polka dots. She appears drained, almost as if she might be ill; there are deep hollows in her eyes and her lips are colorless. Even her hair, which is down again, seems flat. The camera picks up a swatch of freckles on her cheeks and nose.

George is wearing gold-rimmed glasses and his usual blue suit. He leans back in his chair and rests his hands on the edge of the table. An odd smile flickers across his face as Eileen resumes the stand.

She immediately corrects the record: She *did* call George Jr. at one point and ask him not to tell anyone about her hypnosis story, then decided she didn't want to worry about the lie being out there and told him, "Screw it, just tell them the truth."

She also backs off her statement that she wouldn't accept money for book and movie deals. Now she says she is not sure whether or not the money issue is settled between her and Barry.

Horngrad leaves his assigned seat in the jury box and hovers around while grilling her once more on Janice and the van. Tipton rises to protect her witness:

"Back off the witness, please," she commands. "He is practically sitting on top of her."

"Back to number nine, certainly," Horngrad says quickly.

Toward the end of his examination, Horngrad asks her if she has any other recently retrieved memories. She starts to cry, and Horngrad, apparently realizing she is going to mention the godfather rape episode, which he definitely does not want splattered about in the morning papers, backs off immediately.

After hammering her one final time on lying to George Jr. about being hypnotized, he announces he's finished and sits down. With no further question, Tipton waives re-direct and Eileen steps down. She receives a big hug from a friend in the audience and exits tearfully from the courtroom in the protective arms of the detectives.

The prosecution's case is finished. As its first witness, the defense calls Barry, causing a ripple in the local press: finally they will get to see the man who wouldn't stop talking. Barry, smiling and cocky, strides to the stand. Thin brown hair falls on his forehead, and his small, close-set eyes look out confidently over his bushy mustache. Art Wachtel questions him, and Barry, who is quite litigious, is not the least intimidated by him or the setting. If he feels he has already answered the question, he says, "I just told you," or, "I have answered that." When the attorneys are arguing to the judge over the appropriateness of a question, he freely inserts his opinion or steams ahead and answers the question before the judge has ruled. He admits that he has said he would murder Franklin if he thought he could get away with it and pleads with the judge to let him explain why. He manages to mention the godfather rape when Wachtel asks him if Eileen's father was discussed in therapy (which Barry insists on calling "counseling") with Kirk Barrett, thereby setting up the next day's headlines—WITNESS'S HUSBAND: FRANKLIN HELPED RAPE DAUGHTER—and getting his name in the paper. (Eileen is allegedly furious when she finds out Barry mentioned the rape in his testimony. Therapist Barrett will deny that the rape was discussed in therapy.) Barry ascribes their marital problems to the rape.

Wachtel is hesitant, perhaps too careful, in cross-examining Barry. Barry shrugs off his damaging statements to the press—"I don't know why it took her so long to come forward," and, "She knows all the details. Of course she followed it"—as if they are inconsequential. Wachtel reads other damaging newspaper and radio quotes to him—"She started recalling this incident just a few weeks ago"; "She has recalled minute details of the day, even the color of the clothing"; "They've [Janice and Eileen] put their two stories together"—and Barry's response is that he gave so many interviews he doesn't remember what he said. He appears amused by the quibbling of the lawyers, the whole show.

Wachtel nails him down on the fact that before he had called the district attorney's office, Janice told him she had seen Susan get in the car the day of her disappearance. Then Barry wanders incoherently.

"You want me to be specific about that picking her up statement, or okay. Not much more than something to the effect that he had picked up this little girl, and Eileen, or Eileen was there. Picked them up, or Janice was with them; picked them up; one way or another."

In closing, Wachtel asks Barry if he told Eileen that she should make money from book and movie deals because of her ordeal. Barry answers yes.

Tipton, who has experienced Barry's testimony with some trepidation, cautiously passes on the opportunity to question him.

"He really loved the limelight, didn't he," one reporter comments. "He would have been a lot happier if it had been his memory."

A strange and funny moment occurs when Tipton is arguing a point to the judge. Horngrad slides over next to her and, hands folded behind his back and head bent slightly forward, he looks into her eyes.

"Is there some reason why Mr. Horngrad is gazing wistfully . . ." Tipton begins.

Judge Browning finishes the sentence for her:

"Let the record reflect that Mr. Horngrad is gazing wistfully at Ms. Tipton."

"Just paying close attention to what she says," Horngrad explains guilelessly.

The judge expresses his displeasure at the defense for calling Barry, saying Wachtel's examination was purely a fishing expedition. The judge has discretion to limit the extent of the preliminary hearing, and he is considering exercising it, particularly in regard to the upcoming testimony of Janice Franklin. Horngrad mollifies him, explaining that Janice's testimony is critical to his defense and that he will try to keep her examination brief.

May 30, 1990—Wednesday

Janice is waiting in the hallway. When she first arrived, she ran into her mother, who rose from the bench where she was sitting and came over to give her a hug. Janice felt sick—it was her mom faking it again, acting like the good, caring mother she never was. Janice hates both her father and mother. She refers to her mother as "Leah the bitch," and is still bitter about her mother's reaction when she told her in 1978 that she thought her father might have murdered Susan Nason. What sort of a zero scum of a human being would leave her children with a man she suspected of being a child killer? She should have pulled her children out of the house immediately, and her failure to do so made her a complicitor in her husband's crimes against her children. Today Janice allows her mother a short, cold embrace.

Janice is a tall, striking brunette with deep brown eyes and a full red mouth. She is wearing an outfit she has bought just for her court appearance. When she enters, she sits in front of the bar for a few minutes until court reconvenes and she starts to shake. Tears come to her eyes, a friend puts a hand on her shoulder, and the reporters seated behind her wonder sympathetically if she is going to make it through her testimony. Her father enters and walks in front of her, but her head is down, she doesn't see him.

Janice testifies that she remembers the events of the day Susan disappeared and, although she had told the police earlier that she had walked to school with Susan, now she states that she doesn't remember seeing Susan that day and specifically that she doesn't remember seeing her after school. In an odd contradiction, however, she says she remembers that on the day she disappeared Susan was wearing a blue dress with white daisies with yellow centers in them.

Janice reminds herself to stay calm and remember that she is smart and can handle the lawyer, but she shakes the whole time she's on the stand. She tries not to look at her father, but can't help sneaking one or two glances his way. He is looking over her shoulder.

She explains that after school she had gone home and then over to Susan's house to play, but Susan wasn't there. When she returned home, her father was sitting in his chair in the living room having a drink. "Hello, Janice," he said to her in a weird way, and when she stopped to see what was going to happen, he said, "What's the matter, can't I even say hello to you?"

In 1984 she told a sergeant at the Foster City Police Department that she had returned home from Susan's house at approximately 4:00 P.M. and that her father was there and stayed home the rest of the evening. She is aware that if that time stands, she has provided an alibi for her father.

Now, however, she is sure she didn't return home until 5:00 or 6:00 P.M. The change in times had occurred the previous fall when she was in therapy with Kirk Barrett (at Eileen's suggestion) and realized she never went home before 5:00 or 6:00 P.M.

Like Eileen, Janice has changed the time of day, not because her actual memory changed but because she *thought* about it and realized her first version didn't fit with other facts. Her adult mind overrode her ten-year-old's memory.

As to whether she was in the van or not that day, she's not "a hundred percent" sure about it. Even though she has just said that she did not see Susan that day, now she says:

". . . I can visualize my father and the car and Susan being there and my sister Eileen, but I don't know why."

Janice also changes another fact: First she told the police that she thought that her father removed the seat and put a bed in the back of the van sometime after Susan was killed; now she remembers that he put the bed in before her disappearance.

Janice remembers two police officers coming to school after Susan's body was found and showing her two rings—one gold and one silver with a blue stone in it—and asking if they were Susan's. She told them yes, she had seen Susan wearing them. She also told them she had seen Susan riding by her house on her bike around 4:15 P.M.

Janice testifies that a few months after Susan disappeared, she and Eileen had both read an article in the *San Mateo Times* about a red-haired man wearing a brown Pendleton and brown corduroy pants who had tried to molest or abduct a child in San Mateo. The girls had been amazed when they realized that they had independently come to the conclusion that the man sounded like their father. Contradicting both Eileen and Barry, Janice denies that she told Eileen or anyone else in the family about going to the police in 1984 or that she ever told Barry that she had seen Susan get in the van.

The judge, exasperated at the length of Wachtel's questioning, finally shuts off direct examination.

Tipton, her appearance softened somewhat by glasses, runs a hand through her hair as she rises to question Janice. She has little to accomplish on cross except to make sure the judge understands what a bastard George Franklin was to his children. Using the opening Wachtel provided on direct, Elaine asks Janice to explain why she had wanted so badly to stay out of the home until dinner time:

"Yes, it was a combination of alcoholism in the home, physical violence, sexual abuse, physical abuse, mental and emotional abuse."

Janice calmly tells the judge of the incident when her father kicked her in the base of the spine as she walked to the telephone to talk to the Foster City police.

Although he is scoring points, Horngrad is making little headway: it is obvious that Judge Browning likes and believes Eileen, and as long as this is the case, not much else matters. However, Horngrad proceeds with an array of witnesses in an attempt to learn what he can.

Leah testifies briefly that she has believed for a long time that George murdered Susan Nason because that's the sort of man he is, and that when she accused him of it, his only reply was, "You think things like that of me." Kirk Barrett testifies that Eileen suffers from post-traumatic stress syndrome, but that he believes her story. He also gives a radically different version of how Eileen told him she had recovered her memory. Several cops take the stand and recount various aspects of the 1969 investigation, and Horngrad calls numerous neighbors from old Neighborhood One in Foster City in an attempt to stitch together a credible scenario that Susan had been abducted by a man in a blue station wagon.

ON JUNE 1, 1990, THE PRELIM IS CONCLUDED, ELEVEN DAYS AFTER IT began. Judge Browning tells Franklin to rise and announces that in his opinion there is sufficient evidence to believe that he has committed the crime with which he is charged. He orders Franklin to appear for arraignment in Superior Court on June 15, at which time a trial date will be set. He continues the two-million-dollar bond.

The reporters still doubt that Franklin can be convicted on the basis of the evidence presented so far. There must be some other piece of physical evidence to link him to the murder. No one believes Eileen is consciously lying about what she saw (how could she possibly make up those details?), it's more a question of whether some trauma has operated to distort her personality and, through some unconscious need or desire for revenge, created a false memory. One journalist points out that however you cut it, Eileen has to be screwed up: If she did witness the killing and has lived with it buried in her psyche for twenty years, imagine the disastrous effect on her personality; if she didn't see it, what sort of a person would bring such a false charge against her father?

Whatever doubts Horngrad might have had before the hearing about the nature or source of Eileen's misperception have been resolved in his own mind: Eileen Franklin is an out-and-out liar. The trigger, the "I met her gaze" story, was a complete fabrication. She and her sister Janice, at one level or another, concocted the entire story, and Eileen lied all the way through the hearing in order to make the charge stick. His task at trial will be to catch her in the lies. Last fall, when he first got the case, he had jokingly referred around his office to the "Gang of Four": Eileen, Barry, Leah, and Janice. Now he has narrowed it down to the Gang of Two: Eileen and Janice. In fact, the more he thinks about it, the more he sees Janice as the primary force and Eileen as her front person.

Tipton, who had been in charge of the prosecution for only five or six weeks at the time of the prelim, improved substantially in the last few days of the hearing. Although Horngrad might have won the mini-play on points, her cross-examination, particularly of the man-in-the-blue-station-wagon witnesses, was very effective. She feels a lot more optimistic about the case after seeing Eileen on the stand for two days and realizing how strong she is. Her key witness is not about to be carved into pieces or bamboozled by the likes of Doug Horngrad.

On June 15, Franklin is formally arraigned in Superior Court for the murder of Susan Nason and a trial date is set for October 15. A murder case in San Mateo usually takes two years to come to trial, but not this one. The defense will not ask for the usual continuances. George Franklin wants out of jail and twenty years having already elapsed since the alleged offense, his case is not likely to improve over time.

Elaine Tipton is well aware that she has a tremendous amount of work to do in the next five months to demonstrate Franklin's guilt beyond a reasonable doubt.

38

THE CONSENSUS THAT EILEEN IS DAMAGED PSYCHOlogically is probably one of the few undisputed facts in the entire case, one even she does not deny. The differences develop over the source of the damage, the extent its long-term effects on her personality and, ultimately, on the trustworthiness of her memory. Tipton acknowledges that if Eileen suffered only a portion of what she alleges she suffered at the hands of her father, a normal, healthy, integrated personality would be impossible. In fact, if she appears too well put together on the stand, it might well undercut her credibility. From Horngrad's point of view, the source of the damage is not, cannot be, the issue; rather, the issue is whether Eileen's damaged psyche has created, consciously or unconsciously, a story that is not true, is at worst a lie and at best a delusion.

A saying in clinical psychology goes: "Put the mind in an impossible place and it will do the possible." This assumes the mind to be an adaptive, creative force capable of filtering and distorting, forgetting and remembering. Who has not had a dream in which an entire drama unfolds: a story with a beginning and an end, complete with full-blown characters and complex dialogues and places so rich in detail and imagery, so foreign to known reality, that it startles the awakened mind?

The mind strives to make sense out of things, to find order in disorder, to develop explanations for inconsistencies, to resolve conflicts, to make the intolerable tolerable. In Freudian terms, the primary purpose of the ego is to protect and defend and ensure the survival of the self. The ego can employ a range of defense mechanisms to this end, and many of them involve the reshaping or filtering of objective reality to a less threatening form. Daydreaming, floating away in thought for a few minutes, detaches the self from the boring or unpleasant reality of the moment. The mind innocently forgets a bad experience for long periods of time—a favorite pet getting hit by a car—or it can alter certain aspects of the experience to make it more tolerable—someone other than you called the animal to cross the street. Or more aggressively, the mind can deny that anything happened at all. *Suppression,* probably the most conscious of the defense mechanisms, involves active or intentional forgetting. In *denial,* the mind pushes an unpleasant memory and its associated feelings away and keeps them at a distance. At the other end of the spectrum, the mind may distort the entire thought system to deal with a trauma, thus creating a *psychotic delusion.*

When the human psyche is faced with an impossible situation, the possible may require a mental break with reality in order to survive. If the threat to the self appears overwhelming, the ego, in order to avoid a psychotic fracture or the disintegration of self, will protect the self by separating from the experience. In *dissociation,* the conscious mind is completely separated from the traumatic experience; it's as if the trauma never occurred.

A little girl who is being sexually abused suddenly finds herself wandering in a sunny meadow picking flowers, or playing with her favorite dolls in her bedroom, or watching from the corner of her room as another little girl is abused. The trauma is not felt; the pain is not experienced. In such instances, the ability to dissociate is seen as a blessing or a gift, because it allows the self to survive. In the long run, however, the trauma and fragmentation in consciousness can lead to the creation of a range of psychopathologies and, in children, may lead to permanent impairment of the central nervous system, cognitive processes and, it is suspected, the chemistry of the brain.

The *Diagnostic and Statistical Manual of the American Psychiatric Association, Version III Revised,* sets forth several types of dissociative disorders: psychogenic amnesia, which is an inability to recall important events or personal information; a psychogenic fugue, in which an individual travels from home and establishes a new identity with no recollection of his or her previous identity; depersonalization disorder, in which the person has sensations of self-estrangement or unreality; and multiple personality disorder (MPD), which involves the existence of two or more distinct personalities within the same individual. The creation of multiple personalities is the most extreme dissociative reaction to trauma, and it involves the creation of a new ego or egos within distinct personalities to contain and isolate the traumatic experiences. Some recent studies show that over ninety percent of people diagnosed with MPD have suffered physical or sexual abuse as children.

Sigmund Freud's contribution to the psychology of trauma has been both immense and controversial. An underpinning of psychoanalytic theory is the existence of the unconscious mind as an active storehouse of memories, fantasies, thoughts, and dreams from childhood, which affects and influences the feelings and evolution of the adult personality. A function of the ego is to repress unwelcome fantasies and wishes, such as the Oedipal urge. Around the turn of the century, Freud noted the high incidence of hysteric reactions in his Viennese female patients and listened with great interest to their stories that as little girls they had been seduced by their fathers. Initially he believed them, and he adopted the incidents as the causes of the hysteria and expanded his theory of repression to include the repression of such traumatic childhood experiences. Within a year, however, he repudiated the seduction theory and concluded instead that the memories of abuse were really the women's repressed wishes and fantasies. (Recent evidence suggests that Freud continued to believe that the incidents happened as his female clients related them but abandoned the seduction theory because he had been ostracized professionally and suffered financially after it became known.)

Due to the dominance of Freudian psychoanalytic thinking in the American psychiatric community during this century, the effect of external trauma, including incest, on the development of the personality was largely ignored. It wasn't until severely impaired vets came home from Viet Nam in the early seventies that the effect of stress or trauma on the personality began to receive attention in this country. And it wasn't until the early eighties that the therapeutic community focused on the existence and impact of psychic childhood traumas.

Children who successfully wall off traumatic experiences may eventually pay a terrible price for the dissociation. While it allows a part of them to go on living, perhaps normally, another part of them is lost. A black hole develops in their personality, a place where they cannot think or feel. Although isolated, the unfelt experiences seethe beneath the conscious mind, constricting and affecting emotional, physiological, and cognitive development.

Post-traumatic stress disorder (PTSD) is the current diagnostic category for the global response of the human organism to trauma; and it frequently co-exists with a dissociative disorder. The primary characteristics of the syndrome are a reliving or re-enactment of the trauma and the emergence of a numbing response, or a social isolation and a sense of estrangement from others. Re-enactment is a derivative of the repetition compulsion, in which, according to Freud, "The patient . . . is obliged to *repeat* the repressed material as contemporary experience, instead of remembering it as something belonging to the past." Re-enactment of the original trauma plays out in a range of forms, including, in the case of abused children, continued attempts to obtain love from the abusing parent or the eventual substitution of an abusive adult male.

Some people subjected to extreme stress also often have difficulty developing intimate relationships and controlling or modulating their emotions, particularly anger. They are hypersensitive and subject to extreme emotional responses. Typically, they are also subject to intrusive recollections or flashbacks of the actual traumas.

Research indicates that when children suffer traumas at the hands of one or both of their parents, the results can be devastating. Children are instinctively aware of their extreme vulnerability and their dependency on parents to provide a safe and secure place for them in the world. When children are abused by their parents, the realization of their helplessness can be so terrifying that they modify their perceptions to see a bad parent as good and themselves as bad. This distorted version of the relationship is more acceptable to children because it does not entail the vilification or potential loss of the parent. It can set up, however, an enduring sense of badness and guilt in the child, a belief that the child is responsible for what has happened to him or her.

If a parent *sexually* abuses a child, the perception of the self and the parent may become even more twisted. In this distorted version, the child is receiving the attention and affection that he or she desires and needs, and the child may even enjoy some of the feelings of the sexual encounters. While the child may initially experience the sex as normal, feelings of violation and anger toward the abusing parent will eventually surface. This ambivalence toward the parent—loving on one hand and hating on the other—can create a pool of rage that grows with the child into adulthood.

As the child develops, the maturing personality will often repeat and re-enact the confusion caused by the mixture of love and pain. The anger or rage can be acted out in aggression against others or against the self. In women, the aggression is more often directed at themselves, such as self-mutilating or suicidal behavior. In men, the aggression is often directed at others. The defiled sense of sexuality in a female often leads to a permanent self-stigmatization, promiscuity, and prostitution. The familiar is always more comfortable than the unknown, and sex is one way a sexually abused woman has learned to get what she needs. She may have affairs with older, married men as a way of re-experiencing an incestuous relationship with her father. She may become a lesbian. She may feel isolated and be subject to bouts of depression and often attempt self-medication through alcohol or drugs. She may have an inherent distrust of any relationship and have difficulty going beyond the superficial level. She expects abandonment and betrayal at every turn and she finds it.

Not all sexually abused or traumatized children dissociate or repress the abusive experiences. Some, like Janice and Kate Franklin, never forget them. And some abused children, occasionally referred to as "transcenders," are, for reasons not fully understood, less vulnerable to the lasting effects of the childhood traumas. They lead apparently normal lives and obtain substantial levels of success in education and careers, and enter into stable and nurturing relationships with members of the opposite sex. The re-enactment compulsion is not the driving force in their evolution of self.

However, an abused female child is usually a sitting duck for revictimization as an adult; she is likely to walk right into the hands of abusive males and return again and again to the abuser in a repetition or re-enactment of the original trauma. The sense of helplessness coupled with a desire for intimacy may lead to a re-enactment of the trauma in the selection of a partner.

The abused child may also develop a chronic sense of victimization as an adult. The acute feelings of helplessness that accompanied the childhood abuse continue and she feels that she has no more control over her life now than she did then. She may be unable to accept responsibility for anything in her life; whatever bad happens is someone else's fault. As a chronic victim, she may combine her rage with her need to blame others. Recent research indicates that a victim may even become physiologically addicted to the trauma experience.

The wall that so effectively isolated the terrifying experience and its accompanying feelings from the consciousness of the child may last a lifetime, in which case the person will probably compulsively re-enact the trauma without understanding why. Or at some point in her life, perhaps when she is older and the world is safer, the wall may leak, and bits and pieces of the memory or memories may slip through the crack into consciousness. Eventually enough bits and pieces may emerge to form an accurate representation of the traumatic incident, a true memory. Or the fragments may be scrambled together with other contents of the unconscious to create a false memory, a visualization sincerely believed by the patient but not true.

The renowned Swiss psychologist Jean Piaget wrote of his own experience with the ability of the mind to create a false memory. He remembered and talked about for years an incident in which a man tried to kidnap him at age two from his pram in the presence of his nurse. When Piaget was fifteen, his nurse returned to his parents and confessed that the story was false, there never had been an attempted abduction, and that she had made up the incident in order to win their approval. Piaget had heard the incident recounted from his earliest consciousness and had incorporated the details into a visual memory which he believed to be real and recounted as factual for years.

The experts in this field don't deny there are both true traumatic memories and false traumatic memories. What they don't agree on is how to tell one from the other, or whether that is even possible.

39

THE DRAMA OF A CRIMINAL TRIAL IS MORE LIKE PER-formance art than a traditional play: there is no common script and certainly no set ending. In fact, different scripts designed to achieve different endings are pursued simultaneously and, in a good trial, much is left to the resources of the actors to do what they can with the material they're given. However, the action is not free-form: all the actors have well-established roles which have been carefully crafted and defined by statute, case law, and custom. The role of the defendant, whose fate is the subject of the drama, is naturally filled first, albeit unwillingly, and then the two major combatants, the prosecutor and defense lawyer, are selected. Like gladiators, trial lawyers fight for a living, moving from one arena to the next, usually until they wear out, go on the bench, or die. Next comes the judge, whose job it is to define and enforce the rules by which the drama will be performed. The judge sits high above everyone else, cloaked in a dark robe of power and neutrality, and supposedly without emotion or bias, untainted by personal feelings or concerns. The judge issues edicts designed to ensure the fairness of the struggle and the rightness of the result. The judge can scold like a parent, thunder like a god, pound like a football coach, or reason like a professor, but in the end the judge's word is law and must be obeyed.

The presiding criminal judge of the Superior Court contacted Superior Court Judge Thomas McGinn Smith and asked if he would be willing to try the Franklin case. Anticipating that the case would be interesting and an intellectual challenge, Smith readily agreed. Pre-trial motions were scheduled to be heard on September 18, 1990, by Judge Smith.

Judge Smith had turned fifty-three a few weeks earlier, and despite graying hair, his unlined face and boyish good looks make him appear to be in his early forties. Smith comes from an affluent, old-line, Republican Redwood City family and he speaks softly but mellifluously, which adds to his patrician bearing. Friendly and easygoing off the bench, he is cool and clipped on it. He can be abrupt and abrasive, and in some courthouse quarters he is referred to respectfully as "the Ice Man." Others call him "Chuckles," because of his stern demeanor on the bench. He is thought of as smart and very conservative.

Judge Smith graduated from the University of Santa Clara Law School in 1963, where he was managing editor of the law review and in the top twenty percent of his class. He joined the district attorney's office in 1965 and went into private practice as a criminal defense attorney in 1967. Active in Republican politics and in community affairs, Smith was appointed to the municipal bench in 1972, where he served until his election to Superior Court in 1985. In the fall of 1990, he had served on the bench for eighteen years. Judge Smith will not seek elevation to the appellate bench: he loves the action of the courtroom too much.

Judge Smith knows the law and the procedures, and he makes sure from the beginning of a case that both lawyers understand that he is in control of the courtroom. He makes up his mind quickly and seldom changes it—once he has ruled, particularly in front of a jury, he tolerates no further argument from the lawyers.

Smith has a well-known soft spot for animals. A few years back, a defendant in his court had been charged with a misdemeanor charge of cruelty to animals for kicking a litter of puppies who had awoken him. Several of the puppies had subsequently died. The defendant, obviously anticipating a lecture and a fine, appeared without a lawyer and pled guilty. Smith sentenced him on the spot to one year in jail. In another case, a woman had starved a dog to the point where the flesh had grown around its collar. Smith asked the vet how long he thought the dog had suffered, and when the vet answered four months, Smith sentenced the woman to four months in the county jail.

Judge Smith's courtroom is at the top of the escalator on the second floor of the Hall of Justice. The courtroom is modern with dark wood and recessed lighting, but small and windowless. The judge's bench is in the left-hand corner of the far wall as you enter and the jury box is along the right wall. The witness stand is in the center, so the witness can look either at the judge or the jury, but not both. The back wall is decorated with the American and Californian flags. The spectator section consists of only five rows of ten seats each. The defense and prosecution tables sit end to end facing the witness stand.

On Judge Smith's first entrance of the day, Deputy Sheriff Vince Nocon pops through a door along the far wall and calls out, "Please rise. Court is now in session!" a split second before Judge Smith enters from a door behind the bench. After that, Smith comes in and sits down without ceremony. Vince, a balding and hefty Filipino who lifts weights during the lunch hour, sits just inside the bar along the right wall, where he can keep an eye on both the jury and the courtroom entrance. Across the room sits the clerk, Peggy Gensel, a matronly woman only a few months from retirement who swears in the witnesses, marks and keeps track of the exhibits, and conducts court business over the phone which rings loudly and incessantly.

Franklin is housed in the jail on the fourth floor of the Hall of Justice. In the morning a deputy escorts him in chains down a back elevator to a small receiving room and removes his shackles and handcuffs. When court is ready to begin, Vince signals the deputy, who brings Franklin into the courtroom through a rear door and walks him to the defense table. The deputy sits in a chair against the wall a few feet away from his charge. Franklin must always be seated before the jury is brought in to avoid any implication of guilt from being seen in custody. During recesses, Franklin is usually returned to the receiving room.

In the center of the courtroom sits the stenographer, Gloria ("Glo") Bell, a thin, quiet woman, poised over her machine to record each and every word of the drama.

ON THE MORNING OF SEPTEMBER 18, HORNGRAD ARRIVES PREPARED to argue pre-trial motions. He rises from behind his table as his client enters and greets him warmly. He knows George is having a hard time. Over the past ten months George has participated actively in his defense, but now he seems to be backing off. Horngrad senses that he is becoming frightened.

Pre-trial motions are supposed to raise and decide critical matters of evidence and procedure, such as venue and the admissibility of disputed evidence, before the actual trial begins. The court attempts to settle all of these issues before the jury is empaneled so that disputes don't erupt during the trial and contaminate the minds of the jurors or disrupt the orderly progress of the drama. A judge's rulings on pre-trial motions often determine the outcome of the trial.

Horngrad has filed a slew of motions. First, he requests disclosure of Eileen Franklin's misdemeanor conviction. Second, he argues that since Eileen has been interviewed by a prosecution psychiatrist, Dr. Lenore Terr, the defense is entitled to have her evaluated by an independent psychiatrist. Both motions are denied. He seeks dismissal of the case because the prosecution failed to tell the defense about the trip to search for Franklin's diary and failed to turn over 178 pages of the detectives' notes until only two days before the hearing. These motions are also denied, as are his requests that all conversations between Eileen and the prosecution be recorded and that all evidence obtained in the search of Franklin's apartments be suppressed. Judge Smith does, however, grant his request to delay the trial until October 22.

NBC has filed a motion to televise the proceedings and Smith denies the request without argument or hearing. He doesn't like cameras in courtrooms, doesn't think they promote the cause of justice in any fashion, and routinely bars them. He watched the cameras turn the prelim into a circus—lenses snapping so loud the witnesses couldn't be heard—and he will not have it in his courtroom. NBC appeals.

During a break in the pre-trial motions, reporters ask Tipton about the misdemeanor conviction and she says, in an obvious attempt to sidetrack them, that it is not at all clear that the misdemeanor conviction relates to Eileen. One reporter guesses that it is probably a traffic conviction. Somebody heads to municipal court to check the records. No one thinks of checking in San Jose.

Tipton had talked earlier to Eileen about the possibility of the prosecution introducing the prostitution conviction into evidence. Dr. Terr, the prosecution psychiatrist, would like very much to mention Eileen's prostitution in her testimony as further evidence of her psychopathology. Prostitution is a classic re-enactment of childhood sexual abuse and trauma. Eileen, however, is determined to keep this part of her past from the public eye.

Horngrad is convinced that Eileen is not only lying but that she is intentionally hiding things from the defense. She withheld the name of the second therapist, Katherine Rieder, for several months in spite of the fact that it was clearly called for by the subpoena, and she tried to shield information about her movie deals behind an attorney-client privilege, which was disallowed by Judge Smith.

Eileen also seemed to have spent the summer cooking up additional allegations against her father based on new "memories." In July she had given a taped statement to the cops alleging that when she was five or six her father had attempted to sodomize her in the bathtub. She also, quite incredibly, told the cops that she had remembered seeing her father commit *another* murder. On August 1, she had given a taped statement on the second murder to Morse and Cassandro. Although she would later tell Dr. Terr that she had begun remembering this murder in December of 1988, *before* the return of the memory of Susan's murder, she told the detectives that she had just recently begun remembering it. The statement is confused, and in many places, barely coherent:

Eileen: . . . I started to remember . . . being with my dad and he, we were in his car and he picked up a woman in his car . . . what I remembered just seeing him placing her body, which she wasn't alive any more and that he was holding her up, upside down and holding her around her, like her hip area . . . made me stand somewhere, and I, and I was, I think holding a flashlight . . . she was laying on the ground and he was like straddling on top of her across her stomach area and he took her belt off of her, at least that's what I think he was doing . . . another thing that I remember, which, I would guess happened before this, she was running, and this is in a wooded area, but she ran by where it was in my, my vision and that across her, her left breast was what I think was blood, it looked like there was a series of scratches and then there was blood coming down off the breast. . . . I don't think that she had a top on. . . . Then I became very upset and I, I can't quite figure it out why that he was, something, it had something to do with her left breast that it was very bloody or something that was very just horrific. When, where, the way he put the body was like lowering it, that he had the body lifted with his arms around the thigh area. And I don't know how to describe this, there's a recessed area. And there's something across the top like, I think it's what a storm drain would be like, or a creek bed or a tree that had fallen across the top . . . it's just a bit further on, not a great distance, a very close distance. And I, I just remember him trying to put this body down and that I had to stand there with the flashlight and that I was thinking to myself that I was glad that it was almost over, that it was a relief that he was putting her down.

Morse: You say you were in a car, well which car was that?

Eileen: Well, now, I think it was the Volkswagen because, it's very, when she got into the car, now he picked her up somewhere that is very familiar to me. . . . And the two places that come to mind, now I can't say definitely that either one is it, one was the El Camino Real, and the other was CSM [College of San Mateo], and it just seemed to me that it was somewhere that was real familiar to me and not a foreign place at all.

Morse: What time frame are we talking about in as far as your age?

Eileen: . . . I think that, that my hair was long and that, that it was much longer when I was a little bit older than then [when Susan disappeared]. And I just remembered being really cold, that my feet were really cold. And there's something about the belt. And I think it's her belt. But something about it that, that I think that I remember that it, it was really tight when it was around her. That it was pulling on her.

Morse: Do you remember where she got into the van?

Eileen: She got into, on the passenger side. She was reluctant to get in, and this is what I remember that she was reluctant to get in, and then what my dad said to her was, he said, well, come on now, you don't think I'd try anything with my pretty red-haired girl here in the car. And, she looked at me and he looked at me and she kind of smiled at me, not like a huge grin but she smiled at me, you know, in an acknowledging way and got into the car.

Eileen remembered that the woman was pretty and had dark hair, probably about twenty years old, but she couldn't remember how she was dressed. It was light when they started out and dark when it was over and Eileen sat in the back while they drove and she listened to them talk.

Morse: What ultimately happened to the woman?

Eileen: Well I, it just seemed to me that, that he killed her. And then he put, put her body in this recessed . . .

Morse: Like a little gully?

Eileen: Yeah, it could be a gully, it could be a ditch, it could be a . . .

Cassandro: Storm drain?

Eileen: Storm drain, it, I, I just can't say clearly enough what it was. But it was very peculiar because he was carrying her upside down, it was very peculiar . . .

Morse: But you can't remember him inflicting any injuries upon her?

Eileen: I don't know, but that, the belt really, it seems to me that he did something with the belt that, that I think that it's, it's possible that he strangled her with it.

Eileen didn't remember any struggling, but she did remember hearing the woman scream.

In an attempt to link Franklin with other crimes, Morse and Cassandro had previously reviewed the San Mateo coroner's files for unsolved murders. After Eileen's August 1 statement, they teletyped surrounding jurisdictions for information on unsolved murders of young females in the early and mid-1970s. They received information back on two girls, eighteen and fourteen, who had been sexually assaulted and stabbed to death in Pacifica, a coastal town just south of San Francisco, in 1975. One girl's body had been found at the bottom of a six-foot gully on the edge of a golf course. Semen samples had been recovered in both cases.

Horngrad was outraged when he learned of the new allegations against George Franklin based on another "memory" of Eileen. When the prosecution asks for blood and hair samples from George Franklin, Horngrad immediately agrees. He is not surprised when the tests results from the county laboratory exclude his client as a suspect in the two cases. He is not amused when he learns that Tipton, unwilling to accept the results, forwarded the evidence to the FBI laboratory for additional analysis. He thinks seriously about introducing the statement into evidence to reveal the hallucinatory qualities of her mind to the jury.

SINCE THE END OF THE PRELIMINARY HEARING, TIPTON HAS PLUNGED headfirst into the Franklin case. She is slightly obsessive in her attention to detail anyway, and she has worked the case backwards and forwards, twelve hours a day, seven days a week. Everything else—her social life, her family, her duties as a supervisor—has been put on hold. She knows that she is in for the toughest fight of her life, and, to the consternation of the two detectives, has insisted on checking and recheking each and every detail of the case, going over every line of each 1969 police report, examining each piece of physical evidence, talking personally to every 1969 and 1989 witness, reading each pornographic and pedophilic item seized from Franklin's residences. She has an excellent memory, and she intends to use it.

Over the summer, Tipton visited the crime scene several times by herself, casting about for ways to tighten down her case. At one point, she thought of having Cassandro videotape the crime scene from 3:00 to 5:00 P.M. on September 22 so they could see exactly what the lighting was like at the time of the murder, but she changed her mind. If the experiment turned out badly, she would have to turn the tape over to the defense, and why should she do their work for them?

On one occasion she had been driving on Highway 280 past the reservoir when she glanced to her left in the direction of the spot where Susan's body was found and burst into tears at the sheer awfulness of what had happened there. In her mind, George Franklin is some sort of hybrid monster who has committed unspeakable acts—holding his daughter down so a friend could rape her is almost worse than the murder—and she will do whatever it takes to make him pay for his horrible crimes.

Tipton knows she can be hard when she has to be (although she is careful not to come across as a ballbuster in front of a jury), but she also considers herself a soft touch. She has handled hundreds of sex crime cases and she cares greatly for the victims and the pain they have suffered. In this case, she has learned to be careful not to get overwhelmed by Eileen's pain, which seems inexhaustible.

Morse and Cassandro would fall on their swords for Tipton. She is as tough as they come in a courtroom, never yielding an inch, battling every step of the way, and when she goes into the arena she is thoroughly prepared on the law and the facts. But they also appreciate her good nature, the part of her that cares for people, jokes around, and organizes office social functions.

40

THE SITE FOR THE PERFORMANCE OF AN ORDINARY drama may have some effect on the success of the play, but nothing like the effect the location has on the outcome of a trial, for here the local townspeople are more than the general audience—twelve of them become players themselves, and in the final scene they will sit solemnly in their seats and vote yes or no.

The prosecution was counting on bringing George Franklin to trial before the citizens of San Mateo County. Morse knew he would be begging the D.A. to dismiss the case if it had been filed in San Francisco or some of the northern counties. When Horngrad filed his motion for a change of venue, the prosecution wasn't too worried: in the last ten years, only one case had been moved out of San Mateo County.

October 11, 1990—Thursday

The hearing on the venue motion begins today and Smith puts smiles on the faces of the defense team when he announces that the trial will begin next week either in San Mateo

County, Los Angeles County, San Diego County, Imperial County, or Riverside County. He startles everyone even more when he announces that "I've already advised the clerk, the bailiff, the court reporter, and my wife that if I grant it [the motion] we're going to commence trial the next day in one of those counties."

Observers chuckle at the strange colloquy between Smith and Wachtel. "But your honor, I have a dog," Wachtel objects, perhaps aware of Smith's fondness for animals.

"I've got six cats," Smith replies, not to be outdone. "So?"

At the break, Morse is clearly worried—there is no bullshitting with the press in the hallway this morning. Horngrad tries not to get too excited. The local "cops and courts reporters" are concerned. They have been waiting for this trial for almost a year, and while it might be fun to go to a new location, they are not at all sure that their editors will pay for six weeks room and board in Southern California.

The defense has the burden of showing that there is a reasonable possibility that Mr. Franklin cannot get a fair trial in San Mateo County because of the pre-trial publicity. The court is required to consider the nature and extent of the publicity, the size of the community, the nature and gravity of the offense, the status of the victim, and the status of the accused. Wachtel, impeccably dressed in a gray suit, his hair a little shaggy, argues for the defense. He intends to prove that the county has been saturated by television, radio, and print journalism, and that a recent survey reveals that a substantial bias already exists against his client.

Wachtel introduces into evidence a listing of 174 newspaper articles and 13 television segments dealing with the case. A marketing research analyst testifies about a public opinion survey conducted in San Mateo County. The testimony on the methodology of the survey is deadly boring and most reporters soon drift out of the room to check on a trial across the hall. The upshot of the expert's testimony is that phone interviews had been conducted with jury-eligible voters in the county, and of the 374 respondents, 73 percent were familiar with the case and of those, 46 percent believed that Franklin was probably or definitely guilty. Only five percent thought he was innocent. On cross-examination, Tipton points out several flaws in the methodology.

October 15, 1990—Monday

George Franklin finally wears something other than his blue suit to court: a beige sport coat and khaki pants. The strange smile flits across his face as he strides into the courtroom clutching his files. Elaine Tipton is wearing a flowered skirt, red blouse, black jacket, and red lipstick. The look softens her a little, makes her more feminine. Both sides keep track of who comes and goes, turning and looking each time the door opens. Judge Smith adds Orange County to the list of possible sites, further heightening everyone's expectation of a transfer.

Wachtel calls a psychology professor to the stand and he testifies that this very dramatic and emotional story has generated a tremendous amount of publicity, much of which is potentially prejudicial to the defense. However, he says the newspaper articles were much more balanced than usual. (The reporters love this remark and most manage to work a version of it into their next article.)

The professor states that the level of prejudgment is tremendously high, and he is not at all sure that the prejudice can be cured by voir dire (questioning of the potential jurors) or appropriate judicial instructions. But, he adds, a careful and sensitive voir dire may remedy the problem.

After Tipton's cross-examination and the testimony of her expert witness, Judge Smith gives his decision. Going beyond his usual one-sentence rulings, he quotes the psychology professor's statements that the press was unusually balanced in this case and that any prejudgment could be cured by careful voir dire and denies the motion to change venue.

The defense might have done better if the professor had stayed in school. The prosecution is greatly relieved at retaining the home field advantage.

* * *

ACROSS THE HALL FROM FRANKLIN, THE STATE IS TRYING VERY HARD to put two men to death. In April 1990, Ramon Salcido went on a three-hour bloody rampage in the wine country of Sonoma County to the north. The twenty-nine-year-old winery worker from Los Mochis, Mexico, is charged with seven counts of murder for shooting to death his Anglo wife, who had just left him and whom he suspected of being involved with another man, and a winery co-worker, and of stabbing to death his two daughters, ages four and one, his wife's mother, and his two sisters-in-law, ages twelve and eight. He slashed the throat of a third daughter, Carmina, and tossed her body in the Dumpster with the other two daughters, but she survived, perhaps because earlier she had slumped forward and closed the slit in her throat. He fled to his mother's home in Mexico, but two Sonoma County cops tracked him down and he confessed in the airplane on the way back.

The defense attorney won a motion to have the trial moved out of Sonoma County, but the victory turned to disaster when the judge sent the case to San Mateo County, known even in Sonoma County as a hanging county.

The Salcido trial had begun about six weeks earlier. The large courtroom is packed every day and a bank of television cameras, barred from the room, are lined up outside the door. Each time the door opens, their lights flash on and their metallic black snouts focus in on Salcido seated at the defense table.

Salcido's defense does not deny his bloody acts, nor is it claiming that he is mentally ill; rather, his lawyer argues that he exploded in a psychotic episode resulting from an array of stresses and excessive use of alcohol and cocaine, and was therefore incapable of forming the intent necessary for first-degree murder. Salcido cries when a picture of Carmina, now four, is shown to the jury.

In the courtroom next to Salcido, a jury is deciding the fate of Raymond Gurule, on trial in the 1982 murder of a fifteen-year-old boy. After emptying the cash register of the gas station where the boy worked, Gurule held the youth on the ground, cradled his head in his lap, and drew the blade across his throat, severing his jugular, carotid artery, and trachea, cutting through almost to his backbone. Blood had spurted five feet high on the walls. Gurule got away with the crime until a few years later when his male companion confessed and named Gurule as the killer. By then Gurule was serving a life sentence for killing an eighty-one-year-old Oakland woman during a mugging. Gurule had been convicted of the boy's murder in a previous trial, but the jury had deadlocked 10–2 on the death penalty. Now a second jury is trying to decide if he should be put to death.

Gurule has tattoos on his hands and face and he reeks of unmitigated evil. His features are thick and heavy, as if carved inexpertly out of wax, and his eyes tell you he could cut the heart from his grandmother and feel nothing.

Two women walk into the Salcido hearing and find seats in the very last row. The local reporters recognize the attractive brunette in the sunglasses from the preliminary hearing as Janice Franklin. The tall, slender woman with the lustrous red hair causes a stir when she enters; heads turn in her direction and eyes linger on her for a moment as she finds a seat. This must be Diana.

Morse has been baby-sitting the two sisters in the hallway while Judge Smith, during breaks in the venue testimony, conducts a series of hearings which have been closed at the request of both the prosecution and defense. The frustrated press objects to their exclusion, but Smith refuses their request for a hearing on the issue. The reporters have picked up bits and pieces and, with the appearance of two of Eileen's sisters, figure that the judge is deciding what other heinous acts of George Franklin will come before the jury.

October 16, 1990—Tuesday

Today Judge Smith hears arguments on the admissibility of the uncharged conduct evidence. For Tipton, the moment of truth has finally arrived. She is convinced that without the admission of at least some of the uncharged conduct she cannot convict George Franklin of murder. Unless the jury sees evidence of his sexual interest in children and his horribly violent nature, unless they can comprehend what sort of a vile human being he really is, they won't convict him. She also wants Smith to see all of the evidence: it never hurts for the judge to think the defendant is guilty. Tipton is worried: Judge Smith is notoriously strict on admitting uncharged conduct. She understands the possibility that if she does get in some or all of the uncharged conduct and Franklin is convicted, the admission could set up a reversal on appeal. She and Murray had talked about this risk at length and finally decided they had to go for the conviction first and worry about the appeal later. Without a guilty verdict, there would be no appeal to worry about.

In preparing for Eileen's testimony that she had been raped by her godfather, the cops figured they had better find Stan Smith. They tracked him to the Napa State Hospital, where he had been since 1970. He had been married and teaching school and one day he just snapped. He had been diagnosed as a paranoid schizophrenic and fifteen years ago was placed under a conservatorship. When Morse and Cassandro interviewed him, he said that he had gone to high school with Leah and he remembered George and his three daughters. He had never seen "Hair," nor had he ever owned a poster of Jimi Hendrix.

Tipton has organized her evidence of uncharged conduct into three exhibits. Exhibit A summarizes the testimony of Eileen Franklin that when she was five or six years old her father had attempted to anally penetrate her in the bathtub, that when she was six or seven he digitally penetrated her, that when she was nine or ten he held her down while another man raped her, that in 1984 she had come into a room and found her father with both thumbs pulling her young daughter's labia apart while he looked into her vagina, and that on one occasion he had described his granddaughter as "sexy"; the testimony of Janice Franklin that when she was nine or ten her father had intruded upon her in the bathroom and demanded that she wipe herself in his presence, that when she was eleven he had inserted his hands inside her panties and fondled her, that when she was twelve or thirteen he raped her and forced her to orally copulate him; the testimony of Diana that when she was five or six her father had demanded that she uncover her chest, and up until she was twelve he had put his tongue in her mouth when he kissed her; the testimony of Susan DeBernardi that when she was seventeen George Franklin had grabbed both of her arms by the wrists and held them over her head and fondled her breasts; the testimony of Jean DeBernardi that when she was seventeen Franklin had kissed her roughly and put his hand inside her blouse and fondled her breasts; the testimony of the two baby-sitters that he had asked them about their sexual activities with boys.

Exhibit B summarizes the testimony of Elizabeth, a former girlfriend, that Franklin had told her that he and some other men had had group sex with fourteen- and fifteen-year-old girls; the testimony of Carolyn Adams that Franklin was obsessed with sex, that he called her his "little girl," and that in 1987 he had told her he had sex with one or more of his daughters; the testimony of Pamela, a former girlfriend, that Franklin insisted that she tell him of the details of her molestation by her father when they were having sex because it sexually aroused him, that Franklin asked her to procure little girls with whom he could have sex, that Franklin asked her to take pictures of her eight-year-old daughter's vagina and give them to him, that Franklin told her he belonged to an organization that believed children should have "Sex before eight, or else it's too late," that Franklin asked her if he could have sex with her eight-year-old daughter, claiming that it would be beneficial for the girl; the testimony of Carol, a former girlfriend, that during sexual relations with Franklin he would say, "Daughter, do you like that?" and when he asked her how old she was she was to answer eight or nine, that during sexual relations Franklin often would grab her wrists with one hand and pin them down over her head while he tickled her and told her "to be quiet and do what Daddy says," that Franklin had told her young girls had sexual urges and that he had had sex with ten-year-old girls, that Franklin asked her if her father had expressed a sexual interest in her, that Franklin spoke to her about having sex with a dog; the testimony of Frances, a former girlfriend, that Franklin had sent her a picture of himself masturbating and had discussed with her the possibility of her having sex with a dog; the testimony of Chrissy, a former "phone contact," that Franklin had told her he had been seduced by his twelve-year-old niece at a wedding, that Franklin had asked her if she had been molested as a child and about her willingness to have sex with a dog; the testimony of Elena, a former girlfriend, that during sex with Franklin she called him "Daddy" and he referred to her as his "Naughty Little Girl," that Franklin asked her to have sex with a dog in his presence and that he said he was attracted to teenage girls; the testimony of Lad, an associate, that Franklin had suggested that they pick up young female hitchhikers and rape them, that Franklin would say things like "The younger they are, the sweeter the meat," and "There's no substitute for youth," that Franklin had asked to perform oral sex on Lad's seventeen-year-old girlfriend.

Exhibit C consisted of the items Morse seized from Franklin's two apartments and storage locker, including copies of the father-daughter incest stories, sexually explicit letters from several of the girlfriends, a book entitled *Animals as Sex Partners*, a photo of a naked girl in a bathtub, a photo of a woman in a sequined mask pointing a dildo toward a girl doll, photos of Franklin with dildos and porno books, photos of a nude black woman, photos of the lamb and the dildos, and the photo of the German shepherd apparently having sex with a woman.

Tipton argues quite persuasively to the judge a number of different theories as to why the various items of uncharged conduct evidence should be admitted. She offers the testimony of Sue DeBernardi and former girlfriend Carol to establish George Franklin's "signature": in both instances he used one hand to hold the wrists over the head of a young girl (he called Carol his "incestuous little girl") while he performed real or simulated sex acts with the other, just as he had allegedly done with Susan Nason. This evidence would thus be relevant in establishing the identity of Franklin as Susan Nason's killer.

She argues that the bulk of the uncharged conduct evidence

should be allowed in to establish the element of intent. Under the felony murder charge, the prosecution must prove that George Franklin touched Susan with lewd intent. Under the straight murder charge, the prosecution is entitled to prove motive, and in this case the motive was to avoid discovery and prosecution as a child molester. To establish this motive, the prosecution is entitled to prove that he had in fact molested Susan, that he had touched her with lewd intent. This evidence would also allow the prosecution to establish the premeditation element of straight first-degree murder: If he killed her to cover up his crime, he obviously thought about the act beforehand.

Thus, the uncharged conduct would establish that George Franklin has a sexual interest in little girls and that fact would go to prove that he had a sexual interest when he touched Susan Nason. Tipton relies on the 1988 California case of *People* v. *Robbins,* which discussed the "doctrine of chances." This doctrine states roughly that the more instances you have of similar results, the more likely it is they were produced by the same cause. If a person has had lewd intent in touching young girls in five other instances, the more likely it is he had lewd intent in touching the girl in the sixth instance. The more instances there are, the less likely there is an innocent explanation for the current instance. Under this theory of admissibility, all of Franklin's written or oral statements and behavior evidencing a lewd interest in young girls should be admitted.

In opposing the "signature" evidence, Wachtel argues that the two previous instances did not contain enough identifying marks to establish a signature that could be matched with the current alleged crime. He also argues vigorously that the only time evidence of similar acts is admissible to establish the intent of the defendant is when the *defendant* has placed intent in issue. In *Robbins,* the defendant was charged with picking up, sodomizing, and then killing a young boy, and the prosecution sought to admit evidence that the defendant had previously molested and killed another boy in similar circumstances. The defendant admitted the killing but said that he had done it in a frustrated rage when the boy had kicked his motorcycle. In *Robbins,* intent *was* the issue: Did the defendant mean to do it or was it accidental? In this case, the defendant has not placed his intent in issue. George Franklin isn't admitting the act but denying the intent. He is saying that he hadn't touched Susan at all, that he hadn't killed her.

Tipton argues that Eileen is going to testify that she saw her father in a crouching position, holding Susan's arms over her head and moving his pelvis, and it is absolutely essential for the prosecution to be allowed to eliminate a variety of theories which could explain this conduct: that his conduct was innocent touching or playing that had escalated into wrestling or horseplay; or that he was disciplining her, trying to stop her from doing something in the back of the van; or that he was assaulting her, hitting her, but without any lewd intent. The uncharged conduct is necessary to *disprove* these alternate theories of why he was doing what he was doing. Since Eileen did not see any penetration or any fondling, his conduct was ambiguous and his intent needs to be established by this circumstantial evidence. If Franklin behaved in a way in the past that showed he had a deviant and lewd interest in children, then it is more likely than not that he had the same intent in his behavior toward Susan Nason on the afternoon of September 22, 1969.

In a closed hearing, Tipton calls Janice and Diana to testify before the judge on the instances of abuse. Eileen and Barry moved to Switzerland in August (to sit in their Swiss chalet and collect their royalties, Horngrad would quip in the hallway) and she will testify when she arrives in the country for the trial. Diana testifies that her mother was in the room when her father ordered her to take her arms down and that it had been humiliating. She has only a vague recollection of her father putting his tongue in her mouth when he kissed her. Janice says that during the several instances in which her father put his hands in her panties and fondled her genitals, he asked her if it felt good. After he unsuccessfully tried to penetrate her, he played with himself and made her kneel in front of him, then ejaculated in her mouth. Horngrad has a few questions for Diana, but leaves Janice alone.

Even after hearing this evidence, Judge Smith has no feelings toward George Franklin. On the bench, he has developed a cold detachment to the participants and the process. George Franklin could have been on trial for spitting on the sidewalk for all the difference it made to him as a jurist. He didn't let himself feel pain over the death of Susan Nason either, although he had felt sad when he realized that Susan Nason would have been the same age his son was when he was killed in a car accident.

He understands Tipton's theory of admissibility on the uncharged conduct, and he is inclined to go along with it to a limited degree. In order for the evidence to be admitted, he must determine that the probative value of the evidence—the strength of the inference that it raises—outweighs the prejudicial effect it might have on the jury. He announces that he will exclude all of Diana's testimony as too removed and lacking in probative value. He will admit all of Janice's testimony except for the bathroom incident. Sue DeBernardi and Carol will be allowed to give the signature evidence that Franklin held their hands over their heads while tickling or fondling them, but Jean DeBernardi will not be allowed to testify about Franklin accosting her. The baby-sitters' statements will be excluded. Carolyn Adams can testify that Franklin told her he had sex with his daughter, but not about the violence. None of the girlfriends will be allowed to testify about sex with a dog or bestiality. But Pamela can testify about Franklin's sexual interests in her daughter and his belief in "Sex before eight, or else it's too late." Likewise, Elena is allowed to testify about Franklin's requests that he call her "Daddy" while he called her "Daughter" during sex and his comments about his sexual urges for young girls. Chrissy will be allowed to repeat for the jury Franklin's story that he had sex with a twelve-year-old niece at a wedding and that when she had said, "But she was only twelve years old," he had said, "Yeah, that's the fun part of it!" None of the material seized in the search warrant will be admitted.

After the ruling, Morse comes out into the hall and walks

over to the reporters, who are speculating about what is going on inside.

"You won't be disappointed," he says, a small grin crossing his face, his left eyebrow dancing up and down. "We're doing all right in there."

Horngrad is blown away. Not only does he think the judge is dead wrong on the law, he knows that his client won't have a chance if this evidence comes in. George Franklin is on trial for murder, not child molestation, but this stuff will most certainly convict him of murder. If the judge's ruling stands, his client is doomed.

Horngrad takes up the cause himself and argues to the judge that his research indicates there is not a single reported case in California allowing "other crimes" evidence to prove intent when the defendant has not admitted being at the scene of the crime. He asks the judge for permission to re-argue the issue and says he will prepare an additional brief on the question over the weekend and submit it to the judge for his consideration Monday morning. Smith listens to Horngrad and is sufficiently impressed to grant him a rehearing on the issue, an unusual move for a judge who almost never changes his mind.

Judge Smith is pleased so far with the lawyering in the case. It is difficult when one lawyer is better than the other, because then he feels some need to balance the scales, which is tricky business for a judge. Tipton is, in his opinion, one of the best prosecutors in the county, very thorough and well prepared. In the many cases she has tried in front of him, he has learned to read her face. She can speak a whole paragraph without even opening her mouth.

Horngrad has never appeared in his court before, but he is impressed with him. He is intelligent and tenacious: he raises every possible issue and argues it again and again from every angle. His briefs are excellent, his objections well presented. He also did a damn good job of cleaning his client up and making him presentable for the jury.

Neither lawyer seems too emotionally involved with their case, which is good.

October 17, 1990—Wednesday

Judge Smith takes up other pre-trial motions. Tipton asks to be allowed to show the jury photos of the body at the scene and the autopsy during her opening argument. She also wants to be able to show the jury pictures of Susan Nason and Jessica Lipsker in her opening in order to explain how Eileen's memory was "triggered." Smith rules that she may do so.

Tipton also seeks a ruling that Morse and Cassandro be allowed to testify as to what Franklin said the day he was arrested. Horngrad argues that the statement—"Have you talked to my daughter?"—should be excluded because Franklin had not been given his Miranda warnings and it is hearsay. Tipton argues that the statement indicates a "consciousness of guilt." Smith rules the statement admissible.

The appellate court has stayed the commencement of the trial until it disposes of NBC's appeal, so court is adjourned until Monday.

October 18, 1990—Thursday

The Court of Appeals dissolves the stay. Word circulates that NBC will file an immediate appeal to the State Supreme Court.

The Gurule jury retires to decide whether the throat slasher should live or die. Forty-four minutes later, word whips around the courthouse that the jury is back. Clerks from other courtrooms, defense lawyers from other cases, prosecutors from other trials, deputies from the jail, longtime Gurule-watchers, and miscellaneous press gather in the courtroom. Seven deputies keep an eye on the twice-convicted murderer. Gurule, empty-eyed and thick-featured, looks nowhere. The clerk stands and impassively reads the verdict: "We the jury, in the above captioned case, do hereby determine the penalty to be imposed on defendant shall be death." Gurule doesn't twitch. The judge dismisses the jury with thanks and leaves the courtroom. The prosecutor hugs the boy's mother, who is crying, and his sisters. Marty Murray, and six or seven other prosecutors, who have been sitting together in the fourth row, go up to the winner and congratulate him, pumping his hand vigorously, slapping his shoulder. Tipton walks up and gives him a big hug.

The prosecutors and the cops will celebrate their victory tonight. Beer and shots of tequila at the Broadway.

41

October 22, 1990—Monday

JUDGE SMITH HAS REVIEWED THE BRIEFS ON UN-charged conduct and is gradually beginning to see things Horngrad's way. The evidence will paint George Franklin as such a dirty old man it will be impossible for a jury to turn him loose. It's not a logical jump from molestation to murder. The guy might well deserve to burn at the stake for what he did to his children, but he's on trial for murder, not his past life, horrible as it appears to have been. There is no way the jury could separate out the uncharged conduct from the murder charge.

What, he asks Tipton, if the defense stipulated that intent was not an issue? What if the defense agreed on the record that *whoever* killed Susan Nason committed a lewd and lascivious act upon her and is therefore guilty of first-degree murder? What if the only issue was the identity of the killer? Would there be any basis for the uncharged conduct evidence then?

The judge has put Tipton in a difficult spot. She argues that it's absurd for the defense to stipulate that even though George Franklin is not the killer, if he were the killer, he had touched Susan with lewd intent. But she can feel the judicial wind starting to shift, so she goes for the strongest possible stipulation: "The killer is guilty of first-degree murder in that the murder was committed in the course of child molestation under the felony murder rule and the killer acted with premeditation and deliberation."

Horngrad isn't happy either. By stipulating that Susan's murderer had first molested her and then killed her to cover it up, he will be implicitly endorsing Eileen Franklin's story of what happened that day. The stipulation will affirm her otherwise uncorroborated, free-standing story and give her unearned credibility with the jury. He has been given a Hobson's choice: Stipulate to first-degree murder or watch a loathsome parade of horribles about his client march in front of the jury. He agrees to the stipulation under protest, noting his objection in the record as grounds for appeal if his client is convicted.

"I can't believe this," a devastated Morse says to Tipton after Smith's ruling. This is absolutely the low point in the trial for him. He realizes, perhaps for the first time, that they might lose the case.

But Tipton has Plan B, a fallback position for the admission of at least some of the uncharged conduct. Assuming that the evidence can't be admitted to prove that Franklin had murdered Susan Nason, she argues to Smith that it should still be admitted to explain and support the prosecution's theory of repressed memory. Dr. Lenore Terr, the prosecution's expert, will testify that it is highly unusual, if not unheard of, for children to repress a single traumatic incident, regardless of how severe the trauma is. She will say that repression is more likely to occur when the child is exposed to multiple traumas. If the jury is left with the impression that the only traumatic incident Eileen experienced was witnessing her best friend's murder, then they will not understand how she could have repressed the memory. For the purpose of repression, the murder trauma needs to be viewed in context of the continuing traumas experienced by Eileen in the Franklin household.

Horngrad argues eloquently that the prosecution is trying to bootstrap in highly prejudicial and otherwise inadmissible evidence, but Judge Smith rules in Tipton's favor: Eileen will be allowed to testify about the digital penetration, the godfather rape, the bathtub sodomy, and Jessica's molestation by George Franklin. Additionally, Carolyn Adams will be allowed to testify about Franklin's comment to her because it corroborates Eileen's testimony of multiple traumas. Smith will instruct the jury not to consider this testimony as proof that Franklin is a child molester or a murderer, but only to substantiate the proposition that Eileen could have repressed the memory of Susan's murder for twenty years.

Tipton's victory is laced with irony. Both she and Murray initially doubted Eileen's story that she had repressed the memory for twenty years and Tipton had been worried that a jury would also have a hard time accepting the idea. Now, Eileen's claim of repression has provided the legal opening through which Tipton will funnel the evidence to reveal the wickedness of George Franklin.

AFTER THE UNCHARGED CONDUCT HAS BEEN RULED ON, JURY SELECTION begins. Soon the last members of the cast will be chosen and the curtain will rise. Twelve unsuspecting souls, all nonfelons and registered voters, will be selected to enter the strange theater of criminal justice as observer-participants and watch and listen to a play staged and performed for their benefit. Their lives will be suspended and transformed as day after day they sit in their designated places and try to sift fact from fantasy, truth from fiction, promises from performances, knowing in the end they will have to write and perform the final scene. Unlike all the other players, except for the defendant, the jurors have no training for their role, nor do they come to it voluntarily. All have been taught since grade school that serving on a jury is the civic duty of every American and some of them look forward to service while others bitterly resent the inconvenience. The jurors are supposed to be ordinary folks, people with no more than the usual turns and twists in their emotional history, the normal range of prejudices and biases, likes and dislikes; they are supposed to be reasonably intelligent, fair-minded people like you and me. George Franklin's peers.

Some lawyers use "experts" to help them select the jury,

sociologists who combine knowledge of the jurors' background with their answers to questions—along with body language, facial expressions, and the like—to determine what sort of jurors they would make. Other lawyers follow a few basic rules and rely on their instincts, honed and tested in previous struggles. Neither Tipton nor Horngrad use experts. Tipton wants jurors who can understand and accept the theory of repression, intelligent jurors who will not be put off by psychiatric testimony on elusive processes of the human mind. Horngrad wants an intelligent jury too, a jury that will think and use their minds to sort through the conglomeration of lies and distortions that will make up the bulk of Eileen Franklin's testimony. He wants a smart, cynical jury that, when the time comes, will think and reason and not simply react emotionally or out of sympathy for Susan Nason.

At 1:30 P.M. the first panel of thirty-two jurors is brought into the courtroom. The atmosphere is more formal now, Vince, the bailiff, speaks with a little more authority when he announces the judge's entrance, and the attorneys and cops and Franklin sit straighter in their chairs. Everyone looks at the prospective jurors as they enter. Tipton is wearing a conservative gray suit, Morse has on glasses, Cassandro, who has been wearing a sports coat, is now in a suit and has a fresh haircut, as does Franklin, who is back in his blue suit. The creases around Franklin's mouth seem deeper, his nose fleshier. His thick fingers scribble across pads of paper. Peggy stands and calls out the names of the prospective jurors, and only one fails to answer. Smith establishes his authority immediately by directing Tipton to issue a contempt order for the missing juror. Peggy swears in the others en masse.

The voir dire serves two purposes: To disqualify those jurors who admit to a bias or prejudice that would prevent them being fair, and to allow the court and the lawyers to begin educating the prospective jurors on the rules and themes of the play. Smith assumes the role of the father, the caring but stern parent, telling the panelists they can answer the questions in private if they choose. He questions them about their background and turns up an IBM consultant, a psychiatric nurse, a surveyor, four teachers, an executive secretary, a real estate broker, an engineer, a fireman, two nurses, a widow, a biochemist, a housewife, a roofing contractor, a savings and loan examiner, a banker, several students, a college instructor, a quality assurance manager, a technical writer, a sales manager, and a collections manager.

In his questions, Smith gives a summary of the play's ground rules to the panelists: They must apply the law as he gives it to them, decide the case based solely on the evidence, and presume the defendant to be innocent until his guilt is established beyond a reasonable doubt. Smith also begins to set the parameters for their decision process, how they must think: They must banish from their minds anything they already know about the case, decide the case on the basis of reason, not talk about the case with anybody else or even among themselves before retiring to deliberate, keep an open mind all the way through the process and not make up their mind before deliberations, and even if they do enter the jury room with an opinion about the guilt or innocence of the defendant, they must listen to the arguments of other jurors and allow their opinion to change if so warranted. On the other hand, if they truly believe they are right, they shouldn't allow themselves to be pushed around, even if it's eleven to one.

A current of rebellion runs through the first panel. The executive secretary says that she has read about the case and has already made up her mind. Smith excuses her. The next juror, perhaps noting how easily one can get excused, says almost the same thing: she simply could not be fair and impartial. Smith excuses her too. Then he tries to close the door by explaining to the panel that certainly everybody feels bad and upset that an eight-year-old-girl was murdered, but we must be able to put our pain aside and determine the guilt or innocence of the man charged with the crime. Another juror says he doesn't believe in the exclusionary rule and might not be able to follow the judge's instructions. Others give the judge letters from employers and principals asking that they be excused. Smith denies these requests on the spot.

Smith begins to focus on the facts of this case and asks the panel members what they think of psychiatrists. The biochemist says he would bow to their scientific expertise, a teacher says they contradict each other all the time, a sales manager says he thinks they're all wacky and hopes he never has to be treated by one, another says his mother was under psychiatric care all of her adult life and never seemed to get any better. Two other prospective jurors admit that someone close to them has been molested and they don't think they could give Franklin a fair chance. Smith excuses them.

Several sketch artists have come into the courtroom, most of them already in the building for Salcido and looking for a chance to double up, and during a recess they tape their sketches of the judge and jurors on a wall outside the courtroom. Television cameras move in to capture the images for their picture-deprived audiences and reporters intone solemnly into microphones that jury selection has begun today in the Franklin case. Several panelists are drawn to the light and crane their necks to look at the colored depictions of themselves on the wall. Smith hears about the incident and is not at all happy and reminds the panel sternly that they should talk to no one, including the reporters in the courtroom, about the case. The reporters get the message too.

October 24, 1990—Wednesday

Horngrad makes a number of motions before the jury is brought in, all of which Smith denies outright. Most of the press is across the hall watching the closing arguments in the Salcido case, where the Sonoma County prosecutor, pointing to the gruesome photographs of the youthful victims on the wall, is arguing stridently that the defendant was on a "mission to kill," and even Salcido's attorney describes his client as a "mad, crazy killer."

So far the attorneys in Franklin have been mute, attentively watching the panel members respond to the judge's questions. Today they begin questioning the prospective jurors in panels of twelve, not only to discover those who should be excused for cause but to determine who to strike when that time comes.

Tipton goes first. She sees voir dire, as do most lawyers, as an opportunity to establish rapport with the prospective jurors and to begin to educate (or indoctrinate) them on her theory of the case. She stands and introduces herself and Morse and Cassandro, who also rise and, hands clasped in front of them, look pleasantly at the panel. Then she moves over in front of the jury box and, in the guise of questions, begins talking to them about her case. Her presence is commanding: she is poised and self-assured, but not arrogant; her voice is strong and smooth, yet, at moments, almost supplicative. She looks each juror in the eye in turn, as if for an instant it is just the two of them in the courtroom. She calmly asks them if they can handle a case involving a murder of a young girl, if they will hold it against her if she asks questions about oral copulation and sexual misconduct and private parts, and whether they think it's unfair that there doesn't have to be sexual intercourse to constitute a lewd and lascivious act. She is asking them to trust her to get them through this horrible nightmare not of their (or her) making; she is apologizing in advance for the pain they are going to feel.

Then Tipton turns to the source of her greatest worry: Do any of them have a hard time believing that a person could remember an incident after having forgotten it for twenty years? She is looking for a juror who will talk about repression and educate the other jurors, who will start building a consensus in favor of the concept. Nancy Salazar, a young, prematurely gray-haired, plump psychiatric nurse, explains that the mind blocks out memories when they are too painful. She unhesitatingly believes these memories can be reliable when they return. Tipton nods encouragingly as Nancy talks, then asks other panelists one by one if they agree with Nancy.

Tipton asks the panel members if they think it would be impossible for an adult to recall what they saw at age eight or nine, whether a child's memory is any less reliable than an adult's. Nancy Salazar says that kids are basically honest and that observations of a child, while they might be remembered differently, are not less credible than those of an adult. Tipton obtains agreement from the panel that if a boy and a man at a baseball game witness the same home run, they could both recall it accurately twenty years later.

Then she turns to the other half of her equation: a repressed memory probably won't have all the details or specifics of a normal memory. She wants it both ways: a repressed memory is as credible as a normal memory, but you shouldn't expect as much clarity or specificity in it as in a normal memory. She asks the panel to affirm that just because someone has a repressed memory for twenty years doesn't mean she is crazy.

Tipton asks if the jurors believe that child molesters can come in all shapes, colors, and sizes, and Horngrad objects. Smith sustains the objection, but her point is made: Don't be deceived by Franklin's appearance.

Horngrad now rises and introduces himself, his partner, and the defendant, George Franklin. As usual, he is unfailingly polite, the ultimate gentleman, addressing Peggy as "Madam Clerk," speaking courteously to Tipton, deferentially to the judge.

Through questions he begins to educate the panel on the alternate theories of his case: Isn't it possible that a person might have a motive to fabricate a charge such as this for reasons personal to herself? For financial reasons? Isn't it possible that a person could believe the memory to be true but in fact have created a false memory? Hasn't everybody on the panel had an experience where their mind played a trick on them, where they thought something had happened to them and it really hadn't? Can't kids make accusations that are not true?

Horngrad varies the baseball example: What if the boy was too small to actually see the home run but heard his father talk about the hit over the years? Isn't it possible that as an adult he could come to believe he had seen the home run and describe the blast as if he had actually seen it?

Horngrad works in his humor: Is there anyone on the panel who has any trouble with lawyers? Everyone laughs, including the judge and Franklin.

The panel members agree with Horngrad that a memory may be affected by subsequent life experiences.

One panelist replies with great candor that he has heard of the case and has a gut feeling that the woman is telling the truth: Why would a daughter make up a charge like this against her father if it weren't true? He would have to hear an answer to this question before he would change his mind. Smith excuses him on the spot.

Judge Smith asks if anyone needs more than fifty minutes for lunch, and one panelist responds nastily that yeah, she needs about four hours because she needs to go to the office and do some work, she has a business to run. Others on the panel snicker in sympathy and admiration for her guts.

October 25, 1990—Thursday

The process continues. Panels of twelve are brought in and the same questions asked over again although at one point Smith indicates he will take over the questioning if the lawyers don't speed it up.

Horngrad hammers away at the presumption of innocence, making each panel member agree that his client is cloaked in this presumption and will continue to wear this cloak throughout the trial until the very end. Some jurors glance over at Franklin, as if expecting to see the cloak around his shoulders. Horngrad brings them back to the Rule of Reason: Decisions must be based on the evidence, on rational analysis, not on emotions or feelings.

Horngrad tiptoes around the false memory theory. He admits that the children were raised by poor parents in a tumultuous, fractious household and suggests that the false memory might have been created out of a conscious or unconscious desire to get even. Every time he says "fractious," Tipton thinks sarcastically, "Don't you mean fractured? As in George Jr.'s broken nose?"

In the hallway, Morse jests with a local female reporter that they need to get a "looker" on the jury to keep the men happy.

The reporter snorts. Morse is pissed about an elderly woman on a panel who said that she thinks that child molestation shouldn't be dealt with in the courts. "Hey," he asks sarcastically, "maybe it shouldn't be against the law to rape eighty-one-year-old ladies either."

Tipton continues to ask about the shapes and sizes of child molesters, until finally Wachtel asks the judge to declare a mistrial or cite her for misconduct. Smith chides her and she stops, but she's established that it takes two, or three, men to handle her. Of the main players so far, she is the only woman. The others, except for Horngrad, are gray-haired men. When her eyes narrow in concentration, she resembles a wolverine. One local male reporter refers to her respectfully as a "tough broad"; a female says she is actually quite friendly but has an "icy streak in her."

October 29, 1990—Monday

Court is not in session on Friday, so questioning of the prospective jurors continues on Monday. The word in the press room is that the jury will be selected on Wednesday morning and that opening statements will follow immediately thereafter. Mary Jane Larkin, Susan's teacher, is rumored to be the leadoff witness for the prosecution.

Smith announces that he is going on a two-week vacation beginning December 4 and if the case isn't finished by then he intends to declare a two-week recess. If they choose, the parties can have another judge assigned at this time. Both lawyers are shocked, rolling their eyes at the press as they walk back to their tables. Tipton, the most visibly upset, tries to propose other options, but Smith won't hear them. Neither side wants to risk the hazards of going through the pre-trial motions again, so they both agree to keep Smith.

Smith also announces he intends to unseal all the records once the jury is seated. Both Horngrad and Tipton protest vigorously. Smith agrees to ABC's request to allow a pool camera one shot of George Franklin entering the courtroom.

The betting in the press room is for a hung jury. No one can envision how twelve people could reach the same conclusion in this bizarre case. Eileen was damn credible at the prelim, particularly when she said, "I've always loved my father"—that's just the sort of sick twist that smacks of reality—but there are just too many loose ends, imponderables. Now, if the prosecution can corroborate her testimony or link Franklin through physical evidence, or if there is testimony that he sexually abused his daughters, that would be a different matter. If they try him for incest, they might be able to convict him of murder.

The press is also running a "ghoul pool" on Salcido: reporters buy chances on when the jury will return and what the verdict will be.

From the bench, Judge Smith anticipates an interesting trial and is particularly looking forward to the psychiatric testimony. If he had to predict at this point, he would guess a guilty verdict.

October 31, 1990—Wednesday

The trial begins on Halloween. The day fails to break over the site where Susan Nason's body was found; the dark, thick fog hovers at the top of the ridge, close to the entrance to Skylawn Memorial Park, and spills down the hillside past the gravel pulloff and the grove of cypress trees toward the reservoir, enfolding everything on the way in a black, watery embrace.

Opening day brings a plethora of reporters to the Hall of Justice and they begin lining up outside the courtroom at 7:30 A.M. Vince has allocated thirteen seats for the press, but three times that number are in attendance. Places in line are saved while coffee and doughnuts are retrieved. Stringers for east coast papers arrive and try to catch up on what's going on. Members of the interested public begin to show up around 8:00 and Vince forms them into a separate line.

In keeping with tradition, the employees in the clerk's office come to work in their Halloween costumes: ghouls, cowgirls, fireflies, Neil Sedaka's calendar girls, witches, coconuts, and spider people.

At a few minutes after 9:00, Peggy calls the roll of the fifty-nine jurors and all but two are present. Vince searches for them unsuccessfully in the hallway. Peggy calls the names of twelve jurors and they file one by one into the jury box. The prosecution has the first strike. Tipton, in consultation with Morse, who is seated next to her, strikes an engineer who said he was skeptical about repression. Cecilia Cordero, a secretary from Daly City, replaces him in the jury box. Horngrad strikes a woman with language problems. Mary Dolan, a middle-aged loan analyst who has sat on two previous juries and is obviously displeased about being here, is called to replace her.

Tipton excuses a biochemist. She is way too opinionated. Pamela Doughton, a black woman from East Palo Alto, replaces her.

Horngrad then stuns the courtroom by announcing that he is satisfied with the jury and will not exercise a challenge, even though he has nineteen left. It is a bold move: he is in effect saying to the world, to the jurors in particular, I am so confident of our case that I believe that almost any twelve reasonable people will find my client innocent. This case is about justice, not psychology. His high-risk strategy is also designed to make Tipton appear insecure about her case if she continues to strike jurors while Horngrad stands pat.

In one sense, Horngrad's task is the less difficult of the two. He has only to convince one juror of George Franklin's innocence and Franklin cannot be convicted. Tipton, on the other hand, has to convince all twelve people of Franklin's guilt in order to convict him. Horngrad looks to the black woman as a possible defense juror. Minorities and poor people are generally considered to be more sympathetic to the defense, and as the only black on the panel, it would be difficult for Tipton to strike her. Horngrad also stands pat because he doesn't see the remaining panel members as being any more favorable to his client than the ones in the box.

Tipton is clearly taken aback by Horngrad's move. She cannot match it: there are several other panelists that must go.

She consults hurriedly with Morse, then excuses juror number twelve, the CPA. A computer programmer takes the accountant's place.

Horngrad announces again that he is satisfied with the jury.

Tipton strikes number one, a computer consultant. He looks disappointed, personally offended. Michelle Merrill, an attractive woman in her thirties from well-to-do Woodside, takes his place. Merrill, a graphic designer, teacher, and Buddhist lay priest, has been very outspoken in favor of the theory of repression.

Horngrad passes again.

Tipton strikes the savings and loan examiner who doesn't believe in repression. Beth Anderson*, a registered nurse with red hair, takes her place. Tipton strikes the computer programmer and Robert Folger, a quality assurance manager, takes her place. So far Tipton is striking those in highly analytical professions.

Horngrad passes again.

Tipton excuses a man with a pregnant wife and a newborn at home, much to everyone's relief. A firefighter takes his place.

Horngrad passes again.

Tipton excuses the firefighter. Oliver Scholle takes his place.

Ollie Scholle (both names rhyme with "trolley") works as the senior vice-president of a major bank in San Francisco and lives in Hillsborough, a wealthy city south of San Francisco. He has never served on a jury before and looks forward to the service as a challenge and a new experience.

Tipton hesitates over Scholle. Normally, a banker would be a good juror in a criminal case, but she's not sure about him for a murder case. Morse urges her to keep him. Tipton also hesitates over Merrill, the lay priest, who she sees as a definite wild card. Merrill could go either way, and whichever way she went, she would most probably not be budged. She could easily hold out 11–1 and probably take others along with her.

Despite her reservations, Tipton accepts the jury. Heads turn toward the jury box, eyes pass over the newly anointed: one doctor, two nurses, three teachers, one banker, one securities analyst, one quality assurance manager, one loan analyst, one claims analyst, and an executive secretary. Eight women and four men. Eleven whites and one black. All solid middle class, most with children. No gas station attendants or truck drivers or welfare recipients; no self-made men, no cowboys or painters. Four alternates are quickly selected.

The press, forever second-guessing, is amazed that Horngrad has left on Nancy Salazar, the psychiatric nurse, and Alger Chapman, the pediatrician who admitted that someone in his family had been molested as a child. Most predict the doctor will be the foreman, or perhaps the lay priest.

Judge Smith is pleased with the jury. The jurors all seem intelligent, without a loser among them. He swears them in, sealing them to their duty. Now they are members of the cast, starring members in a way, except that they cannot speak again until the very end unless they raise their hand or write a note. When they say, "I will," to the oath, they are irrevocably committed to the long, strange journey which lies ahead.

Smith outlines the scenes of the play for the jurors, from opening to closing arguments, then admonishes them not to form an opinion as to the guilt or innocence during the course of the trial—their job now is simply to ingest all the information, not process it. And they shouldn't even say hello to the lawyers in the elevator. Court will be in session Monday through Thursday, 9:00 A.M. to 5:00 P.M., one morning recess and one afternoon recess for fifteen minutes each. If they have any problems, let the bailiff know.

Smith recesses the court until 10:00 A.M., at which time the opening statements will begin.

ACROSS THE HALL, THE SALCIDO JURY COMES IN: GUILTY ON SEVEN counts of first-degree murder. In a few days the penalty phase will begin. The Sonoma County prosecutor speaks into the lights and microphones downstairs and proclaims his determination to have Salcido put to death. "If not now," he demands of the cameras, "when?"

Child murderers and molesters are at the bottom of the jail's social ladder, and Salcido gets knocked around by the other inmates within hours of his conviction.

THE SPECTATORS ARE SEATED AND QUIET WHEN THE judge finally directs Vince to bring the jury in. "Jurors for department nine!" he yells into the hallway. Slowly they file in: Margie Lee, the schoolteacher, on the far end of the first row, Michelle Merrill, the lay priest, behind her, Nancy Salazar, the psychiatric nurse, in the second row next to banker Ollie Scholle, the pediatrician, Alger Chapman, in the middle of the front row, Robert Folger, the middle-aged quality assurance manager, and Peter Nori, the handsome securities analyst, close to the door. Mary Dolan, the loan analyst, is missing and Vince has to go find her. Half of the first row of the gallery has been reserved for the victim's family: a minister sits with Margaret, Don, and Shirley Nason. They know few actual details of the killing. In 1969 Margaret begged the cops to stop when they began describing the specifics.

For opening arguments, Tipton is wearing a trim, navy blue suit and a blouse with a bow. The Dianne Feinstein look, a reporter quips. Her blonde hair is neatly feathered back around her ears and a few bangs fall loosely on her forehead. Her mouth is set in determination. She is ready. She has been working fourteen-hour days for three months and at last the preparation is over, the action at hand. She enjoys arguing in front of a jury, laying out the central themes of the struggle and arranging the facts into persuasive patterns. She is very pleased with this jury.

"Are you prepared to make your opening statement at this time, Miss Tipton?" Judge Smith asks, looking directly down at her without expression.

"Yes, your honor, I am," she replies, rising from her seat.

She walks slowly, deliberately, over to the jury box, stopping only a few feet short of the rail.

"I ask each of you to come with me," she begins in a low, smooth voice, "to come back with me twenty-one years ago and meet two little girls, Susan Nason and Eileen Franklin. Two little girls who in 1969 were best of friends, playmates, and who on September 22nd of 1969, played together for the very last time. Because on September 22nd, 1969, one of those two little girls, Susan Nason, was brutally molested and murdered. And the other little girl was forced to witness that molestation and murder committed by her father, George Thomas Franklin."

The spectators have grown quiet. It is almost impossible to hear Tipton. She is talking only to the twelve people right in front of her—even the judge has difficulty hearing her—as if nothing exists outside their shared space. Her voice, her manner, are soothing but compelling, commanding but seductive, as if she is a teacher telling her students a story, a fairy tale, as if she is trying to open their minds to their imaginations, their hearts. One almost expects to hear the words, *Once upon a time, there were two little girls* . . .

She introduces the first little girl.

"Susie was born on September 27, 1960," Tipton begins. "So, on the 22nd of September, 1969, she was five days shy of her ninth birthday. She was about four feet five inches tall, weighed about sixty pounds. Had brownish blond hair with a little bit of reddish tinge and a lot of freckles across her nose. Her teacher in fourth grade was Mrs. Larkin."

Then she introduces the second little girl, who will become the heroine. "Eileen was an eight-year-old girl with bright red hair, lots of freckles, in the fourth grade of Foster City Elementary School, but not in the same class as Susan."

Tipton pauses and walks to Peggy's table, picks something up, and returns. The jury's eyes follow her closely.

"I would like to show you Susan Nason," she says, holding up a photo to the jurors, slowly turning it so they can all see the young girl with the freckles and gap-toothed smile. She wants her audience to see and feel the youthful innocence, the goodness, the smallness, the sweetness of the little girl, just before her death. She wants to imprint the image in their minds.

"This is Susan as she looked before she was murdered. And this is the child whose murder trial we are here for today."

The tale continues: *On that day some twenty years ago the first little girl had gone to school and when it was time to go home, she noticed that another girl had forgotten her shoes. In those days, little girls wore their good shoes to school and brought their tennis shoes with them for gym.*

"Well, Celia had forgotten to take her shoes home and Susie thought it would be nice to take them to her. So she said to her teacher, Mrs. Larkin, 'Can I bring Celia's shoes to her?' Mrs. Larkin said, 'Sure, as long as you go home first.'"

When the little girl got home, her mother was there to greet her, and the little girl asked her mother if she could take her friend's shoes home to her. Believing that her daughter knew where her friend lived, her mother said, "Yes, you may," but warned her to come right home afterwards.

The little girl, who was wearing a blue print dress with jean shorts underneath and little brown shoes and white socks and a silver ring, took the bag and started happily for her friend's house. But the little girl was mistaken about where her friend lived and walked up to the wrong door. A nice lady there gave her directions, and finally the little girl found the right house.

"She rang the doorbell," Tipton says ominously. "Celia answered. She gave Celia the shoes and then she left. This was the last good deed Susan Nason would do."

Franklin is sitting still, staring without expression. When he turns to look at someone or something, his head rotates as if on a swivel.

The second little girl lived right around the corner from the first little girl, and the two girls were best friends and played together all the time. On that very afternoon the second little girl was out playing, but not alone. She was with her father, and they were going for a ride in his van which had a platform and mattress in the back. You see, her father was a fireman, and he was around home a lot on his days off and he often took his favorite daughter with him on errands.

"And as Eileen and her father drove around the corner, Eileen spotted her little friend Susie and she was excited and she said" (here Tipton imitates a little girl's voice), "Daddy, there's Susie, can we stop and pick her up? Can Susie come with us?"

The father stopped the van and Eileen called and motioned excitedly for her best friend to come in the van with her, and the little girl got in.

Tipton's voice takes on a childish lilt as she describes the girls playing and romping on the mattress in the van as it drove into the hills.

The second little girl watched as they drove past the blue lakes, which she had seen many times before and which she thought were very, very pretty. The girls were having so much fun they didn't notice when the father pulled over and parked the van and they continued to play.

Then the father got out and stood outside the van and smoked a cigarette and the next thing the little girl saw was her father laying on top of her best friend. Susie was on her back, her dress pulled up, her arms pinned over her head and her little legs spread apart as the evil father thrust back and forth on top of her.

"She heard her little friend whimpering and crying" (here Tipton's voice breaks), "and she heard her say, 'Stop, no.' And then Eileen heard her father say, 'Now, Susie. Now, Susie.' What she saw terrified her and she rolled up in a ball and hid her head. She didn't want to look."

Susan's grandmother's hand flies up to her mouth as if she wants Tipton to stop talking, and then she turns and stares long and hard at George Franklin, as if she would pierce his heart with a thousand daggers.

"What was happening to Susan Nason was the last time, the last time that Susan Nason would feel the touch of human hands. And the touch she felt was not one of love and affection or playfulness." Here Tipton pauses and turns slowly to look at George Franklin, inviting the jury to see for themselves the monster/troll in the white hair and glasses and blue suit. "It was a touch of lust and perversion."

The first little girl fled the van, crying and upset, and ran down a trail to a small open space. The evil father, realizing the little girl would tell on him, followed her down. The daughter watched from beside the van as her father picked up a rock and walked to where her friend was crouching. The daughter cried out and her friend looked over at her and their eyes met and then her friend looked up and saw the father holding the rock and raised her hand to protect herself.

Margaret Nason lowers her head and begins to cry. The minister puts his arms around her shoulders.

But "Susie's fate was sealed."

The second little girl turned away but heard the sound of the rock crushing her friend's skull.

"For Eileen the terror had just begun," Tipton continues, forcing the jury to deal with the specifics. "She saw what her father had done. She saw the blood. She saw the human tissue. She saw the crushed skull. She saw the hair, the clump of hair, and she saw the limp, lifeless body of her friend. She also saw her friend's hand, her right hand, and on that hand she saw both damage to the hand and she saw her middle finger of that hand, the little silver ring which had been crushed as well."

Margaret's shoulders are heaving and she is sobbing. Don is looking down and away, his heavy brows pulled down as if to contain a wild fury. Tipton is now pacing slowly back and forth in front of the jury box, holding each juror's eyes for half a second, as if to force them to accept the reality of her words. The jurors' heads move back and forth with her as she paces.

The second little girl began to run, but her fiendish father caught her and told her if she told what she saw people would blame her and think she was crazy and they would lock her up like they had her mother and he would have to kill her.

As the little girl and her wicked father drove away in the van she thought of her friend alone in the dark, so cold and scared. When the little girl got home, she was shaking and felt sick and went straight to bed. From that day until a short time ago, that little girl buried deep in her mind the horror of what she had seen that day.

The first little girl's ninth birthday came and went and nobody knew what had happened to her, except of course the evil father, who wasn't saying, and his daughter, but she had forgotten all about it.

"No one, it seemed, had witnessed her disappearance. It was as though she had vanished into thin air."

Finally, two months later, a forester was poking around on the side of a hill and found the little girl's body hidden beneath a mattress.

"All that was left of Susan was her skull, her skeletal remains and a small amount of mummified skin on her hips, her hands, and one foot."

Franklin has stopped writing and is sitting back in his chair, staring. Occasionally the corners of his mouth twitch up in that strange smile.

Twenty years went by and no one ever found out who killed the little girl. Then one day, when the little girl's friend had grown up and married and had two children of her own, she was sitting on a couch with her baby boy on her lap and she looked over at her daughter who had blue eyes and freckles just like Susie and saw her father standing over her with a rock in his hands.

Tipton holds the pictures of Susan and of Eileen's daughter side by side in front of the jury, then lays them down on the rail of the jury box. She tells the jury how Eileen had gradually recovered more details of the memory and begun telling people. She had lied to her brother and mother, but that was because she was confused. Finally, her husband had called the police.

Tipton describes how George Franklin, the defendant, had damned himself with his own behavior: He gave his wife a bloody shirt and asked her to wash it, and in a grisly celebration of his horrible deed, he drove to the little girl's grave on the one-year anniversary of her death.

Tipton stops pacing and stands squarely in front of the jury box, pausing, the storyteller coming to the end of her story. Her voice drops almost to a whisper.

This horrible tale has spun on for twenty years now, twenty years in which the second little girl has carried the horror of the deed deep in her mind; twenty years in which the murdered girl's parents have lived without knowing what happened to her; twenty years in which the monster has roamed wild and free; and now it is time to bring the tale to a close, for the jury to write an ending in which right and justice finally prevail; to convict the fiend of the crime and seal him away in a dark cave forever.

"Thank you," she says quietly and walks back to her seat. Morse, who has been watching closely, catches her eye with a look of approval. The jury sits stock still.

Smith declares a five-minute recess.

Few of the reporters leave their seats. Vince, who is trying hard to deal fairly with the press, has decreed that the media seats can't be saved during the breaks, so bladders and editors will have to wait. The excluded reporters, hovering in the doorway like predators, have already complained loudly to Vince and their editors. The seated scribes complain about how softly Tipton spoke and they compare notes on Franklin's graveside visit: this is the first anyone has heard the story and it will make a juicy headline for tomorrow's article. While the visit is certainly odd, no one can quite put a finger on the nature of the inference it raises about Franklin's guilt.

HORNGRAD, DRESSED IN A DARK GRAY SUIT, RISES TO ADDRESS THE jury. He does not approach the jury box, but stands back by the defense table. The courtroom is still heavy with the tale of death and evil and perversion and pain, and one wonders how he can hope to dispel it, how he can rise in good faith to defend the monster at his side.

Horngrad tries to wean the jury from the tale. Certainly it is horrible that a young girl was murdered, but that doesn't mean George Franklin did it. The jury must bring their rational processes to bear on the evidence to be presented, they must analyze the evidence piece by piece. They must think, not feel. Don't believe in fairy tales, believe in facts.

The whole case against his client, he argues, is an "improbable tale" by a single witness of an event she claimed to have witnessed twenty-one years ago. There will be no other evidence tying Mr. Franklin to this charge.

Her story is constantly changing to suit the evidence and to meet the requirements of the law and she tells different versions to different people at different times. And the reason for the different versions is because she wants to persuade her listener of the truth of the story.

Horngrad proceeds, calmly and methodically, to give a series of examples of how Eileen's story evolved and why it evolved as it did. First, she supposedly recovered the memory in January 1989, and although she is in therapy with two therapists at the time, she doesn't tell one (Katherine Rieder) at all and when she tells the other (Kirk Barrett) in March or May, depending on which version of Eileen's you believe, she asks him, "If I tell you something, do you promise you will believe me?" and then tells him that she saw her father kill Susan Nason; but Kirk Barrett will say that when she told him of the killing, *she could not make out the face of the killer.*

In the next version of the story, she tells her brother George in August that she had recovered the story under hypnosis, then in September or October she tells the same story to her mother, and when her mother, an attorney, tells her that hypnosis would disable her as a witness, she drops the hypnosis from the story.

That's that way the story evolves: she learns something that contradicts what she has said, so she changes the story to fit the new fact.

The most telling example of how Eileen changes the story involves her older sister Janice. Originally, Eileen said she was alone in the van with her father when she spotted Susan. In the next version, Janice was in the van with them and her father told her to get out of the van when they stopped to pick up Susan. In the third version, Janice is outside the van. Why is Janice now out of the van? Eileen testified that Janice told her in 1986 that she had gone to the police in 1984 about her belief that her father killed Susan and that she, Eileen, had scoffed at her older sister. When Janice is told in 1989 that there is a police report about the 1984 incident, Eileen drops Janice back out of the story because obviously Janice would have told the police in 1984 that she had been in the van and she had never done that.

Horngrad goes round and round with Janice-in-the-van, Janice-out-of-the-van, until he almost appears confused himself about the number of versions of Janice's whereabouts. He mocks the claim that the two sisters have not discussed the case.

Horngrad insists that every fact that Eileen will give about the killing—the crushed ring, Susan's clothes, the injuries to the head—each and every one of them was in the public domain. So the two primary supports relied on by the prosecution—a second witness and facts only a witness could know—don't exist, and all you have is a free-floating, constantly changing story.

Horngrad talks about the "Today Show" and the changes Eileen made in her story after that was aired: suddenly morning changed to afternoon, before school to after school; the bumpy road becomes Highway 92; the deep dark forest becomes a pulloff with a few trees in front of it; the "I remember Dad taking the mattress out of the van" becomes "I kind of remember Dad maybe trying to take the mattress out of the van, but I'm not sure," because the "Today Show" showed old footage of a box spring obviously too large to fit in a van.

Don't you see? Horngrad is saying. Everything changes as she learns new facts. *Think* about it, *think* about it, he urges. Can this free-floating, unstable, shifting, uncorroborated memory possibly constitute proof beyond a reasonable doubt?

Why all the changes? Well, now Eileen is a celebrity, giving interviews on television and to the *San Francisco Chronicle* and the *Los Angeles Times,* and she is besieged with so many book and movie offers that she has to hire an L.A. entertainment attorney to handle them. The movie deal is worth half a million dollars if her father is convicted, nothing if he is found innocent. She and Barry, who is refusing to come to the trial for some reason, are right now in Switzerland quarreling about what they are going to do with all the money.

Horngrad mocks Leah's story of the bloody shirt: she had no

memory of a bloody shirt at the preliminary hearing and now suddenly she does. Just an embittered wife after a fractious divorce.

The graveside visit?

"If the prosecution attempts to introduce that kind of evidence, I assure you," he says confidently, almost arrogantly, "we will meet it and we'll defeat it. That never happened, ladies and gentlemen. That never happened."

Then Horngrad suggests a reason besides greed that Eileen has come forward with this improbable tale. He won't argue with the psychiatrist for the prosecution that a person can repress a memory, but any psychiatrist who tells you that a repressed memory is possible will also tell you that it is equally true that one can harbor a false memory.

In 1969 there was plenty of information to seep into Eileen's unconscious. In those days, Foster City was a small community and it had been saturated for weeks, months, with information about the crime, first after Susan disappeared, then again after she was found.

Now Horngrad introduces the jury, without any particular force, to his alternate theory of the murder: the man in the blue station wagon. A few days before Susan disappeared, a young girl named Ann Hobbs was approached by a man in a blue station wagon who wanted to kidnap and molest her. On September 22, 1969, a man in a blue station wagon was seen lurking in Susan's neighborhood. He was never found.

In conclusion, Horngrad comes back to the beginning: This memory of Eileen's stands all alone and every fact in it has been in the public domain for twenty years. She is either lying or her story is a false memory, a trick of the mind. Either way, her testimony cannot stand as proof beyond a reasonable doubt of George Franklin's guilt.

"Mr. Franklin is not the killer."

"LADIES AND GENTLEMEN," JUDGE SMITH INTONES TO THE JURY AFter Horngrad has finished, "remember that you heard absolutely no evidence. You heard the attorneys tell you how they think the case will progress."

* * *

THE CONSENSUS IN THE PRESS ROOM FAVORS HORNGRAD, ALTHOUGH opinions vary dramatically. Two reporters change their predictions from a hung jury to not guilty. Tipton was good, but Horngrad superbly exploited all the weak points of her case and planted the seeds of doubt. One San Francisco reporter comments that Tipton gave a very powerful, emotional argument because she has no physical evidence to back herself up, which was also why she knocked all the scientific types off the jury. Another reporter thinks Tipton's tone of voice was perfect, particularly when she imitated the voice of an eight-year-old girl, and that Horngrad sounded defensive. Two other reporters, one from a Sacramento paper and the other from a wire service, think Tipton clearly carried the day.

Judge Smith wasn't impressed with Tipton's approach. She appeared nervous and her voice was way too low. He understands the idea of the personal conversation between lawyer and jury, but her presentation came out sounding like she was talking to a wall. Horngrad began poorly, but improved.

Ollie the banker was impressed with the prosecutor. She is obviously convinced of Franklin's guilt and intends to do her darndest in a very professional way to convince the jury of that fact. Horngrad seemed to be trying to slant things a little.

Nancy Salazar was also impressed with Tipton's presentation, but she is determined to keep an open mind.

43

October 31, 1990—Wednesday, continued

MARY JANE LARKIN ARRIVES AT THE COURTHOUSE at 9:00 A.M. sharp and waits in the hallway all morning. Elaine Tipton has asked her not to talk to anyone, so she stays away from the cafeteria to avoid any familiar faces. She is excited about the trial, but sorry that she will have to miss her favorite holiday at school. Her costume was all ready—a clown suit made by her daughter who teaches home economics. The other teachers joked how lucky she was to miss all the extra work, but she sees it as missing all the fun.

Bryan Cassandro has talked to her several times on the phone and visited her once in the classroom. She thinks he's cute with his blue eyes and gray hair. She likes Tipton, finds her warm and reassuring and very competent. She has never wavered in her belief that George Franklin is guilty—why else would that little girl have gotten in a car? She has kept her class up to date on the progress of the case, and when she had her red hair brightened a little for her court appearance, the kids noticed and teased her. This is her last year teaching and she is sad already.

Tipton is leading off with Mary Jane because she wants Susan to be alive and present in the courtroom an instant or two before she is murdered. What better person to breathe life into the little victim than her fourth-grade teacher?

When Cassandro steps into the corridor and motions Mary Jane into the courtroom, she is very nervous. She pauses in front of the clerk's desk to be sworn in and Peggy asks her to spell her name. "Capital M-a-r-y, capital J-a-n-e, capital L-a-r-k-i-n." "My God," she thinks when she sits down, "I spelled it just like a fourth-grader." She looks over at the Nasons in the first row. Don is shocking: she remembers him as tall and thin and handsome in the three-piece suit he wore when he came to school, and now he is so fat she barely recognizes him. Margaret looks the same, except older. She told herself she wasn't going to look at George Franklin—she remembers the young fireman with the brownish-red hair coming to school when Janice was in her class—but she can't help herself and steals a glance his way the minute she sits down. He is staring at her blankly; she sees nothing there to suggest he's not a murderer. He looks much older than fifty-one.

Mary Jane sits too close to the microphone and her voice rattles the courtroom; Tipton asks her to move back a little. Mary Jane explains that she has been a teacher since 1948 and was Susan's teacher in the fall of 1969. She points to Foster City Elementary School on a color-coded diagram of the neighborhood. Then Tipton hands her Exhibit 3, previously shown to the jury, and Mary Jane identifies the girl in the photograph as Susan Nason. Tipton establishes that school let out at 3:00 P.M. in those days, and then asks her a key question: Did Mary Jane talk to her class about strangers?

"Yes," Mary Jane says emphatically, "we always instructed our children to never talk to strangers and never to get into strangers' cars."

Mary Jane relates the events of the afternoon Susan disappeared, and describes coming to school that evening with the other teachers and searching the grounds and bushes around the building and finding no trace of Susan.

Tipton's last question: Were any of her students, or any fourth-graders for that matter, ever interviewed by the police? No, she says, not to her knowledge.

On cross-examination, Wachtel asks Mary Jane if she can say for sure what time school let out that day twenty years ago. No, she can't, she has to admit, not for sure. He asks her about the vividness of her memory, and whether her students in 1969 talked about the murder. The adults did, Mary Jane says, but she doesn't remember any of children talking about Susan after she was gone.

On re-direct, edging in the door that Wachtel has opened, Tipton asks why her memory of that day is so vivid. Mary Jane pauses for a second, searching for a way to explain what seems so obvious.

"Well, you know, in all my years of teaching I have never had a child disappear before or never had anything happen to a child in my classroom."

She tells the jury that every time she opened her grade book after Susan disappeared, she marked an absent by Susan's name until her body was found. When she started a new page in January, she dropped her name altogether.

After Mary Jane leaves the stand, she frets a little about her equivocation over the time school let out. At school the next day, she gives a full report of her courtroom experience to the teachers and her students.

Tipton's next witness is Susan's mother. In the past several months Tipton has developed tremendous respect and admiration for Margaret Nason. The woman's wound, while not as raw as it must have been twenty years ago, is still very present and deep. Margaret has been very good to Tipton, always supportive, never questioning why something had or hadn't happened. "Just tell me what I can do," she would say, "and I'll do it." During the course of the trial, Tipton would come back to her office at the end of the day and find messages of praise and encouragement from Margaret on her answering machine.

Tipton sensed that Margaret's basic approach to life was somewhat compliant: Put up with everything you can possibly put up with and eventually something good will come out of it. Closure for Margaret seemed to have come when Eileen made her charge. The inexplicable became explicable. She seemed immensely relieved that there was nothing she could have done to prevent the horrible fate that befell her daughter. The verdict wasn't going to make or break Margaret.

Wearing a pearl necklace and the same turquoise dress she wore at the prelim, Margaret rises from her seat and walks with a fragile dignity to the witness stand. She folds her hands in her lap and a nervous, lopsided smile plays across her face as Tipton asks her questions. She describes Susan's hair as blonde to light brown and begins crying when Tipton hands her Exhibit 3, the photo of Susan. Tipton gets her a glass of water. Margaret identifies her old house in Foster City, the one where Don still lives, and the vacant lot across the street, on the diagram. She talks about how she had kept track of her daughters' whereabouts and how often and adamantly she and her husband had warned them not to talk to strangers. Over Wachtel's objections, she says that as far as she knew, Susie had never taken a ride with a stranger.

Margaret relaxes a little as she recounts Susie coming home from school and leaving to take Celia's tennis shoes to her, but her nose reddens and her eyes glisten when she describes how devastated she was when, after riding her bike around the neighborhood for an hour, she finally found Celia home alone.

Tipton wants the jury to feel the depth of the mother's pain and continues to probe the wound. What was Margaret's state of mind after Susie was missing but before she was found?

"Well, it's almost indescribable—to have a child that's missing. To not know if she is hurting, if she is warm, if she is cold, what is happening. It leaves you feeling devastated, absolutely numb, numb with the pain of it."

She weeps again when she describes the crushed condition of her daughter's silver ring when the police showed it to her on December 2, 1969.

On cross-examination, Margaret recovers and has almost a friendly attitude toward Wachtel, answering his questions clearly and precisely in her small, thin voice, as if she would like to help him with his task.

Wachtel is in charge of the blue station wagon theory for the defense, and he must dispel the notion that Susan would never have gotten in a stranger's car. He needs a shadowy stranger lurking around the stage. It is a delicate chore, because if he pushes this woman too hard, if her eyes tear up one more time, everyone in the courtroom, including the jury, will hate him.

Isn't it true that a few days after her daughter had disappeared she said to a reporter that she might go with someone if she thought he was a friend and had something to show her? Yes, but that was after the psychic had come to her house and suggested that answer to her. Isn't it true that she told the police that Susie would go with anybody who had a good little story? Yes.

Wachtel wisely leaves well enough alone, and on re-direct, Tipton has only one question for her: Had she ever suspected, either before or after the body was found, that a friend or neighbor had killed her daughter? The firmness with which Margaret says, "Never," reveals her abandonment of that belief.

All eyes in the jury box watch as Margaret, weeping, walks unsteadily from the stand over to Tipton, who holds her and whispers something comforting to her, then slowly sits her down in her seat in the front row.

Judge Smith declares a recess. When the jury reassembles, he asks them to let Vince know if the television cameras outside the courtroom bother them and he will take care of it.

Celia Oakley enters the courtroom wearing slacks and a man's dress shirt. Her brown hair is shoulder length and straight, her face pleasant. She walks over to Peggy with a determined gait and responds firmly.

Celia has lived up to the promise she showed in Mary Jane Larkin's class when she received all A's. She graduated from Berkeley and is within months of receiving a Ph.D. in mechanical engineering from Stanford University. She lives in a house in the hills above Redwood City with the man she intends to marry after finishing school. Celia has not thought much about Susan Nason over the years; she hasn't wondered what she would be like if she had lived or if her killer would ever be caught. Although Eileen Franklin says that Celia was one of the kids who picked on her and Susan, Celia feels no responsibility for what happened to Susan Nason. She doesn't wonder if Susan might still be alive if she had asked her to come in and play rather than simply accepting the shoes from her. Celia has gone ahead with her life.

Her testimony is brief. She identifies her house on the map which she indicates, to everyone's amusement, is not quite to scale. She tells how Susan came to her house, rang the bell, gave her the shoes, and walked down the sidewalk. It was the last time she saw her. To other questions, she says clearly and firmly, "I don't know," or, "I don't recall."

Now that the jury has visualized Susan carrying out the last good deed of her life and seen in the flesh the beneficiary of that deed, Tipton leaves Susan and moves to the site where her body was allegedly desecrated a short time later. The details of what happened in between will be told later by the leading lady.

Ephe Ray Bottimore hopes this is his last appearance. He has become slightly exasperated at the number of times he has had to come to Redwood City in the past year. Lawyers for both sides took him out to the turnoff and walked down to the small clearing where he found the body and went over everything in great detail with him.

He lumbers past the jury and is sworn in and sits down with a sigh. His bad ears don't pick up Tipton's low, throaty voice, so she has to speak up. The jury laughs when he says that he was nine months old when he first visited the watershed in 1923. The jury likes him. He is a good man in the midst of all this sad, pained craziness.

Tipton wants the jury to have a clear picture of the killing site. She pins to the wall a map of the entire watershed and Bottimore traces the boundaries, the ridges, the lakes, and then marks the location of Highway 92. He points to the turnoff where people frequently stopped to admire the view and describes the day he walked down the trail littered with junk and decided to take a closer look at the box spring. He identifies a series of eleven photographs of various views of the area, including the clearing and the pulloff. Tipton lays the pictures down on the front rail of the jury box. The jurors lean forward to look at them.

Then Tipton brings the grisly crime to center stage. She holds up an enlarged color photograph of the box spring as it lay when Bottimore walked over to it. Through the coils and brush two large black holes in a brownish skull peer out grotesquely. Yes, Bottimore says, that's what he saw when he leaned over for a look. Tipton posts the photograph on a bulletin board on the wall behind him, giving the dark sockets a good view of the proceedings. The press worries about Margaret, who has averted her eyes. Don looks straight ahead into nowhere. Several of the women in the front row of the jury box look shaky.

On cross, Wachtel establishes that traffic was heavy on Highway 92 back in 1969 and that cars drove by the site regularly and there were no trees close to the area.

Bottimore is the last witness of the day. Judge Smith, noting that three members of the jury live on the coast and probably drive on 92 to and from court, admonishes them not to do any independent investigation; i.e., don't stop at the pulloff and look around.

CHILDREN DON'T TRICK OR TREAT IN THE NEIGHBORHOODS OF FOSTER City on Halloween anymore. The Rotary Club sponsors Safe Streets in which several blocks are cordoned off and the kids knock on specific doors and go through haunted houses with their parents.

44

November 1, 1990—Thursday

GEORGE FRANKLIN'S SWAGGER IS STARTING TO IRRI-tate the reporters almost as much as his twitchy smile. He strides into the courtroom, back straight, chin up, rolling slightly from side to side like a sailor. A man in his situation, particularly after yesterday's testimony, should be humble, slow-gaited, staring at the floor. When the jury enters the room, he is one of the first people on his feet.

Tipton is dressed dramatically in a bright red suit and a string of pearls. The blonde on red lends an air of passion to her fierceness. She has bought two new suits for the trial. Unlike Horngrad and his basic blue and gray, she will seldom wear the same outfit twice.

The day begins badly for the defense. Juror Doughton, the black woman, is not present and has informed the court she has a family emergency. Judge Smith recesses for an hour, and at 10:00 A.M. announces that Doughton has called and told the clerk she will come at 12:00. When he suggests that they take lunch now and reconvene at noon, Tipton protests that she is supposed to meet with a witness at 12:00. Smith slaps her down: "Would you suggest I rearrange the affairs of man-kind?"

By 12:06 the juror hasn't arrived and Smith, determined to stay on schedule, announces he is going to select a replacement from the pool of four alternates. Horngrad, seeing his strongest possibility for a holdout (and a hung jury) slipping away, springs to his feet and, reminding the judge he exercised only one peremptory challenge, asks him to try and keep the jury intact. Wouldn't it be too bad, he asks, if they impanel a new juror and Doughton walks in five minutes later? At Horngrad's urging, the judge leaves the bench and tries calling Doughton again, without success. Over Horngrad's objection, Smith directs Peggy to randomly select a new juror.

Wendy Canning is forty-one and a widowed mother of two. She works in a warehouse for a sportswear manufacturer and has short brown hair. A few years back she sat on a jury and voted to impose the death penalty on a man who killed his best friend and his best friend's girlfriend in a drug deal. Wendy has listened carefully to the opening statements: she liked Tipton and thought her very clear and straightforward about what she was going to prove, but Horngrad has definitely made her think maybe the daughter was doing this out of revenge. When Peggy calls her name, Wendy takes the empty seat in the jury box.

The Nason family seats are empty for scene two.

Tipton begins educating the jury in the particulars of the killing. She calls the first two cops on the scene, who describe the initial investigation and the collection of evidence. One cop identifies a rock in a plastic bag as the one found close to the body and holds it up for view. Franklin stares at it intently.

A coroner's investigator testifies that he had put the bones in a body bag for transportation to the morgue. He identifies a clump of light brownish-red hair, a brown child's shoe, and a sock as items recovered at the scene. The items are added to the growing evidence pile on Peggy's desk.

Next Tipton calls Dr. Peter Benson, the pathologist. Just as he is seated, Margaret and Shirley Nason enter the courtroom, causing a stir in the press corps. Tipton, hearing the whispering, turns around, sees the women, and tells them they should leave. Morse follows them out to explain what is about to happen.

Benson's European-tailored blue suit seems to suck the last of the color out of his sallow face. But his voice is loud and clear, stronger than at the prelim. Slowly, efficiently, he and Tipton re-create his autopsy of Susan Nason for the jury. Benson describes opening the body bag containing the remains and identifies a series of color photos of what he saw. In one, the skull is disconnected from the spinal column and lies in the skeleton's lap, and the right hand is sticking forlornly up in the air; the dress is bunched on the upper torso and the tops of the underpants are visible around the edges of the tattered denim cutoffs; the right foot is drawn up close to the right hand, and the left leg is stretched out. A second photo shows the gaping black hole in the back of the skull and a clump of hair lying next to the bone. A third is a closeup of the smashed ring and the right hand without any fingertips. A fourth is a closeup of the left foot with a white bobby sock on it. Benson explains that the skull was empty and the body devoid of organs; he notes the insect and animal damage to what little tissue remained on the skeleton.

One by one Tipton holds up clear plastic bags containing various items found on or near the body and Benson identifies them: the multicolored dress, the cutoff shorts, a pair of white underpants, a white sock, a brown buckle shoe, the distorted ring, a gray rock with jagged edges, and a mass of hair containing a fingernail.

Before showing an item to Benson, Tipton takes the evidence over to the defense table for Wachtel's inspection, her deliberate moves being tracked by every eye in the courtroom (except Peggy, who is organizing exhibits and answering the phone, which rings shrilly). On one occasion, Judge Smith observes Franklin leering at the female district attorney as she lays the evidence on the table. He is so struck by the strange sight of a man on trial for the murder of a young girl leering at the female prosecutor that he makes a note of it in his trial notebook.

Almost whispering, Wachtel says, "No objection," as each

item is offered. After the evidence is admitted, Tipton lays it on the rail in front of the jury, trapping the jurors in their box with the grisly evidence of the crime. The retired school-teacher in the first row shrinks back in her chair.

If all that is not enough, Tipton has Benson come down from the stand and identify a plastic, anatomical model of Susan's head which he has constructed from the photographs. The black area at the right rear of the skull represents the dumbbell-shaped hole in her skull. Without being asked, he holds his creation up for the jury to see.

Dr. Benson resumes his seat and opines that either of the two rocks could have caused the injury if it were brought down with sufficient force and that there were most likely two blows to the skull. He identifies photographs showing the injury to the right hand and says that it is very likely that the hand was raised in a defensive gesture to protect the head. The location of the skull injury suggests that Susan's head was bent down when struck and also makes it unlikely that the injury was incurred in a fall. Benson also found bruises on the right hip, which would be consistent with her falling over on her right side after being struck by the rock. Cause of death: accelera-tion and torsion injuries to the brain. Susan probably lost con-sciousness immediately.

On cross, Wachtel asks Benson if he can say what the mini-mum or maximum size of the object causing the injury was, and Benson, slipping out of his usual dour demeanor, cracks: "Well, it wasn't an ice pick and it wasn't a 747." A wave of laughter washes over the courtroom, followed by a deafening silence.

Smith declares a recess, and the press and spectators mill around behind the bar glancing longingly at the grisly photo-graphs on the wall and the bagged items on the rail of the jury box. A few local reporters gingerly slip through the gate and cross into the combat zone, chat with Peggy for a second or two, and walk casually over to the jury box. Other reporters watch to see if Vince is going to call out to them or if Tipton will swoop down to protect her valuable evidence. Nothing happens. Gradually, others follow, somewhat self-consciously.

Hands pick up the vial with the crushed ring and hold it up to the light; a soft female voice comments that the little buckle shoe with the stitching on the strap is like the shoes she wore as a little girl; a man picks up the large rock and says to another reporter, "This must weigh, what, ten pounds?" then holds it high over his head. Others go over to hold the rock and run their fingers along the jagged edges. The discolored underpants lie undisturbed, as does the clump of hair with the fingernail. Somebody pokes cautiously at the blue dress, which is shredded and faded. Conversation stops in front of the photographs: the brown skull with the black sockets looks like a Martian landscape pocked with mysterious explosions; the gray-brown bones look like those of a 1,000-year-old mummy; the right hand is wrinkled and dry like parchment, and the boneless fingers stick out at crooked angles; tiny teeth poke out from the skull peering through the bed springs; the legs look like old turkey bones. This creature can't possibly be the young girl shown in Exhibit 3.

The model skull is mounted on a red plastic stand and sits on Peggy's exhibit table staring straight ahead at the jury. Each half details different parts of the head. The eye on the right half is open, has a black iris, and is surrounded by strips of red muscle which run down the cheeks, over the chin, along the jaw line, and down the neck. On the left side, the red eye is closed, and black and red veins sprout from the top of the skull and flow down the side of the skull and around the ear. Arteries course along the side of the chin and curve up in between the nose and left eye. A thick black carotid artery streaks down the left side of the neck. The nose and the ears are flesh-colored. A jagged black hole in the rear replicates the fracture. A small latch at the top of the skull unhooks and the head swings open to reveal the inside of the brain and brain stem.

In a reversal of positions, Tipton and her cops and Horngrad and his detective mill around in the spectator section watching the reporters pick through the gruesome evidence in a crafts-fair-like atmosphere.

Tipton isn't finished with her gruesome parade. She calls to the stand the dentist who made Susan's retainer. Horngrad had previously argued that there was no need for the dentist since he was willing to concede that the body found below the pulloff on December 2, 1969, was that of Susan Nason, but Tipton wants to put him on anyway.

The dentist testifies that in 1969 he found a match between the casts he made of Susan's jaws and the jaws recovered at the grave site. Tipton hands him the retainer and he identifies it as the one he made for Susan and says that in 1969 he had fitted it onto the skull. The small retainer is admitted into evidence.

Gordon Penfold, chief of the Foster City Department of Public Safety in 1969 and currently sales manager for a security company, testifies that he took the ring, a piece from the dress, and a shoe to the Nasons, and Margaret Nason identified them as belonging to her daughter.

At 4:00 P.M. Tipton tells the judge that she has no further witnesses for the day. In a bench conference, Smith chastises her for not having witnesses ready to testify and warns her not to let it happen again. With Smith's permission, she then passes around to the jury all the photographs that have been admitted in the past two days.

Smith recesses the case until Monday morning.

Juror Mary Dolan is irritated that the prosecution doesn't have additional testimony ready and that court is not in session on Friday. She wants to get the case over with and return to work.

Ollie Scholle is shaken up by the physical evidence; the remains have left him feeling bad. He welcomes the three-day break.

November 2, 1990—Friday

The word went out late yesterday that Eileen Franklin will take the stand Monday morning and the press room is humming with anticipation. People are concerned about the seating—can you imagine telling your editor that you missed the star witness's testimony? At what unholy hour will they have to show up Monday morning to get a seat? Some complain about the bailiff Vince, others stick up for him.

The door swings open and in walks Judge Smith, dressed in a blue suit and flowery tie. He greets everyone pleasantly, many by name. He has received calls from angry editors and has decided to lift the seating problem from the shoulders of his beleaguered bailiff. How can we resolve this seating problem? he asks congenially in his soft, gentlemanly voice. After overcoming an initial reticence—judges don't often come into the press room—the reporters toss out their ideas, which add up to: more reserved seats for the press. Smith leads the reporters up to the courtroom to talk about the specifics. Finally, everyone agrees: half of the seats will be reserved for the press *and* reporters will be allowed to sit in any empty public seats.

45

Tipton spent Friday, Saturday, and Sunday with Eileen. She wanted to go over the details of her sexual abuse with her and prepare her for cross-examination, which she knew would be brutal. She could tell Eileen was putting a tremendous amount of energy into just holding herself together, and recounting the Stan Smith rape was especially agonizing for her. Tipton almost fell apart when Eileen said that after the rape she got up from the table, found her panties, and went looking for her father.

On Friday and Saturday the two women went to dinner together after working most of the day in Tipton's office. They also made appointments with Tipton's hairdresser and, on the way to the shop, they listened to a spiritual by the Neville Brothers on the car radio. Eileen talked a lot about God and putting Him back in her life, and on Sunday the two women attended Tipton's church. Eileen felt they were both praying for the same thing.

Eileen had flown over alone from Zurich a few days earlier. She had stayed with Barry's relatives in Los Angeles before driving up to the bay area in her big green Mercedes, the car which, with its CD playing and its roof open, made her feel like the "Queen of the Road." According to her, she thought about her brother and sisters as she drove, deciding which of them had let her down and which were going to be in or out of her life in the future: Kate was definitely out—she was despicable, as was her husband; after what her brother had done, she wasn't sure she wanted his friendship anymore; she wanted to be close to Diana after the trial, but could not accept her indecision or her friendliness with George Jr.

November 5, 1990—Monday

On the first day of trial, Tipton showed the jury the live Susan Nason, on the second day the dead Susan Nason; now she is going to lay out the facts of what happened in between. She knows that her case will most likely turn on what transpires in scene three: If the jury believes Eileen, Tipton has a damn good shot at a conviction; if the jury doesn't, her case is finished. She has no other evidence linking George Franklin to the crime.

Strategically, Tipton needs to present Eileen in just the right light as the damaged victim. If she appears too impaired, too shaky or confused or unstable, the jury may find it difficult to believe her story, at least beyond a reasonable doubt. If she appears too normal, an ordinary thirty-year-old wife and mother of two, the jury may doubt her accounts of physical and sexual abuse or, more importantly, that she witnessed a brutal murder of her best friend.

Tipton is glad that Barry isn't here to mess with Eileen's mind. Horngrad sent him a letter requesting his appearance and promising airfare, but Barry replied that he was too busy working and taking care of his children to attend the trial.

The press starts lining up outside the door shortly after 7:00 A.M. Eileen's author, a New York writer with whom she has signed an agreement to write "The Eileen Franklin-Lipsker Story," is there, as is her screenwriter, who works for MGM and who for some reason insists on using a false name in the courthouse. The *Los Angeles Times* is present as well as a stringer for the *New York Times* and four sketch artists. Television cameras are on their way.

It is going to be a long wait. Although Judge Smith previously read Eileen's accounts of sexual abuse in Exhibit A, Horngrad is entitled to have her testify to the specifics under oath before the judge issues a final ruling on the admissibility of this testimony. Outside the presence of the jury and the public, Eileen will testify to four instances of uncharged conduct: the digital penetration, the Stan Smith rape, the bathtub sodomy, and Franklin's abuse of Eileen's daughter. If Smith affirms his earlier ruling, she will testify to the same incidents a few hours later in front of the jury and the press.

At 8:25 Eileen appears in the hallway with Morse and Cassandro. She is wearing an emerald green silk dress with an ivory lace bib that spreads out over her front and back like a giant doily. Her hair is thoroughly brushed out behind a white headband and falls the width and length of her back. She appears thinner. Her heavily made-up eyes look plaintively into space as she walks by the cameras. According to Eileen, she purposely and carefully thought out this new look. She didn't want the jury to see a powerful woman of beauty, fashion, and sophistication; she wanted them to see a plain woman, a vulnerable, soft woman who had once had a best friend and then lost her. She doesn't want a look that will mask or hide her pain from the jury.

In the hallway, a female reporter snipes at the contrivance of Eileen's childlike Victorian look, which she considers to be a major departure from the sophisticated Chanel look so evident at the preliminary hearing. Another reporter says Eileen looks just like Alice in Wonderland. There is a definite resemblance.

Margaret and Don and Shirley are in the front row. The two

counsel tables have been moved apart. The men are dressed in blues and grays and Tipton, in sharp contrast to Eileen, is wearing a severely cut black suit. Franklin's closely trimmed hair makes his big ears even larger. The lines in his face are now symmetrical fissures arcing from the rise of his cheekbones to his chin.

After being sworn in, Eileen sits in the witness chair and looks straight ahead. Tipton comes out from behind the table and, after a few preliminaries, asks Eileen to identify her house and her school on the diagram. Then she asks her what she looked like in fourth grade. With a beguiling smile, Eileen says: "I was a goofy-looking redhead with lots of freckles and buck teeth." Her fourth-grade school picture is admitted into evidence.

In great detail, Eileen describes the van her father was driving on September 22, 1969. She uses her hands and looks directly at the jury, as if she's been coached. Eileen also remembers the license plate: VXJ 707. Pictures of the inside and outside of the van are admitted into evidence.

In her steady, husky voice Tipton asks Eileen if her father is present in the courtroom. Eileen looks directly at him and smiles as she describes him as the man in the dark suit and striped tie and adds that, even with his gray hair, he looks similar to the way he did in 1969 when he was thirty years old.

What was your relationship with your father, Tipton asks.

"I was his favorite," Eileen says after a solemn pause, but with the barest hint of pride. "I went a lot of places with him that he didn't take my sisters and brother. I spent a lot more time with him."

"Did he ever tell you why you were his favorite?"

"Well," Eileen begins, her head tilted down, looking up at Tipton shyly from under her brow, "he told me that when I was born and he first saw me and I had red hair on my head, he just thought I was a beautiful baby and that he fell in love with me."

Tipton leads Eileen through the beginning of her story. She says she doesn't know where they were going in the van when they saw Susie on the sidewalk and she also doesn't remember if Janice was in the van with them or not, although, when Tipton asks her a second time, she says she has a vague recollection of seeing or speaking with Janice, she's just not sure.

As Eileen describes seeing Susie on the sidewalk that day she is excited, then her voice wavers and drops as she describes her father stopping to pick Susie up. She looks down and slightly to her left. Her eyes come to rest on her lap.

Eileen goes to the map and describes in specific detail the route they drove after picking up Susie: up Balclutha and around in front of Foster City School and on to Foster City Boulevard. Tipton asks if her father said anything when they passed the school.

"I remember him saying something about 'hooky.' . . ."

". . . Do you know whether this excursion took place in the morning or afternoon?" Tipton asks, intentionally exposing a weakness.

"Well, I think it happened in the afternoon."

"Why is that?"

Eileen's pause this time is long and dramatic. Finally she says quietly: "Because of what happened afterward."

Tipton lets the words hang in the air for a few seconds before continuing the journey up the hill toward the lakes.

Eileen transforms into an eight-year-old girl when she describes the activities in the back of the van while her father drove and drank beer: "Susie and I were bouncing on the bed in the back and just playing," she says lightly; and again when she describes driving by Crystal Springs Reservoir, which she had seen many times as a child when her father would drive her to Half Moon Bay: "I used to think that the reservoirs were the most beautiful color, just a beautiful color, and so I liked to look at them."

Then the vehicle came to a stop and Eileen remembers "feeling the ground underneath the van become bumpy." She didn't look out the window to see where they were and she and Susie kept playing, bouncing on the mattress.

"What happened after your father stopped the van?" Tipton asks.

". . . I remember looking out and seeing him standing off

in the distance, drinking beer and, I think, smoking a cigarette, and the—the sliding door was opened."

The girls kept playing, bouncing on the mattress, until her father got in and starting playing with them in the back. Then Eileen went to the front seat and looked at them.

"Who was on the mattress?"

Eileen's face falls and she pauses dramatically.

"Susan was."

"Where was your father?"

"He was on top of her."

"Can you describe for us what he was doing?"

Eileen pauses again. Her eyes drop, she looks down at her hands, then up at the ceiling, then back down at her lap; finally, her head still down, she glances up at Tipton.

"He had her little arms up above her head, and he was holding them with one of his hands. He was holding them at the wrists with one of his hands. And she was laying down. He had his elbows on either side of her, and her legs were open and hanging off the edge of the mattress and the platform; and her legs were dangling down, but not reaching the floor."

"Was just the upper part of her torso lying back on the mattress?"

"Yes."

"Where was your father's body?"

"He was on top of her and between her legs."

"When you say he had her arms above her head, what do you mean by that? Where were her arms in relation to the mattress?"

"Her arms were all the way up, like this," Eileen says, crossing her arms over her head, "and he was holding them down against the mattress."

"Was he using one hand or two?"

"He was using one hand."

"Was his body moving in any way?"

"Yes," she says very softly.

"Can you describe the way his body was moving?"

"He was pushing his pelvis against hers, back and forth."

"Was he in between her legs?"

"Yes."

"Did you notice anything about her clothing at that time?"

"I noticed that her dress was up. I noticed that there was something white underneath her dress."

Eileen remembers that he kept his pants on.

"Do you recall whether or not you observed his zipper being zipped or unzipped?"

"I saw him fastening his pants afterwards."

The account is compelling in its detail, mesmerizing in its rhythm, and Horngrad moves to interrupt the flow by objecting to Tipton's next question as vague. Smith overrules him.

"What if anything was Susie doing with her arms?"

"She was struggling."

"Was she able to get free?"

"No."

"Did you hear her making any noises?"

Eileen's eyes redden and become moist, her voice wavers.

"She was sort of whimpering, just . . ."

"Did you hear her say anything?"

"She said, 'No, don't.' And she said, 'Stop.' "

"Did you hear your father say anything?"

"He said, 'Now, Susie.' "

"Can you repeat for us whatever inflection you recall your father using when he said that?"

Eileen pauses as if to practice in her head, then says in an admonishing tone, *"Now,* Susie."

Horngrad finally gets an objection sustained. Eileen looks at him coolly when he rises to argue.

Tipton asks her what she did after she had walked over behind the driver's seat. Her voice drops to a whisper.

"I curled up in a ball on the floor."

"You curled up in a ball—I'm sorry, you'll have to keep your—"

Eileen cuts her off and repeats slowly, angrily, "I-curled-up-in-a-ball-on-the-floor."

Tipton asks her how she felt. "Scared," she replies shakily. Tipton brings her a glass of water.

Eileen continues: she sat in the van and watched Susie "walking very cautiously, not surefootedly," down a decline. Then she got out of the van and stood on an unpaved surface by the door and saw her father down to her left. She is very specific about the view:

"If I looked straight ahead, I could see a road curving around. To my right, I could see a decline. There was a little hill to the right. There were trees. Off in the distance, there were three trees in a row—it was very rural—and a hill with more trees all around and that panoramic type of setting." She does not mention the lakes she liked so much as a child and which would have dominated the view from where she was standing.

Tipton asks Eileen to stand and draw the van on a large piece of paper on the wall behind her. She details in the doors and windows and the positions of everybody during the molestation. Then she draws in Susie and her father down the hill and herself by the door. Tipton asks her what position Susie was in.

"Susie was sitting down, but in a hunched position, with her knees up closer to her chest. She was on a little—a little—a bump, a rock—something that was down below, but was slightly elevated."

Eileen estimated her to be about fifteen or twenty feet away.

"What was she doing as she sat crouched in the position you've described?"

"She was crying."

"Crying?"

"She was crying."

"What was the next thing you saw?"

Eileen closes her eyes for a second or two, as if gathering strength.

"The next thing I saw was my father approaching Susan. He had his hands up above his head, with a rock in his hands, and I screamed or I yelled. I did something which caused Susie to look up at me."

"Do you recall that moment when she looked up at you?" Tipton asks gently.

Eileen lowers her eyes: "Yes," she says softly.

"Can you describe it?"

"My eyes meshed with hers."

Tipton asks her what happened next.

"She looked over at my father, and she just—she—just, her hands flew up," Eileen says in a wavering voice, and at that moment her own hands fly up to her head. Her father was striding toward Susie.

"I saw his right leg leading and his arms up and then start to come down, and I either turned away or closed my eyes."

"What was the next thing you saw or heard?"

"The next thing that I heard was two blows."

"What did that sound like, Eileen?"

Eileen pauses, her eyes closed in indescribable pain.

"It was terrible," she says, crying. "It sounded like a crack and a splat."

"Were there two separate sounds that you heard?" Tipton asks, needing to corroborate Benson's testimony about two blows.

"Yes."

The last question was clearly improper as leading, but Horngrad held his peace, obviously not wanting to risk alienating the jury by appearing insensitive to Eileen's pain.

Then, almost as dramatic relief, Tipton creates a play within the play. She has Eileen direct the killing scene in front of the witness stand. A chair is the van, Eileen plays herself, Morse plays Franklin, and Tipton plays Susie. Eileen directs everyone to the right spot and describes what happened up to the moment of the killing. The press twitters over Morse playing Franklin.

Eileen describes briefly how she looked at Susan's head and saw unattached hair and blood and something whitish. As she tells how she also saw Susan's bloody hand and a smashed ring, her voice drops so low that Smith, only a few feet away, has to ask her to speak up.

The sight was so terrifying, she says, that she ran screaming up the hill toward the van and her father grabbed her and knocked her down and her face hit the ground.

"You've got to stop this," he commanded. "It's over now."

Then he put her on his knee and told her she would have to forget what had happened because it had been her idea for Susie to get in the van and people would blame her. Her screaming turned to crying.

"He said that no one would ever believe me," Eileen says, turning away slowly from the mike to face the jury, her voice rising dramatically. "He said that they would put me away; and he said, 'If you don't stop this, then I'll have to kill you.' He said I couldn't tell anyone."

What was your reaction to the threats, Tipton asks.

"Well, I was terrified," Eileen says in a strong and earnest voice, "but I absolutely believed him."

Eileen tells how she went back to the van and her father came and got a small shovel and she heard it striking the dirt down the hill to the left of Susie's body. He came back to the van and tried to pull a mattress or a mattress pad out of the back. He got angry when she wouldn't help him.

"Do you remember what he said?"

"Yes. He said, 'God damn it, Eileen.'"

"Was that a phrase that he used with you often?"

"I would say the 'God damn it,' he used often; but he rarely called me 'Eileen.'"

"What did he usually call you?"

"He usually called me 'Pooh,' as in Winnie-the-Pooh, Pooh Bear." Her eyes flutter when she says "Pooh."

She watched him take the "bulky rectangular object" down below. She saw him crouching or bending over near Susan's body and it looked like he was picking up rocks and putting them on or next to her. He said something like "I know I can make it look like she fell," or "I know it will look like she fell."

Tipton asks if Eileen remembers anything about what Susie was wearing.

Eileen turns and looks directly at the jury. "She was wearing, I think, a dress. I would describe it as an A-line dress, which is . . . like a triangular type of shape, and it was only when I could remember seeing her walk down the hill that I could remember seeing her with that dress. Before that, I don't remember if it was a dress or a skirt."

Does Eileen recall any clothing on any other part of her body? Yes, she says, looking down and to her left again, Susie had on white socks and shoes. "What color were the shoes?"

"They were brown." Then, apparently figuring out what Tipton is after, Eileen adds: "I thought that—I thought that he threw her shoe or her shoes."

Tipton moves to clean up the morning-to-afternoon change and asks Eileen what time of day this happened. It was "in the late afternoon because the sun was coming down," Eileen responds. She knows she had originally told the investigators it happened in the morning, but in fact she had been very unsure and "I stated at least once, if not repeatedly, that I just did not know what time it was."

Her current explanation for changing from morning to afternoon is different from the one offered at the preliminary hearing. Now she says that she really didn't remember what time it was, but she did remember her father saying the word "hooky" as they drove by the school, which made her think as an adult that they must have been on their way to school.

She thinks the police came to her door that night. She saw them when her father opened the door, and she turned around and went back to her bed. The police never questioned her about Susie's disappearance.

Tipton introduces the repression theme by asking Eileen whether during her childhood, adolescence, or early adulthood she has ever remembered the murder of Susan Nason. No, replies Eileen without hesitation.

Now that the tale is told, Tipton needs to anchor it, put it in a setting that makes sense, so that her story is not, as Horngrad would say, a "free-floating memory." The setting is the Franklin family, a family that was, as George Jr. had said to Bob Morse in an interview, "The Family from Hell." Tipton wants to introduce the jury to a critical underlying theme of the drama, one whose dimensions and variations will play out in the courtroom over the next few weeks as the mother and children walk in to face the father and take the stand and describe, or demonstrate, the results of their membership in that family. One reporter will quip that this subtext has all the elements of a John Bradshaw Special: alcoholism, violence, abuse, denial, co-dependence, secrecy, etc. What it all has to do with whether George Franklin murdered Susan Nason is another question, but it makes for compelling theater.

Eileen testifies that the Franklin household was very violent and scary and most of the violence was perpetrated by her father, but also occasionally by her mother. Before the murder, she probably received less abuse than anyone with the exception of Diana, and after the murder she was beaten only once. When she was eleven, a newscaster used the words "electoral vote," and she asked her father what an "electrical vote" was. He started yelling at her and she ran up the stairs and he pulled her down and punched her and said never to call it an electrical vote again.

Janice and George received the worst beatings.

"I remember one [time] in particular with George, that he just kept screaming and screaming and screaming, and my father wouldn't stop. I remember one with Janice, in the house on Beach Park," she continues, her face starting to shake, "where she was screaming inhumanly—she was screaming so much and so loudly—and I could hear her—her body being slammed into the wall."

George Franklin is looking down and writing on his pad as Eileen describes the beatings. Smith refuses Horngrad's request to approach the bench for a conference.

Leah was the recipient of the violence only "on a few occasions." Once her face was bloodied and another time when Eileen was six or seven she walked into her parents' bedroom and saw her father holding a handgun to her mother's head. Eileen's eyes close as she relates the gun incident.

As for Leah, her mothering during this time period was "nonexistent." Eileen recalls how her mother went into a mental hospital because, as her father had told her, the children had given her a nervous breakdown.

Eileen describes the effects of all this violence and neglect on her. Her lips quiver and her eyes cloud over with pain as she recalls that she was "very much alone" after Susan died and she didn't have a real friend again until seventh grade, and then she made lots of friends as a junior in high school.

When Tipton asks her if she hid anywhere as a child, Eileen is curiously amused: she looks up and laughs and recounts how a few times a week she would hide in "closets, behind pieces of furniture, under the laundry pile, in cupboards, anywhere that looked like the right size to hide."

Eileen also used to count on her fingers walking home from school, over and over again. Tipton asks her to demonstrate.

"Do I have to?" she asks, in amused embarrassment. She turns to the jury, smiling like a little girl, and almost flirtatiously taps out a rhythm on her thumb and fingers for them.

She also used to pull her hair out in grade school when she felt bored, anxious, or nervous, and (here she turns and looks straight at the jury, biting her lip) she tried to commit suicide in high school by taking an overdose of Seconal. She looks down in shame when she admits she never graduated from high school.

Tipton is finished with the generic family violence and physical abuse and is now ready to completely unmask the evil hybrid sitting only a few feet away from her. She warns Eileen, and the jury, that she is going to ask about sexual abuse. She proceeds through the incidents chronologically.

The first incident occurred when she was five.

"I was in the bathtub with him [her father], and there was bubble bath in there, and we were playing. And he lifted me and sat me on his lap, and I felt something hard; and then he moved me and positioned me, and I felt it—I felt him trying to push something hard into my bottom." Her voice rises when she says "bottom," in a note of challenge.

"Do you know what that was?"

"Yes."

"As an adult?"

"Yes."

"What was it?" Tipton demands of her.

Eileen suddenly flares and she leans forward and demands

bitterly of Tipton, as if she is now the torturer, the betrayer: "Do I *have* to?"

"If you can," Tipton responds coolly. "What part of his anatomy?"

"It was his penis," Eileen says flatly, suddenly recovered.

Several of the female jurors are looking away from her, at the far wall.

"What did you do when that happened?"

"I yelped."

"And what did he do?"

"Took the back of my head and pushed it under the water."

"What happened next?"

"When I came up my mother came into the room."

"Did she do anything about it?"

"No."

The next incident occurred when she was seven; her father was having a drink and tickling her, and he put his hand into her underwear and his finger into her vagina.

Finally, the rape episode. She was with her father and Stan Smith, her godfather, in a room or a flat somewhere. As she begins to tell what happened, she shuts her eyes for a few seconds, then forces them open. Her face is congested, her eyes full of tears.

"I remember laying down on something like a table. My dad was standing above me, behind. He had one of his hands across my mouth and had my head pinned facing to my left, and with his other hand he was holding my shoulder down. But I couldn't move my arms, and I couldn't move my legs. Somehow my legs were forced open."

She was wearing a dress or a skirt and she could see Stan Smith standing without clothes between her legs.

"Did you see his penis?"

"Yes."

"As an adult, can you describe: Was it erect or not?"

"Yes, it was."

Tipton asks her if Stan Smith said anything, and she looks away and down and begins crying, using a Kleenex for her tears. Yes, she heard him say: "She's going to like this, huh, George?", and both of them had laughed.

George Franklin is absolutely still, except for his head which tilts for an instant to look at the jury and then back at Eileen.

Then Stan raped her while her father held her mouth closed and pushed her shoulder down.

"Can you describe what you experienced physically at that time?"

"It's the most excruciating pain, intense excruciating pain of just being ripped open."

Tipton, not willing to settle for just that, asks: "Do you know what orifice of your body was being penetrated?"

"I don't know. It was so painful, I couldn't—I can't associate it with anything except the pain."

"Do you recall the next thing that you remember after the pain?"

"I remember it being over, but I don't know how I got from the point of feeling this terrible pain and then it was over."

Looking straight at the jury, Eileen describes in low tones how she had put on her shoes and underwear and gone looking for her father.

The sketchers stop sketching and stare at Eileen as she tells the details of her rape; but the scribblers keep scribbling, and the minute she finishes, several of them slip out to transmit their stories.

Elaine Tipton is now convinced that the jury will not acquit George Franklin of the murder of Susan Nason. Like all good trial attorneys, she has been keeping an eye on the jurors, reading their reaction to various witnesses and items of evidence, to herself. She wants to know who in the box is getting it and who isn't. She had glanced over at the jurors as Eileen gave her account of the Stan Smith rape. Juror number twelve, Robert Folger, the soft-looking quality assurance manager and the one closest to her, whom Tipton figured was at best a lukewarm juror for the prosecution, was leaning forward in his seat glaring angrily at George Franklin; when Eileen finished her account, he sat back with a look of complete revulsion on his face. Tipton knows he will never vote to find Franklin innocent, to declare him a free man and turn him loose in society. At the very worst, she will have an 11–1 hung jury.

As he listened to the story of the rape, Ollie Scholle, the Republican banker, thought back on the way Eileen had smiled at her father and he was a little taken aback: How could she possibly have any good feelings toward a father who had done all those things to her? But he believes her. For one thing, it would have to be terribly difficult to get up on the stand and reveal those details in front of strangers, and why would anyone tell those horrible stories if they weren't true? It just doesn't seem like she was faking it; her appearance, her strained voice, the pained expression on her face, she was obviously agonizing over what she was saying. She could have been acting, but Ollie just didn't think so.

Ollie studies Franklin and is bothered by the lack of any expression on his face. "Could he have committed this horrible crime?" he asks himself. "Absolutely!"

During the sexual abuse testimony Judge Smith glanced at juror Mary Dolan, the woman who had been horrified about being on the jury in the first place, and wondered how well she was handling the testimony. Actually, she was doing okay. At first, Dolan thought Eileen was a little too controlled, but then she loosened up. She is impressed with the way Eileen's story matches the forensic evidence: the ring, the rock, the dress, everything fits.

When Mary looks at George Franklin, she doesn't like what she sees either, which is nothing. A couple of times during Eileen's testimony, she noticed a more pleasant expression in his eyes, but he was blank when the pictures of the little girl, either alive or dead, were shown. He looked up at the jurors occasionally, and Mary tried to read him, to see inside him, but she could see nothing except the complete lack of any feeling. She knows some of the other female jurors get scared when he looks at them, but not her; she just looks right back.

Tipton has Eileen explain the change in the rape story. Drawing a circle in the air, Eileen says that during the rape she had seen a Jimi Hendrix poster on the wall and focused on the outline of his big afro and assumed that it was a black person.

When she tried to fill in the details, the pain would become so intense she would have to stop thinking about it. As the months passed, she realized that it probably wasn't a black man because her father didn't have any black friends. As she concentrated, the details of the face filled in.

"And whose face was it?"

"It was my godfather."

"Is he black or white?"

"White."

Tipton now returns to the last critical piece of the puzzle: How had Eileen remembered the murder? Why had it come back to her after twenty years? Eileen turns to face the jury and explains that she had been sitting on a sofa in the family room giving her son a bottle while her daughter and two friends were huddled on the floor coloring. Her daughter said something like, "Isn't that right, Mommy?"

"That caused me to look down at her, and she looked up at me; and when our eyes met, I remembered seeing my father with the rock above his head and seeing Susan sitting there."

"What is it that you remember seeing Susan do in that first initial memory you've described?"

"I remember her eyes meeting mine," Eileen says smiling, "her blue eyes meeting mine."

It's a few minutes before noon and Tipton asks permission to show the jury the photographs of Susan and Jessica before the lunch recess. Smith assents and the two photographs are passed among the jury. Eileen closes her eyes, holds still for a moment, then has a drink of water. Franklin and Horngrad confer while the jurors study the photographs.

Smith declares a recess until 2:00 P.M. and warns the jury not to talk to anybody they don't know.

A few minutes before 2:00, six cameras are waiting for Eileen to enter the courtroom, but she slips in the back way. She sits in front of the bar and her father leans back in his chair and glances at her.

Eileen tells the jury that, although she couldn't see the features of the man holding the rock, she knew it was her father from the silhouette, the shape of his body. The image frightened and confused her and, as more pieces of the memory came back to her in random fashion over the next several months, she resisted remembering them. She didn't know that it was humanly possible for a person to have a memory of something so significant that she hadn't remembered before.

Tipton shifts her focus to an area of some vulnerability for the prosecution: What and whom she had told about the memory and its recovery.

Eileen tells the jury that in June she told Kirk Barrett, her therapist, of the memory. She was scared she might be a little crazy and have to be locked up like her mother had been, so she made him promise that he would not question her in any way. Barrett told her she should trust and believe her memory and not be afraid because she had already survived the trauma.

In August, she told George Jr. of the memory and said that she had recovered it while under hypnosis. She told Janice about what she saw in September, and in October she told her mother of the memory. When her mother appeared baffled, she explained that she had been hypnotized. Later, Eileen called her and told her she hadn't really been hypnotized.

Horngrad punctuates the narrative with a litany of hearsay objections. At first, Eileen appears irritated with him, then she drops her chin in her hand in a doleful pose while the attorneys argue and the judge rules.

She explains that, on her mother's advice, she contacted a criminal attorney in Los Angeles who told her if she had been hypnotized she would be an invalid witness.

In mid-November she told Barry of her murder memory and he contacted the San Mateo County District Attorney's Office.

After her father's arrest, she called George Jr. and said she really hadn't been hypnotized and asked him not to tell the cops she said she had. Then she said, "Screw it!" She wanted the truth out so there would be nothing to worry about.

Having dealt with the fact that Eileen lied to her mother and her brother, Tipton turns to her last area of weakness, perhaps the most serious in her view: the book and movie deals. She needs to give the jury some reason why a woman in Eileen's situation would tell her story on national television and enter into book and movie deals for her life story, some reason other than fame and fortune. In each case the rationale is the same: Eileen didn't want to do it, but someone else talked her into it by convincing her that it would give her control of the situation.

With an edge in her voice, Eileen describes for the jury the barrage of phone calls and unwanted visitors and television crews on her doorstep and how it had been such a terrible invasion of her privacy. Her face fills with disgust as she describes the authors, agents, personal managers, and literary agents who pursued her, and how she had had to hire a lawyer to handle them all. As for the movie people, she had learned that they could make a movie about her saying anything they wanted, but that if she gave the rights to one production company the others would go away and she would then have control over the production and be able to stop the movie from exploiting her, her family, the Nasons, and *her father*. Eileen is no longer the vulnerable violated victim who had just wanted to do the right thing: now her teeth are bared, and when she talks about docudramas her voice is dripping venom and reeking of hatred. She never, ever wanted a book or movie made; she simply had no choice.

When Tipton asks her about money, her voice suddenly turns soft and weary, as if to emphasize how horribly misunderstood she is. Of the $50,000 advance for the book, she paid $5,000 in attorneys' fees and gave $45,000 to a charity called Children of the Night. Of the $10,000 option money on the movie, she gave $5,000 to Children of the Night and $5,000 to the Children's Home Society.

Horngrad is objecting to every other question and is winning at least half, substantially better than his average.

Eileen stakes out the moral high ground with a vengeance when Tipton asks her if she intends to make any money from having witnessed the death of Susan Nason.

"No," she says dramatically, "because it's wrong, because it —it's putting a price on the truth. It's putting a price on Susan Nason's life. It's putting a price on my relationship with my father, and it's wrong."

She insists that she had never envisioned her story would generate this amount of publicity; perhaps an article in the *San Mateo Times*, the Foster City paper, a little something in the *L.A. Times*, nothing more.

Tipton is close to finishing, but she returns to the confused relationship between Eileen and her father to emphasize that the daughter did not come forward out of a desire for revenge or hatred for her father.

"I—I felt like I loved him," Eileen explains. "I was worried about him. I was sad for him. I was afraid of him."

Now Tipton plays her trump card: the visit by the still-loving daughter to see her murderous father in jail.

Eileen recounts how she told her father that he wasn't a terrible ogre and that she knew he loved her. She describes in a low voice how she urged her father to tell the truth.

"I told him that when I was a child he had always told me that the truth shall set you free and that I think that he meant that for both of us, not just for me, and that I thought that he should tell the truth."

His only response to her plea to confess had been to point silently to a sign on the wall saying that calls could be monitored.

Then Tipton brings out her hammer.

"Did your father ever during this visit insist that you withdraw or recant this false accusation?"

"No."

"Did he ever express any anger or outrage at what you had done?"

"No."

"Did he ever deny to you that he had committed this murder?"

"No."

"What else did you say to him before you left?"

"I said, 'Is there anything that I can do for you?'"

"And what was his response?"

"'There's only—there's one thing that only you can do.'"

"And what were the last words that were spoken between the two of you before you left?"

"He asked me if I would come visit him again."

"Thank you," Tipton says evenly as she turns back to her table, "nothing further."

46

THE PRESS REACTION TO EILEEN'S TESTIMONY VARIES widely. An author from San Francisco finds her very stagey and overly sincere, but admits he is cynical anyway. A newspaper journalist finds Eileen credible and a very good witness. A magazine writer and a daily reporter both agree that Eileen sounds rehearsed on the killing, but much more credible on the molestations. One woman finds her refusal to say the word "penis" to be a contrivance; another thinks it quite natural. One writer for a local daily describes Eileen as having a "moue" face like Brigitte Bardot; she concocts the look of the petulant, pained little girl. She finds her good at playing for the jury, turning and talking to them sincerely at key moments.

Several reporters describe as pure bullshit Eileen's testimony about how violated and put-upon she was by the press. If there ever was a woman who was easy to get hold of, who returned their calls instantly, and who seemed eager to talk, anxious for the attention, it was Eileen Franklin.

While the papers report Eileen's story of the killing in great detail the next day, they are very circumspect about the specifics of the violence and sexual abuse. They report in general terms her claims that she was beaten and sexually abused by her father and raped by her godfather.

"THAT'S A LIE!" JEFF MUNSON SAID TO HIMSELF WHEN HE READ IN the paper that Eileen claimed to have repressed the memory of Susan's murder for twenty years.

Jeff Munson, the gay bank teller who had lived with Eileen in the early eighties, had moved to Southern California and lived with Eileen and Barry for a few months in 1984–85 in Manhattan Beach. In exchange for his board, he did laundry and cleaned house and baby-sat Jessica. Barry had sent most of Eileen's other gay friends packing, but Jeff and Eileen had managed to stay in touch over the years. She was very nice to him, frequently buying him presents and looking out for him. But she complained constantly about her marriage, about how she didn't love Barry—she didn't even like him—and how miserable she was. Jeff begged her to leave her husband, but Eileen, who had been born again, or at least so she claimed, argued that the Bible forbade a woman to leave her husband. Jeff called several ministers and reported back to Eileen that the Bible contained no such prohibition, but she wouldn't budge. She was using religion as an excuse for not leaving, Jeff figured.

Since Eileen had become a mother, she had completely given up drugs and alcohol, and she and Jeff had attended Adult Children of Alcoholics meetings together. She wanted very much to be a good mother, but she spoiled her poor daughter terribly and her house was an absolute pigsty. Jeff found Barry to be a complete jerk: selfish, demanding, arrogant, rude, lacking in the most basic courtesies. Barry was extremely mean to Eileen and the two of them yelled at each other constantly.

Gradually, the tension between Jeff and Eileen grew; from his perspective, she was no longer the person he had known and liked so much in Foster City. She wouldn't leave Barry because she loved the money and the home and the car and the security and the identity it all gave her. She could buy whatever she wanted now. She had sold out. Equally important, she needed someone to hold responsible for her life, and Barry was a perfect scapegoat. The two of them needed each other. She talked one way and acted another, and after a while Jeff couldn't handle the hypocrisy any more. Finally, he moved to his own apartment, and their friendship terminated shortly thereafter when Barry came storming into the restaurant where Jeff worked and yelled at him, calling him a thief in front of customers for not having paid his share of the phone bill.

Now, as Jeff read the articles about Eileen, he remembered quite distinctly an afternoon in December 1985 when he and Eileen were in her house in Manhattan Beach and he was folding clothes while they watched a television talk show. They were talking about their past, their families, and Eileen began telling the story of a childhood friend of hers who had been kidnapped and murdered. Then she said: "I think my father killed her." Just like that. His reaction at the time had been "Wow! Those are bad thoughts and feelings to have about your father," but he hadn't taken her comment too terribly seriously. Now she was saying that she had repressed the memory the whole time and never had even the slightest suspicion over the years that her father had killed her friend. He knew that to be a lie.

Jeff wasn't sure what to do. He didn't want to get involved, but his conscience was nagging at him. She was, after all, lying in a court of law.

AFTER LISTENING TO EILEEN'S TESTIMONY ON DIRECT, HORNGRAD is more convinced than ever that she is backing and filling and concocting in order to strengthen the case against her father. The seventeen hours that she and Tipton supposedly spent together over the weekend were probably more like thirty-five, and it was clear that the two women had done some serious work around the edges to clean up her story. The business about seeing her father put the rock on top of the body, for example: today was the first time that detail ever came up, and wasn't it a coincidence that this new piece of the memory just happened to match Benson's testimony about what he found in the folds of Susan's dress? And now, for the first time, Eileen remembers seeing Susan walking "very cautiously" down the slope in an A-line dress. Horngrad doubts that Tipton actually fed her the specifics, but he can imagine some serious coaching going on; God knows Eileen was desperate to be believed and to have her father convicted and she certainly had a malleable personality. Like the "other murder," he could imagine Morse or Cassandro one day asking Eileen if in fact she hadn't seen her father murder anybody else, and a little while later Eileen comes back and says, Hey guys, guess what?

Horngrad was also convinced that not only did Eileen try to hide Katherine Rieder, the first psychologist, and conceal her statements about hypnosis, but that she had done her best to make her former au pair unavailable. If he was ever going to be able to contradict Eileen on her story of the memory retrieval, he needed to get to someone who had lived with her, and he had looked high and low for the former nanny. He finally tracked her to Switzerland and then North Carolina, but by then she was gone. In Horngrad's mind, Eileen was covering her tracks; God only knows what other games she'd played.

He believes even more strongly in the Gang of Two: in Eileen and Janice sitting down to put this thing together to nail their father. Janice had tried once before and failed because of a lack of evidence and now she was operating from behind her sister. Everyone knows there is no stronger evidence than an eyewitness.

He sees Barry as compulsive and Eileen as hysterical, a natural fit. The hysteric needs someone to take care of her and the compulsive is more than happy to do it. Barry obviously hated George and had a rivalry with him and blamed him for his screwed-up marriage. But while Barry had tried to feed information to Eileen later on, Horngrad didn't see him as part of the original plan. No, it had been Janice and Eileen who got together and said: Okay, this is what we're going to do. He speculates that the two of them had actively worked on conforming Eileen's memory to the known facts.

That is what he believes, but from a strategic point of view, he will have a tough time proving it. His most immediate task is to cross-examine Eileen. Both he and Wachtel felt she had been strong and convincing on direct, and since she is, in effect, the prosecution's whole case, he has to go after her hard to convince the jury that she is simply not worthy of belief. But as in most cases where the eyewitness is the victim, if he pushes too hard he runs the risk of creating sympathy for her. Another problem, this one not so common, is that if he is *too* effective on cross, if he succeeds in turning her into a basket case on the stand, he will end up validating her story through the back door and confirming the damage supposedly done to her by his client. The more pathetic she appears, the more credible her story becomes. It is a nasty dilemma.

In addition to Eileen's statement about the "other murder," Horngrad is thinking of introducing the clip of the television interview Eileen gave in 1979 on her attempted suicide so the jury can see for themselves how anxious she is for attention, how willing she is to reveal her pain to get it, and how accomplished she is in front of a lens, even at age nineteen. But he hesitates, because that pain had to come from somewhere, she would have to have some reason to be so screwed up.

Horngrad is absolutely convinced that Eileen was never molested by her father. Ever. It just didn't happen. But if he ends up disputing the molestations, challenging them directly, and he loses, the jury, by having resolved those issues against him, will be that much more likely to resolve the ultimate issue of the murder against him as well. In terms of the revenge motive, there was certainly enough dysfunction in the family to give her reason to hate her father.

In any event, a direct challenge to the molestations would require putting the defendant on the stand, a risk he can't take. There's always the chance Franklin would put his character in issue and all the rest of the uncharged conduct and pornography would come crashing down on him and then the jury would nail him without hesitation. Smith was too damn close to letting all that stuff in a few weeks ago for Horngrad to give him another opportunity.

Another problem Horngrad has is the constantly evolving nature of Eileen's memory. In the usual case, the witness is stuck with what she says the first time out and any subsequent changes in or inconsistencies with that original version can be used to undermine her entire credibility. Here, though, under the prosecution's theory of the repressed memory, the memory is allowed, or almost expected, to come back in bits and pieces.

It fades and sharpens, is added to and subtracted from. This makes it impossible to wed Eileen to a particular version of the story: when it changes, she can always say, well, it became clearer, or she tried harder to visualize it and saw more or different details. Witness the black man/white man switch. How in the hell do you cross-examine under those circumstances? The only way is to demonstrate that the facts changed whenever another indisputable fact became known to her. Like the time of day. The mattress. The dirt road. Janice in the van, out of the van.

Horngrad has one safety net. He will prove to the jury that everything Eileen told them about the murder is in the public domain. Certainly when the jury sees every fact of her story indexed against the 1969 newspaper articles, they will have a reasonable doubt or two.

47

November 5, 1990—Monday, continued

TIPTON FINISHES HER DIRECT EXAMINATION AROUND 3:30 P.M., leaving little time for Horngrad to get his cross-examination fully under way. He begins by establishing a few apparently stray facts: Eileen hasn't seen her father since 1986, but she and Jessica visited him in Hawaii in 1984 and 1985 and also traveled to Las Vegas with him in 1985. In 1978, Eileen traveled with him to Ensenada in the tan van that is pictured on the wall, license plates VXJ707, and that van with the platform in it had been their living quarters.

Then he abruptly changes direction: Isn't it true that she told her sister Kate that the memory of the murder had come to her in a dream?

"No," Eileen responds emphatically, leaning forward in amazement.

"You never told Kate or her husband that the memory came to you in a dream?"

"No," Eileen replies, "I would never say that," seeming to resent the suggestion that she would ever lie about how the memory came back to her.

Then Horngrad turns to the repression. Eileen testifies that she went into individual therapy with Kirk Barrett in June 1989 because she didn't understand why or how she was having the memory of the murder. She had started therapy with Katherine Rieder in June 1988, but had not told her of the murder memory in several sessions in January after she had recovered it. Eileen had, however, told Rieder in December 1988 of her recently recovered memory of the digital penetration and asked her if it was possible to remember something without ever having remembered it before, and Rieder told her yes, it was possible. How then, Horngrad wants to know, can she claim that the recovery of a repressed memory was a new topic, one she didn't understand, when she asked Kirk Barrett about it in June 1989?

"Actually," Eileen says, "I don't think, until just right now and here, that I ever associated the two."

Judge Smith declares a recess until 9:30 the next morning to give the jurors time to vote in local elections.

November 6, 1990—Tuesday

Today Eileen is wearing a rust-colored pleated skirt and a cream blouse with black buttons, a white velvet belt, and a black headband. It is a different look from Alice in Wonderland, but slightly Victorian, hinting of repressed femininity. One of the reporters thinks she looks like Fergie. Eileen has developed a look of pained tolerance for the cameras.

Tipton is dressed in a mauve suit with a slight western cut and a round collar and a pink blouse and a bow tie. All the male players are in gray suits today, except for Smith in his black robe.

Vince has become strict on press seating, demanding passes

from those he doesn't know. Yesterday a few people had sneaked in and sat in press seats.

On the table in front of Peggy are boxes of all the evidence that has been introduced. The plastic model of Susan's head with one black eye and one red eye sits upright staring straight at the jury.

In what will undoubtedly be the longest, most grueling day of the trial, Horngrad begins slowly by going over the same ground regarding Katherine Rieder. Eileen's consternation over Horngrad's picking, jabbing questions begins to show, but for the most part she stays composed. Her mood shifts continually. When Horngrad hands her a flier from Rieder's office, she looks at him with a big, wide smile and says sweetly, "What do you want me to look at?" When Horngrad pushes too hard, she looks to the judge for help, saying, "I don't understand the question." Sometimes, when Horngrad gets to her, her voice rises to a weak childlike tone. Other times she is cocky and combative.

Soon the questioning becomes tedious and the jurors' attention begins to drift. Horngrad scores with Rieder, but the point is a small one, and the press wonders impatiently when he will roll over the big guns.

Horngrad spends the rest of the morning pounding on one of his strongest points: Eileen is a liar, and the reason she lies is so people will believe her.

Eileen recounts how when her brother had come to visit they joked about the "poor parenting" they had received, and then one day in the kitchen she told him what she had seen.

"Oh, he reacted very strongly," she explains. "He looked shocked, disbelieving. He moved back from me; his mouth fell open."

Eileen had "panicked," and, searching for a way to make the story believable to him, asked, "What if I told you I had remembered it under hypnosis?"

After her father's arrest, she had called Georgie, as she begins to refer to him, and said she had learned that a hypnotically induced statement would be inadmissible and that she hadn't really been hypnotized and would he please not tell anyone that she had said she had been. Then: "Screw it, just tell the truth." Horngrad reads out loud her testimony at the prelim in which she denied ever asking George to lie.

As for the lie to her mother, she still didn't know how to explain her lack of memory of the murder for two decades. Horngrad presses: After two therapists had explained it to her, she still didn't understand? As Eileen explains, her composure begins to crack.

"Well, he [Kirk Barrett] didn't explain it to me. He told me it was possible. But he didn't say: 'This happens all the time or happens to some percentage of the population,' like it's an everyday occurrence.

"I didn't know if I was the third person in the entire civilization of man that had had this thing happen or the three millionth person. I didn't know."

Why had she picked hypnosis as an explanation?

Her answer rushes forth defensively, almost pleadingly. "I think that anything was a better story than saying: 'Here I am, a freak of nature that has this memory.' "

Another reason she lied to her mother was so that both her mother and George Jr. would have the same story.

When Horngrad pauses to flip through his notebook to find a previous quote of hers, she looks beseechingly at the jury, as if to ask, "Can you believe this man?"

Horngrad, as always, is polite in his questioning, never hostile or abusive. His style is to follow up on her answers wherever they might lead and, although he always finds his way back to the beginning, his central point sometimes gets lost in the confusion. The back and forth on hypnosis and lying is tedious, and the question still remains: How serious is the damage? Will the jury decide that if she lied twice in order to be believed, she'll lie again?

Judge Smith excuses the jury for the lunch recess, except for the red-haired nurse who has indicated she wants to speak with him. In private she tells him that she has picked up a bacterial infection in Mexico and is not feeling well. Smith suggests Lomotil and a visit to her doctor over the lunch hour.

Juror Nancy Salazar isn't bothered by the fact that Eileen

lied to her mother and brother about hypnosis. It's something she's seen for years in clinical situations. Eileen was a victim and victims desperately need validation, and so it was completely natural for her to say whatever she needed to say to get her mother and brother to believe her. That's the way victims work.

Salazar is worried about the elderly schoolteacher a few seats away from her who nods off a few minutes after she sits down every day. Another juror has even heard her snore. Nancy thinks of nudging her or mentioning it to someone, but then decides it's not her place. Vince has begun passing the sleeping lady cups of water in an attempt to keep her awake.

Salazar knows that the red-haired nurse was shaken by Eileen's testimony that her father had fallen in love with her the minute he saw her red hair. "I have red hair like hers and I just can't stand it when he looks at me," she told Salazar. The nurse had been taking Kaopectate for diarrhea before Eileen came on the stand and seemed to have it under control; after Eileen's testimony about the red hair, she began taking Maalox.

During his questioning, Horngrad has been standing in various locations in the pit, the area encircled by the witness stand, the jury box, Peggy's table, counsel tables, and the bench. He often stands with his hands behind his back and, tilting forward slightly like an inquiring professor, does a slow dance: one step to the left, pause, one step to the right, pause, one step to the left, hold. Repeat.

Now he is leaning up against a filing cabinet in the far corner of the room, as far away from Eileen as he can get and still be in the pit. The relentless struggle continues at a new distance.

He asks her somewhat innocuously if she believed she had reached a safe point in her life when the murder memory returned in January. Yes, she says, that had been a safe, settled period in her life. In December, when she recovered the digital penetration memory, she had also felt safe. That "peculiar memory" had come to her one afternoon when she was with her children and there was a momentary lull in the activity.

She explains that she has concentrated on the details of the murder memory to make them clearer and that her memory has evolved since the preliminary hearing, some details becoming clearer, some less clear. Horngrad tries, without much success, to establish that this evolution took place during the numerous meetings with the prosecutor in which she had reviewed her transcripts and interviews, particularly the three-day period she spent with Tipton just before her testimony.

Then he turns to an extremely sore point for Eileen. He knows her author is in the audience and he suspects he has been telling her what has been transpiring in the hearings. Hasn't she signed a contract for an authorized biography, he asks.

"Unfortunately, yes," she says with disgust.

Won't the authorship read, "Eileen Franklin and . . ."

"Unfortunately, that's true, yes," she says scornfully.

Horngrad asks when she last spoke to him, unwittingly provoking her into an angry attack on her own writer.

"On Tuesday Mr. Wright revealed to me that he had given an interview to ABC News, and I told him that I considered that to be a betrayal of my trust"—here her voice sharpens with bitterness—"and that I considered it to be dangerous to the prosecution of this case."

"I take it you were annoyed at Mr. Wright?" Horngrad asks.

"Oh, I would say so, yes," she says mockingly.

UP UNTIL NOW, MORSE AND CASSANDRO HAVE BEEN ON THE STAGE every day but they have had only minor, functionary roles: tacking photos on the wall, running the television monitor, playing Franklin in the murder scene, looking after witnesses, keeping track of Tipton's cartful of notebooks, whispering advice, generally supporting their warrior in battle. Sooner or later everyone knows the cops will be in the spotlight. It finally happens when Horngrad asks Eileen about Morse's efforts to allay her concerns about coming forward. He directs her attention to her conversations with the cops last November.

"And when Inspector Morse told you, talking of your father:

'We're more powerful than he is. He wouldn't make a pimple on our butt,' did that address your concerns?"

Eileen laughs an instant before the entire courtroom breaks up. Judge Smith, the jury, Vince, the press, Tipton, everyone chuckles. Even Cassandro allows a small smile to cross his face. All eyes turn to Morse who is looking straight ahead in his serpentine deadpan. Finally it happens: His left eyebrow jumps, arches ever so slightly for a fraction of a second, then drops.

Perhaps feeling his quarry sufficiently weakened or worn down by a full day of relentless but to a large extent peripheral questioning, Horngrad ceases his circling and jabbing and moves in to hit the vulnerable areas.

First, Janice. Eileen continues to insist that, despite the fact that Janice has lived at her house for the past year, she never once asked her where she was when Susan got in the van. He reminds her of her original unequivocal statement to the cops that her father was driving her and Janice to school and that he told Janice to get out of the van when they stopped to pick up Susan.

Eileen hedges:

". . . I think that I said then that—that Janice was in the car or something—that she was in the car or that I knew that there was some sort of interaction with her." She asks to see her original statement, but Horngrad won't give it to her.

When he asks her again about it, she is clearer: "I think that I said that I *thought* Janice was in the car."

Horngrad asks when her memory of Janice and the van changed. Eileen says that while she didn't tell the prosecution of the change until May, that's not necessarily when the memory changed. She can't say when the memory changed. She also can't say whether she ever told Janice she was part of the memory.

Pushing on, Horngrad inquires whether she ever *asked* Janice if she was in the van. Eileen, slipping into a tone of self-pity, says maybe she *should* have asked Janice if she was in the van because then she wouldn't be so confused and could tell the jury whether or not Janice was in the van. Horngrad responds: If Janice told you she was in the van, would you now tell the jury she was in the van? Eileen finally sees the implication of her statement—that she would have incorporated Janice's statement into her memory—and backs off.

Then Eileen gives a startling admission as to the instability of her memories:

"I really can't say. I had so many new memories, and memories become more clear and memories change in the first few months after my dad was arrested."

"Did the memory of Janice being in the van become more clear or less clear?"

"The memory of Janice being in the van became less clear."

Still, Horngrad won't drop it.

"And as you sit here now, Mrs. Lipsker, can you tell us, was there another witness to the fact that Susan Nason got in the van September 22nd, 1969?"

"I don't know. I know that somehow I saw Janice or I talked to Janice or she saw me or she was in the van or she was out of the van. I don't know. I can't say definitively whether she was there or not. But I just have this memory of—of her being there."

Horngrad knows Eileen has told yet another version of Janice's location. He has obtained copies of Dr. Lenore Terr's notes of her two August interviews with Eileen, and in those notes Terr indicated that Eileen told her that when the van stopped, she saw Janice in a field and Janice approached the van and asked if she could go back to school and play tetherball with Terry Dalmau. When Horngrad read this statement, he immediately dispatched Steve Schwartz, his private investigator, to locate Terry Dalmau. Schwartz learned that Janice had already been to visit Terry Dalmau and asked her whether she remembered playing tetherball with her the afternoon Susan disappeared. Dalmau said she hadn't.

In her direct testimony and so far on cross, Eileen hasn't mentioned Dalmau, tetherball, or the field. So, to Horngrad, it was a classic example of the two sisters working on Eileen's memory: Janice tells Eileen she was in the field and came to the van door and asked her father if she could play tetherball with Terry Dalmau; Eileen incorporates this fact into her memory and tells it to Dr. Terr; Janice does her detective work and finds out Dalmau will deny playing tetherball with Janice, tells this to Eileen, and all of a sudden Eileen drops the field/tetherball fact from the story, never to be heard again. The two sisters had conformed Eileen's memory to the known facts.

Horngrad asks her again about Janice's location and, as if sensing a trap, Eileen says that her current memory is that, when the van stopped, she saw Janice in the field. Originally she thought that Janice had asked her father if she could go back to the school to play tetherball with one of her classmates, but now she is no longer certain that Janice said anything.

Eileen is getting weary. Horngrad, his elbow resting on the filing cabinet in the far corner, won't let up. When she changed her story and told the prosecutors in May that Janice was no longer in the van, she didn't mention Janice in the field, did she? No, Eileen answers, because she was uncertain about the field. In a wandering soliloquy, she explains further:

"I think that because I have felt so uncertain that I didn't want to—make a statement and say: This is what happened—because, obviously that's what I've done. I said here: Janice was in the van with me, and then I have to come back and say: Oh, gee, she wasn't in the van with me. And not only was she not in the van with me, I don't remember exactly where she was."

Suddenly, Eileen recovers. "So when I—if I become definite enough to be certain," she says mockingly to Horngrad, "I'm more than happy to tell you; but I'm not."

Eileen is smiling, but weariness has mixed in with a combative anger, a dangerous solution.

Tipton, who may well not have heard of Dalmau and the field before, finally starts objecting as Horngrad probes and pushes the field memory. When he asks for the name of the friend, Tipton shotguns it: "Same objection: again, assumes facts not in evidence, asked and answered, irrelevant."

At 3:00 P.M. Smith declares the afternoon recess. Eileen usually leaves the courtroom in Morse's company and they often go for walks around the block, but today she collapses in a chair just inside the bar. The pit empties of lawyers and cops, everyone, and Eileen is left alone with her father, who is seated at the defense table only a few feet away. For three or four tense minutes, father and daughter are alone on the stage, both staring straight ahead into the air still thick with the struggle. Their physical resemblance is remarkable. Finally, Franklin glances over his shoulder at his daughter, but she holds her gaze.

At 3:10 Vince walks into the hallway and calls out, "Jurors for Department Nine!" The jurors are starting to look wrung out.

Horngrad finishes with Dalmau quickly and starts probing Eileen's statement that she and Janice have never discussed the events of September 22, 1969.

She admits that she did talk to Janice about her having identified Susan's rings, but argues that that discussion did not involve the events of that day and that, anyway, Janice had only talked about Susan's "jewelry," not her rings. As she has done from the beginning, Eileen takes Horngrad round and round the mulberry bush before giving him anything. The tedium of the chase tends to obscure whatever points he scores.

Horngrad asks her about the change in her story on the mattress, and she says she doesn't remember when the story changed. Then he asks if 1969 footage of an old box spring was shown on the "Today Show."

"How would I know?" she shoots back sarcastically.

She insists that she had watched only a couple seconds of the show—when she was on—and had seen neither the box spring nor the picture of the turnout off Highway 92. Barry had taped the show, but she had never played the tape.

Haven't you ever been tempted to watch it, he presses. She comes back full force, throwing her pain and her suffering in his face.

"About the murder of my best friend?"

"That . . ." Horngrad begins.

"Why would I want to watch that on television?" she demands, her taut voice rising in righteous anger at his refusal to acknowledge her anguish.

"No, the—" Horngrad tries again.

"No."

"What I'm asking is that the interview of you talking about your memory of the murder—"

"About seeing my best friend murdered?" Eileen shouts at him. "No!"

Didn't she change the time from morning to afternoon after she learned from the show or Barry's clipping file that Susan disappeared after school that day? Hadn't she ever peeked in the folder? She's never peeked, Eileen says, her voice now wavering with self-pity, because if "I want to know about that, I can think about it."

Horngrad walks her through the litany of her efforts to stifle publicity by creating it: She gave the "Today Show" interview in order to protect her privacy, she signed a contract to write a book in order to prevent a book being written about it, and she signed a movie contract in order to prevent a movie being made about it.

For his final strike of the day, Horngrad turns to the location of the molestation and killing. In her original statement Eileen said they had driven "into the woods" and bumped along on a dirt road for several minutes, and had seen no other cars. At the prelim she said that, in response to questions by Elaine Tipton a few days earlier, she had realized that the van was parked off a paved road. She also remembered seeing cars go by. Now Eileen says that "into the woods" wasn't the best wording; what she had meant was going past the reservoir (on a paved road) where there were a lot of trees.

As for the dirt road turning into a paved road, Eileen says her memory now is that they were "driving on an unpaved dirt 'area,'" implying that her recollection hadn't changed at all.

"Ah. Well," Horngrad asks, pursuing the latest version, "is there a difference between 'road' and 'an area'?"

"I think that—that now that my memory has evolved, I think that there is. I think that what I was trying to express a year ago and what I can express now, that definitely the memory is more clear; and possibly, a year from now, it will be even more clear—only I hope not."

"Why do you hope not?"

"I don't want to remember this any more," Eileen says, slipping again into her pain. "I've remembered enough detail. I don't want to live with this. I would just like it to go away."

Horngrad reads aloud two questions from Morse in the November 25 interview in which he suggests that the van had been parked on a turnout along a paved roadway and asks her if it isn't true that her memory changed after she heard those questions.

Eileen reveals a new fallback position: She just really hadn't given the location of the murder much thought.

"Really?" Horngrad asks incredulously.

"Really," Eileen answers.

Horngrad begins questioning Eileen about the diary and the digging in the woods, but at 4:40 Smith mercifully closes off the testimony for the day.

George Franklin stands up and waits silently, expressionlessly, for the deputy to lead him from the courtroom, and it's as if the forgotten man had suddenly reappeared. People had come and gone and argued and cried and shouted and in the midst of it all the white-haired man in the blue suit seemed to have become almost beside the point, a bit player who just happened to set the drama in motion. The struggle between Horngrad and Eileen has become so intense, so volatile and absorbing, that its resolution seemed to have become the very point of the play.

Horngrad is exhausted at the end of the day, barely able to manage a friendly quip or two with reporters. A friend sees a picture of him on television that evening and tells him he looked like he had been dead for a week.

48

November 7, 1990—Wednesday

THE PENALTY PHASE IN SALCIDO STARTS TODAY AND the cameras swing away from Franklin and point across the hall. Salcido's mother and brother are supposedly arriving from Mexico and producers and editors are demanding visuals. The two stories make it a big day for the "cops and courts" reporters and, worried about missing tomorrow's leads, they will shuttle back and forth between the courtrooms all day.

Competition is fierce on all fronts. Two well-dressed elderly ladies, one gray- and the other orange-haired, stand in the Franklin line and argue about the appropriate sentence for somebody who was involved in a murder but did not pull the trigger: one argues for life without parole, the other insists on death. Then they argue about whether to watch Salcido or Franklin. They decided to split up: one will watch Salcido, the other Franklin, then they will switch at midday. They chatter until the Salcido door swings open and the orange-haired lady scuttles off excitedly across the hall.

Eileen appears wearing an expensive copper coatdress trimmed with large black buttons. She looks pale, weak, washed out. While waiting for court to start she sits with the Nasons in the front row.

At 9:00 A.M. Smith announces that the red-haired juror is ill and has a 9:30 appointment at the hospital. Court will reconvene at 10:00 A.M.

The talk among the reporters is that Horngrad scored heavily yesterday. It wasn't any one point in particular, but more the accumulation of facts that have changed or faded or appeared or disappeared since Eileen's original story. She had even remembered one scene—Susan walking cautiously down the slope in an A-line dress—the very night before her testimony! What would she come up with tomorrow? When would the memory ever stabilize? How could you possibly convict on a story whose facts shifted like the ocean sands? Even Eileen had admitted that the memory was continuing to evolve.

It is obvious that Horngrad understands how to exploit Eileen's need to explain and justify herself, to portray herself as the victim-turned-heroine, and how to lure her out from behind the poses of the calm-adult-doing-the right-thing or the suffering-little-girl-paying-the-price-of-her-father's-horrible-misdeed, and tap the anger and rage that lay behind those personas, but one reporter wonders if in doing so he might not be creating more sympathy for her.

Judge Smith is informed that the doctors do not think that the red-haired juror will be able to go forward with the case because the testimony is too emotional for her. She has been referred to a psychiatrist because of the suspicion that her bowel problem is emotionally related.

The second alternate juror is selected: Joyce Beard, a black woman in her mid-fifties from Foster City. Joyce and her husband moved into their house on a lagoon in 1970 when the neighborhood was still mainly windswept vacant lots. They were one of the first three black families in Foster City and she operates a dry cleaner in San Mateo. Joyce is ambivalent about being on the jury: she realizes she has a civic duty, but she is also very uncomfortable with sitting in judgment on another human being. That, she thinks, is more properly God's place.

Joyce has, however, listened and watched Eileen carefully and she has serious doubts about her story. In fact, she is not sure she believes her at all. She also wonders about George Franklin sitting there writing steadily day after day without any expression on his face. Will he ever get up and say anything? Will he ever defend himself?

Horngrad begins this morning by zeroing in on the question of repression. When did Eileen forget the killing of Susan Nason? Eileen first says that she had forgotten the killing by the time she returned to school and then agrees with an earlier statement she had given the prosecution that the memory stopped when she looked down at Susan and saw her hand. She is hesitant and unsure of herself and apologizes when she forgets the question. Her face says: "I'm really hurting, but I'll do my best."

Horngrad presses her on her failure to tell the cops in her early statements that she had forgotten the killing for twenty years. After the body was found, she told Etter she was afraid for a while, but then had to get on with her life and keep functioning in order to keep "the lie going." What was the lie? Her answer—that everything was fine in the Franklin family—sounds made up on the spot. She explained that she hadn't told the cops she had forgotten the memory in the taped conversations because Barry told her he already had told them that. She denies telling Marty Murray that she hadn't come forward all these years because of threats to the family or that she had recovered the memory over twenty years of therapy, despite his statement to the contrary; she denies telling the "Today Show" interviewer in January that she had recovered the memory three months earlier, as the show had broadcast; and she denies telling Lenore Terr that the memory had developed in a month, as Terr had noted in her interview. Her voice falters as she denies saying what all these people said she had said, and after Horngrad takes her through her three different statements on the mattress, she definitely appears weakened and dispirited.

Like a bullfighter who sees the bull tiring, his head dropping low from fatigue, Horngrad slices in for the kill.

"Was there ever, Mrs. Lipsker, anybody else in the back of the van when Susan was attacked? Was there anybody else there who is a witness, who can now tell us what happened, other than yourself?"

It is a serious misjudgment. Eileen's head lifts, her eyes flash, she pauses for an instant, then in one swift move she leans forward and hooks her tormentor cleanly in the heart:

"I would think my father could."

It is a stunning, spontaneous moment, and Eileen's face is swept with a look of satisfaction and triumph. She struggles not to appear too exultant.

Horngrad recovers quickly and shifts back to the buried diary and asks her when she remembered the burying. In answering, Eileen either becomes confused and runs the diary memory together with the "other murder," or she intentionally tries to suck Horngrad into asking about the "other murder" so she can tell the jury about her image of her father carrying a girl upside down with blood pouring from her left breast.

"It was in December of 1988 that I had the memory of my father burying or concealing something."

"In December of 1988?" Horngrad asks, knowing that at the prelim she had said she recovered the *burying* memory in March 1990 and that she had told Lenore Terr of recovering the "other murder" in December 1988. For some reason, Eileen is now remembering the time when she recalled that scene.

Horngrad does not, cannot, straighten out the confusion of her memories, although if he could it would be a telling illustration of the seepage between her many memories. If he opens the door on the "other murder" memory, Smith might well allow her to tell the complete story to the jury.

Horngrad brings her back to the diary memory, and she is instantly calm and composed, dabbing lightly at her eyes with a Kleenex. For almost twenty minutes Horngrad questions her on conflicts between what she now says about the diary and the burying and earlier statements, and Eileen becomes more and more confused. Twice she slips back into the "other murder" memory, and twice Horngrad carefully brings her back and keeps prodding. Finally, when Smith directs her to answer a question, she bursts into tears and turns to him and asks, like a bullied child pleading with her father for help, "How can I answer this, if I can't go on to explain my answer?" Tipton interrupts Smith's response and asks if she can approach the bench, giving Eileen a chance to recover. As the attorneys confer with Smith, Eileen, her eyes wet with tears, her mouth turned down, appears the bewildered girl overcome with a sense of her own vulnerability.

Horngrad keeps hitting on the diary memory, trying to demonstrate the similarity between it and the Susan Nason memory: in both cases she and her father pulled off a paved road onto an unpaved portion; in both cases she saw a clump of three trees off in the distance; in both cases there was digging. His main point—that the diary memory, so similar to the murder memory, had obviously been planted and therefore the murder memory could have been planted too—gets lost in the midst of Eileen's confusion and pain.

Horngrad retreats to the filing cabinet and continues jabbing away, largely at peripheral, minor inconsistencies or changes. Eileen has recovered and is now testy and argumentative. She addresses her tormentor as "Mr. Horngrad," and when he won't let up on a subject, when he picks and jabs and picks and jabs, she shakes her head slowly in mock disbelief at his stubbornness, his tediousness, his obtuseness. Smith begins sustaining Tipton's objections regularly and cutting off Horngrad abruptly.

Eileen smiles when she recounts how, when Barry tried to feed her information on the case, she said to him, "Barry, shut up!" Horngrad pokes around in the relationship between Barry and Janice, seeking to pry an admission from her that Barry had repeated to her things that Janice told him. Eileen is firm that he hadn't and jabs back at Horngrad. He does get her to admit that after Barry called the police initially she did not feel that the decision to go forward was within her control any more.

He returns to Kirk Barrett.

"Why did you mention the death of Susan Nason to Kirk Barrett in March of 1989 in the first place?"

His question provokes another outburst of self-pity.

"Well, I guess the only way that I can explain my childhood to people is to let them know that, yes, one time I did have a best friend. And other than that," she says, punching out the words one by one, "I was an outcast and a misfit child that was *tortured* for having bright red hair, and that I didn't really make friends after my best friend was murdered." She looks away in pained exasperation and then collects herself and lectures Horngrad severely: "And I think that that is probably significant in describing me as a child."

Her outburst has revealed once again the depths of her feelings of sorrow for herself and the inexhaustible supply of her righteous anger, but again it doesn't seem to advance the cause of the defense.

Horngrad revisits several issues he has covered before about Rieder, and Eileen easily slips the jabs and becomes more confident and aggressive. When Horngrad refers to Rieder as a psychologist, she reminds him with a scornful smile that "I thought you told me at the preliminary hearing that she wasn't a psychologist."

When Smith finally breaks for lunch, it seems like the play has become stuck, locked in an immutable configuration of characters and emotions: Eileen on the stand passing, like a changeling, through a range of emotions, from vicious anger to coquettishness to sarcasm to little-girl vulnerability; Horngrad standing back in the corner, leaning up against the filing cabinet, relentlessly, coolly, poking and prodding her wounds; Tipton popping up and down with objections trying to protect her witness; the gray-haired but youthful judge mumbling one-word rulings; the exhausted jury watching silently from their assigned seats. The feeling is: When is somebody going to change the music, the scene? We've had enough of this dance. It's gotten too heavy in here. The press seats are more than half empty.

George Franklin has been writing more and looking up at Eileen less. Occasionally his head rotates and he looks over his shoulder and scans the audience. Sometimes when he sits back in his chair, his mouth flops open and he seems to gasp for air, like a fish out of water.

After lunch, Horngrad asks Eileen whether she read an article a few weeks after the killing about a man dressed in tan Levi pants, a wool Pendleton, and a white T-shirt trying to abduct a small girl. She doesn't remember reading the article or discussing it with Janice.

Horngrad takes Eileen through a list of inconsistencies and changes in her story, looking to turn a small opening into a large one, scratching around for an advantage, waiting for Eileen to make a mistake.

Then he returns to the absent Barry and asks about the time he set up the appointment with an L.A. attorney to convince Eileen to accept money for her book and movie rights.

"Isn't it true that you told Barry that you followed it [the murder of Susan Nason] in the newspapers?"

Eileen, apparently tired of talking about Barry, snaps back viciously at Horngrad:

"No! And why don't you subpoena him and ask him!" Her face flashes a gleeful sneer.

Judge Smith, for the first time showing irritation with the witness, moves immediately to close the door: "The jury will disregard the last comment by the witness."

Horngrad tries to wedge the door open—he wants badly to show that Eileen had talked Barry into not coming to trial because she knew he would hurt the case—but Smith cuts him off. Later, outside the presence of the jury, Horngrad argues forcefully that he should be allowed to explore the possibility that the key witness in the case is counseling another witness not to testify.

Smith is brusque with Horngrad, describing his position as a "beautiful example of a bootstrap argument." The press twitters when Smith, after all this time, addresses defense counsel as "Mr. Hornstein." A few minutes later, Smith responds sarcastically to one of Horngrad's points: "If the world was not round Christopher Columbus would have had a real problem." Nonplussed, Horngrad continues to argue his point, without success.

Horngrad asks Eileen if she is aware that Barry has an intense dislike for her father. She smirks at Barry's name, like he's a boob and she doesn't care who knows it. She admits that he is a controlling person.

Smith won't allow Horngrad to explore similarities between Eileen's father and Barry. Horngrad turns back to the rape, a move he knows is fraught with danger, but he wants to hear again about the change from black to white.

Wasn't the rapist originally black and didn't she change his color to white because she realized that it was illogical for him to be black?

Eileen suddenly leans forward, her eyes flash in anger, her voice whips back at her tormentor.

"And it still is part of my memory of having my head forced over to look at a poster of a black man, who I think is Jimi Hendrix.

"Yes, that is still part of my memory. Yes," she says emphatically, bitterly. She will make Horngrad pay a price for resurrecting her pain, her rage. He and the monster beside him.

"But now, as you think about it, you believe that you merged your memory of the true event with a poster you saw on the wall. Is that fair to say?"

"I do."

"Merging" is a new and dangerous word for Eileen's memory processes and Tipton breaks the rhythm with a series of objections, all of which are sustained.

"How did it come to pass that your memory changed?"

Now Eileen's anger changes to tears; she begins crying as she explains how she forced herself to complete the memory.

Horngrad waits and watches patiently, then picks up where he left off, asking her again if she hadn't thought the first version to be illogical.

Eileen shakes her head in disbelief that this terrible man can continue on in the face of her agony. She dabs her eyes with a Kleenex, then, in a barely coherent response, adds a new detail to support the change.

"Once I realized that not only could I not see the face of this person, but that the edges of the afro were *iridescent,* that they were colors, that the—just on top of not being able to see the face and having these—the *iridescent* colors of it, but being able to remember the other details, that it just struck me as being highly illogical and highly unlikely that it would have been."

She testifies that sometime after November but before May, she had seen the face very clearly and realized that the man laughing at the end of the table was Stan Smith.

Horngrad returns to the changes in her story of the murder: originally her father was drinking beer, but that got dropped from the story; originally she thought she saw Susan carrying something in her hand, but that also was dropped; she told Etter that Susan was wearing a lavender or blue sweater, but that has disappeared; originally there was no dress, and now there is one; originally there was no rock on the body, now there is one; originally there were no shoes, now she remembers her father throwing one or two.

Eileen is no longer intimidated or angry but very calm and balanced. She works with Horngrad on his questions; if they are not clear, or he is confused in his facts, she works to clear up the question and his confusion. He has her read a document, then she asks politely, helpfully: "And so you are asking me?"

This cooperative effort dissipates when Horngrad turns once again to the books and movies. Horngrad has in his hand a document entitled "Collaboration Agreement," which sets forth the terms of her agreement with her writer to co-author a book. It is dated May 14, 1990, fourteen days before Eileen testified at the prelim that she had not signed a book deal and that in fact she wasn't even in the process of negotiating a book deal. Eileen explains that while the contract is dated May 14, she hadn't signed it until the end of June or early July.

Eileen, now bristling with righteous anger, denies knowing that the book is to be called "The Eileen Franklin-Lipsker Story," and when she reads that title on the first page of the agreement, she blames it on whoever drew up the agreement and insists she was never consulted on the "tentative" title.

"Well, but you signed that contract, did you not?"

"Mr. Horngrad," she begins harshly, "I signed this contract under the advisement of my attorney, who is trying to protect my rights. So, yes."

She refuses to admit that the book will be worth more if her father is convicted. Horngrad goes over the terms of the contract with her: She is to provide photos; she is to obtain releases from Barry, Leah, Diana, and Janice; royalties will be split 50–50 (although she will get 100 percent of the existing movie deal); she is to write her first-person account; and she will have control of the content of the book as it relates to her, Barry, Leah, Diana, and Janice.

Suddenly, without warning, Smith cuts off questioning on the contract, saying the document is in evidence and that under the relevancy provision of the evidence code he doesn't want to hear any more about it. Horngrad manages to slide in a few more questions.

"The contract also provides that you can still give lectures and television appearances?"

"Yeah," Eileen responds sarcastically, sneeringly, "isn't that nice?"

She doesn't remember the amount of money her attorney estimated she could make from the book, because she is not interested in money and plans on giving it away. She only signed the contract to protect herself.

Smith declares an unusual second afternoon recess, despite Horngrad's request that he be allowed to ask his final few questions. After the break, Horngrad comes back determined to leave the jury with one central point.

"Mrs. Lipsker, can you assure this jury that there will never be any other changes in your memory?"

"Objection."

"Sustained."

"Do you believe that there could be any more versions that you recall?"

"Objection."

"Sustained."

"Mrs. Lipsker," Horngrad persists, trying to make his point with the question if not the answer, "are you sure that there will be no more changes in your memory?"

Smith sustains Tipton's objection again and tells Horngrad not to ask the question any more.

"Very well," Horngrad says politely, his voice dropping slightly in disappointment. "I have nothing further, your honor."

The end is so sudden, so abrupt, that the tones of Horngrad's now-familiar voice hang suspended in the heavy air, with no one moving or coughing or whispering, as if waiting to make sure he isn't going to rise again and steal over to the filing cabinet and say, "Mrs. Lipsker, this business about . . ."

But he holds his seat, and finally Tipton rises to ask a few rebuttal questions. The relief over the dissolution of the configuration is palpable: Thank God we can finally move on to the next scene.

"Eileen, can you describe for us your tolerance for pain?" Tipton asks from nowhere.

Horngrad objects but is overruled.

"It seems that I have a very high tolerance for pain," she says majestically.

"What, if any, plans, dreams, ideas, did you have for yourself as a child and adolescent for your future?"

"I thought that I had no future. I thought that I would end up being murdered."

It is a nice, dramatic finish, and Eileen, when she is told she can step down, seems almost to float from the courtroom.

49

JUDGE SMITH IS COMPLETELY DRAINED AFTER EIleen's testimony. For three days she has taken everybody in the courtroom on an emotional roller coaster, up and down and round and round, and by the end of it even he, the cool, imperturbable jurist, is exhausted. He sees Eileen as part actress and guesses she testified in part from her own recollection and in part from what she had learned from reviewing her own interviews and transcripts. Smith is curious about why Tipton didn't ask Eileen about the time her father had allegedly abused her daughter Jessica. She had fought so hard to get this item of uncharged conduct admitted. He feels that Horngrad did an excellent job cross-examining Eileen and getting his points across without bullying her.

Vince believes Eileen. She is like a child; the manner in

which she swings from happiness to sadness reminds him of his kids when he disciplines them: one second they're crying and the next they're happy and laughing.

Peggy, watching the show stone-faced from behind her table stacked with exhibits, thinks Eileen handled herself very well on the stand. That Horngrad is slick: there was never a mean look that crossed his face and he maintained an attitude that he was just trying to do his job and get to the bottom of things. Like Vince, she thinks Franklin is guilty.

Nancy Salazar thinks Eileen is telling the truth. Either that or she is an incredible actress and deserves an Academy Award for her performance. She worries, though, that some of the jurors will be put off by the bland, almost mechanical way in which Eileen described her incest. Nancy has no doubt that George Franklin sexually abused Eileen. Her anger, her rage boiling just beneath the surface, bubbling up at the slightest provocation, is undoubtedly born of feelings of shame and guilt. Nancy noted that Franklin didn't show any anger or hostility toward his favorite daughter and sensed that the bond they shared when she was a child still exists. The incest is still continuing. Which may well account for the intensity of Eileen's rage.

Joyce Beard, the black woman, doesn't like Eileen Franklin. While her story seemed plausible, Joyce's intuitive reaction to her is very negative. She is bothered by the book and movie deals and the money that Eileen will make from Susan's death.

Wendy Canning, the juror who had voted for the death penalty in a previous case, isn't troubled that Eileen switched the time of the killing from morning to afternoon because both times were during the day. She also finds Eileen's lapses in memory to be believable: If she had made the story up, she would have memorized the details in order to be more convincing; instead, when Tipton asked her a question, she would pause and think and search in her mind, and then say, yes, she could see Susan down the hill on the left, or some clutter off to the right. She remembered some details and not others, which would be normal for a twenty-year-old memory.

November 7, 1990—Wednesday, continued

It's 4:30 when Eileen leaves the stand and everyone, including Judge Smith, is convinced that the hearing is over for the day. But Tipton has other ideas: she figured Eileen would be on the stand for only two days, so mindful of Smith's chastisement for not having witnesses ready, she has had Carolyn Adams waiting in the wings for over a day. Carolyn is getting antsy and Tipton wants to get her on the stand before she changes her mind about testifying. At the bench Smith tells the attorneys he is going to recess for the day, but Tipton pleads with him to allow her to put on one short, out-of-state witness. Reluctantly, he agrees.

The few reporters who remain—Salcido has most of them—shift uncomfortably in their seats when Vince calls out the the the name of Carolyn Adams.

Carolyn, a heavyset Hispanic woman in her late forties, is very down to earth and Tipton is convinced she will be a strong witness. She is right. After Carolyn testifies that she had a romantic relationship with George Franklin from 1983 to 1987, Tipton asks her:

"And was there something that the defendant said to you shortly before the end of the relationship that contributed to you—to the end of that relationship?"

"Yes."

"What was that?"

"The statement that was made, that he had sex with a daughter."

After another question or two, Tipton sits down.

"I have no questions," Horngrad says quickly.

In one sentence, twelve words, Carolyn Adams sucked the oxygen from the fire of two and a half days of cross-examination. As Carolyn Adams steps down, Nancy turns to Ollie Scholle and comments how refreshing it is to have such a brief witness. Ollie agrees: he found Carolyn to be very convincing.

Joyce Beard understands why Horngrad didn't ask Carolyn Adams any questions: He got her off the stand before she could do any more damage.

*   *   *

CAROLYN ADAMS COULD HAVE TOLD THE JURY MUCH MORE ABOUT George Franklin. In 1983, George sold his apartment building in Sacramento and moved to Hawaii. With the help of a friend, a former fireman who owned his own real estate company, he invested in several condos on the island of Maui. Carolyn joined him and they lived in one of the condos close to the beach. She soon learned that George Franklin was a Jekyll and Hyde: out in the world, he was charming and intelligent and considerate; inside the house, he was a strange, violent man. He drank constantly and smoked vast amounts of pot and ate psychedelic mushrooms.

He almost killed her more than once. One Sunday morning in December 1984, he was drinking Kahlúa and coffee and everything seemed fine and he announced he was going into town because he had run low on pot. She was cleaning the condo when he returned and burst through the door in a rage and began hitting her viciously about the head and shoulders. She eventually escaped and went to the police and found safety in a women's shelter. He tried to charm his way out of what he had done, but the cops believed her story—how could they ignore her swollen face and the black and blue marks all over her?—and she filed assault charges against George. He found her on Christmas Eve and apologized and said he had been wrong and she shouldn't have to spend the holiday in the shelter. She left with him, and he talked her into dropping the charges. Still scared for her life, she told him she was leaving. When he took her to the airport, he cried and seemed to know that he had hit rock bottom with nowhere to turn. He told her about how he and his mother had suffered at the hands of his drunken and abusive father. Carolyn often suspected, although he never said it, that he had been sexually abused as a child.

On February 8, 1985, George attended his first meeting of Alcoholics Anonymous and went stone-cold sober. He returned to Sacramento and Carolyn moved back in with him. He had found religion and was making amends to people in the AA way, but he still had a tendency toward mental and physical abuse and he still hated women. One day he got on top of her and whacked her head with his fists, banging her face on the floor. He stopped before he killed her, but it left her with horrible headaches.

She sold her condo and left town right after he made the remark about having sex with his daughter. Actually, she thinks he said "daughters."

50

November 8, 1990—Thursday

As HE DOES EVERY MORNING, BOB MORSE APPEARS twenty minutes before court convenes pushing a three-tiered cart laden with thick black notebooks filled with carefully organized Franklin facts. Morse takes his trial role quite seriously. He shows up early at Tipton's office and begins energizing her for battle. "Okay, boss," he will say, "we're going to go in there today and nail them; there is absolutely no doubt you are going to seriously kick ass today." He also insists on knowing if there is anything, anything at all, he can do for her. (He ironed Eileen's dress before she testified at the prelim.) If Tipton isn't fired up and ready for action when she comes to work, she is when Morse is through.

At the end of the day, Morse corners other lawyers and investigators in the hallway of the D.A.'s office and brags about Tipton's feats in the courtroom, how she really snookered Horngrad or got a great ruling from Smith. When things have gone badly for them, he minimizes the problems, often with humor, and reassures her that no real ground was lost, certainly nothing she won't easily make up in the arena the next day. His aggressive high spirits, his relentless cheerleading, have always worked on Tipton. One afternoon, after a particularly successful day when Morse had really been blowing her horn, she turned to him and said, jokingly, "Jesus

Christ, Bob, I love the way you love to revel in the afterglow at the end of every day, and come to think of it your foreplay isn't too bad either."

The testimony of Carolyn Adams at the close of yesterday was a master stroke worthy of such reveling, but today holds no such promise. Today is FBI day, and Morse's cart is heavily laden with hundreds of vials and envelopes to be identified by three special agents. Tipton must go about the tedious task of proving what would appear to be an element of the defense: that there is absolutely no forensic or scientific evidence to connect George Franklin to the killing of Susan Nason. She has to demonstrate to the jury that the failure to connect him through physical evidence isn't because the prosecution didn't try. She can't have Horngrad standing up in his closing argument saying, "Why didn't the prosecution check this for fingerprints or that for fibers?" implying that she has done a sloppy job and possibly overlooked evidence that could have exculpated his client.

Before getting to the agents, Tipton calls a criminalist with the San Mateo County Sheriff's lab. After being qualified as an expert, the witness testifies that she unsuccessfully tested a broken pair of sunglasses recovered from the crime scene in 1969 for fingerprints. In August, she cut seventeen samples from the many layers of carpets and seat covers and collected one paint sample from the passenger door of the 1968 Volkswagen van license VXJ707. Tipton has her identify each sample in sequence and they are marked and entered into evidence.

Next, Bryan Cassandro takes the stand and testifies that at four o'clock on October 30 he drove the most likely route from where Susan was picked up to the pullout along 92 and it took him seventeen minutes and six-tenths of a second. He testifies that he sent all of the physical evidence in the case—the rocks, dress, denim cutoffs, panties, socks, brown shoe, ring, nail scrapings from Susan's left hand, the lock of hair, the carpet and paint samples—to the FBI in Washington, D.C.

Special Agent Douglas Deedrick, in his gray slacks and gray hair, could be a spin-off character from "Twin Peaks." He is completely devoid of all affect as his squirrely voice explains the functions of a hair and fiber specialist at the Bureau. After two hours of mind-numbing testimony and over 100 exhibits (Vince, who enjoys forensic evidence, was leaning back in his chair, his eyes varying between closed and glazed), he concludes lifelessly that all of the hairs on Susan's clothing were hers, that there was no pubic hair on her clothes, that the broken hairs on the small rock indicated it was probably the murder weapon, that the two rocks were not originally one rock, and that none of the fibers from Susan's clothing matched any of the fibers or the debris taken from the van. In sum, there is absolutely *no* evidence that Susan Nason had ever been in van VXJ707 or that she had been in physical contact with George Franklin.

A young, attractive wire reporter is so moved by Deedrick's methodical performance that she passes a note to a local female reporter, saying, "I'll bet this guy's great in the sack!"

Robert Spalding, the second gray man, is a serology expert, and he testifies in detail that he found neither blood nor semen on any of the items submitted to the Bureau. This is not surprising, he opines solemnly, because the items were exposed to natural elements and were on or next to a decomposing body and subjected to insect and animal activity for ten weeks.

William Tobin, the third gray man, is a forensic metallurgist, and he describes his job somewhat grandiosely as applying "the principles of metallurgy to the interests of justice." He is here to talk about the damage to the silver ring, and he has considerably more difficulty speaking in English than his two colleagues. After wandering about in the laws of physics, he opines that the damage to the ring was most likely caused by a rock brought down on it with a severe amount of force. Either of the two rocks could have done the damage.

When Horngrad announces he has no questions for Tobin, the last gray man strides purposefully from the room.

Judge Smith is surprised that Tipton has taken so long with the forensic witnesses. For what their testimony offered to prove, she should have had them on and off the stand in a fraction of the time. He is worried about finishing the trial on schedule and he has been thinking about continuing into the evening. He asks the jury to think about whether they would be willing to spend a few more hours in trial every day.

"Does this [thinking about extras hours] include counsel?" Horngrad asks, setting Smith up. "No," Smith replies immediately, and the jury looks at Horngrad, who is wearing a small smile, and laughs. They like Horngrad, his pleasantness, his self-deprecating humor, his willingness to play the clown now and again. Once Horngrad was looking in vain for some photographic exhibits which lay on the rail of the jury box. Finally, two of the female jurors in the first row pointed to them and said with indulgent smiles: "Here they are, Mr. Horngrad." Thank you, he said, thank you very much.

The sleeping juror passes Vince a note for the judge saying she is having slight chest pains. Smith confers with her privately before the noon recess and she decides to see her doctor. Outside the presence of the jury, Smith says he has received a note from somebody in prison confessing to the killing. The local reporters chuckle: they know this guy, he confesses to every notorious crime.

"Janice Franklin." The name catches the few reporters in the courtroom by surprise, stirring them from their gray torpor. Tipton has had to juggle her witnesses to make sure she didn't bring Janice and Leah to the courthouse on the same day. Janice is a problem and an enigma to Tipton, but she accepts her as another casualty of George Franklin's brutality and Leah's neglect. Cassandro has been baby-sitting her in the hallway while the gray men testified.

JANICE, THE ANGRY REBEL, THE SHIT-KICKER, THE GIRL WHO DIDN'T belong even in her own family, the least favorite child of both parents who was beaten horribly; the tough girl who smoked and threw dirt clods at other kids in grade school and wore lipstick and liked fast boys in high school and had a reputation for being fast herself; the teenager with a terrible temper who fought viciously with her mother and was called "Lady Cunt" by her and who called her "Leah the Bitch" in return, has had a hard life.

Janice didn't graduate from high school, and she moved in with her maternal grandparents for a while, then with her father in Mountain View. She and Eileen shared an apartment for several months. Her first job when she dropped out of school was in customer service with the San Mateo phone company. She rented an apartment in Burlingame and seemed to be doing fine and then, after eight or nine months, she quit for no apparent reason. That seemed to be her pattern: She would get things going okay, and then blow them up or simply walk away. Like all the Franklin sisters, she loved clothes, and she ran up charge accounts and then had trouble paying the bills. She always seems to be broke and borrowing money from people, particularly her sister Kate. She had a dream—she wanted to design fancy dresses and own her own shop—but she could never translate the fantasy into reality.

Janice has been plagued with severe medical problems. She had a tumor on her pituitary gland and after several methods of reduction failed, she had the growth surgically removed in the mid-eighties. Kate drove her to the hospital for the operation. Then she developed kidney problems, and was eventually diagnosed as having lupus. After she moved in with Eileen and Barry, Barry would tell others she was dying.

After Janice's involvement with a bus driver, she had two major relationships, one of which almost led to marriage. She rejected two men who loved her and were responsible and stable because, in one observer's view, they weren't hot or fast enough for her.

In addition to seeing Kirk Barrett, Eileen's therapist, Janice has been in therapy on several other occasions, and even attended est, a gift from her father. She feels that one result of her sexual abuse was her inability, for a period at least, to associate the sex act with any emotion or feeling.

Like Eileen, Janice remains locked in the dynamics of the Franklin family dysfunction. She is capable of erupting viciously at any moment. Kate, Diana, and George Jr. view her as extremely moody and unstable, the shakiest of the five children. Unlike Eileen, who can fly into similar rages, Janice seems to lack an emotional anchor. She has no relationship with any sibling except Eileen, and that relationship is plagued, as it has always been, by frequent fights and periods of alienation.

Janice has believed since 1979 or 1980 that her father murdered Susan Nason and is proud of her role in unmasking him and in having "busted his ass." She received $7,500 for her rights in conjunction with Eileen's book and movie, part of which she spent on a new car.

Janice looks stunning. She is wearing a purple, drop-waisted dress with long sleeves and a pearl necklace. Her chestnut hair is short and brushed back. Her slender figure, long neck, and high cheekbones give her a touch of class lacking in Eileen. In the beginning, she speaks so softly she can barely be heard and Tipton has to ask her to move closer to the mike. Often when she pauses before answering a question, she rolls her tongue between her teeth and upper lip. Glaring at her father, she identifies him as the man in the brown jacket.

Tipton moves immediately to defuse the Terry Dalmau issue. Janice testifies that she had a feeling that she was playing tetherball with Terry the afternoon of Susan's disappearance and had contacted her about a month ago to see if she remembered playing with her. Terry didn't remember.

Janice testifies that on the afternoon Susan disappeared, she had come home around 5:30. Her father said hello to her and she was taken aback.

"What was the next comment?" Tipton asks.

"He did say: 'What's the matter? Can't I even say hello to my daughter?' "

"You considered your father saying hello to you unusual?"

"Yes."

Then Tipton asks her about the time her father told her the police were on the phone and wanted to talk to her. Janice says that on the way to the phone, he "kicked me at the base of my spine, and I fell flat in the hallway."

So far, Janice is speaking quietly and a little shakily, but her responses are clear and composed. In the next exchange, she becomes confused and evasive. Tipton asks Janice if, before 1984, Leah had ever told her of her belief that George had murdered Susan Nason. Janice denies that her mother had ever shared any such suspicion with her, even though she has said many times previously, including at the prelim, that her mother did tell her she thought her husband had murdered Susan.

Tipton can't leave her exposed like this and asks her the question again, and again Janice refuses to admit the 1979 conversation. Either Horngrad's objections are rattling her, she has forgotten the conversation, or she is trying to hide it.

"My question is," Tipton begins in a tone more appropriate to cross-examination, "before 1984, had anyone else ever shared with you, told you that they had those same suspicions?"

Horngrad's objection is overruled.

"I don't think so," Janice replies.

Tipton plugs away inartfully at her own witness.

"Had you ever had a conversation with your mother about your father?"

Horngrad's objection is overruled again and finally Janice catches on.

"I recall I did have a conversation with my mother. I just don't recall what year it was."

Tipton asks her if the conversation was before she went to the police in 1984 and Janice says she doesn't remember. She is sure, though, that whenever the conversation took place, it didn't influence her own belief that her father had killed Susan.

Tipton needs to clean up the fact that in her 1984 statement to the Foster City police Janice alibied her father by placing him at home after four o'clock on the day Susan disappeared. At the prelim, Janice explained she had changed the time from 4:00 to 5:30 because she realized in therapy with Kirk Barrett that she never went home before 5:30 or 6:00. Today, she gives the jury a different reason: She told the cops in 1984 that she didn't remember what time she had seen her father that day, but the officer had suggested four o'clock to her and they had kind of agreed on it.

Tipton now moves to deal with another problem related to Janice's 1984 statement to the police. Janice testified at the prelim that she had not told Eileen about her statement, but Eileen had testified just a few days earlier that Janice told her in 1985 that she had gone to the cops the previous year. Now Janice wants to change her testimony on that point.

"As you sit here now, what is your best recollection: that you did or did not tell other family members that you had gone to the police in 1984?"

"I did tell other family members."

Tipton has in fact impeached her own witness. Cross-examination hasn't even started, and Janice looks bad: either confused and unreliable or devious and unreliable. But the jury has heard what Tipton wants them to hear: George Franklin kicked his ten-year-old daughter at the base of the spine to shut her up and she lived in such terror of her father that a simple greeting from him left her speechless. It doesn't take a psychiatrist to suspect that the former might be the cause of the latter.

For the first few minutes of cross, Janice manages to hang back and stay cool. When Judge Smith directs her to speak up, she suggests that he turn up the volume on the mike instead.

Horngrad also begins with the Dalmau incident, and Janice testifies that the first time she ever mentioned Dalmau to the prosecution was in the past seventy-two hours when Tipton asked her about it. She hadn't told her previously because she didn't think it relevant.

"But to you—" Horngrad begins, and suddenly Janice's cool exterior evaporates and her eyes roll toward the ceiling with exasperation.

"To me? I'm not a *lawyer*," she says in a mocking tone.

"But to you it seemed irrelevant?"

"Yeah."

Then Janice contradicts Eileen.

"Did you ever mention that [her conversation with Terry Dalmau] to your sister Eileen?" Horngrad asks her.

"No," Janice says flatly.

Horngrad asks her again, and, perhaps thinking that the only way the Dalmau conversation could have become known was through Eileen, Janice backtracks.

"It's possible that I could have. I don't recall it specifically, but it's possible that I could have."

Within a few seconds, Janice's memory clears completely on this point and she remembers the details of a specific conversation in which she told Eileen about Dalmau. Then she says she only talked to Dalmau about a month ago, which is inconsistent with Terr's notes that Eileen told her about Dalmau in August.

As Horngrad probes lightly, Janice begins lashing back in a style reminiscent of her younger sister, hissing, "I told you that!" when she feels Horngrad is badgering her.

Then Horngrad presses her on her statement that she and Eileen never talked about the events of September 22, 1969. She backtracks again, saying she was just coming off some strong medication in November and she can't swear as to every little thing that she and Eileen might have talked about, and that when she denied talking to Eileen about the facts of the case, she had forgotten she had talked to her about having identified Susan's rings in 1969.

Horngrad tries to pursue this critical line of inquiry—what other facts of the case did she and Eileen talk about?—but Smith, for some reason, cuts him off. Horngrad tries four more questions and is shut down.

Janice, of course, has never claimed that she repressed or forgot memories of the abuse she suffered, so she, unlike Eileen, is not able to explain inconsistencies or changes or shifts in her story by the recent retrieval of additional facts or the emergence of new memories. She must blame it on a faulty memory. At the prelim, she had simply forgotten that she had told Eileen about going to the cops in 1984.

Horngrad twists her hard on this item and gets her to admit that she told Eileen of her suspicions a couple of years ago.

"1986 sound about right?" he asks.

"Your guess is as good as mine," she replies caustically.

Didn't she tell the police in May 1990 that she hadn't discussed her suspicions with Eileen until after Eileen had come forward?

"Yes. I thought we just clarified that."

"Well?" Horngrad bores in on her.

"I'm confused with the same questions over and over and over. No wonder I'm confused: the same question over and over."

Like a referee calling a fight, Smith puts a halt to the pounding. Horngrad pauses, but can't resist one final shot: Hadn't Janice told the cops in August 1990 that she told Eileen about her going to the Foster City police three months before Eileen went forward? When she answers yes to this question, Janice has in effect admitted to four different versions of when she told Eileen she went to the police in 1984.

Janice is clearly not doing well. She glances nervously at the clock on the wall, as if to ask: How long can this abuse continue?

Although she told the cops a year earlier that Susan was wearing a blue dress with white daisies the day she disappeared, now she doesn't remember what she was wearing. She does remember, however, reading the article in the *San Mateo Times* in 1969 about a red-headed man wearing tan corduroys and a Pendleton shirt being sought in the abduction of a young girl and thinking that it sounded like her father; she also remembers talking to Eileen about the article years later and realizing they had both read the same story and reached the same conclusion.

Janice denies watching the "Today Show" tape, except, she explains with a dazzling smile, she had fast-forwarded through the show to watch herself, just as she had read the captions under her pictures in the newspaper articles. She denies ever putting her story together with Eileen and insists that Eileen never once asked her if she remembered seeing Susan get in the van.

Janice glances again at the clock.

Horngrad finishes with her by summarizing in a series of questions her various versions of whether she had been in the van or out of the van. By the time she steps down, her credibility has been thoroughly shredded.

To Judge Smith, Janice's tough appearance was belied by her shakiness on the stand; at one point she was almost quivering, and seemed to be teetering right on the edge of collapse. Horngrad had, in his view, come very close to bullying her.

Nancy Salazar wasn't at all sure that Janice was going to make it through her testimony. She seemed so fragile and so much more emotionally damaged than Eileen. Although Janice hadn't testified to any sexual abuse, Nancy is fairly sure her she had also been sexually abused by her father. During the break, Nancy was riding down the escalator behind Janice and Eileen's author and Janice was very upset because she thought the jury had laughed at something she said. "Was I that bad," she asked him, "that the jury laughed at me?" Nancy felt terrible and wanted to interrupt the poor girl and tell her that the jury wasn't laughing at her, it was the *way* she had said something, not what she had said.

Nancy, for one, does not believe for a second that the two sisters lived in the same house in 1989 and never discussed any details of the murder or Eileen's memory. Surely, Janice would have said whether or not she had seen Susan getting into the van. Surely Eileen, with her desperate need for validation, would have asked her. No, Eileen and Janice were both lying on this issue. Nancy wondered why the sisters thought the dishonesty was necessary; perhaps they thought the defense would twist the truth.

Nancy guessed that Eileen thought Janice probably had repressed memories too and so she sent her to Kirk Barrett in the hope that he could uncover a few of them, hopefully one that would reveal whether or not she had seen Susan get in the van with Eileen and her father.

In the hallway, one reporter comments on the two Franklin women's intense need to be believed and how that need blinds them to the blatant contradictions in their individual testimony, and how exasperated they both get with Horngrad when he doesn't follow their revisionist explanations. Both of them have a problem with the truth, but in their own minds they are not lying, and that's why they are able to present their stories with such conviction. Their memory is selective: they remember details that point to their father's guilt, such as Franklin's "hello" to Janice, but shrug off other facts by saying, "That's twenty years ago."

The day should be over, but it isn't. Tipton wants to establish that George Franklin wasn't working as a fireman on the day Susan disappeared, so she calls Barry Johnson, an assistant fire chief, who appears in full dress uniform pushing a cart stacked high with logbooks.

Barry Johnson never cared for George Franklin; in fact he has had a visceral dislike for him almost since the day he met him. He found him morally offensive, and repulsive, particularly his demeaning, exploitative attitude toward women. He is, in Johnson's mind, a crude, classless asshole, who is undoubtedly guilty of killing Susan Nason.

But Barry Johnson is not asked about his feelings for George Franklin or his opinions of his guilt. He testifies from the records that in 1969 Franklin was assigned as an engine rider on C Platoon at Station 2 in San Mateo and that Franklin was not on duty on September 22 of that year. Johnson also testifies that Franklin was not on duty on September 22, 1970, either. The parties stipulate that Franklin's personnel records indicate he was given family leave during 1967 when Leah was confined to a mental hospital.

It is now 5:00 P.M. Several jurors have objected to running into the evening, mentioning ill spouses, PTA meetings, and the like. Both attorneys—neither one of whom wants an angry jury—have assured Smith they think they are on schedule. Smith relents and adjourns at 5:05. Monday is a holiday, so court is in recess for four days, a welcome break.

51

November 13, 1990—Tuesday

VINCE POPS OUT OF HIS DOOR AND CRIES, "PLEASE rise! Court is now in session, please be seated," and sprints down the first row of the jury box to his place by the door. In a few minutes he leaves to collect the jurors and they walk in looking refreshed; not overjoyed to be back, just refreshed.

Tipton looks colorful and crisp in a cranberry-colored jacket, but her clothes are beginning to hang a little on her already small frame. Other than Fig Newtons and milk for lunch, her "trial food" (it stops her stomach from growling in court), she has stopped eating and lost almost twenty pounds. Morse has begun teasing her, calling her "Mrs. Bones" because of her disappearing rear end.

Tipton is coming down with a cold and she is slightly hoarse this morning. If she has to lose her voice, though, today is the day to do it: her primary witness, Dr. Lenore Terr, will gladly do most of the talking.

Horngrad has fought hard to keep Terr off the stand—her testimony, after all, is the doorway through which all the uncharged conduct has marched—and he argues again today that her testimony is not admissible under California case law. He requests a hearing to determine whether Terr's opinions meet the standards of reliability for new scientific evidence. Smith denies the motion and rules that Dr. Terr will be allowed to testify as to the nature of memory, the mechanisms of repression, and the process of retrieval of lost memories, but that she will not be allowed to opine as to whether Eileen in fact has a repressed memory or whether her story of the killing is a true or false memory. The jury will be instructed that they are not to consider her testimony for either of these purposes.

Dr. Terr's testimony is essential to the prosecution's case: the jury has been told a believable but still rather incredible story, and now they must be taught to view it in the broader context of memory and trauma and the protective processes of the human mind. The jury must also be given the tools for performing their ultimate task: deciding whether Eileen Franklin's memory of the murder is true or false.

Dr. Terr strides into the courtroom looking the academic. She is on the short side, slightly heavy-footed, and her frizzy brown hair looks plastered in place. Rather than the predictable heavy countenance of the self-important intellectual, however, she displays an open, pleasant smile and an easy self-confidence. Tipton leads her through her impressive professional credentials: she is a clinical professor of psychiatry at the University of California at San Francisco and a lecturer in law and psychiatry at the University of California at Berkeley and Davis law schools. She has published over forty professional articles and is on the American Board of Psychiatry and Neurology. She has become known for her work in the field of childhood trauma and the type of memory that is created by the trauma.

Dr. Terr is not modest: in her writings and testimony, she credits herself with being one of the primary people responsible for awakening modern psychiatry to the reality and effects of childhood trauma after the long period of Freudian denial and neglect. Her primary work was with the Chowchilla children, a group of schoolchildren in California who were kidnapped in their school bus which was then submerged in a pit of mud. A summary of her work in psychic trauma has just recently been published in the book *Too Scared to Cry*. She testifies she is being paid $250 per hour as an expert, and although she cannot admit in front of the jury that she interviewed Eileen, which she did twice in August, she testifies that she has spent close to twenty hours familiarizing herself with the facts of the case.

Terr leads off with a lengthy explanation of the six types of memory, and before she is finished it has become apparent exactly how powerful and effective a witness she will be. In the simplest possible terms, using no jargon whatsoever, she explains about immediate memory (the rest of your sentence), short-term memory (what you had for breakfast), knowledge and skill memory (math tables), priming (riding a bicycle), then suddenly she forgets the fifth, and when Tipton reminds her of associative memory, she pokes fun at herself, saying, "Oh yeah, associative memory is the one that you don't even have to think of because"—here the entire courtroom breaks into laughter and she joins in with an impish smile—"this is conditioning memory." The jury settles back: she is not a female version of the gray men, she is a human being who makes mistakes and says, "Oh yeah," just like everyone else. The sixth type, episodic memory, is the story of our life, and she introduces the jury to the complex field of trauma and dissociation by saying simply that "there are certain kinds of problems that can interrupt or hurt episodic memory." A psychic trauma is the "kind of harm or damage . . . that is caused by a terrible external event [or] series of events. . . ." In children, psychic trauma can interrupt episodic memory. Psychic trauma can also interrupt the three processes of memory: perception, storage, and retrieval.

In her folksy, down-home manner she gives a loose, rambling explanation of the term "repression" or "repressed memory," describing it as an active but unconscious process of forgetting or keeping down painful or hurtful memories. Her examples are in the form of clinical experiences, and when she gets to the good part of an anecdote, she leans forward in her chair and looks the jurors in the eye like a good storyteller. She tells of a spinster who, on her first date at the age of fifty-three, unexpectedly orally copulated the man as they sat in his car. It appeared that as a girl she had been forced into oral sex acts, although she has no such memory.

Terr has written a paper soon to be published in the *American Journal of Psychiatry* setting forth her theory on the two types of psychic trauma and now she explains it to the jury: a Type I trauma is caused by a single "blow"; Type II is caused by multiple blows or incidents. In her paper she makes it clear that these are rough categories, theoretical or organizational constructs that she has developed as a way of looking at psychic trauma, but in her testimony she presents them as clear and well-accepted differentiations. Type I is exemplified by the Chowchilla children, none of whom have forgotten the details of the kidnapping, although several of them have tried. The details in these memories may be incorrect and accompanied by hallucinations, and the victims may exhibit the typical characteristics of post-traumatic stress disorder.

In Type II traumas, the child learns to cope by forgetting:

"What happens in Type II trauma is that the child, instead of being surprised by these events, anticipates these events: something more is going to happen; something worse is going to happen. I know that more things can happen. Once a child begins to anticipate events, the child can actually use mechanisms to stop perceiving, even stop the input or stop the storage or stop the retrieval."

In other words, the child *learns* to dissociate or repress the memory in order to avoid the pain.

Terr does not explain to the jury that she believes that Type II traumas leave the person with unremitting feelings of rage ("The rage of the repeatedly abused child cannot safely be underestimated"), and that the rage may become so fearsome to the child that the child could become very aggressive or swing between extreme anger and extreme passivity. She also does not explain that Type II traumas frequently lead to later diagnoses such as borderline, narcissistic, and multiple personality disorders, and to the creation of "chronic victims."

In her written report of her interview with Eileen, Terr did not question the validity of the murder memory. She has also said that she believes Eileen's story. Although she cannot make that statement in court directly, she makes it indirectly by correlating the known facts of Eileen's story, without specifically mentioning them, to the various criteria she espouses for Type II trauma victims. For example, she explains that Type II children will start doing things like hiding, telling themselves they are invisible, and counting.

Tipton ties Eileen's testimony closer to Terr's theory of repression when she asks her what other factors might cause repression and Terr mentions the "loyalty conflict" in which somebody threatens you with what will happen if you remember; the shame and guilt over feeling that you were an accomplice to the terror; the "gore" of the event; the failure of a third party to talk to the child shortly after the event.

Now Tipton poses a hypothetical question which matches Eileen's story perfectly: If a child is subjected to one hideous, violent act coupled with a death threat in the midst of a childhood filled with physical and sexual abuse by a parental figure, would the single act be repressed? It would most likely be, Terr responds.

Having had Terr bury Eileen's murder memory, Tipton now has her unearth it. What would be likely conditions for retrieval of a traumatic memory? she asks. First of all, Terr says, you would have to have a feeling of safety, a sense that you're financially secure and you can count on yourself for survival. Having children of the same age as you were at the time of the trauma would help because that often re-creates feelings of your own childhood. Being in therapy would increase your readiness for retrieval because you have a listening, trusting ear.

As for what could trigger the event, well, many things could: sights, sounds, smells, but certainly seeing somebody who looked just like the victim, or looking at someone who is in a similar posture to another person in the event could trigger the return of the memory.

Terr talks herself dry and Vince, clamping his huge ring of keys to his side to stop the clanking, takes her a cup of water. While she is drinking she casts a glance at Franklin over the rim of the cup, her eyes betraying a cold, professional curiosity.

Terr explains that the return of a repressed memory is often like the bursting of an abscess: initially a huge bolus of memory shoots forth, and then, just as an abscess will continue to drain fluid (if treated correctly), the memory will release more details to the conscious mind. And as an abscess may never be fully cleaned out, so all the details of a repressed memory may never surface. In other words, blank spots in the memory are to be expected.

Tipton turns Dr. Terr to a critical point: How is a false traumatic memory created and how do you tell a false traumatic memory from a true traumatic memory? It is entirely possible, Terr explains, for someone to tell a child again and again that something happened, to keep harping on it, and eventually the child will believe it. Children can be led to make false accusations of sexual abuse, for example.

As for distinguishing between a false and a true memory, Terr looks at three factors: First, the person's symptoms. Although the person may have repressed the memory, a part of them remembers the event and causes them to repeat it again and again through such behaviors as self-mutilation or suicide attempts, which are a result of the repressed rage and feelings of hopelessness. You should also see a "handful" of convincing symptoms, such as nightmares, intense fears, a lack of belief in your own future, or a feeling of emotional numbness. These children prime themselves to be escape artists, to hide, for example, in closets.

Second, a true memory should be rich in detail. A false memory is a child describing her psychiatrist dressing up in leather "G-straps" and lying down on the floor and "having sex" with her. A true memory has details about what it felt like, what it sounded like, a positional sense.

Lastly, a true memory should be told with the appropriate emotion; it should be accompanied by "some weeping or some tightness of the body or some kind of a sign that emotionally that you're wrought up, that you're experiencing something."

In other words, your pain should show.

To illustrate all three of her points, Terr tells in horrible detail a tragic story about one of her patients, a young girl, who sat down on an open drainpipe in a swimming pool and was eviscerated. Two of the girl's siblings were in the pool and witnessed the evisceration and a third, the youngest, was in the adult pool and saw nothing. Two years later, when the girl died, the youngest sister described the tragedy to Terr as if she had actually witnessed it. Terr says she could tell it was a false traumatic memory because the sister gave only the standard details and did not display the appropriate symptoms. The siblings who witnessed the tragedy showed such symptoms: the brother spent time trying to design safe swimming pools with his blocks, and the older sister was connecting everything in her room with a string, representing the intestines. Of course, Terr also knew from the beginning that the young girl's memory was false.

Will the adult's recovered memory of a traumatic childhood trauma be accurate, Tipton asks in her final point. Yes, Terr explains, when the memory pops out of the abscess, it will be as clear as the event itself. The fact that the memory has been repressed may actually enhance its accuracy.

Horngrad has been noticeably quiet at the defense table during direct examination. He can see that the jurors are enthralled with Dr. Terr. Were he to interrupt one of her tales with an objection as to relevance or responsiveness, he would most certainly earn their enmity. But he has work to do on cross: Terr has, in effect, just given her stamp of approval to the processes of Eileen's mind and the truthfulness of her memory.

Horngrad quickly finds Terr to be a worthy adversary. He begins by asking her questions about statements she has made in her book or in articles that appear contrary to her testimony today. Politely, firmly, she argues with him and corrects him on his use of certain terms and keeps on talking when she feels he has interrupted her. When he effectively demonstrates an inconsistency, she will turn and talk to the jury for several minutes about the facts of a particular case, diverting them from Horngrad's point, or she will recount interesting but not particularly relevant anecdotes. Horngrad cannot control her; she is center stage and all eyes are on her. His points are lost in her charisma.

Terr grudgingly admits that she has had very few cases involving repressed memories of murder and that with most of her patients the nature of the trauma is already known.

Horngrad focuses, as he must, on Terr's list of criteria for determining a true memory from a false memory. In one of

Terr's studies on trauma, all of her subjects reported dreams or nightmares, and yet Eileen reports no dream disturbances, not even as an adult. Terr has stressed in her writings that many of the Chowchilla children developed fears of vehicles and school buses. It takes Horngrad ten minutes, but finally Terr admits that the children would be frightened of their kidnappers and unlikely to get on a bus with them.

Tipton seldom objects, perhaps because her voice is disintegrating rapidly, but also because Terr can obviously take care of herself. The jury continues to nod approvingly as the doctor explains concepts or skillfully slides out of Horngrad's pincers.

Aren't some fears and other post-traumatic symptoms contagious, Horngrad asks her. Can't the symptoms be caught like a disease? Terr has written about a brother of one of the Chowchilla children who had picked up his sibling's fears and anxieties and a girl who became terrified of earthquakes after hearing her grandmother describe her experience in an earthquake. Terr has also written of her own daughter becoming distressed playing Ring Around the Rosie because it was a rhyme made up about the great plague in Europe in the fourteenth century. Horngrad is suggesting the possibility that Eileen may have picked up some of her behaviors or symptoms from Janice or Leah. Yes, certainly, Terr answers, you can pick up a symptom or two, but the person will never pick up the terror itself, never the experience of the trauma.

As for Piaget's false memory about someone trying to kidnap him from his pram, yes, he had a very detailed, elaborate visual memory of the incident based on what somebody else told him, but that was all he had. Piaget was a very careful recorder of his experiences and nowhere does he describe any of the post-traumatic symptoms that would have corroborated his memory; i.e., Terr never would have believed him in the first place, because he had no symptoms.

Horngrad now introduces his most delicate theme. He long ago decided he cannot directly propose the revenge theory; that is, that Eileen and Janice, consciously or unconsciously, are accusing their father of murder to get even with him for all the rotten things he did to them as children. First, he doesn't believe Eileen was sexually abused, and second, it would be devastating to make such an admission to the jury. He must, however, suggest an answer to the question of why Eileen would accuse her father of murder if it weren't true. He must suggest the answer without saying it.

Isn't it possible, he asks Terr, to determine that a child has been traumatized but to not know the exact nature of the trauma? In other words, sure Eileen was traumatized, but maybe it was something other than witnessing a murder that traumatized her.

Terr takes his question and runs with it, setting up what is perhaps the best piece of pure theater in the entire drama. She explains that she went to see the movie *Stand by Me,* and when she saw the two boys high up on a trestle running for their lives as a train roared toward them, she turned to her husband and said, "Whoever wrote that scene is playing post-traumatic games with me." She was sure that whoever had written it had almost been hit by a train. When she learned the writer was Stephen King, she researched his past and found out that, although he had repressed the memory, he had in fact seen a friend get hit by a train. King had watched as the pieces were picked up and put in a basket.

Horngrad bites: How do you know King actually saw his friend get killed as opposed to hearing about it afterwards like the little sister of the girl in the swimming pool? Terr's answer is fascinating and revealing.

"As a child psychiatrist, I know that King saw it because I see what he produces, what—he produces these oil rigs that run down people, murderous cars that run down people, fire hydrants that explode in people's faces, miniature armies of toy soldiers that shoot people.

"Everything in King is mechanical and terrifying, and he shows me time and time again what he's doing by—by mowing people down in the same kind of way that his friend was."

Isn't it possible, Horngrad asks, that King walked with his friend up to the tracks and then left and came back or turned away momentarily and only saw what happened to his friend afterwards, when he was picked up and put in a basket?

No, Terr insists, she knows King was exposed to the trauma because of his post-traumatic symptoms.

"King was exposed because King came home with his pants wet. He didn't speak for twenty-four hours to his mother."

King bears another symptom of being traumatized: he keeps reenacting the trauma. "King can't stop doing what he does," she explains.

She personally confirmed this when sitting in a hotel coffee shop one day she heard several people telling someone that he had to stop killing so many people. She realized they were talking about a movie script when one of them said: "You want to kill too many people; and if you do a movie for us, you can only kill one." The other person had replied: "I've got to kill more because it's really part of me. I've got to do it."

"And then I looked at the person really carefully, and it was Stephen King," Terr says in amazement, as if she'd encountered one of her heroes. "He was sitting in my lap in a coffee shop.

"And the problem," Terr says, rolling now, "is one that the —the person who has been traumatized can't stop this kind of behavior; it's a behavior that has to be. And the person may not be aware of why the behavior is linked to the trauma, but it's there, and it has to be repeated."

Dr. Terr's spontaneous description of her encounter with Stephen King in a coffee shop has mesmerized the entire courtroom. The jury looks at her expectantly, as if waiting for the ending of the story, to see if she tapped King on the shoulder and asked him about his childhood encounter with the train. The notion of a psychiatrist of her renown translating complex principles of human psychology through the movies of Stephen King rather than obtuse medical jargon captivates the jury.

For an instant, the stage in Courtroom Nine is haunted by the images of two trauma victims: Stephen King and Eileen Franklin. One re-enacts his trauma by writing books and movie scripts about runaway trains that run over people and cars that kill, and the other re-enacts her traumas by trying to kill herself, becoming a prostitute, marrying a father substitute, and becoming a chronic victim. Unfortunately, according to Terr, the prognosis for either one is not very good. The repetition compulsion, as Freud called it, can lock up a personality.

As to whether or not a therapist can work back from the observed symptoms to discern the nature of the underlying trauma itself, obviously if Terr can watch a movie and reconstruct the specific childhood psychic trauma of the scriptwriter, certainly she can listen to and observe a patient and reconstruct their original trauma or traumas. The symptoms reek of the original event, she says, and symptoms from one trauma will not necessarily mix with the symptoms of another trauma. She makes it clear that she can tell whether a child is telling her a true or a false memory.

Horngrad continues to work on the nature and etiology of a false memory and this time he comes very close to admitting the abuse as a motive for revenge. He asks Terr to explain a "loyalty conflict," and she says it is a conflict in a child who has been stroked and loved by the very person who has repeatedly abused her. Could not a child with reasons to be mad at an abusing parent construct a "compensatory fantasy" and blame that parent for something she didn't do, he asks. He refers to Celeste, one of the Chowchilla children described in Terr's book. Celeste had a fight with her mother the morning of the kidnapping and was pushed from the house by her mother. After the kidnapping, Celeste described one of the kidnappers as a woman with exactly the same features as her mother, although in fact all of the kidnappers were men. Because of her anger, Celeste had converted her mother into one of her kidnappers.

Terr sidesteps this comparison by stating that Celeste was a Type I trauma victim, where misperception is much more common. In cases of repeated abuse, the victim is not likely to mistake the identity of the abuser.

Isn't it possible, Horngrad asks, nudging the unspoken revenge/false memory theory in front of the jury, that a child who has been sexually abused would also show the "I don't have a future" symptom? Terr gives him that one.

At one point Horngrad asks Terr if it's not true, as she has written, that Type II traumas tend to create massive character or personality disorders; when she agrees, Horngrad drops it, perhaps realizing that the jury will hold his client responsible for any character disorders from which Eileen might be suffering.

Horngrad then takes a weak shot: Might verbal violence constitute a Type II trauma? Terr dismisses the possibility out of hand: a terrible household is not a Type II trauma. A trauma is the internal processing of a horrible external event, and being yelled at or cursed is not such an event. So much for Horngrad's "fractious household" theory.

Terr eventually takes over the cross-examination. When Horngrad asks her a question, she turns and give her answer, always interesting but not always responsive, directly to the jury, as if Horngrad weren't even in the room. If Horngrad uses language she doesn't like, she will help him translate it into the correct or acceptable terms, like a good college professor. If he interrupts her, she will say sternly, "I haven't finished yet." Horngrad puts up with her behavior good-naturedly, perhaps because he really has no choice.

Tipton's voice continues to fail. By lunchtime it is raspy. In the early afternoon she is croaking out her objections. She has loaded herself up with tea and cold medicines, determined not to let the cold get the best of her. She could ask for a continuance, but she won't. Who knows, maybe one or two jurors will feel sympathetic and admire her for hanging in there. The advantage is wherever you find it.

The jury is out on Salcido. During lunch several Franklin jurors watch intently as the prosecutor announces to the TV cameras that "Showing mercy to cruelty is equivalent to indifference to good."

Morse spends many of the recesses standing out on the courthouse steps, where he can smoke. Probably a quarter of the people entering or leaving the building—from defense attorneys to politicians to secretaries to janitors to ordinary citizens—say something to him as he stands there smoking, calling him affectionately "Bobbie" or "Bones." A few pull him aside for a quick word or two, most joke with him, and if it's a woman, she usually flirts. Reporters know it's a good place to chat up the detective. Morse, fully aware of what's happening in the courtroom, turns to a journalist who has followed him outside. "Hey," he says, with his lazy half-smile, his left eyebrow arching and falling, "is it all coming together for you now?"

Back in the courtroom, one exchange brings smiles all around. Terr is explaining to Horngrad why there really are no controlled studies of traumatic memory.

"Because you've never had a chance to do it?" Horngrad asks.

"What?"

"You've never had a chance to . . ."

"To traumatize people?" She interrupts in the tone of a Jewish mother scolding her son. "I'm shocked at you." Psychiatrists are not ghouls, she lectures him, and no one would set up an experiment to replicate trauma.

Horngrad scores a solid point by noting that at the time Eileen retrieved the memory she was within days of a hearing on her divorce action. When Terr sees where she's being led, she backpedals rapidly from her earlier testimony that a feeling of being safe was almost a required condition for the return of a repressed memory. A feeling of safety, she now says, is not a *requirement* for the return of a repressed memory, only one of several possible associated conditions.

Tipton asks to approach the bench and quips on the way that maybe she should wear a mask. Not to be out-quipped, Horngrad suggests that Wachtel stand next to her. The jury laughs, Margaret Nason laughs, so does George Franklin. For a moment there is almost a sense of community, the feeling that comes from sharing a long, difficult journey.

Then Terr, possibly seeking to make up lost ground, appears to explicitly endorse the accuracy of Eileen's story. Horngrad has asked her what evidence one can rely on to be *sure* an image is a real memory. Symptoms and signs, she replies, and those must be interpreted by a professional. She offers:

"I thought there was strong evidence also in details, the

richness of detail that the person provided in the telling of the tale and in the accompanying emotion of the tale."

The *person* Terr refers to could only have been Eileen. Horngrad does not object—to do so would only focus the jury's attention on her remark—but he does ask permission to approach the bench, which is denied.

Terr has written about false traumatic memories and how they are created, and Horngrad brings up several instances that would support the proposition that a child who is subject to some sort of trauma can create or imagine entire scenes.

In her book, Terr had told the story of Betsy Ferguson, a young girl who lived with her grandmother. One morning her mother's boyfriend came to the house and her grandmother told her to call the police. Instead, the boyfriend drove Betsy to school and then returned and strangled the grandmother and took the car. When Betsy came home from school, she couldn't get in the door. The police were called and she was told what had happened to her grandmother. She later developed a very distinct, slow-motion visual memory of the boyfriend strangling her grandmother, despite the fact that she hadn't even seen her grandmother's body. Traumatized, Betsy, in Terr's words, had transferred what she had heard (the details of what happened) and felt (guilt over not having called the police) into a visual memory of what she had never seen. She had "experienced a transfer of perceptual impressions."

Betsy Ferguson's experience is similar to Eileen Franklin's: Eileen, traumatized by physical and sexual abuse and the loss of her best friend, and hearing the details of the murder, and reading about a child abductor who looked like her father, creates a visual memory of her best friend being killed. The analogy is not complete, because Betsy's memory was never repressed, but the subsequent surfacing of Eileen's memory could be explained by the fact that the creation and retrieval of the memory were psychologically beneficial to her. If the mind continually strives to make sense of things, this false traumatic memory would make sense of Eileen's unhappy life. It would make her into a victim and victims cannot be held accountable for anything they do. In addition, Eileen would experience what psychologists call "secondary gain": she would receive all the attention she ever wanted.

The jury was a long way from this theory, and they would certainly never hear it from the lips of Dr. Lenore Terr. Horngrad could never propose it outright: the risk was too great that the jury would nail the defendant for the other abuse he inflicted on her.

Terr, tugging at a lock of hair, quickly explains that false memories are very uncommon. She admits she doesn't know everything about false memories because they are so rare. It would, she says, be like "trying to study giraffes in Ohio."

The consensus among the press is that Terr was very convincing and that Horngrad did not shake her on cross. Whatever points he scored were lost in roaring trains and coffee shop-plotted murders. He seemed frustrated at the end.

Nancy Salazar laughed to herself when Terr, rumpled and mismatched, walked in and sat down. How many doctors like this have I worked with over the years, she chuckled. But when Terr began speaking, it was like magic, and Nancy felt like she and the other jurors were having an audience with a special person. She spoke in a language everyone could understand. She was there to *talk* with the jury, not lecture them.

From the bench, Judge Smith found Dr. Terr to be an excellent witness: very disarming in appearance, effective in her use of lay terminology, and absolutely unshakeable on cross-examination. He also found her to be superb entertainment.

HORNGRAD COULD POSSIBLY HAVE DONE A BETTER JOB ON CROSS-examination in differentiating between the concept of truth as it exists in the therapist's office and truth in the criminal justice process. Mental health professionals are not trained fact-finders. It is neither the function nor the goal of the clinician in the normal therapeutic setting to determine the factual reality of what the patient is saying; the purpose of the clinical experience is therapy and, by and large, the truth is whatever the patient says it is. The therapeutic relationship must be based on acceptance and trust, and a therapist is not going to enhance this relationship by challenging or questioning the patient's story when she describes what happened to her as a child. In many instances, the therapist will, instead, assure the patient, as Barrett did Eileen, that he believes her story. The factual truth is not the point in therapy; rather, the point is for the patient to make sense of the experience and to heal. Sometimes this principle is referred to in psychiatry as "the shared delusion." Other psychiatrists sum it up differently: "The patient never lies." Therapists are, by nature and training, healers, not truth-finders.

Horngrad could perhaps have pointed out that Terr's method for determining the truth or falsity of a patient's memory is not based on any scientific data. Her three factors—symptoms, richness of detail, and accompanying emotion—have not been proposed as a hypothesis and proven through a carefully plotted, rigorous field study. Neither are these three factors generally accepted in psychiatry as a method for determining the truth or falsity of a patient's memory. They are nothing more than Terr's educated "hunches," based on her clinical experiences. When she says that she can tell if a child is telling the truth or not, she is making a personal statement, not a scientific one, and one that a great many psychiatrists would seriously disagree with. Recent studies suggest that it is impossible to tell from observing a person whether the person is lying or not.

Likewise, Terr's distinction between Type I and Type II traumas, which she relies on so heavily in her testimony in de facto validation of Eileen's memory, are not diagnostic categories generally accepted in psychiatric literature; although she refers to these traumas as mental disorders, they are not found in the *Diagnostic and Statistical Manual III—Revised,* the generally accepted manual of psychiatric diagnoses. There are no scientific data to support her critical statement that a child must suffer multiple traumas in order to repress a memory. Many therapists have clinical experiences of patients repressing single traumas. Neither are there any data to support her statement that repressed memories are clearer or more pristine than nonrepressed memories. Finally, many therapists would seriously dispute her statement that it is possible to identify the specific underlying trauma simply by looking at the patient's symptoms.

The area of childhood psychic trauma and repressed memories is in its infancy and is to a large extent bereft of carefully collected data and accepted scientific conclusions. For that reason, Dr. Bessel van der Kolk, perhaps the most widely recognized expert in the field, has stated that he would decline to give any expert testimony in this area.

Horngrad could have made these points, but it is unlikely the jury's reaction to Terr and her testimony would have been any different. The fact is, they liked her, and what she said made sense.

52

November 13, 1990—Tuesday, continued

THIS DAY SHOULD END WITH THE EXIT OF THE RUMpled psychiatrist and the pleasant feelings of maternal benevolence that linger in her wake, but it's only 4:00 P.M. and Tipton calls her next witness, Leah Franklin. Within minutes Leah will bring everyone crashing back to the painful reality of the Franklin family.

Tipton won't enjoy what she is about to do: rip open the wounds that Leah has tried so hard to heal, part the curtain of denial that she has lived behind for so long, and bring her face to face, for an instant, with her own responsibility for what happened to her children. Tipton wants the jury to see and feel what life was like in the Franklin household, the good times mingled with the terror, and she knows the complete picture has to include an answer to the question: Where was Mommy while all this was going on?

Dealing with Leah has been a frustrating experience for Tipton. The woman was in massive denial and claims not to remember much of anything about her life with George Frank-lin. When Tipton asked her earlier about her nervous breakdown and hospitalization, Leah said she didn't remember it. She also said she didn't remember the incident in which George allegedly held a gun to her head. In one pre-trial interview Morse asked her what kind of a guy George was.

"That is difficult for me to remember," Leah had replied. "Certainly not a person I wanted to be around. After our marriage ended, I pretty much chose that I would not involve myself with anyone like that again."

"Did George drink during those days?"

"Yes."

"Did he drink to excess?"

"I can't answer that. I am sorry, it is going back twenty years and I cannot really remember it."

Had George abused her?

"Yeah, physically and verbally."

"Could you describe that for us?"

"No. Again, it is so far back. I can't really retrieve it. It has been such a long time."

"Did he ever hit you? With his fist?"

"I can't remember."

"Did he ever choke you or hit you with any objects?"

"I can't remember."

"Did you ever report this abuse to the police?"

"No. Never."

While Leah had a general memory of him abusing the children, she had difficulty coming up with specifics because it all was "so far back in my mind."

Tipton sees Leah as the battered wife, a casualty of George Franklin's brutal inhumanity, but even so she finds it hard to believe that Leah wasn't aware of the sexual abuse suffered by her daughters. While Leah would later remember things her husband had done to her, it wasn't easy for her to admit what he had done to the children, because that meant she would have known what was going on and hadn't done anything about it.

Tipton is sometimes overwhelmed by the extent of the damage George Franklin has inflicted on his wife and children. The saddest part is that the siblings can't really help each other: Janice can't really be there for Eileen, Eileen for George, George for Diana, Kate for Janice; and Leah, Leah can't really be there for anybody. These people have all been torn up in the same way. If one tried to help the other, she would run headfirst into her own pain. Tipton feels more compassion for the children since they had had no control of the situation. When she stops and thinks about what this man had done to his wife and offspring, she's amazed that all of them weren't locked up in mental wards somewhere.

The woman who walks into the courtroom late this afternoon is a long way from the 200-pound housewife and mother of five who wore long hair and bulky dresses and sandals and lived mired in fatigue and depression on Harvester Drive in the mid-sixties. Leah is classy now, a sophisticated professional woman, slender except for the flare of her hips, and she is well dressed in a black jacket with a large gold pin, a pumpkin-colored blouse, and a flowered skirt. Her thick black hair is cut short to frame her finely featured face. Her small red mouth is drawn tight, and the corners of her oval eyes are pulled slightly down in perpetual melancholy. She looks years younger than her white-haired former husband, but her face is strained and her eyes seem to squint as if she has just stepped into bright sunlight.

When Leah enters the room, Tipton and Horngrad are at the bench conferring with Smith, and she hesitates at the bar, waiting for someone to notice her, to signal her what to do. She doesn't see the Nasons, seated only a few feet behind her. The jury and the press stare with fascination at the mother of Eileen and Janice, the former wife of the defendant; as the conference drags on and Leah stands all alone at the rail, everyone finally looks away, as if embarrassed over the intensity of their curiosity.

Finally Morse, sensing the uneasiness in the courtroom, turns around and notices Leah at the bar. He motions for her to sit down and she does.

On the stand Leah's voice is rough, husky. Slight bags puff

beneath her oval eyes. She can't bring herself to say her former husband's name, and refers to him only as "the defendant." She testifies that there had been a mattress in his van in 1969 and that he drove the van exclusively until he gave it to Diana in 1981. She remembers the license plate—VXJ707.

George is not writing on his pad. His puts on his glasses, leans back in his chair, and looks at his former wife intently.

"Can you describe the environment, the atmosphere in the Franklin household during the late sixties?" Tipton asks Leah.

"It was very stressful." Her face begins to tighten. "It was just too much work, too much abuse: verbal abuse, physical abuse. It was living in terror. It was not being safe in my own house. I wasn't safe, and my children weren't safe."

Had her children been in the courtroom, they would certainly have noted with bitter satisfaction their place on her list of concerns. Her first complaint was about *how hard she had had to work,* and her second had been about *how she hadn't been safe.*

"Are there periods of time during those years that you do not recall in full detail?" Tipton asks her.

"I don't have a very complete memory of those years because they were very difficult and when my marriage ended, I worked as long and as hard as I could to get as far away from those memories as I could."

"Were you hospitalized for a nervous breakdown during the sixties?"

"I don't remember."

Leah testifies that the only thing she knew about the murder of Susan Nason was what she read in the newspapers and she hadn't discussed those facts with her children.

When Tipton asks her about the bloody shirt that Franklin had supposedly given her shortly after Susan disappeared, Leah's emotional devastation surfaces. Horngrad had asked her about the shirt at the prelim but she had had no memory of it. Now she says:

"I didn't remember it when it was first asked. When I remembered it was when—at the preliminary hearing, when Mr. Horngrad asked me if I remembered it. At that point I said no,

I was present with the defendant. The questioning was going on, and as the questioning was going on, I realized that I remembered the shirt."

Her explanation is slow and pained.

"And we were asking something else at that point in time and answering other questions. And then, when I left the courtroom, I knew that I had remembered it, and I couldn't recall it again. I think I was asked the same question later by Mr. Morse, and I told him that I had remembered it but that I again couldn't recall it. And then the memory came back to me and I called Mr. Morse and made a statement."

Over strenuous objections by Horngrad, Leah is allowed to testify that for a long time she had suspected that "the defendant" had murdered Susan Nason. When she confronted him with it, he replied only, "Why do you think things like that of me?" She sees his failure to deny the murder to her as an admission of guilt.

One of the reasons Leah suspected George of the murder was that he told her in 1978 that he had written his memoirs and sealed them in wax and buried them on Star Hill Road. She had mentioned her suspicions in one or two conversations with Janice, but never to Eileen.

It is obvious that Leah is not a trial lawyer: several times she rambles on with clearly inadmissible evidence, once or twice after Smith has sustained Horngrad's objection.

It is 4:45 when Tipton completes her direct. Leah will have to come back tomorrow for cross. Smith excuses the jury and then denies Horngrad's motion to dismiss the charge based on Terr's endorsement of the truth of Eileen's memory.

LEAH WAS SITTING AT HER DESK IN HER LAW OFFICE WHEN EILEEN called almost a year ago and told her about Susan Nason. She was shocked. She had tried for twenty years to block George Franklin and those hideous years out of her life, out of her mind, her soul; she had struggled to put together a new life, one that didn't include memories of Harvester and Beach Park, a new life in which she was an attorney with her own office and a Mercedes-Benz, and wife to a successful contractor with a house in the exclusive town of Portola Valley; and now the man had risen out of the dark past to haunt her carefully crafted present.

When Eileen hung up, Leah tried to blank George Franklin from her mind again; she knew something bad was going to happen, that it would inevitably mean pain for her. She worried about what it would do to her life, how she would tell her husband.

Leah has not seen her ex-husband since before he went to Hawaii in the early eighties and when she walked into the courtroom at the prelim she didn't recognize him. She was shocked at his appearance—he looked like hell, and she wondered why. Something must have happened to make him look so horribly old and dead inside.

Leah knows her children harbor grudges against her for not being a better mother. Eileen has confronted her with angry tears over the appendicitis episode. Leah told her that she went to the camp to pick her up as soon as she possibly could, and that she called her father to take her to the hospital because she had four other kids to look after, and that she did visit her in the hospital. But Eileen sees it her own way.

She knows her children are angry at her for not protecting them and for not getting out of the marriage earlier—it was always blame Mom for everything, even after their father left and took up with another woman. She always felt that they directed their anger at their father toward her, and she hopes some day they can resolve those feelings. Her children don't understand how it was back then, what her life was like. Maybe they will have more understanding and compassion when they are a little older. Certainly none of her daughters are shouldering the burdens that she had as a young woman.

Growing up in her family you didn't question authority, either your parents or the church. You lived with what life handed you and made the best of it. Sure, now she wishes she had gotten out of her marriage years before she did, but she hadn't understood what was happening back then. Who would she have turned to? Nobody had heard of a battered spouse— she hadn't even heard the term when she graduated from law school in 1981—and there were no shelters for battered wives, no support groups, no laws to protect her. In the sixties people didn't believe men beat their wives and abused their children. She had no employment skills: How would she make it with five children on three dollars an hour? She's not the only woman who sat back helpless in a rotten marriage for longer than she should have, but how was she supposed to have made the break? The Catholic Church prohibited divorce, and her parents hadn't supported her. The helplessness, the hopelessness—it was all she could do just to survive herself. God knows, if she had seen a way out back then, she would have taken it.

She is especially bitter about the church. It should offer options instead of being a party to the abuse of women and children through rigid adherence to dogma. As she sees it now, her life was being destroyed while the church looked the other way. Maybe in a thousand years the church will get around to thinking about marriage a bit more sensibly, but it won't do her any good. A few years ago, she had figured, "Okay, I may not be able to change the past, but I am going to make sure that the church acknowledges that this marriage was not right," and she sought and obtained an annulment. (This had infuriated Janice, who had said, "I suppose this means we're not her children anymore!")

Leah began her recovery in the early seventies when she lost weight, began to care about her appearance, and developed a sense of control over her life. She did have lots of stamina, after all, enough to go to school, raise five kids, and run the rental properties. By the time her marriage finally came apart in 1974, she had been married to George Franklin for half of her life, and his departure brought her tremendous relief. All the energy she had put into surviving she could now put into life, into school and new friends. She began law school about a year and a half later and, although she had her real estate license, decided not to go to work: there was money from the rental properties, which God knows she deserved for all of her past labors, and she wanted to be able to spend more time with her kids, who then ranged from eleven to seventeen.

She never had any idea that her daughters were being sexually abused. She had seen George's collection of pornography at the fire department, but never noticed any perverted or deviant sexual behavior on his part. The first she had known of the sexual abuse was when Janice told her in the late seventies that he had raped her.

People just don't understand how insidious George Franklin was: very charming to everyone outside the family and a monster inside the home. He must have deliberately hid the sexual abuse. She guessed if she matched their schedules in those years, she would find several nights a week when she was in school from 6:30 to 10:00 and he was off-duty. He must have waited until she left to do what he did to them. She knows her daughters think she wasn't there for them, but she never had an inkling, never suspected it. *Nobody in those days thought things like that went on inside the house.*

Beneath all of her children's anger, she knows they love her. She knows Eileen loves her. Didn't Eileen call her to tell her about her memory before she called the district attorney? Children have strange ways of telling their parents that they love them. Most of the time she is on speaking terms with four of her five children; that isn't too bad, is it? Kate lives nearby and they go for walks together. And George Jr. has the most wonderful sense of humor. Diana, her youngest, is still very special to her. If you were to see them, they look polished and loved, as if someone has been tending to them all these years. When they get a little older, they will understand that those were bad years, that's all, everyone was just trying to survive. They'll see that she didn't know herself what was really wrong or what to do about it.

Everything makes sense to her now. Poor Eileen has been keeping this horrible secret inside ever since she was eight and it has always impaired their relationship. This memory prevented her daughter from trusting or confiding in her and naturally she's been angry at her ever since. Now Eileen is saying, I love you, trust me, we've got to work this through. Leah knows, hopes, that there will come a time for healing and forgiving.

After Eileen's phone call, Leah tried to pull herself together but things had gotten worse and she thought she couldn't handle it much longer if everything was always so black. Then one morning on the way to work she thought, *I'm going to be dead for thousands and thousands of years and this is today and I've got something difficult to deal with and I'm going to deal with it. I always have.*

From that moment forward she tried to find something to appreciate in each day—a piece of music, a conversation with a friend. She told herself there was no reason to become overwhelmed with everything that has gone wrong or might go wrong; why not choose to enjoy the good things in life?

As for Doug Horngrad and his questions, Leah knows he is going to try to paint her as the ex-wife with an ax to grind, a co-conspirator with her daughters—which isn't true—and she has no intention of making his job easy for him. She doesn't have a current memory of many things from that time period, and she isn't about to try and reconstruct things, to go running around digging up the pieces and fitting them together. No good could come from that. She will leave the pieces where they lie, and Mr. Horngrad will have to make his case some other way.

53

November 14, 1990—Wednesday

L EAH'S STORY ABOUT THE BLOODY SHIRT CAPTURES the day's headlines. One reporter comments that it's just another Franklin woman with a repressed memory. Maybe it's hereditary, this losing and recovering memories.

The cops and the attorneys and Franklin rise as usual when the judge signals Vince to bring the jury in, but this morning they continue standing and staring off into space long after the jury is seated, zoned out, and finally Smith has to tell them to sit down.

The night has not been good to Leah. She is wobbly, unsure, from the very first word. It's almost as if Tipton primed the pump yesterday afternoon and the pain continued rising overnight.

Horngrad begins with the October 25 phone call in which Eileen asked Leah if she remembered whether Eileen changed after Susan's death. Leah had gone home and looked at family photographs, but nothing came to mind. Eileen called back the next day.

"When Eileen phoned me on October 26th, she told me three things: First was that one day when she was home from school sick, her father took her from the house to another place; that he held her down, and another man raped her. And then she said, 'Do you want me to go on?' and I said, 'Yes.' "

Slowly, Leah begins to lose it. Her voice falters, her eyes close as she speaks.

"And then she said: 'My father murdered Susan Nason. I was there when he'd done it.' And I said, 'Oh, my God,' and it took that long for me to realize that she had been there and that the defendant had done that—" she begins crying and then chokes up, managing to blurt out that "it was an atrocity."

"Do you need a moment?" Horngrad asks solicitously. "Some water or—"

"No, I don't need a moment."

"—or a handkerchief? A Kleenex or something?"

"I'm fine."

Horngrad is only looking for the conversation in which Eileen told her she had been hypnotized. Wasn't that during a phone call, too, he asks. Yes, Leah answers, and then, continuing to unravel, justifies to Horngrad why she and Eileen hadn't spoken in person.

"Because the criminal proceeding was pending, I haven't visited Eileen personally. And I only saw her briefly one day when she was here testifying, up on the third floor, for about thirty seconds. So everything has been a phone conversation."

Horngrad tries to pin her down on the date of the hypnosis phone call, but now Leah's memory has shut down.

"My best estimate was that the mention of—I don't remember. I'm trying to remember. Okay? I can't—"

"Let me ask you—"

"I can't—I just can't—I can't estimate it. I don't remember it."

Was it before George Franklin was arrested?

"I don't remember."

But wouldn't it be fair to say, Horngrad pushes, that it was more than a few days?

"It wasn't, because the first three weeks I felt like someone had dropped a bomb on me. I couldn't sort out which was the most dreadful." Here she starts to shake, and her words rush out in a pitiful torrent of maternal self-reproach.

"I couldn't figure out what I could do to help Eileen. I mean, here—here she needed me more than ever, and I suddenly realized there is a twenty-eight—two—year rift in her telling me between these events, and here she needs me and—I didn't know where to begin to help her."

The jury has looked away from Leah, unable to bear the sight of a mother exorcising her guilt and feelings of inadequacy in public.

So it was at least three weeks, Horngrad continues. But Leah has completely lost the focus of the questions, has floated off into her own disordered reality.

"I was in shock," she continues, almost to herself. "I spent three weeks saying: 'My God, Eileen, how are you going to be able to tell Barry, your husband? How am I going to tell my husband?'"

Finally Horngrad realizes that Leah is unable to continue. After a brief bench conference, he says that he has no further questions. He will recall her during his case.

Leah thanks the judge for being excused and walks woodenly, jerkily, from the courtroom; Margaret Nason rises and follows her out, but returns in a few seconds.

Leah's cross-examination lasted only a few minutes, but its impact is inestimable: the wife, like the daughter, so horribly damaged by the defendant, is laid open on the stand for all to see. Another demolished victim of George Franklin. Horngrad, inadvertently, has done Tipton's work for her.

Judge Smith is moved by Leah's testimony. Whatever else could be said about her, the woman was not acting.

One reporter comments that so far it's the girls versus the boys: Tipton and her string of powerful female witnesses—Eileen, Carolyn Adams, Lenore Terr, Leah Franklin—vs. the boys in the blue and gray suits and gray hair. With eight of the twelve jurors women, it's not a bad lineup for the prosecution.

The Salcido-watchers have descended full force on Franklin. The orange- and gray-haired ladies sit nervously in the back row, ready to bolt when word arrives that the jury is back. A man wearing a sweat-stained blue polyester shirt and too-short brown polyester pants and reeking of body odor leans into reporters' faces to ask questions and argue the facts of the case. Another man, so fat that his stomach spills over the armrests, belches constantly, emanating a horrible garlic cloud.

Because of the unexpected brevity of Leah's testimony, Tipton has to scramble to come up with a witness. She calls Karyn Weis, the second of Ephe Ray Bottimore's two daughters, who has worked at Skylawn Memorial Park for the past twenty years. She verifies an exhibit identifying the location of Susan's grave and testifies from company records that there were no funerals and only two cremations on September 22, 1970, one year after Susan's disappearance.

Tipton now calls Bill Hensel to flesh out her allegation that Franklin visited Susan's grave on that date. Hensel recounts that on September 22, 1970, he and his partner spent the day parked twenty yards from Susan's grave noting the license plate of each and every car that passed by the grave. He gave the list to his superiors for transmission to the Department of Motor Vehicles and a check on the registered owners. He identifies a teletype sent to DMV on October 13, 1970. On the teletype is license number VXJ707. Hensel never received a response to the teletype.

Cross-examination is uneventful, except for Judge Smith's adamant refusal to allow Hensel to testify as to the contents of his 1969 investigative report or to allow the report into evidence. At one point Tipton interrupts Horngrad in the middle of a question and Horngrad objects that he hadn't quite gotten the question out. "You didn't have to," Smith says sternly, "sustained." The jury chuckles at Horngrad's predicament.

Smith also refuses to allow Hensel to testify as to any of the alleged sightings of the blue station wagon, or to what Ann Hobbs told the cops in 1969 about the man who approached her. It's not a good harbinger for Horngrad's intended blue station wagon defense.

Tipton calls the jail guard who arranged Eileen's visit with her father. He identifies five photographs of the jail visiting room, one of which depicts a sign that says: "Conversations may be monitored." Tipton wants to remind the jury that Franklin did not deny the killing to his accuser during her visit.

Tipton has one final witness: Inspector Robert Morse. This is Morse's first time on the stand in front of the jury and he is on his best behavior. Dressed in a gray suit and wearing a pleasantly professional expression, he gives short, clipped answers: over 25 years in law enforcement, over 100 homicide cases. Morse recounts the circumstances of Franklin's arrest and describes how Franklin, after they had told him why they were there, asked: "Have you talked to my daughter?" Morse basically renounces the accuracy of Cassandro's written report which says that Franklin had said "daughters" in the car on the way to the station.

When Horngrad rises to question him, Morse's eyes get flatter, more hooded. He doesn't like Horngrad—the way he persists in asking objectionable questions, the way he waltzes around things, implies that Tipton is not playing it straight, withholding information—but the San Francisco lawyer is giving Franklin a damn good defense and Morse has come to respect his skills. The guy never gives up. The sly smile crosses Morse's face only once, when Smith sustains an objection by Tipton. Morse knows Judge Smith and has no doubt the judge will believe his testimony.

Horngrad, laying the groundwork for a major theme of the defense, quickly goes after Morse for initially telling the prosecutors that Eileen knew facts she couldn't have known unless she had witnessed the killing.

"Detective, after you spoke to Mrs. Lipsker in Canoga Park, you then made a statement that you had examined newspaper articles regarding the discovery of the body, which were in the Coroner's files. Correct?"

"Yes, it was an article in there."

"But your statement was, 'I have examined newspaper articles,' plural. Is that—"

"I believe there was one article," Morse interjects.

"So that your statement 'newspaper articles,' you wish to amend that? Change it?"

"Is that what it says?"

"Would you like to see it for your recollection to be refreshed, if you don't recall?"

Morse declines to have his recollection refreshed.

"And didn't you state: 'I've examined newspaper articles regarding the discovery of the body, in the Coroner's files, and they do not mention the damaged hand or ring?' Did you say that?"

"I believe I did, yes," Morse concedes finally.

Tipton and Horngrad begin squabbling with each other over a question, raising Smith's ire. "Maybe neither of you heard me," he says, "I asked you to stop arguing once you've made an objection." Both appear appropriately chastened.

Horngrad asks Morse if, based on what he knows now, there are any facts that Eileen knew that weren't in the public domain. Tipton's objection is sustained, spelling more trouble for the defense. Horngrad sits down.

With that, Tipton rests her case. Smith denies Horngrad's motion for a verdict of acquittal and calls the lunch recess.

54

THE CURTAIN DROPS ON ACT ONE WHEN BOB MORSE steps down from the stand. The press is almost relieved: the prosecution's case seemed to be slowing down, the actors losing their fire. The reporters anticipate a good show by Horngrad.

Strategically, Tipton always saw her case as simple and straightforward, free of the tactical decisions that bedeviled the defense, and she put it on as cleanly and crisply as she could. Her last shot was the voice of George Franklin (through the mouth of his nemesis, Bob Morse) damn near admitting his guilt, which is probably as close as Franklin will ever get to the stand, and not a bad image to leave in the jury's mind.

Tipton played every card she had, except one. After fighting so hard to have the incident of Franklin abusing his granddaughter Jessica declared admissible, she decided not to bring it up, even though it would have beautifully illustrated Franklin as an *unreformed, unrehabilitated* monster of some twenty years standing. She worried that the jury might have wondered why Eileen continued to be involved with her father after watching him sexually abuse her infant daughter. The jury might also have wondered why that incident didn't trigger the memory of Eileen's own molestation or the molestation, and therefore the murder, of Susan Nason. Lastly, the jury could have viewed the incident as a motive for Eileen to accuse her father of murder.

Now Tipton must relinquish her role as primary storyteller. It is Horngrad's turn to direct the play and Tipton must sit down, watch the action, and prepare to discredit those who would challenge her carefully constructed version of events.

In the defense of any criminal case, there are always two distinct, but not necessarily exclusive, approaches. First, the defense lawyer should attack the prosecution's case, pointing out inconsistencies and lapses and lies and holes, arguing that the fabric is far too flimsy to support a guilty verdict. Second, the lawyer tries to construct an affirmative defense, an alternative version of what happened, such as an alibi—the defendant was in Omaha on the day it happened—which is great if it holds up and disastrous if it fails, or the possibility that *somebody else did it,* which can be effective, except it means the defense lawyer must play prosecutor and solve the case.

Horngrad, who will utilize both strategies, has a difficult task: he must extract the jurors from the storyteller's forum; he must lead them into the laboratory of rational analysis and convince them to view the tale through the eye of the thoughtful skeptic, to think and question and dissect their way through the prosecution's case until they see the story for what it is—either a treacherous lie or a mad delusion. At the bare minimum, his task is to prevent at least one juror from voting guilty. That person need not conclude that George Franklin is innocent, only that there is a serious doubt as to his guilt.

Horngrad's cause is not lost. The jurors, while impressed with Tipton and Eileen, are waiting to hear what the defense has to say, what Horngrad's story will be, to see if George Franklin will stand and explain away his favorite daughter's charges. Was he out of town? Was he insane? Drunk? Did the man in the blue station wagon kill Susan Nason?

Ollie Scholle is definitely ready for the defense. He thought Janice's story about being startled when her father had said hello to her had the ring of truth. And then he had called her to the phone and kicked her in the spine and knocked her down when she walked by. What manner of human being would do that? The time he sodomized Eileen in the bathtub —did those things really go on, for Christ's sake? Did fathers really do those things to their daughters?—and the time he held her down and she looked at a poster of some rock singer while another guy raped her: Ollie can't help but wonder if a guy who could do those things wouldn't also be capable of hitting a little girl on the head with a rock. And there sits Franklin through all of this, immobile, expressionless, as if he was carved out of stone.

Mary Dolan has not made up her mind yet, although, quite frankly, she found the defendant's statement, "Have you talked to my daughter?" to be very incriminating. As for Eileen's story, she isn't bothered by all the changes: none of the essential facts changed, only peripheral ones, such as the type of road or the time of day.

Wendy Canning wasn't that shocked by the abuse testimony, bad as it was; lots of people abuse their wives and children and that doesn't make them murderers. What did get her, though, was Franklin's failure to deny his guilt to Eileen when she visited him in jail. She can think of only one reason he wouldn't have said to her, "I didn't do it."

November 14, 1990—Wednesday, continued

None of the Nasons are present for the opening of the defense. The fat garlic-belcher is back, puffy and red-faced, coughing, flicking his nails, taking big gulps of air, as if about to expire. He is very friendly, but he stinks.

During the break, Horngrad has removed the jail photographs from the bulletin board. Not unexpectedly, he opens up with a quick swipe at Eileen's credibility.

Jay Jaffee is the handsome, well-dressed, slick-looking Los Angeles criminal defense attorney Eileen consulted in the fall of 1989 about the possibility of going forward with her story. Shortly after Jaffee told her he wanted $10,000 to represent her, Eileen decided to tell Barry of her memory. Jaffee testifies that he does not recall Eileen telling him that the memory of the murder had been lost or repressed, and while they may have discussed hypnosis, he can't be sure of that either. He is sure of one thing, though: Eileen told him she had visualized the memory of the murder when she was quite young. She had been on an outing with a friend when she had had an image of "a ring on the little girl's finger that had been crushed." Although this version contradicts Eileen's story, Jaffee's testimony also cuts another way: a woman bent on revenge does not normally consult an attorney on the best way to go about exacting it.

Horngrad calls Kirk Barrett, the Canoga Park therapist who at various times has counseled Eileen, Eileen and Barry, and Janice. Barrett is soft-looking, a mellow Teddy bear, with a tanned, pillowy face. At the prelim his head was wreathed in thick brown curls, but they have since been shorn and today his short brown hair lies flat against his head. He has a master's degree in psychology and is a licensed marriage counselor. With no medical degrees or publications or memberships in professional societies, he pales in comparison with the impressive Dr. Terr.

At the prelim, Barrett testified that he had diagnosed Eileen as suffering from post-traumatic stress disorder, although he does not give that opinion today. He had also testified that Eileen told him that dealing with Barry was the equivalent of dealing with her father, but Smith does not allow him to repeat that statement now. He had said that he believed Eileen's story that she had witnessed the murder, another opinion he is not asked about. He talks so softly that people begin nodding off: first a juror, then Tipton's research assistant, then a reporter.

Barrett's version of how Eileen recovered the murder memory is far different from the one she told the jury. He says that Eileen recovered the memory over five sessions in June and July, beginning with a session in which she mentioned that her childhood best friend had been murdered. Then one day she told him that "(S)he had been having some memories and some pictures of things that were coming into her mind that were really upsetting her, and she didn't know what to make of them." Over the next several sessions she told him of specific images that had been coming to her: a pile of Susan's clothes on the sidewalk, Susan's crushed ring, a tan Volkswagen van, a mattress. Then she told Barrett that one afternoon in her family room she had met her daughter's gaze and pictured someone hitting Susan on the head with a rock, although she could not identify the person. Finally, toward the end of July, the details filled in and she could see that the man standing over Susan with the rock was her father.

This is the *fifth* version of how Eileen said she recovered the memory—in court she testified she had recognized her father in the very first image in January 1989, some six months before she even mentioned it to Barrett—but somehow what should have been a good hit gets lost in the confusion. Horngrad is having a rough time, losing objection after objection, and he wanders around tediously trying to get where he wants to go. When Barrett leaves the stand at 3:30, a sense of "Ho hum, who's next?" pervades the courtroom. The defense is not off to a rousing start.

The next witness, George Franklin Jr., injects some excitement into the proceedings.

GEORGE, IN SPITE OF A WRETCHED CHILDHOOD AS THE ONLY BOY IN A brood of girls and a favorite target of his father's violence, has turned out fairly well. He dropped out of high school and traveled around the country, stopping in Ocala, Florida, to meet his grandmother and aunts, and eventually joined the Army for two years. He returned to Foster City and lived with Diana and Leah while he went to school and worked, and eventually moved to San Francisco where he got a clerical job in an import-export business.

Despite the rumors in high school, George is not gay. He is very much attracted to women. To his sister Kate, he seems very kind and gentle with women and treats them with respect and affection, a remarkable feat, she thinks, in view of his primary role model. Different as a child, he is also different as an adult. He still comes at life from an odd angle and enjoys taking the absurd view of human behavior. He does things like buying a cotton plant in the central valley and growing it in his apartment so he can have the only cotton plantation in San Francisco. He uses his wacky sense of humor to turn everything on its side and keep it at a distance. He is not so much cynical as he is distrusting of his fellow man; he readily assumes the worst about everyone's intentions. He is intelligent and very well read, with an emphasis on Russian literature and offbeat fiction. He is a volunteer usher at a local community theater. George has a solid, very loyal circle of friends whom he enjoys immensely. He loves the outdoors and hates the suburbs.

Over the years, George had little use for either of his parents, maintaining a careful distance from both of them. He hasn't seen or talked to his father in four or five years and only calls his mother on the phone "quarterly." He puts in the briefest possible appearance for Christmas, and characterizes Thanksgiving as the "turkey torture." He puts Barry in the same category as his parents and enjoys parodying him.

People who know George say that for all his intelligence, he has never quite found his groove, that he is still wandering across the landscape of his life. He was completely blown away by the murder charge against his father; the publicity was so intense that he even considered changing his name. He quit his job and for a while had serious problems coping. His close friends were his salvation.

While George hates his father's guts, he doesn't believe he killed Susan Nason. "I know he's a pedophile," he has said to Kate, "but that doesn't mean he's a murderer." Having grown up with Eileen, George finds her totally untrustworthy; she may well believe what she is saying, but her story alone cannot be accepted as proof of his father's guilt.

THE GEORGE FRANKLIN JR. WHO STRIDES INTO THE COURTROOM THIS afternoon is a different person from the one liked and admired by his friends and sisters. He is stiff and has a rigid, intense gaze. When Peggy raises her hand to swear him in, he locks in on her with his eyes and holds her for long moments without blinking, completely unnerving her. He is slender, but he has thick hair, big ears and a broad forehead like his father, and a slightly bent nose. When he talks, his chipped tooth shows. He looks like a farm boy, but speaks like a well-educated man. He is just about the age his father was when Susan Nason was murdered, and he reminds Judge Smith of a picture he has seen of George Sr. as a young man.

George stares straight at Horngrad and gives clipped, one-

and two-word answers to his introductory questions. Then, in softer tones, he describes how Eileen bought him a plane ticket in August 1989 to visit her in Canoga Park, and how after he arrived she had begun disparaging their parents and bragging about how she was doing a better job with her children, how they had private schools, a playroom, better clothing and medical care and more toys. That first night she mentioned that she was in hypnotherapy and analysis. The next night, while they were standing in the kitchen, she told him that while under hypnosis she had remembered her father molesting and killing Susan Nason. Her therapist, she said, would back her all the way. George had not believed her.

Eileen called him shortly after their father was arrested and told him that she had actually recovered the memory during a *psychotherapy* session and asked him to please not tell anyone that she had ever said she had remembered it under hypnosis. He told her he would not lie. Then in February, after she learned he had talked to the defense, she called again and said she had not recovered the memory in therapy but in her nightmares.

Tipton is ready for George on cross. She asks him if he didn't tell Eileen that when she returned from Europe the two of them would "poke at it [the memory] with a stick" and see what it looked like. George bristles and tells her she has taken his words out of context and to please read the complete quote. Apparently sensing the anger in George and how easy it will be to bring it to the surface, Tipton walks out from behind the defense table. She addresses him as "Mr. Franklin" and he leans forward and addresses her through clenched teeth as "Miss Tipton."

Didn't he talk to the defense while refusing to talk to the prosecution, she asks him.

"Yes, *Miss Tipton*, that's true," George responds, his eyes taking on an eerie glint.

Tipton has struck a gold mine—a Franklin male, the son of the accused, expressing anger and hostility toward a female—and she continues to prod him. She asks him if he had told the cops about the psychotherapy statement in their interview:

"Miss Tipton, I believe I answered all your questions. When I left—when I left, you did not give the impression that any of my answers had been unsatisfactory."

"Well, I didn't know what you knew, did I, Mr. Franklin?"

"No," he says, "but I did try and explain it to you, *Miss Tipton."*

George has been placed in an intolerable role. He suffered as badly, if not worse than any of his siblings, at the hand of his father, yet he is the one called to testify on his behalf. Like Kate, he tried to live away from the pain of his childhood, to move on with his life, and now Eileen, who has stayed stuck in the family mess, has spilled her guts in the newspapers and on national television (how she must love the attention!) and made him relive it all in the public eye. Perhaps that accounts for the bristling energy emanating from him on the stand.

Glo, the quiet stenographer staring up at him from a few feet away, can feel the anger and hostility crackling around him. "What a family," she thinks, "what a family. How did it all happen?"

As a boy, George was obedient and always tried to please his father, to earn his affection, and during one vituperative exchange with Tipton, he glances, almost reflexively, over at him with a look like "How am I doing, Dad?"

He denies Eileen's allegation that he was spying for the defense. Anything personal Eileen told him he kept in strict confidence, but he did report facts relevant to the defense, such as when she began changing her story.

In her last question, Tipton asks him if he has a hope or expectation as to the outcome of this case.

"I would not call it a hope," George answers, "I would call it an expectation." George simply cannot imagine his father being convicted on Eileen's word alone.

After Horngrad's brief re-direct, George steps down quickly and marches across the courtroom, looking straight ahead at the door like a soldier.

The courtroom is stunned. The blast of George's anger resonates in his wake. He frightened two female jurors. Nancy Salazar, who feels he was on the verge of losing control, sees him as a direct pipeline into the defendant, a veritable snapshot of his father at the same age.

In Ollie Scholle's view, George was harmful to the defense. His seething rage toward Tipton was completely unprovoked and reminds him of the brutality of his father. He looked at the son raging at Tipton and said to himself, "There's the father."

Mary Dolan, watching George as he storms in and out of the courtroom, finds him so tense and angry as to be almost unreal. He reminds her of a firecracker ready to go off. But she understands why he is that way and she feels sorry for him. The poor guy hasn't done anything to bring this all about, to have this stigma attached to his name, and now here he is in the spotlight defending his father.

Joyce Beard watches the son's sudden mood changes, from calm composure to a rage in an instant, and wonders if maybe he is a multiple personality.

The scene is a startling display of Tipton's ability on cross-examination. She turned Horngrad's sword around and thrust it in his stomach so deftly that it looked like Horngrad did it to himself. The woman leaves no fingerprints.

55

November 14, 1990—Wednesday, continued

Diana Franklin," Vince calls out.

Easily the most gorgeous of any of the Franklin women, Diana looks like a fashion model of the twenties. Long-limbed and slim-hipped, her coppery red hair is piled on top of her head and spills in luxurious waves onto her shoulders. She is wearing a tight black skirt, a black blouse imprinted with bright flowers, a string of pearls, and heels she jokingly refers to as her "come-fuck-me-pumps."

Diana will be Horngrad's last witness of the day. She has been standing outside the courthouse smoking while her brother testified. She is nervous. She had talked to Horngrad briefly at the prelim, and she doesn't really know what he wants from her.

She walks in the door and across the floor with a casual sensuality. On the stand, she seems composed. A slight glimmer of her mother's features, her natural pain, is etched in her large brown eyes.

As Horngrad begins his questions, the scene begins to seem unreal, fuzzy to Diana. When the judge talks, she looks at him but she can barely make out his features. She is uncomfortable, restless.

Horngrad seems to be making a lot out of nothing. In the hallway at the prelim, Diana had said to him and Tipton that Eileen told her that she had called her mother and brother back and corrected her story the day after she told them she had been hypnotized. It is a minor contradiction of Eileen's testimony. Now Diana testifies that those were her words and not Eileen's; she was nervous and wasn't paying that much attention to exactly what she said.

Diana is relieved that Horngrad doesn't ask her whether she and Eileen had ever watched the "Today Show" segment. Tipton has few questions for her.

DIANA HAS NOT GROWN EASILY INTO ADULTHOOD. SHE HAS RECOVERED from a serious cocaine problem, but knows she has an addictive personality and cannot be around people using drugs or alcohol. Like Eileen, she is in many ways reliving or re-enacting the traumas of her childhood.

After dropping out of high school, Diana held various jobs as a waitress and bankteller, but had few plans or ambitions. While living on Beach Park with Leah, she was wild and began hanging around with a restaurant crowd and using cocaine in increasing amounts. Two or three times a week she would stay up all night with her friends, snorting coke and talking and listening to music. The drug seemed to numb her feelings of alienation.

When she was twenty-two, she moved out of the Beach Park house and into her own apartment. A year later, in 1986, she met Guy*, a forty-seven-year-old drug dealer, at a neighbor's house during a drug deal. Guy had money and was a good dresser and bought Diana nice clothes, and soon they were living together. Even in the beginning, he was emotionally abusive to her, constantly yelling and screaming how stupid she was and how her family was nothing but a bunch of "users and losers." The way he intentionally withheld his affection from her reminded Diana of her mother. Her self-esteem, minimal to begin with, withered even further. Living with him, she would say, was the next best thing to living with her parents.

For a long time people told Diana that Guy looked like her father, but it wasn't until he beat her that she saw the resemblance. They were in the car and Diana said something that irritated him and he began smacking her in the face and neck. He pulled over and continued to beat her, striking her over twenty times in the head. Her face puffed up and her eyes turned black and blue. She walked unsteadily for weeks. She filed charges against him, but dropped them when he threatened to tell the cops about her drug history.

Diana has always wanted the family to work. She wanted all of her siblings to love her the way she loved them. It wasn't easy to love her mom. She usually talked with her on the phone every couple of days and visited her once a week, but since Eileen's allegation, she has been unable to communicate with her. She has heard her mother's explanation of what went on when her children were young, but she can't accept it. Sometimes she views Leah as having been simply comatose in those years, but most of the time she sees her as too weak to take care of her children.

"I don't know how she could have lived a day with herself watching her children getting beaten up," she says. "Even if you take her background and the circumstances into consideration, the human thing to do is to protect your children, get them out of the house. She is going to make excuses for the rest of her life and I just don't buy it."

Several times in recent years Diana has turned to her

mother for help. Leah bailed Diana out of a couple of legal jams, and when Diana realized that her cocaine problem was completely out of control, she sat down and told her mother about her addiction. Leah let her cry and listened to her story carefully and without judgment. She was very supportive and gave Diana sound advice on seeking help.

When she thinks of those times, Diana realizes that she loves her mom. But when Leah gives her one of her cold, stiff embraces, bitter memories of her childhood flood through her and she pulls away.

Diana wishes she could love her father, just as she wishes he could love her. She dreams of sitting down and talking to him about her life. That's why she stayed involved with him after he left home, visiting him and his girlfriends in Mountain View, San Francisco, and Sacramento—she kept hoping that someday she would finally get from him what she needed. She knows her painful involvement with Guy is another version of the continuing search for her father's love and acceptance.

Except for vague recollections of her father french-kissing her, she has no memory of him molesting her, and she prays to God that horrible images won't begin popping up in her mind some day.

Diana doesn't remember much about Susan Nason, although she does recall asking Eileen about her best friend one day when they were walking home from school, about a year after Susan disappeared. Eileen became very uncomfortable and said that Susan had been found under a mattress and that her fingernails had been torn off.

She and Eileen have had problems in the past several years. After the uproar about who had told Barry about her prostitution conviction, Eileen stopped talking to her. Diana waited and kept her peace, knowing one day she and Eileen would come back together. It was inevitable. They shared the same soul.

She had forgiven Eileen for waiting until the last minute to tell her about her father's arrest—she would always forgive Eileen anything—and in the ensuing months she had visited her several times in Canoga Park. Rude Barry hadn't been there most of the time, thank God, and she and Janice and Eileen had some good times, like the afternoon they watched the tape of the "Today Show" together and laughed over Janice's mannerisms. Or the time they had a girls' night out and the three of them dressed up in black without any underwear and took the cop who lived next door out dining and dancing.

Eileen had asked her to come stay with her at her hotel during the trial and Diana had delightedly accepted. Eileen explained that Barry must never know that Diana was staying with her. She had convinced him to stay at home in Switzerland by telling him that she wanted to be alone during the trial. If he heard that Diana was staying with her he would jump on the first plane and fly over, and Eileen definitely did not want that.

Her visit didn't work out the way Diana expected. Eileen would come into the room after court and spend the whole evening on the phone talking to Barry and various other people. Eileen had new "friends" now—her author, the screenwriter, the movie producer—and she preferred talking to them about the various projects and the trial. Some of her new friends were staying in the same hotel, and one evening at dinner they began advising Eileen on how she should handle herself on the stand. One said she should quit looking at her father so much; another agreed, but said she shouldn't stop too abruptly because *that* would look funny. After a few days of being ignored, Diana felt hurt and angry. *Why am I here? Eileen picks me up and then drops me again, and I don't like being treated that way.*

The problem came to a head three days later. Eileen was on the phone talking to Barry and Diana had walked over to her motioning a message. Eileen brusquely pushed her away. Diana burst into tears and became furious and the two of them argued until finally Diana stormed out of the room. She hasn't spoken to Eileen since.

* * *

Tipton snaps her fingers and the judge's head jerks up.

"That was an inadvertent snap," she says quickly, "sorry, your honor."

"Yeah," Smith replies.

"But I just thought about this evening's television program."

"I understand. I'm going to tell them about it."

Smith explains to the jury that "A Current Affair" is featuring the trial tonight and the jurors are not to watch it. Juror Robert Folger asks if that means that people in the courtroom will be on the show. Smith assures them they will not.

"I don't know what they do; but certainly, you're the people who are going to make the decision, not some television producers. Lord knows we've had enough problems with them so far in this trial."

56

November 15, 1990—Thursday

Judge Smith tells the jurors that he expects the testimony to be completed on the 27th and they will get the case the next day, so "the end is in sight." The sleeping juror asks if next Wednesday, the day before Thanksgiving, will be a full day, and Smith says it will. The voice from the jury box startles everyone.

Today is the day of the Blue Station Wagon Alternative. Finally, the defense will present its theory of the case: Somebody Else Did It. Wachtel has scheduled ten witnesses for the morning with the hope of creating in the jurors' minds the image of a blue station wagon and Susan Nason converging on the same place at the same time on the afternoon of September 22, 1969. The defense can't, and won't, try to prove that the driver of the car actually abducted Susan. The defense wants only to create the reasonable possibility that it happened; it wants the jury to be able to visualize someone other than George Franklin luring the little girl into a vehicle.

The first witness is Sharon Fuls, the blonde girl who was riding up Balclutha on her bike and called out, "Na-na-na-na-na!" to Susan on the sidewalk. Sharon, now a beautiful blonde with a flawless complexion, had long since put Susan Nason out of her mind until one day she turned on the "Today Show" and saw Eileen talking about the murder. Images of Eileen as a whiny, emotional girl always seeking attention and Susan as a frail, shy girl came immediately back to her. Sharon, who had been a good friend of Celia Oakley, didn't enjoy remembering how she and the others had teased and picked on Susan, and now she wondered why they had. Perhaps because Susan had been such easy prey.

Sitting in the hallway with the other witnesses from 1969, Sharon tries to visualize them with twenty years wiped off their faces. A few seem familiar, but she can't place any of them. Waiting in the hallway to be called reminds her of waiting to go into the dentist's office as a little girl.

Wachtel leads Sharon through the day of Susan's disappearance. She recounts how she and her friend passed Susan on their bikes as she walked up Balclutha around 3:30. She admits, under Wachtel's questioning, that it might have been 4:00. Wachtel tries for 4:30, but Tipton objects and is sustained.

On cross, Tipton establishes only that the sighting probably occurred closer to 3:30 than 4:00. Sharon is relieved when the ordeal is over. She is particularly happy that no one asked her if she had said anything to Susan as she zipped past her on the street.

The next two witnesses are crucial to the viability of the Blue Station Wagon Alternative. Suzanne Darois was Suzanne Banks when she lived on the corner of Matsonia and Balclutha and answered a little girl's knock on the door and showed her the way to Celia Oakley's house. Her daughter, now Linda Mutoza, had been playing in a fort in a lot across Matsonia when her mother called her home. Both mother and daughter saw a man in a blue station wagon parked on Matsonia directly in Susan's path.

Mrs. Darois is a heavy woman who wears lots of makeup and speaks in a rough voice. On direct, everything goes smoothly. She tells how she watched Susan walk up to the Oakley house and then turned around and began walking home. Calling to her daughter across the street to come home, she saw an unfamiliar, light-colored car parked in front of her house. A man was sitting inside. A few minutes after entering her house, she heard her dog barking in her backyard and looked out her kitchen window, which faced down Matsonia in the direction of the Oakley house. The dog was barking at the side fence, where the car was, and through the fence at the rear of the yard she could see a small child with strawberry blond hair who looked like Susan standing in the driveway. When the dog continued barking and banging against the fence, she stepped out on the patio and heard the sounds of a car pulling away.

Quickly, almost effortlessly, Tipton shreds Mrs. Darois.

The woman admits that the vehicle could have been blue, although at the prelim she said it had been green, and that it could have been a station wagon, although at the prelim she said it had been a large sedan. Tipton has her repeat that she was looking through the kitchen window when she saw Susan standing in the neighbor's driveway, and then shows her a series of recently taken photographs of the view from the kitchen window in her old house. In several of the pictures, Morse is standing in front of the fence, which is six inches or a foot taller than he is. It is obvious that from this viewpoint one could neither see through the fence—the slats are too close together—nor over it into the neighbor's driveway, although Mrs. Darois insists that she could do both.

At the prelim, Mrs. Darois said she could only see the top of Susan's head. Now she says that while she couldn't see a "whole person," she could tell that someone was on the other side. At the prelim she said she had been standing on the patio when she saw and heard the car pull away, now she says she had been standing "real close" to the fence, perhaps as close as Morse in the picture. Then, looking closely at the picture, she decides that maybe the fence in the picture isn't the same fence as in 1969.

Tipton moves in to finish her off. At the prelim Mrs. Darois testified that when she saw Susan on the other side of the fence, she thought to herself, "Why is Susan there? She should get on home for her birthday." She says the same thing today, and when Tipton asks her how she knew it was Susan's birthday, she replies that when Margaret came to her house looking for Susan, she said it was Susan's birthday and that her grandmother was at her house waiting for her to come home and frost her cake. Seeing her obvious error, Mrs. Darois admits she is confused and mixed up and that she must have had that thought sometime later.

Finally, Mrs. Darois testifies that she can't remember whether she told Margaret in 1969 about the man in the car and the barking dog, and although she is sure she told Gordon Penfold, the chief of police back then, about the car and the dog, she isn't sure whether she told Morse and Cassandro about them when they interviewed her several months earlier.

On re-direct, Wachtel completes the destruction of his witness when he asks her if she is positive about her own testimony. She says that now she thinks she was standing in the living room when she looked out the window, not the kitchen.

Tipton, with a little help from Wachtel, has shown Mrs. Darois to be a witness who reconstructs events with later-acquired facts and changes her story when it no longer seems plausible. Not a firm foundation for the Blue Station Wagon Alternative.

Wachtel now calls Linda Mutoza, Mrs. Darois's daughter. Linda is another attractive former acquaintance of the dead girl; she has a full figure and a head of shiny, streaked brunette hair that bounces like a Breck girl's when she nods or turns her head. She gives Wachtel a broad, wholesome smile when she sits down and a bubbly "Hi" when he says good morning to her. She tells her story of that day with an innocent effervescence. When she comes to the part about the man in the car saying something to her as she walked by, she is, for a moment, the little girl who got away.

As it did for her mother, cross-examination goes badly for Linda. First she says that she and Susan were seven-year-olds and in second grade together when Susan disappeared. Tipton then reads to her several statements she made previously to Morse over the phone to the effect that she wasn't sure whether she actually remembered the facts in her story or was repeating what she had heard and been told over the years. After first saying that she and her mother hadn't talked about the killing over the years, Linda admits that she made a statement at the preliminary hearing that it is possible what she was remembering about that afternoon is a reconstruction of what her mom has told her. As Tipton leads her through conflicting statements about whether she saw Susan walking to or from the Oakley house, the smile disappears from her face, the bubbliness evaporates.

On re-direct, Wachtel tries hard to rehabilitate Linda. She says that she is able to separate out the facts she remembers on her own and those told to her by her mother and she has testified only to those from her own memory. On re-cross, Tipton asks her if she is certain that the man in the car actually said something to her, and when she says yes, Tipton reads out loud her statement from the prelim that she is not certain whether that fact is something she remembers or one she has been told. Linda's pretty face has now fallen. As she steps down from the stand, she is no longer the girl who got away, but the daughter of the mother who could see through fences.

Tipton was neither cruel nor repetitious in destroying the credibility of the mother and daughter. She found the weak points, took clean, swift shots, and sat down. It is a style that will become familiar.

Judge Smith adjourns for the morning. Several jurors lobby Vince to ask the judge for an early recess next Wednesday, and after the lunch break Smith announces that he will grant their request, but that they should be prepared to go late Tuesday night.

Wachtel calls Annette DeNunzio, a next door neighbor of

the Oakleys in 1969, to try to shore up the collapsing foundation of the Blue Station Wagon Alternative. Mrs. DeNunzio, a San Francisco matron, testifies that around 3:30 on the afternoon of September 22, 1969, she was standing in her window, waiting for her decorator to arrive. She saw a girl with long blonde hair carrying tennis shoes in her hand stroll by and turn up the walk to the Oakley house. Mrs. DeNunzio turned away briefly, and when she returned to the window, she saw the little girl walking back the way she had come. At the same moment she saw a man in a blue station wagon with long cardboard boxes in the rear drive by in the same direction as the little girl. She estimated the speed of the car at twenty-five or thirty miles an hour. When she later saw a picture of the little girl, she realized it was Susan Nason.

Tipton is able to accomplish little on cross. Mrs. DeNunzio says she did not notice the car slowing down as it passed Susan, nor did she hear any yelling or dogs barking after Susan passed by her window.

A few snickers arise from the press as the name "Penny Stocks" is called out. Who would give that name to their child, one reporter asks. Penny, a woman with droopy brown hair and broad shoulders, has a strange story to tell. Shortly after coming home from school on September 22, she went to the Nason household looking for her friend Shirley. Both Susan and Shirley were at home, but only Shirley returned home with Penny to play catch with a friend's football. Around five o'clock Susan called out to them from across the street, "Hey, Shirley, hey, Penny, I want to play."

"We don't want to play with you," Shirley had replied to her sister. "We want to play by ourselves."

Penny becomes visibly upset as she describes how she went across the street and told Susan that she and Shirley were playing by themselves that day and she should go home. Wachtel asks her if she remembers the dress Susan was wearing that day.

"It was kind of black and red; but it was kind of flowing together, and it had little white dotted lines that squared off the dress.

"I went to twenty different fabric stores," Penny continues on her own, "trying to find the material this last week so I could bring it to court today."

Heads in the press gallery turn to look at each other as if to say, "This woman is not in good shape."

The two girls continued playing until Shirley's father came and told her to go home because they couldn't find Susan. Penny talked to the police that evening, and when they came to the school a few days later, another girl said to her, "You'd better not say nothing, that you sent her away. They'll lock you up." Penny had been scared to death.

On cross, Penny testifies that after Susan disappeared, she and Shirley weren't close friends any more. She figured that Shirley's parents wouldn't let Shirley play with her because they blamed her for what happened to Susan.

Tipton catches Penny in a number of contradictions about what she said to the cops in 1969, at the preliminary hearing, and in court today. In 1969 she told the police she was unsure of whether she sent Susan home that day or some other day. She has thought about that day a lot since then.

"Well, how much thinking have you done since May?" Tipton asks her.

"I've done a lot of drilling in my brain about what went on that day because I wanted to be sure. I know for a fact I saw her that day. I know for a fact what—I remember what she was wearing. I know for a fact I've carried the guilt for twenty-some-odd years that I sent her away. She never made it back home. These things I know for a fact."

When Penny states that she is positive that Susan wasn't wearing a blue dress on the day she disappeared, the last thread of credibility snaps and she becomes merely another victim of whoever killed Susan Nason, a victim who for some reason seems determined to hold herself accountable for Susan's death, despite evidence to the contrary.

The next witness is Ann Hobbs, the Foster City girl who reported being accosted by a man in a blue station wagon five days before Susan disappeared. She previously told both the defense and the prosecution that she had absolutely no recollection of the incident. Wachtel wants to put her 1969 statement into evidence, and in order to do that he has to demonstrate her lack of recollection. On the stand, she again denies any memory of a blue station wagon, which, from the jury's point of view, makes the defense look silly.

The next witness is Danny Munier, the ballet teacher's son. As with many of the other defense witnesses, he sounds good on direct. He testifies that he and a friend were riding bikes after school and had just turned off Matsonia onto Balclutha when they saw a blue station wagon with cardboard taped to the inside of the windows traveling at a low rate of speed. The two boys tried to ride up to the station wagon, but it picked up speed and drove away. Danny figures the time of the sighting to be close to 5:45 P.M.

Tipton asks Munier whether he had been on the lookout for something suspicious because of Susan's disappearance. He replies that he doesn't think so, and she reads to him from his statement to Cassandro that he and his friend might have been riding around after Susan's abduction. After much wrangling, it becomes apparent that he doesn't remember when he saw the blue station wagon: it could have been after the Ann Hobbs incident or after the Susan Nason incident. His testimony is of little, if any, value.

Wachtel calls Jerry Steele, who lived on a cul-de-sac a block past the Oakley house on Matsonia. He testifies that on the Friday before Susan disappeared he spotted a 1958 or '59 light blue Ford station wagon parked across the street facing the wrong way. The next Monday he spotted the car again when he returned home around four o'clock. After Margaret Nason came by that evening looking for Susan, he wondered if the car might have had anything to do with her disappearance and he called the police.

On cross, Tipton establishes only that Steele hadn't seen anyone inside the car or any unusual activity around it.

Steele's testimony, along with DeNunzio's, could have been extremely helpful in establishing the Blue Station Wagon Alternative, but the potential value is lost in the midst of so many witnesses who have recanted, revised, forgotten, or possibly, for some unknown reason, confabulated their testimony. By putting on so many weak witnesses, the defense has obscured the few strong ones. In the press room, the Blue Station Wagon Alternative is seen as a bust.

At 3:43, the jurors are excused until Monday morning. Many in the audience join the throng of people and television cameras waiting in the hall for the Salcido verdict. The jury has been out three days and expectations are building. One observer notes that the television cameras are here in hopes of recording the look on a man's face when he gets the death sentence. At five o'clock the Salcido jury is sent home.

November 16, 1990—Friday

The Salcido jury comes back. The defense attorney predicted publicly that the jury would come back today and the hard-core Salcido-watchers have been lingering in the hallways.

Death.

The jury ignored the mother's plea for her son's life. Downstairs the prosecutor holds a press conference. TV cameras are everywhere and reporters are throwing elbows into each other and yelling questions at the winner. He says Salcido was not a mad dog, but a fox. The defense attorney is also here and he talks fervently to whoever will interview him. Several jurors are also present and reporters ask them questions like, "How does it feel?" And the jurors say things like, "It wasn't an easy thing," and, "You just have to get some people off the street." One says the fact that Salcido took his children's bodies to the garbage dump was the final point for him. One juror, a short chubby woman, walks away crying.

San Mateo County juries are now two for two on the death penalty in as many months.

57

November 19, 1990—Monday

Sᴀʟᴄɪᴅᴏ ɪs ɢᴏɴᴇ. Hᴇ ᴡᴀs ᴛᴀᴋᴇɴ ᴛᴏ Sᴀɴ Qᴜᴇɴᴛɪɴ Saturday morning.

George Franklin, who is dressed like a businessman in a gray suit and red tie, is escorted into the courtroom this morning by a young female deputy who walks a few feet behind her white-haired charge. She is new and unsure where to sit in the courtroom. Franklin seems uncomfortable in her presence, perhaps because she had been chaining and unchaining him.

Steve Schwartz, Horngrad's private detective, appears in faded blue jeans and a sports coat. His attire irritates Morse, who thinks it shows disrespect for the court.

Before the jury comes in, Tipton and Horngrad squabble over Barry Lipsker. He has refused Horngrad's request to appear, and Horngrad has asked to have his prelim testimony read to the jury. Tipton objects, arguing that Horngrad hasn't made a diligent effort to secure his presence. In a brief filed the previous week, Tipton laid out the proper way to serve a witness overseas and, somewhat to her irritation, Horngrad followed her advice and served Barry. Smith delays a ruling.

The jury walks in single file, except for Chapman, the pediatrician, who is missing. Vince goes looking for him. He shows up ten minutes late. Juror Merrill, the lay priest who stretches out on the benches and meditates during breaks, has a new haircut.

The plastic head is now jammed facedown in the exhibit box on Peggy's desk.

Horngrad calls Leah Franklin. Wearing a black suit, pink blouse, and gold chain necklace, Leah is once again left standing at the gate for several minutes. Finally Horngrad tells her to sit down. Her forehead and eyes are tight and strained.

Horngrad hits her with a series of small points: the family subscribed to the *San Mateo Times* in 1969; Leah visited the defendant in jail; Leah thought Eileen was a happy child in 1969 and 1970 and saw no change in her after Susan's disappearance. Then he tries to establish that the platform and mattress weren't put in the van VXJ707 until George went on a cross-country trip to Florida, months after Susan's disappearance. Leah gives him no help whatsoever: some of her answers are evasive, some just don't make sense, and several times she seems to slip off somewhere else and Horngrad has to bring her back. As she and Horngrad stumble around together, she begins to appear very weary. Somewhere inside, however, is a thread of strength that resists Horngrad's probing.

Horngrad has difficulty with the bloody shirt. He laboriously extracts from her the changing memories of the shirt—first she didn't remember the shirt, then she did, then she forgot it, and finally she remembered it again—but her explanations are so tortured and confusing that his point—that she probably made it up out of a desire to get even with her former husband—gets lost.

Horngrad has heard that Leah was offered $15,000 for her book and movie rights but that she refused the offer because it wasn't enough money. He tries to ask her about the offer, but Smith won't allow it.

He asks her if she went to the chapel for Susan's service.

"Yes."

"And up to the burial?"

"Up to Skylawn, yes."

"And did you go alone or were you in someone else's company?"

"I was with the defendant."

George Franklin tilts his head quizzically like the RCA dog as he looks up at his former wife.

On cross, Tipton asks Leah why she might have had trouble noticing everything that went on in the household in the sixties and seventies. It is a clever ploy to allow Leah to repeat for the jury her testimony about the defendant's violent nature, and over Horngrad's strenuous objection, Smith allows it. Shrugging off her weariness, Leah comes alive and recounts how she and her children weren't safe in their own home and the defendant knew that he could get away with whatever he wanted because she wouldn't seek a divorce. Her hands fly dramatically in the air as she describes the outbursts of violence which followed periods of calm. She steps down from the stand a renewed victim.

HORNGRAD CALLS TWO DETECTIVES WHO WORKED THE CASE IN 1969, both of whom are old, balding, and retired, and neither of whom can remember anything about the investigation, even after Horngrad shows them their reports. Peggy reads two parts of one detective's report out loud to the jury: in the first one he recounts that on December 10, 1969, Janice Franklin told the detectives that she had seen Susan Nason riding her bike on Harvester around 4:15 on September 22 and she identified a yellow metal ring with blue stones as belonging to Susan; in the second one he says that officers had noted the license plates of the cars at Susan's funeral.

Horngrad tries to weave in another strand of the Blue Station Wagon Alternative by calling Gordon Penfold, the Foster City police chief in 1969. He identifies the widely circulated flier with a picture of Susan and a description of a blue station wagon with cardboard cartons in the rear window. Penfold testifies that, despite the widespread publicity given the case, no one ever came forward and admitted to having driven such a car in the area that afternoon. The flier is admitted into evidence. Horngrad tries to ask him about the arrest of Aaron Patterson, the owner of a blue station wagon, but Judge Smith won't allow Penfold to testify about any arrests in 1969 in connection with the Susan Nason case.

OVER THE LUNCHEON RECESS THE PLASTIC HEAD HAS CHANGED POSItion in the exhibit box: now it's now lying on its side, red neck muscles bulging, the open eye staring balefully out at the spectators.

Horngrad's next witness is Dr. David Spiegel, professor of psychiatry at Stanford University. Spiegel is the defense's answer to Lenore Terr: his testimony is designed to throw doubt on the validity of Eileen's story and to discredit several of Terr's propositions, such as that you can discern the nature of the underlying trauma by looking at the symptoms and that it is possible to tell a true memory from a false memory. He wants Spiegel to present the jury with the intellectual framework to view Eileen's memory as unreliable.

Spiegel's credentials are every bit as impressive as Terr's: besides being a tenured professor, he is an examiner for the American Board of Psychiatry and Neurology, an editor on several psychiatric publications, including the *Journal of Traumatic Stress*, he has published sixty-five papers in scientific journals and chapters in thirty-five books, and he is on the committee of the American Psychiatric Association that is reviewing dissociative disorders for the *Diagnostic and Statistical Manual IV.*

On the stand, however, Spiegel appears the antithesis of Terr. He is tall and balding, and he speaks in a deep, authoritative voice. He is not arrogant, but he is very self-assured. He sounds and looks like a professor, a typical scientist, not a storyteller. And of course he is male.

Although Spiegel has reviewed Eileen's various statements to the authorities and the transcripts and videos of her testimony at the prelim, he has not, pursuant to Smith's ruling, been allowed to interview her.

Horngrad leads Spiegel through a discussion of post-traumatic stress disorder (PTSD), and the doctor explains that the disorder is caused by a serious trauma that results in symptoms which fall into three categories: a reliving or intrusive recollection of the traumas, such as nightmares; a numbing or loss of pleasure in life; and a sensitivity to a stimulus connected with the event, such as a rape victim's avoidance of the scene of the rape. A person who suffered repeated traumas early in life would most likely show evidence of dissociating; that is, a detaching of one's self from the trauma as a protective measure with the resulting loss of memory of that event.

Horngrad asks: Suppose a person reports having witnessed a murder twenty years earlier and that person hasn't had any nightmares about the murder or about the perpetrator—is that consistent or inconsistent with PTSD? Inconsistent, Spiegel testifies. Additionally, if the person had an ongoing relationship with the perpetrator, that would also be inconsistent with PTSD.

If the person were somehow responsible for luring the victim to her death, wouldn't that person assume some responsibility for the result and express feelings of guilt when recounting the trauma, Horngrad asks. Yes, replies Spiegel, he would expect more than the normal feelings of guilt.

The logic of Horngrad's approach seems to be that if the person's behavior doesn't match the symptom criteria for PTSD, then the underlying trauma must not have occurred; i.e., Eileen didn't witness the murder.

Mindful of Eileen's continued closeness to and involvement with her father after Susan's death, including her trip to Mexico with him in the very van that transported Susan to her death, Horngrad brings Spiegel back to the stimulus sensitivity criteria. Spiegel explains, "Since stimuli that are reminiscent of the trauma set off painful feelings or memories, very often trauma victims consciously or unconsciously avoid a contact with the place or the instrument or the person who represented the trauma to them; so they will engage in strategies to avoid having further contact with things that remind them of the trauma."

So, Horngrad asks, if a person suffered a trauma at the hands of a pilot in an airplane, would it be inconsistent with PTSD for that person to get back in the airplane with that person? Yes, Spiegel replies. Edging up to the actual facts, Horngrad asks if it wouldn't also be inconsistent with PTSD for the person to go on a pleasure trip with the pilot to Hawaii or Las Vegas. It would be, Spiegel answers.

Horngrad switches to his second major theme: Eileen's memory of the killing is *a false memory*. Laying out his building blocks carefully and methodically, he asks whether a psychiatrist can distinguish a false memory from a true one. Unlike

Terr, who had three criteria by which she claims she can make such a distinction, Spiegel says it is often quite difficult to tell the difference between the two. Particularly with events that occurred many years ago, it is very hard to distinguish a memory from a fantasy. In fact, the older a memory is, the more likely it is to be a combination of fact *and* fantasy.

Next, Spiegel explains that memories can be influenced by suggestion; what people tell you about an event, or the type of behavior you expect from a person involved in the event, can affect the way you remember it. Studies have also shown, Spiegel testifies, that children are more suggestible than adults, and that both traumatized children and traumatized adults are more suggestible than nontraumatized adults and children. Finally, and here Spiegel takes the defense into dangerous waters, individuals who have suffered *repeated* traumas, who have sustained more psychological and physical damage, are more likely to have later events colored by the earlier traumas.

Although there are no studies on the point, he says persons with "repeated traumatic experiences might be more likely to have a false memory."

Horngrad's point: The more abuse Eileen suffered at the hands of her father, the more susceptible she was to having had a false memory of him killing Susan Nason.

Horngrad takes it one step further. Spiegel explains that children who have endured repeated physical abuse may suffer delayed cognitive development and their personal view of the world may be affected by their interactions with the abuser. Sexually abused children might feel guilty because they think they brought the abuse upon themselves; they tell the story in such a way that they are the author, not the victim, of the experience.

"So they tend," Spiegel explains, "in the way that they remember the trauma, to overemphasize their control and their central authorship in the events that happened and underemphasize how much they were a victim of events."

Horngrad tries to bring this "authorship" concept to bear on the facts at hand and asks if traumatized children will have a skewed view of outside events.

"They will be no less likely—and sometimes more likely—to place themselves at the center of stories that occur outside the home as well, to figure that since I'm an especially bad child who is always doing things wrong and getting punished for it, if something else goes on outside that they're marginally associated with it, they may assume that they're responsible for that, as well."

"Or have a role in it?" Horngrad asks.

"Yes."

Horngrad's point: Eileen, who sees herself as the center and author of her own abusive situation, is traumatized by the death of a friend and assumes that she is the center and author of that event which also involves her abuser. Since Eileen's friend was killed, Eileen's abuser must have killed her.

Attempting to connect Leah, and possibly Janice, with the construction of the false memory, Horngrad asks whether suspicions or beliefs of third parties can have an effect on the memory of a child or a traumatized child?

"Yes," Spiegel answers without hesitation.

Horngrad can't dispute the existence of some of Eileen's symptoms, but he can dispute that they resulted from her witnessing a murder. He needs to rebut Terr's assertion that she can tell the nature of the trauma by looking at the symptoms, that she could tell from watching *Stand by Me* that Stephen King had been traumatized by a train. He asks Spiegel if it is possible to describe the trauma by looking at the symptoms.

"As psychiatrists," Spiegel intones professorially, "we do much better reasoning forward than backward; that is, it's a much clearer case where someone is sent to us because they were recently assaulted or raped or injured and then we're clear about what the proximate trauma is, and our task is to help treat the symptoms.

"It is much more difficult and dangerous to reason backwards, to say: Well, this person has the symptoms; therefore, this type of trauma must have occurred, because there can be many reasons to produce a syndrome that looks quite similar."

Horngrad asks Spiegel about the concept of a "triggering event" and Spiegel explains that one condition under which the dissociative powers could weaken and allow the material into consciousness would be if the person had gotten married and had a good relationship with their spouse or if they had a good therapist. But merely because a specific stimulus triggers a certain memory does not mean that that memory is any more likely to be true than false.

In terms of the recovery of the dissociated memory, Spiegel explains further, the more complete the dissociation or loss of the memory, the more likely the memory will return fairly complete into the consciousness.

Then Horngrad turns to the shifting and changing nature of Eileen's memory and asks Spiegel if it is typical for significant details to change in a recovered memory.

"In general, because the memory, in a sense, leaps back into consciousness rather than it being a kind of process of accretion, where additional details are added—my experience is, it's relatively unusual for details to change. New material may be added, but it is relatively unusual for the story, as it comes back into consciousness, to change in major ways."

"How about for details to be discarded by the reporting person as wrong?"

"That is also comparatively unusual."

In concluding, Horngrad asks whether it is possible to distinguish a repressed fantasy from a true repressed memory. One explores it with a patient, Spiegel explains, one looks to see if it is plausible in light of what one knows about the patient, and one looks for outside corroboration, but one can never be absolutely sure if the memory is true or false.

Horngrad's point: If a psychiatrist of Spiegel's training, stature, and experience cannot tell the difference between a false memory and a true memory, how can you, the jury? At least beyond a reasonable doubt?

Juror Merrill, one of the most attentive jurors, yawns during Spiegel's testimony. If Terr's scientific testimony is open to debate, it is nonetheless good theater. While Spiegel's testimony is more grounded in traditional theory, it is poor theater. Spiegel, while pleasant and amiable enough, speaks as though he were in a lecture hall. There are no anecdotes, no stories, no encounters with famous authors to illustrate his points and enthrall his audience.

Spiegel proves extremely difficult for Tipton to handle on cross. She gets off to a bad start by engaging him in an extended debate about the difference between repression and dissociation. "Repression" was the word Terr used for the lost memory, and Tipton prefers that term apparently because it does not imply the existence of any personality disorders. "Dissociation," on the other hand, refers to a range of character disorders, the most extreme of which is multiple personality. Spiegel does not budge: repression refers to an inability to remember feelings or wishes which are "disturbing," while dissociation is defined as a mechanism in which the person sustains a temporary alteration in the integrative functions of consciousness or identity as a result of a severe trauma or multiple traumas. In dissociation, the entire experience, from beginning to end, is blocked or isolated from consciousness.

Having lost the battle to have Eileen's loss of memory defined as the more benign repression, Tipton digs herself in deeper by asking if it's not true that many patients suffer severe traumas without developing dissociative disorders.

"The majority of the patients who I see who have experienced either physical or sexual abuse or who have witnessed the murder of someone have dissociative disorders," Spiegel responds calmly.

Tipton moves on. She tries to get Spiegel to agree that it is more likely that memories of childhood traumas are true than false. Spiegel replies that, unlike Terr, "I am rarely fortunate enough to be able to determine in a sense that would satisfy a court of law whether or not those memories are accurate. I make every effort to interview family members or acquire other corroborating evidence, but it is rare that I have the absolute answer to that question."

Tipton retreats and, seeking to salvage something, asks if it isn't at least true that repression doesn't necessarily equate with false memory. True, Spiegel says, but "when events are kept out of awareness and kept unconscious, there's certainly opportunity for transformation of the events to occur." Unlike

Terr, who said that repressed memories are likely to be more pristine, Spiegel says that repressed or dissociated memories are always interacting and changing in the unconscious.

Tipton questions him about the tendency of a traumatized person to avoid the place where the trauma occurred, the nature of the conditions under which a trigger will stimulate the return of the memory, and whether a repressed memory will come back in a chunk or pieces, and makes little headway. Finally the debate returns once again to the difference between repression and dissociation, and Spiegel insists that you cannot repress major traumas, you dissociate from them, and that dissociated memories do not come back in bits and pieces.

In the end, Tipton has to settle for an agreement by Spiegel that he would give more credibility to a recovered memory if it were corroborated by outside details.

Tipton asks him if he is going to be paid for his testimony and he says, "Hopefully," and the jury laughs. Horngrad dryly says he'll keep the rates in mind on re-direct, and the jury laughs again.

Spiegel agrees with Horngrad that the corroborating details would be more persuasive if the details were known only to the patient.

Tipton is not at all pleased with her cross-examination of Dr. Spiegel.

Court adjourns at 4:48. Horngrad catches Franklin's eye as he is being escorted out by the deputy and holds a finger to his lips.

58

November 20, 1990—Tuesday

GEORGE FRANKLIN STRIDES INTO THE COURTROOM with his usual swagger, folder in hand, a pleasant but blank look on his face. He glances at each member of the audience in turn as he approaches the defense table. It is too much for one reporter, who comments, "God, I'm so sick of that smile!"

Vince steps into the hallway and calls: "Jurors for Department Nine!", but he has forgotten to unlock the judge's door and Smith is stymied in the hallway. Vince hurriedly retreats to open it, and the judge walks out to the bench while the jurors are coming in.

Tipton looks striking in an emerald green suit, print blouse, and gold hoop earrings. She is still coughing. The breather is back, wheezing his garlic breath in clouds around the press section. He explains that he is retired and plays a lot of golf. He is in court today because it is women's day on the course.

"I think the sonofabitch is guilty," the breather says to no one in particular. "He did it. I'm not sure they can prove the case, but the sonofabitch did it, I just know it."

"Bill Mann!" Vince shouts in the hallway. George Franklin smiles at Bill as he walks by on his way to the stand. Finally, after all the enemies, a friend.

Bill, who is still a fireman, hasn't seen his mentor from Station 2 in almost twelve years and didn't recognize him when he first saw him on television. A student owes his teacher something, Bill thought, and went to visit George in jail. George, who had very few visitors, was glad to see him. They talked little about the case, but George did profess his innocence.

"I say to you, Bill," he had said in that odd formal way of

his, "I am innocent of this charge and the other charges levied against me."

George was convinced he would be found innocent.

"All they have is a story from my daughter," he explained. "It will all be over soon."

Bill remembered that George always thrived on adversity, and now with his strong mind he seems to be trying hard to turn this nightmare into something positive. He reads constantly and has lost lots of weight. "They have my body, Bill, but not my mind," he told him.

Bill wasn't sure what he thought about the murder charge: George could have done it, but he didn't think so. He had been startled, though, when he read Eileen's quote in the paper that George had said, "Now, Susie," when the little girl was struggling, because that sounded just like him. Whatever the case, he still felt bonded to George and was willing to be his friend.

Steve Schwartz had contacted Bill a few weeks ago and asked him what he remembered about van VXJ707. Bill remembered the vehicle well. George bought it in 1968 or 1969 after he had gotten drunk one evening and run the first one into a bridge embankment and ended up in a hospital with his jaw wired shut.

Bill doesn't look at George as he testifies, but out of the corner of his eye he can see him smiling up at him. Bill explains to the jury that George was the cook at the station in 1969 and that Bill became familiar with the inside of the van because he helped him carry groceries inside on many occasions. He testifies that the curtains, the platform, and the mattress weren't put in the van until some time in 1970, after George had had it for a year or so.

On cross, Tipton asks Bill if he considers Mr. Franklin a friend, and he hesitates.

"He was a friend at one time, and I think he is—yeah, I still consider him my friend."

Tipton establishes that Mann started his four-week training period on September 16, 1969, and that he wasn't actually assigned to a platoon at Station 2 until October 16 of that year.

Mann insists that he became acquainted with Franklin during the training period and noticed then that the rear seat was still in the van. Tipton will need more than this to discredit his testimony, however, because even if he didn't see the rear seat in the van until October or November of 1969, it still means the platform wasn't in the van at the time of the killing. Tipton questions him on why he would remember the details of the inside of the van so clearly, but she gets nowhere.

Horngrad next calls Katherine Rieder, the psychologist whom Eileen saw in 1988 and 1989. Rieder, who appears in her mid-thirties and is short with permed hair, saw Eileen fifty times between June 1988 and June 1989, and Horngrad wants the jury to hear that Eileen told her therapist of her just-recovered memory of the digital penetration in December 1988, but failed to tell her a few weeks later of her just-recovered memory of the murder of her best friend. Another key fact for the defense is that Rieder confirmed for Eileen in December that recovery of such a repressed memory was possible.

During her testimony Rieder nods her head continually like a therapist reassuring and encouraging a hesitant patient. Initially, she will only say that she had probably told Eileen that it's possible that a repressed memory of abuse could be recovered. Early in her therapy, Eileen told her about Susan being murdered, but as far as Rieder knows Eileen did not recover a memory of Susan Nason being murdered while in therapy with her. She did feel like Eileen was open and honest with her and that they had a good exchange.

On cross, Tipton elicits from her that often patients choose not to discuss certain things with their therapists. On re-direct, Rieder expands on her earlier statement and says she "probably" discussed with Eileen the fact that when people experience a traumatic event such as incest or murder, they push it down and don't look at it and sometimes something triggers it and it comes up later.

Since Eileen claims to have recovered the murder memory only a few weeks after hearing this, Rieder's statement suggests that she might have planted the idea of the repression and recovery of traumatic memories in the conscious or un-conscious mind of her patient.

As her last question, Tipton asks the therapist if Eileen showed any signs of mental disease or disorder. Although the question is far beyond the scope of direct examination, and no foundation has been laid for Rieder to render such an opinion, and although the defense was denied the right to have its own expert give such an opinion, and over Horngrad's strenuous objection, Smith allows Rieder to testify that she saw no signs of mental disease or disorder in Eileen.

Horngrad calls Dr. Elizabeth Loftus. Finally, a female ex-pert witness for the defense. Loftus is a professor of psychol-ogy at the University of Washington and a nationally recog-nized expert on human memory. She has written 14 books and over 200 articles on the processes of memory and her specialty is the fallibility of eyewitness identifications in criminal cases. Dr. Loftus is an experimental psychologist and, based on her research, she believes that a memory is not a static image but an ongoing, integrative process. Memories decay with time and they change or grow as new information is received. Her re-search also shows that memories can be implanted in the mind and believed by the perceiver to be true. She calls them "cre-ated memories."

Although Loftus will not be allowed to give an opinion as to the truth or falsity of Eileen's memory, Horngrad hopes that her testimony about the instability, fluidity, and suggestibility of memory will, when viewed in light of the facts of this case, seriously weaken the credibility of Eileen's story.

Loftus is a trim woman with a full head of black hair and large black-rimmed glasses. She is clearly at ease in the court-room: after Peggy swears her in, she spells her name as she walks to the witness chair.

Horngrad runs her through the generally accepted theory of the three stages of memory: acquisition, retention, and re-trieval. Memory is not like a videotape recorder, she explains in a calm, confident voice, and various factors can influence the accuracy of each stage. The acquisition of memory can be affected by such things as the lighting or the mental state of the perceiver. Usually, the more shocking the event, the fewer details recorded by the perceiver.

As for retention, not only do memories fade with time, the older the memory the more vulnerable it is to being distorted or contaminated by post-event information. Her studies indicate that witnesses will incorporate newly acquired facts into an old memory and then repeat them as if they were part of the original memory. She has conducted an experiment in which people were shown a film of a robbery and shooting and were later exposed to television accounts of the event containing inaccurate details. In later tellings the subjects had incorporated the television details. Witnesses can also absorb and integrate facts told to them by other people.

In terms of retrieval, once people have absorbed post-event information, they will repeat it quite confidently and in great detail. When they are told that these facts are wrong, they resist as strongly as they would if the details were accurate. People also gain confidence in erroneous memories each time they repeat them, and positive feedback can also strengthen an erroneous memory.

Loftus's testimony, on its face, is devastating for the prosecution. In essence she is saying that memories are unreliable, and the more traumatic and older they are the more subject they are to distortion and contamination. Horngrad has already demonstrated in great detail how Eileen's twenty-year-old memory evolves and changes in the telling, and now Loftus has explained why.

After listening to Loftus, Tipton is morally offended. To her, the psychologist is nothing more than a "whore" who is testifying in favor of George Franklin solely for the money. Her expertise and opinions have nothing to do with this case and Tipton means to make that clear. In her highly focused, brief, step-by-step style she proceeds to isolate Loftus and her expertise from the case at hand.

Tipton establishes quickly that Loftus has appeared for the defense in all of the 113 criminal cases in which she has testified. Then she establishes that Loftus is a researcher who conducts studies on memories and does not see patients in a clinical setting. Many of her studies are based on simulations of real events in front of college students who are being paid or are receiving credit for participating. Her studies usually involve questions of whether or not the subject accurately remembers if the robber had a mustache or in which hand he held the gun. They deal with the discrete *details* of a given event, not questions of whether the event occurred at all; i.e., she hasn't found people who claim to have witnessed a murder when what they really saw was a ball game.

It's true that some of the cases in which she has testified involved the identification of the perpetrator, but she has never testified in a case in which the question was whether or not the victim could recognize her own father. She hasn't, of course, conducted studies which involve real live traumatic situations, because such studies are forbidden by research ethics. Her subjects are normal, untraumatized people.

"You don't recruit your subjects from a pool of people that have been documented victims of psychic trauma, do you?"

"No."

Then Tipton asks, "Children are not your area of expertise, correct?"

"That's correct. I've done only five studies or so with children, and the bulk of my research is with adults."

"You've never done a study, have you, wherein you've recruited a group of subjects to view an event in which the main actor was a relative of the group of subjects? Have you?"

"No, not that I recall."

Tipton makes her final distinction.

"Let me just ask you this: You have conducted no study, have you, in which you tested a person's ability to retrieve and describe an event that they witnessed twenty years later. Isn't that true?"

"I don't recall personally doing such a study, and there aren't very many studies with that long an interval of time in the literature."

"And in fact, none of the studies that you have done involve the subject's having repressed the memory of the event that they witnessed prior to the retrieval; isn't that true?"

"I have to assume that is true; that I study in these experiments the distortions of memories that were not repressed."

To wrap up her questioning, Tipton establishes that Loftus bills her time at $250 an hour and expects to make approximately $5,000 in this case.

Tipton sits down, satisfied that she has rendered Loftus's expertise and testimony irrelevant to this case.

Smith tells the jurors that the trial has moved faster than anticipated and that they won't have to return in the afternoon.

"We're going home?" a juror asks excitedly.

"You're going home," the judge assures her.

Judge Smith noticed the sleeping juror dozing off during Loftus's testimony and he asks her and the two alternates to remain. On several occasions he has seen jurors nudging her to keep her awake. Worried that her sleeping might create grounds for appeal if Franklin is convicted, he has decided to speak with her about it privately. First, he asks the defendant if he is agreeable to waiving his appearance in chambers. When Franklin stands and says in a husky voice, "I am," it is as if a stone statue has suddenly come to life. Of all the words in all the days of this trial, these are the first spoken by the man whose freedom is at stake.

Judge Smith feels bad about the sleeping juror. She had said on voir dire that she had trouble keeping awake in the afternoon, but she had been kept on the jury anyway.

"Are you catching everything?" he asked her in chambers with the two lawyers.

"No, I can't say I'm hearing everything," she answered.

"We're going to have to excuse you. I'm very, very sorry."

"I'm sorry too, Judge, I really thought I could do it."

Only two alternates remain. Patrick Carbullido, a San Jose State student, is selected to take the sleeping juror's place.

One local reporter changes her prediction from a hung jury to outright acquittal. The defense has bombarded the jury with lots of witnesses and planted many seeds of doubt.

Judge Smith sees it differently. He thinks the prosecution put on a good case and the defense lost its rhythm with the blue station wagon evidence. Wachtel did a poor job of trying to convict the man in the blue station wagon of the murder. You could tell he had never been a prosecutor. He called way too many witnesses: he should have put on two or three—Boom!—and then moved on. Tipton was superb on cross, just the opposite of Wachtel. She found the primary weakness in each witness, exposed it quickly and cleanly, then sat down. Tipton is ahead on points.

59

November 21, 1990—Wednesday

THE UPCOMING HOLIDAY CREATES AN ALMOST FESTIVE atmosphere in the courtroom. Horngrad, wearing a colorful Thanksgiving tie, cracks jokes with the reporters in the hallway. Peggy notices that he seems exuberant, wired.

"Kate Franklin!" Vince calls out, and an audible gasp arises from the press. Rumors have been floating for the past several days about a mystery guest, perhaps an alibi witness, or another expert psychiatrist, or even George Franklin himself. But no one had guessed Kate. The word is that she is married to a successful lawyer and lives in one of the wealthy mountain suburbs, but no one has spoken with her. The TV reporters, always undereducated on the facts, jab the print reporters and ask who she is. "Kate," someone finally tells them, "the oldest daughter." In the doorway stands the last of five siblings, the final member of the Franklin family to enter the courtroom and take center stage.

KATE WAS THE ONLY ONE OF THE FRANKLIN CHILDREN TO GRADUATE from high school and she finished a semester early. She immediately enrolled in a two-year community college and began studying psychology. Her plans to leave home on her eighteenth birthday were moved up a couple of months after a horrible fight she had with Leah. Her mother had accused her of not helping enough with George Jr. and Diana, and Kate had accused her of letting them run wild. Leah told her to leave and never come back. For the rest of the year she lived like a gypsy, moving from one friend's house to another, until she finally rented an apartment. She and her mother eventually made up.

Kate also fell in love when she was eighteen. Leah had enrolled in San Mateo Law School that same year, 1976, and she joined a study group that often gathered at her house. One of the students who came over was Allen, a man eight years older than Kate. She found him smart and handsome, and for both of them, it was love at first sight. Their first date was on Halloween, and they went to see *Night of the Living Dead*. She eventually proposed marriage to Allen, but he insisted on waiting until he finished law school, so they lived together instead.

George Franklin was extremely proud of his oldest daughter for finishing high school and going to college and marrying an intelligent, educated man. He lost thirty pounds for her wedding and clipped the hair between his eyebrows because he thought the hair made him look like a Neanderthal. Unlike Leah, he contributed a thousand dollars for their wedding, and he went out of his way to make a good impression on his daughter's new in-laws.

Kate tolerated her father. He would come over with a girlfriend or by himself and they would have a brief, amiable visit and that would be that. She had never forgotten the sexual abuse she had suffered at his hands, but she had developed an aggressive attitude of trying to get on with her life. Unlike Eileen, she had never been her father's favorite, nor had she ever thrived on his attention. She never experienced the "loyalty conflict" described by Lenore Terr, because she never felt affection for her father, nor did she think what he was doing to her was right or an expression of love. She always knew it was wrong and she loathed him for it. What had happened wasn't her fault and she never believed for a minute that she had invited or enjoyed it.

Kate understood that she hadn't been in control of her life as a child, but she was in control now, and she would not let the past destroy her future. She was determined to make her own decisions and try to live a happy, normal life. Her childhood was over, and the challenge was to convert that liability into an asset. She had survived, after all. Every good choice she made now reinforced her belief that she was in control of her destiny.

Maintaining this attitude wasn't easy. Although she seldom saw her father, and her mother had a new life, the family dysfunction continued and there was a constant risk of getting sucked into it. After the brouhaha about Allen supposedly flirting with Diana, Leah had inserted herself into the situation and called Allen and yelled at him, "How dare you do this to my daughter?" Then Eileen had called in a rage and accused Kate and Allen of telling Barry about her prostitution conviction, when in fact they hadn't known about it until Barry had told them. When these things happened, Kate swore off the family, at one point severing communications with them altogether. But they always found her. Janice would stop by to borrow money and talk about how their father had sexually abused them or Eileen would invite her down to Canoga Park under some false pretense. She saw Janice and Eileen as continuing to act out their terrible childhoods, unable or unwilling to let go of their rage and anger over what had happened to them. It was almost as if they *needed* the turbulence and pain. Kate seriously doubted whether Eileen had been sexually abused by their father—Kate and Janice and George had been the expendable kids, Eileen and Diana the favored ones—but still she understood her pain. Her compassion for her sisters dwindled, however, when they tried to pull her into their craziness.

When Allen graduated from law school, he and Kate moved to Spokane for a year, then back to the peninsula where he worked for a law firm. Later he took a job in Paris and Kate resumed her schooling. When they returned to the peninsula in 1988, she finally received her degree in economics from the University of San Francisco.

Her relationship with Allen has had its ups and downs, but they truly love each other, and when Eileen called her to tell her of her dream of Susan's murder, Kate was happily seven and a half months pregnant. She hadn't spoken with Eileen since she called her to wish her Happy Birthday.

Kate worked at maintaining a relationship with her mother. She had supported Leah in her decision to go to law school, and she had a party for her when she graduated and gave her an expensive set of antique diamond earrings. Leah was still Leah, though. She held her grandson as if he were a foreign object. After she saw her former husband on TV and at the prelim, she said to Kate with great satisfaction, "I look so much better than he does!" She wallowed in bitterness toward him, and saw the murder charge as a vindication of herself.

Leah might have felt vindicated, but the murder charge also knocked her way off balance. She had finally escaped her past and put together the pieces of a life, then *boom!* her past exploded in her face, and her name and personal history were laid out in every paper on the peninsula. She had gone into psychotherapy immediately after Eileen told her the story, and after a few sessions she had proudly told Kate several times that the doctor had said she was normal.

Kate and Leah had talked about the case before the trial. Leah told her she was going to say on the stand that she didn't remember anything about her mental breakdowns. Kate told her that Allen's grandmother, Helen, who had always liked George, was probably going to attend the trial.

Kate had learned of her father's arrest when Janice left a message on her answering machine saying Kate should wear her sunglasses to work because it was going to be the biggest case San Mateo County had ever seen. Kate had wanted as little to do with the case as possible. She didn't know whether her father had killed Susan Nason or not—part of her thought it was her two sisters acting out their crazy rage in public—but she figured the truth would come out at trial and there was little she could add one way or another. While Eileen sought the spotlight, Kate sought the shadows.

The prosecution had talked to her the Friday before the

prelim for over an hour and a half, but tape-recorded only the last fifteen minutes of the conversation. Tipton was quite pleasant to her, but seemed disappointed when Kate said she wasn't sure she believed Eileen's story. Janice, Kate said, was a pathological liar and Eileen's credibility was no better than fifty percent.

The defense pestered Kate through the summer for an interview, but she told them she didn't know anything and didn't want to talk to them. Finally, she agreed to answer two or three questions if they promised to leave her alone. Schwartz asked her if Eileen had told her that she had recovered the memory under hypnosis. No, Kate said.

"How did she tell you she recovered it?"

"She said she had been having nightmares and then it came to her one night in a dream."

Since Kate had never heard any other version of how Eileen claimed to have recovered the memory, she didn't realize her answer had any particular significance. Tipton had asked her in the interview what Eileen had told her, but when Kate began to describe how exhilarated Eileen had sounded on the phone, Tipton suddenly changed the subject.

Kate thought she had slipped through the net until one evening during the trial, Schwartz called her and said Eileen had denied under oath telling Kate that she had recovered the memory in a dream. Was she sure? he asked. She was sure, Kate responded. Then she would have to testify, Schwartz said.

VINCE HOLDS THE DOOR FOR KATE AS SHE ENTERS AND LOOKS around hesitantly for the witness stand. She is wearing a well-cut gray wool suit and a large flowered shawl, set off by a string of pearls. Her dark, wild hair is cut short, accentuating her soft face, sea green eyes, and porcelain complexion. Other than the faint swish of her walking, the courtroom is silent as she passes through the gate in the wooden railing.

On the stand, Kate feels numb, disoriented. She has never been in a courtroom before. Her mouth is dry and she wonders if her voice will work when she tries to speak. She hears a small cry in the back of the courtroom and sees her husband pick up her small boy and carry him out. She wants to look at her father—it has been eight years since she has seen him—but she is concerned that the jurors might see some sort of complicity. Finally, she steals a glance and is shocked by the change. The white hair and deep creases make him look ancient. She thinks of what life in jail must be like and feels a moment of compassion for him. In his eyes she sees a look of love. Keep a stiff upper lip, she tries to communicate, you'll get through it.

Direct examination is short but explosive. In a calm, composed voice Kate recounts the telephone call a year earlier in which Eileen told her that she and Janice had been riding in her father's van on the way to school when she saw Susan walking on the sidewalk. She imitates Eileen's voice—"Please, Dad, pick up Susan. Please, please." He had stopped and made Janice get out of the van and Susan got in. When Eileen had described how they had driven into the woods, Kate had interrupted her. "Eileen, stop. I don't want to hear any more."

Eileen had told her she had had a series of recurring nightmares in which she saw flashes or images of a murder, and that they frightened her. As a result she went back into therapy. Later, Eileen had said, she had had a dream in which she saw their father murdering Susan Nason.

"Miss Franklin, do you have any doubt that your sister told you that she had a series of nightmares about it?"

"No, no doubt."

"Do you have any doubt that your sister Eileen told you that the fact that your dad was the killer came to her in a dream?"

"No doubt."

"Thank you. I have nothing further."

Tipton had been watching Kate closely. She had known since Eileen's cross-examination that this moment would arrive. Eileen and Leah had told Tipton that Kate had been very upset and angry over Eileen coming forward and tried to discourage her from pursuing the case because it would upset her life. Leah had also told Tipton that Kate had told her that Allen's grandmother, Helen, had come to the trial and reported back to Kate on Eileen's testimony. Leah said Kate told her Eileen was lying and had called up Horngrad and offered to testify. One thing Tipton is certain about: Kate hadn't told them in the interviews what she had just said on the stand about dreams and nightmares. She had obviously thrown in with the defense. Tipton intends to discredit her by demonstrating bias and prior inconsistent statements.

Tipton begins by asking if Allen's grandmother had sat through the trial. Kate replies that she isn't sure, that Helen had said she was going to attend, but she didn't know if she had or not. Hardening her tone and addressing Kate by her married name, Tipton asks her if it's not true that her husband's grandmother had been in court while Eileen testified and reported back to Kate.

"No, that's not true."

"You never had a conversation during the course of this trial with your husband's grandmother in which she reported back to you Eileen's testimony?"

"No, I did not. I do not discuss the details of this case with any of my husband's family members."

Tipton, realizing that either Leah or her daughter is lying, asks the same question again, and Kate, in a steady, solid voice, answers the same way.

Tipton shifts to her bias.

"You're angry at her [Eileen], aren't you?"

"No, I'm not."

"Isn't it true that you urged her and begged her not to come forward with this information, that it would bring shame on the Franklin name?"

"No, I didn't say that."

"Isn't it true that you told her that, if she came forward with this information, it would make it impossible for your child to grow up without a cloud over his head?"

Kate had never said any of this to Eileen, and she is shocked at Tipton's attacking style. The prosecutor had been so pleasant in the interviews and now she is obviously gunning for her.

Kate doesn't weaken or wobble under the barrage, however, but leans forward slightly in her chair and addresses Tipton in a firm tone.

"No, I never said that. What I told Eileen, Elaine, is that she and Barry are adults and that they have to do what they think is right. And I did say that to her."

It would have been ludicrous, Kate says, to urge Eileen not to go forward, since by that time she already had.

"Didn't you tell her that, with this much time having passed, what was the point of doing this? The Nasons have probably forgotten about Susan after all?"

"No."

Tipton turns to the dream.

"Do you recall being interviewed in May of this year by Inspector Morse and myself?"

"Yes, I do."

"And you didn't tell us at that time anything about Eileen stating that she had nightmares about the murder, did you?"

"Correct."

"Nor did you tell us anything about Eileen having this come to her in a dream, did you?"

"Correct."

"Nor did you tell us anything about Eileen claiming that, because of these recurring nightmares, she had returned to therapy."

"Correct."

"And in fact, you never told us that Eileen had mentioned anything about driving into the woods. Isn't that true?"

"Correct."

"Nor did you in that statement ever say anything about Eileen claiming that Janice was in the van. Isn't that true?"

"Correct."

The rhythm of the questions and one-word answers is gripping. As Kate responds, Morse flips through the pages of her earlier statements looking for contradictions. Tipton and Kate continue in this odd sing-song style through the litany of facts Kate hadn't told them in the interview. Kate, unlike many witnesses, does not try to explain or qualify her answer. She answers only what she is asked. Tipton appears to have scored heavily on cross once again.

On re-direct, however, Horngrad rehabilitates her.

"And when you talked to the prosecutor in May, why didn't you mention the nightmares and the dreams?"

"They never asked me. I was never asked: 'What was the nature of Eileen's recollection?' " ·

Kate explains that she hadn't been trying to hide anything from the prosecution, she simply had no idea that Eileen's statement about the dreams had any particular significance or bearing.

Tipton thinks differently: She remembers telling Kate after the interview that George Jr. would testify that Eileen told him she had recovered the memory under hypnosis, so she had to be aware that the manner of retrieval was significant.

The struggle between the two women is a draw.

BONNIE CURB NOW TAKES THE STAND. SHE TESTIFIES THAT SHE LIVES in Modesto, but in 1969 she worked as a bookkeeper in Vallejo for the Skylawn Memorial Park. She recalls driving one day that year to the cemetery in San Mateo to check some computer records. Horngrad asks her if she remembers the car she drove in 1969, and when she says she doesn't, he hands her a copy of her motor vehicle registration record.

"USK897," she reads. "This sounds familiar. Pontiac."

Horngrad has pinned on the wall Prosecutor's Exhibit 51, which is the list Hensel and Morgan compiled at the cemetery of the cars which approached the area of Susan's grave on September 22, 1970, and which contains plate VXJ707. He asks the witness to look on the list and see if she spots her plate number, and when she finds it, he has her circle it in red.

"Oh, after you stopped working for Skylawn cemetery," Horngrad adds, almost as an afterthought, "did you ever go back to the San Mateo office again?"

"No."

For the better part of Mrs. Curb's testimony, Tipton has been looking down at the papers in front of her. When Horngrad finishes, she says abruptly, "No questions."

The next witness, Linda Lythgoe, went to work for Skylawn cemetery in October 1969. She circles her license plate number on Exhibit 51 and testifies that she never returned to the cemetery after she quit in February 1970. Tipton has no questions for her either.

Horngrad offers a stipulation that one T. C. Merney attended the funeral of Susan Nason on December 9, 1969, and that his license plate at that time was CSH107, which is also on the list.

"So stipulated," Tipton says, without looking up.

Juror Chapman, the pediatrician, points to the list on the wall and whispers to Peter Nori, the securities analyst. Nori looks confused for a second, then nods knowingly. At the same time the press finally gets it: "They've got the wrong list," someone says. "That's the 1969 funeral list on the board."

Horngrad discovered the prosecution's error only a month earlier. The prosecution had given him the list of license plate numbers months before, but it wasn't until he received Morse's notes mentioning a visit to Skylawn cemetery that he suspected the cops thought they had found a one-year anniversary graveside visit by his client. He asked Tipton and she confirmed his suspicion. He told Schwartz to drop everything and get on the list immediately because there had been no such visit by George Franklin. As he began tracking down the people on the list, Schwartz found that none of them had been at the cemetery on September 22, 1970, but they had been there for various reasons on December 9, 1969.

Tipton didn't realize her error until midnight the previous evening. At the end of the day, Horngrad had given her the names of his next five witnesses, but she didn't figure out their significance until Margaret Nason told her that one of the names on the list was her father and that he had attended the funeral but had definitely not made an anniversary visit to the grave. Tipton feels responsible for failing to direct Morse or Cassandro to check out the list. Hensel had been so sure, and on the side of the list is typed "October 13, 1970," which would seem to verify his recollection. She and Hensel and Morse even went to Susan's grave and Hensel showed them where he had been parked on September 22, 1970, when he jotted down the plate numbers. (Before they left, the three of them stood over Susan's grave and joined hands and Morse said, "We finally got him and we're going to take care of him for you, honey.")

During the break, reporters crowd around Horngrad to make sure they understand the impact of the evidence. He is ebullient. In a burst of enthusiastic overstatement, he asks rhetorically, "Can you believe they have charged this man with murder?" It has been a good day for the defense, maybe the best so far. Kate, a strong and so far unimpeached witness, had confirmed yet another version by Eileen of how she recovered the memory, and the cemetery incident revealed the ineptness and out-of-control zeal of the prosecution. Not bad impressions to leave in the minds of the jurors over the four-day Thanksgiving break.

At 10:15 the judge announces that the defense has only two more witnesses and dismisses the jury until Monday morning. Tipton and Horngrad argue again about Barry Lipsker. Smith rules that the defense has exercised due diligence in trying to obtain Lipsker's presence and that he will allow portions of his transcript to be read to the jury.

In the press room the reporters are busily writing the story of the nonexistent graveside visit when Tipton stops in. Since she is in their territory, they are more relaxed and they chide her about the rough day she had.

"The fat lady hasn't sung yet," she says good-naturedly. No one doubts that the tough prosecutor has another surprise or two up her sleeve.

60

November 26, 1990—Monday

AN AIR OF CONGENIALITY PERVADES THE COURTROOM this morning, probably due to the long break and everyone's sense that only a few scenes remain to be played. Tipton is wearing an attractive black suit, and the flair to her hair suggests she had it done over the weekend. The jury is chatting amiably among themselves, almost like old friends. Joyce Beard has a purple outfit on, and Ollie Scholle is wearing a yellow golf sweater. Peter Nori is wearing a suit, leading Tipton to comment jokingly to Morse that maybe he is lobbying for election as foreman. The plastic head is facing harmlessly into a corner.

Horngrad calls William Hensel to the stand, not to explain the cemetery screw-up (he knows Tipton will call him for that purpose) but to further develop the Blue Station Wagon Alternative. He tries again to introduce Hensel's report indicating that Aaron Patterson was booked (but not arrested) for investigation of homicide in the Susan Nason case, but Smith refuses to admit the report. The judge does allow in, however, Hensel's report of his interview with Ann Hobbs, who had testified a few days earlier that she remembered nothing of the incident. In the report, Ann says that the blue car had cardboard in the window.

On cross, Tipton uses Hensel to her own advantage. She establishes that, although the Ann Hobbs incident occurred three days before Susan disappeared, she didn't come forward and make her claim about the man in the blue car until three days *after* Susan Nason disappeared, and that prior to her statement there had been nothing to link Susan's disappearance to a blue station wagon. The description of the car in the flier was based only on Hobbs's statement, and it was the flier that had generated all the blue car sightings. For example, the statement of Mrs. DeNunzio, who had seen a blue car while watching for her decorator, was given on October 6, at least two weeks after the flier had been distributed.

After Hensel's testimony, it is time for Glo, the court stenographer, to read portions of Barry Lipsker's prelim transcript to the jury. Glo is personally convinced that George Franklin is guilty of the murder of Susan Nason and she is convinced he won't go anywhere near the witness stand. He so unnerves her that she has asked the deputy not to walk him by her on their way to the defense table. Glo stands and reads

Barry's testimony rapidly and without any inflection. George Franklin is tracking a transcript on the table, a finger to his mouth. None of Barry's surliness or arrogance comes through in Glo's flat, rote reading, and within minutes the jury has lost interest.

When Glo finishes, the breather comments, "That husband sure deserves a lot of credit."

Horngrad calls Helen, Allen's grandmother, who, according to Leah, sat through the trial and reported Eileen's testimony to Kate. Helen, quite elderly, hands Horngrad her purse on the way to the stand. When Horngrad asks the frail woman if she has been to the trial before, she says adamantly, "No way." She thought the trial was in the city of San Mateo and her eyes are too bad to drive this far anyway. She has in fact never been in this building before. She certainly didn't tell anybody that she had come to the trial. Tipton has no questions for her. On leaving the stand, she angles straight toward George Franklin, and for a second it looks as if she is going to say something nasty or even whack him. Instead, she comes close, pauses momentarily, and gives Franklin a big smile. Helen has liked George Franklin since she met him at Allen and Kate's wedding years ago. She retrieves her purse from Horngrad and totters out.

AFTER THE NOON RECESS, HORNGRAD IS READY TO PLAY HIS TRUMP card: The 1969 newspaper articles which prove conclusively that every key fact that Eileen recited about the killing was in the public domain. Before the trial began, Horngrad had little doubt that the articles would be admitted into evidence. As the trial progressed, however, and he saw the whimsical nature of many of Smith's rulings, he became concerned. He has had the articles prepared in three different formats to ward off any procedural objections by Tipton or the judge: first, poster-size blowups of the complete articles; second, articles with misleading or irrelevant items crossed out; and third, a listing of the 1969 articles and the key facts that they contained. Horngrad will settle for any of the three versions, but he prefers the posters, because he wants to circle the key facts—the smashed ring, the brown shoe, the mattress, the rock—in red for the jury.

With the jury out of the room, Horngrad argues to the judge that the articles are the very "heart of the defense," and stresses that he is not required to prove that Eileen actually read the articles for them to be relevant and admissible. Several experts have testified that people absorb into their memory information picked up from outside sources, and the evidence shows that the Franklin household received the *San Mateo Times* in 1969 and that the facts of the case were widely disseminated and talked about in the community. Even Barry was quoted in a newspaper article as saying that of course Eileen had followed the details of the case back then. If the articles are not admitted, the jury will be left with a false impression and allowed to speculate that the only way Eileen could have known those facts was if she was at the scene of the crime.

Tipton strenuously objects to the admission of the articles. An argument similar to Horngrad's could be made in any case involving eyewitness testimony, she tells the judge, and the fact is that Eileen testified that she didn't read the newspapers in 1969 and did not hear the case discussed in the house. It is preposterous to think that the information she is reciting now is based on what she heard twenty years ago. Any relevance the articles might have is outweighed by the likelihood they will mislead or confuse the jury.

The judge rejects the articles without explanation. Horngrad is shocked, and, glancing at Tipton, sees what he takes to be a look of surprise on her face.

"Your honor, could I just be heard very briefly?" he asks, almost pleadingly.

"No. You've already made your argument, Mr. Horngrad. We've got to get on with the trial."

"I understand, your honor, but just—I would just like to respond to one point the prosecutor made."

"I've ruled. Please bring the jurors in."

The next witness is Cinde Chorness, the reporter for the *San Mateo Times*. She interviewed Barry (because he wouldn't call

Eileen to the phone) for an article in which he said that Eileen and Janice had put their stories together before Eileen came forward, and that Janice had seen her father and Eileen together the day Susan disappeared. The import is that the two sisters and Barry were talking and sharing facts about the case, which contradicts Janice's and Eileen's testimony. Horngrad has a hard time getting Chorness's article into evidence, perhaps because he's still recovering from the last ruling, and Tipton interrupts with enough objections to diffuse the article's impact.

Horngrad has one witness left, a pathologist, but he is not available until tomorrow, so the defense rests its case until then. If the prosecution's case had ended on a low note, the defense ends on no note at all. Tipton begins her rebuttal before it sinks in that the defense has shown everything it has. No alibi. No George Franklin. No other killer. Nothing.

Rebuttal is the prosecution's opportunity to regain the momentum and begin recasting the drama in a light favorable to it. Tipton calls Shirley Nason, the dead girl's sister. Shirley, who has been sitting through much of the trial, has a thin face like her mother, but she lacks Margaret's softness. Shirley denies knowing Penny Stocks and says that, after passing Susan on her way to take the shoes to Celia that afternoon, she waited in the house for her sister so they could play together. She did not send Susan away as Penny testified.

Continuing to remind the jury of the victim, Tipton recalls Margaret Nason. Margaret tells how she had gone to the Banks home looking for Susan, and Mrs. Banks (now Mrs. Darois) told her she had pointed the way to the Oakley house and watched Susan through her kitchen window. Mrs. Banks had not told her that she had seen Susan walking back from the Oakleys, that she had seen a strange man parked in a blue car, that the man in the car had tried to talk to her daughter, or that she heard her dog barking and a car pull away.

Now Tipton recalls William Hensel. She phoned him immediately when she discovered the mistake in the two lists of license plates. He felt horrible, and he knew he would have to come in and perform a mea culpa in front of the jury. On the stand Hensel explains that he thought the document was the 1970 list because it had October 13, 1970, printed on the side of it and he assumed that was the date of the transmission of the plate numbers to the Department of Motor Vehicles.

Continuing her relentless decimation of the Blue Station Wagon Alternative, Tipton has Hensel recount how when he interviewed Mrs. Banks in October 1969, she showed him how she had been looking out her kitchen window when she saw the top of a red-headed girl through her fence. She had said nothing then about a man in a blue station wagon or her dog barking ferociously. Hensel testified that he looked out the window and couldn't see through the fence. Hensel also recalls that Penny Stocks told him she was playing with her brother, not Shirley, when Susan approached her.

On cross, Horngrad hammers Hensel as long and hard as he can about the cemetery list before Smith mercifully puts a stop to it.

During the break, Smith addresses Horngrad's motion to admit Eileen's divorce papers into evidence. Horngrad argues that Dr. Terr testified that a person is likely to retrieve a memory when the person is in a safe period in life and that divorce proceedings would not be considered a safe time. He also points out that in her divorce affidavit Eileen had said she was afraid Barry would dissolve the corporation and take the money and abscond with one of the children. Smith accepts the documents, but orders them sealed.

In the press room, the reporters are shocked by the exclusion of the newspaper articles. They are also curious about Smith's bad mood. "God, he's letting everybody have it," one big city reporter says.

TIPTON, UNWILLING TO LET UP ON MRS. DAROIS AND THE BLUE STATION wagon, calls Morse to the stand and has him identify the photographs of her backyard and the fence. Morse testifies that from the kitchen window it would be impossible to see a car on the street or a girl on the walk.

Tipton's next witness is George Franklin Jr. Wearing a gray pinstripe suit, he strides in and out of the courtroom as rapidly and stiffly as before. He testifies that he has visited his father in jail three times. Over Horngrad's objection that the testimony is improper rebuttal, Tipton asks George Jr. whether he asked his father if he committed the crime. Yes, says George, and his father denied the killing. George looks confused when he steps down from the stand.

The question Tipton wants the jury to consider is: Why would Franklin deny the charge to his son and not to his daughter?

TIPTON DOES NOT FEEL GOOD ABOUT THE NEXT SCENE. SHE IS GOING to complete the ruination of one of the few existing relationships in the splattered constellation of the Franklin family. She recalls Leah Franklin to the stand to impeach the testimony of her oldest daughter.

Leah has trouble talking as she disowns her once-favorite daughter. She refers to her as Cathleen, although it's been Kate or Katie for twenty-five years. She tells how she stopped by Cathleen's house on her way to meet with the prosecutor on the last day of Eileen's testimony and that Cathleen told her that her husband's grandmother had been in the courtroom and reported back to her that Eileen denied on the stand that she had told Cathleen she had recovered the memory in a dream. Cathleen told Leah that she didn't believe Eileen was telling the truth, and a few days later Cathleen called and said she was going to call Mr. Horngrad and tell him that.

Leah's face barely works, as if all the elasticity has been sucked out of it. Her voice vibrates with pain and her words, once out, seem to hang and quiver in the air. She drops her head, shakes it slowly, and closes her eyes for several seconds as she talks. Soon she is whispering her answers. She begins referring to her daughter as Kate, then reverts back to Cathleen.

Cathleen, Leah testifies, always felt that Eileen shouldn't have gone forward because it was so difficult for everyone in the family. Cathleen was pregnant and humiliated and took early maternity leave from her job. She was so ashamed she has been unable to go back to work.

Smith sustains one of Horngrad's objections and Horngrad is so startled that he turns to the judge and says, "Pardon me?"

On cross, Leah testifies that she doesn't remember Kate ever saying that Eileen told her she had recovered the memory in a dream. Leah purses her lips, stands slowly, and walks out one last time.

Margaret Nason follows Leah out and catches her at the bottom of the escalator. Leah is in tears and Margaret pats her on the shoulder and consoles her quietly. "It's just so awful," she says, and Leah turns and gives her a hug and Margaret hugs her back.

"Poor soul!" thinks Mary Dolan as Leah exits, "It must have been a horrible life." The woman was out to lunch emotionally and mentally. "I don't remember" seems to be her mantra.

Joyce Beard finds the mother unstable and is surprised she is an attorney. She would not want Leah representing her on a case.

Wendy Canning can't figure Leah out. Here is a woman who could get a law degree but couldn't protect her own children. She was right there and had to know what was going on: why didn't she grab her children and leave the first time he smacked them? It almost seemed like she had two lives, one as the passive, dependent wife and mother and the other as the strong woman getting an education and taking care of herself.

THE DAY SEEMS ENDLESS. THE LAST WITNESS IS MARTY MURRAY, who is trying a case on another floor. He testifies that he never told Eileen any of the facts of the case or showed her any photographs or physical evidence. He told her it was critical that she not get any information about the case from an outside source.

On cross, Horngrad establishes that in one of the early conversations Eileen told Murray that Janice was in the van when they stopped to pick up Susan. Murray also testifies that he told Eileen that he believed her because she had information only an eyewitness could know, but he is not allowed to testify if he subsequently learned otherwise.

*　　　*　　　*

JUDGE SMITH IS WORRIED ABOUT THE JURY BEING CONTAMINATED BY the publicity during deliberations—he had observed the Salcido circus—and he tells the jurors that he expects to give them the case on Wednesday night and that he is thinking of sequestering them. The jurors are not pleased.

61

November 27, 1990—Tuesday

TIPTON IS WEARING A CRANBERRY RED SUIT. A small gold pin flashes on the lapel of her jacket. George Franklin, in his gray suit, is laughing and joking with Horngrad. He believes he will be acquitted. The plastic head, looking wide-eyed, almost startled, is staring straight at the jury. The Nasons are present, but very few reporters.

The last day of testimony begins gruesomely. Wachtel calls Dr. Paul Herrmann, the defense witness who was unavailable yesterday. Herrmann, a pathologist, looks as if he has stepped off a plane from Vienna: he has a mustache and Vandyke beard, is wearing a three-piece gray suit, and has a distinct bearing of self-importance. As soon as Morse hears the word "pathologist," he walks back to the first row of seats and tells the Nasons they probably want to leave.

It quickly becomes apparent that Herrmann, who has reviewed the photographs, the physical evidence, the autopsy, and Dr. Benson's prelim testimony, is here to challenge scientifically the prosecution's theory of how Susan died. If the physical evidence doesn't fit Eileen's memory of how the death occurred, then the entire memory is untrustworthy, including the identity of the perpetrator. Herrmann's appearance is unfortunate timing for the defense, however: his testimony will make the jury relive the horror of Susan's death all over again, only a day before they begin deliberations.

Herrmann holds up the plastic head and points to numerous rounded areas of the fracture and opines that anywhere from two to four blows could have caused the damage. Then he holds the small rock splotched with the blood and hair in his hands and says that while he can't say for sure, he would be very surprised if it caused the damage: it is too small and its irregular contours do not match the rounded areas of the fracture. The blood and hair on the rock don't really mean anything because the victim could have fallen or been lying on the rock. He takes the large rock out of the bag and looks at it and says that while it is has enough mass, he is very "suspicious" of it because it too has irregular edges.

Wachtel asks him about the injuries to the hand, and he says it is impossible to tell whether they occurred before or after death. There were no fractures to the right hand, which doesn't support a conclusion that the hand was involved in the injury. Additionally, if the hand had been over the head, it is unlikely that the skull would have been injured in the way it was.

Herrmann also opines that, based on the physical evidence, it is not possible to say what position the body was in when the injury occurred, or whether the girl was killed where the body was found.

When Wachtel steps down, Herrmann appears to have served his purpose. While he didn't prove that the injuries *did* occur in some other way, he at least demonstrated the possibility that they did.

Tipton, in a brilliant display, demonstrates how to stand an expert witness on his head and send him spinning off into the ionosphere. Given that she had no idea who the witness was or what he was going to say before he took the stand, her performance is even more remarkable.

First, she loosens Herrmann up a little by getting him to agree that the person who performed the autopsy on Susan, Dr. Benson, is in a much better position to render an expert opinion than someone who has just looked at photographs. Then she engages him in a debate over whether the skull injuries are in a dumbbell shape or not, and his nitpicking stuffiness quickly becomes apparent. He implies that the plastic head, which has been replaced on Peggy's table and is staring directly at him, is an imperfect replica. She tries to get him to admit that the small rock could have been the weapon, but he will only say that he would be "very, very surprised" if the large rock had caused the injury and that "it's very unlikely" that the small rock was involved.

Tipton then engages him in a physics debate over the proper factors to consider in determining whether a particular object in fact caused the damage, getting him to admit that the strength of the person wielding the object is important, causing two jurors to glance at the stocky white-haired figure sitting at the defense table. As Tipton keeps coming at him from slightly different angles, he maintains his attitude: I am the scientist, you are the layperson.

Tipton leads Herrmann into a maze from which he never escapes. His "science" begins to look silly and contrary to common sense. By refusing to give any ground, his expertise is reduced to arrogance.

Didn't he consider the numerous broken hairs in rendering his opinion that the small rock was an unlikely weapon?

"Certainly that's an interesting finding, but I think that crushed hairs and blood can get on a rock for other reasons than having been used as the instrument to cause this damage."

The reason the large rock is devoid of hairs, he explains, could be that by the time the body was dragged over the large rock all of the hairs had been rubbed off onto something else, like the small rock.

"But," Tipton asks him, "a very direct and likely explanation would be that the rock was used to actually crush the hairs and the crushed hairs remained attached to the rock; correct?"

"Well, that would be very nice and would make a nice story. But I, first of all, think that rock is unlikely because it is so small and not very heavy. And I think there are other ways this would happen."

Tipton, working with a steady determination, turns to the injury to the hand and the crushed ring. The doctor admits that it is certainly a possibility that the right hand could have been held in a defensive position, but the fact that the right hand and the right side of the skull are injured doesn't prove anything. Who knows how the hand was injured? There were no fractures in the hand, after all, he points out. Isn't it possible, Tipton asks, that the animals, attracted to the damaged area, took away the fractured bones? Herrmann mocks her, and in the process displays an incredible insensitivity to the victim.

"Oh, yes. But animals took away lots of this body. They have taken away almost the whole front of the chest wall, they have taken these bones out of this hand.

"These parts of the skull are missing. Did animals take them away? We don't know. There are practically no internal organs, they have all been taken away. Does that mean they were injured?

"I don't know. Animals carry bones away and we don't know why."

He explains patronizingly that he doesn't look for zebras when he hears hoofbeats.

Herrmann has now not only insulted Tipton, whom the jury likes, he has offended the memory of Susan Nason.

Tipton presses him on whether both the ring and finger may have been smashed by a blunt object. He foolishly refuses to give her even that, insisting that it could have been an animal who came along and tried to bite the ring and crushed it.

"There are—there are animals who are attracted to bright shiny objects, particularly birds and perhaps some other animals, I don't know."

Tipton pauses for a long moment.

"Do you think a bird did that?" she asks incredulously, but with a straight face.

His denial is drowned out by laughter. Almost unintentionally, it seems, Tipton has the jury laughing at the defense's expert.

Are these facts mere coincidences? she asks. These findings don't mean anything, he insists, they could be part of some phenomenon that occurred after the child was dead.

"Doctor, wouldn't it be a fairly reasonable explanation that the ring was on the middle finger of that little girl's hand when she put her hand to her head and saw what was coming at her shortly, within moments of being struck by a rock on the right side of her head?"

"Well, that makes a very good story," he says derisively, "but I don't know whether it is true or not."

In denying the likelihood of the obvious, Herrmann has destroyed his own credibility.

On re-direct, Herrmann finishes himself off by suggesting the possibility that Susan could have been "struck on the head by a rock thrown out of a Piper Cub flying at 3,000 feet."

In the hallway, Morse is gleeful. "Christ," he says, both eyebrows jumping, "she really chewed him up, didn't she? He was fuming when he left the stand!"

THE JURY IS EXCUSED AND HORNGRAD, EVER PERSISTENT, RAISES again the admissibility of the newspaper articles. Uncharacteristically, Smith indicates he is reconsidering his ruling.

"Oh good," says the surprised but pleased Horngrad. He and Tipton argue their positions back and forth again. The judge appears ready to rule in Horngrad's favor, until Tipton points him in another direction: Horngrad is not prohibited from arguing to the jury that Eileen *may have* learned the information from external sources. Many people testified about the wide dissemination of the facts of the case in 1969, and he can argue the inference, she insists.

Smith takes the matter under advisement.

FINISHING HER REBUTTAL, TIPTON CALLS BARRY JOHNSON, THE ASSIStant fire chief who thoroughly loathed George Franklin when he was a fireman. Tipton is out to undercut the testimony of Bill Mann, who testified that he saw the van without the platform and mattress in the fall of 1969. Johnson says first that Mann told him a couple of days before that he wasn't really sure when he noted the condition of Franklin's van; it could have been in 1974 when he and George were working together. Additionally, Johnson has reviewed the fire department records and found only one day—October 27, 1969—in 1969 and the first six months of 1970 in which Mann and Franklin were working the same shift at the same station.

TIPTON HAS THOUGHT LONG AND HARD ABOUT RECALLING EILEEN Franklin to the stand. Eileen has returned from Switzerland for that possibility, as well as to be present for the verdict, and Tipton could have her testify to rebut an array of statements introduced by the defense. Tipton decides against it: it might be good to have the jury see her one more time, but she doesn't want to unnecessarily expose her to additional cross-examination.

Instead, Tipton will introduce Eileen's voice. The tape of the phone call in which Eileen first related her story to Inspector Charles Etter is powerful. She offers it as a prior consistent statement by Eileen. Horngrad objects, but Smith allows the tape into evidence.

Inspector Etter, the man who had handled Eileen and Barry so skillfully in the beginning, takes the stand to identify and provide the context for the tape. When he is finished, the tape is played and Eileen's disembodied voice fills the room. The jury listens raptly as she coyly asks Etter if he has figured out yet what case it is and as she and Barry argue loudly over what she is going to tell Etter. Without identifying herself, she haltingly gives an abbreviated version of the story. Her reluctance to reveal her name or the name of the perpetrator is evident throughout the entire conversation. She explains how afraid she is that if she comes forward there will be no evidence but her word and that basically means nothing. The thin voice of an eight-year-old girl says, "Thank you," at the end.

The courtroom remains silent for a few seconds after the conversation ends. The tape is an unequivocal masterstroke for the prosecution. The woman behind the voice was *scared* to give her name. She only gave the information she did because a cop was pulling on one end and her husband was pushing on the other.

With the star performer's credibility apparently restored and intact, the prosecution rests.

Judge Smith originally said he was not going to allow the defense any surrebuttal, but he has relented, and Horngrad calls a retired deputy sheriff who worked on the case in 1969. He identifies a report of an interview with Margaret Nason in which Margaret says that on the day Susan disappeared, Shirley went out and played with a friend. It is an attempt to shore up the testimony of a thoroughly discredited Penny Stocks, and it looks particularly weak following the high drama of the tape recording.

The last witness of this drama packs more of a punch. Kate has been recalled by the defense to rebut her mother's testimony. She is wearing a suit with a dark blue sweater and a long strand of pearls which swings slightly as she walks to the stand. Speaking in even, measured tones, Kate explains once again that Eileen told her the memory had returned in a dream and that she told her mother that about a week after the call from Eileen. She commented to Leah that the dream was pretty unbelievable and they talked about it in the context of the child development theories of Bruno Bettelheim. Discrediting Leah's testimony that Kate had gone on maternity leave early because of shame and embarrassment, Kate testifies that she went on maternity leave on January 12, 1990, only two weeks before her baby was due.

Tipton is determined to paint Kate as hostile to Eileen and a partisan of the defense. For once, she has little success. Tipton starts to badger Kate over why she told the defense and not the prosecution about the dream, and Kate explains patiently and firmly that the prosecutor hadn't asked her about it.

"In your conversation with your mother two weeks ago during Eileen's testimony, you never told your mother that Helen had told you that she had heard Eileen's testimony?"

"Correct."

"So if your mother has testified to that, then that is untrue; is that correct?"

Kate pauses. "Yes."

"And is it similarly untrue that you were opposed to Eileen going forward with this information because of the embarrassment and shame this whole case has caused you?"

Kate leans forward in her chair, looks Tipton in the eye, and says evenly:

"Elaine, it hasn't caused me any embarrassment or shame whatsoever."

"Isn't it true," Tipton continues, shifting angles, "that you have on many occasions told your mother that all you have to do is pray for an acquittal in this case?"

"No, Elaine, that's not true."

"That's not what you are doing?" Tipton presses her, perhaps hoping for an outburst, "You are not hoping for an acquittal?"

In one of the most compelling and spontaneous moments of the drama, Kate pauses, then leans forward and addresses Tipton forcefully on the purpose of the criminal justice system.

"I am praying—Elaine, we're all here and we all share the same objective, and that's to see that the truth comes out and that it's known. That's all I am doing here is participating, just like you are participating in that process. I pray that the truth be known."

There's not much Tipton can do with that, except back off and go with the flow.

"And you don't know what the truth is of the events of September 22, 1969, do you?" she asks.

"No, Elaine, I don't," Kate responds, uttering the final four words of live testimony in the trial of George Franklin.

KATE HAD NOT WANTED TO CALL HER MOTHER A LIAR IN COURT, BUT she had had no choice. She wasn't surprised by what her mother had done—she had seen similar behavior over the years—but it was still hard to accept that in Leah's desperate need to convict her former husband she would lie and repudiate her oldest daughter in the eyes of the world.

THERE IS ONE LAST MATTER BEFORE THE JURY CAN BE EXCUSED FOR the morning. In pre-trial motions, Horngrad agreed, in order to keep the bulk of the uncharged conduct out of evidence, to stipulate that whoever murdered Susan was guilty of first-degree murder. Smith reads the stipulation to the jury:

"Both parties in this case, People and the Defendant, hereby stipulate and agree that the killer of Susan Nason is guilty of murder in the first degree in that the murder was:

"One, committed during the commission or attempted commission of a lewd and lascivious act upon a child under the age of fourteen, child molestation, and; Two, that the murder was premeditated and deliberate."

The reporters, who have heard nothing of this issue before, are both confused and startled by the stipulation. If they understand it right, Horngrad has admitted that Susan was molested and then killed with premeditation, thus putting a stamp of veracity on Eileen's story of what happened that afternoon. How can the defense claim it is a false memory if they admit that critical parts of it are true?

Smith asks if any jurors have problems with sequestration. In his chambers, Alger Chapman, the pediatrician, explains that he has a six-month-old baby at home, and Mary Dolan says she has an elderly husband who needs constant care and would not be happy having a nurse in the house. Neither side wants sequestration because nobody wants unhappy jurors. Smith decides against it.

Smith excuses the jurors until 3:00 P.M., at which time he will read the instructions. Closing arguments will begin tomorrow.

ACT TWO CONCLUDES ON A FAINT NOTE. EXCEPT FOR THE JUDGE AND the adversaries, all of the players have exited the stage, but without celebration or fanfare, not even a gradual dimming of the lights. Soon the jury will be center stage, and the lawyers will tell the jurors how to make sense of what they have just seen and heard. In the instructions the judge will tell the jurors how to think, how to process the information, how to be fair in reaching their decision, how not to be unfair. In some ways the system treats jurors as children, in others it asks them to do the impossible.

While the jury is gone, the judge and the lawyers dispose of the remaining exhibits and resolve questions regarding the instructions. Smith asks to see Horngrad's latest version of the newspaper articles, and Horngrad shows him a sheet of paper on which he has noted seven facts from two *San Mateo Times* articles that he would like the jury to see: Susan's body found under a mattress, Susan's body found with one shoe, the injury to Susan's head, Susan's body found in the dump area, Susan's hand being used defensively, a reference to Susan's crushed ring, and references to a rock as the murder weapon. Smith seems ready to accept the exhibit on the spot, but courteously asks Tipton her position. Tipton makes it clear that if the extracts are allowed in, she will introduce articles containing *erroneous* information—the ring was found the day after the body, Susan was found with two shoes—to prove that Eileen hadn't learned the facts from the articles.

Smith declares that he will not conduct a trial by newspaper and rejects the amended offer. Horngrad, sensing that victory has just slipped from his grasp, asks to be allowed to respond. He repeats his arguments eloquently and at some length, insisting that the absence of the articles could be "fatal" to his case, but to no avail. Smith will not allow a battle of the newspapers.

The judge and lawyers argue over the wording of the instructions, and at the end Horngrad, seeing the slightest opening, says:

"And one last thing. While we were finishing, you said something else was going through your mind. If you had a second thought about the newspaper articles, I am here to ask you to hold that thought."

The courtroom erupts in laughter and Smith, dangling hope in front of Horngrad, says that he has until tomorrow morning to change his mind.

"Great," Horngrad says. "Hope you do. Thank you, your honor."

62

IN THE HALLWAY, BEFORE THE JURY IS BROUGHT IN, the press chews over the day's events. Most still can't believe that the jury won't be allowed to see the newspaper articles. The colloquy between Kate and Tipton was strange, almost as if no one else was in the room. Kate was strong and convincing, but why would Leah make that stuff up?

A local reporter comments that the tape recording was classic Eileen: she begins coyly, beguilingly, then pulls back and withholds information, then chokes up with pain, and finally becomes the little girl who only wants to be believed.

In court, the judge informs the jury that they will not be sequestered and assures them that while they are deliberating they will be in the charge of the bailiff. "He will protect you," he says. Vince smiles and everyone chuckles.

Vince thought the tape was very effective. Eileen sounded just like she did on the stand—laughing one minute, in tears the next—and she couldn't be that skilled an actress to pull it off the same way both times. Vince is convinced the jury is going to nail George Franklin.

Peggy doesn't know what the jury *will* do, but she knows what it *should* do. She can't even stand to look at Franklin any more, that smug look on his face, sitting there thinking he's going to get out of this.

Smith, now the lawgiver, instructs the jury that, in deciding the facts and applying the law, they must not be influenced by "mere sentiment," passion, or sympathy; they must not pay attention to questions that are not answered and must forget any evidence that was stricken by the court, even though they heard it. They are to decide who is telling the truth and who isn't, and in doing that, they may consider the fact that a witness has previously lied or made inconsistent statements; in fact, if a witness lies in one material part of her testimony, her testimony is to be distrusted in others.

A defendant is presumed innocent, and his guilt must be established beyond a reasonable doubt, which doesn't mean "a mere possible doubt, because everything relating to human affairs depending upon moral evidence is open to some possible or imaginary doubt," but means that in the minds of the jurors, "they cannot say they feel an abiding conviction, to a moral certainty, of the truth of the charge." In judging the accuracy of eyewitness testimony, the jury should consider, among other things, the period of time between the alleged act and the identification and whether the identification is in fact a product of the witness's own recollection.

The jury *must not* draw any negative inference from the failure of the defendant to testify: the jury must not "permit it to enter into your deliberations in any way." However, if the defendant is accused of a crime and fails to deny it, his silence may be construed against him.

Certain testimony has been admitted for limited purposes and must be considered only for that purpose; for example, the testimony about acts of physical and sexual abuse by the defendant against his daughter and others cannot be considered in deciding whether or not he physically or sexually assaulted Susan Nason, but only for the limited purpose of determining the effect the abuse would have on the witness's motive or memory; likewise, the testimony of the experts, Terr, Spiegel, and Loftus, cannot be considered on the issue of whether Mrs. Lipsker's claim of a repressed memory is true.

He, the judge, has not intended, by anything he has done or said, to suggest what the jury should do. The jury has only two choices: guilty or innocent.

The jury is dismissed until 9:45 tomorrow morning, at which time closing arguments will begin.

JUDGE SMITH THOUGHT UP TO THE LAST MINUTE THAT HORNGRAD might put Franklin on the stand. Smith understands the risks, but he also knows the jurors will wonder why Franklin didn't testify. If someone accuses you of something, it's human nature to stand up and deny it.

The judge can imagine Franklin getting up on the stand and saying, "You know, Eileen has been like this since she was a child, she's always angry, always pointing a finger at me and saying, 'Daddy, stop doing it,' and she's been coached by her mother, who hates me, and frankly I'm getting tired of it. I told Hensel and Penfold back then, watch out for my daughters, they might tell you stories about me." Or Franklin could have said, "I'm a pedophile and I'm trying to correct it. It's a heavy cross I've had to bear all my life, and now I've found religion. I'm straightened out, and now these kids are accusing me of murder because of what happened to them twenty years ago. I might have been a bad father, but I'm not a murderer."

Franklin needed to get up on the stand and say *something* so the jury would have a basis to find him innocent. As it was, Horngrad could only argue that the prosecution had failed to prove him guilty. If Franklin wasn't going to take the stand, he should have pled to manslaughter.

Smith figures the jurors will elect Chapman, the young pediatrician, foreman, which will be helpful to the prosecution. He can envision Chapman sitting down with Joyce Beard, the black woman, and dealing with her concerns patiently and rationally, rather than arguing with her. The outcome might very well turn on the closing statements.

HORNGRAD HAD CONSIDERED PUTTING FRANKLIN ON THE STAND, BUT he abandoned the idea earlier when he saw how close Smith came to letting in all of the uncharged conduct. If he opened the door an inch, Smith would open it the rest of the way and Tipton would come in with guns blazing. Horngrad had no doubt that if his client testified, everything, including the pornography, would be admitted.

Look at Smith's preposterous, pigheaded ruling on the newspaper articles, for example. Horngrad figured that Smith knew the defense was still in the running and he didn't want to be the person responsible for an acquittal, so he kept the articles out. What did he have to lose? If Franklin gets convicted, then he ought to get convicted. If the case gets reversed on appeal, Smith can still say, "Well, I didn't eviscerate the prosecution's case."

Horngrad has to give Tipton credit for knowing how to manipulate the judge. Her message was: "Look, Judge, you owe us this. You kept eighty percent of the uncharged conduct out and you've done everything you need to for the defense, now give us this one. You worked in the prosecutor's office, everyone knows you here—don't do this to the prosecution."

DOWN IN LONG BEACH, JEFF MUNSON HAS BEEN READING ABOUT THE case in the *San Mateo Times*. He is confused and conflicted— he has a very clear memory of Eileen telling him years earlier that she thought her father had murdered her best friend, but in the paper and on TV she denies ever having suspected him until a year ago. Sometimes he feels sorry for her and thinks, "Poor thing, she must be going through hell," and other times he wonders, if she's lying about this, what else is she lying about? He always suspected that maybe she and Barry cooked this whole thing up for the money. Part of him doesn't want to get involved, another part wants to do the right thing. Finally, his conscience gets the better of him and he decides to give Doug Horngrad a call.

63

November 28, 1990—Wednesday

THE SUN IS SHINING BRIGHTLY OVER THE RIDGE ON THE morning of the opening scene of Act Three. The newly cut green grass of the cemetery rises to meet an unusually blue sky, and white clouds sail aimlessly over a calm Pacific. Down the road, past the pulloff, a thick fog, brightly lit on top by the overhead sun, has settled in over the Crystal Springs Reservoir. The road disappears into the dark underside and cars run their windshield wipers for half a mile or more before ascending into the lighted foothills.

INSIDE THE COURTHOUSE, AT THE TOP OF THE STAIRS ON THE SECOND floor, it's like old times. The closing statements have drawn the national press and the hallway has been filling with reporters and TV crews since 7:30 A.M. Even the sketch artists have returned, arguing as usual for their right to front-row seats. Everyone automatically forms a line outside the door just the way Vince taught them almost a month earlier. A few reporters sit on the floor drinking coffee and reading morning editions; generally the talk is loud, the energy high. The drama is almost over and the writers are visualizing their wrap-up stories: FRANKLIN CONVICTED. Or, FRANKLIN ACQUITTED. Or, FRANKLIN JURY DEADLOCKED. A Sacramento reporter calls it 12–0 for acquittal; a local calls it 7–5 for acquittal, a hung jury. No one predicts a quick verdict. The general feeling is that the closing statements could make the difference.

Morse arrives around 8:30 in a good mood, amused at seeing such a well-behaved press corps. He jokingly offers to arrange good seats for $5.50 a pop.

Inside, Tipton and Cassandro have carefully arranged the stage for the final scene. The evidence table, laden with rocks, the dress, the underpants, the brown shoe, and the crushed ring, has been pushed close to the jury box. The plastic head stands on the edge of the table, posed to watch the jury file in and take their seats. Photos have been tacked up on the bulletin board. In the right-hand corner, closest to the jury box, the fleshless skull with gaping black eyeholes gazes down; in the left-hand corner, closest to the judge, is the photograph of van VXJ707.

All three Nasons are present in the front row.

The breather, better dressed than usual, is sitting and wheezing in the press section, as if he belongs.

Judge Smith announces that his ruling excluding the newspaper articles will stand and directs Vince to bring in the jury.

Vince steps into the hallway and yells, "Jurors for Department Nine," and holds the door as they file in solemnly, very much aware that their hour is finally at hand, and put on their badges. Vince is a little puffed up this morning, officious. He knows soon the jury will be put in his charge. He has already ejected one observer for disorderliness.

MANY LAWYERS WRITE THEIR CLOSING STATEMENTS BEFORE THE JURY is even selected. If they understand their case, they know at the beginning what they will want to say at the end, and they try their case so they can say it. Of course, they add to, subtract from, and modify the final address as the play progresses, but if the drama has gone well, if their themes have held up, they can relate their last statement to their first, they can say to the jury, "Remember what I originally said I was going to do? Now, look, I've done it."

Tipton knows it has been a long, emotional, and sometimes confusing trial for the jurors, and she intends to lead them from the chaos of conflict and lies and accusations back into the storyteller's circle of truth. She will tell them once again the story about the evil man and his red-headed daughter and her innocent friend and what horror transpired on that sunny afternoon twenty-one years ago. She will ask them to write the final scene and seal the monster in the cave so the good, decent people can get on with their lives and be safe in their homes.

She walks over to the jury box and lays down three photos on the rail and begins.

"We are all here for a very important reason, and it's three little girls that brought us here together, three little girls, two of whom never knew each other at all, although they could have almost been sisters or twins. Those two never knew each other because one of them died fifteen years before the other was even born.

"Yet these lives, these three little girls, were inextricably intertwined by the acts, the criminal acts of one man: the defendant in this case, George Thomas Franklin.

"These three little girls are Susan, Eileen, and Jessica.

"Susan," she says, holding up Susan's photograph to the jurors, "she's the one who died, and she died because she trusted the defendant. That was the price she paid for trusting her best friend's father.

"Eileen," she says, holding up Eileen's fourth-grade picture, "is the little girl who survived. She survived only by burying, for twenty years, the memory of what her father had done.

"And Jessica," she says, holding up the third picture, "is the little girl who unwittingly came twenty years later to remind the survivor of the one who had died.

"We're here," she continues, "because twenty-one years ago George Franklin chose to murder an innocent girl rather than be identified and punished as a child molester, and we are here because twenty years later that little girl's best friend had the courage, the strength to come forward and identify her father as the killer."

Standing three or four feet in front of the jury box, speaking in her soft yet firm storytelling voice, pacing slowly back and forth, Tipton finishes her opening flourish.

"The road that brings us to this trial is a long and a winding one. It's a road that travels through the memory, the repression of the memory, and the retrieval of the memory of a horrible, horrible crime: The molestation and the murder of an eight-year-old girl.

"This trial," she says solemnly, "is as stark, as sorrowfully simple and straightforward as a desert highway."

Jurors Salazar and Merrill, the lay priest, are not looking at her. Nori, the securities analyst, smiles at the metaphor. Robert Folger, whom Tipton sees as her guarantee against an acquittal, is following her with a look of deep concern.

Reminding the jurors in stark terms of their duty, Tipton makes their choice absolutely clear: there will be no compromise verdicts, no splitting the difference. Because of the stipulation, George Franklin must either be found guilty of first-degree murder or innocent.

Then Tipton turns to the star of the drama, Eileen Franklin, and asks the jurors to give her credit for her willingness to admit her lies when they judge her credibility. Bragging about how well Eileen stood up under three days of questioning, Tipton points to a gaping hole in Horngrad's cross-examination of her: In over two days of questioning, he didn't ask her one question about the molestation or the murder. Isn't this trial about whether or not George Franklin murdered Susan Nason on September 22, 1969, and isn't Eileen the only witness to this murder, she demands. "Then, why? Why, ladies and gentlemen, in over two days of cross-examination, why did the defendant, through his attorney, not ask her one single question about the actual murder?"

Don't be distracted, she insists, by all the red herrings—the dreams, therapists, books, movies, marital relationships, attorneys, fractious households—but ask yourself instead why Horngrad didn't question Eileen about the one thing that really mattered—the murder. It's George Franklin on trial here, not Eileen. Several jurors nod their head approvingly at Tipton's point.

Having set the emotional tone, Tipton moves to the central theme of her case: corroboration. Under the judge's instructions, she tells the jury, you can convict George Franklin on Eileen's word alone if you choose, but it's not necessary to do that because of the mass of evidence that *corroborates* her story. On a chart she has listed the facts of Eileen's story next to the corroborating evidence. She knows she has to tie Eileen's memory to concrete facts in the jurors' minds, and she reviews the corroborating evidence in great detail: the photographs of the scene substantiate Eileen's statement that Susan was sitting down and to the left from her and that the road curved from that perspective; Eileen said the site was "cluttered" and other witnesses testified to the debris in the area; Eileen's description of the dress, the brown shoe, white sock, and white underpants matches the evidence; Eileen's description of the murder weapon fits the rock with the crushed hairs on it; Eileen's description of the killing is corroborated by the nature of the injuries and the damage to the silver ring. She holds the rock up for the jury to see, then picks up the plastic head and traces the two wounds caused by the rock.

Tipton gives us, for the first time, the official version of the mattress: Franklin tried to pull one out of the van, but when he couldn't get it out, he used the box spring which he found in the clearing. She also explains Eileen's original statement that she had bumped along a dirt road for several minutes by saying that Franklin had probably turned the vehicle around at a pulloff a few yards up the road before parking.

Then, to demonstrate Eileen's impressive recall for detail, Tipton recreates and makes the jury live through every instant of the molestation and murder one more time. She imitates Susan saying, "No, stop. Please don't," when Franklin is "humping" her. When Eileen sees her father with a rock and screams, Tipton's hands fly up to her head an instant before the rock would crash into her skull. She tries to imitate Franklin when he threatens to kill Eileen, but she's not a convincing monster. For an instant her voice falters as if she is about to break down, but it passes quickly. During the molestation, Morse casts a surreptitious but obvious glance over at Franklin as if to remind the jurors of who is responsible for the pain and disgust they must be feeling.

Just after Tipton recounts how Eileen saw the cars driving by after the murder, Smith declares a recess. In the hallway, Morse is ecstatic: "Christ, did you see Franklin's face, that guilty look?" he asks. "We got him." Before the jury returns, Morse moves the charts to the side so the jury can have an unobstructed view of Franklin.

Tipton reminds the jury again of the pain of the little girl and the hideous consequences of her evil father's deed.

"She only knew that her father had done something terrible and that he was compounding it by leaving Susie there alone, alone for ten weeks, alone in a coffin that was nothing more than the hard rocky ground of a ravine, with a rusty old bed spring for a gravestone. The only visitors to Susie Nason's grave were wild animals, rats, and insects."

She reminds the jury of the judge's instruction that they can consider the failure of a defendant to deny a crime in the face of a direct accusation as an admission that the accusation is true. What innocent man, she asks the jury, would not deny his guilt to his daughter/accuser when she visits him in jail? Why wouldn't he say, "Eileen, why are you doing this? You know it's not true. Whatever it is, we'll talk about it. Don't do this to me. You know it's wrong. You're lying. Are you sick? Are you angry? What is going on? Why are you falsely accusing me?"

Does he say any of these things? Tipton demands.

"He knows"—here Tipton the avenging angel whirls and points at the monster—"he knows that she knows because they were together."

She waits until the jurors' eyes have returned to her before reminding them of Franklin's parting remark to Eileen, the person who is supposedly falsely accusing him of murder: "Will you come back and see me?"

Tipton decimates the blue station wagon witnesses one by one before moving to the uncharged conduct, the "monster evidence." She knows she can argue it only in terms of the repressed memory, but in recounting Eileen's repeated traumas, she lets herself fill with loathing for the defendant.

"Her childhood was, quite obviously, a relentless series of really sickening, distressing, dehumanizing acts perpetrated upon her by her father, a *monster* who has so defiled the name 'father' that he does not deserve to be called her father."

Tipton reviews the many traumas Franklin perpetrated on his favorite daughter, including the bathtub sodomy, beatings, holding a gun to her mother's head in front of her, and the Stan Smith episode, "the ultimate rape of his child's body and soul as he held her down and muffled her screams and laughed as he watched his friend ravage and tear his nine-year-old daughter, his own nine-year old daughter."

At this image, Michele Merrill looks down and away from the prosecutor; Folger stares at Franklin with disgust; Ollie Scholle looks like he's had enough too.

"And," she asks, her voice rising in indignation as she points to the defendant's silence, "has there been one iota of evidence presented that refutes this testimony? Absolutely not. Not one iota." This is as close as she can come to pointing out Franklin's failure to take the stand and defend himself.

In spite of all the sick, despicable things her father did to her, this courageous little girl survived, and the way she sur vived was to forget what had been done to her or in front of her. To make it all worse, Tipton argues, Franklin is now arguing that his daughter is either mentally deranged or a cunning liar. As she recounts the defense's attempt to discredit Eileen, she becomes visibly worked up and launches a personal attack on Doug Horngrad, painting him as little better than his client.

"The very simple truth is that it is incomprehensible that anybody would go through what she has gone through to wrench her life apart, the lives of her children, her own family, her siblings, her privacy, to have to expose to the world that her own father held her down when she was nine years old and laughed while another man raped her—to go through all of that, to be cross-examined, humiliated, pried, probed, violated, harangued, harassed."

There is no question who the violator and the prober is, and this highly improper characterization of Horngrad reveals an avenging angel who, for the moment, has lost her balance and been overwhelmed by her feelings of personal outrage over the crimes of the defendant.

Horngrad objects and asks the judge to admonish the jury to disregard the violator remark. Instead, Smith tells the jury to ignore Horngrad's comments.

Tipton closes by describing Eileen as a woman of honesty and courage who came forward because she felt she owed it to the Nasons to tell them how their daughter had died.

Although a verdict of guilty will not recapture the twenty years Franklin has stolen from society, Tipton tells the jury, it will resolve twenty years of unanswered questions and fear and establish the truth once and for all. George Franklin must be held accountable for his horrible crime.

Holding a picture of Susan in front of them, standing absolutely still, she says, after a pause, "It's never too late for justice."

FOR SOME REASON JUDGE SMITH STANDS BEHIND THE BENCH AS HE gives the jurors the normal admonishment not to speak about the case or read any newspapers. Vince takes them out the rear door to lunch. Horngrad requests a mistrial because Tipton improperly referred to his client as a monster, used the uncharged conduct evidence as evidence of Franklin's character, and cast aspersions on defense counsel's character. He also asks once again that the articles be allowed in to refute Tipton's emphasis that Eileen's richness of detail supports the validity of her memory. The rich details could all have come from the newspapers, he argues. Smith denies the motions.

64

November 28, 1990—Wednesday, continued

DOUG HORNGRAD IS NOT A HAPPY LAWYER. HE intended a major theme of his closing argument to be the affirmative proof that everything Eileen testified to was in the public domain, and now the judge has taken that from him. His closing argument will have to be based almost completely on the failure of the prosecution to prove its case beyond a reasonable doubt, and any defense that stands on that alone rests on a shaky foundation. Although he firmly believes that the man in the blue station wagon abducted Susan Nason and dumped her body below the pulloff, he also knows that the blue station wagon theory did not come off well. He will mention it, but he can't hang his hat on it. He must argue as persuasively as he can that the government's evidence has failed to erase all reasonable doubts as to his client's guilt, and the way to demonstrate that is to discredit Eileen Franklin.

He knows, and he knows that Tipton knows, the answer to her question: Why didn't the defense cross-examine Eileen on the details of the molestation or the murder? You cross-examine someone about facts you can contradict. There was no way he could contradict her testimony about the two girls playing in the back of the van, or where she was sitting while Susan was supposedly molested, or what Susan had said. He had nailed Eileen on facts that he could contradict through other evidence, such as the supposed mattress, the dirt road, the time of day, and Janice's location, but he couldn't grill her on the details of what went on inside the van or only in her head. He had very little to gain by going over the facts of the crime itself, except to give Eileen one more opportunity to act out the horrible scene for the jury.

He has to go after Eileen on the fact that she is a self-confessed liar and that her story on the known details shifted and changed constantly as she received new information. He firmly believes that Eileen's testimony on direct was a lie, but the question is how hard he can hit her, the victim, in his closing argument without arousing sympathy for her and confirming for the jury the damage that someone (his client) has inflicted on her.

AFTER COURT IS ADJOURNED FOR LUNCH, THE PRESS WANDERS INTO the pit and examines the evidence that Tipton has so carefully laid out in front of the jury. Before court reconvenes, Horngrad gains access to the courtroom and cleans up the stage. All of the evidence—the photos, ring, rocks, cutoffs, underpants—is removed from view and placed out of sight. Even the plastic head is hidden away.

A few moments before Horngrad is to begin his closing statement, Steve Schwartz rushes in and hands him a note. Jeff Munson, a friend of Eileen's from the early eighties, has called and said that Eileen was lying about her repressed memory. "Too late now," Horngrad thinks ruefully, as he stands to make his argument.

The jurors seem cold to Horngrad, except for the retired schoolteacher, who smiles benevolently at him. Nori, the securities analyst, and Chapman, the pediatrician, are looking elsewhere.

Horngrad sorts through a stack of red and blue cards in front of him. After the obligatory thank you to the jurors, he immediately brings them back to the point of origin: they must follow their oaths and view the case dispassionately and logically, not emotionally. They must adhere to the standard of reasonable doubt, which the judge has defined as the lack of "an abiding conviction, to a moral certainty, of the truth of the charge." What does that really mean? He points to a chart in which he has laid out the four different burdens of proof in the law: the lowest is prima facie, which means "just a little"; the next is preponderance of the evidence, which means fifty percent "plus a drop"; the next is clear and convincing, which is one step higher; the highest is beyond a reasonable doubt, a much higher standard than a person uses even in making major life decisions. An abiding conviction means that tomorrow, after you've thought it over some, you won't change your mind. An abiding conviction is unshaken by time.

All of the jurors are listening to him now. Not warmly, but attentively.

Horngrad lays out a dangerous proposition: It is obvious, he explains, that if a juror is convinced that Eileen saw her father murder Susan Nason, the juror must convict; if, on the other hand, the juror believes that Eileen has lied from the beginning, the juror must acquit. If the answer is anywhere in between—*maybe* George Franklin was there, *possibly* George Franklin was there, or *probably* George Franklin was there— the jury must *still* acquit. He is right, of course, but his statement that the jury could find that Franklin was *probably* at the murder scene seems a form of admission.

Horngrad begins setting up the false memory theory. The facts of the case as Eileen told them were well known in 1969: in addition to extensive newspaper, radio, and television coverage, the town was literally drenched in the fliers which described Susan and her clothes, the blue dress, white socks and brown shoes; the murder was talked about at school and in the homes; Janice, who identified the crushed ring in 1969, even remembered the mattress and the color of Susan's dress. Then, hinting at his revenge/conspiracy theory, he admits that, as a child, Eileen "lived in an unpleasant, violent, and scary environment . . . the kind of environment where Janice and Leah, possibly together, harbored the suspicion that George Franklin might have been responsible for the killing. . . ." We don't know, he insists, whether Eileen's story was a false memory, a fantasy, a visual illusion, or a reconstructed memory, and we'll never know for sure because we weren't there, but we can make our best judgment based on the credibility and character of Eileen Franklin, who is the entire case.

With this, Horngrad moves around to the front of the defense table. He glances at his cards like a concerned professor, then lays them on the table. He opens with his best shot: the numerous lies and versions Eileen has given of how she recovered the memory. If you cannot believe what she told people in the last two years, he demands of the jury, how can you believe what she says happened twenty years ago? Start from the beginning. She says she told her therapist, Kirk Barrett, during a session in June of 1989, of her image of her father murdering Susan Nason. Barrett, on the other hand, says that over the course of several sessions she first told him about bits and pieces of images, a pile of clothes on a sidewalk, a crushed ring, a Volkswagen van, until finally six weeks after the images began she recognized her father killing Susan Nason.

Next she told George Jr. that she recovered the image under hypnosis, then she told him it was under therapy, finally in a dream. When she changed her story, she also urged him to lie about her lie to him. She repeats the same lie to her mother and gives a variety of reasons why: she didn't think her mother would believe her, she wanted the story to be consistent with what she told George Jr., she didn't want to get caught in a lie, she was afraid of the memory. In yet another version to Jay Jaffee, the Los Angeles attorney, she fails to say that the memory was repressed at all. To her sister Kate, Eileen says that she had images in a nightmare and then saw the killing in a dream. When she tells the story to Detective Etter in November, she makes no mention of a lost memory, and when Morse and Cassandro visit her a few days later, she also fails to mention to them that she had just recovered the memory some ten months earlier. In some of the versions, Janice was in the van; in other ones, after Janice moved in with Eileen and Eileen realized that that version would be contradicted by Janice's 1984 statement to the cops, Janice is suddenly out of the van. Finally there is the version given in court, which surfaced for the first time just prior to the preliminary hearing last May, which is the one in which she met her daughter's gaze and suddenly visualized her father standing over Susan Nason with a rock.

Horngrad is now doing his solo dance: sidestep left, hold, sidestep right, hold. He's pulled the jurors in. They are following him closely.

Throughout the recounting, Horngrad mocks Eileen's testimony that she never discussed the details of her memory with Janice. Is it possible, he asks, that when she was having so much trouble remembering where Janice was, when she was struggling with these horrible images, she wouldn't turn to her sister and ask: Janice, where were you? And he attacks Leah for not telling anyone until the prelim that Eileen told her the memory came to her in hypnosis. Is it possible, he asks, that Leah made the pact that George Jr. refused to make? Is it possible that Janice, who never mentioned hypnosis, also made that same pact with her?

If you apply the instructions on judging a witness's credibility, particularly an eyewitness's testimony, these six versions of the memory make her unbelievable not just on this point, but on the very truth of the memory itself.

Struggling to answer the question of why Eileen would level this charge if it weren't true, Horngrad returns to the concept of a false memory. In an effort to make the concept credible and concrete, he admits, or almost admits, that his client sexually abused his children. Remember when Dr. Spiegel said that children are suggestible, and that traumatized children are even more suggestible? Remember how children see themselves as the central actors in all of these traumas?

" 'Mommy's sick; I made her sick. Mom and Dad got divorced; it was my fault.'

"Children think that way.

"When you live in a home where there is a bad guy in the home—Dad—and you associate him with acts of sex and violence and something happens to your best friend, where she disappears and turns up dead and is the victim of a violent sexual act . . . how many bad guys are there in your universe? In your home? Well, Dad is a bad guy. Did Dad do this, too? Did Dad take away my friend? Is it Dad's fault?"

Dr. Spiegel told us, Horngrad reminds the jury, that you can't reason backward, that you can't look at the current behavior and divine the specific trauma behind it. And it was Dr. Terr herself who told us about people who make sensational accusations based on false traumatic memories. Remember the Chowchilla girl who identified her mother as one of the kidnappers? And the girl who swore she saw her sister eviscerated? They all believed in their memories, but they were false.

Certainly Eileen was traumatized, but there is no way we can tell beyond a reasonable doubt *what* traumatized her. Spiegel told us it's impossible to distinguish a memory from a fantasy after twenty years. Spiegel also said that if it's a true memory, you don't take a wrong fact and discard it and replace it with another fact. We also learned that if Eileen had been traumatized in or around the van, she would not have traveled and slept in it with the very man who supposedly committed the horrible deed in front of her.

At 3:30 P.M. Judge Smith declares a fifteen-minute recess. The blue and red cards are moving one by one from the unused to the used pile.

So far Horngrad has focused mainly on Eileen and her unbelievability. After the recess, he goes after the prosecution for bringing the case in the first place.

The prosecution told you in their opening that Eileen Franklin was not their whole case, that they were going to present other evidence. Where is it? he asks. Where is the other evidence? Were they thinking of the alleged cemetery visit by the defendant? The so-called "jailhouse admission"? That amounts to nothing. George Franklin was suspicious of his daughter when she visited him in jail, as well he should have been. If he was as cunning as Tipton says he is, why didn't he just stand up and deny the crime to her? You certainly can't take seriously Leah's testimony about the bloody shirt, not after she forgot it and remembered it so many times.

You may not, he reminds the jury, look to the uncharged conduct—the evidence of molestation and violence—as proof of this crime. The judge instructed you that it is to be considered only for the effect it might have had on Eileen's memory.

In stressing this point, Horngrad seems to admit once again the truth of the uncharged conduct.

"It is beyond dispute that to abuse a child in any way is unforgivable. We don't dispute that.

"In this case, however, with this charge, George Franklin does not seek your forgiveness for the kind of father he was in 1969. He is not on trial for the kind of father he was in 1969. He is on trial for murder. And that's what you have to render a verdict on, not what kind of guy he was in 1969."

Certainly a central question in this case should be: Did Eileen know anything that wasn't in the newspapers?

"Why hasn't the prosecution come in here and shown you that there was one thing that she's saying that wasn't in the public domain? . . . They showed you no evidence that was not in the public domain. Not one thing. Not one shred of evidence. . . ."

He comes back again, as he must, to Eileen's credibility. He has prepared a chart which lists all of the facts of her constantly evolving story and demonstrates how they drop out, get added, or change as she learns new information. Pointing at the items on the chart, he goes through the litany of new or changing facts. He seems to get caught up in the recitation and begins repeating himself and dropping verbs and nouns in a rush to force the jury to see the undeniable pattern of calculated deceit by Eileen. Eileen, Janice, Barry—they all tell different stories, how can you possibly tell *who* is telling the truth and *who* is lying?

The retired schoolteacher drifts away during his repetition of the Janice/Eileen flip-flops. Nancy Salazar is staring off into space. Peggy's eyes are almost closed. Horngrad seems to be struggling for a way to conclude his argument.

He takes a shot at Eileen over the book and movie deals. Sure, Eileen gave away the first $60,000, but that's only the advance. Did she tell you what she is going to do with the royalties or the money from the movie deal?

Eileen lies constantly, he says again, and who knows

whether this murder story is another lie. Or perhaps it's a false memory. The jury doesn't have to choose. All the jury has to find is that her story is so shaky that it can't be believed to a moral certainty.

Horngrad pauses, and then tries to defuse the sympathy he knows the jury will have for Eileen.

"And for that pain—she's entitled to have the pain. She's entitled to that. Of course, she's entitled to that.

"But that's not your job to ease her pain, you see. That's not your job. . . . She's entitled to it, Lord knows. But this is not the time and place—not a murder charge, ladies and gentlemen."

She is entitled to her rage, too, he admits, but that's more properly dealt with in therapy.

Horngrad can't dwell on the Stan Smith story—Eileen's telling was too vivid and disturbing—but he can't let it pass unquestioned either.

The change in her memory, he tells the jury, came after she realized she had superimposed the image of Jimi Hendrix onto the rapist. "What is important, ladies and gentlemen, is that we can say to ourselves: Thank God that Jimi Hendrix wasn't on trial for that rape during the one year she believed it was a black man who raped her."

Horngrad skillfully turns the story around as a classic example of how Eileen constructs false repressed memories.

"That's what's important to our analysis—not whether it happened or not, but how she, in a belief she has, can take an image off—a face off the wall, superimpose it on a person, and believe in her heart that that's who did this crime to her."

Horngrad saves his final shot for the prosecution. The case is an example of a system that has failed, he insists. In their rush to charge and convict, the cops and the D.A. made three big mistakes: They believed that Eileen knew facts only an eyewitness could know, when she didn't; they relied on the fact that there was a second eyewitness, when there wasn't; they alleged an anniversary cemetery visit, which never happened.

On the last point, Horngrad gets vicious for the first time. Whirling, he points at Morse and Cassandro and says:

"You had fifty years of experience sitting at this table—thirty years in homicide investigations—and they come in here and they tell you that that's a list from a year later and George Franklin visited the cemetery a year later?"

It's not poor Bill Hensel's fault, Horngrad says, it was Morse and Cassandro who screwed up.

"They wanted you to believe that that would help shore up an unshorable case. That's what they wanted you to believe."

Certainly the community and the Nasons are entitled to a resolution, but not based on mistaken assumptions, bad facts, and poor investigation. When you cut Eileen's statement from these moorings, it is nothing more than a free-floating, totally uncorroborated memory.

Horngrad, perhaps sensing that the jurors will not be able to declare Franklin an innocent man, shows them a side door.

"A finding of not guilty is not a finding of factual innocence, ladies and gentlemen. It's not a finding he's innocent. It's a finding that the case is not proven. That's what it means. It's a finding that they haven't proven their case beyond a reasonable doubt."

Tipton will have the last word, he says in a nice finishing touch, but while she's talking he will be sitting at his table like a schoolboy who knows the answer but can't get called on. Two female jurors smile benevolently, almost affectionately, at Horngrad, perhaps imagining him at age thirteen jabbing his hand in the air for attention.

If the jurors vote on the evidence, he tells them, they must render a verdict of not guilty.

George Franklin gives Horngrad a brief smile when he returns to his seat.

It is five o'clock and everyone in the courtroom is tired. Smith dismisses the jurors, warning them not to read newspapers or watch TV. Horngrad, who has been arguing for three hours, is wrung out but animated in chatting with the press. His job is finished. He has done all he can.

The breather says, "That guy did all right, but Franklin is still guilty as hell. There's no way he didn't kill that little girl."

The reporters chatter over Horngrad's great line about Jimi

Hendrix being charged with rape. A national television reporter says she would be scared to bring in a verdict of guilty after Horngrad's lecture. She is irritated by the repetition in his argument, but it does create doubts. She expresses a commonly felt paradox: She thinks Eileen was at the scene, but she doesn't find her believable. Tipton has the more relaxed, organized style and she always knows where she's going, while Horngrad seems to wander. The reporters give Horngrad the edge.

One journalist wonders why, in three hours, Horngrad never once said his client was innocent, never once insisted to the jury that George Franklin did not murder Susan Nason.

65

November 29, 1990—Thursday

Morse and Cassandro were pissed at the way Horngrad attacked them in court during his closing and they railed about it at the Broadway Bar afterwards. Word of Horngrad's fingerpointing chastisement had spread in the courthouse and the two received a good share of ribbing from the other cops in the lounge.

"Jesus Christ," one of them had said, "I'm amazed you guys have the guts to go back into the courtroom without bags over your head."

Morse comes to work this morning with two brown paper bags. Sitting in his office, he carefully cuts eyeholes in them. Cassandro makes sure Tipton is in her office, then the two best homicide detectives in San Mateo County, or perhaps the state as Marty Murray and many others would argue, place the bags over their heads, adjust them so they can see, and walk down the hall toward her office, attracting a following of curious secretaries and attorneys along the way. They stand quietly in her doorway until she looks up at them and bursts out laughing. She knows what they are up to—boosting her spirits for her final foray into battle—and she loves them for it. She has a folder of memorabilia from cases she has worked with Morse and Cassandro—one item is a picture of her with a surprised look on her face and the caption: "You want a sample from where?"—and the bags will go in this special folder.

Tipton knows the two detectives have been feeling badly about the cemetery list, and on the way to court she assures them that she will take care of them in her rebuttal.

Inside the courtroom, Tipton immediately puts the physical evidence back out on the table and up on the bulletin board. The skull is up in one corner, the van in the other, the crushed, fingerless hand in the middle; the ring is on the table, as is the model head, which is upright and staring at the jury box. If Horngrad wants to know where all of the evidence is, by God, she'll show him. She thought Horngrad's closing was a joke; he said in essence, "You may think he's guilty, you may believe he's guilty, you may feel he's guilty, but you can't find him guilty because the prosecution didn't prove it."

GEORGE FRANKLIN WALKS INTO THE COURTROOM AND LOOKS AT HIS two lawyers, who are conferring. He sits down and still they don't look at him. The forgotten man.

Vince charges in through his door and yells, "Please rise!" A few reporters grumble. The jurors file in, almost self-consciously, and pin on their name tags.

Tipton begins where she left off, holding a picture of Susan Nason in front of the jury. Seeking to rehabilitate Eileen, which she must in light of Horngrad's devastating recitations of her lies and inconsistencies, she urges the jurors to listen to the tape again and note the reluctance, hesitation, the *fear* in her voice about coming forward. As for the various versions of how Eileen disclosed her memory, all that really proves is how terrified she was of the consequences. "Who can say," Tipton asks the jury, "what the proper etiquette is for disclosing that one's father murdered one's childhood friend and that one witnessed that?" The blame for her lying should be placed on the defendant, for he was the one who placed her in this impossible moral predicament.

Give Eileen credit, Tipton insists, for admitting her lies. How easy it would have been for her to deny her lie to George Jr. As for George Jr. and Kate, they are simply embittered, resentful siblings who really don't believe their father is innocent but are ashamed and angry at Eileen for disrupting their lives.

Tipton's voice seems to lack conviction, force, this morning. The retired schoolteacher and securities analyst are refusing to look at her. Salazar is glancing around the room.

Tipton stresses her theme that Eileen's memory is more believable because of its flaws. If she had researched this case, the first fact she would have learned was that Susan was wearing a blue dress. The second easiest fact to learn was that Susan disappeared in the afternoon.

As for Barry, don't pay any attention to him as an impeaching witness. Barry talked up a storm and gave interviews and offered baseless interpretations of things Eileen had said.

In reviewing the defense experts, Tipton can't help but mock Dr. Hermann, the goateed pathologist who said, "Well, that makes a nice little story, doesn't it?" Tipton doesn't think this is a nice story at all. This is the same man who suggested that Susan's ring could have been damaged by a bird.

Sure, the cops screwed up on the license plates, but didn't the defense also screw up by putting on the stand completely discredited people like Mrs. Darois, Penny Stocks, and Bill Mann? The defense hit the anniversary visit so hard because they don't have anything else to talk about.

Juror Beard is staring at her lap. Other jurors are looking everywhere but at the blonde woman in front of them. Perhaps they already agree with her and don't want to hear any more, or perhaps they have decided her case has failed and are embarrassed for her. Either way, her words seem to be sailing by them.

Tipton folds her arms and smiles and takes a shot at Horngrad. Remember when he asked, "Where is all the evidence?"

Well, he hid all the evidence from you; just before his closing, he put it all away!

Tipton makes Horngrad pay a horrible price for admitting (or seeming to admit) in his closing that his client perpetrated the various acts of physical and sexual abuse on Eileen. First, she says, Horngrad questions whether Franklin really did these things, then when he needs an explanation for why Eileen might be confusing what her father did to Susan with what he did to her, he says, "Yes, this man did molest his daughter." It is, she says, "disgusting and appalling" for the defendant to do these base things to his daughter and then use them as an explanation for what he claims is a false memory. The defendant is asking the jury to reward him for all the horrible things he did to his daughter with a not guilty verdict.

"Forget it," Tipton says indignantly.

Tipton responds to Horngrad's analysis of reasonable doubt. Don't let him confuse you: If you believe Eileen, then the case is proven beyond a reasonable doubt. If you find she is telling the truth, he is guilty. Period.

Tipton closes by comparing her case to an oak tree rooted firmly in the earth. The defense comes along and pushes and pulls the tree until a few leaves fall to the ground—the leaves of the cemetery visit, Eileen's lie to George Jr.—and then they throw some mud at the tree and ask you to find that the tree is not a tree but a house. Don't fall for it. The tree may be missing a few leaves, but the roots and trunk and the branches are still there. This is a tree of truth.

Tipton reminds the jurors that she is speaking on behalf of Susan Nason and the citizens of the county and state when she asks them to use their courage and common sense to convict George Franklin of first-degree murder. "No one will ever second-guess your decision," she assures them. "Thank you," she says softly and sits down.

Judge Smith announces that the jurors have now heard all the evidence. In considering the case, think for yourself, he tells them. Do not hesitate to change your opinion if you become convinced you are wrong, but not just because a majority believe otherwise. It is not helpful to express an emphatic opinion at the outset, because a sense of pride may attach and make it difficult to change your mind. Do not talk about the penalty. You will retire now, he says, and select a foreman and begin deliberations.

He calls Vince front and center and places the jury in his charge. Hand raised, bearing erect, Vince promises solemnly to keep the jury safe and sound in a quiet and convenient place. At 10:15 A.M. Vince strides forcefully through the rear door of the courtroom with the jurors following single file like ducklings. The remaining alternate juror is sent to a room by herself.

Horngrad makes another motion for a mistrial based on Tipton's statement in her rebuttal that his comments were "disgusting and appalling." Smith denies the motion. Horngrad requests that the tape recording not be allowed into the jury room, insisting that he didn't realize until this morning that it was in evidence and noting he had made a mistake in not objecting earlier. Smith tells him that the tape is in evidence. Well, Horngrad jokes, he won't object to the tape going into the jury room as long as the tape recorder doesn't go along with it. George Franklin laughs and slaps him on the back when he sits down. It's the most emotion Franklin has shown in six weeks. Franklin is led away and court is recessed at 10:25.

JUDGE SMITH DIDN'T LIKE TIPTON'S OAK TREE METAPHOR, BUT HE thought even less of Horngrad's closing, which he found way too repetitious. In Smith's view, counsel should address jurors in opening and closing statements as if they were high school students: make short and clear arguments and sit down. He thinks the jury will stay out for a while and review the facts, but that it will likely come in with a guilty verdict. In not putting Franklin on the stand, Horngrad didn't give the jury a real choice.

The reporters retreat to the press room to wait. "Franklin looked at me with kind of a leer," one female reporter says. "It gave me the shivers." After lunch a few reporters gather in the courtroom, which has been left open, just to make sure they don't miss anything. Horngrad wanders in and tells jokes and war stories. The reporters like and respect him. Earlier a friend of Franklin's had given him candy and knickknacks for Franklin and when the deputy wouldn't let Franklin accept them, he passed out the items to the reporters. One L.A. reporter tells Horngrad that the press is almost unanimous in their prediction of an acquittal. The only problem is, he says, the press is almost always wrong.

Horngrad continues to believe his client is innocent and that the jury will do the right thing. Wachtel, his partner, is less sanguine. He recalls the power of Eileen's testimony on direct. He hopes, at best, for a hung jury.

Tipton waits upstairs in her office. She is worried, not at all sure of the verdict. Eileen Franklin waits with her.

George Franklin mentions to one of his jailers that it is a fascinating experience to have your fate in the hands of twelve jurors. He is confident of an acquittal. He plans to be lolling on the beaches of Hawaii soon.

66

VINCE TAKES THE JURORS INTO A SMALL ROOM IN A hallway of offices and judges' chambers. Several jurors complain that the room is too small and Vince takes them down the hall to a larger one, which has a long conference table and a bathroom, but no windows. Vince brings in the boxes of evidence, sets them on the table, and tells the jurors to let him know if they need anything. He closes the door and sits on a chair outside, guarding his brood. Vince doesn't take any chances: in one case a juror got loose and was spotted talking to one of the witnesses in the cafeteria and the judge declared a mistrial.

The jurors sit at the table amidst a general feeling of relief. The performance is finally over. No more watching and listening and sitting silently. Now it is their turn to talk and think and, ultimately, to act. Several jurors ask Wendy Canning to serve as foreman because of her past experience, but she declines. Once was enough, she says pleasantly. Alger Chapman, the pediatrician, Peter Nori, the securities analyst, Ollie Scholle, the banker, and Michele Merrill, the lay priest, indicate their willingness to serve. Joyce Beard finds Alger Chapman a fine, decent young man and strongly urges his selection. Chapman is elected.

Chapman suggests an immediate, nonbinding vote in order to get an idea of where they are and what sort of a road lies ahead of them. Choices are guilty, not sure, not guilty. Pieces of paper are passed out.

Nancy Salazar, the psychiatric nurse, ponders her vote. Her belief in Eileen has never wavered. Because she understands victims, she is not bothered by Eileen's lies about how she retrieved the memory. Even Eileen's marriage to a controlling, exploitive man fits the profile of someone who was abused and traumatized as a child. She doesn't doubt that both Eileen and Janice perjured themselves on the stand when they said they didn't talk about the case while living together, but those lies are also a result of the victim's need to be believed. The black man/white man switch doesn't bother her; in fact it makes sense that Eileen, the victim, would resist the memory and deceive herself about the true identity of the rapist. Still, she wants to study the evidence and see if anything refutes or contradicts it before she makes up her mind. She votes unsure.

Wendy Canning didn't let go of the revenge theory until almost three-quarters of the way through the trial. The testimony of Dr. Terr swayed her. Her testimony validated Eileen's memory for Canning, made it credible. Canning had waited in vain for the defense to present an alibi or witness to say Franklin was drinking beer or bowling or that Eileen was playing at a friend's house that afternoon. As for Franklin, she would have expected him to get up on the stand and deny the killing if he hadn't done it. Why would an innocent man remain silent in the face of such a charge? His silence when Eileen came to the jail was probably the final straw. Still, as she sits around the table now, she is only eighty percent convinced of his guilt. She wants to go over the evidence and see if any doubts surface. She wants to be double sure, triple sure. She wants to see if there are any facts that Eileen knew that she couldn't have known unless she was a witness. She votes unsure.

Ollie Scholle, the banker, doesn't have any doubts as he enters the jury room. His intuition still tells him Eileen's story is the truth. Her appearance on the stand, the agonized expression on her face, the difficulty she had remembering things, her obvious pain at retelling the story, all gave it the ring of truth. Dr. Terr was impressive and explained for him how Eileen could still feel love for her father after everything he had done to her. Her behavior of staying involved with him, traveling to Mexico with him, visiting him in Hawaii, didn't seem to be the behavior of a woman bent on revenge. As for George Franklin, during the entire trial he never showed any inkling of remorse over what he had done to his daughters and family. He just sat there and wrote and smiled that quirky smile, without the tiniest glimmer of human decency. When Scholle listened to the testimony about how he had sodomized Eileen in the bathtub and kicked Janice in the spine, he couldn't help but think that a man who could do that could also smash a little girl's head in with a rock.

Still, he wants to see if any of the evidence contradicts his intuitive response. He also doesn't think it will take a great deal of time to find that out. He wants to be finished by the weekend. Scholle votes guilty.

Mary Dolan is leaning toward guilty. When Eileen first started testifying, she seemed too controlled and Dolan had some doubts about her, but as she continued, she loosened up and showed emotion and became more credible. All of the inconsistencies and changes didn't bother her: the core facts about the murder didn't shift. Dolan had moved to guilty after listening to the tape of the phone call. Eileen never would have concocted this story without knowing whether or not her father had an alibi. Franklin's girlfriend's testimony substantiated Eileen's stories of abuse. If you abuse your daughter, you could also molest her best friend. If you use a child for sex, couldn't you just as easily destroy her? The man had no feeling or moral appreciation for people as human beings. Mary Dolan votes guilty.

Joyce Beard didn't believe Eileen when she testified and she is still disgusted with her. Maybe she is telling the truth, but maybe she is acting. The fact that she was making money from the books and movies bothers her a great deal. Joyce Beard votes not guilty.

Chapman tallies the votes: six guilty, five unsure, one not guilty. Nancy Salazar is shocked. Without any discussion or deliberation, six people believe Franklin guilty. If the unsures are leaning the way she is, deliberations could be over very fast.

Chapman admits to the others that he has gone back and forth during the trial. During the closing arguments Tipton would convince him of Franklin's guilt, then he would listen to Horngrad and he would think, yes, there are some reasonable doubts. Others agree that Horngrad's closing, when he described the meaning of a reasonable doubt, was perhaps the most powerful moment of his case.

It soon becomes apparent that most of the jurors entered the room believing Eileen Franklin. With the exception of Joyce Beard, no one even suggests that she might be lying. They discuss Horngrad's impeachment efforts, and Nancy Salazar says he went over and over the same areas trying to run the jury in circles so they wouldn't know where they were. "What's the point?" she says, referring to his hammering of all the minor inconsistencies and changes. Mary Dolan agrees: the impeachment was all on peripheral facts not related to the murder itself. Stan Smith is not on trial, George Franklin is. Ollie Scholle wonders who among them could keep such details straight after twenty years. In some jurors' minds, Eileen's omissions and mistakes in the details increase, rather than decrease, her credibility.

Scholle argues that financial motives should be dismissed and everyone, with the exception of Joyce Beard, agrees.

Wendy Canning thinks that Eileen and her husband already seem to have plenty of money, and in any event, she can't believe that someone would put themselves through this horrible ordeal for *any* amount of money. As unsavory as Eileen's behavior might have been, it's absurd, others agree, to think that she cooked this whole story up so she could get rich. Joyce Beard shakes her head. She believes Eileen was interested in the money from the beginning.

The atmosphere in the room is cooperative and congenial. It is quickly apparent that this deliberative process will not dissolve into some version of *Twelve Angry Men*. Chapman suggests that they review and discuss the evidence piece by piece until they are satisfied with its meaning. Michelle Merrill and Nancy Salazar have taken copious notes with elaborate time-lines and they refer to them during the course of the discussion. Many jurors are interested in trying to determine if Eileen knew any facts she couldn't have known unless she had been a witness to the murder.

The jury breaks for lunch and Vince takes them to a restaurant several blocks away, which he has predetermined has vegetarian meals to fit Merrill's diet. He and Merrill walk at the front of the pack and joke and tease each other.

After lunch, they ask Vince for a blackboard and Peter Nori, the securities analyst, begins to list the items of evidence on the blackboard as Nancy Salazar removes them from the box and spreads them out on the conference table. Chapman, in a deliberate, methodical fashion, leads a discussion of each item until everyone is satisfied with its meaning and impact. Several times Mrs. Beard has an objection or a problem and the others stop and go over the item again for her. Mary Dolan finds her questions helpful.

One by one the items are demonstrated to corroborate Eileen's testimony: The photographs of the crime scene show a clearing down and to the left of the van; photos also show debris or "clutter"; and the ring looks like it could certainly have been smashed by a rock.

Several jurors want to hear the tape of the phone conversation and see the video of the 1969 crime scene. Chapman writes a note to the judge requesting these items. In it he also thanks the bailiff for providing them with a good lunch.

WHEN THEY HEAR OF THE JURY'S REQUEST, THE REPORTERS SWARM up to the courtroom. Horngrad, fully aware of the power of the tape, argues strongly against its being given to the jury. As a compromise, he suggests the jury be given a transcript. When Smith rules that the jury is entitled to hear the tape, Horngrad argues that it be played only once for them in open court. Smith says the jury can play the tape as many times as it wants and directs that both audio and videotapes and players be supplied to them.

On learning that Alger Chapman is the jury foreman, Smith is even more convinced of a guilty verdict. He predicts the jury will come back tomorrow.

THE JURY LISTENS TO THE TAPE AND SEVERAL MEMBERS NOTE HOW the details Eileen gives in that conversation match several of the items of evidence on the blackboard. If that woman had been bent on revenge, Ollie thinks, she would have been angrily calling her father a dirty SOB. The video shows the debris on the trail and the clearing down the hill and to the left.

Some of the jurors express concern over the murder weapon, and Salazar removes the two rocks from their bags. The one found in the folds of the dress looks almost too small and hard to hold to make such a blow. Wendy Canning recalls that Franklin was left-handed and Merrill, who is taking a leadership role, points out that if the rock were held in the left hand the edges would be coming down on the head at the perfect angle. She holds the rock up and brings it down on the dumbbell-shaped black area of the plastic head to show how it would fit. Mary Dolan worries that the rock is too small to hold with two hands, and someone demonstrates how you could hold the right hand over the left. Nancy Salazar explains that the rock probably worked more like a chisel or a screwdriver. The narrow end fits perfectly in the black hole of the plastic head. At one point Scholle and Chapman re-enact the killing, with Scholle playing Susan Nason and raising his right hand to his head to ward off Chapman's blow.

Nancy Salazar opens three bags and takes out Susan's dress, cutoffs, and underpants. When she holds the dress up, she is struck by how small Susan was compared to her own daughter. There is some concern about the purple or lavender jacket or sweater that Eileen originally said she saw Susan wearing. Merrill explains that Eileen testified that the dress, which is blue with touches of yellow and green, was bunched up around Susan's midriff during the molestation, and in that position it could easily have appeared lavender or purple. Salazar holds up the cutoffs and points out that the jeans have an elastic, gathered waist rather than a zipper or buttons. It would have been easy for Franklin to pull them down and reveal the white underpants that Eileen said she saw. To Dolan's discomfort, the items of clothing are passed around the table.

On another blackboard, the jury tries to isolate those facts that Eileen could only have known if she were a witness. As a reference for what was known, the jurors refer to the flier, the television footage, and facts that Leah or Janice knew and might have told her. Nancy Salazar points out that Eileen testified that the dress was an A-line, a fact not mentioned in the flier. The evidence showed that Susan had on one white sock and a brown shoe, and Eileen testified that she thought she saw her father throw a brown shoe. Salazar speculates that when Franklin threw the sock and brown shoe, the shoe went further than the sock, which landed in the bushes. How could Eileen have known that only one shoe was found? Also, how could she have known about the white underpants? Lastly, she said that she saw her father place a rock on the body and Dr. Benson testified that he found the small rock in the folds of Susan's dress.

The jury is working smoothly, cohesively. No one is arguing for or against conviction; in fact no one is arguing at all. Under Chapman's direction, the jurors are calmly and dispassionately going over each item and seeing where it points. "Is everybody satisfied?" the doctor asks before moving on. If Joyce Beard has a problem, he goes over it with her in a supportive and understanding manner. Several times the deliberations resolve down to an amicable discussion between the two of them.

Most agree that Franklin's failure to deny his guilt to Eileen in jail is incredibly damning. A guilty man would have begged and pleaded with his daughter to recant her false accusation instead of mutely pointing to a sign. Joyce Beard objects that maybe Franklin's lawyers told him not to speak about the case to Eileen or anyone else who visited him. Another time, Beard points out that Franklin would have been busy the afternoon of the killing because he painted on his days off and someone explains to her that he didn't paint *every* day off. She seems stuck on the fact that Eileen is going to make money from the book and movie deals.

"You're probably right, Joyce, there probably is going to be a lot more money," Chapman reportedly said to her, "but it has nothing to do with Susan Nason being killed. It has nothing to do with what happened twenty years ago."

Canning thinks Beard has missed several points and suggests to Chapman that he might want to go over them again with her, which he does, more slowly. Gradually she seems to be coming around.

The jury talks a lot about Franklin's question "Have you talked to my daughter?" when the detectives came to his door, and agree that a man with nothing to hide would have said, "Why are you here talking to me about this?" or, "Have you found who did it?" not "Have you talked to my daughter?" There was no evidence that he knew that Janice had accused him of the crime in 1984.

The changes in time of day do not bother the jury. Eileen probably became confused when she remembered hearing her dad say the word "hooky" and thought it must have been morning. Maybe he meant he was going to play hooky from a painting job. As for the road, the girls were in the van playing, and when the defendant turned around on a gravel pulloff and then parked on another gravel pulloff a few seconds later, it probably seemed like they were on a dirt road.

George Jr. comes up frequently. Wendy Canning says that if looks could kill, he would have killed Elaine Tipton. He didn't give her one civil answer. Some of the jurors admit they were even worried for Tipton's safety as he walked by her. Most felt that his blast of anger was a snapshot of his father at the same age, and a few wonder about their safety if they convict his father. Perhaps he might follow them as they leave the courthouse.

The Blue Station Wagon Alternative becomes an object of ridicule. Jurors refer to it as the "blue station wagon myth." Despite all the witnesses, the vehicle could never be reliably placed in the right place at the right time. Nancy Salazar believes that the mother and daughter who said they saw the car were getting off on the publicity; not that they had made the story up, but they had talked about it over the years and confirmed a version that didn't really happen. Ollie Scholle found their story reasonably credible until he saw the pictures of the fence. Why would the defense put a witness on the stand who claimed to have seen something through a solid fence? To Scholle, it looked like Horngrad was grasping at straws, that he was desperate for any sort of a defense. The jurors have tremendous admiration and respect, and in some cases affection, for Elaine Tipton, and they cite her cross-examination of the blue station wagon witnesses as an example of her incredible skills.

Tipton also demolished the testimony of Elizabeth Loftus, the psychologist who tested college students for altered memories and who had never worked with children. Loftus was impressive on direct, but Tipton made it clear that her experience and background had nothing to do with this case. "What's the point?" Salazar asked the other jurors.

Dr. Lenore Terr is another matter. The jurors talk about how interesting and entertaining her testimony was. She made sense of Eileen's experience and put a stamp of approval on her memory. Dr. Spiegel, the Stanford psychiatrist, is barely mentioned.

As for the swearing match between Kate and Leah, it wasn't a serious factor; it was a side show, more machinations of the screwy, dysfunctional family created by George Franklin. Lies are everywhere in the family, and sorting them out would be an impossibility. No one believes that Janice and Eileen didn't discuss the case while they were living together, and it's understandable why Kate would want to stay out of the family craziness. Mary Dolan lost a little respect for Elaine Tipton when she went out of her way to call Kate by her married name, thus identifying her to the press. That was uncalled for.

Everyone agrees the cops screwed up on the cemetery visit. Mary Dolan thinks it is the low point of the prosecution's case because it suggests that the prosecution might have been concocting evidence. Others see it as just a simple mistake and think Horngrad made way too much of it. Overall the cops did a good job.

Despite their opinion that Horngrad's questioning could get tedious and occasionally obfuscating, the jurors respect and like him, especially his sense of humor, and think he did the best he could with what he had. Nancy Salazar jokes that she checked every morning to make sure his shoes matched. Several jurors resented Horngrad for talking to his client during Tipton's rebuttal argument. She didn't talk while he was arguing.

Dr. Herrmann, the defense pathologist, is ridiculed for saying that the injury to Susan's skull could have been caused by a bird falling out of the sky. Jurors resented his referring to the death of Susan Nason as "an interesting story." His testimony is another example of Tipton's ability to turn a witness around.

There is much talk of the lack of any alibi for George Franklin, of the failure of the defense to even *try* to build an alternative scenario for his whereabouts on the afternoon Susan disappeared. Why somebody didn't get on the stand and say, "George and I were drinking that afternoon," or why Franklin didn't take the stand himself and say, "I went fishing that afternoon." He wasn't working that day and he and Eileen usually spent a lot of time together, so the prosecution version makes sense.

At 4:30 P.M. the jury is ready to quit for the day. Slips are passed out and another vote is taken. Alger Chapman announces the new tally: eleven guilty, one unsure. Five people, including Wendy Canning and Nancy Salazar, have moved from unsure to guilty, and Joyce Beard has moved from not guilty to unsure.

REPORTERS WANDER IN AND OUT OF THE COURTROOM, CHATTING with each other and with Horngrad and Wachtel. The sketch artists are here, not only to record the verdict but to peddle their sketches. Horngrad buys one of himself, and Peggy and Vince buy one of the judge for Christmas. One lone camera waits outside. Horngrad says he still believes the jury will do the right thing.

AT THE BROADWAY AFTER WORK, MORSE REPEATS HIS BELIEF THAT Franklin is "going down." He has studied the jury closely and doesn't see a real problem anywhere. Chapman's selection as jury foreman has him even more convinced of the verdict. Tipton's closing was brilliant, and none of Horngrad's mud stuck. It's not time for the shots of tequila yet, but damn close.

JOYCE BEARD IS STILL UNCOMFORTABLE WITH SITTING IN JUDGMENT on another human being, but that night she ponders the situation and goes over the pluses and minuses in her mind again and again. She has difficulty believing Eileen. She doesn't know what the truth is. As she goes to sleep, she prays to the Lord for guidance.

67

November 30, 1990—Friday

GUILTY.

The instant Joyce Beard opens her eyes this morning she knows the Lord has answered her prayers. George Franklin murdered Susan Nason. She feels grateful for the clarity and the certainty and knows she will never look back. Now she is anxious to get on with the process and put the whole experience behind her. She practically missed Thanksgiving and Christmas is coming right up.

MICHELE MERRILL BRINGS DANISH INTO THE JURY ROOM FOR EVERYone and Vince brings in fresh coffee. Several people suggest that they take another ballot to see if there has been any change overnight. The vote is the same: eleven guilty, one unsure. Beard is surprised, since she switched to guilty. Someone must have moved from the guilty to the unsure.

Yesterday everybody kept the same seats, but today Beard is unexplainedly sitting next to Alger Chapman. As they begin reviewing the evidence, Chapman and others direct their explanations to her as if she is the holdout. Finally she sends a note to him saying she isn't the "unsure."

The jurors repeat the exercise on the blackboard. They list the physical evidence and demonstrate how it matches Eileen's testimony. Ollie Scholle even plays devil's advocate to see if he can find any facts that don't fit. Eileen was probably confused when she said she saw her father take a mattress from the van and put it over the body. She saw him *trying* to take it from the van and merged that with seeing him put the box spring on top of her. Several jurors still don't like her use of the word "clutter" to describe what she saw in the area, but one figures that Barry the blabbermouth probably fed it to her.

The review picks up speed. There are fewer objections and questions. A feeling develops that everyone is in the same flow and that they are quickly closing on their destination. The room grows quieter. A feeling of sadness blends uneasily with the sense of inevitability.

No one has spoken a word in George Franklin's favor. No one has carried his banner even for an instant, arguing even faintly the possibility of his innocence, or suggesting that maybe he, a fireman, isn't the sort of man who would do this. He is probably worse than they know. The most Nancy Salazar can give him is that maybe he was so drunk that he didn't remember killing Susan. Horngrad might have shaken their minds a few times and made them wonder, but in the end they come back to Tipton the storyteller who pointed to Eileen Franklin and said, so convincingly, *"Believe her!"*

At 11:15 the discussion comes to a standstill. There is nothing more to do or say. Another vote is taken. Chapman reads the tally: 12–0.

The room is stunned silent. "Thank God!" Joyce Beard thinks. Some jurors who thought they might have a holdout and be in the room for days are frightened at the enormity of what they have just done. "What do we do now?" someone finally asks. They decide not to act, but to go to lunch and take a fifth ballot when they return. When Vince leads them to lunch they are not their usual talkative, joking selves, and Nancy Salazar wonders if the deputy can tell the difference. Things loosen up a little at the table and they chat about their families and jobs. They return at 1:15 and take their fifth secret ballot. Chapman announces the results: again 12–0. Some jurors begin putting the evidence back in the sacks and boxes, erasing the blackboards and straightening up the room.

"Do you want me to tell Vince now?" the young, brown-haired doctor asks his fellow jurors. He waits a few minutes, just to make sure. It would be horrible if someone changed their mind in the jury box. Chapman fills out the verdict form and knocks on the door. Vince opens it and Chapman tells him they have a verdict. "Wait here," Vince says, and hurries off.

Vince finds the judge, who is just returning from his usual Friday afternoon lunch with a group of judges and lawyers. Smith tells Peggy to call Tipton and Horngrad and have Franklin brought to the courtroom.

TIPTON HAS JUST RETURNED FROM LUNCH WITH EILEEN WHEN PEGGY calls. She tells Eileen the jury has a verdict and Eileen becomes so anxious she almost throws up. Tipton reaches Morse and Cassandro in a restaurant and calls Margaret Nason at home. She will stall for twenty minutes to give Margaret a chance to get here. Tipton hadn't figured on a verdict today and she is wearing a black and white print dress rather than a suit. She is excited: you can never tell, but a quick verdict usually means guilty.

She and Eileen go to the bathroom and Eileen is shaking so badly she can barely stand up. Tipton warns her of the possibility of a not guilty verdict.

"You never promised me a guilty verdict," Eileen admits. "I can handle a hung jury, but not an acquittal." Be ready for one, Tipton warns her again. Eileen changes clothes for the verdict. The two women embrace.

Some of the reporters are in the press room, while others, including Eileen's scriptwriter and author, are lounging on the benches outside the courtroom. Several cameras are present. The press room empties in a second when Peggy calls to say the jury is back. The murmur in the press section is of an acquittal.

Slowly the courtroom fills with the players. Margaret Nason arrives alone and sits in her usual place in the first row. Cassandro enters and, seeing Margaret by herself, sits down beside her. His heart is thumping in his chest, but he manages to assure her that it's usually a good sign when the jury comes back early.

Morse is keeping an eye out for Donald Nason. Hensel has warned him that Nason had said if the jury doesn't nail the sonofabitch he might have to take care of him himself. When Nason shows up, however, he's wearing a tight short-sleeved shirt that couldn't conceal a gun.

Horngrad waits by Vince's door for George to be brought in. He greets his client and they walk to the counsel table together, conferring. Wachtel is nowhere to be seen.

The room is now packed with reporters, secretaries, assistant D.A.'s, and hangers-on. Seven deputies line the walls. The minutes tick by with a heavy stillness as the audience waits for the final scene. The slightest sound, a rustling of a coat, flipping of a sketch pad, a cough, crashes around the courtroom. Finally, Tipton and Eileen enter. The audience turns to watch as Cassandro rises and moves to the defense table and Eileen sits next to Margaret Nason. The two women murmur a greeting.

Tipton sits at the table, then turns around and searches the faces for Marty Murray. Although he has been trying his own case upstairs, Marty has been dreaming about this trial, practicing a closing argument in his sleep. Tipton spots him sitting in the back row and motions him up to the table.

"Sit up here with me," she says as he approaches.

"It's your case," he replies.

"I know, but if I go down, you're going down with me," she jokes. He chuckles nervously and pulls up a chair next to her. She is so shaky that she holds Murray's hand with her right hand and Morse's with her left.

During the forty-minute wait, the jurors have been chatting in the jury room. "Some of you people didn't keep open minds like the judge said," Merrill says, teasing those who voted guilty on the first ballot. Ollie Scholle protests that there really wasn't any choice. They chat about Christmas, what sort of a sentence Franklin is likely to receive, whether he is broke and who paid for his expert witnesses, none of whom did him any good. They speculate about which reporters in the audience work for which paper and decide that Steve Schwartz, Horngrad's private detective, is a reporter for the *San Francisco Chronicle*. Several jurors are adamant that they do not want to speak with the press. They want to go home and be left alone. A few are also worried about George Jr. following them out of the building. Vince assures them he will take them out a back door immediately after the verdict.

When the courtroom is ready and the judge is on the bench, Vince gathers his charges for their final entrance. He checks the bathroom to make sure no one is left behind. As the jurors file in, Vince scans the courtroom: no one should be standing but the deputies.

Franklin glances at the jurors, a small smile flitting across his face. Cassandro is so nervous he grabs Morse's hand under the table. When the jurors won't look at Franklin, he is ninety percent sure of a conviction. Tipton's face is completely drained of color.

At 2:09, Judge Smith announces that all parties are present and asks Dr. Chapman if the jury has reached a verdict. Unlike most judges, Smith doesn't have the clerk bring him the slip of paper—he doesn't know why he should know the verdict before anyone else—but instead directs the foreman to read it out loud. Chapman stands.

"We, the jury in the above-entitled case, find the defendant, George Thomas Franklin Sr., guilty of the crime of first-degree murder, in violation of Penal Code Section 187, as alleged in Count 1 of the Information filed herein."

At the word "guilty," Tipton cries and slumps toward Marty Murray, who holds her. Eileen and Margaret Nason turn and hug each other and begin crying. Horngrad's face drops in his hands. Franklin, whose face is impassive, pats him on the shoulder and says, "That's all right."

The jury is polled, the judge thanks them, and Vince escorts them through the back door. Smith tells counsel that they did an excellent job and assures Franklin that it's not his lawyer's fault that he lost.

Morse escorts Eileen from the courtroom while Cassandro takes charge of Margaret Nason and Murray stays with Tipton. The hallway is chaos, reporters pushing, shouting questions in each other's ears. The cameras fight for a shot of Margaret Nason's face, and one cameraman trips over another and goes down cursing loudly. As Margaret and Cassandro wait at the elevator, she turns to him and says, weeping, "Thank God there is a God." Leah and Aunt Sue join the rest of the prosecution team in Tipton's office and a strange pathos of joy and pain, happiness and tragedy, swirls around the hugging and crying people. Eileen calls Barry and tells him of the conviction. Then she and Morse go downstairs to talk to the press.

The reporters are busy interviewing Margaret and Shirley Nason and Elaine Tipton, and Eileen sits forlornly on a bench outside the press room waiting for them to come to her. Finally, someone spots her and the cameras swing hungrily on her and Morse.

"I can't be happy," she says with a sad, pained look on her face, "he's still my father."

"It's the jurors of San Mateo County who deserve the credit," Morse tells the reporters.

*   *   *

AFTER FRANKLIN IS ESCORTED FROM THE COURTROOM, HORNGRAD slips through the crowd to a phone booth at the end of the hallway. First he calls Hattie Franklin to tell her of her son's conviction. Then he calls Dennis Riordan, an excellent San Francisco appellate criminal defense lawyer, to tell him of the verdict and urge him to take the case on appeal. He takes the elevator up to the jail to see his client and to tell him he's arranged to have the best criminal lawyer in the state handle his appeal.

"You're the best criminal lawyer in the state," Franklin tells him.

Wachtel is rushing up the escalator when a reporter, seeing the question in his eyes, says, "Guilty." Wachtel wobbles backward as if slapped in the face, then turns around and hurries away.

Within a few minutes, the theater is disturbingly empty. Vince, responsible for security, comes in, glances around, and locks the outside doors. He goes to the jury room and checks on the boxes of evidence, which Peggy will inventory before putting away. He locks the door and returns to his seat in the courtroom to wait out the few remaining hours of Friday afternoon by himself.

IN THE MIDDLE OF THE BROADWAY BAR, TABLES ARE ENCIRCLED BY wooden cafeteria chairs. The floor is carpeted in red and the cement posts are covered chest high with fake wood paneling.

The cops and prosecutors start gathering around three o'clock and the mood is high. Morse and Cassandro, their jackets off and sleeves rolled up for a long night of celebrating with their brethren, are the stars of the hour. "Goddamn it, Bones, you guys did it!" rings out again and again. Cassandro is slapped on the back so heartily that he almost swallows his beer bottle. Voices rise each time another cop or prosecutor comes in the door, and the mood swings back and forth from joviality to amazement: "Fucking Bones actually nailed the bastard!" Someone dissents: "Hey, and Cassandro!" Another cop agrees: "Yeah, day in and day out he's the best fucking homicide dick on the unit!" Beer and shots of tequila occupy the tabletop, and loud, aggressive toasts are made to the two detectives and to the extinction of the murderous soul of George Franklin.

As he drinks, Cassandro becomes more loquacious and he repeats the story of how he was so nervous at the table that he grabbed Morse's hand. "Everybody says I'm so cold and unemotional," he explains, "but Christ was I a mess waiting for that jury!" Morse's eyes twinkle in response and he throws an arm around Cassandro and toasts their partnership. Marty Murray shows up and has a shot and a beer or two before heading home. By five o'clock, the celebrating cops have completely taken over the place. The few non-cops are huddled at the far end of the bar. The waitress, who knows and likes Morse and Cassandro, keeps the shots and beers coming, putting everything on a tab. Reporters wander in and join the party.

When Tipton walks in the door, a loud cheer rings out. Morse and Cassandro rise hurriedly and greet her with big smooches on the mouth and long hugs. The other cops gather round for their turn to kiss the successful prosecutor. Shots of tequila and beers are handed to her and she gulps down one shot.

Tipton knew she had to show up at the Broadway, but she also knows what the scene will be like if she stays: Everyone will get roaring drunk and then she will go home to a dark and empty house and crash hard. Besides, she has promised her sisters she will go to her cousin's fiftieth birthday party in Sacramento. She leaves the Broadway after the one shot and returns to the courthouse for an interview with Channel 2, then walks to her car. She changes into party clothes in the bathroom of a nearby gas station and heads for Sacramento. During the two-hour drive she listens to music and relaxes and enjoys her euphoria. She knows it is the most dramatic moment of her life, an experience she will never have again. She arrives at the banquet two hours late. When she walks into the room, the place breaks into applause, which surrounds her as she crosses the room to greet her cousin. The moment feels good.

* * *

BY MIDNIGHT, THE CROWD AT THE BROADWAY HAS DWINDLED TO Morse and Cassandro and a few others. The stale air is saturated with smoke and the smell of beer, and the ashtrays are stuffed with butts. Several tables are still pushed together in the center of the room, and chairs are scattered aimlessly about. Morse's tie is at half-mast, as are his eyes. The two detectives, leaning up against the bar, have become maudlin. They are telling stories about Sheriff Brendon Maguire, a legendary figure in San Mateo County and Morse's personal hero, who died unexpectedly a few years earlier. With tears in their eyes and shots in their hands, they toast their mentor whose portrait stares down at them from the post a few feet away, and salute him in the hour of their greatest victory.

There is another melancholy strain in the song of victory. This is the last case Morse and Cassandro will work together. Because of a personal problem with the sheriff, Morse has moved to the district attorney's office as an inspector, which means the long and successful partnership is over. Up to now, Cassandro has seemed less bothered by its demise than Morse, but now he begins lamenting it. When Morse is in the bathroom, Cassandro buys two roses from a flower girl who has just come in. On his return, Cassandro holds the flowers behind his back and, tears in his eyes and a slight slur in his voice, gives a long (for Cassandro) and moving speech about Bob Morse, what a great cop he is, how much he will miss him, how much he loves him. During the speech both of Morse's eyebrows slide up as he beams affectionately at his partner. Under the picture of their beloved sheriff, Cassandro presents Morse with the roses, kisses him, and the two cops embrace. For once, Morse is speechless.

After another round, Morse pays the tab for 144 shots of tequila and 105 bottles of beer and the two detectives, wasted and happy, go home.

68

MARY JANE LARKIN WORRIED FROM THE BEGINNING whether the jury would convict George Franklin. She had continued to pray for his conviction and had even sent Elaine Tipton a bouquet of flowers during the trial to keep her spirits up. Mary Jane was in her room at school when Susan's former second-grade teacher burst into her room and said she heard on her car radio that George Franklin had been found guilty. Mary Jane was euphoric. At the dentist's office she was so excited she chattered away while the dentist was trying to work. She rushed home to tell her husband, George, who had attended the last two weeks of the trial and had predicted a hung jury. He had already heard the news and had prepared a surprise for his wife. When she opened the door, she was greeted by a banner made up of paper towels emblazoned with the word "GUILTY!"

HATTIE FRANKLIN WAS SADDENED WHEN HER SON'S LAWYER CALLED and said George had been convicted. She doesn't have any bad feelings toward Eileen or Janice; she loves George and all of his children too deeply to be angry. She thinks Eileen made a mistake, that's all. Her hurt deepens with the passing days.

"My heart's broke," is how she put it.

NANCY SALAZAR SUFFERED A SEVERE LETDOWN AFTER THE TRIAL. After so many weeks of holding it all in and not being able to talk about it, suddenly it was over and she could talk, but who could she talk to and what could she say? She would begin telling someone about the trial and suddenly burst into tears. It would be nice, she thought, if someone provided psychological counseling for jurors who have had to decide a difficult case.

Salazar heard that Stan Smith had been diagnosed as schizophrenic and was at Napa State Hospital and she asked a friend of hers who worked there about him. Bad news, her friend reported. He'd been there for fifteen years and was currently in an isolated section of the hospital for violent patients, a ward where restraints were commonly used. He had come up behind a nurse and decked her.

Ollie Scholle didn't lose any sleep or suffer any emotional reverberations over the Franklin case. After the verdict he drove to the bank in San Francisco and put in a few hours work. He had no regrets or misgivings: the jurors had done what they had been asked to do. Actually, Scholle thought the whole experience had been quite interesting, particularly the testimony of the expert witnesses, and he enjoyed talking about the trial with friends at holiday parties. He had never encountered someone like George Franklin and he had no sympathy or pity for him. If allowed, he would have voted to impose the death penalty.

After receiving God's guidance, Joyce Beard never suffered another doubt, although she hoped she would never have to sit on another jury. She watched Franklin's face when the verdict was read and he didn't look surprised, as if he knew what was coming. She felt sorry for Horngrad, who had worked so hard for his client. A few weeks after the trial she had been in the Wells Fargo Bank in Foster City and Margaret Nason had come over and spoken to her. The poor girl's mother had thanked her and said she wished she could thank all of the jurors personally. She said she could finally put her daughter to rest now.

JUDGE SMITH HAD SET GEORGE FRANKLIN'S SENTENCING FOR JANUary 29, 1991. Horngrad filed a motion to delay the hearing, alleging that he had uncovered new evidence and needed additional time to research it. At a hearing on this motion on January 22, Tipton rose and angrily denounced the request, saying Margaret Nason and Eileen wanted the matter concluded as soon as possible and it would be unfair to them to continue the matter any further. Smith denied Horngrad's motion.

The new evidence referred to by Horngrad was the allegation by Jeff Munson that Eileen had told him several years earlier that she thought her father had killed Susan Nason. When Horngrad first spoke with Munson, he had been upset by Munson's failure to come forward earlier. "Do you realize," he had said testily, "that I just gave my closing statement today?" Munson, put off by Horngrad's attitude—it hadn't been easy for him to come forward, after all—almost backed away altogether. But Horngrad apologized, and eventually Munson signed an affidavit setting forth the specifics of the incident.

Horngrad filed a motion for a new trial, attaching the affidavit and alleging, among other things, that the court had erred in excluding the newspaper articles and in admitting the uncharged conduct, and that Tipton was guilty of prosecutorial misconduct.

Prior to the sentencing, the probation department conducted an investigation of George Franklin. The report, which was released to the press, contained detailed references to the uncharged conduct and pornography, as well as statements by various friends and foes. The probation officer recommended that George Franklin be denied probation because "his seeming lack of conscience and remorse, and his aberrant sexual proclivities, especially as regards defenseless children, make him an ominous and ongoing threat in the community." A few papers carried references to Franklin's interest in bestiality, incest, and pedophilia, and one quoted his statement to the probation officer that he was innocent and that the abuses he had committed on his family had led them "to either dream, imagine, fantasize [or] fabricate . . . that I had murdered Susan Nason in order that they could vent their rage."

Judge Smith agrees with the jury verdict. He regrets that he doesn't have much discretion in sentencing. Under the mandatory sentence of life with the possibility of parole, Franklin will be eligible for parole in six years.

January 29, 1991—Tuesday

This play has a hard time closing. There always seems to be one more scene. Most of the regular players are here today, except for Eileen and the jury. The media is present en masse for their wrap-up stories. The reporters and radio and TV people line up against the wall under Vince's direction.

Inside, the breather, wreathed in garlic, sits as usual in the press section; he has come to see Franklin receive his punishment and is in a good mood. The blue-haired lady is here, but without her orange-haired companion, who always preferred Salcido anyway. Don and Margaret Nason are also present. Tipton, wearing a crisp blue suit, looks a little tired. Horngrad, in a baggy blue suit, seems chipper.

Today, for the first time, George Franklin sits in the courtroom a convicted murderer, wrapped in a heavy cloak of guilt rather than innocence. It doesn't seem to bother him. He chats amiably, almost happily, with Horngrad.

The probation officer is sitting at the prosecution table with Tipton and Cassandro. Morse sits alone in the first row of the audience. He is wearing slacks and a leather jacket and a bored, slightly bemused expression on his face. Occasionally he turns around and jokes with the local reporters. After the hearing, he is leaving for Sacramento for a robbery convention. He doesn't worry about Franklin getting out on parole. The sonofabitch will never see the light of day.

Smith asks Horngrad if he has anything to say in addition to his written brief. Horngrad explains that he hadn't learned of Munson's allegation until right before his closing and could not, in good conscience, have asked the court to reopen the trial without having looked into the matter. Tipton argues that Horngrad had the opportunity to raise the issue before the conclusion of the trial, but failed to do so. Smith denies Horngrad's motion for a new trial, saying that Munson's testimony "would in no way affect the outcome of the trial."

Since the sentence is automatic, there is little reason for Tipton to say anything, but she rises anyway. She feels compelled to say that George Franklin received an eminently fair trial and that his punishment is moral and just.

"The only injustice in this case is one that this Court cannot address or undo and that is that this punishment comes twenty-one years too late."

Tipton pauses, then says shakily that while she never knew Susan Nason, "I wish I could have. If she had lived, she would be a thirty-some-odd-year-old woman and I'm sure she would have been a delightful person."

Horngrad quibbles with a few items in the report, then the room falls silent. Smith looks directly at Franklin.

"Mr. Franklin, do you have anything you would like to say at this time? This is your last chance to say anything."

Horngrad and Wachtel lean into Franklin and confer with him. Franklin rises and, hands clasped front of him, shoulders square, looks at the judge and says in a rough voice:

"I am innocent of that for which I have been convicted."

He starts to sit down, but Smith's voice cuts the air like a lash and jerks him upright.

"You will stand, sir. The evidence will indicate that you are a depraved and wicked man. An anomaly prevents me from providing you with a just sentence.

"Your application for probation is denied, and you are committed to the Department of Corrections for the rest of your life."

Smith truly regrets that the law prevents him from directing the jury to go into the penalty phase of the trial to determine if George Franklin should be executed. He feels strongly that society is entitled to demand death for such a heinous crime as this.

SHORTLY AFTER HIS SENTENCING, GEORGE FRANKLIN RECEIVES HIS initiation into the club of convicted child molesters and killers. Two inmates order Franklin's cellmate to rough him up a little. When he refuses, the inmates smack him, then hit Franklin in the face.

Epilogue

The JURY WAS WRONG IN ITS CONCLUSION THAT Eileen knew facts only a witness to the crime could have known. Everything that Eileen testified to was either unverifiable—something Susan said while she was being molested, for example, or Eileen's thoughts as they drove away from the pulloff—or in the public domain. The jury relied on Eileen's recollection that only one shoe was found at the scene. In fact, Eileen only said that she saw her father throw something brown, *a shoe or shoes,* which is obviously quite different from saying only one shoe had been located. The fact that a sock was found in the bushes may support her statement that he threw a shoe or shoes, but it doesn't validate the fact that only one shoe was found. In addition, one of the 1969 newspaper articles actually mentioned the finding of a single shoe.

The jury was impressed that Eileen knew Susan was wearing an A-line dress the day she was killed, apparently forgetting that Eileen claimed to have recovered this fact only a few hours before her testimony. By the time Eileen testified, the style of Susan's dress was clearly in the public arena. Margaret Nason had testified to the A-line both at the preliminary hearing in May and at the trial only a few days before Eileen took the stand. Any one of a number of people could easily have reported this fact to her.

Lastly, the jury correlated Eileen's testimony that she saw her father place a rock on Susan's body after he killed her with Dr. Benson's testimony that he found a rock in the folds of her dress. Eileen also recovered this fact just before trial, and her testimony was only that she saw her father place a rock near or next to the body. Also, the rock was not found in the folds of the dress at the scene, but only at the hospital after the remains had been loaded into and out of a body bag and an ambulance.

The jury was handicapped in its analysis because it did not have the 1969 articles to compare with Eileen's statements. A reporter for a San Francisco legal newspaper later sent a compilation of the 1969 articles to each juror in an attempt to determine if the articles would have made a difference in their decision. Nancy Salazar read every one of the articles, but was skeptical that a different result would have been reached had the articles been in evidence. Ollie Scholle skimmed them and felt the same way. Mary Dolan became quite upset when, after reading the articles, she realized that, in fact, most of Eileen's details were in the public domain. She suspected that the jury would have discussed the facts more closely, but she was not sure that the outcome would have been different.

The uncharged conduct impacted the jury's decision in several ways. When the jury heard the testimony about the digital penetration, the bathtub sodomy, the Stan Smith rape, Franklin beating and kicking his children, his admission to Carolyn Adams that he had sex with his daughter, and all the rest, he became subhuman. Seeing him as a monster, the jurors were relieved of the normal anxiety one might have about making a mistake; if they incorrectly convicted him of the murder, he certainly had committed other sufficiently heinous crimes to warrant serious punishment.

Although Judge Smith had instructed the jurors that they were to consider this testimony only as it related to Eileen's memory and not as proof of commission of the crime itself, no one in the courtroom believed they would be capable of making that distinction, and they weren't. In addition to the possible unconscious effects of this material on the jurors' minds, several jurors logically but improperly reasoned that any man who would do these horrible things to his own daughter would also do them to his daughter's best friend, and then kill her to cover it up. A monster does monstrous things.

The third impact of this material was to explain or excuse what should have been Eileen's tremendous failings as a witness. The way Nancy Salazar and others on the jury saw it, all of the lying and instability were understandable, perhaps predictable, because of what her father had done to her. What would you expect of someone who had suffered this sort of violent physical and sexual abuse? To get up and tell a completely rational, unchanging, coherent story like a normal person with normal parents?

In the final, ironic twist on the uncharged conduct, Eileen's lying and instability came full circle to validate and confirm her testimony about the abuse she said she had suffered at the hands of her father. The damaged psyche that rambled around on the stand had to be the result of *some* traumatic acts or experiences, undoubtedly committed by her father.

In essence, the uncharged conduct evidence provided Eileen with the cloak of victimhood, and that cloak immunized her from the effects of her lying and constantly shifting and changing stories. The cloak made her into a Teflon witness: Nothing Horngrad threw at her stuck, and in fact the more he threw, the more he validated her victimhood and seemingly enhanced her credibility.

One senior judge in the county believed that George Franklin was a dead man the instant Smith decided to allow in the uncharged conduct. Several jurors admitted they would have had a very hard time reaching a guilty verdict if they had heard none of the uncharged conduct evidence.

The question that has haunted this case from the beginning, and one the jury was never able to answer, was: Why would Eileen make up this horrible charge? What motive could she possibly have to concoct a story about seeing her father murder her best friend? Certainly she wouldn't consciously level a false charge—she would have to be an awfully good actress to make such a story stick—which meant she must in fact believe the story herself. How could the mind construct a false memory so complete and rich in detail? How could she tell a false story with such agonizing emotion?

It was, of course, the task of the defense to answer these questions, a task which, for many reasons, turned out to be almost impossible. In addition to the dilemma of having to admit his client's abuse to provide a revenge motive for Eileen, Horngrad was faced with having to articulate a very elusive, hard-to-grasp concept about the fabricative abilities of the human mind. The concept of repression is simple—one buries a traumatic experience and then one day it pops up—in comparison to the theory of how a false memory is constructed.

The field of repressed memories of traumatic events is relatively new in psychology and one in which very little formal work has been done. Other psychiatrists would not testify with the certainty of Dr. Terr that she can tell a false memory from a true memory by listening to and watching the patient, or that she can discern the nature of the trauma by the symptomatology, or that a single traumatic event can't be repressed. Her testimony that false memories are as rare as trying to study giraffes in Ohio is not a scientific statement, but an educated hunch.

In Eileen's case, the first building block in the construction of a false memory of the murder would be the availability of the facts of the event itself. There is little doubt that Eileen was exposed to the essential details of Susan's murder in 1969. The killing was talked about in the community, which was still quite small then, at school, and, according to Kate, in the Franklin household. It is quite likely that Eileen read an account of the murder in the *San Mateo Times,* which was delivered to the home and which gave the story front-page coverage. Reading was stressed in the Franklin household, and local television stations covered the story for days after the body was found. Janice, who continued to play with Shirley, was interviewed twice by the police in 1969, and on the second occasion the police showed her Susan's crushed ring. Eileen knew the facts well enough only a few years after the crime to describe Susan's crushed hand to Diana and tell her that her body had been found under a mattress.

Secondly, if Eileen's vision is in fact a false memory, the idea of her father as the murderer would not be an idea that leapt into her mind from nowhere. George Franklin's involvement in the killing of Susan Nason had been something close to a rumor in the Franklin family almost from the time of her disappearance to the moment Eileen told her story to the cops. Janice testified that both she and Eileen read an account in the newspaper of a child molester and talked about how the description sounded like their father. Janice says she began suspecting her father of killing Susan when she was around ten years old. Leah was suspicious of her husband for many years and her suspicions grew when he told her he had buried a diary in the woods. Leah, whose mother also believed George had killed Susan, finally accused George to his face of the killing in 1978. Not long after that, both Janice and Leah agreed that they thought he had killed Susan.

According to Jeff Munson, Eileen told him in 1983 that she thought her father had killed Susan. In 1984, Janice told the Foster City police of her belief that her father had killed Susan. After initially denying any knowledge of Janice's 1984 accusation, Eileen finally admitted that Janice *had* told her she had gone to the police, although she gave conflicting dates as to when she was told. The idea of George Franklin as Susan's murderer was so well developed that when Eileen finally told Barry of her newly recovered memory, his first reaction was, "I knew that was what you were going to say!"

Thirdly, Eileen, by her own words, has a very active, aggressive mind, capable of adding and dropping facts, reshaping scenes, and merging images. In fact, if she is to be believed, her mind has admittedly created at least one very critical false fact in a traumatic memory. In the rape scene where her father held her down, she believed her assailant to be a black man for around six months, until finally she took a closer look and realized that he was white. Not only did his skin color change, he became someone she knew.

Eileen constructed a false image, created an identity around the Jimi Hendrix poster that wasn't true; she took one image and merged it with another inside her mind, and became so convinced of the reality of her confabulation that she repeated it as fact to family members and law enforcement. Kate recalls Leah telling her that when Eileen told her that she couldn't recognize the assailant, Leah suggested to Eileen that the rapist might be her godfather, Stan Smith.

Nowhere are the constructive abilities of Eileen's mind under stress more apparent than in the instance of the buried diary. A short time after learning from her aunt that her father had buried a diary, she suddenly visualized him digging and burying something in the woods. Perhaps desperate to have her story corroborated and anxious to avoid a trial, she merged the facts her mother and aunt had provided with this new image into a memory of her father burying a diary. She was sufficiently confident of the validity of this memory to take Morse and Barry into the hills and point to a specific spot on Star Hill Road (which had been suggested by her mother) to begin digging for the diary. The fact that both this location and the location of the murder memory have three trees in the foreground suggests leakage between or duplication of some details in the two memories. At the trial, Eileen confused the memory of the diary with memories of terror she experienced while running through the woods in Switzerland in 1988.

Eileen also came to believe that her father used her as bait to attract young women into his car so he could rape and murder them. In her August 1990 statement to the cops about her father stuffing a woman with a bloody left breast into a recessed area, her narrative wanders and rambles incoherently, taking on in many instances the qualities of a hallucination. The statement certainly was not sufficiently integrated to form the basis for any prosecution, or even be used in evidence, for that matter.

Still, if Eileen did not witness the murder, the question remains: *Why* would she have created a false memory? The answer might lie in the status of Eileen's life in the fall of 1988, shortly before her memory allegedly returned. Her life was a mess, and it held few prospects of improving. She was living the results of her Faustian bargain. She had married a man whom she didn't love in exchange for financial security and comfort and now she had all those things and she was still miserable. Her husband was a jerk and an embarrassment. He was abusive, insensitive, domineering, and controlling. Life with him consisted of one long screaming match. In many ways she had married her father. Barry had driven off her dad, so now she was even deprived of the joy of that renewed relationship. She had been in therapy for several months, but she didn't feel comfortable with the therapist. She could buy whatever she wanted, but it was her husband who made the money. She had no education. She was trapped. She had tried to escape several times, but Barry had always blackmailed her into returning. She had filed for divorce, but was so terrified that Barry would take the money and Jessica that she backed off. She had had a miscarriage and felt that everyone—including her husband and mother and mother-in-law—was insensitive to her pain. She had arrived at her class reunion as the swan, only to feel the stings of her classmates' arrows and leave as the ugly duckling. And what sort of a mother was she if after witnessing her father molest her daughter she had continued to allow him around her?

The psychic pressures had become intolerable. She needed a solution, a safety valve, a way to explain how she had ended up in this mess, to clear herself of any responsibility for her miserable situation, a new way to understand and look at her life, before she went crazy. She couldn't unload on Barry. Part of her deal with him had always been that in exchange for giving him control of her life she could blame him for her unhappiness, but that equation wasn't working anymore. And she still needed him financially and emotionally. Her father, on the other hand, was safe. She didn't need him at all, didn't even see him anymore. Probably never would.

In her conscious or unconscious mind smoldered plenty of material to connect him to the crime. She knew his violence firsthand. Although as his favorite she had been beaten less than most of her siblings, she had experienced his rage and seen his blows rain down on the heads of Janice, George Jr., and Kate. She knew of his sexual interest in young girls: not only had she seen him molest her daughter Jessica, Janice had told her about the time he had raped her, and she remembered overhearing Janice and Kate talk about what he had done to them. Eileen was as close as Janice came to having a friend in the family, and Janice had been jealous for years of Eileen's close relationship with their father. Janice had hammered her sister for years about what an unrehabilitated bastard he was, insisting that he was as mean and immoral as he always had been. Finally, Eileen knew that her father liked Susan Nason. Eileen and Susan used to play the belly-button game with him.

Suddenly, in December, Eileen has a memory of her father digitally penetrating her as a child. She tells her therapist, who explains to her that indeed, someone can repress a painful or traumatic event and that that event can lie buried in the person's psyche, ready to surface when the time is right.

Now everything is in her mind: the raw material, the need, the mechanism. Only a stimulus is needed. A few weeks later, she is looking at her daughter, who had been molested by George, and Jessica reminds her of her best friend, Susan, who had been ripped from her long ago, and gradually she sees an outline of a figure, her father, who had been a source of so much pain in her life, standing over her friend with a rock in his hand. It is a horrible image and she shudders and turns her mind away. The image returns, arousing intensely painful feelings, and she resists it, but the door is open and the path lies before her, irresistible. Things begin to sort out: Her suicide attempt, her heavy drug use, her prostitution, her loveless marriage, all take on a new meaning. Gradually, as the days pass, the details of the crime begin to fill in: she sees herself calling to Susie from the van window; she visualizes Susie's crushed ring and bloody hand; she hears her cry out; she imagines what she would be thinking as they drove away. The pain is horrible, but the internal pressure begins to subside. She now has a focus, a target, for her rage. Her self gradually begins to make sense.

An alternative explanation would be that the murder memory operated as a "screen" for more painful memories. Under this theory, the digital penetration memory in December 1988 was the first sign of leakage from walled-off memories of sexual abuse, and it threatened horrible, perhaps intolerable pain for Eileen. The murder memory was created to screen these memories, because horrible as that memory might be, at least the event didn't happen to her.

Both of the above hypothetical explanations for the origin of Eileen's memory assume the validity of her sixth and final version of how the memory returned to her. There is no reason to credit that version any more than any of the five earlier ones, but the dream memory and the hypnotically induced memory could have served the same purpose.

Several other of Eileen's dominant psychological traits would mesh easily with the first explanation. Although Eileen was never formally psychologically evaluated in the judicial proceedings, her lifelong need for attention, to be the center of the situation, is not inconsistent with a narcissistic personality. Once she went forward with her story, or more accurately, once Barry went forward, she was suddenly the center of attention, not only in her own family, but in the eyes of the world. Everybody wanted to talk to her, take her picture, put her on television. A producer for Connie Chung, whom she has always admired, sought her out for an interview. The largest newspapers in the country called her. Perhaps it was a horrible storm to be in the middle of, but it was *her* storm and she could grant and withhold favors as she saw fit. The world is now defined for her, and anyone who really cares about her sees her in terms of her trauma, her pain. She finally has an identity.

Eileen also evidences some characteristics of the borderline personality, particularly a trait referred to as "splitting." Everyone is either good or bad, a friend or enemy, and the slightest behavior can move a person from one category to another. Eileen sees betrayal everywhere: God, Elaine Tipton, her brother, her sisters, her author, anyone who seems for a moment to question her story, her pain, or her. Another characteristic of the borderline personality is intermittent rage. Eileen is capable of flying into a screaming rage in an instant, and then cooling off immediately. Now, as a victim of this horrible trauma, her rage is understandable and evokes understanding, sympathy, not critical judgment. However she behaves, whatever she does, must now be seen in the light of what she has endured and survived. Even Barry, even her *mother,* must accept her anger and treat her with more respect.

She has, after all, solved not only her personal mystery, but the family mystery as well.

Whether or not a formal evaluation of Eileen would lead to a diagnosis of post-traumatic stress disorder, as Kirk Barrett suggested, or some other psychiatric disorder, there can be little doubt that she was severely traumatized as a child and that these traumas involved a neglectful mother and a chronically abusive father. Her identification with her father, her continuing love for him (on "60 Minutes" her eyes lit up joyfully when she described going places with him as a little girl, startling interviewer Lesley Stahl), reflects the confusion she experienced as a child between love and pain, caring and shame. Her adult life has been spent repeating and re-enacting these traumas. The promiscuity, self-destructive behavior, prostitution, drug abuse, her marriage to an obviously controlling and abusive male, her mimicking of her mother's life, are, according to one psychiatric theory, compulsive repetitions of the early traumas. This pattern is considered by some experts to be nearly intractable, her prognosis bleak; absent intensive and long-term treatment, Eileen may be doomed to continue her self-destructive patterns.

The benefit, or detriment, depending on how you look at it, of the trial and verdict to her personality could be that it has created for her the right to a perpetual, chronic victimhood. The jury verdict (which is nothing less than twelve strangers saying they believe her story beyond a reasonable doubt), the adulation and uncritical attention from the national press and from other survivors of childhood abuse, have confirmed for her that she is a victim, apparently leaving her blind to her own impact on events and allowing her to escape responsibility for the consequences of her behavior. She has an unchallengeable *right* to her unrelenting, inexhaustible rage, a *right* to point the finger at others as the cause of all her misfortunes. Her anger is the righteous anger of the suffering, doomed heroine. The cloak that protected her in trial has now become an emotional straitjacket.

None of which means that she didn't see her father murder Susan Nason.

* * *

ON A LARGER STAGE, THE DRAMA CONTINUES:

Long after the trial was over, the DNA analysis came back from the FBI excluding Eileen's father as a suspect in the 1974 Pacifica murder.

In the summer of 1991, Barry had quadruple bypass heart surgery in Switzerland, and a few months later the family moved to Seattle to obtain better medical care for him. Eileen's book came out in October of that year and she toured the country aggressively promoting it, appearing within a few weeks on "60 Minutes," "Oprah Winfrey," "Larry King Live," "Good Morning America," and countless television panels and radio talk shows. On "60 Minutes," after lashing out at Lesley Stahl for seeming to minimize the depth of her pain, she talked bitterly of the remaining cases she expected to be brought against her father the serial murderer, hinting at how much pain was still in store for her. Within days of the broadcast, the D.A.'s office announced that the cases had been dropped for lack of evidence. In a *People* magazine article, which contains several pictures of her children, she revealed a new incident of sexual abuse by her father which she says occurred when she was three years old. Her book, which is both a victim's story and a payback to all those who have wronged her (she removed several statements about Kate and Allen and a photograph of Kate's wedding after they threatened to sue), including her fifth-grade teacher, was riddled with factual errors and, for all the massive publicity it received, sold poorly. Her movie, *Fatal Memories,* over which she had fought to maintain creative control, finally went into production in 1992 and was shown on television in the fall of that year.

Barry didn't live to see himself depicted on the screen. He died on Labor Day 1992 of heart disease. Of Eileen's immediate family, only Janice attended the funeral. One sibling remarked that now Eileen can eat her cake and have it too: her father is in jail, her husband is dead, and she has all the money from the movie and the book. Another sibling remembered how she and Eileen used to joke about the Heart Attack Specials—high cholesterol meals—Eileen prepared for Barry.

Still, the last frame of Eileen's movie reads: "In Loving Memory of Barry Lipsker 1947–1992."

IN DECEMBER 1990, BRYAN CASSANDRO WAS PROMOTED TO SERgeant and in 1992 moved from the detective bureau to the county jail. Morse, who accompanied Eileen on her book tour in California as a paid bodyguard, continues to work cases for the district attorney's office. A photograph of Morse and Cassandro hangs on the post in the Broadway below the portrait of their mentor, Sheriff Maguire.

As a supervisor, Elaine Tipton does not try cases anymore. She is very happy. In August 1992, she married an attorney she had known for many years who works in the civil division of the district attorney's office. She had a large Catholic wedding, which Eileen and Barry attended, and a fall honeymoon in Europe. Keeping her eye on the pending appeal, Tipton sometimes wonders if maybe it wouldn't have been wiser to allow the newspaper articles into evidence. The jury would have convicted Franklin anyway.

Mary Jane Larkin retired in the spring of 1991. After graduation ceremonies in which she was honored, students and their parents gathered in her classroom and thanked her with gifts and flowers. Now, she substitute teaches and travels with her husband.

The Nason divorce became final during the trial. Don left his job and began his own construction business and Margaret took a position working as a secretary in the district attorney's office. Then she fell in love with a man from her Baptist church, married him, and the two of them moved to North Carolina to do church work.

The jar containing Susan Nason's hand eventually disappeared from the evidence room of the Foster City Police Department. Rumor has it that a departing officer took it with him as a souvenir.

Doug Horngrad's private practice has been building rapidly. He remains resolutely convinced of George Franklin's innocence and his failure to receive a fair trial, and even though he is not formally representing him anymore, continues to visit him in prison in San Luis Obispo. Horngrad thinks back on the mistakes he made in the trial—he should never have cross-examined Eileen the second day, for example—and the tricks, the deceit, practiced by the prosecution, and he aches for a chance to try the case again.

Elaine Tipton, suspecting that George Franklin has money secreted away, objected to his claim of indigency and the Court of Appeals' appointment of Dennis Riordan to handle his appeal, but the court appointed him anyway. Riordan's brief hits hard on the exclusion of the newspaper articles, admission of the uncharged conduct evidence, and prosecutorial misconduct. Material contained in Eileen's book provides several new grounds for appeal. A decision is expected some time in 1993.

Elizabeth Loftus, the defense psychologist whose testimony was ignored by the jury because her expertise did not relate to repressed or traumatic memories, has, in partial response to the Franklin case, launched a major research effort at the University of Washington in the area of repressed memories. A preliminary study, which she described in an address at the annual meeting of the American Psychological Association in August 1992, indicated that it is possible to implant false memories of traumatic childhood incidents in adults. The formal study is under way. Her research also indicates that in some instances therapists may be instrumental in suggesting or creating repressed memories of sexual abuse in their patients. She has been appointed to an American Psychological Association taskforce to study repressed memories, and has testified in many of the civil and criminal repressed memory cases filed around the country since the Franklin verdict.

FROM THE CALIFORNIA MEN'S COLONY IN SAN LUIS OBISPO, George Franklin writes steamy, erotic love letters to Tish Tyler, the Sacramento hairdresser. He often opens with "Greetings of peace from the land of the free," and talks easily of life in prison. The other prisoners, he says, are a bunch of sadistic misfits. He spends most of his free time alone or in the library. He works in the kitchen serving breakfast and lunch and attends business school five days a week, taking courses in business law, accounting principles, and microeconomics. He also studied Civil War history and introduction to theater. He has earned straight A's.

To Tish, he seems as strong and positive as ever. He expresses belief in God as his higher power, a force within each person, and he keeps his mind focused on the positive. When Tish is down, he advises her, "Don't let despair rule your life." He works hard at letting go of painful thoughts and feelings, for fear they will limit his personal growth.

George berates the tabloid press and the public's willingness to believe the sensational misinformation it spreads. The hysteria around his case, or "this bizarre situation," as he calls it, reminds him of the Salem witch trials, which he has been studying. In every letter he writes: "Visualize Peace," and often he recites sayings or poems. In one he said:

> The passing of all time
> Changes all lines of
> My memories.

Down the side of another letter he wrote:

> To remember
> Pleasures past
> To recall
> Places gone
> To remake
> Plans forgotten
> To give
> A chance taken
> To relive memories.

"My body," he tells her, "is caged, but my mind and spirit are at one with the center of the universe." He writes that his appellate lawyer is optimistic that he will one day receive the fair trial to which he is entitled. George admits to Tish that he was a bastard to his children and that only his son still communicates with him. He tells her that he is innocent and that his trial was a miscarriage of justice. The truth, he remarks, is inconvenient to a lot of people. Most folks just don't think for themselves. He suggests that he and Tish, whom he refers to as "my precious" and "my princess," should think about collaborating on a book one day. "Life is a comedy for those who think," he tells her, "and a tragedy for those who feel." He always signs off, "Aloha."

After following the trial in the newspapers, Tish decided that George was probably innocent. Too many things simply didn't add up. She thinks about visiting him—he has sent her applications and suggested a conjugal visit, which is impossible unless they were to be married—but she hesitates. He'll look so different from the way she remembers him. She still cares about him, though, and there's one thing she knows for sure: George, a strange mixture of machismo and sensitivity, was always a gentleman and he treated her a lot better than most of the men in her life.

OF ALL THE FRANKLIN CHILDREN, KATE WAS THE ONLY ONE WHO hadn't visited her father in jail. The idea never occurred to her. When Janice went to see him, her father turned around and left when he saw her in the waiting room. "That's the one I don't want to see," he complained harshly to the guard.

Diana went with George Jr. to San Quentin in early January 1991, a few months after the conviction. She felt horrible about her father being in jail and cried for hours before the visit. It wasn't that she loved him. She didn't. Most of the time she loathed him. But she also felt sorry for him. Going to see him, she felt, would be like paying her last respects.

In the visiting room, she and George Jr. each had a phone and her father held a handset to each ear. He told her he was innocent. Diana replied that even if he was guilty, she knew they hadn't arrested the man he was twenty years ago. She had imagined him old and lonely and had hoped that he felt some remorse, but she soon learned otherwise. He was as angry and arrogant as ever. At one point he said mockingly to her,

"Jesus, Diana, where were you when the civics books were passed out!"

"Look," she had told him, "you need all of the friends you can get right now. I don't think you're in any position to be an asshole." Her brother had interrupted, "Dad, can't you see that she cares? She came to see you." He had been nicer to her after that, but it was still awkward. She couldn't think of anything to say. It had always been hard to talk to him, and she sure didn't want to fill him in on the details of her life for the past five years.

Toward the end she asked if he needed anything, if she could bring him some books. He said no, he had friends who were helping him out. She rose to leave and was walking to the door when he said, "I love you, Diana." It was so unexpected, it caught her off guard. All she could think was it wouldn't hurt her to say those three words to him, even if she didn't mean them. She still *wished* she could love her father. She turned and, regretting the words as they slipped from her mouth, said, "I love you." She caught his eye. He had been staring at her rear end. *Jesus,* she thought, *he's cruising me. His own daughter, from behind bars. How pathetic.* As she walked from the jail she could feel the pity inside her evaporate. She realized she never wanted to see him again.

Diana's life has taken a dramatic upturn since the trial. Completely off cocaine, she enrolled in aesthetician school in San Francisco and received her license in the summer of 1991. She finally left her abusive relationship with Guy, who had quit drugs, and found an apartment and a job in a salon. She is excited about her fresh start and the feeling of being in control of life. She is determined to look forward, not backward. She knows her weakness with men and is determined to avoid another abusive relationship, but she worries that somehow she'll get fooled, miss the warning signs, and get sucked in again. She has decided not to get serious about anyone for a while.

Eileen has been the main confusion in her life. Her sister is angrier now than before the trial, and she gets angrier and angrier. She sees betrayal everywhere. If you don't toe her line one hundred percent, then you are a false friend. In spite of the fact that Diana has supported her from the beginning, Eileen called her a traitor because she talked to George Jr. and Kate. She even said that George and Kate's failure to support her was the same as "condoning Susan Nason's murder." It's as if Eileen feels that because of the damage she has suffered, she has a license to inflict pain on others, particularly her family. She has told others that Diana is suffering from fetal alcohol syndrome and that George Jr. is illegitimate.

Eileen can talk of nothing but "IT" and how bad her pain is. "I'm dead inside," she tells Diana dramatically, "I don't even have it for my children." She has always been skilled at making people feel sorry for her, and Diana has always played right into it. When Eileen told her therapist in Switzerland about what had happened to her, the therapist broke down and cried. "You can't imagine the smell of murder, the sound of murder," Eileen told her younger sister. She talks about other murders.

Diana has come to realize that Eileen has become someone other than the sister she has loved all these years. She had called Eileen in Switzerland and, after she had admitted that she was still talking to George Jr., Barry began yelling in the background, "Diana, you're an asshole!"

"Barry warned me about you," Eileen said viciously, "and you know what really pisses me off about this more than anything? This makes him right!" When Diana admitted that she had spoken to an author other than Eileen's writer about the case, Eileen began wailing so loudly that her words were almost incomprehensible. "Did he pay you?" she screeched. She insisted that she had spent over $20,000 in legal fees protecting the Franklin family, which infuriated Diana because Eileen had in fact exploited the family. Eileen swore that she would cancel the $7,500 movie consulting contract she had arranged for Diana, but Diana had long since decided that, broke as she was, she wasn't going to accept the money or have anything to do with the movie.

"Diana, fuck you!" Eileen screamed and hung up the phone.

Diana stood there. She didn't feel any of the usual hurt. She knew she would always love Eileen and would miss her, but it would never be the way it was, accepting her no matter what she said or did. She would learn to live without her. It felt as if a great burden had been lifted from her.

Early Summer, 1991—Sunday

Kate bustles around in the kitchen getting everything ready for brunch while keeping an eye on her son, Daniel, now one and a half. She is serving frittatas, corn bread, fruit salad, and fresh juice. Diana and George Jr. are expected around 11:00, just a few minutes away, and she wants to spend the time talking with them. It is a bright, sunny morning and the light flows in through the many windows of her cottage, casting a warm glow everywhere. From the kitchen and dining area she can look out over the green hills to a park and beyond to the waters of San Francisco Bay. The pink geraniums are vivid in her window boxes and a warm wind brushes the rose bushes alongside the deck.

Kate hasn't really been close to either George Jr. or Diana over the years, partly because she was older, but also because of the family craziness. She lost touch with Diana when she fell into the cocaine hole and an abusive relationship. She talked to George Jr. on the phone occasionally, but in keeping with the unwritten rules of the Franklin family, they kept a safe distance, wary of touching their common pool of pain.

This isn't the first Sunday she and her husband have had George Jr. and Diana for brunch. They came once before the trial. Diana, who lives in Marin County, stops in San Francisco and picks up her brother and drives to Kate's house. Diana and George Jr. developed a close relationship in the years they lived with Leah on Beach Park and have become even closer in the past few years.

Leah, who lives around the bend from Kate, is not invited to the brunch. Although George Jr. still calls his mother quarterly and Diana visits her every couple of weeks, Kate hasn't spoken to her since the trial. Eileen also doesn't communicate with her mother, and Janice calls her mainly to yell and tell her how much she hates her. Diana could forgive Leah if only she would *admit* that she hadn't been a good mother, but she never will. Kate can't imagine herself ever speaking to her mother again.

George Jr. and Diana arrive and there are hugs and kisses and everyone sits in the living room for coffee and talks about things normal families talk about: how big Kate's child is getting, the rearrangement of the furniture, Diana's hairdo. George and Kate tease Diana good-naturedly about how early she had to get up to put herself together. The sisters tease George about the cotton plantation in his apartment.

At the table, the feeling is lighthearted, natural, devoid of any of the intense uneasiness so common to Franklin family gatherings. Everyone is glad to be here. Kate serves the omelets and the conversation bounces from books to movies to local politics. Occasionally the subject of Eileen, their father, the trial, comes up—Diana will report the latest news in the paper or George Jr., the pundit, will make a pithy remark about Eileen or Barry—but the siblings don't dwell on the family traumas. All three have taken different positions on whether their father killed Susan Nason—George Jr. thinks he's innocent, Diana thinks he's guilty (although she now believes Eileen lied about the memory being repressed), and Kate isn't sure—but they don't debate the issue. Mainly they talk about their lives, their jobs, their friends, and their futures. The only sad note sounds when George Jr. says he wishes Kate would make up with their mother. Kate promises to think about it.

Afterwards, Kate and Diana clear the table while George Jr. and Allen walk outside. Talk in the kitchen turns to Diana's loss of her relationship with Eileen, then to the good things that are flowing from the tragedy. Diana is blooming and she and Kate talk three or four times a week on the phone, and are closer than they have ever been. The way they feel now is the way sisters are supposed to feel.

A few hours later, after more hugs and kisses and promises to return, Diana and George Jr. depart, Diana carrying a plant Kate has given her from her garden. Kate stands in her doorway, feeling the warm afternoon sun on her face, and watches her brother and sister walk down the steep drive to the car. As the older sister, she can't help but worry. She hopes Diana will finish school and find a job and meet a good man and that George Jr. will go back to school and begin to realize his incredible potential. Diana and George wave gaily to her as their car disappears around the bend, and Kate finds herself already looking forward to the next gathering.

Afterword

GEORGE FRANKLIN'S APPEAL WAS DENIED BY THE
California Court of Appeals in April 1993. The Court held that
Eileen's testimony about her father's failure to deny the killing
when she visited him in jail violated his Fifth Amendment
rights, but decided that the record demonstrated beyond a reasonable doubt that the testimony was harmless error. The
Court found that neither Judge Smith's refusal to allow into
evidence the 1969 newspaper articles nor his admission of the
uncharged conduct constituted error. The California Supreme
Court refused to hear the appeal. The case is currently before
the federal district court on a petition for a writ of habeas
corpus.

If the charge against George Franklin were tried today, it
would almost certainly be a remarkably different trial. In 1990,
the use of a repressed memory in a court of law was extremely
rare; in criminal cases it was virtually unheard of. In the psychological community there was still very little debate about
the validity of repressed memories or about the concept of
repression itself, because such memories were so infrequently
presented as literal replicas of actual, lost events.

Suddenly all of that changed. A man was convicted of murder based almost solely on a repressed memory; adults around
the country began suing their parents based on recovered
memories of childhood sexual abuse; people were recovering
memories of bizarre, unverifiable stories of satanic ritual abuse
and off-planet experiences. As the phenomenon gained visibil-
ity, a common denominator became apparent: most, if not all,
of the people who claimed to recover memories of childhood
trauma had been in therapy at the time of the recovery. Many

of the therapists were using highly questionable techniques and advising their patients to read nonprofessional books on the subject that contained statements like: "If you think you might have been sexually abused, then you were."

The mental health community woke up with a start. Leading psychiatrists and psychologists from major universities began to speak up and point out that there was no scientific basis to presume the validity of these memories; that truth in the clinical setting was a radically different concept from truth in the courtroom; that the data indicated that memory was a process and that it didn't function like a camcorder; that false memories of childhood trauma could be implanted in adult subjects. The American Psychiatric Association issued a warning against the use of recovered memory techniques.

The clinical community struck back, charging that those who challenged these memories were perpetuating male domination and exploitation of women, that they were either perpetrators themselves or defenders of perpetrators. The debate became more fierce with the formation of the False Memory Syndrome Foundation, many of whose members are parents accused of sexual abuse by adult children on the basis of repressed memories. The chairman of the department of psychiatry at Johns Hopkins University became one of the leading spokespersons. Meetings of the American Psychological Association and the American Psychiatric Association were dominated by debates over the validity of repressed memories. The debates were punctuated by name calling and hissing.

On the larger scene, the validity of repressed memories has become one of the hottest issues in our society. The subject has been the topic of endless "Oprah" and "Donahue" and "Sonia Live" shows. A new player has surfaced: "recanters," women who are claiming that memories recovered in therapy and once believed to be true are in fact false, that they were created in the therapeutic process. Lawyers, ever ready to feed on conflict and confusion, are suing everybody in sight, including the therapists. The public perception in favor of these memories has turned around: *Time* magazine proclaims them to be "Lies of the Mind," and Ann Landers denounces them as "character assassinations." Other writers denounce the repressed memory phenomenon as nothing more than a wave of cultural hysteria comparable to the Salem witch trials and the McCarthy era.

All pendulums by their nature come to rest in the middle, and someday this one will too. One can only hope that in the near future, before too many more lives are destroyed, science catches up with the law and we learn the real nature of these memories, whether they represent actual traumatic events or are instead confabulations, mixtures of fact and fantasy, bubbling up from active but disturbed unconscious minds.